SUBSIDIA MEDIAEVALIA

7

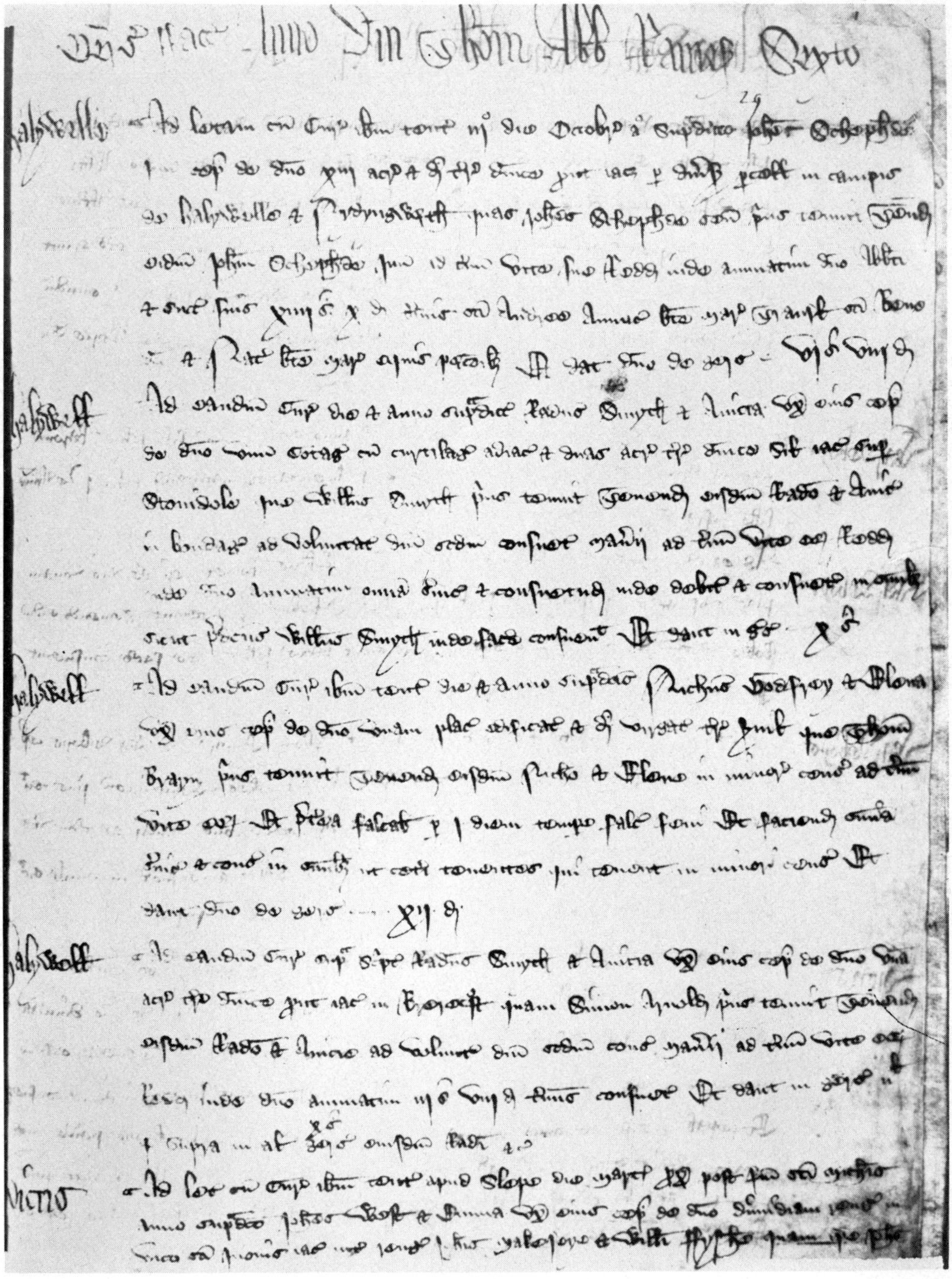

B.L. Harl. MS. 445, f. 29r. (See infra, nos. 288-92).

THE *LIBER GERSUMARUM*
OF RAMSEY ABBEY

A Calendar and Index of B.L. Harley MS 445

BY

EDWIN BREZETTE DEWINDT

PONTIFICAL INSTITUTE OF MEDIAEVAL STUDIES
TORONTO, CANADA
1976

ACKNOWLEDGMENT

This book has been published with a grant
in aid of publication from
the De Rancé Foundation.

CANADIAN CATALOGUING IN PUBLICATION DATA

DeWindt, Edwin Brezette, 1941-
    The Liber Gersumarum of Ramsey Abbey

(Subsidia mediaevalia ; 7 ISSN 0316-0769)

Bibliography: p.
Includes indexes.
ISBN 0-88844-356-0 pa.

1. Land tenure — England — History. 2. Registers of birth, etc. —
England. I. Ramsey Abbey. Liber Gersumarum. II. Pontifical Institute of Mediaeval Studies. III. Title. IV. Series.

HD604.D5   333.3'22'0942   C76-017096-7

PRINTED BY UNIVERSA PRESS, WETTEREN (BELGIUM)

*For my Father
Joseph Constant DeWindt
who always began
a story by giving
its sources*

LIST OF PLATES

TABLE OF CONTENTS

PREFACE

The world of the Middle Ages was predominantly a world founded on and penetrated by peasants. The peasantry formed the single largest population group in mediaeval society. It was the peasants who, by their labour, primarily produced the necessities of life for society as a whole, and who supplied considerable raw human material for the urban explosion of post eleventh-century Europe, both in its economic and academic guises. The Christian Church, throughout its turbulent mediaeval pilgrimage, never forgot — or escaped — its agrarian roots, neither in its personnel, in such men as Hadrian IV, Grosseteste or Pecham, in its forms of public worship and liturgical calendar, nor in the heavy rural emphasis of its institutions of the *cura animarum*. Wherever one looks in the Middle Ages, the essentially agrarian stamp of society is apparent, and the peasant himself is seldom far from view. Yet, for all its admitted importance to a full understanding of mediaeval civilisation, the world of the peasant is one of the most difficult to penetrate. Rarely literate themselves, the peasants have most frequently been perceived through the words of landlords, as set down in manorial surveys, extents and accounts. Only recently has a new perspective been brought to bear on the peasantry by the exploitation of the wealth of data and personal information on thousands of mediaeval men and women contained in surviving English village court rolls.

My own involvement with the use of the court roll in the study of the mediaeval English peasant began ten years ago, while a graduate student under the direction of Professor J. Ambrose Raftis of the Pontifical Institute of Mediaeval Studies and the Graduate Centre for Medieval Studies, University of Toronto. In the course of examining several aspects of the society of the village of Holywell-cum-Needingworth (co. Hunts.), I became convinced of the crucial role of local court materials in extending understanding of peasant life. Unfortunately, the vast amount of mediaeval English village court records preserved in national and local archives is not readily available to a wide variety of scholars. Most are still unedited, and although it is to be hoped that the editing and publication of series of court rolls will be actively encouraged and supported, the task of preparing an edition of a good series of rolls for even one village is neither easy nor enviable. In the meantime, there exists a smaller body of local, court-related records — e.g. charters, wills, court books — which can be profitably edited or calendared and subsequently made available to scholars desirous of expanding investigation of the society of the mediaeval

English countryside. Among this latter group, one of the most remarkable collections is the *Liber Gersumarum* of Ramsey Abbey (B. L. Harl. MS. 445).

I first became aware of the *Liber Gersumarum* in 1964. Its use in my own research soon convinced me that it was a manuscript, the contents of which deserved a wider circulation. In 1968, I began preparing the text for publication. However, because of the demands of full-time teaching, it was not until 1972 that any real progress on the project could be made. In that year, while receiving financial support from the Kellogg Foundation and an appointment as a Research Associate at the Pontifical Institute of Mediaeval Studies, I was granted a term's leave of absence from teaching by the University of Detroit, enabling me to work on a calendar of the *Liber Gersumarum* while participating in the establishment of the Regional Data Bank at the Institute, a project funded by a Research Grant of the Canada Council. The calendar itself was finally completed on 1 November, 1973, the indices on 1 September, 1974.

In the six years that have passed since beginning the project, I have benefited, both directly and indirectly, from the help of many people and institutions. I am especially grateful to the British Library, for affording me the opportunity to inspect Harley MS. 445 personally, for permission to reproduce plates of folios, and to quote from Ramsey court rolls preserved in the Department of Manuscripts. Similarly, I wish to thank the Public Record Office, London, for permission to quote extracts from Crown copyright materials.

Among the staff at the Pontifical Institute, I am grateful to: Professor J. Ambrose Raftis, for his encouragement from the start; Professor Michael M. Sheehan, for his valuable criticisms and suggestions, as well as for help in deciphering legal points arising in the text; and Professor Leonard E. Boyle, O.P., for his unswerving belief in the practicality of the calendar, his readiness to give advice on methods of presenting the text, and his assistance with palaeographical problems. Errors and shortcomings that remain are solely my responsibility.

Further, I wish to thank my colleagues in the Regional Data Bank project — especially Edward Britton, M. Patricia Hogan, Ellen Wedemeyer Moore and Beryl Wells — for their willingness to share with me the results of their own research.

At the University of Detroit, I owe much to many: to the University itself, for a grant to aid in publication; to Professor John Mahoney, former Dean of the College of Arts and Sciences, for his constant and strong support of my work in all its phases: to Professor Thomas Porter, S.J., Dean of the College of Arts and Sciences, for his sympathetic promotion of my research; to Professor Edmund Miller, S.J., of the Department of Classics, for his eagerness to discuss questions of Latin terminology; to my colleagues in the Department of Religious Studies, in particular Professors George W. Pickering, John F. Porter and T. K. Venkateswaran, for their continuous encouragement and faith in the value of this project, and most especially Fr. Arthur E. Loveley, S.J., for help I can never adequately repay. Further, I have derived much benefit from students — both past and present — at the University, in particular : Patricia Alwin DeLeeuw, Sharon and Marilyn Fucinari, Susan McKay, Theresa Darwish, Mary Lynn Stabile, Maureen Harmon, Joan Miranda, John T. Greene, and Michael Evans. Their enthusiasm for mediaeval social history has been a source of stimulation and encouragement to me while engaged on the calendar.

Finally, I wish to thank my wife, Anne, for just being herself, during what, at times, must have seemed an endless process.

University of Detroit,
Michaelmas, 1975.

INTRODUCTION

I
The *Liber Gersumarum*: the Manuscript

The *Liber Gersumarum* of Ramsey Abbey is preserved in the British Library as Harley Manuscript 445. Acquired from Peter le Neve (1661-1729), it is a single, bound volume measuring 22 cm. by 33 cm. Its 256 numbered parchment folios contain Latin transcripts of land transfers, marriage licences and exodus fines from 42 manorial villages of the monastery in the counties of Huntingdon, Cambridge, Bedford, Hertford, and Northampton, from the third year of Abbot Thomas Butterwyk (1398) through the twenty-second year of Abbot John Stowe (1458). The manuscript itself is nearly contemporary with its contents, being written in at least 17 clearly distinct fifteenth-century hands. Since its acquisition by the British Museum (now British Library), the book has received little attention from mediaevalists, although it has not gone completely unnoticed. In fact, virtually its entire history in scholarship has stemmed from an attempt to give the manuscript a name. A hand-written description of the book, contained on its first, unnumbered folio, labels it a "Registram ... continens extractas e rotulis curiarum diversorum maneriorum ..."[1] Since 1957, it has been customary to refer to it as the "Ramsey Abbey Court Book".[2]

An exhaustive examination of the text, however, raises doubts about its being a Court Book, at least in the sense in which that term has come to be understood since Professor A. E. Levett's pioneer investigations of the St. Alban's court books.[3] Firstly, the entries are tightly restricted to land, marriage and exodus cases and do not reflect the variety normally found in court books.[4]

---

[1] B.L. Harl. MS. 445.

[2] A description coined by J. Ambrose Raftis, *The Estates of Ramsey Abbey* (Toronto, 1957; hereafter cited *Estates*), p. 321. As far as I can determine, Professor Raftis was the first scholar to devote any serious attention to the manuscript, and in an appendix to the *Estates* he published an edition of sample entries. The existence of the manuscript was noted in the 19th century by Hart and Lyons in their introduction to the Ramsey cartulary, where it is described as a "fine manuscript". (*Cartularium Monasterii de Rameseia*, [London, 1884: Rolls Series 79], I:xi. Hereafter cited, *Carts.*) It was also noted by W. Dunn Macray, (*Chronicon Abbatiae Rameseiensis*, [London, 1886: Rolls Series 83], p. liv). For later use of the text, see my *Land and People in Holywell-cum-Needingworth* (Toronto, 1972), Chapter 2. (Hereafter, *Land and People.*)

[3] See *Studies in Manorial History*, (Oxford, 1938).

[4] *Ibid.*, pp. 79 ff., 134 ff. Extracts, pp. 224 ff., 300 ff.

Secondly, and most interestingly, although the majority of the entries begin by noting the date and location of a court or view of frankpledge, in those cases where court rolls survive for the places and dates recorded, the entries are not to be found.[5]

A solution to the question of a title, however, appears to lie in the text of the manuscript itself. In two cases, reference is made to land transfers enrolled in the *Liber Gersumarum* for specific abbatial years.[6] When examination of Harley 445 for the years noted is made, the specific entries are found. Hence, I have concluded that Harley 445 is itself the *Liber Gersumarum*, a conclusion strengthened by the survival for the Ramsey town of St. Ives of a partial, so-called "Gersuma roll" from the middle of the fourteenth century, whose entries are virtually identical in language to those of Harley 445.[7]

Having a name for the manuscript, however, does not solve all its problems. Firstly, there is a question of its completeness. The text itself begins in the third year of Abbot Thomas and stops in the twenty-second year of Abbot John Stowe.[8] But an apparent index of exodus and marriage fines early in the

[5] This lack of correspondence between the court rolls and Harley 445 has been indicated in the notes accompanying the calendar . This, in fact, raises a question — which cannot be answered here — as to whether, by the late 14th century, there had been a policy-change in Ramsey administration, with land, marriage and exodus matters being treated independently of the village courts. There are, for example, cellarers' rolls from 1389 to 1508 (see B.L. Add. MSS. 33447, 33448), which contain land entries for several Ramsey villages that are not contained in any other source. Apparently the abbey cellarer was responsible for specific, independent properties. On the other hand, land entries and exodus licenses do not disappear from 15th-century court rolls, although those that are in the rolls are not found in the *Liber Gersumarum*. (For an indication of land and exodus entries in Ramsey court rolls from the 13th to the 15th century, see J. A. Raftis, *Tenure and Mobility* (Toronto, 1964), *passim*, and DeWindt, *Land and People*, Chapters 1-3.) This question is further complicated, however, by the unique case of King's Ripton (co. Hunts.). This Ramsey village, from its earliest extant court roll of 1279, boasts court rolls crowded with land cases, while it is one of the most poorly represented villages in Harley 445. For King's Ripton, see Anne Reiber DeWindt, "Society and Change in a Fourteenth-Century English Village: King's Ripton, 1250-1400," unpublished Ph.D. thesis, University of Toronto, 1972.

[6] See infra, nos. 1082, 1320.

[7] PRO 178/95. I owe this reference to Ellen Wedemeyer Moore.

[8] Although entries in the *Liber Gersumarum* are dated by abbatial years, the method employed is not traditional. In normal instances of dating documents by regnal, episcopal or abbatial years, the date of coronation, election, installation or consecration is usually taken as the beginning of the "year", which would then run for the subsequent 364 day period. In the *Liber Gersumarum*, however, a curious variation of this method was used. Specifically, abbatial years were made to correspond with the accounting years employed on Ramsey manors — i.e. from one Michaelmas (29 September) to the subsequent Michaelmas. Thus, four years actually begin on Michaelmas in the manuscript: 4 Thomas, 5 Thomas, 3 John Tychemersh, and 9 John Tychemersh. Twenty-eight years have their initial dates in the month of October (Thomas: 6, 10, 12, 13, 15, 17, 21; John Tychemersh: 6, 7, 10, 13, 14, 15; John Croyland: 2; John Stowe: 2, 3, 6, 8, 9, 10, 11, 12, 13, 14, 15, 17, 18, 19). Remaining years begin with imprecise or unindicated monthly dates.

For the actual dates of Ramsey abbots during the period covered by the *Liber Gersumarum*, see Appendix 1.

manuscript[9] implies that the book should continue into the abbacy of William Witlesey (1468-1473). Furthermore, there is a total gap of two years in the text — years 7 and 8 of Abbot Thomas are missing. Given the condition of the present binding, which is tight and prevents examination of the inner margins of the folios, it is impossible to determine if these years were once present and subsequently lost, or never included at all.[10]

Despite the missing two years, the remainder of the book appears to be intact.[11] It is excellently preserved, and the writing is clearly legible almost throughout.[12] It still remains uncertain, however, whether the *Liber Gersumarum* as we now have it actually began in 1398 and ended in 1458, forming part of a continuing series of such books, other volumes of which are now lost or misplaced, or whether it was originally a more complete book, covering the full abbacies of Thomas Butterwyk through William Witlesey, of which only 256 folios have survived.[13]

Finally, the actual arrangement of entries in the manuscript is haphazard. There was apparently no attempt to group vills according to any plan — alphabetical, geographical or topical. Nor do the entries follow the "travel circuit" of Ramsey seneschals in presiding over local courts — as is clear from simply a glance at the order of entries under 4 Thomas. An impression is left of the abbey scribes choosing entries from some original source — now lost — and making their choices rather clumsily at times.[14]

Whatever may be the final solution to the question of its original condition, the *Liber Gersumarum* in its present form is a unique collection of information for the student of the Ramsey Abbey estates in particular and of the fifteenth-century English countryside in general.

[9] See infra, pp. 43-49.

[10] It is difficult to believe that there was a complete cessation of land transfers, marriages or emigration on Ramsey villages in those years, or, for that matter, that the normally scrupulous abbey book keepers suddenly decided to take no note of them.

One further complication regarding the completeness of the text is the homage received from William Holcott (see infra, no. 4115), which dates from the time of abbot John Warboys II (1507-1539).

[11] The folios are numbered consecutively, although it cannot be determined exactly when the Arabic numerals were added to the upper right-hand corners of the folios. The hand appears to be post-mediaeval, which is a conclusion strengthened by the fact that the apparent index (see infra, pp. 43-49) locates entries by abbatial years, not by folio numbers.

[12] Only four folios are bound badly, cutting off the final words of as many entries. See infra, nos. 2877, 2915, 3472, 3588; see also no. 4271.

[13] That the *Liber Gersumarum*, whatever its original status, was part of some kind of continuing series is difficult to doubt. The fragmentary St. Ives Gersuma Roll (see supra, note 7) indicates a similar practice in the mid-14th century, while early 14th-century court rolls have references to a "Gersuma roll" (*Rotula de gersumis*) kept at the monastery at Ramsey. (See infra, p. 85, note 31, for a similar reference in a fifteenth-century court roll.)

[14] For example, in 4 Thomas, not even all the entries from one vill are grouped together. Thus, Hemingford and Holywell entries occur in three different places, while Abbots Ripton and Wistow are found in four different places.

II
The *Liber Gersumarum*: Contents and Uses

Although it does not include a record of *every* land transfer, marriage or exodus occurring in Ramsey villages in the first half of the fifteenth century,[15] what the *Liber Gersumarum* does include is highly significant and valuable for mediaevalists representing a variety of orientations.

Forty-two Ramsey vills are represented in the book, the total number of entries being 4374 with a spread among villages of from one to two entries (seven vills) to over 300 (three vills). In addition, the entries are normally so detailed that, in the cases of land transfers, it can frequently be learned what the conditions of tenure were, the amounts of rents, the dates for payments, supplementary obligations, the condition of the land itself (arable or pasture, with or without buildings), and, especially with respect to towns such as St. Ives and Ramsey, the location of properties in relation to other tenements or local landmarks.

Land clearly dominates the *Liber Gersumarum*, but there are also over 50 exodus licenses, 402 marriage licenses, and 40 miscellaneous entries, ranging from employment relationships to fines for making waste and disrepair of properties.

The sheer volume of information in the *Liber Gersumarum* gives some broad outlines of tenurial practices and peasant behavior that call for more detailed and specialized examination. It underlines the existence of a wide-scale peasant land market in customary properties over the first half of the fifteenth century. The phenomenon of a peasant land market is, of course, not unknown to specialists,[16] but the turn-over in properties recorded here is of much greater frequency than would be seen if rentals, surveys or account rolls were the sole source of information.[17] Indeed, so fluid does the market appear that it can be wondered if tenurial continuity was even a major factor in the lives of Ramsey peasant families by the early fifteenth century. It is possible to investigate this problem more closely, since the entries in the text often record the identities of at least two previous tenants of a property in a transaction. Thus, the descent of specific parcels of land through several hands can be

[15] For example, the manuscript all but ignores free-hold properties. For other omissions, see supra, note 5.

[16] For the 13th century, see M. M. Postan and C. N. L. Brooke, *Carte Nativorum* (Northamptonshire Record Society, 22: Oxford, 1960); for the 14th century, see Anne DeWindt, "Society and Change"; for the 15th century, see Andrew Jones, "Land and People at Leighton Buzzard in the Later Fifteenth Century," *Economic History Review*, 2nd series, 25 (1972): 18-27.

[17] For an example of the modification of a more traditional picture of land dealings by a peasant family as reflected by the *Liber Gersumarum*, see my *Land and People*, pp. 132-33.

traced, and the intensity of familial land-holding as opposed to non-familial tenure is capable of assessment.[18]

In addition to the magnitude of the land market, there are the terms of tenure themselves. Over 3600 of the land entries are life-leases. What effect, if any, does the ubiquity of the limited leasehold have on the peasant and his attitude towards tenurial committments?[19] As for the obligations of tenure, over 1700 cases are definitely monetary, with 351 being specified as ad censum and arentatio tenures.[20] Less than one per cent of the land cases involves work services. The remaining entries do not specify services, but the bulk would seem to involve money rents. Even though this surely can be said to have limited landholding — and especially extensive landholding — to persons able to pay rent, a study is needed of the exact extent of the rents, as well as of the opportunities available to the peasant to accumulate capital to take on such obligations. Although individual rent packages could be high, an extended sampling of the rents recorded indicates a general equation of a shilling to the acre, with nominal entry fines and frequent discounts for repairs or maintenance obligations. The initial impression is that, although land was not necessarily cheap, neither was it discouragingly expensive, and this impression is given further substance by the existence in the *Liber Gersumarum* of a considerable number of peasants not only accumulating large blocs of property in one village, but in several villages simultaneously.[21]

As provocative as the *Liber Gersumarum* is in itself, its value as a source and tool for examining mediaeval English peasant life can be most fully realized by its use in conjunction with other contemporary materials, especially village court rolls. The exploitation of village court roll series has only recently begun,[22] but their utilization by the social historian has opened new doors to

[18] For familial and non-familial tenurial patterns in one village, see *Land and People in Holywell-cum-Needingworth*, pp. 130-35.

[19] For suggestions on this problem, see *Land and People*, pp. 134-35.

[20] The *ad censum* involved a commutation of work obligations, but, apparently, still required customary rent payments. It was present on Ramsey estates as early as the 12th century. The *arentatio* (*arentatum*), was introduced in the middle of the fourteenth century and seems to have involved a more complete schedule of commutation. For discussion of these arrangements, see Raftis, *Estates*, p. 251 et seq.; and *Land and People*, pp. 95-97.

[21] For discussion of the prosperity levels of peasant families in Holywell, see *Land and People*, pp. 193-205, 278-79. Further discussion of the so-called "standard of living" question can be found in R. H. Hilton, *A Medieval Society* (London, 1967), p. 114; J. Z. Titow, *English Rural Society* (London, 1969), Chap. 3; and M. Patricia Hogan, "Wistow: A Social and Economic Reconstitution in the Fourteenth Century," unpublished Ph.D. thesis, University of Toronto, 1971.

[22] The pioneer study of the court roll can be found in F. W. Maitland, *Select Pleas in Manorial and other Seignorial Courts* (Selden Society, 2, London, 1889), and *The Court Baron* (Selden Society, IV, London, 1891). It was not until the 1920's that serious attention was again given to this source, with the publication of W. O. Ault of *The Court Rolls of the Abbey of Ramsey and of the Honor of Clare* (New Haven, 1928), followed by G. C. Homans, *English*

the peasant world.[23] A methodology of the court roll is still incomplete,[24] but
it is already apparent that its use by the historian greatly amplifies the
meaning and application of more traditional manorial sources by locating them
in the context of peasant village society. This is especially true of the *Liber
Gersumarum*, which covers a period in the history of Ramsey Abbey when
more classic and specifically manorial sources are either lacking or deficient.[25]
Consequently, the court rolls and the *Liber Gersumarum* both complement and
supplement each other. On the one hand the latter often supplies crucial
tenurial, marital and mobility data on peasants appearing in the court rolls that
is not found in any other source. On the other hand, the court rolls give fuller
meaning to the transfers and licenses of the *Liber Gersumarum*, by relocating

Villagers of the Thirteenth Century (Cambridge, Mass., 1941). For over twenty years, Ault and
Homans were the sole defenders of the study of the court roll (see Ault, *Open-Field Husbandry
and the Village Community* (Philadelphia, 1965)). Since 1964, the court roll has won a place for
itself alongside extents and account rolls as a key source for mediaeval English society,
primarily resulting from the studies of J. A. Raftis. See, for example: "Peasant Mobility and
Freedom in Mediaeval England," *Report of the Canadian Historical Association*, 1965, 117-
130. *Tenure and Mobility* (Toronto, 1964); "The Concentration of Responsibility in Five
Villages," *Mediaeval Studies* 28 (1966): 92-118.

[23] Among areas of peasant experience recently emphasized by court rolls, for mobility see
Raftis, *Tenure and Mobility*, and a forthcoming volume of individual mobility studies, edited by
Raftis and containing contributions by Edward Britton, Ellen Wedemeyer Moore and Ann
Reiber DeWindt, *Regional Aspects of Some Peasantry in Late Thirteenth and Early Fourteenth-
Century England*.

For settlement and survival patterns of individual families, see my *Land and People*, chapter
3. For social groupings, see Ellen Wedemeyer (Moore), "Social Groupings at the Fair of St.
Ives (1275-1303)," *Mediaeval Studies*, 32 (1970): 27-59. Village violence has been probed by
Raftis in "Changes in an English Village after the Black Death", *Mediaeval Studies* 29 (1967):
158-177, while a recent article by Alfred N. May discusses the problem of peasant economic
levels from the evidence of court fines. (See "An Index of Thirteenth-Century Peasant Impoverishment? Manor Court Fines," *Economic History Review*, 2nd series, 26 (1973): 389-
402.

[24] One of the most important problems posed by court rolls is that of peasant identification.
The immense number of named peasants appearing in the records is certainly a welcome change
from the near anonymity of 12th and 13th-century manorial documents, but the precise identification of many men and women is complicated by the sheer volume of names forthcoming,
the fluctuation of surnames, the frequency of aliases, the relatively small number of Christian
names, and the haphazardness of scribes in specifying blood ties between specific peasants. A
consideration of this problem, especially concerning surnames reflecting trades or occupations,
is currently being prepared by J. A. Raftis.

Another factor contributing to the care needed in establishing a methodology is the lack of
uniformity among the extant court rolls. Not all rolls are alike, not even within the same administrative system. Among Ramsey rolls, for example, the King's Ripton rolls are rich in land
material, the Broughton rolls record information on peasant marriages not found elsewhere, the
rolls of Hemingford Abbots, Upwood and Ramsey are especially interesting for the student of
mediaeval violence. A survey of the contents of extant court rolls in England is badly needed, as
are editions of complete series of rolls.

[25] The last complete extents or surveys of Ramsey manors date from the 13th century (see
Carts., vols. I-III), while the majority of 15th-century account rolls omit tenants' lists and are
less detailed than 14th-century rolls.

them in their original, local setting, so that they are no longer isolated incidents but rather moments in the continuing histories of specific families and individuals. As examples of this broadening of the book by court rolls, the following have been chosen at random.[26]

The *Liber Gersumarum* contains seven entries involving four members of the Aylmer family of Hemingford Abbot's: John, Jr., Robert, Thomas and William.[27] The initial impression is of four men modestly involved in land; one a virgater, the others as semi-virgaters. When attention is directed to the surviving Hemingford court rolls,[28] not only is a total of nine members of the family encountered between 1400 and 1450, but the family is seen to be one of the more active ones in the village. Already resident for a century by 1400, the Aylmers display consistent involvement in both the economic and administrative life of the community. Between 1409 and 1433, two female members are regularly among the ale-brewers (*sc.* Johanna, 1409-22; Beatrix, 1423-33). John Jr., initially encountered in 1402 as a butcher, begins an administrative career in 1419 by serving on the local jury. He will be found on subsequent juries for 1422, 1423, 1428, 1429, 1432 and 1433. In the last year, he is also ale-taster, and, with his election as beadle, enters into the manorial — as distinct from the village — administration that will culminate in his serving as both reeve and tax collector in 1445 and 1446. Furthermore, it is seen that in these various roles he is but following in the footsteps of his father, John, Sr., a regular juror and taster from 1395 to 1440, constable in 1419, 1423 and 1432, beadle in 1433 and 1437, and also a butcher.[29] About Robert and William Aylmer nothing is known from the court rolls, but Thomas is recorded from 1400 through 1440. Like John Sr. and Jr., he too is a butcher, as well as an active administrator: he serves on at least nine juries and is elected reeve in 1405. Another Thomas — Jr., — is noted as a butcher, selling bad meat in 1429.

A John Newman of Ramsey is mentioned in the *Liber Gersumarum* in 1438,[30] taking up a toft and three selions of land previously held by Robert

---

[26] The subsequent sketches have been aided by the use of the Regional Data Bank at the Pontifical Institute of Mediaeval Studies, Toronto. Established under the direction of J. A. Raftis and funded by a Killam award of the Canada Council, (1972-73), the Regional Data Bank consists of an index of 4" × 6" cards containing all the known biographical information on over 10,000 peasants in 15 Huntingdonshire Ramsey villages from the mid-13th century to ca. 1450.

[27] See infra, nos. 2905, 3133, 3592, 3731, 3819, 3893.

[28] For lists of extant Ramsey court rolls, consult Raftis, *Tenure and Mobility*, pp. 289-99. For the towns of St. Ives and Ramsey, see the "Court Rolls" volume of the *Lists and Indexes of the Public Record Office* (London, 1896), pp. 210-222, and the *Index to Additional Charters and Rolls in the British Museum*, 2 vols. (London, 1900, 1912).

[29] From 1419 through 1440, John Sr. was fined 10 times for selling bad meat or charging high prices.

[30] See infra, no. 3118.

Couper. When the court rolls for Ramsey are examined, an interesting picture emerges. First of all, John Newman is the step-son of Robert Couper, whose wife, Emma, was John's mother. John enters the rolls in 1414, paying a 1d. fine for being a common dice-player. Whether he was a victim of prolonged adolescence or simply had a curious sense of humor is not known, but in 1423 he and a comrade were fined 12d. for putting willows and nettlecloth in the windows and doorways of village houses at night. He had apparently learned to control himself somewhat by 1425, for in that year he is on the local jury. In that year he is also fined for selling meat at high prices in his capacity as butcher. He is not on any subsequent juries, but he continues in his excessive demands for his products: between 1430 and 1443, he is fined three times for high prices.

The Coupers, John's relatives through his mother's marriage, constituted a modest family in the vill. John's step-father, Robert, a juror in 1430, is otherwise noted as a trespasser. Between 1389 and 1430, he is fined nine times for obstructing the common gutter and stream, polluting the stream with his latrine and with ashes, and for causing obstructions in public pathways. A Henry Couper -— possibly Robert's brother and who took up woodland in 1414[31] — was primarily remembered for not fulfilling his obligations. Between 1401 and 1422, he is fined four times for default, once for failing to come to a special investigation in which he was involved as a juror, and between 1395 and 1410 it was necessary for the court to require him on four occasions to pay his debts.

Clearly, the court roll data on the Coupers and Newmans of Ramsey is not of the same calibre as that on the Aylmers of Hemingford, but it is still informative. In the case of John Newman, a family connection is established between him and the previous tenant of his property. As for Henry, it is perhaps not insignificant that when he did take up land, it is land that would not commit him to heavy labor, such as ploughing.

Three members of the Gosse family of Little Stukeley are mentioned a total of six times in the *Liber Gersumarum*.[32] A reading of the court rolls reveals a family whose members were involved in business and personal affairs in several villages in the northern Huntingdonshire region. Thus, John Gosse, appears in the *Liber Gersumarum* in 1424 obtaining a license to marry Margaret Robbys of Abbots Ripton. Margaret is a member of a family in Abbots Ripton that, at the end of the fourteenth century, controlled over one and a half virgates of land, while John Gosse, by the date of his marriage, had already established a pattern of multi-village activity. As early as 1408 he had interests in Ramsey, being fined for default in that year and again in 1414. By

---

[31] See infra, no. 1219.
[32] See infra, nos. 267, 2059, 2148, 2198, 2521, 3138, 3293, 3679.

1430, both he and Margaret seem to have moved to Ramsey, and in 1437 they are joined by John's son, John Jr. Ramsey, in fact, attracted more than these members of the family. Richard Gosse was briefly in the vill as a butcher in 1422. He is back in Little Stukeley in 1429, but from 1437 he has abandoned the village, being off the manor with the rector of Little Stukeley. In 1454, he is noted as being at Dennys, apparently employed by monks.

Thomas Gosse, a semi-virgater in Little Stukeley, was involved in trespasses in Abbots Ripton from 1410 to 1430, while other members of the family continue the practice of multi-village activity or mobility. John, son of Thomas, is living at Wolle in 1437. William Gosse is recorded in the rolls of Little Stukeley, Abbots Ripton and Ramsey between 1386 and 1432, invariably as a trouble-maker. In Little Stukeley, for example, he has left a record of frequent assaults, breaking-and-enterings, unpaid debts and trespasses. In Abbots Ripton, he is the object of a suit by a local villager, and in Ramsey he is fined in 1422 for refusing to keep the watch. Given his apparent anti-social tendencies, it is hardly surprising to find that his son, John, has left Stukeley for Wennington by 1437.

The Gosses are a family with frequent contacts in several villages. The Martyns of Abbots Ripton, on the other hand, are an example of a family whose mobility seems to have been precipitated by a tragedy. The *Liber Gersumarum* has a brief concentration of items on the family around 1400, when William Martyn and Andrew Martyn are noted as having been virgaters, and when Thomas and John Martyn surrender their properties to other villagers.[33] In the case of Thomas Martyn, his transfer of his lands to John Green is apparently a transfer to a son-in-law.[34] In the cases of John, Andrew and William Martyn, however, another factor is involved. Specifically, in 1394 William Martyn was responsible for the violent death of Andrew Outy. He abjured the realm in that year, his property and chattels being confiscated. Within six years, the remaining members of his direct family have all left the village: John, his son, after relinquishing his virgate in 1401, is at Swavesey by 1405. Andrew and Richard, two other sons, have similarly left the vill — for parts unknown — as has a daughter, Agnes. It is possible that the homicides committed by William had resulted in social pressures on the children that made it impossible for them to continue in residence, and hence the family dispersed.

The above examples serve to illustrate the use of court rolls in expanding the context of entries in the *Liber Gersumarum*. For the Aylmers, their dominance of the village butchering trade helps clarify their modest investment in land. John Newman's land activity in Ramsey is seen as an example of familial continuity in landholding. The Gosses of Little Stukeley are a

---

[33] See infra, nos. 96, 360.
[34] See infra, no. 95.

regularly mobile family group, while the mobility of the Martyns seems to have been triggered by a murder. Additional cases could be cited,[35] but it is sufficient to emphasize the value of seeing the *Liber Gersumarum* as being extracted from a multi-faceted background of village life.

A combination of the *Liber Gersumarum* and court rolls provides opportunities for several different studies on the English peasantry in the early fifteenth century. For example, in addition to questions raised by the land entries,[36] the marriage and exodus licenses suggest areas of investigation for the social historian. The marriage licences, firstly, frequently assist in the matter of peasant identification, since marital and paternal ties are not always clear in the court rolls. In addition, the marriage licenses demand investigation of the question of whether or not there was a pattern of inter-marriage between families of similar social or economic positions.[37] Finally, the fact that approximately 12% of the marriages recorded are mixed marriages — between freemen and villeins — is worth noting, and invites closer examination of the entire marriage question through the evidence of village sources as well as ecclesiastical court rolls.[38]

In addition to peasant marriage patterns, the *Liber Gersumarum* affords a good opportunity for probing the question of peasant mobility. There are over 1600 individual surnames in the text, more than half of which are present in two or more villages. It remains to be determined how many of these represented multi-village families, and, once established, what the actual blood and social ties were. Finally, there is the major question of the regionalism of peasant experience. This is a phenomenon already noted by Professor DuBoulay for the Canterbury estates,[39] but it was not unique to south-east England. The fact that there were two market towns among the Ramsey Huntingdonshire estates alone — St. Ives and Ramsey itself — raises questions about the relation of the countryside to these towns,[40] while virtually un-

---

[35] For a study of land holding in the *Liber Gersumarum* in light of the social positions of its participants from one village, see my *Land and People*, Chapter 2.

[36] It should be noted that almost one-quarter of the transfers involve dilapidated properties. In addition, approximately one-fifth of the properties are described as having buildings. This, coupled with the rapid turnover in land, suggests that the peasant economy was shifting from direct cultivation to real estate speculation and pastoral activities. A detailed investigation is needed.

[37] This problem is already under investigation for the Hungtingdonshire region by Edward Britton.

[38] For ecclesiastical court rolls, see especially Michael M. Sheehan, "The Formation and Stability of Marriage in Fourteenth-Century England: Evidence of an Ely Register," *Mediaeval Studies*, 33 (1971): 228-263. For recent work on the Canterbury courts, see Charles Donahue Jr. and Jeanne P. Gordus, "A Case From Archbishop Stratford's Audience Act Book," *Bulletin of Medieval Canon Law*, 2nd series, 2 (1972), 45-59.

[39] See F. R. H. DuBoulay, *The Lordship of Canterbury* (New York, 1966).

[40] Among rural families active in the towns, the Aungewyns of Hemingford Abbots appear

touched are the relationships between Ramsey peasants and the two non-Ramsey urban centers of Huntingdon and Godmanchester.[41] There is much, therefore, that needs to be investigated in the matter of peasant regionalism. Especially important as regards peasant regionalism is the extent to which the lives of Ramsey peasants by the fifteenth century were focused less on one vill than on a multiplicity of villages and towns.[42] Only a thorough exploitation of all available Ramsey sources can help answer these questions, and the *Liber Gersumarum*, being the major repository of tenurial information, occupies an important place among these sources.

III
The *Liber Gersumarum*: the Format of the Calendar

It has not been the purpose of the present writer to present a full and detailed analysis of the *Liber Gersumarum*, or to conduct an exhaustive study of the implications of its contents for Ramsey estate management or the social and economic history of the monastery's peasants. To do full justice to the volume requires a mastery of several disciplines. Certainly it will require the talents of more than one person before its potential is exhausted. Consequently, because the text is both an object of research in itself and a tool for broader historical research, a calendar of its contents has been produced, so that it may have as wide as possible a circulation among scholars.

Originally, it was intended to produce a critical edition of the full Latin text.[43] However, it soon became apparent that a complete edition was unnecessary. Firstly, the text has no inherent literary value. Secondly, the entries in the manuscript are *formulae*, and only five basic *formulae* are employed

in St. Ives as landlords; the Wests of Abbots Ripton are in Ramsey as tenants; and the Outys, present in several northern Huntingdonshire vills, function in Ramsey as tradesmen. For a recent examination of the connection between urban centers and their rural surroundings in the Middle Ages, see J. C. Russell, *Medieval Regions and their Cities* (Bloomington, 1972).

Of the Ramsey towns in question, St. Ives is currently being investigated by Ellen Wedemeyer Moore, while a study of Ramsey, from 1250 to 1450, will shortly be undertaken by the present writer and his wife.

[41] The court rolls of mediaeval Godmanchester are in the process of being incorporated into the Regional Data Bank at the Pontifical Institute. Court rolls for Huntingdon from the second half of the 14th century through the reign of Henry VI are currently preserved in Huntingdon, at the Borough Archives. I owe this information to Mr. P. G. M. Dickinson.

[42] A preliminary examination of regional activities of Ramsey peasants in Huntingdonshire in the 14th century is being prepared by Anne Reiber DeWindt. Also see her "The King's Ripton Land Market," *Mediaeval Studies* (in press).

[43] Prof. J. A. Raftis announced an edition of the manuscript in 1957 (See *Estates*, p. 322). Unfortunately, the project had to be abandoned by him due to other urgent demands. In 1968, I received permission from Prof. Raftis to take over the project.

throughout the text. Variations within them are minimal, either concerning the omission of a phrase or word, the addition of a co-tenant, or minor changes in word order.[44] What is important about the text, in fact, is not so much its language as the data to be extracted from it, and this can be transmitted by a calendar just as well as by an edition.

In preparing the following calendar, I have sought to faithfully reproduce the contents of each entry. All material of a biographical, financial and statistical nature has been retained. The only exclusions have been repetitive and standardized *formulae*. In the cases of entries from St. Ives and Ramsey, where the standard *formulae* for land transfers are distinct, a full summary has been given at their first appearance, with an abbreviated notation employed thereafter.[45]

Concerning the spellings of personal and place-names, I have decided to leave unaltered all variant spellings of personal names or field names in the manuscript. Firstly, it is hazardous to arbitrarily settle on one spelling over several others when the scribes themselves were inconsistent. Secondly, I am aware of the possible interest of the text to surname and linguistic scholars, for whom the spelling of a name is frequently an aide to understanding its pronunciation. Consequently, such names have been left in their original forms. A process of standardization has been employed for them only in the Index, and even there I have not used the modern form of a name as basic, but rather the form most often employed by the scribes.

Regarding place-names of villages and towns, since the work of the Place-Name Society has virtually exhausted the various forms of these names for the Ramsey estate regions, I have standardized them, using the publications of the Place-Name Society and the *Concise Oxford Dictionary of English Place-Names* as my guides.

Concerning the dates of individual entries, I have modernized them when possible, substituting the day, date and month for the manuscript's dating by feast-days.

---

[44] One distinctive formula is confined to land entries for St. Ives (see infra, p. 22, note 5), another for Ramsy (see infra, p. 37, note 13). The remaining villages are characterized by one basic formula, with slight variations. (In the following example, I have indicated the variations in brackets).

"(N) cepit de domino (....) que (N) nuper [quondam, prius] tenuit, tenendum eidem [et (N) uxori ejus] ad voluntatem domini secundum consuetudinem manerii ad terminum vite, reddendo et faciendo inde domino per annum [in omnibus sicut (N) prius reddere et facere consuevit] [omnia servitia et consuetudines inde debita et consueta]. Et dat in gersuma (....)."

A fourth formula is employed for marriage (e.g. "(N) dat domino pro licentia se maritandi (N)" or "cuicumque voluerit". The fifth formula is for exodus licenses: "(N) dat domino pro licentia manendi extra feudum [apud (N)] ..., reddendo domino annuatim (N), et veniet ad letam annuatim."

[45] See infra, p. 22, note 5 and p. 37, n. 13.

Finally, because the calendar is basically a summary of data, I have kept the notes to a minimum, confined to indicating whether entries are reflected in surviving court rolls, and to the explication of unusual terms or phrases. *Lacunae* in the text have been indicated in the calendar by parentheses.

Three indices — of places, of persons and of selected subjects — have been appended to the calendar to facilitate its use.

THE *LIBER GERSUMARUM* (B.L. HARLEY MS. 445)

Calendar

3 THOMAS BUTTERWYK (1398-1399)

1r **1** CRANFIELD (May 1399) John Berford: surrender, through Thomas Jaye, bailiff, of one messuage and one virgate of servile land, previously held by William (of the Feld?)[1], to the use of Thomas Aleyn of Estende and his wife, Alicia, in bondage for life, rendering annually in all things as John had done. G.[2]: 12d., and no more, because the tenement is in ruins.

2 CRANFIELD (18 May) Walter Rydeler: one messuage and one half-virgate of servile land, previously held by Matillis Rydeler, his mother, to be held by him in bondage for life, rendering annually in all things as did his mother: 12d., and no more, because he is a pauper.

3 WARBOYS (June) Thomas Barbat, his wife, Alicia, and son, Thomas: one tenement previously held by John Hygh, together with nine rods, two and a half acres in Lowefurlong, and one acre of demesne in Stokkyng, to be held by them in bondage, saving the right of anyone, for life, rendering annually in all things as did John.

4 CHATTERIS (June) John Bocher: surrender of one cote, to the use of John Cut of Ely, for life, rendering annually in all things as did John Bocher.

5 CHATTERIS (June) Katerina, widow of John Thomesson: surrender of one cote previously held by her husband, to the use of her son, John, for life, rendering all services and customs owed therein.

1v **6** WISTOW (26 June: court) Nicholas Martyn of Little Raveley: one plot with building and one virgate of servile land in Little Raveley previously held by Stephen Hyche, in *arentatio*[3] rendering annually 16s. at the customary times, as well as performing boon ploughing and autumn boon works, sheep-shearing, and mowing of the lord's meadow in Thornbriggemede, as do certain of his peers. G.: 12d.

7 HEMINGFORD ABBOTS (Early May) John Baker: two messuages and two virgates of servile land, previously held by William Baroun, to be held in bondage for life, rendering annually in all things as did William. G.: 10s.

8 ABBOTS RIPTON (July) William Ledde: one plot with building and a virgate of servile land, previously held by his father, Philip Ledde, to be held in bondage for life, rendering annually in all things as did his father.

9 ABBOTS RIPTON (July) Same William Ledde the same day and same year: one empty plot and one virgate of servile land previously held by his father, Philip Ledde, in *arentatio*, for life, rendering annually 14s. at the customary times. G.: 12d.

10 ABBOTS RIPTON (5 July) John Haulond Sr.: one parcel of one vacant plot and one quarter of servile land, previously held by Roger Godmer, in *arentatio*, for life, rendering annually 4s. at the customary times. G.: 12d.

11 ABBOTS RIPTON (5 July) Thomas Wattes: one built up cote, previously held by his father, for as long as he is in the lord's service as shepherd, rendering annually 12d. as new rent and two hens at the terms of Easter and the Nativity of Blessed Mary,

---

[1] The name is partially obliterated in the manuscript.
[2] G. = *Gersuma*.
[3] See supra, p. 9, note 20, for a discussion of *ad censum* and *arentatio* tenures.

as his father was accustomed to render. The same Thomas also receives three acres of demesne land, for the same terms as above, rendering annually (*blank*). G.: one capon.

2r **12** St. Ives (10 July) John Makeseye, his wife, Alicia, and daughter, Alicia: one half-row next to the pillory, previously held by William Tadelowe, for life, rendering annually 24s. at the customary times. Further, they will repair and maintain all buildings and houses well and competently, both in carpentry and roofing and in all other necessities, at their own expense, and they will be obedient to the abbot and his successors and his bailiffs in the observation of all articles posited and listed in the *gersumae* of other tenants of St. Ives effected in the time of abbot Robert.[4] G.: 40d.

13 St. Ives (9 July) Thomas Freman, his wife, Margaret, and their daughter, Alicia: one half-row lying between the tenement of John Chamberleyn and that of Isabella Martyn and previously held by John Makeseye and his wife, Alicia, for life, rendering annually 20s. at the customary times. Further, they will repair and maintain all buildings and houses well and competently, both in carpentry and roofing and in all other necessities, at their own expense. Nor will they put themselves under the protection of any other lord to the prejudice of the lord abbot or to the damage of their neighbors under penalty of confiscation of the property. They will also be obedient to the lord and his successors in the observation of all articles posited and listed in the *gersumae* of other tenants of St. Ives effected in the time of abbot Robert, and if, in the future, they are rebellious to any of the articles, they will be expelled from the property, this *gersuma* not withstanding. Further, Margaret, should she survive her husband, shall not be permitted to take another husband without the lord's license, under penalty of confiscation. Further, the front of the half-row shall be reserved to the lord during the time of the fair.[5] G.: one half-mark and no more because of a rent increase of 2s.

2v **14** St. Ives (9 July) John Edenham, chaplain, William Edenham and his wife, Johanna: one and a half rows, previously held by Thomas Baa, for life, rendering annually 32s. at the customary times, with the obligation to maintain all buildings on the property in good repair at their own expense. Et non licebit, etc. G.: 2s., and no more, because they have paid other *gersumae*.

15 St. Ives (9 July) John Bailly, Sr., his wife, Katerina, and their daughters, Alicia and Anota: a half-row previously held by Ambrose Newynton and recently burned, for life, rendering annually 5s., with the first payment due at the next Easter, and with the obligation to rebuild the property within one year from Michaelmas. *Et non licebit*, etc. G.: excused, because of repairs.

---

[4] Robert Nassington, abbot of Ramsey, January, 1342-July, 1349.

[5] The latter part of this entry (i.e. beginning "Nor will they", etc.) consists of a formula that will be repeated, with but the slightest variations (i.e. omissions or abbreviations to "etc.") in St. Ives entries throughout the remainder of the manuscript. The full Latin text is: "Et non licebit eis ponere se in advocacione alterius domini in preiudicium domini abbatis seu ad nocementum vicinorum suorum sub pena amissionis dimidie rengie predicte, set quod de cetero erunt obedientes domino abbati at successoribus suis in observatione omnium articulorum positorum et nominatorum in gersumis aliorum tenencium de vico sancti Ivonis factis tempore domini Robert abbatis. Et si rebelles in aliquo articulo in posterum inveniantur de predicta dimidia rengia expellantur hac gersuma in aliquo non obstante. Et non licebit in posterum prefate (Margarete) si supervixerit eundem (Thomam) maritum accipere sine licencia domini sub pena predicta. Frons vero dicte dimidie rengie tempore ferie domino reservetur."

Henceforth, this formula will be indicated by the phrase: *Et non licebit*.

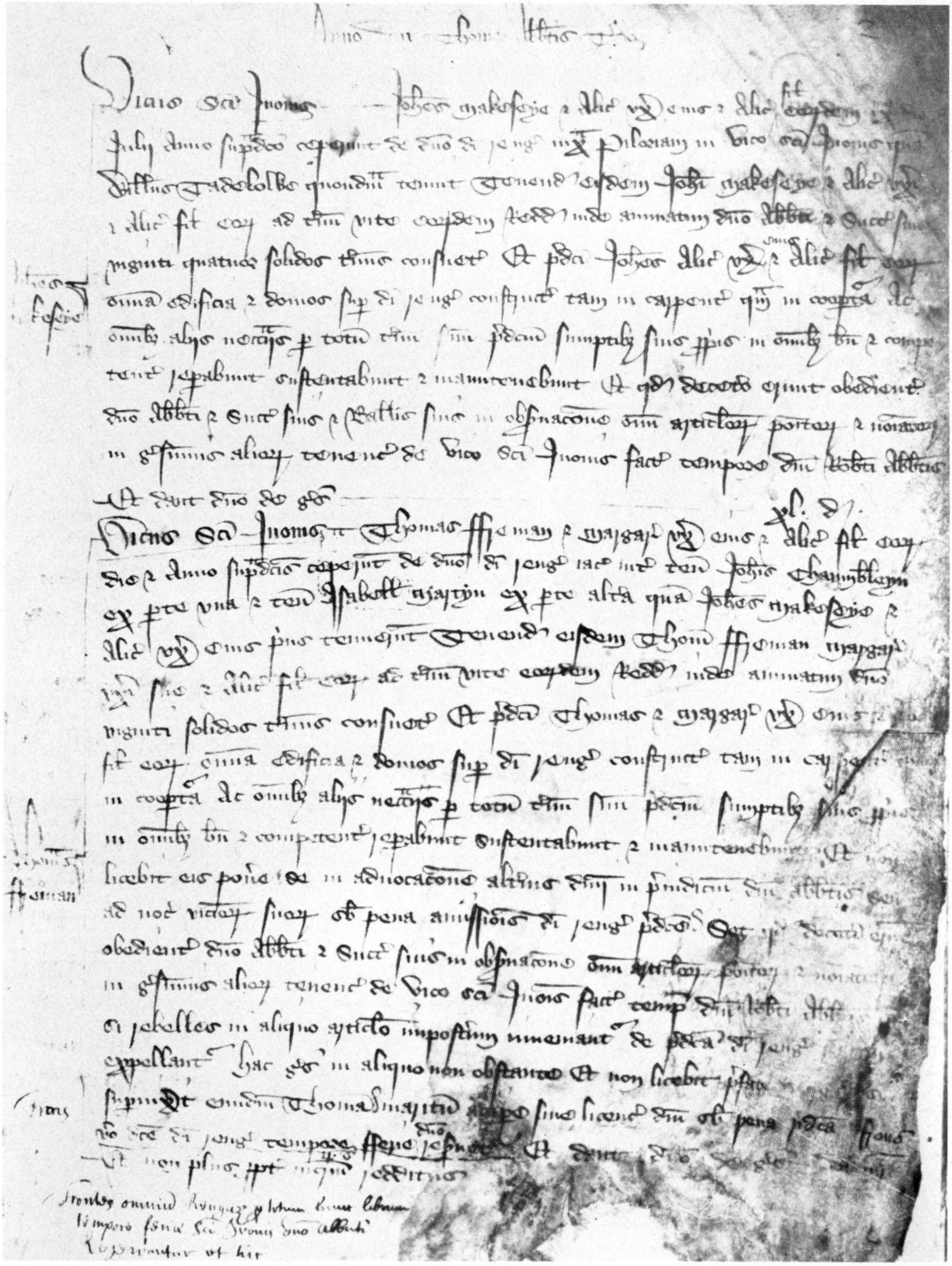

B.L. Harl. MS. 445, f. 2r. (See infra, nos. 13-14).

3r **16** St. Ives (July) John Wyllymot: a half-row previously held by William Bernewell, with his wife, Alicia, and their daughter, Johanna, for life, rendering annually 10s., with the obligation to maintain the property in good repair. *Et non licebit*, etc. G.: 40d.

17 Therfield (11 July) Johanna, daughter of Robert AtteWode and naif of the lord, pays 40d. for license to marry Thomas Wyngor, Jr., naif of the lord. Further, Johanna and Thomas: one messuage and one half-virgate previously held by Thomas Wyngor, Sr., in bondage, rendering annually in all things as did Thomas Sr. G.: a half-mark.

18 Barton (22 July: court) Andrew Chauncellor and his wife, Isabella: one croftland[6] and one cotland previously held by John Stonle, for life, saving the right of anyone, rendering annually in all things as did John. G.: 40d.

3v **19** Barton (22 July) Johanna, daughter of Edmund Barnard: one cote with curtilage and one acre of servile land previously held by Alicia Wyse, in bondage for life, rendering annually in all things as did Alicia. G.: 12d.

20 Barton (22 July: court) Isabella, daughter of Henry Atte Grene: one messuage and one virgate of servile land previously held by Johanna Wodeward, in bondage for life, rendering annually in all things as did Johanna. G.: 13s.4d.

21 Shillington (23 July: court) Amicia, daughter of John Wyldefowle and naif of the lord, pays 40d. for license to marry John Catelyne, freeman.

22 Shillington (23 July) Peter Breton, alias Cook: one messuage recently held by Nicholas othe Abbeye, for life, rendering annually 40d. Also: three acres of demesne land in le Stockyng, recently held by the same Nicholas, for life, rendering annually 12d. per acre. G.: 20d., and no more, because Peter will build up the tenement at his own expense.

23 Shillington (23 July: court) Emma, daughter of Thomas West and naif of the lord, pays 6s. for license to marry whomever she wishes.

24 Shillington (23 July) Margeria, daughter of Richard Atte Grene and naif of the lord, pays 6s.8d. for license to marry Adam Iryssheman, freeman.

25 Shillington (23 July) Thomas Bradefan: five acres of demesne land lying at Chirchehill and parcelled out of eight acres previously held by Robert Stonle, from the previous Michaelmas for twenty years, rendering annually 6d. per acre at the customary times. G.: excused by the seneschal.

4r **26** Shillington (23 July) John Kychener: one cotland previously held by Nicholas othe Abbeye, for life, rendering annually 3s. G.: 2s.

27 Shillington (23 July) John Waryn: one messuage and half of one virgate of servile land, the other half of which is held by William Coche, in bondage, for life, rendering annually all services and customs previously rendered, with the condition that if anyone later wants to dwell on that messuage and, in the judgment of the court and his neighbors, can pay John for his expenses on the property, he shall be allowed to take possession of the land, without any contradiction from the said John. G.: 2s.

28 Shillington (23 July) Robert Atte Grene and his son, John: one plot with building in the common, for life, rendering annually 8d. at the feast of the Annunciation. G.: 8d.

29 Shillington (23 July) Nicholas Laurence: two messuages, one of them with a building, two virgates of servile land, and all the demesne land previously held by Thomas Atte Made and surrendered by him to the said Nicholas, together with nine

---

[6] See Appendix 2 for the known acreages of customary land units (i.e. virgates, cotlands, crofts) on Ramsey estates.

acres of demesne in Newmanlond recently held by the same Thomas, in bondage, for life, rendering annually in all things as did Thomas. G.: excused, because of new repairs to be done to a house by Nicholas. Pledges for repairs: John Laurence and John Beeston.

30 SHILLINGTON (23 July: court) William Coche: one meadow, recently in the lord's hands, called Milnemade, for as long as he serves in the office of bailiff, rendering annually 6d. at the feast of St. Peter in Chains, with the obligation of supplying hay for the horses of the lord, his seneschals and his clerks for one day and one night when they come, as well as for the *famuli* of the lord, whenever they come. Further, he will supply hay sufficient for two carts to John Tydy, as John was accustomed to receive before, as set down in his charter. Further, the lord will be kept free from damages regarding both the said John and all others during the aforesaid time. G.: one capon.

4v   **31** THERFIELD (25 July: court) William, son of John Waryn, and Isabella, daughter of John Noke: one messuage and a half-virgate and one quarter of servile land previously held by John Jankyn, Sr., in bondage, for life, rendering annually in all things as did John. G.: 100s., of which 20s. are relaxed at the request of the rector of Therfield and others.

32 THERFIELD (25 July: court) John Ordemare and his wife, Agnes: 10 acres of demesne land lying in various parcels and previously held by Henry Thurrene, for life, rendering annually in all things as did Henry. G.: 2s.

33 BURWELL (2 August: court) William Taillor, alias Poket, and John Toys: the fishpond of la Nesse, with adjoining meadows and ponds and the mill-dam, previously held by Richard Fr13aunceys, from the previous Michaelmas for 10 years, rendering this year 10s., and each year thereafter 11s.4d. at the customary times. Further, they will maintain the properties, both regarding ditches and all other necessities, at their own expense, with the exception that the bailiff will assign 20 *opera* of the customaries of the lord in assistance, and the customaries will be suitably rewarded by the *firmarii* when they come. Further, the lord will be kept free of damage regarding anyone by them during the aforesaid time. G.: excused, because of a rent increase of 40d.

34 BURWELL (2 August: same court) Helena, daughter of Thomas Sparwe and naif of the lord, pays 5s. for license to marry whomever she wishes, this time.[7]

35 BURWELL (2 August: same court) William Ideygne: one tenement of 15 acres of servile land without buildings, once held by his father, located next to Tyceshous, *ad censum* from the previous Michaelmas for life, rendering annually all services and customs rendered by other tenants who hold *ad censum*.

5r   **35a** ELTON (7 August: court) Henry Balle: one messuage with building and a half-virgate of servile land previously held by John Purcas, in bondage for life, rendering annually in all things as did John. G.: two capons.

36 HOLYWELL (11 August: court) William Prykke: the windmill from the previous Michaelmas for seven years, rendering annually 20s. at the feast of the Annunciation, the first payment already being due. Further, he will repair and maintain the windmill at his own expense during the whole period, with the exception of heavy timber and its transport and six oak boards for repairing and improving the walls of the mill supplied by the lord.

37 RAMSEY (13 September) John Bonde: during the time of Thomas de Pilton, sub-cellarer of Ramsey, one messuage with appurtenances in Ramsey lying in the Whyte and previously held by John Schirwode, from the next Michaelmas for a term of 40

---

[7] MS.: "*hac vice*".

years, rendering annually 10s. in equal portions at the feasts of the Annunciation and the Nativity of Blessed Mary. Further, he will repair and maintain well and competently all buildings and houses on the messuage, both in carpentry and roofing and in all other necessities during the whole term, at his own expense, except for timber being supplied by the lord when necessary.

38 RAMSEY (13 September) John Bonde: one piece of demesne meadow called "Lytilhydyke" previously held by Laurence Mildecombe, for 40 years, rendering annually 3s. in equal portions at the feasts of the Annunciation and the Nativity of Blessed Mary. Further, he will not relinquish or dismiss the tenement during the aforesaid time to anyone without having sought and obtained the lord's permission. Further, if the rent at any term is either totally or partially in arrears for seven weeks,[8] or if he does not observe any of the said conditions, then the lord, his ministers or attornies can take back all the tenements with their appurtenances and hold them in their original state without contradiction. G.: 2s.

5v **39** RAMSEY (14 September) John Borell, his wife, Beatrix and their son, John: through the hands of Thomas de Pilton, sub-cellarer, one newly built up plot with its appurtenances, previously held by John Smuddyng and lying in the Whyte next to the tenement now held by Thomas Wayte, John, for life, rendering annually 8s. in equal portions at the feasts of the Annunciation and the Nativity of Blessed Mary. Further, he will not relinquish or dismiss, etc. *Et si predictus redditus* (seven weeks' arrears). G.: 3s.4d.

40 RAMSEY (14 September) Simon Milnere: one-half of one messuage in Bridge Street previously held by Katerina Clerk, the other half of which is now held by Richard Betele, for life, rendering annually 12s. in equal portions at the feasts of the Annunciation and the Nativity of Blessed Mary. Further, he will not relinquish or dismiss, etc. *Et si predictus redditus* (7 weeks' arrears). G: 2s.

41 RAMSEY (14 September) John Orfreyser, alias Pryouresclerk: one messuage in Bridge Street previously held by Alan Colewyck, for life, rendering annually 12s. in equal portions at the feasts of the Annunciation and the Nativity of Blessed Mary. Further, he will repair and maintain the property and will not relinquish or dismiss it without license. *Et si predictus redditus* (7 weeks' arrears). G.: 3s.4d.

6r *Blank*

4 THOMAS BUTTERWYK (1399-1400)

6v **42** HOUGHTON and HEMINGFORD ABBOTS (29 September 1399: leet with court) William, son of Galfridus Smyth of Houghton, and Stephen Fuller of Hemingford Abbot's: the water mill of Houghton and Hemingford from the previous Michaelmas for 10 years, rendering annually 20 marks in equal portions at the feasts of the Annunciation and the Nativity of Blessed Mary. Further they will repair and maintain the mill and all that pertains to it for the whole term, in stones, iron work, timber, roofing, carpentry, and all other necessities, with the lord supplying timber and its transport and an allocation of *opera* of his customaries for supplying water when necessary. Further, they will not give away the mill to anyone without the lord's license, and they will also receive a half-mark annually from the manor of Huntingdon and one small boat supplied by the lord for transport. In addition they receive the whole fishpond in Houghton and Hemingford for 10 years, rendering annually 13s. Pledge: Galfridus Smyth.

---

[8] This condition reappears regularly in Ramsey entries, differences being in the amount of time allowed, and in the penalty: seizure or the imposition of distraints. Henceforth, this formula will be expressed as *Et si predictus redditus*.

43   BURWELL (6 October: leet without court) Richard Spencer: five acres of demesne land, of which three acres lie in Dychefeld at Galewhyll and two acres in Estfeld at Buntynges Paath, from the previous Michaelmas for nine years, rendering annually 5s. at the customary times. G.: excused.

44   BURWELL (6 October) Margaret, daughter of Simon Styward and naif of the lord, pays 5s. for license to marry whomever she wishes, this time.

45   BURWELL (6 October) William Westmorland pays 8d. for license to marry Agnes, daughter of Thomas Swyn and naif of the lord. And he pays no more because he is a pauper.

46   BURWELL (6 October) Richard Gardener: one cote with croft previously held *ad censum* by Thomas Sawyer, in *arentatio* from Michaelmas for 10 years, rendering annually 6s. at the customary times. G.: 6d.

47   SHILLINGTON (10 October: leet with court) William Coche, his wife, Margeria, and their son, Matthew: the hall with adjoining rooms, the kitchen, bake house, kiln, and other buildings within the manor of Shillington, namely: Abbot's Dower, the dovecote with adjacent garden, and a certain parcel of the large garden lying at the pasture as meted and bounded, together with other sections of garden and pasture, for 7r   life, rendering annually 6s.8d. Further, the hall, with the principal room, kitchen and all other buildings within the manor reserved to the lord, his seneschal and others of the lord's household when they come. Further, the said *firmarii* are obligated to repair and maintain the property, except that they will reasonably have *housbote, haybote* and *firbote* from the lord, as much and as often as is necessary.

48   SHILLINGTON (10 October: leet with court) William Coche, and his wife, Margeria: as much demesne land, with meadow and pasture, as the two other *firmarii* now hold, for life, rendering annually all services and customs owed therein. G.: two capons.

49   SHILLINGTON John Barfoot, son of John Sr., and Walter, his brother, naifs of the lord, pay 6d. for license to live off the fief, rendering annually 12d. as chevage at the leet, which they will attend yearly. Pledge: John Barfoot, their father.

50   BARTON (11 October: General Court) Johanna Child: one messuage and one virgate of servile land previously held by her husband, Richard Child, for life. G.: 5s.

51   BARTON (11 October) Same Johanna Child: one cotland previously held by her husband, for life, rendering annually all services and customs owed therein. G.: 20d.

52   CRANFIELD (13 October: leet with court) John Sare: surrender of one quarter of servile land to the use of John Aleyn of Wodend for life, rendering annually all services and customs owed therein. G.: 18d. John Sare is to pay 2s. as heriot.

53   CRANFIELD (13 October: same leet) Thomas othe Hirst: surrender of one messuage and one half-virgate of servile land to the use of John Sare for life, on condition that he maintains Thomas in food and clothing for the rest of his life. G.: 2s. Thomas is to pay 8d. as heriot.

54   CRANFIELD (13 October: same leet) John Cook pays the fine for license to grant Thomas Terry one messuage and one half-virgate of servile land from Michaelmas for 12 years, rendering annually all services and customs owed therein.

7v   **55**   BYTHORNE (15 October: leet with court) Stephen othe Hill: one messuage, one quarter and a half of one quarter of servile land, previously held by William othe Hill, for life, rendering annually all services and customs owed therein. G.: excused, because the land pertains to the farm.

56   ELTON (16 October: leet with court) Richard Abbot: surrender of one empty plot of one quarter of servile, once held by Stephen Wryghte to the use of Richard Best, in *arentatio*, for life, rendering annually all services and customs owed therein. G.: one capon.

57 ELTON (16 October: same court) Roger Milnere: one messuage and one half-virgate of land once held by Adam Godeswayn and recently surrendered back to the lord by John Barker, for life, rendering annually in all things as did John. G.: 12d.

58 WISTOW (23 October: leet with court) Peter Wakyr: surrender of one quarter of servile land parcelled out of a virgate once held by Walter Gernoun, to the use of John Chartres of St. Ives, from the next Michaelmas in *arentatio*, for life, rendering annually in all things as did Peter. G.: 6d.

59 UPWOOD (22 October: leet with court) William Hacoun: surrender of all his lands and tenements in Upwood, to the use of Nicholas Hendesson of Hemingford Grey and his wife, Johanna, for life, rendering annually in all things as did William, with the condition that one *camera* in the manse called "le Schopp" and one acre of arable in two fields be reserved to William and his wife, Cristina, for life. G.: one capon, and no more, because the tenements are in ruins.

8r **60** HOLYWELL (25 October: leet with court) John Scot and John Schephird, Jr.: the reversion of the demesne meadow called Dryhirst, now held by Roger Houghton and John Schephird Sr., for life, rendering annually 15s. at the feast of the Translation of St. Benedict. G.: 2s.

61 HOLYWELL (25 October: same court) John Hemyngton: one acre of demesne land in Brerecroft previously held by John Porter, for life, rendering annually 18d. at the customary times. G.: 3d.

62 HOLYWELL (25 October: same court) John Shepperd, Sr.: two acres of demesne land in Brerecroft, for life, rendering annually 18d. per acre at the customary times. G.: 6d.

62a HOLYWELL (25 October: same court) Radulph Muryell: one acre of demesne land in Netherbrerecroft, for life, rendering annually 14d. at the customary times. G.: 3d.

63 HOLYWELL (25 October: same court) John Cartere: one cote with adjacent croft once held by William Baroun, for life, rendering annually in all things as did William. G.: 3d.

64 GRAVELEY (28 October: leet with court)[9] Robert Danyell: one messuage and one semi-virgate of servile land previously held by Galfridus Benet, in bondage for life, with the obligation to maintain the capital messuage and the bake house built upon it in good repair at his own expense, rendering annually all services and customs owed therein. G.: 6d.

8v **65** ELSWORTH (29 October: leet with court) Walter Bale of Yelling, his wife and son: one plot with building and one quarter of servile land once held by Roger Lucas, together with another plot with building and one quarter of servile land once held by William Dryvere, and one quarter of servile land called Sewyneslond previously held by Thomas Newman Sr., for life, rendering annually all services and customs that the previous tenants rendered. G.: 13s.4d.

66 ELSWORTH (29 October: same court) Thomas Smart: surrender of one croft and one quarter of servile land in le Grane once held by Robert Catelynesson, one croft lying next to the aforesaid croft and another croft lying next to a croft held by John Gagge, also in le Grave, together with one cote with a building on it once held by Alan Smart, to the use of Robert Swynford, for life, rendering annually 12s.6d. at the customary times. G.: nothing.

[9] See B.L. Add. Roll. 39476. The entry is not in the roll.

67 GRAVELEY (October)[10] Walter Newman: one empty plot and a half virgate of servile land called Cacheslond previously held by John Harveys, in *arentatio*, for life, rendering annually 6s.8d. at the customary times. G.: six capons.

9r **68** HEMINGFORD ABBOTS (7 November) Agnes, daughter of Henry Cok through the hands of William Baroun, pays the seneschal of Ramsey 6s.8d., for license to live off the manor and to marry whomever she wishes, this time.

69 WISTOW (November) Katerina, daughter of Thomas Outy, pays 4s. for license to marry John Gouler, freeman and bastard.

70 RAMSEY (9 November) John Merywedir and his wife, Isabella: during the time of Brother Thomas de Pilketon, sub-cellarer, the reversion of a certain messuage with all its appurtenances in Ramsey, built next to the lane called Koolane and now held for life by Alan Fyne and previously held by John Grigge, for life, rendering annually 6s., with the obligation to maintain the property in good repair at their own expense. G.: four capons.

71 ST. IVES (November) John Wyllymot, his wife, Alicia, and their son, John: one row recently burned and previously held by Ambrose Newington and once held by Nicholas Hayward, from the previous Michaelmas for life, rendering annually 5s. at the customary times, with the first payment due next Easter. Further, they will build up the front of the row with proper buildings at their own expense within two years. *Et non licebit*, etc. G.: 2s.

9v **72** BIGGING (15 November) William Edward of Upwood: during the time of Brother Thomas de Pilketon, sub-cellarer, a certain piece of meadow called "Tunstedemedowe," for life, rendering annually 3s. in equal portions at the feasts of the Annunciation and the Nativity of Blessed Mary, with the condition he cannot relinquish or grant out that land to anyone without the lord's permission. G.: two capons.

73 WARBOYS (November) John Edward: and his son, Thomas: two tenements previously held by John Stapilford, in bondage, rendering annually in all things as did John Stapilford. G.: 10s.

74 ABBOTS RIPTON (November) John Swon: surrender of one cote with two butts of adjacent land, to the use of William Smyth, in bondage, for life, rendering annually in all things as did John. G.: 12d.

75 WARBOYS (November) John Wattesson: one mondayland previously held by Thomas Hunte and seven acres of demesne land in diverse parcels also held by Thomas Hunte, for life, rendering annually in things as did Thomas. Pledges for maintaining the property: Richard Berenger and Henry Norburgh. G.: 3s.

76 ELSWORTH (3 December) Nicholas Cook: surrender of one messuage, three quarters of servile land in le Juhom and one quarter of land in Grave, to the use of John Elyot Smyth, in bondage, for life, rendering annually in all things as did Nicholas. G.: 5s.

10r **77** SLEPE (December) William Herrof, his wife, Juliana, and daughter, Emma: one plot with building with adjacent curtilage previously held by Simon Herrof, in bondage for life, rendering annually 13s.4d. in equal portions at the customary times. G.: excused by the seneschal.

78 CRANFIELD (December) Walter Rideler: surrender, through the hands of Thomas Joye, bailiff, of one quarter of servile land, to the use of Thomas Mons, in bondage, for life, rendering annually in all things as did Walter. G.: 18d.

---

[10] Ibid., entry not in roll.

79 BYTHORNE (December) Margaret, daughter of John Sachebien and naif of the lord, pays 2s. for license to marry Thomas Bole, freeman, within the domain.

80 BYTHORNE (December) Thomas Bole: one messuage and one quarter of servile land previously held by John Sachebien, in bondage, for life, rendering annually in all things as did John. G.: 2s.

81 ABBOTS RIPTON (December) John Houlot: one messuage and one quarter of servile land in Wennington previously held by William Smyth, in *arentatio* for life, rendering annually 4s.6d. at the customary times. G.: 2s.

82 ABBOTS RIPTON (December) Same John Houlot and Andrew Swon: one toft and one quarter of servile land previously held by Roger Godmar, in *arentatio* for life, rendering annually 3s. at the customary times. G.: 6d.

83 ELSWORTH (December) John Neweman: one cote with building previously held by Alan Taillor and more recently held by Thomas Neweman, together with the third part of one virgate once of St. Luke's land and recently held by the same Thomas, in bondage, for life, rendering annually in all things as did Thomas. G.: 3s., to be paid to the seneschal of Ramsey.

10v **84** ELSWORTH (December) John Aleynesson: one cote called "Baldewynesyerd," previously held by Thomas Newman, in bondage for life, rendering annually in all things as did Thomas, with the obligation to rebuild the cote with proper buildings at his own expense within two years, lumber being supplied by the lord. G.: 6d.

85 WISTOW (4 January) Stephen de Ely: one plot with building and adjoining forge previously held by Walter Smyth, for life, rendering annually 3s.4d. at the customary times. G.: 6d.

86 WISTOW (4 January) Same Stephen de Ely: one acre of demesne land in le Lowefeld, previously held by John atte Gate, for life, rendering annually 8d. at the customary times. G.: excused by the seneschal.

87 BROUGHTON (4 January) William Clerc: one cotman's tenement previously held by John Clerc, for life, rendering annually in all things as did John. G.: 6d.

88 BROUGHTON (4 January) John Cabe: one messuage and one virgate of servile land previously held by John Coupere, in bondage *ad censa*, rendering annually 12s. at the customary times, with the first payment due at Michaelmas after one complete year. G.: 6d.

89 WISTOW (6 January) John Asplond: surrender, in the presence of Brother Richard, seneschal of Ramsey, of one quarter of servile land in Little Raveley, to the use of Thomas Cook, *in arentatio* for life, rendering annually 5s. G.: 6d.

90 UPWOOD (11 January) Richard de Freeston: one plot with two buildings and one quarter of servile land in Little Raveley previously held by William Chaumberleyn, in *arentatio*, rendering annually 4s. at the customary times. G.: 12d.

11r **91** WISTOW (19 January) Agnes, daughter of John Gouler and naif of the land, pays a half-mark for license to marry John Outy, freeman, within the domain. Further John Outy and the said Agnes: the reversion of one messuage and a half-virgate of servile land, one-half of a vacant plot with one quarter of land and all other lands which John Gouler now holds, in bondage for life, rendering annually in all things as does John Gouler. G.: 40d.

92 ELLINGTON (January) Alicia, daughter of Thomas Gerold and naif of the lord, pays 10s. for license to marry Thomas Turnor, freeman, within the domain.

93 ELSWORTH (January) John Cook: one cote and one quarter of servile land previously held by Thomas Smart, in bondage for life, rendering annually in all things as did Thomas. Further, one croft at Grave previously held by the same Thomas Smart. G.: 6d.

94 St. Ives (February) Thomas Clerc Glovere, his wife, Johanna, and their daughter, Semanna: one half-row, as meted and bounded, previously held by John Belleman and surrendered by him, in the presence of Brother Richard, seneschal of Ramsey, and the other half of which is now held for life by the same John Belleman; for life, rendering annually 8s. at the customary times, and all other services and customs owed therein, with the obligation to repair and maintain the property at their own expense. *Et non licebit*, etc. G.: a half-mark.

95 Abbots Ripton (March) Alicia, daughter of Thomas Martyn and naif of the lord, of Wennington, pays 10s. for license to marry John Grene, freeman, on the fief of the lord. Pledge: Thomas Martyn.

96 Abbots Ripton (9 March) Thomas Martyn: surrender of one messuage, a half-virgate, another messuage and half-virgate, one quarter of servile land and one cote, to the use of John Grene, in bondage for life, rendering annually in all things as did Thomas, with the obligation to repair and maintain the property at his own expense. Pledge for repairs: Thomas Martyn. G.: 2s.

11v **97** Abbots Ripton (9 March) Simon Califer, alias Simon Smyth, of Wennington: one messuage and a half-virgate of servile land previously held by Nicholas Hoberd, in *arentatio* for life, rendering annually 10s. at the customary times. G.: 6d.

98 Abbots Ripton (9 March) Same Simon Califer: two acres of demesne at Catteshegge previously held by the same Nicholas, for life, rendering annually 16d. at the customary times. G.: 6d.

99 Warboys (21 March) Roger Muryel: one messuage and one quarter of servile land previously held by Thomas Hunte, in bondage for life, rendering annually in all things as did Thomas. Further, a certain parcel of demesne land at Bascroft previously held by the same Thomas, for life, rendering annually 16d. at the customary times. G.: 12d.

100 Slepe John Roger: one cote with adjacent land and meadow previously held by Thomas Morlee, in bondage for life, rendering annually in all things as did Thomas. G.: 4d.

101 Houghton (April) John Kebbe: surrender through the hands of Galfridus Smyth, bailiff, of one plot with buildings and a half-virgate of servile land, to the use of John Abbot, in *arentatio* for life, with a small space for a bed reserved in a proper place to John Kebbe for life. G.: 12d.

102 Elton (April) William Frettere: surrender of one plot with building and one virgate of servile land, to the use of John Deche, for life, rendering annually in all things as did William. G.: 18d.

103 Elton (April) John Deche: surrender of one tenement recently held by Richard Hoberd and once held by William Heymes, to the use of William Frettere, in *arentatio* for life, rendering annually 4s. at the customary times. Further, John Deche to the same William: one quarter of servile land, for life, rendering annually in all things as did John. G.: 12d.

12r **104** Slepe (April) Thomas Trover: one plot with building and one virgate of servile land in Woodhurst previously held by William Brunne, in *arentatio* for life, rendering annually 24s. at the customary times. G.: 6d.

105 Wistow (21 April) Robert Rede: one plot with building and a half-virgate of servile land recently held by William Waryn and previously held by Thomas Waryn, from the next Michaelmas *ad opus*, for life; another plot with building, adjoining the above property on the north, with a half-virgate of servile land recently held by William Waryn and once held by Thomas Haukyn, from the next Michaelmas, *ad censum*, for life; the reversion of four acres of demesne land called "Nynetene", now held for life by Emma, widow of William Waryn, for life, rendering annually 4s.8d. at the customary times; the reversion of one acre of demesne land lying at Toftdole, for life, rendering annually 12d., the reversion of three acres of demesne land called "Godefreyslond", now held by Emma Waryn, for life, rendering annually 3s. at the customary times; the reversion of a certain parcel of meadow called "Aldeburyslade", and the reversion of a certain parcel of meadow called "le Redyng", rendering annually 13s.ob. for Aldeburyslade and 14d. for le Redyng at the customary times. G.: 13s.4d.

106 SLEPE (16 May) John Edenham, Sr: one capital plot with building and half of one virgate of land once held by John in the Hirn in Woodhurst, the other half of which is now held by William othe Helle, in *arentatio* for life, rendering annually 10s. at the customary times, with the first payment due at the feast of St. Andrew after one full year, and with the obligation to maintain the property in good repair, including carpentry and roofing, at his own expense. G.: excused, because the property is in ruins.

12v   **107** CHATTERIS (18 May: court) Stephen atte Brigge and his wife, Beatrix: one tenement of eight acres with one plot with building recently held by Simon Piroun, in bondage, for life, rendering annually all services and customs owed therein. G.: 12d.

108 CHATTERIS (18 May: same court) Agnes Drynge: surrender of one tenement of eight acres with one grange and its appurtenances, to the use of her son, John, the son of John Drynge Bocher Sr., in bondage for life, rendering annually in all things as did Agnes, with one *camera* in the aforesaid reserved to Agnes for life, together with easement in the grange for her grain, and one and a half-acres of land, namely: a half-acre in any field and one rod in a croft. G.: one half-mark.

109 CHATTERIS (18 May: same court) William Dobyn: four acres of servile land with adjacent meadow parcelled out of one tenement of eight acres held by John Edenham, for life, rendering annually all services and customs owed therein. G.: 40d.

110 CHATTERIS (18 May: same court) John Cut of Hythé: four acres of meadow in Crowlode previously held by William Rede, for life, rendering annually in all things as did William. G.: 6d.

111 CHATTERIS (18 May: same court) Stephen Lytholf: surrender of half of one tenement of eight acres with appurtenances and meadow, and half of one cote with appurtenances, to the use of John Lytholf, his son, for life, rendering annually in all things as did Stephen. G.: 40d.

112 CHATTERIS (18 May: same court) John, son of Stephen Howesson: surrender of one cotland with appurtenances, to the use of John Lawe, for life, rendering annually in all things as did John Howesson. G.: 2s.

113 CHATTERIS (18 May: same court) John Swetemelk: surrender of one plot with building, to the use of John Trumpor, for life, rendering annually in all things as did John Swetemelk. G.: 12d.

114 CHATTERIS (18 May: same court) Robert Reder: surrender of one rod of servile land parcelled out of his tenement of eight acres lying next to the tenement of John, son of Simon Howesson, to the use of the said John Howesson, in exchange for another rod of land of John's, lying in the same furlong next to the land of John Swetemelk, in perpetuity for services and customs. G.: excused, because John Howesson is to build a new grange on that rod.

13r   **115** CHATTERIS (18 May: same court) Thomas Rede: one parcel of meadow in Hollode next to Ousedych once pertaining to the office of the custodian of Hollode, for seven years, rendering annually 6s.8d. at the customary times. G.: 12d., but excused by the seneschal.

116 CHATTERIS (18 May: same court) John Masstly: a certain parcel of meadow called Brodestlode, and one parcel at Longdole previously held by Thomas Sempool, for as long as it pleases the lord, rendering annually 10d. at the customary times. G.: 6d.

117 HOLYWELL (May) Johanna, daughter of John AtteWelle of Needingworth and naif of the lord, pays 3s.4d. for license to marry John Bate, freeman.

118 UPWOOD (30 May) William Herryng Jr.: surrender of one cotland of two acres with the buildings once held by William Cook, to the use of William Aleyn from the next Michaelmas for life, rendering annually as did Herryng.

119 UPWOOD (30 May) Same William Alcyn: one acre of demesne land lying in Fenhill and previously held by William Herryng, from the next Michaelmas for life, rendering annually 12d. at the customary times. G.: two capons.

120 SLEPE (30 May) William atte Halle: half of one virgate once held by John in the Hirne in Woodhurst, the other half of which is held by John Edenham together with the capital messuage, in *arentatio* for life, rendering annually 10s., with the first payment at the feast of St. Andrew after one full year, and with the obligation of building a *camera* of six posts on the property at his own expense within two years. Pledges for repairs: Nicholas Hunneye and John Lawe. G.: one capon.

121 ELSWORTH (May) John Seberne, outside the court: currender through the hands of William Kelleshull, bailiff, of one plot with building and a half-virgate of servile land once held by William Muryell, to the use of William Poonde, for life, rendering annually all services and customs owed therein. G.: 2s.

122 WISTOW (20 June) Robert Rede Sr.: one acre lying in Nomaneslond, for life, rendering annually 12d. at the customary times. G.: one capon.

13v **123** SLEPE (June) John Colle and his wife, Rosa: one empty plot recently burned and one virgate of servile land with appurtenances in Woodhurst once held by Robert Lord, in *arentatio* for life, rendering annually 20s. at the customary times. G.: excused, because they will rebuild the property.

124 ST. IVES (2 July: court of Slepe) Thomas Draper, his wife, Agnes, and son, John: one row previously held by John Stodele and once held by John Pykeler, for life, with a certain parcel of the row, as meted and bounded, reserved to Nicholas Chikesond for life. During Nicholas' lifetime, they will render to the lord annually 12s.8d. After his death, they will render annually 13s.4d., as well as all things rendered by Stodele, in addition to rendering and performing as certain tenants of St. Ives are held to do, and which is more fully contained in the Gersuma Book of abbot Robert. G.: 6s.8d.

125 ST. IVES (same court) John West, his wife, Agnes, and son, John: all that row that John Ellesworth held, for life, rendering annually 14s. at the customary times, with the obligation to repair and maintain the property at their own expense. *Et non licebit*, etc. G.: 40d., and no more because of an increase of 8d. in rent.

126 SLEPE (2 July: court) John West: one cotland previously held by Simon Love, in *arentatio* for life, rendering annually 13s.4d. at the customary times. G.: three capons.

127 SLEPE (2 July: court) Nicholas Bernard and his wife, Agnes: one ruined plot and a half-virgate of servile land previously held by Simon Love, in *arentatio* for life, rendering annually 10s. at the customary times. G.: two capons.

128 SLEPE (2 July: court) Benedict Boner and his wife, Lucia: one cote with adjoining toft and croft in Woodhurst previously held by Nicholas Oky, for life, rendering 3s.4d. this year, 4s. next year, and 5s. each year thereafter, at the customary times; G.: excused, because he is in the lord's service.

14r **129** HOLYWELL (3 July: court) Nicholas, son of Nicholas Scharp: one cote with adjacent croft previously held by Nicholas, his father, in bondage for life, rendering annually in all things as did his father.

130 HOLYWELL (3 July: court) Same Nicholas Scharp Jr.: three acres of demesne land previously held by his father, of which one acre lies in Schepenfurlong, one in Oxhowe, and the other at the end of the village of Needingworth, for life, rendering annually 3s. at the customary times. G. : 40d.

131 WARBOYS (5 July: court) Walter Erby Taillor: one mondayland previously held by Roger Emperour, in *arentatio* for life, rendering annually 5s. at the customary times and all other services, except suit to court, with the first payment due at Michaelmas after one full year. Further, Walter will repair the tenement, which is in ruins. G.: excused by the seneschal because of repairs. And Walter swears fealty to the lord.

132 WARBOYS (5 July: court) John Brennewater and his wife, Alicia: one cote previously of the tenement of Roger de Hirst, together with another cote next to it also from Roger's tenement previously held by John Pappeworth, for life, rendering annually 4s. at the customary times, with the condition that within the next three years they will build a "cross chamber" on one cote and a new bake house on the other, at their own expense. G.: six capons.

133 WARBOYS (5 July: court) John Levot Jr.: surrender of one cote with curtilage from the tenement once held by Roger de Hirst and recently held by Richard Taillor, to the use of John Harefeye, for life, rendering annually 4s. and all other services and customs as did John, with the obligation to repair and maintain the property at his own expense. G.: 12d.

134 BROUGHTON (6 July: court) William Broughton: one plot and one quarter of servile land previously held by John Robyn, *ad censa* for life, rendering 3s. annually at the customary times, with the first payment at Michaelmas after one full year. G.: excused, because he will rebuild the property at his own expense within three years.

135 HEMINGFORD ABBOTS (7 July) Richard Brekepot: one cote with adjacent croft previously held by John Fermer, for life, rendering annually in all things as did John. G.: 2s.

14v **136** HEMINGFORD ABBOTS (7 July) Matillis, widow of Thomas Koke Jr.: two acres of meadow previously held by Richard Ive, for life, for services and customs. After her death the property will revert to their sons, John and Nicholas, naifs of the lord, in bondage for the same services, for life. G.: 12d.

137 HOUGHTON (7 July: court) John atte Cros: one plot with building and a half-virgate of servile land previously held by John Thressher, in *arentatio* for life, rendering annually 8s. at the customary times. G.: 12d.

138 ABBOTS RIPTON (8 July: court) John Ropere: one plot with building in Wennington and half of one virgate of servile land, the other half of which William Halsham still retains after surrendering the other half to John Ropere, in *arentatio* for life, rendering annualy 11s. at the customary times, with the obligation to repair and maintain the property, including carpentry and roofing for all buildings and houses. G.: 12d.

139 ABBOTS RIPTON (8 July: court)[11] John Atte Chirche: one half-virgate of free land previously held by John Goothird, in *arentatio* for life, rendering annually a half-mark. G.: two capons.

140 ELSWORTH (12 July: court) John Howesson: one quarter of servile land in Elsworth recently held by John Yntte, for life, rendering annually in all things as did John. G.: 6d.

---

[11] See PRO-SC2-179/45. Entry not in roll.

141 ELSWORTH (12 July: court) Alicia Atte Brook: surrender of the sixth part of one virgate of servile land in Elsworth, to the use of John Brigge "Gallicus", for life, rendering annually in all things as did Alicia. G.: 12d.

142 ELSWORTH (12 July: court) Andrew Merton and his wife, Katerina: one built up cote with adjacent croft previously held by William Brigge, for life, rendering annually all services and customs owed therein. G.: one capon.

15r **143** ELSWORTH (12 July: court) John Ynttes: one cote in Grave previously held by Thomas Smart, for life, rendering annually in all things as did Thomas. G.: one capon.

144 ELSWORTH (12 July: court) Henry Porter: one built up cote previously held by Simon Smart in Elsworth and one quarter of servile land in Grave, previously held by John Cowhird, for life, rendering annually in all things as did Simon and John. G.: 12d.

145 ELSWORTH (12 July: court) Nicholas Cook, naif of the lord, pays 12d. for license to live off the manor. He will attend the leet annually and pay 12d., the first payment being due at the next leet. Pledge: John Yntte.

146 ELSWORTH (12 July: court) John Thatchere: one quarter of servile land previously held by John Cook, for life, rendering annually in all things as did Cook. G.: 12d.

147 CRANFIELD (August) Alicia, daughter of John Aleyn and naif of the lord, pays 12d. for license to marry Thomas Catelyn, naif of the lord.

148 CRANFIELD (August) Margaret, daughter of John Frost and naif of the lord, pays 12d. for license to marry Thomas Aleyn, naif of the lord.

149 BYTHORNE (September) Johanna, daughter of Thomas Bachiller and naif of the lord, pays 12d. to marry William Spaygne, freeman. Also received: G. for 12d. from Johanna and William for one quarter of land.

15v *Blank*

5 THOMAS BUTTERWYK (1400-1401)

16r **150** SLEPE (29 September: leet with court) Thomas Baldewyn and Thomas, son of John Baldewyne: one half-row previously held by Thomas Gamelyn, for life, rendering annually 10s. in equal portions at the customary times, with the obligation to repair and maintain the property, as well as rendering annually in all things as did Gamelyn. *Et non licebit*, etc. (except for remarriage of wives). G.: 10s.

151 HEMINGFORD ABBOTS (2 October: leet with court) Richard Botiller: one cote with adjacent curtilage previously held by John Cademan, in bondage for life. G.: 6d.

152 CRANFIELD (4 October: leet with court) John Skynnere pays 12d. for license to marry Johanna Aleyn, widow and tenant of one messuage and a half-virgate of servile land, which land is to be held by John for the life of Johanna, rendering annually all services and customs owed therein.

153 BARTON (6 October: General Court)[12] William Prior: one messuage and one virgate of servile land previously held by Petronilla, widow of Thomas Child, in bondage rendering annually all services and customs owed therein. G.: 10s.

154 SHILLINGTON (7 October: leet with court) John Atte Well: one plot with building and one virgate of servile land in Pegsdown previously held by Thomas Atte Well, for life, rendering annually in all things as did Thomas. G.: 3s.4d.

155 SHILLINGTON (7 October: leet with court) Johanna Godard, naif of the lord, pays 6s.8d. for license to marry Richard Atte Halle of Langford, freeman.

16v **156** SHILLINGTON (7 October: court) Thomas Sweyn: one long, tiled cattle-shed located within the manor, together with one adjacent curtilage, as meted and bounded,

---

[12] Ibid., entry not in roll.

and one lot of demesne land, for life, with the condition that he will dwell on the tenement, rendering annually 10s. at the customary times. G.: 2s.

157 SHILLINGTON (7 October: court) Richard Atte Halle pays 16d. for permission to marry Johanna Godard, naif of the lord, and tenant of one messuage and a half-virgate of servile land in Stondon, to be held for the lifetime of Johanna, rendering services and customs annually.

158 SHILLINGTON (7 October: court) Isabella, daughter of Robert Cartere and naif of the lord, pays 3s.4d. for license to marry whomever she wishes, this time.

159 SHILLINGTON (7 October: court) Agnes, daughter of John Smyth of Grenende and naif of the lord, pays 2s. for license to marry William, garçon of the rector's household, freeman. Pledge: John Smyth of Grenende.

160 SHILLINGTON (7 October: court) Alicia, widow of John Atte Wode Jr., of Stondon: one plot with building and one half-virgate of servile land previously held by Johanna Atte Wode, together with a parcel of meadow land also held by Johanna, for life, rendering annually in all things as did Johanna. G.: a half-mark.

161 SHILLINGTON (7 October: court) John, son of William Atte Hill Sr., of Pegsdon: the whole site of the manor of Pegsdon, with all surrounding hedges and ditches, one building, and one virgate of servile land previously held by Henry Herper and John Barfoot, for life, rendering to the farmer of the manor annually 12d. for the site, and services for the building and virgate, with the obligation to repair and maintain the property after building up the site of the manor. Further, he will abide there. And, free access to the dovecote is reserved to the farmer. G.: 40d.

162 SHILLINGTON (7 October: court) John Ede pays 2s. for permission to marry Margaret Hamund, tenant of two messuages and one and a half virgates of servile land previously held by her late husband, Thomas Hamund, to be held for the lifetime of Margaret, rendering annually in all things as did Thomas. G.: 2s.

163 SHILLINGTON (7 October: court) John Atte Brook: 10 acres of demesne land in the fields of Hanscomb previously held by Gilbert Atte Brook, and four and a half acres of demesne land at Chirchehill in Shillington previously held by John Dyer, for life, rendering annually 12s. at the customary times. G.: one capon.

17r   **164** THERFIELD (9 October: leet with court) John Taillor of Royston: surrender through the hands of William Angtill, bailiff, of 12 acres of demesne land parcelled out of Newelond, lying near the village of Therfield, opposite the mount there and on both sides of the King's road, to the use of John Patoun of Royston, from the previous Michaelmas for 20 years, rendering annually 6s. in equal portions at Michaelmas and Easter. G.: 8d.

165 THERFIELD (9 October: leet with court) John Hattele: surrender of one parcel of a certain croft containing four acres and located at the western end of the village of Royston, recently called Branncestree, lying between the land John Adam holds from the lord, on the one side, and the croft pertaining to the village of Royston, on the other, and extending from the western end of Peter Hiltoft's croft to Bruer', the other part of which croft the said John Hattele and his wife, Katerina, hold from the lord, to the use of John Patoun of Royston, from the previous Michaelmas for 20 years, rendering annually 4s. in equal portions at Easter and Michaelmas. G.: 8d.

166 THERFIELD (9 October: leet with court) John Hattele and his wife, Katerina: one toft lying at the western end of the village of Royston, called Branncestres, and one perch of land in the croft of that toft containing one acre, which parcel lies, in width, between the road leading from Royston to Therfield and the croft pertaining to Royston, and extends, in legth, from the aforesaid toft eastward to the end of Peter Hiltoft's croft, for life and a year beyond, rendering annually 12d. in equal portions at Michaelmas and Easter. G.: 4d.

167 THERFIELD (9 October: leet with court) William Wymer, naif of the lord, pays 12d. for marrying Felicia, daughter of William Watte and naif of the lord, without license.

168 THERFIELD (9 October: leet with court) The said Felicia pays 12d. for marrying the said William without license.

169 THERFIELD (9 October: leet with court) Thomas Tottehale, alias Doke, and his wife, Katerina: a manse previously held by Peter Branncestre in Therfield, with all pertaining buildings and houses recently erected by William Kymble, with a certain portion of the adjacent garden, together with the reversion of the other part of the garden now held by Nicholas Adam as meted and bounded, for life, rendering annually 10s. during the lifetime of Nicholas Adam, and 13s.4d. annually after his death, at the customary times. G.: two capons.

17v **170** BURWELL (11 October: leet with court) Thomas Bosoun, chaplain: eight acres of demesne land lying at le Nesse, four acres of demesne land at "Bynnges" and "Rebynes hanedlond", four acres of demesne at Estfeld previously held by John Walden, two acres of demesne at Ayllyhanedlond recently held by John Walden, two acres of demesne in Dychfeld at Galowhyll and one rod of demesne in Northfeld at Braddeye touching upon Gyllescroft, and three acres of demesne in le Braach, from the previous Michaelmas for 20 years, rendering annually 20s.6d. at the customary times. G.: excused by the seneschal.

171 BURWELL (11 October: leet with court) Thomas Schipwreyght: one tenement with one building and 15 acres previously held by Alexander Sparwe, in *arentatio* from the previous Michaelmas for 10 years, rendering annually 20s., with 4d. for *capitagium*, at the customary times. G.: two capons.

172 BURWELL (11 October: leet with court) John Rolf: one tenement of 15 acres with one croft previously held by Robert Wyot, in *arentatio* from the previous Michaelmas for 20 years, rendering annually 15s. at the customary times. G.: one capon.

173 BURWELL (11 October: leet with court) John Jemes: one croftland containing three acres, previously held by himself, and four acres of land lying in the fields of Reche, once held by Thomas Swasham.

174 HOLYWELL (15 October: leet with court) John in the Lane: surrender of one plot with building and one virgate of servile land, to the use of John Beaumeys Jr., in bondage for life, rendering annually in all things as did Lane.

175 HOLYWELL (15 October: leet with court) John Beaumeys Jr.: one acre of demesne land previously held by John in the Lane, for life, rendering annually 12d. at the customary times. G.: 2s.

176 HOLYWELL (15 October: leet with court) Robert Atte Welle: surrender of one plot with building, one virgate and one quarter of servile land, together with three acres of Penilond, to the use of his son, John, for life, rendering annually in all things as did Robert. G.: 40d.

18r **177** WARBOYS (16 October: leet with court) John Boys and his wife, Juliana: one plot with building and 10 acres of land from a tenement previously held by Robert de Hirst and once held by Radulph Boys, father of John, for life, rendering annually in all things as did his father. G.: 40d.

178 WARBOYS (18 October: leet with court) Thomas Bele and his wife, Johanna: one mondayland previously held by William Squyer, in *arentatio* for life, rendering annually 4s. at the customary times and one autumn *precaria*. G.: excused, because the tenement is in ruins.

179 WARBOYS (18 October: leet with court) Robert Cole, chaplain, and John Levot: 11 selions of demesne land in Lowefurlong previously held by John othe Hyll, for

life, rendering annually 2s.6d. at the customary times. G.: excused by the seneschal.
180 Warboys (18 October: leet with court) William Derworth and his wife, Johanna: one mondayland previously held by Edmund Webster, together with one acre of demesne at the end of his croft previously held by Hugo Derworthe, in *arentatio* for life, rendering annually 4s.6d. at the customary times, one autumn *precaria*, hay in Chevereth, and other customs, as do certain of his peers who hold in *arentatio*. G.: 6d.
181 Warboys (16 October: leet with court) William Smart: one plot with building and a half-virgate of servile land previously held by Hugo Webster, in *arentatio* for life, rendering annually 8s. at the customary times, one autumn *precaria* and other services. G.: excused by the seneschal.
182 Bythorne (19 October: court at Weston) Emma, daughter of John Randolf, will pay 40d., if naifty is proved, for license to marry John Preston of Keston, freeman.
183 Bythorne (19 October: court at Weston) William Randolf: one servile plot with half of three quarters of servile land previously held by Robert Rande, the other half of which is now held by Matilda Rande, in bondage for life, rendering annually in all things as did Robert. Also: the reversion of the other half of the aforesaid tenement, now held by Matilda Rande, for life, rendering annually in all things as Matilda does now. G.: excused, because it pertains to the vill.
18v **184** Brington (19 October: court at Weston) William Faukes: one plot with building and three quarters of servile land previously held by William Revesson, for life, rendering annually in all things as did William. G.: 40d.
185 Elton (20 October: leet with court) John, son of Henry Hobbesson: one empty plot and a half-virgate of land previously held by John Bryd, for life, rendering annually 6s.8d. for the first six years, at the customary times, and for the remaining years as do others who hold such property. G.: 6d.
186 Elton (20 October: leet with court) Thomas Robyn: one cote *ad opus* previously held by John Grene, for life, rendering annually in all things as did John. G.: 6d.
187 Elton (20 October: leet with court) Henry Hobbessone: four acres of land of the akirman's tenement, for 12 years, rendering annually 12d. and in all other things as did the previous tenant. G.: one capon.
188 Abbots Ripton (22 October: leet with court) William Atte Stylle: surrender of one empty plot and one virgate of servile land previously held by William Martyn, to the use of John Falnon, in *arentatio* for life, rendering annually 20s. at the customary times. G.: 2s.
189 Abbots Ripton (22 October: leet with court) John Baylly: two quarters of servile land previously held by Nicholas Tayllour and Alicia Cartere, in *arentatio* for life, rendering 5s. this year and 6s.8d. each year thereafter, at the customary times. G.: 6d.
190 Broughton (27 October: leet with court) Robert Grymmysby: one quarter of servile land previously held by John Swon, in *arentatio* for life, rendering annually 3s. at the customary times. G.: excused by the seneschal.
191 Barton (1 November) Abbot Thomas grants William, son of William atte Chirche, naif of the lord, license to receive all holy orders from any English or any other Catholic bishop. Further, the said William will, in the future, not denigrate the abbey, but he will stand in the service of the abbot and his successors, if required,
19r because he is not manumitted by this.[13] Payment: 20s.

[13] The full text is as follows:
"Thomas permissione divina abbas monasterii Rameseye primo die mensis Novembris anno

192 CHATTERIS (4 December) John, son of John Wyllessone: one messuage and a half-cote with meadow previously held by his father, for life, rendering annually in all things as did his father. G.: 4s.

193 ST. IVES (4 December) Thomas, son of Loretta Foster: the reversion of half of a certain row in Bridge Street, on the east side, which the aforesaid Loretta now holds for life, rendering annually 14s. in equal portions at the customary times, and in all things as did his mother, with repairs at his own expense. *Et non licebit*, etc. (except for remarriage of wife). G.: 6d., and no more, because of an increase of 8d. in rent.

194 ST. IVES (4 December) Margaret, daughter of the aforesaid Loretta: the reversion of the other half of the row held by her mother, for life, rendering annually 14s. at the customary times and in all things as did her mother, with repairs at her own expense. *Et non licebit*, etc. (except for remarriage). G.: 6d.

19v **195** POPENHOE (11 December) Richard, son of John atte Mere of Walsoken, carpenter and naif of the lord, pays for license to live off the manor. He will render to the *receptor* of the abbot annually 2s. at Christmas, at Ramsey, and he will be a naif as before.

196 BROUGHTON (12 December) William Gotte: one plot with building called Gybonnesplace, with adjacent garden, previously held by Thomas Peny, in bondage for life, rendering annually 4s. at the customary times. G.: excused by the seneschal, because he is a pauper.

197 WARBOYS (19 December) Galfridus Broun: one empty plot and a half-virgate of servile land previously held by John Wylkes, for life, rendering annually in all things as did John. Also: one acre of demesne land at Bascroft previously held by William Sande, for life, rendering annually 8d. G.: 6d.

198 WISTOW (19 December) John Elmeslee: nine acres of demesne land in le Braach previously held by John Wenyngton, for life, rendering annually 10d. per acre, in two installments, at the feast of the Annunciation and the feast of the Translation of St. Benedict, with the first payment due at the next feast of the Annunciation. G.: excused by the seneschal.

199 WARBOYS (19 December) John Broun: one dichmanland previously held by John Edward and lying between the tenements of Richard Horwod and John Hych, for life, rendering annually in all things as did Edward. G.: 40d.

200 ELLINGTON (20 December) John Wynter: one plot with building and three quarters of servile land previously held by John atte Nook, for life, rendering annually in all things as did Nook. G.: 6s.

20r **201** ELLINGTON (20 December) John West: one plot with building and one quarter of servile land previously held by John Lethenard, in bondage for life, rendering annually in all things as did Lethenard. G.: 2s.

---

supradicto caritatis intuitu et ad instanciam amicorum concessit et licenciam dedit specialem Willelmo filio Willelmi atte Chirche nativo dicti Abbatis de manerio de Barton in comitatu Bedfordie ad recipiendos omnes sacros ordines a quocumque seu a quibuscumque episcopis Anglie vel a quocumque episcopo catholico celebrandos ita quod dictus Willelmus filius Willelmi ecclesie Rameseye in futurum denegare non existat sed quod stet in obsequio dicti abbatis et successorum suorum/(f. 19r) in servicio pro etate suo congruo et competenti/si ad hoc fuerit requisitus hac concessione in aliquo non obstante quia per hoc non manumissus. Et dictus Willelmus filius Willelmi dat domino pro fine pro irrotulatione viginti solidos."

Despite the general prohibition of the ordination of the unfree, an exception is found in Gratian for *servi monasterii*. See Dist. LIV, Part IV, c. 22. (*Corpus Juris Canonici*, ed. Friedberg, I, 213-14.)

202 BURWELL (21 December) John Sparwe Jr.: three croftlands in Reche previously held by Robert Rede, in *arentatio* from the previous Michaelmas for life, rendering 10s. this year and 12s. each year thereafter, at the customary times. G.: excused by the seneschal.

203 ELTON (21 December) John Hykkessone: one empty plot and a half-virgate of servile land previously held by Henry Balle, and one quarter of servile land previously held by Henry Balle, and one quarter of servile land previously held by John Bythorne Sr., in *arentatio* for life, rendering annually 15s. at the customary times. Also: one cote called Belesyerd, next to Berygate, for life, rendering annually 4s. at the feast of the Nativity of Blessed Mary. G.: 12d.

204 ELTON (21 December) Hugo Hoberd: one plot with building and 10 acres of land and meadow once held by Thomas de Lye and previously held by Hykkesson, for life, rendering annually 10s. at the customary times. G.: 12d.

205 HOUGHTON (3 January) Galfridus Smyth: half of one messuage with croft, 26 acres, one rod of land and one rod of meadow once held by Richard Twywell, alias Dykes, and one virgate in Houghton, for as long as the manor is in his hands as *firmarius*, rendering annually 20s. at the customary times, with the first payment due at the next feast of St. Andrew. G.: excused by the seneschal.

206 HOUGHTON (3 January) Robert Roger: one empty plot and a half-virgate of servile land once belonging to Peters, in bondage for life, rendering annually 5s. at the customary times, with the first payment due at the next feast of St. Andrew. G.: excused by the seneschal.

20v **207** HOLYWELL (4 January) William Thudeby: one cote with croft previously held by Nicholas Fannell, in bondage for life, rendering annually in all things as did Nicholas. G.: 12d., and no more because the tenement is in ruins.

208 CHATTERIS (9 January) William Lyfle: surrender through the hands of Thomas Rede, bailiff, of one half of one tenement of eight acres without plot, to the use of John Herford Jr., in bondage for life, rendering annually in all things as did William. G.: 40d.

209 WISTOW (12 January) John Waryn: surrender through the hands of Brother Richard Schenyngdon, seneschal of Ramsey, of one plot with building and a half-virgate of servile land in Wistow, to the use of John, son of Nicholas Schepherde Jr., and his wife, Johanna, *ad censa*, for life, rendering all services and customs rendered by other tenants *ad censum*. G.: 20d.

210 GRAVELEY (21 March) William Slow: one plot with building and one virgate of servile land previously held by his father, John Slow, in bondage, for life, rendering annually in all things as did his father. G.: 40d.

211 ELSWORTH (22 March) John Howesson: one cote with adjacent croft previously held by Henry Porter, in bondage for life, rendering annually in all things as did Henry. G.: 3d., and no more, because the property is in ruins.

21r **212** ELSWORTH (22 March) Thomas Peek: one quarter of servile land with a parcel of a certain croft in le Grave previously held by Henry Porter, in bondage, rendering annually in all things as did Henry. G.: 6d.

213 ELSWORTH (22 March) John Wymond: one half-virgate of servile land previously held by William Ponde, in bondage, for life, rendering in all things as did William. G.: 2s.

214 ELSWORTH (22 March) Johanna, daughter of William Aleynnesson and naif of the lord, pays 13s.4d. for license to live off the fief for one year and as long as it pleases the lord, and for permission to marry whomever she wishes, the first time.[14]

---

[14] MS.: "prima vice."

215 ELSWORTH (22 March) William Mychell: one cote with croft, together with five selions of adjacent land previously held by William Muryell, in bondage, for life, rendering annually 40d., one *precaria* of mowing the hay, and one autumn *precaria*, with the first payment due next Christmas. G.: 12d.

216 SLEPE (22 March) Margaret, daughter of Simon Love and naif of the lord, pays 10s. for license to marry Robert Bate of Stanton, freeman.

217 BROUGHTON (5 April) William Botiller: one plot with a ruined building, and a half-virgate of servile land previously held by Simon Fysshere, *ad censa* for life, rendering annually 6s. at the customary times, and all other services and customs rendered by those *ad censum*, with the first payment due at the next feast of the Annunciation. G.: excused by the seneschal, because the property is in ruins.

21v **218** WISTOW (6 April) Robert Randolf Jr.: one plot with building and a half-virgate of servile land previously held by John Kyng, together with the reversion of another quarter of the aforesaid virgate which John Kyng holds for life, in bondage, for life, rendering annually in all things as John. G.: excused, because the property is in ruins.

219 CHATTERIS (10 April) John Wartir: one built up cote with adjacent croft and meadow previously held by William Joseph, for life, rendering annually in all things as did William. G.: 4s.

220 CHATTERIS (10 April) John Austyn Jr.: one cotland with building previously held by John Austyn Sr., his father, for life, rendering annually in all things as did his father. G.: 5s.

221 CRANFIELD (16 April) Agnes, daughter of Richard Catelyn and naif of the lord, pays 40d. for license to marry Simon Leveneth, freeman.

222 CRANFIELD (16 April) Alicia Herton: surrender through the hands of Thomas Joye, bailiff, of one messuage and one quarter of servile land, to the use of her son, John Herton, for life, rendering annually in all things as did Alicia. G.: 12d.

223 WARBOYS (19 April) Katerina, daughter of John Hersene and naif of the lord, pays 6s.8d. for license to marry John Crystemasse of Needingworth, freeman.

224 BRINGTON (8 May) Felicia, daughter of Walter Lucas and naif of the lord, pays 4s. for license to marry William Wryghte, freeman, within the domain.

22r **225** ABBOTS RIPTON (19 April) Andrew Swon: one plot with building and a half-virgate of servile land previously held by John atte Chirche and once held by John Outy, in *arentatio* from the next Michaelmas, for life, rendering annually 12s. at the customary times. G.: one capon, and no more because the tenement is in ruins.

226 WARBOYS (May) Beatrix, daughter of Hugo Rolf and naif of the lord, pays 6s.8d. for license to marry William Michell of Hartford, freeman, outside the fief of the lord.

227 WARBOYS (15 May) Richard Bennesson and Nicholas, his son: one plot with building and one quarter of servile land previously held by John Wylkes, in bondage from the next feast of St. Peter in Chains, for life, rendering annually in all things as did John. G.: 4s.

228 WISTOW (15 May) John Randolf: six acres of demesne land at Busshoppeswong, for life, rendering annually 6d. per acre at the customary times. Also: the adjoining capital meadow, as meted and bounded in length and breadth; and one acre of demesne land previously held by William Sabyn, for life, rendering annually 12d. at the customary times. G.: 6d.

229 CHATTERIS (22 May) William Neuman and John Neuman: half of a certain meadow in Oldehalf, on the north side, the other half of which is held by Robert Aylleward, on the south, for life, rendering annually as does Robert. G.: 2s.

22v **230** WISTOW (29 May) Margaret, daughter of John Love and naif of the lord, pays 6s.8d. for license to marry Robert Ely, freeman, within the fief of the lord.

231 WISTOW (29 May) same Robert and Margaret: the reversion of one messuage and one virgate of servile land now held for life by John Love, in bondage for life, rendering annually in all things as John. G.: 3s.4d.

232 SLEPE (2 June) William Wryghte and his wife, Alicia: a certain built up tenement in Woodhurst previously held by Thomas Wynnegoode and once held by David de Brounfeld, for life, rendering annually 5s. in equal portions at the feasts of St. Andrew, and the Nativity of Blessed Mary, and in all things as did Thomas. G.: 20d.

233 BROUGHTON (3 June) William Boteler and his son, Thomas: one ruined house and a quarter of one virgate of servile land previously held by Simon Fysshere, another quarter of which virgate is already rented by the said William, in *arentatio* for life, rendering annually in all things as did Simon. G.: excused, because the tenement is in ruins.

234 BURWELL (July) William Ideyne, naif of the lord, pays 2s. for license to marry his daughter, Margaret, to Radulph Lane, freeman, this time.

23r **235** BURWELL (July) Richard Chapman Barkere: one plot with building with 15 acres of land once held by William Swyn, in bondage for 20 years, rendering annually 20s. as rent at the customary times, and 4d. as common fine. G.: 2s.

236 BURWELL (July) John Peyntour: one plot with building with 15 acres of land once held by Robert atte Brygge, in bondage for 20 years, rendering annually 16s. at the customary times and in all things as did Robert. G.: 6d.

237 WISTOW Margaret, daughter of Nicholas Martyn and naif of the lord, pays 10s. for license to marry Richard, son of John Baroun, freeman, this time.

238 WISTOW (13 July: court) John Baroun: surrender of one plot with building and a half-virgate of servile land in Raveley, to the use of his son Richard and wife, Margaret, in bondage, for life, rendering annually in all things as did John. G.: 2s.

239 ST. IVES (22 July) William Martyn, his wife, Margaret, and their daughter, Margaret: two half-rows in St. Ives previously held by Hugo Porthos, for life, rendering annually 30s. at the customary times and in all things as did Hugo, with the obligation to repair and maintain the property. *Et non licebit*, etc. G.: excused by the seneschal because the tenements are in ruins.

23v **240** SLEPE (22 July) Robert Wryghte: a certain part of the manor, i.e. one wall called Pyndefoldeyerd, as meted and bounded, for life, rendering annually 12d. at the customary times. G.: two capons.

241 ST. IVES (22 July) William Fonne, his wife, Elena, and their daughter, Alicia: one row previously held by John Ellesworth, for life, rendering annually 13s.4d. and in all things as did John, with the obligation to repair and maintain the property. *Et non licebit*, etc. G.: 20d., and no more because of an increase of 8d. in rent.

242 ST. IVES (22 July: court) Richard Nicholl and his wife, Agnes: a half-row in Bridge Street previously held by Thomas Netman, for life, rendering annually 20s. at the customary times and in all things as did Thomas, with the obligation to repair and maintain the property. *Et non licebit*, etc. G.: (*blank*).

24r **243** UPWOOD (23 July) William Chaumberleyn and his wife, Johanna: one plot with building, one virgate and one quarter virgate of servile land previously held by John Love, a half-virgate of which is to be held *ad censum*, the remaining three quarters to be held in *arentatio*, for life, rendering annually 13s.4d. at the customary times and all other services and customs rendered by other tenants *ad censum*, with repairs at their own expense. G.: 20d.

244 WARBOYS (7 August) John Hygh Jr.: one mondayland previously held by John Peverell, for life, rendering annually in all things as did Peverell, with the first payment due at Michaelmas after one full year.

245 WARBOYS (7 August) John Hygh Jr.: four acres of demesne land lying in Stokkyng previously held by John Peverell, for life, rendering annually 8d. per acre at the customary times, with the first payment due at Michaelmas after one full year. G.: nothing.

246 WARBOYS (7 August) John Hygh Sr.: one windmill, from the next Michaelmas for 10 years, rendering annually 40s. in equal portions at the feasts of St. Andrew, the Annunciation, the Translation of St. Benedict and the Nativity of Blessed Mary, with the obligation to maintain the mill in good repair, both in carpentry and in lumber. He will supply roof timbers and make cogs and rungs from lumber supplied by the lord, and he will maintain the mill and keep it safe from damage, from heavy winds and storms.

247 ST. IVES (8 August) William Martyn, and his wife, Margaret: surrender of one empty row next to the row of William Fysshere and once held by Simon Flechere, to the use of Henry Spicher, alias Okam, and his wife, Elena, for life, rendering annually 3s.4d. and all other services, and customs owed therein, with the obligation to rebuild the row at their own expense within one year. *Et non licebit*, etc. G.: excused by the seneschal because of repairs.

24v

248 WISTOW (14 August) Richar Broun of Raveley: one plot with two houses and a half-virgate of servile land previously held by Robert Tryppelowe, for life, rendering annually in all things as did Robert. G.: excused, because the capital messuage pertaining to the tenement was recently burned and Richard is obligated to rebuild it at his own expense within a year.

249 BROUGHTON (15 August) Henry Deche and his wife, Agnes: one plot with building and a half-virgate of servile land, one empty plot and a quarter of servile land, and one other quarter of land, without a plot, previously held by Richard Deche, Henry's father, for life, rendering annually in all things as did Richard. G.: 12d.

250 CRANFIELD (August) Agnes, daughter of (blank) Terry and naif of the lord, pays 2s. for license to marry Richard Othefeld, freeman, within the fief of the lord, this time.

251 BROUGHTON (17 September) John Schepherde Jr.: one cote with croft, together with one selion of land previously held by William Swon, for life, rendering annually in all things as did William. G.: excused by the seneschal, because the property is in ruins.

25r

252 BROUGHTON (September) Edward Justice: surrender of one plot with building, one virgate of servile land, one other plot with building, in ruined condition, a half-virgate of servile land and a quarter of Cleryvauxlonde, to the use of his son, John Justice, for life, rendering annually in all things as did his father. G.: 6d.

253 WESTON Johanna, daughter of Richard Buncy and naif of the lord, pays 6s.8d. for license to marry whomever she wishes outside the fief of the lord. Pledge: John Hacoun.

254 THERFIELD (September) Johanna, daughter of Robert atte Wode and naif of the lord, pays 13s.4d. for license to marry John Waryn, freeman, within the fief of the lord, this time.

255 THERFIELD (September) John Waryn and Johanna, daughter of Robert atte Wode: one plot with building and a half-virgate of servile land previously held by Thomas Wynnegor Jr., late husband of the aforesaid Johanna, to be held by them saving the right of anyone, until Thomas, son and heir of the aforesaid Thomas, reaches full and legitimate age, rendering annually, in the meantime, in all things as did Thomas. G.: 6s.8d.

256 SLEPE (22 July: court) John West Bocher: one plot with building at Grene, with a grange in "Coulane" and one virgate of servile land previously held by Thomas Wryght, in *arentatio* for life, from the previous Michaelmas, rendering 22s. this year and 24s. each year thereafter, at the customary times, with the obligation to keep and maintain the grange at his own expense in as good — or better — condition as when he received it. G.: 12d.

25v 257 SLEPE (22 July: court) Simon Brunne and his wife, Alicia: one cotland at Grene recently held by John Iryssh and once held by John Godeman, in *arentatio* for life, rendering annually 13s.4d. and in all things as did Iryssh. G.: excused, because Simon is a carter within the manor.

258 ST. IVES (22 July: same court) John Burman, his wife, Alicia, and their son, John: a half-row previously held by Maia Smyth, for life, rendering annually 13s.4d. at the customary times, and all other services and customs owed therein, with the obligation to maintain the property in good repair. *Et non licebit*, etc. G.: 16d.

259 ST. IVES (22 July: same court) John Raven, his wife, Emma, and their son, Thomas: two half-rows previously held by William Dunton, for life, rendering annually 20s. at the customary times, with the obligation to maintain the property in good repair. *Et non licebit*, etc. G.: 12d.

26r 260 ST. IVES (22 July: same court) John Raven, his wife, Emma, and their daughter, Agnes: a half-row previously held by John Hunne, for life, rendering annually 13s.4d. and all services and customs owed therein, with the obligation to maintain the property in good repair. *Et non licebit*, etc. G.: 13s.4d.

26v 261 NAMES OF THE NAIFS OF BARTON.
William at Chyrche. (Thomas 5)
Elias Dowkys. (Thomas 8)
John Atfan. (Thomas 9)
Edmund Barnard. (Thomas 14)
William Roger (Thomas 14, John 5 and 8)
Alan Mathew. (Thomas 13 and 16)
Adam Taylor. (14)
John Stonley. (Thomas 19, John Stowe 10)
Walter Wudward (John 1)
William Reveson (John 2 and 9).
Thomas Willimott (John 8 and 9, John Stowe 7).
John Shalever (John 13).
John Burnard, alias Hilari (John 15, John Stowe 9 and 16).
John Grene (John Crowland 1 and 2, John Stowe 2).
John Bonde (John Stowe 3 and 16).
John Lillye (John Stowe 6).
William Roger Plow wryth (John Stowe 7).
John Pryor (John Stowe 8 — twice).
John Mathew, alias Colman (John Stowe 5 and 16).
Thomas Chyld (John Stowe 18).
William Fabyon (John Stowe 23).
Thomas Corulman (William Witlesey 2).
262 NAMES OF THE NAIFS OF THERFIELD.
William Watt (Thomas 5).
Robert at Wood (Thomas 5).
John Sperver (Thomas 6, John 9, John Stowe 12).
John Adam (Thomas 7 and 10, John 5, and 10).
John Fryer (Thomas 7 and 10, John 6, 9 and 14).

William Waryn (Thomas 10, John 4, John Crowland 1, John Stowe 11 and 12).
John Wynmer (Thomas 13, John Stowe 5).
Thomas Frost (Thomas 19).
John Wood and John Waryn (John Stowe 5).
John Colle (John Stowe 4, 8 and 14).
William Wyngore (John Stowe 6).
263 BYTHORNE.
John Sachebien (Thomas 4).
Thomas Bachyllar (Thomas 4, 10 and 14).
John Randolf (Thomas 5, John Stowe 3).
John Athyll (Thomas 8).
Simon Collesson (Thomas 8).
John Baron (Thomas 10).
John Hacon (Thomas 16).
John Bocher (John Stowe 1).
John Watson, alias Schepherd (Thomas 3 and 5).
John Kemp (John Stowe 13).
264 ELTON.
John Saldyn (Thomas 7, John Stowe 7, 19 and 20).
John Hobson, alias Clerk (Thomas 13).
William Beche (John 13, John Stowe 10, William Witlesey 5).
John Atgate (John Stowe 4, 18, William Witlesey 2).
265 WESTON.
Richard Buncy (Thomas 5).
Adam Carter (Thomas 5, 8, 9 and John Stowe 11).
Roger Jamysson (Thomas 8).
Simon Hacoun (Thomas 8, John 3, John Stowe 3, 7, and 33).
Margaret Man (Thomas 9, 13, John 3).
John Felis (Thomas 9).
William Myller (Thomas 9, 10, John Stowe 13).
Walter Flessher (Thomas 13, 18, John 5, John Stowe 15, 32, William Witlesey 4).
John Watson (Thomas 14).
John Barton (Thomas 22, John 9).
John Randolf (John 1).
Johanna Wryght (John Stowe 2).
John Flesshall (John Stowe 14).
Walter Kyng (John Stowe 15 and 16).
William Booney (William Witlesey 4) — lives at Keston.
John Hacon (William Witlesey 4) — lives at Godmanchester twice.
266 BRINGTON.
Walter Lucas (Thomas 5).
William Perye (Thomas 6).
John Purye (John 2).
Thomas Austyn (Thomas 7).
Elizabeth Baron (Thomas 13).
Richard Howesson (Thomas 19) — twice.
William Sawnder (John 2).
John Beveriche (John 4).
Thomas Thressher (John Stowe 19).
John Bachyller (John Stowe 19).

267 ABBOTS RIPTON
Thomas Martyn (Thomas 4).
John Howlot (Thomas 8).
John Robbys (Thomas 9, John 5).
William West (Thomas 10, 12, John Stowe 7).
William Wattys (John Stowe 16).
Robert Ivell (Thomas 10).
William Howe (Thomas 11, John 1).
John Nicholl (Thomas 22).
Robert Jurdon (John 5).
John Gosse (John 5) — lives in Little Stukeley.
John Hyche of Catthorpe (John Stowe 4, 17) — twice.
Robert Curteys (John Stowe 6).
268 ELLINGTON.
Thomas Gerowld (Thomas 4).
John Alenson (Thomas 7).
Robert Mok (Thomas 6, John 12, John Stowe 16 and 18).
Thomas Hikeson (Thomas 15, 16, John Stowe 9, William Witlesey 3).
Thomas Fote, alias Coper (Thomas 19, 21).
Thomas Burgeys (John 1, 5, 11, John Crowland 1, John Stowe 3).
Thomas Buk (John 14).
Thomas Bateman (John Stowe 3).
Thomas Peinell of Sibthorp (John Stowe 18).
John Baron (John Stowe 33) — twice.
27r **269** NAMES OF THE NAIFS OF HOLYWELL.
John At Well (Thomas 4, John Stowe 14).
Thomas Hunney (Thomas 10, 16, 20 and 22).
Roger Hunney (John Stowe 18).
John Grey (Thomas 8).
John Deye (Thomas 16).
Nicholas Skott (Thomas 20, 21, John 6, John Stowe 31).
Alice Sander (Thomas 22, John Stowe 9).
Thomas Nicholas (John 3 and 9).
Thomas Edward (John 4 and 8).
John Elyett (John Stowe 9).
John Gere (John Stowe 17, and 19).
270 ELSWORTH.
William Alynson (Thomas 5).
John West (Thomas 8 and 13, John 5)
Robert Boner (Thomas 10 and 16, John Stowe 14, 18, 22 and 23).
John Yntte (Thomas 13, 15, John 8, John Stowe 19).
John Elyett (Thomas 14, 18, John Stowe 14).
Agnes Hebbe (Thomas 14).
Agnes Flesshewer (Thomas 21).
John Attwod (John Crowland 1, John Stowe 5, 8 and 16).
John Smyth (John Stowe 3).
Robert Yolt (John Stowe 31).
271 WARBOYS.
John Harsene (Thomas 5).
Hugo Rolf (Thomas 2).
John Baron (Thomas 6).

Thomas Semar (Thomas 7, 12).
William Sande (Thomas 7, 21).
John Wilkys (Thomas 7, John Stowe 23).
William Berynger (Thomas 8, 10, 11, 13 and 20).
Richard Benson (Thomas 9, John Stowe 6, 25, 26 and 33).
Thomas Eyer (Thomas 10 and 17).
John Flemyng (Thomas 10).
Agnes Brounyng (Thomas 10).
Thomas Edward (Thomas 11).
Thomas Molt (Thomas 12, 13 and John 2).
John Woolt (Thomas 13).
John Bennytt (Thomas 16, John 1, John Stowe 1 and 5).
Alicia Freman (Thomas 22).
John Berynger (John 2, John Stowe 4, 5 — twice, and 17).
Richard Margarete (John 2).
John Plumbe (John 5, John Stowe 5).
John Wylson (John 13).
John Benessun (John Croyland 2).
William Scutt (John Stowe 2).
William Raveley (John Stowe 6 and 10).
John Newman (Thomas 28, William Witlesey 3).
John Justice (William Witlesey 3).
John Barynger (John Warboys 3).
272 SLEPE.
Simon Koc (Thomas 5).
Henry Sewyn (Thomas 7).
Simon Brunne (Thomas 8 and 20).
Emma Turster (Thomas 8).
John Wro of Woodhurst (Thomas 8).
Thomas Hunnye (Thomas 8).
Simon Herroff (Thomas 14, 16, John 2).
John Pokys (Thomas 15).
John Ravyn (Thomas 16).
Thomas Cutt (John 4, 6, 8, John Stowe 8 and 32).
Johanna Grene (John Stowe 18).
273 SHILLINGTON.
John Wyldfowle (Thomas 3).
Thomas West (Thomas 3, 18, John Stowe 9).
Richard Attgrene (Thomas 3, 18).
John Barfott (Thomas 4, 23, John 13).
Johanna Goddard (Thomas 5).
Robert Carter (Thomas 5).
John Smyth (Thomas 5, 16 and 12).
John Atmede (Thomas 5 and 12).
John Sparrow and Adam Sparrow (Thomas 9).
Nicholas Grave (Thomas 10, John Stowe 8 and 23).
John Atwood (Thomas 10, 16, and 19 — twice).
Richard Attgrave (Thomas 10).
Thomas Stonleye (Thomas 14, John Stowe 12).
William Pryouor (Thomas 14).

Isabella Howghton (Thomas 14).
Gilbert Attbroke (Thomas 16).
William Atthyll of Pegsdon (John 3, John Stowe 6).
William Chybbele, alias Atfan (John 5, 12, John Stowe 8).
Henry Hamond (John 6, John Stowe 12).
Gilbert del Hyll (John Crowland 2, John Stowe 9).
John Grene (John Stowe 1 and 10).
William Herberd (Thomas 2).
William Howesson, alias Smyth (Thomas 6).
John Colman (Thomas 23 — twice; William Witlesey 4).
274 CRANFIELD.
John Abeyn (Thomas 4).
John Frost (Thomas 4, John Stowe 1).
Richard Catlyn (Thomas 5, 18).
John Terry (Thomas 5, John 10, John Stowe 3).
Thomas Catlyn (Thomas 6, John 6).
John Alyn (Thomas 6, John 5, 10, John Stowe 3).
John Athyrst (Thomas 6).
Edmund Chyld and Richard at Rede (Thomas 6).
Thomas of the Hyll (Thomas 7, John 1).
Henry of the Mede (Thomas 7, John 15, John Stowe 6).
John Gudwyn (Thomas 14).
Matilda Rydeler (Thomas 20, John 1).
Henry Hamond (John 1).
John Sare (John 2 and 6).
William Joye (Thomas 6).
Richard Alyn (Thomas 11, John Crowland 1, John Stowe 9, 16, 19; William Witlesey 5).
Thomas Dunwud (John 11, 15, John Stowe 3).
Richard Curteys (John Stowe 3, 24, William Witlesey 1).
Thomas Berell (John Stowe 24).
27v   **275** WISTOW CUM RAVELEY.
Thomas Owty (Thomas 4, 13, 14, 21, John Stowe 8, 9, 13, 14, 20, 24).
John Gowler (Thomas 4).
Nicholas Martyn (Thomas 5 and 10).
Robert Attgate (Thomas 11, John 3, John Stowe 8, 10).
William Hyche (Thomas 12, 13 — twice; John Stowe 4).
John Frawnce (Thomas 18, John Stowe 4).
Robert Randolf (John 7, John Stowe 4).
Thomas Asplond (John 7, John Stowe 17, 24).
John Aylmer (John 11, John Stowe 12).
Richard Willson (John 13, John Stowe 3, 19, 27 and 29).
Thomas Boone (William Witlesey 2).
276 HEMINGFORD ABBOTS.
Robert Marchall (John 14, John Stowe 11).
Henry Cok (Thomas 4).
William Osmond (Thomas 6).
John Seld (John Stowe 7).
Thomas Hyrd (Thomas 6, 13, William Witlesey 5).
Alicia Trap (Thomas 11, 15).

John Heyne (Thomas 11, 12, John 6).
Emma Newman (Thomas 18, John Stowe 29).
Alicia Yngell (Thomas 18, John Stowe 20).
William Martyn (Thomas 23).
Robert Bryndhowse (John 3).
277 BURWELL.
Thomas Sparwe (Thomas 3).
Simon Styward (Thomas 4, 8, 20).
Thomas Swyne (Thomas 4).
William Ideyn (Thomas 5).
Thomas Plumbe (Thomas 8, 14, John Stowe 9).
William Howghton (Thomas 15).
Thomas Rower (John 2).
278 GRAVELEY.
William Essex, alias Franceys (Thomas 6).
Robert Newman (Thomas 6, 10, 23, John 1, 4).
John Algar (Thomas 7, 10).
Thomas Poleyard (Thomas 8, 20).
Walter Benyt (Thomas 9).
John Dyke (Thomas 11).
Robert Danyel (Thomas 11).
John Rabat (Thomas 15, John Stowe 2, 16, 30).
William Robet (John 1).
Richard Smyth (John Crowland 2, John Stowe 4, 8, 11).
Thomas Barton (John Stowe 10, 12).
John Rolf (Thomas 12, 28).
John Baron (Thomas 13, 21, 27).
279 WALSOKEN CUM POPENHOE.
John Hunt (John Stowe 10).
Jacob Palmer (John Stowe 33).
280 BROUGHTON.
Robert Balde (Thomas 8, 12).
William Butler and John Butteler (Thomas 13).
John Barnwel (Thomas 10, William Witlesey 1).
William Asplond (Thomas 10).
Richard Wilson (Thomas 13).
William Justyce (John 4, 6, John Stowe 2).
John Poole (John 6).
Johanna Wryght (Thomas 8).
Richard Cabe (Thomas 9, John Stowe 3, 6, 7, 15, 18).
William Nele (John Stowe 30, 32).
Thomas Boone (William Witlesey 3).
281 HOUGHTON.
John Sawnder (Thomas 8, 9).
Roger Elyott (Thomas 8, John 5, John Stowe 3).
William Atkyn (Thomas 19, John 1, John Stowe 14).
John Andrew (Thomas 20, John Stowe 8, 10).
John Roger (Thomas 22).
Robert Upton (John 7, John Stowe 13).
Richard Poole (John Crowland 2, John Stowe 5).
Robert Harveys (John Stowe 2).

Thomas Robyn (John Stowe 4).
John Carter (Thomas 4, 14).
John Newman (Thomas 10).
John Gottys (Thomas 10).
John Merchall (Thomas 13).
William Weythe (Thomas 13).
John Alyn (Thomas 32).
282 UPWOOD CUM GREAT RAVELEY.
Richard Albyn (Thomas 8, John Stowe 4, 13).
William Heryng (Thomas 10, 17, 19).
William Symon (Thomas 11).
Richard Peyn (Thomas 11).
Robert Mylys (John 8).
John Andrew (John Stowe 15).
Thomas Gowlar (Thomas 19, 22, 28, 29).
John Pope (Thomas 23).
Thomas Rede (Thomas 33).
283 CHATTERIS.
John Danherd (Thomas 9).
John Byllar (John 2).
John Fythyon (John 14).
Thomas Gere (John Stowe 19).
Peter Asplond (Thomas 24).
284 GIDDING.
John West (Thomas 10).
285 KNAPWELL.
Andrew Boykyn (John 6, 14).
John Lawe (John Stowe 6, 8, 13).
Roger and Jacob Denyell (Thomas 9).
28r   **286** LITTLE STUKELEY.
Beatrix Foote (John 11).
287 RAMSEY.
Agnes Freman (Thomas 11).
28v   *Blank*

6 THOMAS BUTTERWYK (1401-1402)

29r   **288** HOLYWELL (3 October: leet with court) John Schepherde Jr.: 13 and a half acres of demesne in the fields of Holywell and Needingworth previously held by John Schepherde Sr., for life, rendering annually 14s.10d. in equal portions at the feasts of the Annunciation, St. Andrew, the Translation of St. Benedict and the Nativity of Blessed Mary. G.: 6s.8d.

289 HOLYWELL (3 October: leet with court) Radulph Smyth and his wife, Amicia: one cote with adjacent curtilage and two acres of demesne in Stonydole previously held by William Smyth, for life, rendering annually in all things as did William. G.: 10s.

290 HOLYWELL (3 October: leet with court) Nicholas Godfrey and his wife, Elena: one plot with building and a half-virgate of servile land previously held by Thomas Brayn, in *minor censum* for life, rendering annually all services and customs rendered by other tenants in *minor censum*, with mowing service for one day at the time of the mowing of the fen. G.: 12d.

291 HOLYWELL (3 October: leet with court) Radulph Smyth and his wife, Amicia: one acre of demesne in Brerecroft previously held by Simon Arnold, for life, rendering annually 3s.8d. at the customary times. G.: excused, because of the payment of another gersuma by Radulph.

292 ST. IVES (4 October: leet with court). John West, and his wife, Emma: a half-row between the row of John Makeseye and William Fyshere and previously held by John West himself and once held by Alexander Eugen, for life, rendering annually 14s. at the customary times, with the obligation to maintain the property in good repair. *Et non licebit*, etc. G.: 2s.8d.

29v

293 WARBOYS (5 October: leet with court). Agnes, daughter of John Baroun and naif of the lord, pays 4s. for license to marry John Nedham, freeman, within the fief of the lord, this time.

294 WARBOYS (5 October: leet with court) Robert Benet: one plot with building and three quarters of servile land previously held by John Othehyll, for life, rendering annually in all things as did John. G.: 40d.

295 WARBOYS (5 October: leet with court) Thomas Eduard of Warboys: one plot with building and one virgate of servile land previously held by John Wenyngton, in bondage, for life, rendering annually in all things as did John. G.: 12d.

296 ST. IVES (4 October: leet with court, at Slepe) Robert Takell, his wife, Elena, and their son, John: a half-row next to the row of John Peyntour and previously held by John Bocher, for life, rendering annually 10s. at the customary times, with the obligation to maintain the property in good repairs. *Et non licebit*, etc. G.: 20d.

30r

297 CRANFIELD (10 October: leet with court) Alicia, daughter of Thomas Catelyn and naif of the lord, pays 40d. for license to live off the fief and marry whomever she wishes.

298 CRANFIELD (10 October: leet with court) Thomas Joye: one acre of demesne in the fields of Pirye previously held by John Dekene, for life, rendering annually in all things as did John. G.: 2d.

299 CRANFIELD (10 October: leet with court) Margeria, daughter of John Aleyn of Woodend and naif of the lord, pays 2s. for license to marry John atte Hyrst, within the fief.

300 CRANFIELD (10 October: leet with court) William, son of Thomas Baylly: one messuage and a half-virgate of servile land previously held by his father, in bondage, for life, rendering annually in all things as did his father. However, until the said William reaches full age, the land will be in the custody of William Borell and John Perye. G.: 2s.

301 CRANFIELD (10 October: leet with court) Thomas Catelyn Jr. one cote with adjacent curtilage previously held by John Groby, for life, rendering in all things as did John. G.: 2s.

302 BARTON (12 October: General Court) Margaret, daughter of Edmund Chyld and naif of the lord, pays 5s. for license to marry Galfridus atte Wode, freeman, within the fief.

303 BARTON (12 October: General Court) Galfridus atte Wode: one croftland once held by John Homely and now held for life by Margaret Chyld, for life. G.: 20d.

30v

304 BARTON (12 October: General Court) Peter Boys: one cotland previously held by William Roger, for life, rendering annually in all things as did William. G.: 2s.

305 BARTON (12 October: General Court) Richard, son of John Stonle: one cotland and one croftland previously held by Andrew Chaunceller, in bondage, for life, rendering annually in all things as did Andrew. G.: 40d.

306 SHILLINGTON (13 October: leet with court) John Beston: one plot in ruins and a half-virgate of servile land previously held by Nicholas Piers, in bondage, from the previous Michaelmas for 12 years, rendering annually in all things as did Nicholas, with the condition that he will rebuild the plot with a new house 40 feet long and 14 feet wide within four years. G.: 2s.

307 SHILLINGTON (13 October: leet with court) Alicia Bonker and Simon Thomhyll: one messuage and a half-virgate of servile land previously held by Thomas Bonker, late husband of Alicia and which as is more fully contained in the court roll, for life, rendering annually in all things as did Thomas. G.: 40d. Heriot: recorded in the court roll.

308 THERFIELD (15 October: leet with court) Isabella, widow of Robert Piers, and her daughter, Agnes: one pithel within the site of the manor called Bernewyk, together with one messuage previously held by Richard Bullok, and 12 acres of servile land previously held by Robert Gerveys, in bondage, for life, rendering annually 16s. at the customary times. G.: one capon.

31r   **309** THERFIELD (15 October: leet with court) William Frere: one plot with building and 15 acres of servile land previously held by his father, John Frere, together with another plot with building and 15 acres of servile land previously held by Robert Stevene, and one toft with 10 acres of servile land previously held by the same Robert, in bondage for life, rendering annually all services and customs owed therein. G.: 10s.

310 THERFIELD (15 October: leet with court) Katerina, daughter of John Sperver and naif of the lord, pays 12d. for license to marry John, son of William Watte, naif of the lord, within the fief of the lord, this time.

311 BURWELL (17 October: leet with court) Constancia, widow of John Kyng, and her son, John: half of one tenement of 24 acres once held by Edmund Poul and recently held by her husband, the other half of which is now held by John Aylwynne, in *arentatio*, from the previous Michaelmas for 20 years, rendering annually 11s. at the customary times, as rent, and 2d. as common fine.

312 BURWELL (17 October: leet with court) Same Constancia and John: one toft of one croft previously held by John Kyng and once held by Robert Bocher, in *arentatio* from the previous Michaelmas for 20 years, rendering annually 6d. at the customary times. G.: 2s.

313 BURWELL (17 October: same court) John Aillesham and his wife, Maria: one cote with croft pertaining to a tenement of 20 acres lying in Northstrete next to the tenement of John Baret, on the east, and previously held by John atte Hyll, together with the aforesaid 20 acres, in *arentatio* from the previous Michaelmas for 20 years, rendering annually 5s. at the customary times. G.: 6d.

31v   **314** BURWELL (17 October: leet with court) Nicholas, son of John atte Hyll: one built up tenement of 20 acres previously held by John atte Hyll, in *arentatio* for 20 years, rendering annually 15s. at the customary times, 4d. as common fine, and reaping, binding, and tribute of two acres of grain of the demesne land. Pledge for maintaining the property: William Poket. G.: 2s.

315 BYTHORNE (25 October: leet with court) John Bywerth: one plot with building and one quarter of servile land previously held by John Bocher, in bondage, for life, rendering annually in all things as did Bocher. G.: 12d.

316 BYTHORNE (25 October: leet with court) John Randolf, chaplain: one cote with curtilage and one adjacent acre previously held by William Barbour, for life, rendering annually in all things as did William. G.: 12d.

317 BYTHORNE (25 October: leet with court) Richard Evesham: half of one built up messuage and a half-virgate of servile land previously held by William Barbour, for life, rendering annually in all things as did William. G.: 12d.

318 FITON (26 October: leet with court) John Holm: one built up cote with a built up curtilage and croft previously held by John Best, in bondage, for life, rendering annually in all things as did Best. G.: 4d.

32r **319** Elton (26 October: leet with court) Galfridus Webster: one plot with building with adjoining croft and garden previously held by John Germyn, in bondage, for life, rendering annually 4s. and in all things as did John. G.: 4d.

320 Elton (26 October: leet with court) Robert Ferour: one plot with building and one virgate of servile land previously held by William Forster, in bondage for life, rendering annually in all things as did William. G.: 12d.

321 Warboys (30 October) John Nunne: one tenement called dichmanland previously held by Juliana Packerell, for life, rendering annually in all things as did Juliana. G.: 4s.

322 Wistow (30 October) William Heryng Jr.: five acres and a half-acre of demesne at Kynggeslond previously held by William Chaumberleyn, for life, rendering annually 10d. per acre, at the customary times. G.: one capon.

323 Upwood (6 November) William Bracer: those butts in le Stokkyng called a "forland" previously held by William Chaumberleyn, for life, rendering annually 4d. at Michaelmas. G.: excused by the seneschal.

324 Brington (9 November) Thomas Gander: one cote with adjacent croft, together with six acres and a half-rod of land lying in diverse parcels previously held by Roger Berounesson, in bondage for life, rendering annually in all things as did Roger. G.: 40d., paid to the seneschal of Ramsey, and then he is quit.

32v **325** St. Ives (1 December) Benedict Baron Draper: two and a half-rows previously held by Galfridus Bykeleswade and surrendered by him, through the hands of Brother Richard of Schenyngdon, seneschal of Ramsey, to the use of Benedict, from the previous Easter for life, rendering annually 26s. in equal portions at the customary times, with the first payment due at the previous Michaelmas. He will maintain the property in good repair. *Et non licebit*, etc. G.: 10s., and no more because of a rent increase of 4s.

326 Cranfield (5 December) Thomas, son of Hugo Terry: one messuage with one pithel and six acres of demesne previously held by Hugo and surrendered back to the lord by him to the use of Thomas, for life, rendering annually in all things as did Hugo. G.: 20d.

327 Cranfield (5 December) John, son of Hugo Terry: the reversion of one messuage and a half-virgate of servile land now held by Hugo and his wife, Cristiana, for life, rendering annually in all things as did Hugo. G.: 2s.

328 Cranfield (6 December) William Joye: the whole part of a certain hedge called Portenhalehegge, the other part of which the same William now holds, along with a croft called Bryttendenneshyll, for life, from the previous Michaelmas, with all produce and profits and without any waste or destruction, rendering annually one capon at Easter, and all other services owed therein. G.: excused by the seneschal.

33r **329** St. Ives (8 December) John Bate, his wife, Cecilia, and their son, William: two half-rows previously held by Thomas Beteryng, for life, rendering annually 26s.8d. at the customary times, and in all things as did Thomas, with the obligation to maintain the property in good repair. *Et non licebit*, etc. G.: 2s.

330 Therfield (23 December) Maurice Bode, John atte Wode, John Gerveys, Richard atte Wode and William Waryn of Fynehouses: one plot with building, 30 acres of servile land and one toft with another 30 acres of servile land previously held by John Waryn, from the previous Michaelmas until someone else comes who wants to take up that land for an increase of rent in one fixed payment and for services as specified in a certain Rental made in the time of the farming of the village, rendering, in the meantime, annually in all things as did John, with the obligation to repair and maintain the property at their own expense.

331 HOLYWELL (27 December) Agnes, daughter of Thomas Cartere of Needingworth and naif of the lord, pays 40d. for license to marry Nicholas Gybbe, freeman.

332 WARBOYS (1 January) Richard Smyth: one mondayland previously held by John Benet, in *arentatio* from the previous Michaelmas, for life, rendering annually 4s. at the customary times, with the first payment due at the previous feast of St. Andrew. If, in the future, Richard puts lead in the bake oven or installs a hand mill, he will not dismiss them to anyone at the end of the term unless at his own will. G.: 6d.

333 WARBOYS (1 January) John Collessone Jr. of Wistow: one plot with building and one virgate of servile land previously held by William Olyver, in *arentatio*, for life, rendering annually 16s. at the customary times, with the first payment due at the next feast of the Annunciation, together with a ploughing *precaria*, two autumn *precariae*, mowing of the meadow in Chevereth for one day, and carrying of six quarters of grain and barley, whenever summoned, from Warboys to Ramsey. He will contribute to the common fine, as do other tenants in *arentatio*. G.: 2s.

33v **334** HOUGHTON (1 October) William Roger and his son, Robert: one plot with building and two cotlands previously held by John Ede, and a half-virgate of servile land recently held by Ede for 6s., in *arentatio* for life, rendering annually for the cotlands, as did Ede, and for the half-virgate, 5s. at the customary times. G.: 20d.

335 UPWOOD (15 January) Nicholas Alston: one quarter of servile land in Great Raveley recently held by John Cok Sr., in *arentatio* for life, rendering annually 3s.4d. at the customary times, and in all things as did John. G.: 2s.

336 HEMINGFORD ABBOTS (19 January) William Osmunde, naif of the lord, pays 6d. for license to live outside the fief at Hartford, with the obligation to render 6d. annually as chevage at Hemingford, the day of the leet. Payments will cease if, in the future, he resides in Hemingford.

337 WARBOYS (24 January) Robert Cole: one quarter of servile land without messuage previously held by Henry Eduard, in *arentatio* for life, rendering annually 3s.4d. at the customary times, and in all things as did Henry. G.: excused, because of a rent increase of 10d.

338 BROUGHTON (January) John Schepherde Jr.: one plot with building and one quarter of servile land previously held by John Schepherde Sr., for life, rendering annually in all things as did John Sr. G.: 4d.

339 WISTOW (1 February) John Schepherde, son of Nicholas Schepherde, Jr.: surrender of one plot with building and a half-virgate previously held by John Waryn, to the use of John Outy Sr., from the next Michaelmas, for life, rendering annually in 34r all things as did John Schepherde. G.: 20d.

340 WARBOYS (8 February) John Berenger Wryghte: one ruined plot and one quarter of servile land previously held by Thomas Hychesson, in *arentatio* for life, rendering annually 5s. at the customary times, one autumn *precaria*, common fine, and mowing of the lord's meadow in Chevereth, as do certain of his peers. G.: 6d.

341 WARBOYS (8 February) William Berenger: one plot with building and one half-virgate of servile land previously held by Margaret Eduard, for life, rendering annually 8s. at the customary times, ploughing *precariae*, autumn *precariae*, mowing of the lord's meadow in Chevereth, making hay, carrying service at Easter with a wagon, and common fine, as do certain of this peers, for all other services. G.: excused by the seneschal.

342 ST. IVES (24 February) Cristina Joseph and her daughter, Matilda: one row previously held by her husband, Joseph Tayllour, for life, rendering annually all services and customs owed therein and in all other things as did her husband. G.: 40d.

343 ST. IVES (24 February) Richard Eton and his wife, Isabella: one half-row previously held by Robert Iryssh, for life, rendering annually all rents, services and customs as did Robert. G.: 5s.

34v **344** UPWOOD (24 February) William Purquey: one plot with building and a half-virgate of servile lands with appurtenances in Great Raveley previously held by Peter Gray, in *arentatio* for life, rendering annually 10s. at the customary times, and carrying service in summer with his own wagon at the summons of the bailiff. G. excused by the seneschal.

345 WARBOYS (12 March: outside the court) Robert Gildesowe: surrender through the hands of the bailiff, of one cote with appurtenances opposite the gate and previously held by John Gerold, together with two acres of demesne in Ryvelond, to the use of Thomas Asplond, for life, rendering annually in all things as did Robert. G.: 6d.

346 ABBOTS RIPTON (19 March) John Nichol Jr.: one plot with building and one virgate of servile land previously held by John Nichol, his father, together with a lot of Langelond previously held by John Wyllesssone, in *arentatio*, from the next Michaelmas for life, rendering annually 24s. at the customary times, and all other services and customs rendered by those holding in *arentatio*. G.: 40d.

347 GRAVELEY (26 March) Isabella, daughter of William Essex and naif of the lord, pays 10s. for license to marry John Seburgh of Yelling, freeman, this time.

348 HOUGHTON (28 March) Thomas Hervy Jr.: one plot with building and one virgate of servile land previously held by Robert Smyth, in *arentatio* for life, rendering annually 12s. at the customary times. G.: 12d.

349 ELLINGTON (29 March) Robert Payn: surrender through the hands of John Lethenard, bailiff, outside the court, of all his right and status in one plot with building and one virgate of servile land with appurtenances in Coten previously held by Roger Peverell, to the use of William Couper in perpetuity for life, rendering annually in all things as did Robert. G.: one capon, and no more, because he has paid other *gersumae*.

35r **350** ELLINGTON (29 March) John Lethenard, in person and in the presence of the seneschal of Ramsey: surrender of one plot with building and one virgate of servile land in Sibthorp in the parish of Ellington previously held by Walter de Lethenard, to the use of John Penyhill, in bondage for life, rendering annually in all things as did John, with the obligation to support all the burdens regarding the property, and to maintain the property in good repair. Pledge for maintenance: Lethenard. G.: 10s.

351 ELLINGTON (29 March) John Wynter, outside the court: surrender, through the hands of the bailiff, of one plot with building and a half-virgate of servile land, to the use of John Bocher, for life, rendering annually in all things as did Wynter. G.: 2s.

352 WISTOW (2 April) John Asplond Sr.: one cotland previously held by Peter Waker, in *arentatio* for life, rendering annually 2s. at the customary times, and carrying service, with the first payment due at the next feast of the Nativity of Blessed Mary. G.: two capons.

353 HOLYWELL (3 April) Agnes, daughter of Robert Houghton of Needingworth and naif of the lord, pays 40d. for license to marry Thomas Galyon of Hilgay, this time. Pledge: John Robynnesson.

354 CHATTERIS (3 April) Stephen Leche: one plot with building and four adjacent acres previously held by John Leche and his wife, Katerina, in bondage for life, rendering annually in all things as did John and Katerina. One *camera* in the eastern part of the aforesaid plot with building is to be reserved to Katerina for life, together with free access to half of a curtilage pertaining to that building. G.: 6s.8d.

355 CHATTERIS (3 April) Roger Aleyn: one plot with building with four adjacent acres previously held by John Wynewyk, for life, rendering annually in all things as did John. G.: 10s.

35v **356** ST. IVES (5 April) John Revenhale and his wife, Johanna: a half-row in Bridge Street previously held by John Bande Tayllour and once held by William Meyne, for life, rendering annually 24s. at the customary times, with the first payment due at the next Michaelmas, and all other services and customs owed therein. They will maintain the property in good repair. *Et non licebit*, etc. G.: excused by the seneschal because of repairs.

357 HEMINGFORD ABBOTS (9 April) Margaret, daughter of Thomas Hirde and naif of the lord, pays 3s. for license to marry Thomas Lincolne, freeman, on the fief of the lord. Pledge: Thomas Hirde.

358 HEMINGFORD ABBOTS (9 April). Thomas Lincolne and Margaret (Hirde): one cote with appurtenances previously held by Thomas Hirde, for life, rendering annually in all things as did Hirde. G.: 6d.

359 WISTOW (23 April) Robert de Ely: one plot with building and a half-virgate of servile land recently held by John Outy Sr. and once held by John Waryn, for life, rendering annually in all things as did John, with the first payment due at the next feast of St. Andrew. G.: nothing, because the property is in ruins.

360 ABBOTS RIPTON (30 April) John Martyn: in the presence of Brother Richard Schenyngdon, seneschal of Ramsey, surrender of one plot with building and a half-virgate previously held by Philip Beton and a quarter of servile land with appurtenances in Ripton once held by Gilbert de Hurst, to the use of Roger Gardyner, for life, rendering as did John Martyn for the half-virgate, and 4s. annually at the customary times, in *arentatio*, for the quarter of land. The same Roger: the reversion of 11 rods of demesne land calles Suakache, now held for life by Martyn, for life, rendering annually 2s.3d. at the customary times. G.: 6d.

36r **361** ABBOTS RIPTON (30 April) Juliana Thedeware: surrender, in the presence of Brother Richard Schenyngdon, seneschal of Ramsey, of one plot with building, a half-virgate of servile land, one empty plot and a half-virgate of servile land previously held by John Thedeware, to the use of William Thedeware, *ad censa*, until he marries. G.: excused by the senschal, because he is a pauper.

362 SLEPE (30 April) William Herrof: surrender, in the presence of the seneschal, of one plot with building with adjacent curtilage previously held by Simon Herrof, to the use of William Bernewell, his wife, Alicia, and their daughter, Margaret, in bondage, for life, rendering annually 13s.4d. at the customary times, with the first payment due at the feast of the Translation of St. Benedict.

363 SLEPE (30 April) Same William, Alicia and Margaret Bernewell: one empty plot and a half-virgate of servile land previously held by John Slow, in *arentatio* for life, rendering annually 11s. at the customary times, with the first payment due the feast of St. Andrew. G: 4s.

364 ELTON (7 May) John Bythorne Jr.: one plot with building and one quarter of servile land previously held by John Bythorne, his father, for life, rendering annually in all things as did John Sr. G.: excused by the seneschal.

365 ELTON (16 May) John, son of Richard atte Cros: all lands and tenements previously held by John Blachaf and escheated to the lord, and more recently held by Richard atte Cros, for life, rendering annually 11s. at the customary times and all services and customs rendered by his father, with the obligation to repair and maintain the property. Pledges: John Bythorne Jr. and John atte Cros Jr. G.: 6d.

366 CRANFIELD (21 May) Isabella, daughter of Richard atte Rode and naif of the lord, pays 40d. for license to marry whomever she wishes, this time.

367 CRANFIELD (21 May) Henry atte Mede: one cote in ruins containing one acre of land previously held by Richard Brettenden, for life, rendering annually in all things as did Richard. G.: 3d., and no more, because of the ruined condition of the property.

368 BRINGTON (27 May) Emma, daughter of William Pirye and naif of the lord, pays 6s.8d. for license to marry Thomas Gander, freeman, within the fief of the lord.

369 BRINGTON (27 May) Thomas Gander and Emma Pirye: one plot with building and three quarters of servile land with appurtenances previously held by John Beverech, for life, rendering annually in all things as did John. G.: 40d.

36v **370** WISTOW (4 June) John Asplond: surrender of one cotland with appurtenances in Little Ravelcy, previously held by Peter Waker, to the use of the same Peter Waker, in *arentatio* for life, rendering annually 2s. at the customary times, and carrying service. G.: one capon.

371 ELTON (4 June) William Forster: surrender through the hands of John Hobbesson, bailiff, of one plot with building and a half-virgate of servile land with appurtenances in Elton previously held by Robert Ferour, to the use of John Bate, in bondage for life, rendering annually in all things as did Robert, with the obligation to maintain the property in good repair. Pledges for maintenance: William Wakefeld and Richard Couherde. G.: 8d.

372 CHATTERIS (6 June: court) William Newman and John Newman: one plot with building with four acres of land and four acres of meadow previously held by Roger Aleyn and once held by John Wynnewyk, in bondage for life, rendering annually in all things as did Roger. G.: 6s.8d.

373 CHATTERIS (6 June: court) John Lytholf Jr.: one tenement of eight acres and one cote with appurtenances previously held by his father, Stephen Lytholf, for life, rendering annually in all things as did his father, with the western half of a plot, half the adjacent croft, one and a half-acres of Myllefeld, a half-acre in Estfurlong and a half-acre in Hersladefeld reserved for life to Margaret, mother of John Newman. G.: 5s.

374 WESTON (9 June) John Reynold and his wife, Amicia: one plot with building and one quarter of servile land and adjoining demesne land recently dismissed to farm and previously held by Walter Cartere, for life, rendering annually in things as did Walter. G.: 12d.

375 WARBOYS (11 June) Cristina, daughter of John Baron and naif of the lord, pays 18d. for license to marry William Laweman of Hemingford Abbots, naif of the lord, this time.

376 WISTOW (11 June) Richard Rede: two acres and one rod of demesne land lying at Henndhegges previously held by Richard Wodecok, for life, rendering annually 12d. per acre at the customary times, which land used to render 16d. annually. G.: two capons.

37r **377** WARBOYS (18 June) Thomas Fraunceys: surrender of one mondayland previously held by Hugo Webster, to the use of William Sande, for life.

378 ELTON (19 June: court) William Couherde: one empty plot and one quarter of servile land and one cote with appurtenances previously held by his father, Richard Couherde, rendering annually in all things as did Richard, with the obligation to maintain the property in good repair. Pledges for maintenance: Richard Hiche and Richard Abbot. G.: 6d.

379 ELTON (19 June: court) John, son of John Rumbold: one plot with building and one quarter of servile land with appurtenances previously held by his father, rendering annually in all things as did his father. G.: 4d.

380 BRINGTON Surrender by John, in person but outside the court and in the presence of Brother Richard Schenyngdon, seneschal of Ramsey, of one plot with building and a half-virgate of servile land with appurtenances in Brington, together with adjacent land, meadow and pasture of demesne previously held by William Perye, to the use of Thomas Hacoun and his wife, Margeria, in bondage for life, rendering annually in all things as did John. G.: 6d.

381 WESTON Surrender by Beatrix, widow of Roger Barton, in the aforesaid manner, of one plot with building and one virgate of servile land with appurtenances, together with adjacent land and meadow, previously held by Roger Barton, to the use of her son, John Barton, for life, rendering annually in all things as did Beatrix. G.: 6d.

382 WESTON Margaret, daughter of Adam Cartere and naif of the lord, pays 3s.4d. for license to marry Andrew Thatchere, freeman, within the fief, this time.

383 SHILLINGTON (26 June: court) Robert Pole: surrender of one plot with building, one virgate of servile land in Hanscomb, and 10 acres of demesne land at Chalkeshull previously held by Philip Richard, to the use of Gilbert atte Brook, his wife, Lucia, and their son, John, in bondage for life, rendering annually in all things as did Robert, unless any heirs come in the future to claim it and reimburse Gilbert, Lucia and John for their expenses as determined by the judgment of the lord, the court and the tenants elected and sworn for that purpose. G. and heriot: 20s.

37v **384** SHILLINGTON (26 June: court) Robert Lewyn: surrender of one plot with building and one virgate of servile land called Greneslond, with appurtenances in that village, to the use of John Kychener, his wife, Katerina, and their son, John, for life, rendering annually in all things as did Robert and all other services and customs owed therein. Further, if any heir comes to claim that tenement, he shall reimburse them for all their expenses as determined by the lord's court and his tenants elected and sworn to this purpose. G. and heriot: 10s.

385 BARTON (same court) John Stonle: surrender of one croft and one cotland with appurtenances in that village, to the use of Edmund Burnard, in bondage for life, rendering annually in all things as did John. G.: 6s.8d. Heriot: one multon valued at 20d.

386 WARBOYS (1 July: court) William Wodecok: surrender of one and a half mondaylands with appurtenances in that village previously held by Richard Rede, to the use of William Ravele, for life, rendering annually in all things as did William. G.: 12d.

387 WARBOYS (1 July: court) John Molt: surrender of one half-plot and one quarter of servile land with appurtenances in Caldecote previously held by Richard Nunne, to the use of Thomas Asplond, in *arentatio*, for life, rendering annually 4s. at the customary times. G.: excused by the seneschal because of a rent increase.

388 SLEPE (6 July: court)[15] John Wynnegoode: surrender of one plot with building with appurtenances in Woodhurst and one virgate of servile land in Woodhurst previously held by his father, Thomas Wynnegoode, to the use of Roger Waryn of Pidley, in bondage for life, rendering annually all services and customs as are more fully contained in a certain new Rental. G.: 12d.

389 ELSWORTH (13 July: court)[16] Grant by the lord to Katerina Chicheley of one *camera* within a certain cote previously held by her late husband, Simon, and now held by Robert Braughyng, freely, without any burdens, for life, with free access to that *camera* by the King's road. G.: excused, because she is a pauper.

38r **390** GRAVELEY (14 July: court)[17] Elena, daughter of Robert Newman and naif of the lord, pays 4s. for license to marry John atte Chirche, freeman, within the fief.

[15] See PRO 179/47. Entry not in roll.
[16] Ibid., not in roll.
[17] Ibid., not in roll.

391 HOLYWELL (14 July) William Albry of Fen Stanton: one cote with adjacent curtilage in Needingworth and two acres of demesne land in Stonydole once held by Radulph Smyth and recently held by William Smyth, in bondage for life, rendering annually in all things as did William. G.: excused by the seneschal because the property is in ruins.

392 SLEPE (17 July) William Herrof of Woodhurst, plough wright: one plot and one virgate of servile land with appurtenances in Woodhurst, together with a parcel of Bracheslond, previously held by Henry Wryghte, in bondage for life, rendering annually all services and customs owed therein and as are more fully contained in a certain new Rental, with the first payment due at Michaelmas after two full years. G.: excused, because the property is in ruins.

393 HOLYWELL (20 July: court) John Hemyngton: one acre of demesne land in Needingworth at Oxhowe previously held by Thomas Bernewell, for life, rendering annually 12d. at the customary times. G.: 8d.

394 WISTOW (July) William de Wistowe: surrender, outside the court, through the hands of the bailiff, of one cotland with appurtenances previously held by William Webster, to the use of William Stapilton Wodeward, in bondage for life, rendering annually all services and customs owed therein. G.: one capon.

395 ST. IVES (August) John Moryce and his wife, Lucia: the reversion of one row now held by William Botheby and his wife, Agnes, for life, rendering all rents, services and customs owed therein, with the obligation to maintain the property in good repair. *Et non licebit*, etc. G.: 2s.

396 WISTOW (21 September) Richard Fletton, rector of the church of Wistow: eight acres, three rods of demesne land in Stocroft, from the previous Michaelmas for life, rendering annually 4s.4d. in equal portions at the feasts of the Annunciation and the Nativity of Blessed Mary. G.: one capon.

38v **397** ST. IVES (August) John Barker and his wife, Margaret: two half-rows previously held by Richard atte Gate, for life, rendering annually in all things as did Richard, with the obligation to maintain the property in good repair. *Et non licebit*, etc. G.: 6s.8d.

398 RAMSEY (November). William Edward: From Brother Richard Overe, sub-cellarer of Ramsey, 10 acres and one rod lying at a place called "Undyrerodys", on the western side, for life, rendering to the sub-cellarer annually 3s.6d. in equal portions at Michaelmas and Easter, with the first payment due at Easter. G.: 20d.

39r *Blank*

9 THOMAS BUTTERWYK (1404-1405)[18]

39v **399** RAMSEY John Shyrwode, in the time of Richard Schenyngton, sub-cellarer: a certain meadow called "le Mechilhylke" with all appurtenances, a certain part of the meadow with nine acres being reserved to the lord for his own use, for life, rendering annually 6s.8d. in equal portions at Easter and the feast of the Nativity of Blessed Mary. He will repair and keep all the ditches of that meadow during the said time, nor will he relinquish, the property without the lord's license. He may take the willows growing there as often and as much as necessary, provided he plant new ones; he will keep that meadow separate during the said time; and, if the rent is in arrears at any term for one month, or if he impleads the monastery of Ramsey, the lord will reenter, retake and retain that meadow perpetually, without any contradiction. G.: excused.

---

[18] Years 7 and 8 of Thomas are missing. See supra, pp. 6-7.

400 BURWELL (same court, same day) Johanna Perye, widow of Henry Pomeray: one cote and one croft previously held by her husband and once held by John Smart, for life, rendering annually in all things as did Henry. G.: 12d. — 40r

401 BURWELL (same court) John Ayllewyn: one curtilage recently made of a furlong of the lord, at the eastern end, for life, rendering annually 10d. Also: two butts' ends alongside the old furlong of the lord, for life, rendering annually 4d. at the customary times, with the provision that the lord can make a furlong on that land without a reduction of rent. G.: excused, because of a rent increase of 4d.

402 ELSWORTH (24 July: court) Thomas Payn: one quarter of servile land previously held by John Sweyn and once held by Richard Leffeyn, in *arentatio* for life, rendering annually 5s. at the customary times. G.: 40d., and no more because of repairs.

403 ELSWORTH (24 July: court) Richard Brampton: one cote with adjacent croft of servile land previously held by John Pokebrook and once held by John Chyrcheman, in *arentatio*, for life, rendering annually 2s.6d. at the customary times and certain customs that the previous tenants were accustomed to render. G.: 12d., and no more because of repairs.

404 ELSWORTH (24 July: court) John Clerke: one cote and one quarter of servile land previously held by Thomas Pulter and once held by John Howessone, in bondage for life, rendering annually in all things as did Thomas and John. G.: 40d.

405 ELTON (court) John Kybatour: one quarter of servile land recently held by William Blakman Smyth from the tenement of Gamelys, in bondage for life, rendering annually all services and customs owed therein. G.: 6d.

406 ELTON (same court) William Tayllour: one plot with building and a half-virgate of land once held by Henry Balle, in bondage for life, rendering annually in all things as did Henry. Pledge: Thomas Harpe. G.: 2s.

407 ELTON (same court) William (blank): one quarter of servile land once held by Henry Robery, in bondage for life, rendering annually in all things as did Henry. Pledge: Thomas Harpe. G.: two capons. — 40v

408 ELTON (same court) Richard Hoberd, William Pokebrook and Richard Bate: one half-virgate of land in Wedwesplace, three quarters of land once held by Richard Dawys, one quarter of land once held by Maynard, and one virgate of land once held by Robert atte Welle, and a half-virgate of land once held by Allota atte Grene, for as long as it pleases the seneschal to dismiss the land or parcels for the old rent and farm, namely, for 5s. for each quarter of land; and they shall render annually to the lord 33s.4d., with the first payment due at the previous feast of the Nativity of St. John the Baptist. G.: excused, because of repairs.

409 WESTON Adam Cartere, naif of the lord, pays 10s. for license to marry his daughter, Agnes, to Thomas Thernyng, freeman, this time.

410 WESTON William Myllere, naif of the lord, pays 6s.8d. for license to marry his daughter, Beatrix, to John Moryssesman. Pledge: John Morys.

411 WISTOW (July) John Owty Jr.: one plot with building and three quarters of servile land containing two cotlands previously held by Peter Waker, in bondage, for life, rendering annually in all things as did Peter. G.: 10s. — 41r

412 BROUGHTON (August) John Justice: one plot and a half-virgate of servile land in *major censum* previously held by Richard Bowke, for life, rendering annually all services and customs owed therein. Also: one pithel next to "le Brook" opposite the aforementioned plot, for life, rendering annually 6d. at the customary times. G.: two capons.

413 WARBOYS (August) William Laurence: one virgate of servile land with one building previously held by John Colle and once held by William Olyver, in *arentatio*

for life, rendering as did John Colle and also rendering customs calles "Boshull", ploughing *precariae* and autumn *precariae*. G.: 6s.8d.

414 WARBOYS (August) John Wynde: one mondayland with one building once held by John Harsene, in bondage, for life, rendering annually in all things as did John Harsene. Also: one quarter of land in *arentatio* previously held by the same John Harsene, for life, rendering annually in all things as did John. Also: six acres of demesne land lying in le Stokkyng and once held by the same John Harsene, for life, rendering annually in all things as did John. G.: 6s.8d.

415 RAMSEY (August) John Webstere and his wife: in the time of Richard de Schcnyngdon, sub-cellarer, two built up cotes once held by Henry Worm and Thomas Wodeward, together with one empty plot lying in the Wyght next to the plot held by Thomas Wodeward, for life, rendering annually 11s. in equal portions at Easter and Michaelmas, with the first payment due at Michaelmas. Further, they will repair the property, except for thatch and clay supplied by the lord, together with heavy lumber straw and clay if, in the future, they build anything on the property. G.: two capons.

41v **416** RAMSEY (August) John Deynes: eight acres of demesne land called Snapeslond once held by John Brouse, for life, rendering 8s. at the customary times. G.: excused.

10 THOMAS BUTTERWYK (1405-1406)

417 BYTHORNE (October) Roger Baroun and his wife, Johanna: one quarter of land once held by John Baroun, for life, rendering in all things as did John. G.: 3s.4d.

418 BYTHORNE (October) Johanna, daughter of John Baroun and naif of the lord, pays 6s.8d. for license to marry Roger Baroun, freeman.

419 BROUGHTON (November) Richard, son of John Cabe, and his wife, Alicia: one virgate of servile land previously held by John Cabe, in bondage for life, rendering annually in all things as did John. Also: one quarter of land previously held by the same John, in *arentatio* in *major censum* for life, rendering annually in all things as did John. G.: 6s.8d.

420 BROUGHTON (November). Johanna, daughter of John Bernewell Sr. and naif of the lord, pays 6s.8d. for license to marry William of the Wold, freeman, and no more because he resides in the demesne of the lord abbot.

421 ELTON (November) John Waleys and his wife, Alicia: one virgate of servile land recently held by Robert Feror and once held by Henry Collesson, for life, rendering annually in all things as did Robert. G.: 6s.8d.

422 ELTON (November) John Bryan and his wife, Isabella: a half-virgate of land with one built up messuage previously held by John Germyn and once held by Richard de Elyngton, for life, rendering annually in all things as did John. Also: a half-virgate of servile land previously held by John Germyn and once held by Richard de Elyngton, for life, rendering annually in all things as did Germyn. G.: 3s.4d.

42r **423** CHATTERIS (November) Thomas Rede: one parcel of meadow in Hollode next to Ousedych once pertaining to the office of the custodian of Hollode, from the next Michaelmas for 10 years, rendering annually 6s.8d. at the customary times. G.: 12d.

424 CHATTERIS (November) John Howesson: a half building and two acres of servile land with adjoining meadow parcelled out of one tenement of eight acres once held by Richard Collesson, for life, rendering annually in all things as did Richard. G.: 6s.8d.

425 CHATTERIS (November) Simon Tomysson: two messuages lying in Pakersdole containing two acres and once held by John Asse, for life, rendering annually in all things as did John. G.: 3s.4d.

426 ELSWORTH (November) John Swynford, alias Braunghyng: one quarter of servile land of Gravelond once held by William Taillour, for life, rendering annually in all things as did William. G.: 40d.

427 ELSWORTH (November) Robert Barbor, alias Grym: a part of one virgate of Senleeslond once held by Henry Leman, for life, rendering in all things as did Henry. G.: 12d.

428 RAMSEY (February) Agnes, widow of William Freman: from Brother Thomas Pylketon, sub-cellarer, one meadow called Fremannesholm once held by the same William Freman and lying between the meadow called Ferthynges, on the east, and the meadow of the community, on the west, for life, rendering to the sub-cellarer and his successors annually 20d. at the customary times. G.: one capon.

42v **429** RAMSEY (April) William Pakerell and his wife, Agnes: from Brother Thomas Pylketon, sub-cellarer, one plot with building in le Wyght once held by John Borell, from the next Michaelmas for 12 years, rendering annually 8s. at Michaelmas and Easter, with the first payment due at Easter. Further, they will repair the property, except for heavy lumber and thatch supplied by the sub-cellarer. *Et si predictus redditus*, etc. (arrears of one month). G.: three capons.

430 RAMSEY (April) John Borell and William Pakerell: from Brother Thomas Pylketon, the fishpond of le "Swonhousmedsdych" on both sides of "le Wilwerowe" and the fishpond of "le Newmededych" on both sides of Wilwerowe, with ditches, from Michaelmas for 15 years, rendering annually 2s. at Michaelmas and Easter, with the first payment due at Easter. *Et si predictus redditus*, etc. (arrears of one month). G.: four capons.

431 HEIGHMONGROVE (July) John Outy Jr. and his wife, Agnes: from Brother Thomas Pylketon, one plot and 14 acres of land and meadow with all pertaining meadow and hedges once held by his father, Robert Outy, of which land one parcel consists of five acres and three rods and 32 feet of meadow lying at Tylkilne, two acres at Poulescroft and one acre in le Newefeld, three rods in that furlong, one acre in Fremannescroft, one acre in le Longnewefeld and two and a half acres in le Stokkyng, 43r for life, rendering annually 26s.2d.ob. and all services and customs previously rendered by Robert. Further, they will repair, the property, etc. and if they unjustly bring suit against the abbot or the monastery, the lord shall reenter, retake and retain the property in perpetuity. G.: six capons.

432 ELSWORTH (October)[19] John Howesson: one toft with three butts of land once held by Thomas Smart, for life, rendering annually 18d. at the customary times. G.: 4d.

433 ELSWORTH (October) Emma, daughter of Robert Boner and naif of the lord, pays 6s. for license to marry John Bere, freeman.

434 GRAVELEY (October) John atte Chirche: two virgates of servile land once held by John Danyell, for life, rendering annually in all things as did John Danyell. G.: 40d.

435 GRAVELEY (October) Anna, daughter of John Newman and naif of the lord, pays 6s.8d. for license to marry Laurence Scherman, freeman.

436 CRANFIELD (leet)[20] Thomas of the Mede: the reversion of one messuage and a half-virgate of servile land and five acres of demesne land with one pithel annexed to the messuage once held by William of the Leen, in bondage for life, rendering annually in all things as did William. G.: 6s.8d.

[19] See PRO 179/50. Neither this entry, nor the following is in the roll.
[20] See PRO 179/50. Neither this entry, nor the following two entries, is in the roll.

437 CRANFIELD (leet) William Mayhew pays 6s.8d. to marry Isabella, widow of William Ryngge, and to enter into one messuage and a half-virgate of servile land held by Isabella and previously held by her husband, William, rendering to the lord annually in all things as did Ryngge.

43v **438** CRANFIELD (leet) William Catelyn: one messuage and 12 acres of servile land once held by John Berford, for life, rendering annually in all things as did John. G.: 3s.4d.

439 SHILLINGTON (leet) John of the Hill Jr.: one lot once held by William of the Hill, his father, for life, rendering annually in all things as did William. G.: 13s.4d.

440 SHILLINGTON (leet) Richard Goddard: one messuage and a half-virgate of servile land previously held by William Goddard, in bondage for life, rendering annually 6s.8d. annually and in all other things as did William. G.: excused, because the property is in ruins.

441 SHILLINGTON (leet) William Wynter pays 20d. to marry Alicia, widow of William Waryn, and to enter into one messuage and a half-virgate of servile land held by Alicia and previously held by her late husband, for the lifetime of the said Alicia rendering annually in all things as did Waryn.

442 SHILLINGTON (leet) Nicholas Grave, naif of the lord, pays 10s. for license to marry his daughter, Margeria, naif of the lord, to John Hebbe, freeman.

443 THERFIELD Agnes, widow of Nicholas Adam and naif of the lord, pays 33s.4d. for license to marry John Payn of Watton, freeman, this time.

444 THERFIELD (leet) Nicholas Croyser: nine and a half acres of demesne land once held by Thomas Malt, in bondage for life, rendering annually 7s.9d. and all other services and customs rendered by Thomas. G.: excused, because of a rent increase.

445 THERFIELD Johanna, daughter of William Waryn and naif of the lord, pays 2s. for license to marry William Wyngore, naif of the lord.

44r **446** BURWELL (leet) John Roolee Jr.: four acres of servile land lying between Estfeld and le Sowthfeld and previously held by the aforesaid John, for 20 years, rendering annually in all things as he was accustomed to render. G.: 12d.

447 BURWELL (leet with court) John Wryghte: 12 acres of servile land once held by John Frache, for 20 years, rendering annually in all things as did Frache. G.: 3s.4d.

448 BURWELL (same court) Simon Calvesbane pays 3s.4d. to marry Cecilia Wyat, widow of Nicholas Rolf, and to enter into 26 acres of servile land previously held by the aforesaid Nicholas, for the lifetime of Cecilia, rendering annually all services and customs owed therein.

449 HOLYWELL (leet: Thursday after St. Edward) William Wryghte: one acre of demesne land lying in Braynesdole previously held by John Asplond Sr., for life, rendering annually in all things as did John. G.: 20d.

450 HOLYWELL (same court) John Morcie: two and a half acres of demesne land previously held by John Schepperd, in bondage for life, rendering annually in all things as did Schepperd. G.: 12d.

451 HOLYWELL (same court) William Palfreyman: one messuage and a half-virgate of servile land *in opere* once held by John Hunne, in bondage for life, rendering annually in all things as did John. G.: 6s.8d.

452 ELTON (leet) Agnes Burnet: a half-cote previously held by Henry Spencer and
44v Roger Milnere, in bondage for life, rendering annually in all things as did Henry and Roger, with the obligation to repair and maintain the property. Pledges for repairs: John Bythorne and John Pilton.

453 ELTON (leet) John Wycher of Fotheringay one built up messuage and four and a half acres of servile land once held by Galfridus Webstere, in bondage for life, rendering annually 5s., with the obligation to repair and maintain the property. He will fix his dwelling on the messuage before the feast of the Nativity of St. John the Baptist, under penalty of loss of his property and *gersuma*. G.: 2s.

454 BYTHORNE (leet) Roger Walter: surrender of one messuage and one quarter of servile land, to the use of William Lokyn, in bondage for life, rendering annually in all things as did Roger. G.: 3s.4d.

455 BYTHORNE Johanna Bacheler, naif of the lord, pays 3s.4d. for license to marry William Lokyn, this time.

456 WESTON (same leet) John Cartere: one cote and a half-cote of servile land once held by William Miller, in bondage for life, rendering annually in all things as did William. G.: 12d.

457 GIDDING (leet) Amya, daughter of John West and naif of the lord, pays 2s. for license to marry Thomas, son of Robert Gorbat, this time.

458 ABBOTS RIPTON (leet) Johanna, daughter of William West of Wenyngton and naif of the lord, pays 6s.8d. for license to marry William Wodeward, freeman.

459 WARBOYS (court) Alicia, daughter of Thomas Eyr and naif of the lord, pays 20d. for license to marry Robert Soulton.

45r **460** WARBOYS (court) Richard High: one cotland and one quarter of servile land previously held by Thomas Wryghte and once held by Thomas Molt, in bondage for life, rendering annually in all things as did Thomas. G.: 40d.

461 WARBOYS (court) Walter Hert: one cote recently held by Robert Swon and once held by Robert Gildesowe, in bondage for life, rendering annually in all things as did Robert Swon. G.: 12d.

462 WISTOW (same leet) Nicholas Martyn, naif of the lord, pays 13s.4d. for license to marry his daughter Margeria to John Elyngton, freeman, this time.

463 WISTOW (same leet) John Elyngton: one messuage and one virgate of servile land recently held by Nicholas Martyn and once held by Richard Catelyn in bondage for life, rendering annually in all things as did Nicholas. G.: 6s.8d.

464 WISTOW (same leet) Edmund, parish chaplain of Raveley: a half-cote and one quarter of servile land recently held by John Andrew and once held by Henry Hych, in bondage for life, rendering annually in all things as did John. G.: 12d.

465 ELSWORTH (November) William Chapman: one messuage with one virgate of land once held by William Boner, in bondage for life, rendering annually in all things as did William. G.: excused, because of repairs.

466 WARBOYS (November) John Berenger: one empty plot with a half-virgate of servile land once held by Simon Smart, in bondage for life, rendering annually in all things as did Simon. G.: 3s.4d.

45v **467** BROUGHTON (January) William Aspelond, naif of the lord, pays 13s.4d. for license to marry his daughter, Mariota, to John of the Wold, freeman.

468 UPWOOD (January) Richard atte Well, servant of Nicholas Alston: one acre with buildings in Wodestrete, Great Raveley, and four acres of land at Reddole, with seven acres lying in Crosleye, one acre lying at the end of Little Raveley and two acres at Gowleyrsdole, once held by Nicholas Alston, in bondage for life, rendering annually in all things as did Nicholas. G.: 6s.8d.

469 HOLYWELL Thomas Hunne, pays 40d. for license to marry his daughter, Katerina, naif of the lord, to a certain freeman of this region, this time.

470 HOUGHTON (January). John Lyenum and his wife, Cristina: one cote with curtilage once held by Robert Cook, for life, rendering annually 2s. at the customary times, with the obligation to repair and maintain the property at their own expense within one year. G.: 12d.

471 WOODHURST (January) John Blackwell: one virgate of servile land once held by

Nicholas Hunneye, in *novum opus* for life, rendering annually as do others who hold in *novum opus*. G.: 40d.

472 HOUGHTON (January) John Bethere: one virgate of servile land once held by Henry Gatte, for life, rendering annually in all things as did Henry. G.: 12d., and no more because of repairs.

473 HOLYWELL John Goodsowle Jr.: surrender of one built up cote lying between the cote of Robert Rokysdon and that of Nicholas Baroun to the use of Henry Kyng, for life, rendering annually in all things as did John. G.: 8s.

474 WARBOYS (January) John Flemynge, naif of the lord: one mondayland with *(blank)* acres of demesne land once held by John Norbourgh, for life, rendering annually in all things as did John Norbourgh. G.: 2s.

475 WESTON (January) John Miller pays 2s. for license to marry his daughter, Gloria, to Thomas Cool, freeman.

476 WISTOW (February) John Owty Jr.: one quarter of land once held by John Aspelond, in *arentatio* for life, rendering annually 4s. at the customary times and all other services and customs rendered by Aspelond, with the first payment due at the feast of the Assumption. G.: 3s.4d.

477 CHATTERIS (February) Gilbert Strykeland: two built up cotes in Horsheath once held by John Sumpter and recently in the hands of the lord after the death of the said John, because Alicia, widow of John, married John Dryngs Sr. without license; in bondage for life, rendering annually all services and customs therein. G.: 5s.

478 SLEPE (February) Nicholas Chikesand and his wife, Agnes: one messuage with one quarter of servile land once held by John Cartere, for life, rendering annually in all things as did John. G.: 13s.4d.

479 ST. IVES (February) Richard Fuller and his wife, Magota: one row lying between the tenement of John Peyntour and that of John Wryghte and once held by Robert Takyl, for life, rendering annually 13s.4d. at the customary times, with the obligation to maintain the property in good repair. *Et non licebit*, etc. G.: excused, because of a rent increase of 3s.4d.

480 HOLYWELL (February) Thomas Brayn: one cote with adjacent croft and one rod of land once held by John Cartere, rendering annually in all things as did John. G.: 3s.4d.

481 WARBOYS Richard Berenger, naif of the lord, pays 6s.8d. for license to marry his daughter, Katerina, to John atte Wode, freeman.

482 BROUGHTON (January) Thomas Boteler: a half-virgate of servile land once held by Henry Hyrde and recently held by John Clerk, in *arentatio* for life, rendering annually 6s. at the customary times and all other services and customs rendered by John, with the first payment due at the next feast of the Annunciation. G.: one capon.

483 BROUGHTON (January) William Ivet: one quarter of servile land once held by Richard Buk, for life, rendering annually in all things as did Richard. G.: two capons.

484 BROUGHTON (January) John Cabe: one quarter of land once held by Richard Buk, for life, rendering annually in all things as did Richard. G.: two capons.

485 HOUGHTON (January) Richard Sampson: one cote with adjacent croft once held by Robert Beten, for life, rendering annually 3s.4d. for all services and customs. G.: 20d.

486 HOUGHTON (January) Thomas Styward: one plot with building once held by John Woodcok, for life, rendering annually 5s. at Michaelmas, with the obligation to maintain all the buildings on the property in good repair, with the first payment due at the next Michaelmas. G.: 2s., and no more because of repairs.

487 SHILLINGTON (Tuesday: court) Johanna, daughter of John atte Wode of

Nethstondon and naif of the lord, pays 13s.4d. for license to marry a certain freeman, this time.

47r **488** SHILLINGTON (January) William of the Hill of Pegsdon: one messuage and a virgate and a half of servile land with one cote and five acres of servile land and appurtenances, previously held by his father, William, for life, rendering annually in all things as did his father. G.: 26s.8d.

489 SHILLINGTON (court) Richard atte Grene, naif of the lord, pays 10s. for license to marry his daughter, Agnes, to a certain stranger, this time.

490 SHILLINGTON (same court). Richard Cok: seven acres of demesne land once held by Henythorne, for life, rendering annually in all things as did Henythorne. G.: 40d.

491 BARTON (27 April: court) Richard Martyn: one messuage and one virgate of servile land with one croft of the forland pertaining to that messuage and once held by Hugo Hale, for life, rendering annually in all things as did Hugo. G.: 13s.4d.

492 BARTON (same court) William Roger: one messuage and one virgate of servile land once held by John Roger, in bondage for life, rendering annually in all things as did John. G.: 26s.8d.

493 BARTON (same court) Richard Roger: one messuage and one virgate of servile land, together with license to marry Isabella atte Grene, tenant of that land, in bondage for life, rendering annually all services and customs as did John Wodeward. G.: 40d.

494 SHILLINGTON (court) John Warde: one messuage and one virgate of servile land once held by Thomas Sweyn, in bondage for life, rendering annually in all things as did Thomas. G.: 20s., and no more because of a rent increase of 20d.

47v **495** BURWELL (1 May: court) Radulph Calvesbane: one cote with croft and three acres of servile land previously held by Thomas Ideyngne, in bondage for 30 years, rendering annually in all things as did Thomas and suit to court.

496 BURWELL (1 May: court) Same Radulph: eight acres of servile land once held by Thomas Higenye and once held by John Derye, in *arentatio* for 30 years, rendering annually in all things as did Thomas.

497 BURWELL (1 May: court) Same Radulph: eight acres of servile land once held by Thomas Ideygne, in bondage for 30 years, rendering annually in all things as did Thomas and suit to court, with the condition that Radulph will build two houses on the property at his own expense and with his own lumber within the next two years. G.: 2s.4d., and no more because of extensive repairs.

498 BURWELL (1 May: court) Same Radulph: 12 acres of servile land once held by Thomas Ideyngne, in bondage for 30 years, rendering annually in all things as did Thomas.

499 BURWELL (1 May: court) Thomas Stroppe: half of one messuage and 20 acres of servile land, for 20 years, rendering annually 21s. at the customary times and all other services and customs owed therein. G.: 7s.8d.

500 ST. IVES (May) Thomas Markham, alias Taylor, and his wife, Amya: the toll booth once held by Stephen Irynmonger, for life, rendering annually 16s.8d. and all other customs and services owed therein, with the first payment due at Michaelmas, and with the obligation to repair and maintain all the buildings and houses on the property at their own expense. *Et non licebit*, etc. G.: excused, because of a rent in-

48r crease.

501 ST. IVES (May) John Onyon and his wife, Johanna: one row once held by Stephen Eyrmonger, for life, rendering 13s.4d. this year, and 20s. each year thereafter, with the obligation to repair and maintain the property at their own expense. *Et non licebit*, etc. G.: excused because of a rent increase of 6s.8d.

502 St. Ives (May) Richard Baker and his wife, Magota: one row once held by Stephen Eyrmongere lying next to the row of William Botheby, on the west, for life, rendering as did Stephen, with the first payment due at Michaelmas, and with the obligation to repair and maintain all buildings and houses on the property at their own expense. *Et non licebit*, etc. G.: excused, because of a rent increase of 20d.

503 St. Ives (May) Thomas Bocher and his wife, Matilda: one row once held by Thomas Smyth, lying to the east of the row held by William Foun, for life, rendering annually in all things as Thomas Smyth, with the obligation to repair and maintain the property. *Et non licebit*, etc. G.: 3s.4d.

504 Shillington (May) John Edith Jr.: one-half virgate of servile land once held by Roger Edith, for life, rendering annually in all things as did Roger. G.: 6s.8d.

505 Therfield (May) William Wynmer: one cotland with 15 acres of adjacent land once held by Nicholas Adam, in bondage for life, rendering annually all services and customs owed therein. G.: 26s.8d.

48v **506** Therfield (May) John Frere pays 6s.8d. for license to exchange one virgate of servile land, in which he now dwells, with William Wynmer, for one cotland with 15 acres once held by Nicholas Adam, to be held by each according to the form of exchange for life, rendering annually all services and customs owed therein.

507 Therfield (May) John Watte: one cotland with 15 adjacent acres once held by John Piers Sr., in bondage for life, rendering annually all services and customs owed therein. G.: 2s.

508 Chatteris (May) John Thomiesson: one plot with building with adjacent croft and one meadow in the marsh once held by Richard Preston, in bondage for life, rendering annually in all things as did Richard. G.: 40d.

509 Chatteris (May) Adam Cook: one built up messuage with one rod of land once held by John Stokton, in bondage for life, rendering annually in all things as did John. G.: 6s.8d.

510 Wistow (May) William Bracer: four acres of demesne land lying in Kyngeslond, for life, rendering annually 3s.4d. at the customary times. G.: 12d.

511 Warboys (May) John Hygh Jr.: one plot with building with one mondayland once held by John Harsene, for life, rendering annually 5s., one autumn *precaria* and supplying one man for one day for sheep-shearing, and for one day's work in le Cheverethe. G.: 12d.

512 Warboys (May) John Hygh Jr.: three and a half acres of demesne lying in le Stockyng once held by John Harsene, for life, rendering annually 2s.9d. at the customary times. G.: excused.

513 Warboys (May) John High Sr.: three acres of demesne land lying in le Stockyng once held by John Harsene, for life, rendering annually 3s.6d. at the customary times. G.: excused.

49r **514** Warboys (May) William Hoberd: one quarter of servile land once held by John Harsene, for life, rendering annually in all things as did John, with the first payment due at Michaelmas. G.: 2s.

515 Woodhurst (May) John Screvener and his wife, Margaret: one well built up cote with adjacent land and croft once held by William Harrof, for life, rendering annually all services and customs owed therein. G.: excused because of a rent increase.

516 Elsworth (May) Thomas Baker: one quarter of land with adjacent croft in the field of Grenefeld, in bondage for life, rendering annually 6s. and all services previously rendered by Henry Budolf. G.: excused because of a rent increase of 12d.

517 Elsworth (May) Henry atte Brook: one quarter of servile and with adjacent croft once held by Thomas Payn, for life, rendering annually 5s. at the customary times, and in all other things as did Thomas. G.: 40d.

518 ELSWORTH (May) Thomas Payn: one plot with building and a half-virgate and a quarter-virgate of servile land previously held by Henry Isabell, in bondage for life, rendering annually in all things as did Henry. G.: 7s.

519 ELSWORTH (May) William Boner Sr.: one cote with adjacent croft previously held by Thomas Payn, for life, rendering annually in all things as did Thomas. G.: 2s.

520 HOUGHTON (4 August: court) John Marchall: a half-virgate of servile land once held by Richard Upton, for life, rendering annually in all things as did Richard. G.: 2s.

521 HOUGHTON (same court) John Wappelode: a half-virgate of servile land once held by John Lawe, for life, rendering annually in all things as did Lawe. G.: one capon.

49v

522 BROUGHTON (5 August: court) John Hampton: one toft with adjacent croft and one quarter of servile land once held by John Bonde, for life, rendering in all things as did Bonde. G.: 12d.

523 ABBOTS RIPTON (court) John London Jr.: one quarter of servile land previously held by William Scheperd, rendering annually in all things as did William. G.: 2s.

524 WISTOW (court) Thomas Breselaunce: one built up messuage and a half-virgate of servile land previously held by John Aspelond, for life, rendering annually in all things as did John. G.: 6s.8d.

525 WARBOYS Walter Hert: one acre and three rods of demesne land lying at Westfurlong and once held by Robert Swon, for life, rendering annually in all things as did Robert, with the first payment due at Michaelmas. G.: excused.

526 WARBOYS (August) Thomas Benet: two acres and a half-rod of demesne land lying in Hallelond once held by John Brayn, for life, rendering annually in all things as did John, with the first payment due at Michaelmas. G.: 8d.

527 UPWOOD William Heryng pays 2s. for license to marry off his daughter, Cristiana, naif of the lord, this time.

528 WARBOYS (August) Richard High: one quarter of servile land once held by John Martyn, for life, rendering annually 3s.4d. and in all other things as did John. G.: 12d.

50r

529 GRAVELEY (August) Isabella, daughter of John Alcar and naif of the lord, pays 6s.8d. for license to marry a certain freeman, this time.

530 WARBOYS (August) Agnes Brounyng, naif of the lord, pays 12d. for license to marry Thomas Godfrey, this time.

531 ST. IVES John Makeseye and his wife, Alicia: one half-row near the water which the said John rebuilt, for life, rendering annually 2s., with the obligation to maintain the property. *Et non licebit*, etc. G.: excused.

11 THOMAS BUTTERWYK (1406-1407)

50v

532 ST. IVES (leet) John Grantesdene and his wife, Margaret: one row once held by Adam Smyth, for life, rendering annually all rents, services and customs owed therein, with the obligation to repair and maintain all houses, walls and enclosures on the row at their own expense. *Et non licebit*, etc. G.: excused because of repairs.

533 ELSWORTH (leet) John Cook: a half-virgate previously held by John Chircheman Sr., in bondage for life, rendering annually in all things as did John Chircheman. G.: 4s.

534 ELSWORTH (same leet) Thomas Wymond: one cote and one virgate of servile land once held by John Wymond, in bondage for life, rendering annually in all things as did John. G.: 40d.

535 GRAVELEY (leet) William Bukby: one messuage and one virgate and a quarter of servile land once held by William Esex, in bondage for life, with the obligation to repair and maintain all buildings, walls and other necessaries at his own expense, under penalty of a fine of £10. Pledges for repairs: John Clerk and Walter Newman. G.: 20d.

536 WARBOYS (December) John Plumbe Jr.: one virgate of servile land once held by John Foster, for life, rendering annually 13s.4d. ploughing *precariae*, autumn *precariae*, work in le Cheverethe, and suit to court, for all other services. G.: 6s.8d.

537 WARBOYS (December) Robert of the Hill: surrender of one-half of one tenement, to the use of William Sande, for life, rendering annually 10s. and in all other things as did Robert, with the condition that if he wants the other half when it comes into the lord's hands, he will have it and pay *gersuma*. If he does not, the lord will dispose of it. G.: 20d.

51r

538 WARBOYS (December) John Molt: one quarter of servile land once held by John Benet, for life, rendering annually in all things as did John Benet. G.: 2s.

539 BROUGHTON (December) Thomas of the Wold, alias Smyth: one plot and a half-virgate of servile land once held by Henry Hyrde, in *major censum* for life, rendering annually all services and customs owed therein. G.: 40d.

540 ELTON (December) John Bythorne: half of the common farm next to the manor, for life, rendering annually 5s. and all other services and customs owed therein, at the customary times, with the obligation to repair and maintain the property. G.: excused.

541 ST. IVES (December) Robert Belleman and his wife, Margaret: a half-row lying opposite the booth once held by Thomas Belleman, until John, son and heir of Thomas, comes of age, rendering, in the meantime, annually in all things as did Thomas, with the obligation to repair and maintain the property. They will keep the property themselves if John, when he comes of age, relinquishes it. *Et non licebit*, etc. G.: 6s.8d.

542 UPWOOD (December) Nicholas Albyn: one plot with building and three quarters of servile land once held by his father, Richard Albyn, for life, rendering annually 12s. at the customary times, and in all other things as did his father. G.: 3s.4d.

543 CRANFIELD (leet) John Pynnok: 10 selions of demesne land once held by his mother, Johanna, for life, rendering annually 2s.4d. at the customary times, and in all other things as did his mother. G.: 8d.

51v

544 BARTON (General Court) John Cook pays 4s. for license to marry Johanna, widow of John Scut, and for entry into one messuage and one acre of servile land recently held by Johanna's husband, John, for the lifetime of the said Johanna, rendering annually in all things as did Scut.

545 BARTON (same court) Thomas Pope: one cote opposite the gate and once held by Edmund Burnard, for life, rendering annually in all things as did Edmund. G.: 2s.

546 BARTON (same court) Richard Wodeward: one messuage called Roos and one virgate of servile land once held by Richard Benesson, for life, rendering annually in all things as did Benesson. G.: 6s.8d.

547 BARTON (same court) Edmund Roger: one croft containing one acre of servile land once held by Richard Stonlee, for life, rendering annually all services and customs owed therein. G.: 2s.

548 BARTON (same court) William Sare pays 26s.8d. for license to marry his daughter, Agnes, naif of the lord, to Henry Burrych, freeman, this time.

549 THERFIELD (court) William Croyser and his wife, Katerina: one tenement and a half-virgate of servile land once held by Maurice Bode, together with one cote once held by Robert Wattes, half of a virgate once held by John Colyn, and all parcels of demesne land previously held by Maurice Bode and the fifth part of a half-virgate once held by John Waryn, for life, rendering annually all services and customs owed therein and as previously rendered by Bode. William will rebuild the property at his own expense, except that he will receive from the lord eight marks from the rent once from Peter Brancastre, and 54s.10d.ob. for repairs, through the hands of the aforesaid Maurice. Further, the land will be well manured, fallowed and reploughed by Maurice; William will receive from the lord lumber for the repairs, as do certain of his peers; he will have an allowance of his rent at the previous feast of St. Andrew; and he will also have 20s. G.: excused, because of repairs.

550 ELSWORTH (January) John Brook and his wife, Margaret: a half-quarter of servile land with two selions of demesne lying in the field called Woldhill between two marshes abutting Woldeweye and recently held by Alicia atte Brook, for life, rendering annually 4s. at the customary times and in all other things as did Alicia. G.: 20d.

551 ELSWORTH (January) Thomas Peek: one quarter of servile land once held by William Touslond, with one parcel of a croft, for life, rendering annually 5s. and in all other things as did William. He shall receive from William one quarter of barley, four bushels of wheat and one quarter of peas for the sowing of that land. G.: 40d.

552 ST. IVES Richard White: property (unspecified), rendering annually 13s.4d. G.: 20s. (*No other information given*).

553 WARBOYS John Weston pays 6s.8d. for license to marry Johanna Berenger, naif of the lord, this time.

554 WISTOW John Garnoun Jr., freeman, pays 10s. for permission to marry and take up lands previously held by the lord because he was under age.

555 ST. IVES Thomas Cayse and his wife, Johanna: one row previously held by John Bockenham, together with one curtilage at the end of his garden, for life, rendering annually 14s.4d., with the obligation to repair and maintain the property. *Et non licebit*, etc. G.: 3s.4d.

556 ST. IVES John Mows and his wife, Johanna: a half-row once held by Katerina Fishher, for life, rendering annually 20s., with the obligation to repair and maintain the property at their own expense. *Et non licebit*, etc. G.: 6s.8d.

557 ST. IVES Richard of the Gowde and his wife, Agnes: three cotes once held by Thomas Belleman, for life, rendering annually 5s., with the obligation to repair the property at their own expense within two years, and maintain it thereafter. G.: 20s.

558 ST. IVES John Morice: a half-row once held by Margaret Baxtere, for life, rendering annually 16s. at the customary times, with the obligation to repair and maintain the property. *Et non licebit*, etc. G.: 10s.

559 ST. IVES William Grybbe and his wife, Matilda: a half-row once held by William Pardee, for life, rendering annually 24s. at the customary times, with the obligation to repair and maintain the property at their own expense. *Et non licebit*, etc. G.: 20s.

560 HOUGHTON John Clerk Fuller: one holm lying next to the holm of the chamberlain of Ramsey, for life, rendering annually 3s.4d. at the customary times, and all other services and customs previously rendered by John Fuller of Houghton. G.: 2s.

561 ST. IVES John Pulter and his wife, Margaret: one row once held by William Leg, lying next to the free tenement of the aforesaid John, and one row once held by John Eugyn lying next to the aforesaid row, and a half-row lying between Paddelmoor and le Thwertweye, opposite the above free tenement, for life, rendering annually 26s. at the customary times, with the obligation to repair and maintain the property. *Et non licebit*, etc. G.: 13s.4d.

562 SLEPE John Pulter: one empty plot with one virgate of land once held by John Cartere, for life, rendering annually 20s. and all other services and customs rendered by Cartere. G.: 6s.8d.

52r

52v

563 St. Ives John Revenale and his wife, Johanna: one row once held by Thomas Fysscher, for life, rendering annually all services and customs owed therein, with the obligation to repair and maintain the property at their own expense. *Et non licebit*, etc. G.: excused.

564 Elsworth Thomas Newman de Esex and his wife, Margaret: a half-virgate of land once held by Roger Yntte, for life, for works and services as rendered by Roger. G.: 2s.

565 Elsworth John Wymond and Simon Herry: one toft with a half-virgate of land of Gravelond once held by John Baudewyn, for life, rendering annually in all things as did Baudewyn. G.: 12d. and two capons.

566 Warboys John Woldhull and his wife, Oliva: one mondayland once held by John Laushull, for life, rendering annually 5s. at the customary times, and in all other things as did Laushull. G.: 2s.

567 Barton (June) William Falleys: one plot with building and one virgate once held by John Scut Jr., for life, rendering annually in all things as did John. G.: 6s.8d.

568 Graveley John Dyke, naif of the lord, pays 13s.4d. for license to marry his daughter, Elena, to John Bayly of Stanton.

569 Knapwell John Joye: one quarter of land once held by John Pykerell and one quarter of one half-virgate once held by Simon de Graveley, for life, rendering annually in all things as did John and Simon. G.: 8d.

570 Hurst (June) Roger Wareyn: surrender of one virgate, to the use of William Wareyn, alias Webster, for life, rendering annually in all things as did Roger. G.: 6s.8d.

571 Slepe (June) John Cristemasse and his wife, Katerina: one cote once held by John Roger and lying opposite the cross, for life, rendering annually in all things as did Roger. G.: 2s.

572 St. Ives William Edenham and his wife, Johanna: one row and a half once held by John Edenham, for life, rendering annually 32s. and all other services and customs owed therein, with the obligation to repair and maintain the property. *Et non licebit*, etc. G.: 10s.

573 Holywell Thomas Hemyngton: all land and meadow called Smetheslond containing 12 acres and once held by John Palmere, for life, rendering annually in all things as did John. G.: 13s.4d.

574 Warboys Richard Eyr, alias Geffreyesson: one plot with building and one virgate of land once held by William Bukworth, *in opere* for life, rendering annually all services and customs owed therein, with the provision that he hold it for the next two years after the next Michaelmas for "werksilver". G.: 11d.

575 Warboys Thomas Edward pays 10s. for license to marry off his daughter, Alicia, naif of the lord.

576 Hemingford Abbots Alicia Trapp, naif of the lord, pays 13s.4d. for license to marry Robert Wyth, naif of the lord, of Houghton.

577 Hemingford Abbots Emma Heyne, naif of the lord, pays 6s.8d. for license to marry John Gattere, naif of the lord, of Houghton.

578 Houghton (July) Thomas Styward: the water and fulling mill of Houghton and Hemingford, with the whole fishpond, from the next Michaelmas for seven years, rendering annually 24 marks of silver, in equal portions at the feasts of the Annunciation and the Nativity of Blessed Mary, with the obligation to repair and maintain the mill with all its appurtenances, including stones, iron, carpentry, roofing, plastering, ramming, set-stones and all buildings pertaining to the mill, both in and out of the water, as well as the ditches and the dam, at his own expense, except that the lord will supply lumber and its transport. Thomas may not dismiss the mill or any parcel of it to anyone without the lord's license. He will dismiss the mill with all its appurtenances

53r

53v

and buildings and "les Gooles" in as good — or better — condition as when he received it, except that if the mill requires any new repairs, whether in or outside the water, they will be done by the lord. For better security, as well as for paying the annual farm and for keeping and fulfilling all agreements, Thomas, John atte Style, Richard Cartere and John Bedell of Houghton are obligated to John Bekeswell for 40 marks, as is more fully contained in writing, and if Thomas does not default in any payments or other agreements, this obligation will be held null. G.: 12d.

54r

579 ABBOTS RIPTON Robert Ivell, naif of the lord, pays 40d. for license to marry Margaret, daughter of William Hewe, naif of the lord.

580 ABBOTS RIPTON (July) Adam Knavesbourg, rector of the church, and John Chaimpeyn: one piece of demesne land called Wranglond, from the previous Michaelmas for five years, rendering annually 8s. at the Gules of August. G.: excused, because of a rent increase of 6d.

581 ABBOTS RIPTON (July) Thomas Preston, chaplain: all the arable land called Hernedole in le Stokkyng previously held by John Dycon, for life, rendering annually 10s. at the customary times. G.: excused.

582 UPWOOD William Symond, naif of the lord, pays 6s.8d. for license to marry his daughter, Johanna, to William de Eyr of Huntingdon.

583 UPWOOD Richard Payn, naif of the lord, pays 6s.8d. for license to marry his daughter, Agnes, to John Bigge.

584 UPWOOD William Heryng: a half-virgate of land once held by John Haukyn, in *arentatio* for life, rendering annually in all things as did John. G.: 6s.8d.

585 UPWOOD John Baker: one messuage and a half-virgate of land once held by Stephen Pykeler, *in opere* for life, rendering annually in things as did Stephen. Also: three acres and one rod of demesne land at Fenhill, for life, rendering annually 3s. at the customary times. G.: one capon.

586 UPWOOD John Loveday: one plot with one virgate and a half of land once held by John Robyn Sr., for life, rendering annually works and services for the half-virgate and 18s. in *arentatio* for the full virgate. G.: 2s.

587 WISTOW John West and his wife, Margaret: one cote with all adjacent land once held by John Brounote, for life, rendering annually in all things as did Brounote. G.: 12d.

54v

588 WISTOW Thomas Randolf: one acre of demesne land once held by John Brounote, for life, rendering annually 12d. G.: 12d.

589 WISTOW Richard Rede: one cote called Houndheghoo and Longheghoo containing two acres and one rod, for life, rendering annually 2s.3d. G.: 6d.

590 WISTOW Robert atte Gate, naif, pays 10s. for license to marry his daughter, Johanna, to Richard Outy.

591 WARBOYS Richard Hy: one mondayland *in opere* and all the demesne land previously held by John Flemyng, for life, rendering annually all services and customs owed therein and as rendered by John, and with the obligation to find a tenant for the mondayland and customary acres as well as for his plot in Caldecote, namely: Simon Hy. G.: 40d.

592 WARBOYS John Dallyng: one empty plot with a half-virgate of land once held by Henry Norbourgh, for life, rendering annually in all things as did Henry. G.: 3s.4d.

593 ST. IVES. Richard Scharp and his wife, Johanna: one row once held by John Onyon, for life, rendering annually 20s. G.: 13s.4d.

594 SLEPE Richard Scharp and his wife, Johanna: one garden with three acres of land and meadow once held by Stephen Eyrmonger, for life, rendering annually 6s. at the customary times. G.: 13s.4d.

595 ELLINGTON Robert Mokke, naif of the lord, pays 2s. this year — and each year thereafter — for license to live off the manor at Little Stukeley for as long as it pleases the lord, remaining a naif as before.

596 BROUGHTON (25 March) Simon Mawd: surrender of one plot with a half-virgate of land, to the use of Edmund Taylar and his wife, Alicia, for life, rendering for the next four years as do tenants in *major censum*, and works and services thereafter. G.: 12d.

597 WARBOYS William Hoberd: one empty plot with a half-virgate of land once held by Galfridus Baroun, in *arentatio*, rendering annually as did William. G.: (*illegible*).

598 WARBOYS William AltheWerd: one mondayland once held by John Plumbe Jr., for life, rendering annually in all things as did John. G.: 12d.

599 WARBOYS William Semer: one mondayland once held by Thomas Webstere, in return for 4s.6d. annually, sheep-shearing in Cheverethe, and the great autumn *precaria*. G.: 12d.

600 HOUGHTON (February) Peter Andrew: a half-virgate of built up land once held by Robert Snow, in bondage for life, rendering annually 6s. at the customary times and all other works and services owed therein. G.: one capon.

601 HOUGHTON John Andrew Jr.: a half-virgate of land once held by Robert Snow, for life, rendering annually 4s. and works and services. G.: excused.

602 HOLYWELL Richard Edward: one plot and a half-virgate of land *ad censum*, one cotland *in opere*, one acre of demesne in Stonydole, and one rod of land in le Smethe, with meadow in Salmede once held by his father, John, for life, rendering annually in all things as did John. G.: 13s.4d.

603 HOLYWELL Thomas Hunne: one plot with building and a half-virgate of adjacent land once held by John Edward, *ad censum*, rendering annually in all things as did John. G.: excused.

604 HOLYWELL John Selde: one croft in *arentatio* once held by Thomas Pycard, for life, rendering annually 4s. G.: 4d.

605 HOUGHTON Thomas Seyward: three cotes once held by Robert Snow, for life, rendering annually 4s. at the customary times. G.: excused.

606 ST. IVES John Peyntor: surrender of a certain built up manse, to the use of John Fillyngls and his wife, Margaret, for life, rendering annually 9s. and all other services and customs owed therein, with the obligation to repair and maintain the property at their own expense. *Et non licebit*, etc. G.: 3s.4d.

607 CHATTERIS (court) William Taylor: one cotland and a half-acre of servile land and four acres of meadow in Crawlode with all apurtenances once held by Thomas Lawesson, for life, rendering annually in all things as did Thomas. G.: 6s.8d.

608 CHATTERIS (same court) John Peroun: one messuage and one adjacent holt once held by Walter Bocher, for life, rendering annually in all things as did Walter. G.: 10s.

609 CHATTERIS (same court) Thomas Chapman: one cote with a half-acre of servile land once held by John Bele, for life, rendering annually in all things as did John. G.: 6s.8d. and 13s.4d.

610 CHATTERIS (same court) Thomas Tylneye: one cotland once held by Edmund Rede, for life, rendering annually in all things as did Edmund. G.: 10s.

611 CHATTERIS (same court) John Edenham: one cotland once held by John Bele Sr., for life, rendering annually in all things as did John Bele. G.: 13s.4d.

612 CHATTERIS (same court) William Abell: two cotes once held by Simon Piper, for life, rendering annually in all things as did Simon. G.: 10s.

613 CHATTERIS (same court) John Newman: one cotland once held by John Smyth, for life, rendering annually in all things as did John Smyth. G.: 10s.

614 CHATTERIS (same court) Thomas Lawesson: one cote and four acres of land and meadow once held by William Lille, for life, rendering annually in all things as did William. G.: 10s.

56r **615** ABBOTS RIPTON (July) Peter Danne: one cote once held by Roger Gardener, for life, rendering annually in all things as did Roger. G.: 3s.4d.

616 HOUGHTON Adam Fuller: one plot with a parcel of adjacent land previously held by John Fuller, in *arentatio* for life, rendering annually 6s.8d. for all services, with the obligation to maintain the property. G.: 6s.8d.

617 HOUGHTON (September) Stephen Marchall: one plot with building and one virgate of servile land once held by Thomas Hervy Sr., in *arentatio* for life, rendering annually 14s. and all ploughing *precariae* for all customs, with the obligation to repair and maintain the property. G.: 3s.4d.

618 RAMSEY Agnes Freman, naif of the lord, pays one capon for license to marry Thomas Godfrey, this time.

12 THOMAS BUTTERWYK (1407-1408)

56v **619** WARBOYS John Heryng Jr.: one cote once held by Roger Hirst and recently held by Walter Wodeward, for life, rendering annually 3s. and two hens, with the first payment due at Michaelmas. G.: excused because of repairs.

620 CRANFIELD (3 October: leet) Thomas Terry Sr.: one cote and a half-virgate of servile land once held by John Cook, for life, rendering annually in all things as did John. G.: 2s.

621 SHILLINGTON (leet) John Atte Mede, naif of the lord, pays 5s. for license to marry his daughter, Alicia, to whomever she wishes.

622 SHILLINGTON (same leet) Cristiana, wife of Simon Cowherde: surrender of two cotes in le Briggesende, to the use of John atte Brook Jr., for life, rendering annually 6s.8d. at the customary times. G.: 6s.8d.

623 RAMSEY (September) John Maddyngle and John Berdewell: from Thomas Pylketon, sub-cellarer, a certain small land next to Clapercote on the western side, from Michaelmas for five years, rendering annually 2s. at the feast of the Nativity of Blessed Mary. G.: one capon.

624 RAMSEY John Bekeswell and John Cator of Ramsey: the whole fishpond in two ditches recently made at Wilwerowe between the meadow of Bigging and the marsh and extending in breadth to the corner of the marsh next to Bigging, up to the end of the vill of Ramsey, with herbage growing between the ditches, for life, rendering to the

57r receptor of Ramsey annually 6d. at Easter, with the obligation to purge the ditches at their own expense. G.: excused. (*This entire entry is crossed out*).

625 THERFIELD (15 October: leet with court) Henry Gerveys: one cote with 10 acres of servile land once held by Radulph Flynt, for life, rendering annually in all things as did Radulph. G.: 40d.

626 HOUGHTON (13 October: leet with court) William Aleyn: a half-virgate of servile land and one cote once held by Thomas Hervy Sr., for life, rendering annually in all things as did Thomas. G.: 40d.

627 HOUGHTON (same leet) John, son of Alan Andrew: two virgates and a half and one messuage once held by his father, for life, rendering annually in all things as did his father. G.: 6s.8d.

628 HOUGHTON (same leet) Thomas Elyot: two virgates and one messuage once held by Agnes Syre, for life, rendering annually in all things as did Agnes. G.: two capons.

629 BROUGHTON (14 October: leet with court) John Clerk Jr.: one messuage and a half-virgate of servile land once held by Simon Awde, for life, rendering annually in all things as did Simon. G.: 10s.

630 WARBOYS (14 October: leet). Simon Hy Jr: one messuage with certain land called Dichemanland, nine rods of free land with two acres of land in an adjoining croft, once held by Thomas Barbat, in *arentatio* for life, rendering annually 3s.6d. and all other services and customs owed therein. G.: 4s.

57v **631** WARBOYS (leet) Richard Bakester pays 13s.4d. for license to marry Agnes Semar, naif of the lord, this time.

632 ELTON (24 October: leet) John Burnet: one messuage and one virgate of servile land once held by John Hendesson, for life, rendering annually in all things as did John Hendesson, with the first payment due at the feast of St. Andrew after one year. G.: two capons.

633 ELTON (same leet) Richard Smyth: one messuage and one quarter of land with two acres of demesne land once held by Walter Cator, for life, rendering annually 10s. at the customary times. G.: 6s.8d.

634 ELTON (same leet) Alan Aloun: three acres of land lying in various fields, for life, rendering annually 12d. at the customary times. G.: excused, because the land is waste.

635 ELTON (same leet) John Germyn: one messuage and three acres of demesne land once held by Thomas Smyth, for life, rendering annually 4s. at the customary times, with the first payment due at the feast of St. Andrew after one year. G.: 12d.

636 ELTON (same leet) John Person: a half-virgate of land once held by Alicia Peytevyn, for life, rendering annually in all things as did Alicia. G.: 12d.

637 ELTON (same leet) Agnes Burnet: one half-cote with three selions of demesne land once held by Roger Miller, for life, rendering annually 10d. q. and all other services and customs owed therein. G.: excused, because the land is waste.

58r **638** ELTON (same leet) John, son of Richard Cook: one messuage and a half-virgate of servile land with a half-acre of meadow once held by his father, in bondage for life, rendering annually in all things as did his father. G.: 2s.

639 WESTON (18 October: leet) John Repon: one pithel containing one acre of land once held by Walter Burgeys, in bondage rendering annually all services and customs owed therein, with the obligation to build a new *camera* on the pithel. G.: 6s.8d.

640 WESTON (same leet) Henry Possewyk: one messuage and one quarter of land once held by Adam Burgeys, in bondage for life, rendering annually all services and customs owed therein. G.: 6s.8d.

641 ABBOTS RIPTON John Atte Halle pays the fine for license to marry Juliana, daughter of William West, naif of the lord, this time. Fine: excused.

642 WISTOW (27 October: leet) John Outy Jr: one built up messuage and a half-virgate once held by Henry Hiche, in *arentatio* for life, rendering annually all services and customs owed therein. G.: 4s.

643 WISTOW (same leet) John Atte Gate: one messuage and a half-virgate of land once held by John Atte Gate, his father, *in opere* for life, rendering annually in all thingd as did his father. G.: 20d.

644 WISTOW (same leet) John Catelyn Schepperd: one messuage and one quarter of land once held by John Sabyn, *in opere* for life, rendering annually all services and customs owed therein. G.: 5s.

645 WISTOW (same leet) John Sabyn: one cote with one rod of land once held by John Catelyn, for life, rendering annually all services and customs owed therein. G.: 40d.

58v **646** HOUGHTON (13 October: leet) Richard Smyth: one messuage and a half-virgate of land once held by Henry Lawe, for life, rendering annually all services and customs owed therein. G.: 2s.

647 Burwell (12 November: leet) Adam Alot: one cote with adjacent croft once held by Alicia Kirkeby, with one acre of land, for life, rendering annually in all things as did Alicia. G.: 2s.

648 Burwell (same leet) John Fabbe: one half-messuage with 24 acres of land once held by his father, Richard Fabbe, for 30 years, rendering annually all services and customs owed therein. G.: 6s.8d.

649 Burwell (same leet) Robert Wilkyn: 12 acres of demesne land once held by Richard Wilkyn, for serveral years (*unspecified*), rendering annually in all things as did Richard. G.: 6s.8d.

650 Wistow (December) Richard Wyllesson: one plot with a half-virgate of servile land once held by his father, John Wyllesson, *in opere* for life, rendering annually in all things as did his father. Also: another plot with a half-virgate of land once held by the same John, *ad censum* for life, rendering as did his father. Also: one plot with a half-virgate of land once held by the same John and before that by William Benet, in *arentatio* for life, rendering annually 8s. at the customary times. Also: one empty plot with a half-virgate of land once held by William Hiche, in *arentatio*, rendering annually in all things as did John. Also: one croft called Gernouncroft with one cotland called Kedesyerd once held by the same John, for life, rendering annually in all things as did John. G.: excused.

59r **651** Wistow Cum Raveley (December) John Wyllesson: two quarters of land once held by Cristina Hiche and Thomas Gowler, in *arentatio* for life, rendering annually 8s. at the customary times. G.: excused.

652 Broughton Richard Balde pays 13s.4d. for license to marry Agnes, his daughter and naif of the lord, to William Pynchebek, this time.

653 Warboys (April) John Wynde: one mondayland once held by John Heryng Jr., for life, rendering annually 5s., two hens and one rooster, together with carrying services three times a year and supplying one man for one autumn *precaria*. G.: excused.

654 Woodhurst (April) Robert Wrighte: one plot with building with one virgate of land once held by Thomas Sewyn, for life, rendering annually 16s. annually at the customary times, and all other services owed therein in *novum opus*. G.: excused because of repairs.

655 Woodhurst (April) Thomas Trover: one plot with a virgate once held by William Bronne, for life, rendering annually 16s. at the customary times and all other services owed therein in *novum opus*. G.: excused, because the land is *in opere*.

656 Woodhurst (April) Nicholas Oky: one plot and one virgate once held by John Cok, for life, rendering annually in all things as did John. G.: excused.

657 Woodhurst (April) William Cok: one plot with one virgate and a half-virgate once held by Robert Cok, for life, rendering annually 16s. and all other services as does Robert Wrighte. G.: excused.

658 Woodhurst (April) William Pilgrym: one plot with one and a half virgates of land once held by Thomas Nicol, for life, rendering annually 16s. and all other services as does Robert Wrighte. G.: excused.

659 Woodhurst (April) William Boner: a half-virgate of land with one empty plot once held by John Cok, for life, rendering annually 16s. and all other services as does Robert Wrighte. G.: excused.

59v **660** Woodhurst (April) Thomas Filhous: one plot with one virgate once held by John Edenham, for life, rendering annually 16s. and all other services as does Robert Wrighte. G.: excused.

661 Woodhurst (April) John Blakwell: one plot with one virgate of land once held by Nicholas Hunneye, for life, rendering annually 16s. and all other services as does Robert Wrighte. G.: excused.

662 WOODHURST (April) John Boner: a half-virgate of land once held by Thomas Hogge, for life, rendering annually 16s. and all other services as does Robert Wrighte. G.: excused.

663 WOODHURST (April) John Lawe: a half-virgate of land once held by Thomas Rammyng, for life, rendering annually 16s. and all other services as does Robert Wrighte. G.: excused.

664 WOODHURST (April) William Harrof: one plot with building with one virgate of land once held by Henry Wrighte, for life, rendering annually 16s. and all other services as does Robert Wrighte. G.: excused.

665 WOODHURST (April) Nicholas Hunneye: one plot with a half-virgate of land once held by Thomas Hogge, for life, rendering annually 16s. and all other services as does Robert Wrighte. G.: excused.

666 WOODHURST (April) Cristina Canne: two virgates of land with two plots once held by Reginald Canne, for life, rendering annually 16s. and all other services as does Robert Wrighte. G.: excused.

667 WOODHURST (April) Thomas Porter: two buildings with one virgate and a half-virgate once held by Thomas Lefert, for life, rendering annually 16s. and all other services as does Robert Wrighte. G.: excused.

668 WOODHURST (April) Robert Nunne: a half-virgate of land once held by Thomas Hogge, for life, rendering annually 16s. and all other services as does Robert Wrighte. G.: excused.

669 WOODHURST (April) John Broun and John Trover: one empty plot with a half-virgate of land once held by John Colle, for life, rendering annually 16s. and all other services as does Robert Wrighte. G.: excused.

60r **670** HOUGHTON (April) William Ascomb: one empty plot with a half-virgate of land once held by John Atte Pool, for life, rendering annually in all things as did John. G.: 3s.4d.

671 UPWOOD Peter Bray: one messuage and one virgate of land once held by Thomas Sywell, for life, rendering annually 24s. at the customary times, carrying service, one ploughing *precaria*, and one autumn *precaria* with one man for all services, although he will not be liable to be an official. G.: 10s.

672 WARBOYS (April) William Colville and his wife, Alicia: one plot with one virgate of land in Caldecote once held by William Laurence, for life, rendering annually 16s. at the customary times, and all other services and customs pertaining to the village, and in all other things as did Laurence. G.: 6s.8d.

673 WARBOYS (April) William Attehide of Bury and his wife, Katerina: a piece of land lying at Burywode and once held by John Mercher, for life, rendering annually 12s. in equal portions at the feasts of the Annunciation and the Nativity of Blessed Mary. G.: two capons.

674 WARBOYS (April) Thomas Molt pays 6s.8d. for license to marry his daughter, Margaret, naif of the lord, to John Warde of Barham, freeman, this time.

675 WISTOW Thomas Outy, naif of the lord, pays 3s.4d. for license to marry his daughter, Emma, to Stephen Marchal, freeman, this time. (*Notice added*: freedom is obtained).

676 CRANFIELD (18 June: court) John Of the Hill: one cote with adjacent croft once held by Thomas Colet, for life, rendering annually in all things as did Thomas. G.: 40d.

677 CRANFIELD (same court) Alexander Bele: one plot with building recently *in opere*, a half-virgate of land, and one cotland recently *in opere* and once held by Simon Bele, for life, rendering annually in all things as did Simon. G.: 40d.

678 CRANFIELD (same court) Richard Of the Feld: one plot with building and three quarters of land and another plot with building and three quarters of land, one quarter, one cotland and one empty plot with a half-virgate of land once held by Roger Of the Feld, for life, rendering annually in all things as did Roger. G.: 20s.

60v **679** CRANFIELD (same court) Cristina Terry: a half-virgate of land and one messuage with adjacent croft once held by Thomas Colet, for life, rendering annually in all things as did Thomas. G.: 4s.

680 CRANFIELD (same court) Thomas Atte Grene: two acres of demesne land recently held by Richard Burgylon, for life, rendering annually in all things as did Richard. G.: 8d.

681 SHILLINGTON (20 June: court) Thomas Longe and his wife, Alicia: one plot with two houses and one virgate lying in Nethirstond opposite the tenement of John Collesson and once held by John Atte Wode, for life, rendering annually 10s.10d. and in all other things as did John. G.: 13s.4d.

682 KNAPWELL (court) John Lawe: one cote with adjacent croft once held by John Broun, for life, rendering annually in all things as did John Broun. G.: 2s.

683 CHATTERIS (June) John Drynge Jr: one cote once held by Margaret Reynold, for life, rendering annually in all things as did Margaret. G.: 10s.

684 CHATTERIS (June) John Biller Jr: one messuage with three rods of land once held by John Biller, his father, for life, rendering annually in all things as did his father, with the condition that his mother, Agnes Biller, naif of the lord, will have one *camera* in the above messuage and be supported in all things for life by him. G.: 3s.4d.

685 ABBOTS RIPTON (26 July: court) William Reyner: one messuage and one virgate recently held by John West, for life, rendering annually in all things as did John. G.: two capons.

61r **686** KING'S RIPTON (26 July: court) John West and his wife, Agnes: one messuage and 20 acres of land coming to the lord from a forfeit, for life, rendering annually 13s.4d., with the obligation to repair and maintain the property at their own expense with their own lumber within the next three years. They will also render the appropriate rents and services pertaining to that messuage to the King in excess of 13s.4d. in value. G.: excused because of repairs.

687 WISTOW (28 July: court) William Hiche pays 3s.4d. for license to marry Emma, daughter of Robert Randolf and naif of the lord, this time.

688 WISTOW (same court) Stephen de Ely: one plot and one virgate of land recently held by John Elyngton, for life, rendering annually in all things as did John. G.: two capons.

689 WISTOW (same court) John Elys of Raveley pays 10s. for license to marry Alicia Hitche, naif of the lord, this time.

690 WISTOW (same court) Same John Elys: one quarter of land in Raveley once held by John Chrevener, for life, rendering annually in all things as did Chrevener. G.: excused, because of the marriage fine.

691 WISTOW (same court) Stephen de Ely: one garden and a half-virgate of land once held by John Cleryvaux, in *arentatio* for life, rendering annually 8s. and all other services and customs owed therein. G.: 12d.

692 WISTOW (same court) William atte Hide of Bury and his wife, Katerina: a certain piece of land in Stokkyng next to Burywode, for life, rendering annually 2s. at the customary times. They will cut down the undergrowth at the ditch of that property to repair and maintain the enclosure, except for large timber. G.: four capons.

693 CHATTERIS John Peroun and his wife, Agnes: one fishpond called Wolneyeswer and Achenewer with the full fishpond pertaining to it and once held by John Horsethe, rendering annually 13s. in equal portions at the customary times. G.: 10s.

61v **694**   St. Ives John Wilkyn and his wife, Alicia: a half-row once held by John Martyn, for life, with the obligation to repair and maintain the property at their own expense. *Et non licebit*, etc. G.: 6s.8d.

695   St. Ives William Charite and his wife, Isabella: a half-row once held by John
Martyn and located next to the plot held by Nicholas Chikesand, for life, rendering
annually 10s. in equal portions at the customary times, with the obligation to repair
and maintain the property at their own expense. *Et non licebit*, etc. G.: 13s.4d.

696   Grene William Yeman and his wife, Margaret: one plot with a half-virgate of
land once held by Nicholas Bernard, for life, rendering annually in all things as did
Nicholas. G.: 12d.

13 THOMAS BUTTERWYK (1408-1409)

62r **697**   Warboys (6 October: leet) Agnes Hy: one mondayland once held by John Hy
Jr., for life, rendering annually 6s.8d. at the customary times and all other services and
customs owed therein. G.: 20d.

698   Warboys (same leet) John Payn: one mondayland once held by John Dallyng,
for life, rendering annually 9s. at the customary times and all other services and
customs owed therein. G.: two capons.

699   Warboys (same leet). John Dallyng: one mondayland once held by John Hy,
for life, rendering annually 5s. at the customary times and all other services and
customs owed therein. G.: 20d.

700   Elton (15 October: leet) Walter Swythwyk: one cote once held by Isabella atte
Wyche, rendering annually 4s.6d. at the customary times, and all other services and
customs owed therein. G.: 16d.

701   Elton (same leet) Robert Tayllor: one cote with one croft of land once held by
Alicia in le Vale, for life, rendering annually in all things as did Alicia. G.: 8d.

702   Elton (same leet) John Mason: one cote with three acres of land lying fallow
once held by John Honyngham, for life, rendering annually 11d. for the cote, 12d. for
the three acres, and all other services and customs owed therein. G.: 12d.

703   Elton (same leet) John Pilton: one messuage and a half-virgate of land once
held by John Holde, for life, rendering annually in all things as did John Holde. G.:
40d.

704   Elton (same leet) William Kent: one messuage and one quarter and four acres
of land once held by Nicholas Webstere, for life, rendering annually 10s. at the
customary times, and in all other things as did Nicholas. G.: 2s.

62v **705**   Elton (same leet) William Berne: one messuage with one virgate of land once
held by Henry Hobbesson, for life, rendering annually in all things as did Henry. G.:
2s.

706   Weston (9 October: leet) William Penyhill pays 12d. for license to marry
Agnes Fleshewer, naif of the lord, this time.

707   Bythorne (9 October: same leet) John Twe: one messuage with one quarter of
land once held by John Bywode, for life, rendering annually in all things as did
Bywode. G.: 2s.

708   Cranfield (26 November: leet) John Glovere: one cote and one acre of land
once held by John Melkehous, for life, rendering annually in all things as did
Melkehous. G.: 20d.

709   Cranfield (same leet). Thomas Catelyn: one messuage and a half-virgate of
servile land once held by John Joye, for life, rendering annually 10s. and in all other
things as did John. G.: 40d.

710 CRANFIELD (same leet) John DunWode: one messuage and a half-virgate of servile land with eight acres of demesne land called a forland once held by William Vaws, for life, rendering annually in all things as did William. G.: 6s.8d.

711 CRANFIELD (same leet) Alexander Joye, chaplain: one cote with croft once held by Thomas Joye, for life, rendering annually in all things as did Thomas. G.: 20d.

712 BARTON (28 November: General Court) William Sare: surrender of 12 acres of demesne land lying in le Lye and Westcroft once held by William Messanger. The lord subsequently grants the land to William Shepperd and his wife, Margaret, for life, rendering annually in all things as did Sare. G.: 13s.4d.

63r **713** BARTON (same court) John Baron Sr: one toft and a half-virgate of land once held by John Smyth, for life, rendering annually in all things as did John Smyth. G.: 6s.8d.

714 KNAPWELL (28 November: leet) Margeria Smyth: one tenement and a half-virgate of servile land once held by John Smyth, for life, rendering annually in all things as did John. G.: 12d.

715 SHILLINGTON (29 November: leet) John Wymondham: surrender of one virgate of servile land to the use of John Byeston, in bondage, for life, rendering annually in all things as did Wymondham. G.: 40d.

716 ELSWORTH (28 November: leet) Thomas Payn: a half-virgate of servile land once held by Thomas Wymond, for life, rendering annually in all things as did Wymond. G.: 40d.

717 ELSWORTH (same leet) Thomas Pulter pays 40d. for license to marry Johanna Yntte, naif of the lord, to John Newman, this time.

718 ELSWORTH (same leet) Margaret Wymond: one cote with adjacent croft once held by John Wymond, for life, rendering annually in all things as did John G.: 12d.

719 ELSWORTH (same leet) Thomas Newman: one tenement and a half-virgate of land once held by Thomas Bryth, for life, rendering annually in all things as did Bryth. G.: 6s.8d.

720 ELSWORTH (same leet) William Bocher pays 40d. for license to marry Margaret West, naif of the lord, this time.

721 BYTHORNE John Hacoun: one plot with a half-virgate of land once held by William Baron, for life, rendering annually in all things as did William. G.: 3s.4d.

722 BYTHORNE Elizabet Baron pays 3s.4d. for license to marry John Hacoun, this time.

63v **723** WISTOW John Outy Jr: one plot with one quarter of land once held by Thomas Gowler, for life, rendering annually 4s., three ploughing *precariae* and one autumn *precaria*. G.: 12d.

724 HEMINGFORD Walter Lyncolne, one cote once held by John Tynker, for life, rendering annually in all things as did John. G.: 12d.

725 HEMINGFORD John Roseby: one tenement with one virgate of land once held by John Sly, for life, rendering annually in all things as did John Sly. G.: 40d.

726 WARBOYS Richard Plumbe: one plot with a half-virgate of land once held by John Gerold, *in opere* for life, rendering annually in all things as did John. G.: 20s.

727 HEMINGFORD Walter Lyncolne pays 3s. for license to marry Johanna, daughter of Thomas Hirde and naif of the lord, this time.

728 HOUGHTON John Abbot: one plot with one virgate of land once held by Thomas Hervy Jr., in *novum opus* for life, rendering annually in all things as did Thomas. G.: 18d.

729 ELTON Laurence Pokebrook: one plot with a half-virgate of land and one vacant messuage with a half-virgate of land once held by John Clerk, for life, rendering annually in all things as did John. G.: 3s.4d.

730 ELTON Richard Wodeward: one plot with a half-virgate of land once held by John Wodeward, for life, rendering annually in all things as did John, rendering annually in all things as did John. G.: excused because of repairs.

731 ELTON John, son of Henry Hobbesson, alias Clerk, pays three capons for license to live off the manor for as long as it pleases the lord, remaining a naif as before.

732 ELTON John Harper: one quarter of land once held by John Robyn, for life, rendering annually in all things as did John Robyn. G.: 12d.

64r **733** ELTON John Best: one quarter of land once held by John Wodeward, for life, rendering annually in all things as did John Wodeward. G.: 12d.

734 ELTON John Pilketon: a half-virgate of land once held by John Pool, for life, rendering annually in all things as did Pool. G.: 3s.4d.

735 ELTON William Frettere: one plot with one virgate of land and one cote once held by John Frettere, for life, rendering annually in all things as did John. G.: 6s.8d.

736 WARBOYS John Wolle pays 10s. for license to marry Agnes, daughter of John Molt, naif of the lord. Same John and Agnes: one mondayland once held *in opere* by William Altheworld, in *arentatio* for life, rendering annually 5s. at the customary times and all other works and customs rendered by Thomas Berenger. G.: excused, because it is included in the marriage fine. He pays the full rent for this year.

737 WARBOYS Richard Plumbe: surrender of one akirmanland, one mondayland and one maltmanland, to the use of his son, John Plumbe, in bondage for life, rendering annually in all things as did Richard, except that he will have an allowance of 5s. of the rent for the maltmanland in support of his akirmanland for as long as it pleases the lord. Pledges for good maintenance: John Plumbe and Richard Plumbe. G.: 3s.4d.

738 HURST (January) Roger White Jr: one vacant tenement with one virgate of land once held by John Colles, for life, rendering annually all services and customs owed therein, with the first payment due at the feast of St. Andrew after one full year. G.: 3s.4d.

739 BROUGHTON Richard Willesson of Wistow, naif of the lord, pays 3s.4d. for license to marry Agnes, daughter of Benedict Pye, naif of the lord and widow of John Catoun and for entry into one plot with a half-virgate of land once held by John Catoun, *ad censum* until a tenant can be found for that land.

740 WISTOW William Hiche, naif of the lord, receives license from the lord to marry Alicia, daughter of Thomas Outy, naif of the lord, this time. Fine excused because of their poverty.

64v **741** WISTOW Galfridus Hunne: one plot with building with a half-virgate of land and another plot with one quarter of land once held by Robert Randolf Jr., in bondage for life, rendering annually in all things as did Robert. Same Galfridus: license to marry Cristina, daughter of William Heryng of Upwood, naif of the lord. G. and fine: 6s.8d.

742 HOLYWELL (January) John Tayllor: one plot with building and one virgate of land once held by John Beaumeys, and one butt of land in Salmade, for life, rendering annually in all things as did Beaumeys. G.: 3s.4d.

743 WISTOW John Waryn and his wife, Agnes: one plot with a half-virgate of land once held by John Benet, in *arentatio* for life, rendering annually 8s. at the customary times, with the first payment due at the feast of the Nativity of Blessed Mary after one full year. G.: excused.

744 BYTHORNE Richard Wayte: one plot with building and a half-virgate of land once held by John Rokysson, for life, rendering annually in all things as did John. Also Richard pays 10s. for license to marry Margaret, widow of the aforesaid John, naif of the lord, this time.

745 UPWOOD William Jonesson; four acres of demesne land at Schepecotedole and three acres and three rods of land and meadow at Schortasshes once held by John Cary, for life, saving the right of anyone, rendering annually 8d. per acre at Schepecotedole and 18d. for the land at Schortasshes, at the customary times. G.: two capons.

746 UPWOOD Nicholas Alston: two acres of land at Schepecotedole once held by John Cary and Thomas Rolf, for life, rendering annually 8d. per acre. G.: two capons.

747 UPWOOD Thomas Rolf: one cote of two acres once held by himself, for life, rendering annually 3s.4d. at the customary times. G.: two capons.

748 WARBOYS Thomas Benet: one mondayland with land lying in le Stokkyng once held by John Hy Jr., for life, rendering annually in all things as did John. G.: 3s.4d.

65r **749** WISTOW Richard Rede: one plot with building with three quarters of servile land once held by John Gowler, for life, rendering annually in all things as did John. G.: 3s.4d.

750 WISTOW Thomas Randolf: one plot with a half-virgate of land once held by Richard Rede, for life, rendering in all things as did Richard. G.: 3s.4d.

751 WISTOW Walter Savage and his wife, Margaret: one plot with a half-virgate of land in Raveley once held by John West, from Michaelmas in *arentatio* for life, rendering annually 9s. at the customary times. Nor may they dismiss their sheepfold to anyone unless they first offer it to the lord, nor may they overburden the pasture. G.: 40d.

752 WISTOW John Outy: permission from the lord to dismiss a half-virgate of land once held by Henry Hiche to John Gowler, for life. Fine: 40d., to be paid by Gowler.

753 HOLYWELL FEN William Botiller and his son, Thomas: 12 acres of meadow and a half-acre of meadow, namely, one half of Eefurlong next to the meadow of St. Ives, at their own risk from rising water for 10 years, rendering annually 3s.4d. per acre at the feast of the Exaltation of the Cross. G.: excused.

754 WARBOYS Richard Smyth pays 13s.4d. for license to marry Katerina, daughter of Richard Berenger, naif of the lord.

755 ELLINGTON Wiliam Gymbir: surrender of one cote with one quarter of land, to the use of John Gymbir, his son, rendering annually in all things as did John. G.: 5s.

756 BRINGTON William Pykyn: one plot with a half-virgate of land once held by John Atte Chirche, rendering annually in all things as did John. G.: 2s.6d.

757 WESTON John Reynold pays for license to marry Margaret Man, naif of the lord.

758 WISTOW John Hitche pays 3s.4d. for license to marry Johanna, his daughter, to John Plumbe, son of Richard Plumbe.

65v **759** WESTON Edmund Bartilmew: one plot with one quarter of land once held by Long Jon, for life, rendering annually in all things as did Long Jon. G.: 12d.

760 THERFIELD (23 July) William Malt Schepperd: certain lands and tenements once held by Robert Wareyn, for life, rendering annually in all things as did Robert. G.: 12d.

761 THERFIELD (23 July). John Wynmer pays 6s.8d. for license to marry Felicia, his daughter and naif of the lord, to William Stokton, of this village, this time.

762 ELSWORTH John Newman: one plot with a half-virgate of land and one curtilage with one quarter of Gravelond once held by John Yntte, for life, rendering annually in all things as did John Yntte, with the understanding that Newman will pay nothing for the quarter of Gravelond until the feast of St. Andrew after one full year. G.: 12d.

763 ELSWORTH John Pygot of Drayton: one curtilage with one quarter of land and one quarter of land with the third part of one quarter of Gravelond once held by John Cowherde, rendering annually in all things as did Cowherde. G.: 12d.

764 ELSWORTH John, son of William West: one messuage with three quarters of land once held by John Smyth Jr., with one quarter from a half-virgate of Gravelond once held by William West, for life, rendering annually for the messuage 8s.7d. rent and 17d. tallage and ploughing of 10 acres at the will of the bailiff, and for the quarter of Gravelond 5s. G.: 12d.

765 ELSWORTH Richard Swynford, alias Brawghyng: two parts of a capital messuage of one virgate once held by Alrethe, in bondage for life, rendering annually 2s. at the customary times. G.: 12d.

766 ELSWORTH John Collesson: the eighth part of one virgate of St. Luke's land once held by Henry Leman, in bondage for life, rendering annually 2s.6d. at the customary times. G.: 12d.

767 HOUGHTON John Basset: one plot with a half-virgate of servile land once held by William Aleyn, *in opere* for life, rendering annually in all things as did William, with the first payment due at the next feast of St. Andrew. G.: 12d.

66r **768** HOUGHTON William Aleyn: one plot with building with a half-virgate of land previously held by Thomas Hervy Sr., in *arentatio* for life, rendering annually 6s. at the customary times and all other services and customs rendered by Thomas. G.: 12d.

769 HOUGHTON William Fuller: one plot with a half-virgate of land previously held by John Hervy, in *arentatio* for life, rendering annually 4s. at the customary times. G.: 12d.

770 WOODHURST William Walton and his wife, Margaret: one plot with building with one virgate of land once held by John Blakwell and one quarter of land parcelled out of one virgate once held by Nicholas Hunneye and surrendered into the lord's hands, for life, rendering annually in all things as did John and Nicholas. G.: 3s.4d.

771 WOODHURST Thomas Trover: one quarter of land once held by Nicholas Hunneye, for life, rendering annually in all things as did Nicholas. G.: 12d.

772 ELSWORTH Thomas Aleynesson: one cote with croft and one quarter of land of Gravelond once held by Henry atte Wode, with one *forera* in a croft at Grave, for life, rendering annually in all things as did Henry. G.: 12d.

773 WISTOW John Newman: one plot with building with a half-virgate of land once held by Richard Wodcok, in *arentatio* for life, rendering annually 8s. at the customary times, and mowing for one day in the barley for the lord's table. G.: one capon, and no more because of repairs.

774 WARBOYS Thomas Bele Jr: one quarter of land in Caldecote once held by William Brounnote, in *arentatio* for life, rendering annually 3s. at the customary times and all other services and customs owed therein. G.: 6d.

775 WOODHURST John Chaimberleyn and his wife, Agnes: one plot with all adjacent land once held by John Lawman, for life, rendering annually 13s.4d. at the customary times and all other services and customs rendered by Lawman. G.: one capon.

776 BRINGTON Nothing ("nullus").

66v **777** WARBOYS John High Sr. and his wife, Katerina: one plot with building once held by John AtteWode, for life, rendering annually in all things as did John AtteWode. Also: one mondayland once held by William Brounnote, in *arentatio* for life, rendering annually 3s.4d. at the customary times. Also: 12 acres of land of Alsoneslond and six acres in le Stokkyng once held by John AtteWode Sr., for life, rendering annually 12s.8d. at the customary times. Nor will John and Katerina relinquish any part of this agreement, but they will keep it. One house in the aforesaid mondayland, to be repaired and maintained by John, together with one selion in a croft, is reserved to Emma AtteWode for life, and Emma will have access to the kiln and the oven. G.: 12d.

14 THOMAS BUTTERWYK (1409-1410)

67r **778** HOLYWELL (20 April) Adam Sewale and his wife, Rosa: one cote with adjacent croft previously held by Henry Kyng, for life, rendering annually in all things as did Henry. G.: 40d.

779 HOLYWELL (20 April) John Qwernemaker: one plot with one cote and croft once held by John Morice, for life, rendering annually in all things as did Morice. G.: 10s.

780 ELTON John Robury: one cote once held by John Page, with one quarter of land and one and a half acres of Outlond, for life, rendering annually 9s. at the customary times. G.: 6d.

781 ELTON Richard Saundir: one plot with adjacent croft and one acre, a half-rod of land and a half-virgate of land once held by Radulph Smyth, for life, rendering annually 15s. and all other services and customs owed therein. G.: 2s.

782 ELTON John Hikkesson: one quarter of land once held by John Taillour, for life, rendering annually in all things as did Taillor. G.: 12d.

783 BRINGTON Thomas Austyn: surrender of one messuage and a half-virgate of land, to the use of Robert Botiller, for life, rendering annually in all things as did Thomas. G.: 6s.8d.

784 BRINGTON (7 October: court) William Cartere: one messuage and a half-virgate of land recently held by Simon Collesson, for life, rendering annually in all things as did Simon. G.: 6s.8d.

785 BYTHORNE William Spayn pays 2s. for license to marry Johanna, daughter of Thomas Bacheler and naif of the lord, this time.

786 WESTON William, son of John Wattesson, pays 40d. for license to marry Anna, his daughter and naif of the lord, to William Pecok Jr. of Bukworth, this time.

67v **787** ABBOTS RIPTON (11 October: court) John Gedneye and his wife, Emma: one cote with garden, one croft, and one parcel of land and meadow containing one acre lying in Esthorp and recently held by William del Grene, for life, rendering annually in all things as did William. G.: 5s.

788 HOLYWELL (28 October: court)[21] Adam Sewale and his wife, Rosa: one acre of land in Middilfurlong recently held by John Beaumeys, for life, rendering annually in all things as did John. G.: two capons.

789 HOLYWELL (same court) John Schepperd: a half-virgate of land recently held by William Cartere, for life, rendering annually in all things as did William. G.: 2s.

790 HOLYWELL (same court) Thomas Brayn: one acre of land lying in Middilfurlong recently held by John Taillor, for life, rendering annually in all things as did John. G.: two capons.

791 BARTON (4 November: court)[22] John Smyth: one messuage and a half-virgate of land recently held by Emma Smyth, for life, rendering annually in all things as did Emma. G.: 6s.8d.

792 BARTON (same court) Walter Aleyn: one messuage and a half-virgate of land recently held by John Ser, for life, rendering annually in all things as did John. G.: 6s.8d.

---

[21] See PRO 179/52. Neither this entry, nor the following is in the roll.

[22] Ibid. The entry itself is not in the court roll, which, however, records that Emma Smyth surrendered one messuage and a half-virgate to John Smyth. The heriot is recorded as one sheep worth 8d.

793 SHILLINGTON (5 November: court)[23] John Sampson: one messuage and a half-virgate of land recently held by Roger Taillor, for life, rendering annually in all things as did Roger. G.: 6s.8d.

794 SHILLINGTON (same court)[24] John, son of Richard Grene: surrender of one messuage and one virgate of land, to the use of John Ede, for life, rendering annually in all things as did Grene. G. and heriot: 13s.4d.

68r **795** SHILLINGTON (same court)[25] John Ede: one messuage and one virgate of land recently held by John AtteWode, for life, rendering annually in all things as did AtteWode. G.: 13s.4d.

796 SHILLINGTON (same court)[26] William atte Hill of Pegsdon: one acre of land in Pegsdon which he holds in exchange from Robert Cartere and here regains after a decision by the 12 jurors of the court, for life, rendering annually in all things as did Robert. G.: 20d.

797 SHILLINGTON (same court)[27] John Warde: surrender of one messuage and one virgate and one forland in Chibley, to the use of Thomas Stonley, for life, rendering annually in all things as did John. G.: 20s.

798 SHILLINGTON Grant to Thomas Stonley, naif of the lord, of license to marry Agnes, daughter of Henry Hamond. The fine is excused by the seneschal because Thomas is a pauper.

799 SHILLINGTON (same leet)[28] William Priour Jr., naif of the lord, pays 8d. for license to marry Johanna, daughter of John Hughson and naif of the lord.

800 SHILLINGTON (same leet). William Coche: surrender of one toft and one virgate of land called Aleyneslond, to the use of John, son of William Coche, for life, rendering annually in all things as did William. G.: 6s.8d.

801 SHILLINGTON (same leet) Isabella Hughson pays 5s. for license to marry Dionisia, her daughter and naif of the lord, to Taillor of Barton, this time.

802 SHILLINGTON (same leet) Alicia, daughter of John AtteWode: one messuage and one virgate of servile land previously held by William Waryn, in *arentatio* for life, rendering annually in all things as did William. (*This entry is crossed out*).

803 SHILLINGTON (same leet) Same Alicia: one messuage and one virgate of servile land previously held by William Waryn, in *arentatio* for life, rendering annually 13s.4d. at the customary times, with the provision that Johanna, widow of John AtteWode, will have one *camera* in the above property with no rent. G.: 6s.8d.

68v **804** THERFIELD (7 November: leet)[29] John Piers: surrender of one messuage and a half-virgate, to the use of Robert Sewale, for life, rendering annually in all things as did John. G.: 20s.

805 THERFIELD (same leet)[30] Katerina, widow of William Croyser: nine and a half

---

[23] Ibid. The entry is not in the roll, but there is notation of the surrender of land by Juliana Taillor, with a heriot of 2s.

[24] PRO 170/52. Entry not in roll.

[25] Ibid. The entry is not in the roll, but notice is made of John Atte Wode's surrender of his property. The gersuma recorded is 6s.8d.

[26] Ibid. Entry not in roll.

[27] Ibid. The full entry is not in the roll, but John Warde's surrender of property is noted. Heriot: 8s.

[28] Ibid. Entries nos. 799-803 are not in the roll.

[29] Ibid. Entry not in roll.

[30] Ibid. The entry is not in the roll, but notice is made of the death of William, tenant of one messuage, a half-virgate and Fynehouses. The heriot is one horse, valued at 16s.8d.

acres at Brann̄cestre once held by Thomas Malt, for life, rendering annually 7s.8d. in equal portions at the customary times. G.: 12d.

806 ELSWORTH (10 November: court) Isabella Wymond: surrender of one quarter of land recently held by John Wymond, to the use of John Alderman, for life, rendering annually in all things as did Isabella. G.: 12d.

807 GRAVELEY (13 November: leet) Thomas of the Halle: one messuage and one virgate and a half of land recently held by Robert del Halle, for life, rendering annually in all things as did Robert. G.: 4s.

808 GRAVELEY (same leet) John Flayce: one messuage and a half-virgate of land recently held by William William, for life, rendering annually in all things as did William. G.: 12d.

809 WESTON William, son of John Wattesson, naif of the lord, pays 40d. for license to marry Anna, his daughter and naif of the lord, to William Peecok Jr. of Bukworth.

810 UPWOOD Andrew Balle: one virgate of land once held by William Chaumberleyn and one quarter called Snapeslond with one parcel of meadow in Upvalemede, in bondage for life, rendering annually in all things as did William, with the provision that this year he pay for one-half of the tenement. G.: 40d.

69r   **811** WISTOW John Elyngton and his wife, Margaret: one empty plot with a half-virgate of land once held by John Cleryvaux, in *arentatio* for life, rendering annually 8s. and all other services and customs owed therein. G.: excused.

812 WISTOW Robert Hiche: surrender of a half-virgate once held by Henrysson, to the use of William Hiche, *ad censum* for life, rendering annually all services and customs owed therein. G.: two capons.

813 THERFIELD[31] Robert Prest: one plot with all messuages and lands once held by Robert Doke, for life, respecting always the rights and status of Edith Doke. G. and heriot (for the aforesaid Edith): 16s.8d.

814 THERFIELD (leet) William Frost: all lands and tenements with demesne land once held by John Gerveys, in bondage for life, rendering annually in all things as did John, with the first payment due at the feast of St. Andrew after three full years. Further, William will receive at the beginning 9 bushels of wheat, 10 quarters of dredge and 7 quarters of peas, and the grain, straw and chaff are to be restored to the lord at the end of the term. The lord will pay for the land and its winnowing. William will build up the property and maintain it thereafter for life. G.: 40d.

815 THERFIELD (same leet) John Patoun of Royston: 12 acres of demesne parcelled out of Newelond lying near the village of Therfield opposite the hill, on both sides of the King's road, from the previous Michaelmas for 20 years, rendering annually 6s. in equal portions at Michaelmas and Easter.

816 THERFIELD (same leet) John Patoun: one parcel of a certain croft containing four acres of land lying at the western end of the village of Royston recently called Brancester, lying between the land held by John Adam and the croft pertaining to the village of Royston and extending from the western end of the croft recently held by Peter Hiltoft up to the brew house, the other part of which croft is now held by John and Katerina Laneleer, from the previous Michaelmas for 20 years, rendering annually 4s. in equal portions at Michaelmas and Easter.

817 THERFIELD (same leet) Same John Patoun: five acres of land, from the previous

---

[31] Ibid. The entry is not in the roll, although Robert's death is noted. His tenement is described as having been one messuage and a half-virgate. Heriot is one gray horse, the value not being given "quia in libro gersumarum".

Michaelmas for 20 years, rendering annually 8d. per acre at Michaelmas and Easter. G.: 6s.8d.

69v   **818** WOODHURST William Boner Jr. and his wife, Agnes: one cote once held by his father, Benedict Boner, and two messuages with one virgate of land once held by John and Benedict Boner, in *arentatio* for life, rendering 12s. this year and the next and 20s. each year thereafter at the customary times, and all other services and customs owed therein. G.: 2s.

819 HOLYWELL Thomas Hemyngton: one plot with building and one cote with croft once held by John Quyrnemakere, for life, rendering annually in all things as did John. G.: 6s.8d.

820 WARBOYS (November) John Levot and his wife, Johanna: two mondaylands once held by Roger Wethirle, for life, rendering annually as did Wethirle and Robert Cole, chaplain. G.: 40s., to be paid in three installments over the next three years: namely, 13s.4d. at the next feast of the Purification the remaining two years.

821 WOODHURST (November) William Trover: one empty plot with a half-virgate of land once held by John Harrof, in *arentatio* for life, rendering annually 10s. at the customary times. G.: 12d.

822 ELSWORTH John Howesson and his heirs: all the ploughs traditionally belonging to the lands and tenements recently held by Thomas Sperwer, rendering annually 22d., with the provision that if he or any of his heirs default in rendering payments or tallage as owed to the lord by all, or if they do not keep the abbot and his successors free from blame regarding the King for all services and rents pertaining to the King from those lands, this copy will be held null, unless John or his heirs make sufficient amends within a month after Easter. G.: two capons.

823 ELSWORTH John Lounton, alias Schepperd: one cote recently built up on a tenement once held by William Smyth, for life, rendering annually 4s. at the customary times and all other services and customs owed therein. G.: 12d.

824 ELSWORTH John Ynnte: one cotland at le Brokesbrynke once held by John Pycot and one quarter of land once held by John Philipp, in bondage for life, rendering annually 8s. and all other services and customs owed therein. G.: 6d.

70r   **825** ST. IVES William Pope and his wife, Matilda, a half-row once held by John Millere, for life, rendering annually 8s., with the obligation to repair and maintain the property at their own expense. *Et non licebit,* etc. G.: 6s.8d.

826 ST. IVES William Judde: surrender of two half-rows in Bridge Street once held by Thomas Ketryng and recently held by John Bate Mason. The lord returns the property to the said William and his wife, Emma, for life, rendering annually 26s.8d., with the obligation to repair and maintain the property at their own expense. *Et non licebit,* etc. G.: excused because of repairs.

827 ST. IVES Hugo Portos: surrender of a half row, to the use of Thomas Judde, and his wife, Johanna, for life, rendering annually 10s. at the customary times, with the obligation to repair and maintain the property at their own expense. *Et non licebit,* etc. G.: 6s.8d.

828 ST. IVES John Morice: surrender of a half-row once held by Margaret Bakester, to the use of William Horsham and his wife, Katerina, for life, rendering annually 16s. in equal portions at the customary times, with the obligation to repair and maintain the property at their own expense. *Et non licebit,* etc. G.: 14s.

829 SLEPE Richard Scharp and his wife, Johanna: a half-virgate and one cotland once held by John Roger and William Roger, for life, rendering annually all services and customs owed therein, with the provision that if Richard cannot be distrained to observe the agreement, then John and William will make satisfaction to the lord as originally stipulated. G.: 2s.

70v **830** SLEPE Thomas White and his wife, Margaret: one cotland once held by William Cut, for life, rendering annually 12s. for rents, and works and all other services and customs owed therein, with the first payment due at the feast of St. Andrew after one full year. G.: excused because of repairs.

831 SLEPE Henry Sewyn: surrender of two virgates of land, which he receives back from the lord with William Roger, for life, rendering annually all services and customs owed therein. Also: William pays 3s.4d. for *gersuma* as well as for license to marry Margaret, daughter of Henry Sewyn and naif of the lord.

832 SLEPE John Pulter: surrender of one virgate of land with one empty plot, to the use of Nicholas Chykesand and his wife, Agnes, for life, rendering annually 20s. at the customary times and all other services and customs rendered by John. G.: 6s.8d.

833 SLEPE Frederick Skynnere and his wife, Cristina: one quarter of land and one selion once held by Thomas Wrighte, for life, rendering annually 16s. at the customary times, common fine, and all other royal services. G.: 3s.4d.

834 HOUGHTON John Marchal: surrender of one plot with a half-virgate of land, to the use of Nicholas Marchal, for life, rendering annually 7s. and all other services and customs owed therein. G.: 2s.

835 HOUGHTON Robert Mason: half of one virgate of land once held by John Gate, for life, rendering annually 7s. and all other services and customs owed therein, with the first payment due at the feast of St. Andrew after one full year. G.: 2s.

836 HOUGHTON William Adekyn: one ruined plot with one virgate of land once held by John Hervy, for life, rendering annually in all things as did John, with the obligation to repair the plot within the next two years. G.: two capons.

837 WARBOYS John Boys and Radulph Bokeland: one plot with building with 22 acres of a tenement once held by Roger de Hirst, for life, rendering annually 20s. and one hen, which property used to render 27s. annually. They will build one *insathous* and repair the property before the next feast of St. Martin. Pledges: the one for the other. G.: 3s.4d.

838 WARBOYS Walter Wodeward, alias Hirt: one acre of land at Bascroft once held by John (*cut off*), annually in all things as did John. G.: excused, because the land is fallow.

71r **839** GRAVELEY Robert Danyell, naif of the lord, pays 5s. for license to marry Elena, his daughter, to John Geffrey, freeman, this time.

840 CHATTERIS (9 January: court) John Mason: one tenement and eight acres of land and four acres of meadow recently held by William Rede, rendering annually in all things as did William. G.: 5s.

841 CHATTERIS (same court) Stephen Lytholf: one messuage and four acres of land recently held by John Mason, for life, rendering annually in all things as did John. G.: 3s.4d.

842 CHATTERIS (same court) Laurence Heyne: one cotland recently held by Walter Peyte, for life, rendering annually in all things as did Walter. G.: nothing, because the property is in ruins.

843 CHATTERIS (same court) Robert Mathew: one messuage and four acres of land and four acres of meadow recently held by William Heyne, for life, rendering annually in all things as did William. G.: 8s.

844 CHATTERIS (same court) William Crosse: four acres of land once held by John Smyth, for life, rendering annually in all things as did John. G.: 6s.8d.

845 CHATTERIS (same court) Beatrix, wife of Stephen atte Brigge: in Stephen's absence, surrender through the hands of John Bele, bailiff, of one messuage and eight acres of land 19 acres of meadow recently held by Stephen, to the use of Thomas atte Hythe, for life, rendering annually in all things as did Stephen.

846 CHATTERIS (same court) William Newman: surrender of all his status in one tenement of eight acres with one marsh once held by Matilda Keyse, to the use of John Newman, for life, rendering annually all services and customs owed therein. G.: 12d.

847 CHATTERIS (same court) John Frewet: one toft recently held by Simon Pyper, for life, rendering annually in all things as did Simon. G.: 6d.

848 WISTOW Robert Rede: one toft with one quarter of land once held by William Taillor, in bondage, for life, in *arentatio*, rendering annually 4s. G.: 12d.

71v **849** WARBOYS Henry Prestescosyn: surrender of one plot with building with a half-virgate of land, to the use of William Olyver, in bondage for life, rendering annually 8s. and all other services and customs rendered by Henry, with the obligation to rebuild and maintain the property. G.: 2s.

850 BROUGHTON William Pynchebek: one quarter of land once held by Nicholas Schepperd, in bondage, in *minor censum*, for life, with the first payment due at the feast of St. Andrew after one year. Also: one lot of Dammesson once held by John Caton, for life, rendering annually 11d. at the customary times. G.: two capons.

851 BROUGHTON Thomas Styvecle: one toft with one quarter of land once held by William Everard, in bondage in *minor censum* for life. G.: 12d.

852 BROUGHTON Thomas de Broughton: one built up messuage with a half-virgate of land once held by his father, in bondage *in opere* for life. Also: one virgate of land once held by his father, in bondage in *major censum* for life. G.: 3s.4d.

853 ABBOTS RIPTON Thomas Brere: one plot with a half-virgate of land once held by Thedewar, for life, rendering annually 8s. at the customary times, ploughing and certain other services as do all other tenants holding in *nova arentatio*, with the first payment due at the feast of St. Andrew. G.: 12d.

854 WISTOW John Love: one quarter and a half of land, in *arentatio* for life, rendering annually 7s.6d. at the customary times. Also: one hidemanland once held by Roger Paxton, in *arentatio* for life, rendering 2s.6d. annually; three rods of land once held by Andrew Smyth for 6d. and a half-acre of land in Lowefeld, previously worth 6d., for life, rendering annually 12d. at the customary times, with the obligation to rebuild the hidemanland within three years. G.: excused, because of repairs.

855 WARBOYS John Boys and Radulph Bokelond: surrender of half of the land they recently took up from the former tenement of Roger de Hirst, to the use of Simon High, for life, rendering annually 8s. at the customary times. G.: 12d.

856 BROUGHTON John Everard: one cotland once held by Alicia Burman, for life, rendering annually in all things as did Alicia. G.: two capons.

72r **857** CHATTERIS John Swetemelk: one tenement of eight acres once held by John Edenham, in bondage for life, rendering annually in all things as did Edenham. G.: 13s.4d.

858 ELSWORTH John Stapilford: one cote recently held by John Neweman and once held by Alan Taillor, for life, rendering annually 2s. at the customary times, as well as four *opera* between the Gules of August and Michaelmas, one *opus* in hay making, and one hen at Christmas. Also: the sixth part of one virgate of sown land once held by John Neweman, in *arentatio* for life, rendering annually 6s.8d. at the customary times, with the first payment due at the next feast of St. Andrew. G.: 12d., and no more because of great repairs.

859 WISTOW Thomas Fraunsse: one plot with three quarters of land once held by John Love, *in opere* for life, rendering annually all services and customs owed therein. G.: 40d.

860 WISTOW John Fraunsse: a half-cotland once held by Thomas Hacon, in *arentatio* for life, rendering annually 12d. G.: one capon.

861 UPWOOD William Jonesson: one cotland of two acres once held by William

Flemyng, in *arentatio* for life, rendering annually 3s. at the customary times, with the first payment due at the next feast of St. Andrew, and with the obligation to repair the well and maintain a grange built on that cotland, for which he receives one old, ruined house on the same property. G.: one capon.

862 ELSWORTH Thomas Elyot: one quarter of land once held by William Grigge, for life, rendering annually in all things as did William. G.: 12d.

863 ELSWORTH Henry Botolf and his wife, Cecilia: half of one virgate once held by William Towslond, for life, rendering annually 12s. at the customary times, one *opus* with one wagon and one loader in the peas, and other works pertaining to the vill. G.: 2s.

864 ELSWORTH William, son of Henry Hobbesson, pays 7s. for license to marry Margaret, daughter of John Evot and naif of the lord, and for license to hold half of one virgate once held by William Towselond, for life, rendering annually 12s. at the customary times, one *opus* with one wagon and one loader in the peas, and all other works pertaining to the vill.

865 ELSWORTH William William: one plot with a half-virgate of land once held by Thomas Pulter, in bondage for life, rendering annually all services and customs owed therein. G.: excused, because he is a naif of the lord of the manor of Graveley and a pauper.

72v **866** ST. IVES (January) William Horsham and his wife, Margaret: a half-row once held by William Pilgrym, for life, rendering annually 20s. at the customary times, with the obligation to repair the property within one year and maintain it at their own expense, thereafter. *Et non licebit*, etc. G.: excused, because of repairs.

867 ST. IVES Thomas Bocher: surrender of one row once held by John Ellesworth, to the use of John de Welles and his wife, Agnes, for life, rendering annually 14s. at the customary times, with the obligation to repair and maintain the property. *Et non licebit*, etc. G.: 3s.4d.

868 ST. IVES Thomas Glovere and his wife, Anna: a half-row once held by Baldewyn Taillor, for life, rendering 5s. this year and 6s.8d. each year thereafter, in equal portions at Michaelmas and Easter. They will repair and maintain the property at their own expense. *Et non licebit*, etc. G.: 20d.

869 ST. IVES John Wylymot and his wife, Alicia: a half-row once held by John Edynham, for life, rendering annually 10s. in equal portions at Michaelmas and Easter, with the obligation to repair and maintain the property. *Et non licebit*, etc. G.: 12d.

870 ST. IVES Valentine Draper Barkere: a half-row once held by John Edenham, for life, rendering annually 12s. in equal portions at Michaelmas and Easter, with the obligation to repair and maintain the property. *Et non licebit*, etc. G.: 10s.

871 ST. IVES John Sutton and his wife, Margaret: a half-row once held by Thomas Baa, for life, rendering annually 10s. in equal portions at Michaelmas and Easter, with the obligation to repair and maintain the property. *Et non licebit*, etc. G.: 12d., and no more because of repairs.

872 HOLYWELL John Nicolas and Thomas Nicolas: two acres and a half-rod of land at Oxhowe, one acre at Braynesdole and two acres at Malwode once held by John Taillor, for life, rendering annually 2s.1d.ob. for Oxhowe, 14d. for Braynesdole and 2s.4d. for Malwode, in equal portions at the customary times. G.: 2s.

73r **873** SLEPE John Bayly and his wife, Katerina: one messuage at the western end of the church, with one virgate of land once held by John Martyn, for life, rendering annually in all things as did John Martyn. G.: 12d.

874 BURWELL (4 November) Thomas Paxman: one messuage and 15 acres of land once held by Andrew Morice, for life, rendering annually 21s.4d., which land used to render 28s. He will render all other services and customs owed therein, and he will repair and maintain the property at his own expense, through the pledge of William Poket. G.: 6s.8d.

875 CRANFIELD (27 May: leet) John Godewyn pays 8s. for license to marry Alicia Godewyn, his cousin, to John Hode.

876 CRANFIELD (same leet) John Joy pays 20s. for license to marry Margaret, widow of Thomas Godewyn.

877 CRANFIELD (same leet) John Joy: three acres of demesne land, for life, rendering annually all services and customs owed therein. G.: 6d.

878 CRANFIELD (same leet) John Terry, two acres at Stalipras, rendering 16d. annually, and two acres of land at Perifeld, rendering 12d. annually, for life. G.: 2s.

879 CRANFIELD (same leet) John Smyth: one messuage and a half-virgate of land recently held by Elyas Smyth and valued at 13s.4d, another half-virgate of land in Estende formerly worth 8s., now rendering 10s., and one cote with a croft, rendering 4s. annually, for life. G.: 6s.8d.

880 CRANFIELD (same leet) William Godewyn, son of Thomas Godewyn: one messuage and a half-virgate of land recently held by William Godewyn Sr., and 11 and a half acres of land called a forland, for life, rendering annually in all things as did William Sr., with the obligation to repair and maintain the property and faithfully render payments. Pledges: John Godewyn, William del Rede, John Aleyn of Woodend and John Terry. G.: 3s.

881 CRANFIELD (same leet) William Aleyn Jr.: two acres at Peryhill once held by John Aleyn, for life, rendering annually in all things as did John. G.: 12d.

882 CRANFIELD (same leet) William Joye: one messuage and a half-virgate of land called "molelond" and one cote recently held by his father, one croft called "Hellecroft", six acres of servile land at BeryshonthcrWode, a half-virgate of land recently held by Robert Hethewy, and one quarter of land recently held by Thomas Joye and formerly valued at 4s.6d. annually, now rendering 6s., for life. G.: 26s.8d., to be paid in two equal installments at Michaelmas and Easter.

883 CRANFIELD (same leet) John Godewyn Sr.: 11 and a half acres and a half-rod of land from the land called a forland recently held by William Godewyn, for life, rendering annually in all things as did William. G.: 5s.

73v **884** CRANFIELD (same leet) Thomas Curteys: two acres of land recently held by Thomas Terry, for life, rendering annually in all things as did Terry. G.: 12s.

885 CRANFIELD (same leet) John Frost: a certain place in the lord's waste 30 ells long, for the purpose of making a place for dyeing, to be held in return for 6d. annually. G.: 10d.

886 BARTON (2 May: court)[32] Walter Wodeward pays 16s.4d. for license to marry Johanna, widow of Edmund Bernard and naif of the lord.

887 BARTON (same court) William Falley pays 40d. for license to marry Emma, daughter of William Roger and naif of the lord, to John Aleyn of Higham.

888 BARTON (same court). William Falley pays 40d. for license to marry Edith Mathew, naif of the lord, to a certain John Speryour of London.

889 SHILLINGTON (29 May: court)[33] John Warde: one messuage and one virgate of

---

[32] Ibid. "Isabella Hughson alienavit unum messuagium et unam virgatam terre Johanni Warde, et Isabella dabit herietam, videlicet optimum animal suum quod quidem animal est vitulus etatis j anni, precii iiii s."

[33] Ibid. The entry is not in the roll. Edmund's death is noted, also the assumption of his one built up cotland and croft by Johanna for 21d. Heriot: one ox worth 12s.

land recently held by Isabella Hughson, for life, rendering annually in all things as did Isabella. G.: 13s.4d.

890 SHILLINGTON William Sperwe: surrender of one messuage and a half-virgate of land recently held by Nicholas Richard, to the use of John Schepperd Jr., for life, rendering annually in all things as did William. G. and heriot: 7s., and no more because John will rebuild the messuage.

891 WARBOYS (July) John Dallyng and his wife, Emma: two quarters of land once held by John Molt, in *arentatio* for life, rendering annually 6s.8d. at the customary times, common fine in the leet, hay-making in Chevereth and sheep-shearing. G.: two capons.

892 WISTOW Radulph Pelle Miller: the windmill there, for 12 years, rendering annually 20s. in equal portions at the feasts of St. Andrew, the Annunciation, the Nativity of St. John the Baptist and the Nativity of Blessed Mary, with the first payment due at the next feast of St. Andrew. He will repair and maintain the mill and its appurtenances at his own expense, except for timber and splints from the lord's woods and their transport to the Mill Hill; he will restore the mill at the end of his term in as good — or better — condition as when he received it; and he will have mill stones sufficient for one year after the end of his term.

74r **893** BARTON[34] Adam Taillor: surrender of one virgate with forland, to the use of Henry Burrich, in bondage for life, rendering annually all services and customs owed therein. G: 13s.4d.

894 BARTON[35] Adam Taillor, naif of the lord, pays 12d. for license to live at Hitchin from the next Michaelmas to that of the following year.

895 RIPTON Peter Damme: one quarter of land once held by John Haulond Jr., and one quarter of land once held by John Gille, in bondage for life, rendering annually as do those who hold four virgates of demesne land, with the first payment due at the feast of All Saints after one full year. G.: two capons.

896 ELSWORTH Agnes Hebbe, daughter of Alan Hebbe and naif of the lord, pays 6s.8d. for license to marry. Pledge: John Burton of Barnwell.

897 WISTOW John Atte Gate pays 12d. for license to marry Katerina, daughter of Thomas Outy, naif of the lord. Pledge: Robert Waryn.

898 BURWELL Margaret Plumbe, naif of the lord, pays 40d. for license to marry Nicholas Toys, this time.

899 SLEPE Simon Herrof pays 6s.8d. for license to marry Alicia, his daughter and naif of the lord, to William Thressher of Somersham.

900 BIGGING (21 September). John Outy and John Denys: the whole ditch alongside the meadow and land that they hold from the sub-cellarer, lying between "le Tarfen" and the field of Bigging, together with the fishpond and ditches on either side recently held by John Bek, for life, rendering to the sub-cellarer annually 6d. in equal portions at Easter and Michaelmas; namely: 4d. from John Outy and 2d. from John Denys. They will plant willows and later cut them down as often as they wish. G.: two capons.

901 BURWELL (27 September) John Barwe, chaplain, and Robert, his brother: one tenement of 15 acres of land once held by Thomas Swyn at Wakeleysmesgate and once held by John Barwe, their father, for 24 years, rendering annually 17s. at the

---

[34] Ibid. 28 May: "Adam Taillor sursum reddidit in manus domini messuagium suum ut patet in libro gersumarum, et quia nativus domini dat domino de herietto unum equum preciatum ut in capite (40d।)."

[35] Ibid. Entry not in roll.

customary times and all other services and customs rendered by their father; another tenement of 15 acres once held by Robert atte Brigge and once held by their father, for life, rendering 17s. annually at the customary times; one croft once held by John Sadde and adjoining Gilbertescroft, for life, rendering annually 12d. four acres of demesne in Estfeld in one piece once held by Hugo Berker, for life, rendering 4s. annually; two crofts once held by Thomas Plumbe against the lane of the rector, for life, rendering 4s. annually. They will build a new house on the cote once held by Sawyer and also once held by Elena Helewys, at their own expense within the next three years, which cote is now held *per copiam* by Robert Barwe for a term of years. G.: 6s.8d.

74v   **902**   HOLYWELL Thomas Porter: one cotland with all adjacent demesne land, one croft and one acre of land once held by William Reve and once held also by John Taillor, for life, rendering annually all services and customs owed therein. G.: 2s.

903   CHATTERIS Gilbert Strykeland: surrender of two built up cotlands in Horseth and the toll ferry next to Swyneshed once held by John Sumptor, to the use of John Smyth Semor, for life, rendering annually all services and customs owed therein, with the provision that if John does not keep the ferry well and faithfully for ferrying men and beasts, as it was in the time of John Sumptor, the lord can expel him and accept a new *firmarius*, this agreement notwithstanding. G.: 10s.

15 THOMAS BUTTERWYK (1410-1411)

75r   **904**   BROUGHTON (6 October: leet) Thomas del Wold: surrender of one built up messuage next to the tenement of John Justice and one virgate of land, to the use of William Wolde, for life, rendering annually in all things as did Thomas. He will hold one *camera* and the third part of one barn and two acres in four fields free of payments, at his own will for life. G.: 12d. Seisin is delivered to him.

905   BROUGHTON (same leet) Thomas Botiller: surrender of one toft and one quarter of land once held by Stephen Hill, to the use of John Clerk, for life, rendering annually in all things as did Thomas. G.: three capons. He renders fealty and is granted seisin.

906   BROUGHTON (same leet) Alicia Aspelond: surrender of one messuage and a half-virgate of servile land and one quarter of land recently held by Colman, to the use of John del Wold, for life, rendering annually all services and customs owed therein. G.: 40d.

907   BARTON John Bonde and his wife, Alicia: seven acres of demesne land, of which five acres lie in le Stokkyng and two acres lie in le Overley, for life, rendering annually 7s. and all other services and customs owed therein. G.: 2s. Seisin is granted them.

908.   ELTON (20 October: court) John Newton: surrender of one messuage and one virgate of land recently held by John Gosselyn, to the use of William Taillor, for life. G.: 40d.

909   ELTON (same court) William Taillor: surrender of one messuage and one virgate of land once held by Henry Balle, to the use of John Newton, for life, rendering annually in all things as did William. G.: 12d.

910   ELTON (same court) William Cayne: one messuage of one quarter of land recently held by John Irby, chaplain, for life, rendering annually in all things as did John, with the rent for the first year excused. G.: 40d.

911   ELTON (same court) William Martyn: one toft and one quarter of land recently held by John Best, for life, rendering annually in all things as did John. G.: 6d.

912   ELTON (same court) John atte Crosse: one cotland recently held by Richard Couhird and three acres called Akirmanland, for life, rendering annually in all things as did Richard. G.: 12d.

913 ELTON (same court) Thomas Robery: one cotland recently held by Robert Taillor, for life, rendering annually in all things as did Robert. G.: 6d.

914 ELTON John Bate: one quarter of land recently held by John Wakefeld, for life, rendering annually in all things as did John Wakefeld. G.: 2s.

915 ELTON William Faucon: six butts lying inside the end of Arnewsbroke, for life, rendering annually 8d. G.: 6d.

916 ELTON William Nicoll: one messuage and one quarter of land recently held by John Colyn, for life, rendering annually in all things as did John, with the rent excused for the first year. G.: 2s.

75v **917** BYTHORNE (leet at Weston) John Bruce: one cote recently held by William Spayne, for life, rendering annually in all things as did William. G.: 40d.

918 BRINGTON (court at Weston)[36] William atte Chirche: one messuage and one-quarter of land recently held by John atte Chirche, for life, rendering annually in all things as did John. G.: 6s.8d.

919 WESTON (same court)[37] John Carter Jr.: one messuage and one virgate of land recently held by John Barton and now held by Elena, widow of the same John Barton, for life, rendering annually in all things as did John Barton. G. and fine for marrying the said Elena, naif of the lord: 6s.8d.

920 ELLINGTON Thomas Hykesson pays 6s.8d. for license to marry Agnes, his daughter and naif of the lord, to anyone.

921 RIPTON (25 October: leet) Robert Hemyngton: surrender of one plot with one virgate of land once held by Nicholas Hoberd, with land and meadow at Dammede, Hollebroke, Bonbalk, Hallmade and Buttes, to the use of Thomas Hemyngton, for life, rendering annually in all things as did Robert. G.: six capons.

922 RIPTON (same leet) William Smyth: surrender of two cotlands in *arentatio*, to the use of John Bally, for life, rendering annually 4s. and all other services and customs rendered by William. G.: 2s.

923 RIPTON (same leet) William Webster: one messuage and one virgate of land, one lot in Longland, two acres and one rod in Calvercroft once held by John Nicoll Jr., for life, rendering annually 24s.3d. and all other services and customs rendered by John. G.: 40d.

924 RIPTON (same leet) John Houlot: one acre of land at Cateshegge recently held by William Halsham, for life, rendering annually in all things as did William. G.: one capon.

925 BRINGTON Thomas Hacon: surrender of one plot with a half-virgate of land in Burylond once held by William Pyrye, to the use of Simon Beverich, in bondage for life, rendering annually in all things as did Thomas. G.: 6s.8d.

926 RIPTON John atte Persons: surrender of one quarter of land parcelled out of four virgates recently held by 16 customaries of the lord, to the use of John Robbes, for life, rendering annually in all things as did John atte Persons. G.: one capon.

76r **927** ABBOTS RIPTON Thomas Buks: one plot with building and a half-virgate of land at the corner of Burylond once held by Nicholas Taillor, in *arentatio* for life rendering annually 8s. at the customary times, ploughing for one day with his own plough at the summons of the bailiff, and the supplying of one mower with one stacker for one day in autumn at the summons of the bailiff and food supplied by the lord, except for sup-

[36] PRO 179/53. Notice in the court roll that William takes seisin of one quarter recently held by John atte Chirche.
[37] See PRO 170/53 for notice of John Barton's death.

per. Also: a semi-virgate once held by Thomas of the Hill, one plot with one house, one semi-virgate once held by William Martyn and two selions at Angerlond and half of one plot with one quarter of land once held by John atte Lane in *arentatio* and five acres of demesne land at Myddeldole, a half-acre of land once held by Thomas of the Hill, and another half-acre once held by John None, for life, rendering annually 26s.8d. and all other services and customs rendered by Thomas of the Hill. Also: two lots at Langlond once held by Nicholas Taillor, for life, rendering annually 3s.4d. at the customary times. G.: 3s.4d.

928 ABBOTS RIPTON William Alsoun: surrender of two plots and two semi-virgates of land once held by Andrew Martyn, half of one plot with half of one virgate once held by Andrew Coliere, and four acres at Cateshegge, to the use of Reginald Pypwell, for life, rendering annually in all things as did William. Pledge: William Alsoun. G.: 6s.8d.

929 SLEPE John Cartere, alias Wale, and his wife, Alicia: one plot with building in le Barre once held by John Broughton, for life, rendering annually 10s. at the customary times and all other services and customs owed therein. G.: 6s.8d.

930 WOODHURST Radulph Smyth: one quarter of land once held by Peter Herde, for life, rendering annually all services and customs owed therein, although he has an allowance of 12d. the first year. G.: two capons.

931 SLEPE Richard Scharp: surrender of one plot next to Wayeram with certain lands and meadows once held by Stephen Iremongere, to the use of Robert Elyngham, for life, rendering annually in all things as did Richard. G.: two capons.

932 WARBOYS William de Thorp: one quarter of land once held by John Alor, *ad opus* and *ad censum*; one parcel of land called Temesfordeslond, for life, rendering annually 7s. at the customary times and all other services and customs owed therein; a half-virgate of land in Caldecote once held by the same John Alot, for life in *arentatio*, rendering nothing this year and 6s.8d. each year thereafter at the customary times. G. and fine for license to marry Margaret, daughter of John Alot and naif of the lord: 5s.

933 WARBOYS John Hy Millere: one maltland and one mondayland once held by Richard Schepperd, in *arentatio* for life, rendering annually 9s. at the customary times. G.: two capons.

934 ST. IVES (November) William Horsham: surrender of a half-row once held by William Pylgrym, to the use of William Pardee, and his wife, Margaret, for life, rendering annually 20s. in equal portions at the customary times, with the obligation to repair the property at their own expense before Easter. *Et non licebit*, etc. G.: 6s.8d.

935 ST. IVES Richard Baker: surrender of one row once held by Stephen Yremonger next to the row held by William Botheby, to the use of John Meyk, and his wife, Katerina, for life, rendering annually 15s. in equal portions at the customary times, with the obligation to repair and maintain the property. *Et non licebit*, etc. G.: 6s.8d.

936 ST. IVES William Bakere: surrender of a half-row once held by Margaret Baxtere, to the use of Hugo Arthorngh Lystere, and his wife, Agnes, for life, rendering annually 16s. in equal portions at the customary times, with the obligation to repair and maintain the property. *Et non licebit*, etc. G.: 10s.

937 ST. IVES Richard Scharp: surrender of one row once held by Stephen Yremonger, to the use of Robert Elyngham, for life, rendering annually 20s. in equal portions at the customary times, with the obligation to repair and maintain the property. *Et non licebit*, etc. G.: six capons.

938 ST. IVES Henry Barbor and his wife, Johanna: a halfrow once held by Simon Leg, for life, rendering annually 13s.4d. in equal portions at the customary times, with the obligation to repair and maintain the property. *Et non licebit*, etc. G.: excused because of repairs.

939 WARBOYS John Heryng: one quarter of land once held by William Hoberd, in *arentatio* as long as he is in the lord's service, rendering 15d. this year and 2s.6d. each year thereafter. After his term of service is finished, he will hold that quarter *ad censum*, rendering annually in all things as did William Hoberd. G.: excused.

77r **940** HOLYWELL Robert Wrighte of Woodhurst: two gores of meadow in Holywell Fen once held by John Wyngord, for life, rendering annually 3s.6d. at the feast of the Exaltation of the Holy Cross. G.: two capons.

941 HURST John Edynham: surrender of one plot with building and one virgate of land once held by Thomas Canne, to the use of William Boner, and his wife, Margaret, for life, rendering annually in all things as did John. G.: 4s.

942 ELTON (20 November) Thomas Cakyr: one cote once held by John Benet and one plot with one virgate once held by John Dalton, for life, rendering 4s. this year and the next and 24s. each year thereafter at the customary times. G.: two capons.

943 ELTON (20 November) Hugo Hoberd: one plot with one virgate of land once held by William Benne, for life, rendering annually 20s. at the customary times and all other services and customs owed therein, with the first payment due at the feast of St. Andrew after three full years. He will build up that plot within the next three years and maintain it at his own expense. G.: 3s.4d.

944 ELTON (20 November) Richard Hoberd: one cote once held by John Peretre, for life, rendering annually 2s. for all services, with the obligation to the repair the property at his own expense. G.: 6d.

945 THERFIELD John Adam: the third part of Scharesbrigge, four acres at Wittonhill, alias Wolverdonbusch, a half-acre at Newdich, one acre at Wolverdonhill, a half-acre at Breneplot, a half-acre at Carndole, two acres at Pawlowehill, one and a half acres of Mangrave, one and a half acres at Timberlowe, one acre at Scaldene of land once belonging to Brancestre and recently held by Thomas Martyn, for life, rendering annually 6s. 10d.ob. at the customary times and all other services and customs rendered by Thomas. G.: one capon.

946 KNAPWELL (16 December: leet) John Sampson Jr: one messuage and a half-virgate of land once held by John Smyth, for life, rendering annually in all things as did John Smyth. G.: 12d. Seisin is granted.

947 KNAPWELL (same leet) John Creek: one messuage and one quarter of land recently held by Roger Gute, for life, rendering annually in all things as did Roger. G.: 4d. Seisin is granted.

948 ELSWORTH (16 December: leet) Henry Granneby, chaplain: one toft and one quarter of land recently held by William Gregge, for life, rendering annually in all things as did William. G.: three capons.

949 RIPTON Robert Jurdon: one quarter of land once held by Robert Hemyngton, in old *arentatio* for life, rendering nothing this year and the next and 3s.4d. each year thereafter. G.: one capon.

77v **950** BURWELL (8 January: court) John Kent: the capital messuage of one tenement of 15 acres, for 20 years, rendering annually 8s. as rent and 4d. as common fine. G.: two capons.

951 BURWELL (same court) William Houghton, naif of the lord, pays 6s.8d. for license to marry Margaret, his daughter, to Alexander Lyne.

952 BURWELL (same court) Thomas Poule: 15 acres recently held by John Dyry, for 30 years, rendering annually in all things as did John. G.: 6s.8d.

953 BURWELL (same court) John Sperwe: one plot with building with a curtilage recently held by Thomas, his father, for life, rendering annually in all things as did Thomas. G.: 6s.8d.

954 KNAPWELL John Saumpson: one messuage with a half-virgate of land once by Roger Gute, in *arentatio* for life, rendering annually 13s.4d. and one autumn *precaria*, and no more because of repairs, with the first payment due at the feast of the Annunciation. G.: 12d. and two capons.

955 KNAPWELL John Hot: one quarter of land parcelled out of a half-virgate once held by William Marchaund, in *arentatio* for life, rendering 5s. this year and 6s.8d. each year thereafter at the customary times, along with one autumn *precaria*. G.: 6d., one capon.

956 KNAPWELL John Smyth: one quarter of land parcelled out of a half-virgate held by William Marchaund, in *arentatio* for life, rendering 5s. this year, 6s.8d. each year thereafter at the customary times and one autumn *precaria*. G.: 6d., one capon.

957 KNAPWELL John Hoppere: one quarter of land once held by John Arnold, in *arentatio* for life, rendering nothing this year and 3s.4d. each year thereafter at the customary times. G.: two capons.

958 KNAPWELL John Intte pays 3s. 4d. for license to marry Johanna, his daughter and naif of the lord, to Richard Personysman, this time.

959 ELSWORTH Thomas Cheneyn and his wife: a half-virgate of land once held by William Grigge, in *arentatio* for life, rendering nothing this year and 13s.4d. each year thereafter, and all other services and customs owed therein. Also same Thomas: one toft once held by the same William, for life, rendering annually 8d. at the customary times, and no more because of repairs. G.: two capons.

960 ELSWORTH Richard Brawghyng and his wife, Margaret: one messuage and one quarter of land and one parcel of land of Seyntlys once held by John Cowherde, for life, rendering annually 10s. at the customary times and all other services and customs rendered by John. G.: 12s.

78r **961** UPWOOD Robert Aleyn: one built up cote and one quarter of land, together with all the land at Kyngeslond, once held by John Aleyn, in bondage for life, rendering annually in all things as did John. G.: three capons.

962 SLEPE Nicolas Chikesand and his wife, Agnes: one toft with a half-virgate of land once held by John Baldewyn, for life, rendering annually 6s.8d. at the customary times, with the first payment at the feast of St. Andrew after one year. G.: excused.

963 WARBOYS Richard Smyth: one and a half virgates of land once held by Richard Plumbe, for life, rendering annually 10s. for the virgate and 8s. for the half-virgate at the customary times, with the first payment at the feast of St. Andrew. Pledge for payments and maintenance: Richard Berenger. G.: 3s.4d.

964 HOUGHTON Thomas Wrighte: one cotland containing a half-virgate of land once held by Alan Ede, in bondage for life, rendering annually 6s. at the customary times and all other works previously rendered by William Aleyn, with the first payment at the feast of St. Andrew. G.: 6d.

965 CHATTERIS John Revesson: four acres of customary land once held by William Cartere, in bondage for life, rendering annually in all things as did William. G.: 2s.

966 GRAVELEY William Polyerd pays three capons for license to marry Agnes Denyell, daughter of Richard Denyell and naif of the lord.

967 SLEPE William Botheby: one plot with a half-virgate of land once held by John Mabon, for life, rendering annually 8s., with the obligation to build one house on the property at his own expense, and also with the condition that he will hold this half-virgate together with another half-virgate and one cotland which he has held for a long time for an annual payment of 32s., rendered at the feasts of the Annunciation, the Nativity of John the Baptist, the Translation of St. Benedict and the Nativity of Blessed Mary, in equal portions, and rendering all services and customs owed therein. G.: one capon.

968 WARBOYS (February) John Margarete two half-virgates of land in le Burycroft next to Fensyde, together with all land and meadow of demesne recently held by Robert Coll, in *arentatio* for life, rendering annually 15s. and all services pertaining to the lord and village for two half-virgates, in addition to all other services and customs rendered by Robert Coll. He will repair and maintain the property at his own expense, except that he will receive all the land sown with wheat and peas, except for three acres, and all the seed for peas, barley, and all the thatch, timber, hay and straw from the above land, as well as an allowance of rent. Nor will he serve in an office of the lord against his will, but, he will aid in stocking the demesne with sheep at the expense of the customaries and of the seneschal, whenever it pleases the latter. G.: 13s.4d.

969 RIPTON William Reignald: one quarter of land recently held by Robert Millere and once held by Peter de Denne, for life, rendering annually 3s.4d. at the customary times, with the first payment due at the feast of St. Andrew. G.: excused.

970 HOUGHTON John de Lye : a half-virgate of land once held by Robert atte Pool, in *arentatio* for life, rendering annually 5s. at the customary times. G. : 12d.

971 HOUGHTON William Smyth: a half-virgate of land once held by Robert atte Pool, in *arentatio* for life, rendering annually 4s. at the customary times. G.: 2s.

972 HOUGHTON Richard Smyth: a half-virgate of land once held by Henry Lawe, in *arentatio* for life, rendering annually 5s. at the customary times. G.: 12d.

973 GRAVELEY Agnes Robat, daughter of John Robat and naif of the lord, pays 5s. for license to marry John Drew, naif of the lord, this time.

78v **974** SLEPE Agnes, daughter of Simon Bronne, widow of John Ely, pays 6s.8d. for license to marry John Belleman, son of John Belleman.

975 HEMINGFORD Alicia, daughter of John Trap, widow of Robert Wythe of Houghton, pays 6s.8d. for license to marry John Hamond Carpenter.

976 WOODHURST (April) John Lawe: a half-virgate of land once held by William Porter, for life, rendering annually all services and customs owed therein, with the first payment at the feast of St. Andrew after two years. G.: two capons.

977 GRAVELEY John Seberne: one messuage and one virgate and a half of land recently held by Thomas of the Hall, for life, rendering annually in all things as did Thomas. G.: 40d.

978 HOLYWELL Thomas Nicolas and his wife, Margaret : one messuage and one cotland with three acres of land once held by Nicholas Scharp for life, rendering annually in all things as did Nicholas. G.: 5s.

979 WISTOW Richard Musterell: three acres of land at le Brach and four acres of land there, for life, rendering annually 5s.2d. at the customary times, with no payments until Michaelmas. G.: one capon.

980 SLEPE John Dryvere pays six capons for license to marry Agnes, his daughter, to John Cok, naif of the lord.

981 ELTON (15 June: court) Johanna, widow of John Crosse: surrender of all lands and tenements held by her husband, John Crosse, by *gersuma*, to the use of John Crosse Jr., for life, rendering annually in all things as did John Sr., with the obligation to repair and maintain the property, with the following provision : that if John Jr. does not govern himself well, in the estimation of John Deche, or if he withdraws, then John Deche will have the property. Pledges for maintenance: John Deche, Robert Botiller, John Bythorne. G.: 12d.

982 ELTON (same court) John Burnet: one cotland once held by Henry Hobbesson, for life. G.: one hen.

983 ELTON (same court) John Burnet, John Colyn Jr., John Waryn, Richard Rede, John Robery and John Waryn Sr.: three virgates and one quarter of land in le Overton held in the lord's hands this year, for 12 years, from the previous Michaelmas, rendering annually 22s., with the provision that if it pleases the seneschal to dismiss that land to anyone else during that time, he will reimburse them reasonably for their expenses and dismiss six acres of waste to them. G.: nothing, because the land is fallow.

984 ELTON (same court) John Howesson: five acres of akirmanland, of which five rods lie at Rendheden and a half-acre lies at Calencrosse, one acre at Dedmangrave, one acre at Larkesmor, one acre at Arnewesbroke, and one rod at Grenehill, for life, rendering annually 3s.4d., with the first payment at the feast of St. Andrew. G.: one capon. (Note: he will render this year as other tenants of such land).

985 ELTON (same court) John Harper: one quarter of land recently held by Bythorne, from Michaelmas for life, rendering annually all services and customs owed therein. This year he will have the meadow for fallow land, quit of payments. G.: 6d.

79r   **986** ELTON (same court) John Person: one quarter of land recently held by John Colyn, in Raton Row, from Michaelmas for life, rendering annually all services and customs owed therein, with the first payment at the feast of St. Andrew after one year. He will have meadow for a fallow land this year, quit of payments. G.: 12d.

987 ELTON (same court) John Bate: one toft and one quarter of land recently held by Robert Adam, for life, rendering annually all services and customs owed therein, as above. He will have meadow, as above. G.: 2s.

988 ELTON (same court) William Feryby: a half-virgate of land recently held by Robert Adam, for life, rendering as above. He will have meadow, as above. G.: 40d.

989 ELTON (same court) Thomas Gurmecestre: one quarter of land recently held by Bythorne, for life, rendering as above. He will have meadow, as above. G.: 2s.

990 ELTON (same court) Richard Barbour: one quarter of land recently held by John Gamel, for life, rendering as above. He will have meadow, as above. G.: 2s.

991 ELTON (same court) John Bletchehalf, alias Cros: one quarter of land recently held by Bythorne, for life, rendering as above. He will have meadow, as above. G.: 2s.

992 ELTON (same court) Richard Best: one quarter of land recently held by Stephen Wrighte, for life, rendering as above, with the first payment at the feast of St. Andrew after two years. He will have meadow, as above. G.: nothing.

993 ELTON Thomas Robery: one tenement of Oldmol once held by John Cook and a half-virgate of land once held by Richard in the Lane, for life, rendering 3s. this year and next and 12s. each year thereafter (i.e. 2s. for the tenement, 10s. for the half-virgate). G.: 2s.

994 ELTON Richard Barbor: two tofts of Oldmol recently held by Tayntor, for life, rendering annually 2d., with the first payment at the feast of St. Andrew. G.: nothing.

995 ELTON John atte Crosse Sr: one cotland called "cotmanum" recently held by Thomas Swon, for life, rendering annually in all things as did Thomas, with the first payment as the feast of St. Andrew. G.: 6d.

996 ELTON (same court) Richard Abbot and Thomas Aloun: all the lands of akirmanland in the lord's hands this year or not granted to tenants by copy or in support of other lands, (*per copiam*), with the exception of five acres previously granted out to John Hobbesson, certain acres previously granted out to John Germyn, and three acres assigned to the tenement once held by Carleton, from Michaelmas for 12 years, rendering annually 8s. at the customary times. G.: nothing. He will not dismiss any parcel of these lands.

997 RIPTON William West at Burygate: surrender of one plot with building and one virgate of land, to the use of John West Jr., in bondage for life, rendering for the half-virgate as did William, and for the rest as do those recently put in *novum censum*. G.: six capons.

998 ELSWORTH (18 June: court) Henry Hobbes: one messuage and one semi-virgate of land parcelled out of one virgate recently held by Thomas Clerk, in *arentatio* for life, rendering annually 12s. at the customary times and all other customs pertaining to the vill, with the first payment at the feast of St. Andrew, and with the obligation to repair the *insathous* at his own expense, except for timber from the lord. The lord will repair the grange, and afterwards Henry will repair and maintain it in good condition for the whole period. G.: six capons.

999 ELSWORTH (same court) William Holet: one semi-virgate parcelled out of one virgate recently held by Thomas Clerk, without messuage, and with three tofts pertaining to it, in *arentatio* for life, rendering annually 12s. at the customary times and all other customs pertaining to the vill for one of the tofts, with the first payment at the feast of St. Andrew. G.: six capons.

1000 ELSWORTH (same court) John West: one built up plot, once called a mondayland, and once held by Thomas atte Lane, in *arentatio* for life, rendering annually 3s., with the first payment at the feast of St. Andrew. G.: 2s.

1001 ELSWORTH John Chircheman: one cotland recently held by Thomas Smart and once held by his father, for life, rendering annually 2s.6d., one day's work in raising hay and reaping in autumn, with the first payment at the feast of St. Andrew. G.: two capons.

1002 ELSWORTH John Andrew: one quarter of land in Gravelond parcelled out of one virgate once held by Walter atte Wode, and one built up cote once held by Simon Collesson, for life, rendering 6s.6d. this year and 8s. each year thereafter at the customary times, work for one day in the fen, and one day in autumn. G.: 12d.

1003 BRINGTON John Pyrye: surrender of all his lands and tenements, to the use of John Punte, in bondage for life, rendering annually in all things as did John Pyrye. G.: 26s.8d.

1004 BRINGTON John Punte: surrender of one messuage and a half-virgate of land and all demesne lands adjoining it once held by Thomas Hacoun, to the use of Simon Beverich, in bondage, rendering annually in all things as did John. G.: 6s.8d.

1005 BRINGTON John Punte: surrender of one messuage and a half-virgate once held by John Pyrye, to the use of John Thresshere, in bondage for life, rendering annually in all things as did John Punte. G.: 13s.4d.

1006 UPWOOD John Andrew: one plot with a half-virgate of land once held by William Pykeler, in *arentatio* for life, rendering annually 9s. at the customary times, with the first payment at Michaelmas after one year, and with the obligation to build up the property. Pledges for repairs and observance of the terms: Robert Milys and Richard Payn. G.: two capons.

1007 WARBOYS John Wrighte and his wife, Alicia: one quarter of land *in opere* and all demesne land once held by Adam Coupere, for life, rendering annually in all things as did Adam, except that he will have an allowance of 6d. for the demesne land at Bascroft for life. G.: 8d.

1008 WARBOYS William Ravene and John Miller: the windmill there, from next Christmas for 10 years, rendering annually 40s. at the feasts of St. Andrew, the Annunciation and the Nativity of Blessed Mary, with the following obligations: to maintain the mill, within and without, in carpentry and all things, except that the lord will be responsible for iron works, enclosures, timber, splints, cogs and rungs, sawing of wood and its transport, and stones. They will have an allowance of 6s.8d. for repairing the wheel. G.: two capons.

1009 WARBOYS John Everard and his wife, Alicia: one mondayland once held by

John Keye, for life, rendering annually 4s. at the customary times. He will have one house with curtilage for life. G.: 12d.

1010 SLEPE CUM WOODHURST Richard Nunne and his wife, Johanna: a half-virgate of land once held by his father, Robert Nunne, for life, rendering annually in all things as did Robert. G.: 2s.6d.

80r **1011** ST. IVES Richard Bakere and his wife, Margaret: a half-row once held by Roger Belleman, for life, rendering annually 20s. in equal portions at the customary times, with the obligation to repair and maintain the property at their own expense. *Et non licebit*, etc. G.: 6s.8d.

1012 ST. IVES John Catworth and his wife, Isabella: a half-row once held by William Houghton, for life, rendering annually 15s. in equal portions at the customary times, with the obligation to repair and maintain the property. *Et non licebit*, etc. G.: excused.

1013 ST. IVES John Spaldyng and his wife, Agnes: a half-row once held by William Edenham, for life, rendering annually 10s. in equal portions at the customary times, with the obligation to repair and maintain the property. *Et non licebit*, etc. G.: 6s.8d.

1014 ST. IVES Thomas Crowcher and his wife, Johanna: a half-row once held by Richard Brabon, for life, rendering annually as did Richard, with the obligation to repair and maintain the property. *Et non licebit*, etc. G.: 10s.

1015 ST. IVES John atte Wode and his wife, Margaret: a half-row once held by John Burman, for life, rendering annually 13s.4d. in equal portions at the customary times, with the obligation to repair and maintain the property. *Et non licebit*, etc. Pledges for repairs: John Madd and John Wylymot. G.: excused because of repairs.

16 THOMAS BUTTERWYK (1411-1412)

80v **1016** SLEPE Agnes, daughter of John Ravyn, naif of the lord, pays 6s.8d. for license to marry John Spaldyng of Peterborough.

1017 RIPTON John Laveyn and his wife, Johanna: all lands and messuages once held by Andrew Swon, for life, rendering annually in all things as did Andrew. John will remain in his craft with the lord for receiving a stipend from him. G.: 6s.8d.

1018 ELSWORTH Agnes, daughter of Robert Boner, naif of the lord, pays 10s. for license to marry, the first time.

1019 ELSWORTH John Lucas pays six capons for license to marry Isabella, daughter of Robert Boner, naif of the lord by blood, and for entry into one messuage with one quarter of land once held by John Schepperd, rendering to the lord annually 10s. and works, with the first payment at the feast of St. Andrew, and with the obligation to repair and maintain the property at his own expense, except for timber and two wagons of straw from the lord. He receives 6s.8d. for repairs, granted by the wife of John Wareyn. G.: six capons.

1020 ELSWORTH John Howesson: the windmill there, from the previous Michaelmas for 20 years, rendering annually 16s. at the four customary times, with the obligation to maintain the windmill and appurtenances and appendages both within and without, at his own expense, except for timber, splints, cogs and their transport up to Millehirst from the lord. He receives two mill stones, valued at (*blank*). G.: (*missing*).

1021 ELSWORTH John Howesson: one messuage with one virgate of land once held by William Boner, rendering nothing this year, 6s.8d. the next year, and 22s. each year thereafter and all other works called "commonstamus" and with the obligation to repair the property within the next two years, with two wagons of straw from the lord. G.: three capons.

1022 ELSWORTH Robert Broghyng: one quarter of land of Gravelond once held by

John Newman, rendering annually 3s.4d., with the first payment at the feast of St. Andrew. G.: one capon.

1023 Elsworth John Howesson Sr. and John Howesson Jr: one messuage and one virgate of land once held by William Boner, for life, rendering annually 22s. One of them will mow in the meadow and fleece the ewes for one day and shear the sheep for one day. G.: three capons.

1024 Knapwell John Joye:.surrender of one quarter of land recently held by John Pykeler, to the use of John Aubry Jr., for life, rendering annually in all things as did John Joye. G.: 12d.

1025 Holywell Thomas Deye pays 6s.8d. for license to marry Agnes, his daughter, to John Schepperd of Needingworth.

1026 Slepe cum Hurst William Oky and his wife, Johanna: one messuage with one virgate of land once held by Nicholas Oky, for life, rendering annually in all things as did Nicholas. G.: 3s.4d.

81r **1027** Bythorne John Tredegold pays for license to marry Agnes, daughter of John Hacoun, naif of the lord, and for entry into one messuage and a half-virgate of land in Bythorne recently held by Richard Smyth, late husband of Agnes, for life, rendering annually in all things as did Richard. G.: 26s.8d.

1028 Warboys John Dally Sr.: two mondaylands once held by John Dally Jr., in *arentatio* for life, rendering 20d. this year and 4s. each year thereafter and customs of the vill, with the following provision: that he not be burdened with the 6d. assize *redditus* for two mondaylands previously in his tenure. G.: two capons.

1029 Warboys John Dallyng: two quarters of land, for life, rendering annually 6s.8d. at the customary times and other services rendered by his peers. G.: 12d.

1030 Warboys Katerina AtteWode: one dichmanland once held by Juliana Pakerell, for life, rendering annually in all things as did Juliana. Pledges for maintenance: Robert Ravene and William Bonde. G.: 20d.

1031 Warboys John Heryng Jr.: half of one plot and lands once held by Robert atte Hill, for life, rendering annually 6s.8d. at three terms, with the first payment at the feast of St. Andrew. G.: excused.

1032 Warboys John Brantoun: a capital plot with a half-virgate of land once held by Robert Colle and recently held by John Margarete, for life, rendering annually 8s. 4d. at the customary times, customs of the vill, two ploughing *precariae* and one bedrepe, with the obligation to erect a solar and grange on the property at his own expense within the next three years, except that the lord will supply timber and carpentry for the solar and for its construction. Also: all the demesne land previously held by the same Robert, rendering to the lord as did Robert. For the above repairs, he will receive all the crop sown both in the half-virgate and the demesne land, and all hay, thatch, and manure within the plot.

1033 Warboys John Berenger: one plot with a half-virgate of land once held by Flemyng, in *arentatio* for life, rendering annually 6s.8d. at the customary times, all customs of the vill, one bederepe and one ploughing *precaria*, with the obligation to repair one *insathous* with a solar 40 feet long at his own expense within the next two years, except that the lord will supply large timber. He will receive for his repairs all the crop from the above half-virgate. Also: one croft next to Fensyde called Boyscroft, for life, rendering annually 6s.8d. at the customary times. He will receive undergrowth for the enclosure of the croft as Robert Colle recently had. G.: 6s.8d.

1034 Warboys (September) John Berenger Jr.: one mondayland once held by John Heryng, in *arentatio* for life, rendering annually 4s. at the customary times, customs of the vill, supplying one mower with one stacker in autumn for one day at the lord's food. G.: one capon.

1035 WARBOYS Thomas Benet, naif of the lord: license to marry Agnes Baroun, naif of the lord by blood, and to enter into one half-virgate with all other lands recently held by John Nedham, for life, rendering annually in all things as did John. G.: 12d.

1036 HOLYWELL John Warde pays 10s. for license to marry Agnes, daughter of John Hunne and naif of the lord by blood.

1037 HOLYWELL William Hunne: one acre at Oxhowe once held by Agnes Hunne, for life, rendering annually 12d. at the customary times. G.: one capon.

1038 SLEPE William Harrof pays 3s.4d. for license to marry Emma, his daughter and naif of the lord by blood, to Thomas Tyrraunt.

81v **1039** HOUGHTON John Lye: one cotland once held by John atte Style, for life, rendering annually 6s. and all other services rendered by tenants in *arentatio*, with the obligation to build a house on the property, for which he will receive an allowance of 6s. from the lord. G.: two capons.

1040 HOUGHTON John Andrew and John Qwaplode: five and a half cotlands once held by the rector, for life, rendering annually 6s.8d. at the customary times. G.: excused.

1041 UPWOOD William Aleyn and John Aleyn: a half-virgate of land once held by Pykeler, in *arentatio* for life, rendering annually 8s., with the first payment at the feast of St. Andrew, and with the provision that the capital messuage with croft of the property will be reserved to the lord. G.: four capons.

1042 UPWOOD John Mylys: one plot with a half-virgate of land once held by Thomas Wardebusk, in *arentatio* for life, rendering annually in all things as did Thomas. G.: one capon.

1043 UPWOOD Thomas Michell: one plot with one quarter of land once held by John Lane, for life, rendering annually in all things as did John. G.: excused.

1044 UPWOOD William Edward and his wife, Agnes: one plot and one virgate of land once held by Hakyn, for life, rendering annually 20s. at the customary times, one ploughing *precaria*, one bederepe and common fine in the leet, with the obligation to repair the *insathous*, large grange and bakehouse within the next three years, in consideration for which repairs the lord grants William an allowance of the rents for the next two years, until the feast of St. Andrew. G.: two capons.

1045 UPWOOD John Bracer: one cotland of one acre once held by his father, another cotland once held by William Philyp, and three selions of one acre once held by William Baker and half of one virgate once held by John Horwode, with the plot and croft of the virgate reserved to the lord, in *arentatio* for life, rendering annually 12s.3d. for rent, tallage and hens and all other works, together with one ploughing *precaria* and one autumn *precaria*, sheep-shearing and moving in Brennmede. G.: one capon.

1046 ELTON (January) John Waleys: one cotland once held by the rector, with one quarter of land once held by Gamely, for life, rendering annually, for the cotland in all things as did John Gamely, and for the rest 5s., with the first payment at the feast of St. Andrew after one year. G.: 12d.

1047 ELTON John atte Crosse Sr.: one quarter of land once held by Colyn, for life, rendering annually 5s., with the first payment at the feast of St. Andrew after one year. G.: 6d.

1048 ELTON William Sextoun: one cotland of a tenement once held by Pers and one cotland next to the church once held by William Carleton, for life, rendering annually 4s. G.: 6d.

1049 WESTON William Penyell: one plot and one quarter of land once held by Gylys, for life, rendering annually all services and customs owed therein. G.: excused.

1050 GRAVELEY John Webstere: surrender of one plot with building and a half-virgate, to the use of Nicholas Twyny, and his wife, Agnes, rendering annually in all things as did John. G.: 2s.

1051 THERFIELD (May) John Watte and his wife, Katerina: all lands and tenements once held by John Clerk, for life, rendering annually in all things as did John Clerk, with the first payment at the feast of St. Andrew. G.: 12d.

82r **1052** CHATTERIS John Semtpool: one cotland once held by William atte Cross, for life, rendering annually in all things as did William. G.: 5s.

1053 CHATTERIS John Bate: one cotland once held by John Horsethe, for life, rendering all services and customs owed therein. G.: 5s.

1054 CHATTERIS John Hertford Sr.: one cotland once held by John Smyth Jr., for life, rendering all services and customs owed therein. G.: 2s.

1055 CHATTERIS Richard Smyth: a fifth part of one messuage once held by Adam Taillor, for life, rendering annually all services and customs owed therein. G.: 4s.

1056 WISTOW Amicia Baroun: surrender of a half-virgate of land and one cote once held by John Baroun, which she then receives back from the lord with her son, Richard, for life, rendering annually in all things as did John. G.: six capons.

1057 WISTOW John Outy: one quarter of land once held by John Clerk, for life, rendering annually 3s.4d., with the first payment at the feast of St. Andrew. G.: two capons.

1058 WISTOW Thomas Blacwell: one cotland once held by Thomas Hacoun and recently held by the lord, for life, rendering annually 12d., with the first payment at the feast of St. Andrew. He will receive two wagons of undergrowth for maintaining the enclosure. G.: one capon.

1059 WISTOW John Outy: one virgate and a half of land once held by Thomas Outy, for life, rendering annually in all things as did Thomas. G.: two capons.

1060 WISTOW Henry Paxton and his wife, Petronilla: one plot with all adjacent land recently held by John Sabyn, for life, rendering annually 6s.8d. in equal portions at the customary times, with no payments for the first two years following Michaelmas, and with the obligation to repair the property, the lord supplying two wall plates and ten studs. G.: works.

1061 WISTOW Hugo Buthe: one messuage and five quarters of land and all appurtenances, for life, rendering annually as did Thomas Outy, except that for the next year he will not serve as akirman but will render for them at the order of the seneschal. G.: six pullets.

1062 ELLINGTON John Cartere pays 6s.8d. for license to marry Johanna, daughter of Thomas Howesson.

1063 ELLINGTON John Swyft: by license of the court, surrender of one rod of land at Waddon in Millefeld, to th use of Alicia Moke, in exchange for one parcel of a certain croft next to Ferylane, G.: three capons.

1064 ELLINGTON Johanna Bette pays 13s.4d. for license to marry Thomas Gobald, freeman.

1065 ELLINGTON Johanna Bette: surrender of one messuage and one virgate and all lands and tenements once held by her late husband, Simon Bette, to the use of John Hacoun Jr., and his wife, Mariota, for life, rendering annually in all things as did Simon. G.: 3s.4d.

1066 HOUGHTON (20 July) John Heyne: one tenement with one virgate of land once held by William Deyn, for life, rendering this year up to Michaelmas as did William, 5s. the next year, and 10s. each year thereafter at the customary times. G.: three capons.

1067 BARTON William Frost: surrender of one virgate once held by Isabella atte

Chirche, to the use of Thomas Sweyn, for life, rendering annually all services and customs owed therein. G.: 13s.4d.

1068 RIPTON John Sly pays 3s.4d. for waste made by his wife, Agnes, in a tenement once held by John West.

82v **1069** BARTON John Roger and his wife, Emma: one messuage with one virgate and all cotes, enclosures and demesne land once held by William atte Chirche, in bondage for life rendering annually in all things as did William. G.: 23s.4d.

1070 BARTON (April: court) John Richard: surrender of one plot and one virgate to the use of Richard Roger, for life, rendering annually in all things as did John. G.: 26s.8d.

1071 BARTON (same court) William Broun pays 3s.4d. for license to marry Agnes, widow of John atte Chirche, tenant of a half-virgate with forland.

1072 BARTON John Richard: surrender of one cotland to the use of William Broun, for life, rendering annually in all things as did John. G.: 3s.4d.

1073 BARTON John Bond: two and a half-acres once held by William Milleward, for life, rendering annually in all things as did William. G.: 12d.

1074 BARTON John Stacy pays 3s.4d. for license to marry Lucia, daughter of Alan Mathew, naif of the lord.

1074a CRANFIELD (April: leet) John Frost: one plot and a half-virgate of land recently held by William Marchall and once held by Thomas Bernard, and one cotland in Estende for life, rendering annually in all things as did William, with the obligation to rebuild and maintain the property. Pledge for repairs: Richard Curteys. G.: 5s.

1075 CRANFIELD William atte Pyrye: a half-virgate of land with two acres of old demesne at Newhorsfeld once held by the same John, for life, rendering annually in all things as did John. G.: 7s.

1076 CRANFIELD Thomas Catelyn: surrender at one cote once held by John Croby, to the use of Nicholas Wynnegore, for life, rendering annually in all things as did Thomas, with the obligation to rebuild and maintain the property. G.: 3s.4d.

1077 CRANFIELD Thomas Catelyn: one acre and one rod of demesne land recently held by Margaret Horne, for life, rendering annually in all things as did Margaret. G.: 20d.

1078 BURWELL John atte Hill: 20 acres once held by Thomas Stop, for 20 years, rendering annually in all things as did Stop. G.: 40d.

1079 BURWELL Thomas Poul: half of one tenement of 24 acres, for 20 years, rendering annually 13s.4d. and 4d. as common fine. G.: 12d.

1080 BURWELL William Ydeigne: surrender of one built up cote, one croft, one acre of land once held by his father, which he and his wife, Katerina, receive back, for the life of whomever lives longer, rendering as before. G.: two capons.

1081 BURWELL Richard Sowtheman: one tenement of 15 acres and two crofts with one piece of meadow once held by Richard himself, with a half-acre of land in le Nethfeld next to the land of John Prikke, in place of a third croft, from Michaelmas for four years, rendering annually 21s.4d., common fine, reaping of two acres of wheat and ploughing of three acres at the will of the bailiff or *firmarius*. G.: 2s.

83r **1082** SHILLINGTON (April: leet). John Wyngham: one virgate once held by John himself, in bondage, rendering annually all services and customs owed therein, respecting the rights and conventions in that land granted to John Beston and found in the Gersuma Book for 13 Thomas. G.: 6s.8D.

1083 SHILLINGTON John West pays 3s.4d. for license to marry Alicia, daughter of John atte Wode of Uppenende, tenant of one messuage and one virgate once held by William Waryn.

1084 SHILLINGTON Johanna, daughter of John atte Wode, naif of the lord of Stondon, pays 6s.8d. for license to marry whomever she wishes, the first time.

1085 SHILLINGTON Simon Coupere pays 5s. for license to marry Agnes, daughter of William Smyth, naif of the lord.

1086 SHILLINGTON Robert Waleys: a half-virgate of land and one cotland with two acres of demesne at Chirchehill, in bondage for life, rendering annually in all things as did William Malt. G.: 12d.

1087 SHILLINGTON William Raveyn: one cotland with six acres of land at Stokkyng once held by Nicholas of the Abbey, for life, rendering annually in all things as did Nicholas. G.: 2s.

1088 SHILLINGTON Thomas Elys pays 40d. for license to marry Lucia, widow of Gilbert atte Broke, naif of the lord, and for entry into all the land she holds.

1089 SHILLINGTON John atte Brok: one piece of land in Hanscomb once held by Gilbert atte Brok, and four acres of demesne land at Chirchehill once held by John Dier, for life, rendering annually 12s. at the customary times. G.: 4s.

1090 SHILLINGTON John Hento, servant of the parson: a half-virgate of land once held by Ivo Sergaunt, for life, rendering annually in all things as did Ivo. G.: six capons.

1091 SHILLINGTON John Couche and his wife, Margeria: surrender of one plot and one virgate of land once held by Robert atte Grene, to the use of William Cowcher Jr., for life, with the provision that the aforesaid Robert atte Grene will hold the land until next Easter and receive the crop already sown on that land. G.: five marks.

1092 KING'S RIPTON (May) William of the Hill and his wife, Margaret: one empty plot with a half-virgate of land called Warynnyslond, for life, rendering annually 3s.4d. at the customary times, with the first payment at Easter, and all other services and customs owed therein. G.: one capon.

1093 ABBOTS RIPTON William Ormdiche: half of a plot with building and one quarter of land once held by William Smyth, in *arentatio* for life, rendering annually 4s. at the customary times and one ploughing *precaria* at the summons of the bailiff and with sufficient food from the lord. G.: one capon.

1094 ABBOTS RIPTON John Baskyn: one cote once held by Alexander Marchall and recently held by Robert Broun, for life, rendering annually all services and customs owed therein. G.: 2s.

1095 BURWELL Richard Gardyner: one built up cote with one croft once held by Edmund Waleys, next to the land of Thomas Gardener, for 21 years, rendering annually 4s.4d. at the customary times. G.: excused.

1096 BURWELL John Benet and his wife, Agnes: one toft once a cotland recently held by Robert Bocher and two tofts recently in the waynage of the lord for the life of whomever lives longer.

83v **1097** ST. IVES Richard Sutbrythe and his wife, Margaret: surrender of one row, to the use of Richard Nicol and his wife, Agnes, for life, rendering annually 3s.4d. in equal portions at the customary times, with the obligation to repair the front and hall of the property within the next two years at their own expense. *Et non licebit*, etc. G.: excused, because of repairs.

1098 ST. IVES John Milton: surrender of two half-rows next to the water, to the use of Richard Rikener and his wife, Elena, for life, rendering annually 12s. in equal portions at the customary times, with the obligation to repair and maintain the property at their own expense. *Et non licebit*, etc. G.: two capons.

1099 ST. IVES William Bernewell and his wife, Alicia: one row once held by Adam Smyth, for life, rendering annually 13s.4d. in equal portions at the customary times, with the obligation to repair and maintain the property. *Et non licebit*, etc. G.: two capons.

17 THOMAS BUTTERWYK (1412-1413)

84r   **1100**   WISTOW (4 October) Thomas Brecelaunce: one messuage and a half-virgate of land recently held by John Asplond in Raveley, for life, rendering annually 8s. at the customary times, together with all other customs of the vill, except Monkgeld, and with the obligation to repair and maintain the buildings on the property at their own expense. G.: excused.

1101   UPWOOD (3 October) William Thorston: all the demesne land at Schepecotedole once held by William Jonysson, for 10 years, rendering annually 8d. per acre at the customary times. He will dismiss the property to no one. G.: one heron.

1102   UPWOOD (January) Thomas Newman and John Andrew: one plot with a half-virgate of land once held by William Symond, for life, rendering annually 7s. at the customary times, carrying service with one wagon, and one plough *precaria*. If they have wives or servants, they will maintain the *insathous,* with timber supplied by the lord for the first repairs, and they will come to sheep-shearing. G.: one capon.

1103   HOUGHTON. John Abbot: one messuage with a croft and a half-virgate of land recently held by Henry Lawe, for life, rendering annually in all things as did Henry. G.: 12d. and one capon.

1104   HOUGHTON William Roger: surrender of one messuage and a half-virgate recently held by John Geffrey, to the use of Robert Roger, for life, rendering annually in all things as did William. G.: 12 capons.

1105   HOUGHTON William Brampton: one messuage and one virgate of land recently held by John Abbot, for life, rendering annually in all things as did John. G.: 12d.

1106   HOUGHTON William Aleyn: one toftland and a half-virgate recently held by John Donston, for life, rendering annually 5s. G.: three capons.

1107   HOUGHTON Robert Roger: one plot with one virgate of land once held by John Andrew atte Style, for life, rendering annually in all things as did John, with the obligation to repair and maintain the property. G.: two capons.

1108   HOUGHTON William Smyth, Thomas Styward, Robert Andrew and John Andrew Smyth: one toft with one virgate of land once held by John atte Style, for life, rendering 4s. this year and 8s. each year thereafter at the customary times. G.: four capons.

1109   ELTON (17 October: leet) John Hoberd: surrender of one toft and one quarter of land called Batlyneslond, to the use of John Philyp, for life, rendering annually in all things as did Hoberd. G.: 12d.

1110   ELTON Henry Carleton: one cote in Kyrkerow and four acres recently held by William Carleton, for life, rendering annually 4s. and suit to court. G.: 6d.

1111   ELTON Richard Ryde: one cote recently held by Henry Robery, for life, rendering annually 12d. G.: 6d.

1112   ELTON John, son of Thomas Elyot: one messuage and a half-virgate of land recently held by Hugo Hoberd, for life, rendering annually in all things as did Hugo. G.: six white capons.

1113   ELTON William Taillor: one toft and one quarter of land recently held by Thomas del Wroo, for life, rendering annually in all things as did Thomas. G.: 12d.

1114   ELTON William Facoun: one lot recently held by William Facoun, for life, rendering annually in all things as did William. G.: 12d.

1115   ELTON Henry Schepperd: one toft recently one *corcetell* held by John Carleton, for life, rendering annually 4d. G.: 4d.

84v   **1116**   WESTON John Whyte: surrender of one windmill called Brington Miller, to the use of Richard Botiller, from the previous Michaelmas for seven years, rendering annually 20s.

1117 Brington Simon Beverich: surrender of one messuage and one quarter of land, to the use of William Smyth, for life, rendering annually in all things as did Simon. G.: 20d.

1118 Brington William Pykkyn Jr.: one messuage and a half-virgate of land recently held by John Thresshere, for life, rendering annually in all things as did John. G.: 40d.

1119 Slepe Richard Scharp: surrender of one messuage and one virgate of land recently held by William Roger, to the use of William Geffrey, for life, rendering annually in all things as did Richard. G.: six capons.

1120 Slepe John Baudewyne pays 3s.4d. for license to marry Alicia, daughter of John Hogge and naif of the lord by blood.

1121 Warboys Matilda Bennesson: a half-virgate of land once held by Richard Bennesson, for life, rendering annually in all things as did Richard and 8s. G.: excused.

1122 Warboys John Ravele: one and a half acres at Bascroft once held by John Chapman, for life, rendering annually 8d. per acre, with the first payment at the feast of St. Andrew. G.: two capons.

1123 Warboys John Mold: two and a half acres at Brenfurlong once held by John Gerold and William Baroun, and one acre of land at Bascroft once held by John Chapman, for life, rendering annually 8d. per acre, with the first payment at the feast of St. Andrew. G.: two capons.

1124 Warboys. John Webstere and his wife, Agnes: one mondayland once held by John Taillor and also by Bartholomew Swan, for life, rendering annually 2s. G.: 6d.

1125 Warboys John Brynwat: that acre at Lowefurlong recently held by Robert Oliver and another acre recently held by John Chapman, for life.

1126 Warboys Thomas Beronger and his wife, Agnes: one quarter of land once held by John Flemyng, in *arentatio* for life, rendering annually 3s.4d., one autumn *precaria* and sheep-shearing with the vill, with the condition that he continue to hold a mondayland for life, building it up within two years and maintaining it thereafter, rendering for it annually 4s. and other works rendered by similar tenants, which mondayland previously rendered 6s. G.: two capons.

1127 Warboys John Plumbe, son of Richard Plumbe, and his wife, Johanna: one house with one quarter of land once held by John Flemyng, for life, rendering annually 3s.4d. at the customary times, one autumn *precaria*, and sheep-shearing with the vill.

1128 Warboys (January). Richard Bawde: half of one plot with half of one virgate of land in Caldecote once held by John Mold, in *arentatio* for life, rendering annually 2s.6d., with the first payment at the feast of St. Andrew. G.: 6d.

1129 Warboys (3 January) John Bennesson: one toft with a half-virgate of land in Caldecote once held by Henry Norburgh Catere, in *arentatio* for life, rendering annually 6s., with the first payment at the feast of St. Andrew. G.: two capons.

1130 Warboys (February) John Catoun, John Schakestaf and Thomas Bele: one virgate of land in Caldecote once held by Colnyly, for life, rendering annually 10s. at the customary times, the supplying of one mower with one stacker in autumn for one day, and all other customs of the vill, with the first payment at the feast of St. Andrew. G.: nothing.

1131 Warboys William Schakestaf: a half-virgate recently held by him and one mondayland also recently held by him, and one quarter in Caldecote, for life, rendering, annually 4s. for the half-virgate, 2s.6d. for the quarter, the supplying of one mower with one stacker for one day in autumn, three ploughing *precariae*, the Great *Precaria*, and all other customs of the vill. G.: excused.

1132 BURWELL (24 October) William Gelle: 24 acres recently held by Simon Calvesban, for life, rendering annually 22s. and suit to court. G.: two capons.

1133 CRANFIELD Margaret, daughter of Richard Catelyn, pays 40d. for license to marry John Grene of Crowle.

1134 BARTON John Bocher: two cotes and three acres recently held by John Cut, for life, rendering annually in all things as did Cut. G.: 40d.

1135 BARTON Agnes Carpenter: surrender of one cotland lying in Downe ende, to the use of Richard Bereford, for life, rendering annually 7s. and all other services and customs owed therein.

1136 BARTON Same Agnes: surrender of one messuage and one cotland in Chirche ende recently held by Thomas Carpenter to the use of Richard Bereford, for life, rendering annually in all things as did Thomas. G.: 10s.

1137 SHILLINGTON John Messenger: surrender of all the right he has in Wodehallegrene, with yield of undergrowth and trees without waste or destruction, to the use of Laurence Taillor, for life, rendering annually 4s. at the customary times, with the obligation to repair and maintain the property, with undergrowth supplied by the lord. Nor will be make waste there under penalty of 10 marks and forfeiture of his status in the woods. G.: 2s.

1138 SHILLINGTON John Grene and his wife: Isabella: one built up parcel of the manor with one grange and other houses once held by John Smyth, one garden called Perywyk and one lot once held by the same John Smyth, for life, rendering annually in all things as did John Smyth together with the full crop from John Smyth, as he received from the lord, and with the obligation of building a solar on the property with timber supplied by the lord, and with the top floor reserved to the lord. G.: 2s.

1139 RIPTON (January) Walter Schepperd, alias Savage, and Richard Weston: three semi-virgates of land with 10 acres at Catteshegge once held by John Ivell, in *arentatio* for life, rendering annually 32s. at the customary times, with the first payment at the feast of St. Andrew after one year. They will not be akirmen, but they will pay the common fine and the hundred geld, and they — or one of them — will come to the sheep-shearing, and one ploughing *precaria*, rendering as do others. G.: two capons.

1140 RIPTON John Bailly: one plot with building and a half-virgate of land once held by William West and recently held by Colier, and one toft with a half-virgate of land once held by the same William and recently held by Saby, for life, rendering nothing until Michaelmas, and 16s., the supplying of one mower with one stacker in autumn, common fine, hundred geld and sheep-shearing thereafter, annually. Also: two acres at Catteshegge once held by the same William, for life, rendering annually 16d. at the customary times. G.: 3s. 4d.

1141 RIPTON (October) John Boner and his wife, Agnes: one and a half-virgates and all demesne land once held by William Alfsun, for life, rendering annually for the virgate as do others, for the half-virgate — in *arentatio* — 10s. at the feast of the Annunciation, and for the demesne land, one mower in the meadow for one day. Also: four bushels of wheat, three quarters of barley and three quarters of peas through the hands of Reginald Pypperwell, together with one horse, valued at 3s. 4d., one wagon with wooden wheels, one coulter and one plough-share, one bee-hive, and all the waste and reploughed land, four acres manured with a wagon, and one hand-mill for malt, with two stones. G.: 6s. 8d.

1142 HOLYWELL William Hunne and his wife, Margaret: one croft once held by William Dammesson, for life, rendering annually in all things as did Dammesson. G. : 2s.

1143 HOLYWELL John Merton: one acre at Nethbrerecroft once held by John Hemyngton, for life, rendering annually 14d. G.: one capon.

1144 HOLYWELL John Hemyngton: surrender of one cotland with newly appurtenant demesne land, to the use of Thomas Hemyngton, for life, rendering annually in all things as did John, with the obligation to repair the *insathous* within the next three years and to maintain other houses there. G.: one capon.

1145 ELLINGTON John Broun: one plot with a half-virgate of land and all adjacent demesne land once held by John Wysenell, for life, rendering annually in all things as did John Wysenell. G.: (*blank*).

85v **1146** RAMSEY Robert Coupere and his wife, Emma: from Brother Robert Moordon, sub-cellarer, one vacant toft with two butts of land in a croft once held by John Austyn Sr. and lying between the messuage held by him and the messuage of the said John Austyn, for life, rendering to the sub-cellarer annually 20d. in equal portions at the feasts of the Annunciation and Nativity of Blessed Mary. G.: two capons.

1147 THERFIELD Thomas Waryn and his wife, Elena: all lands and tenements with demesne land held by William Croy, for life, rendering annually in all things as did William, with the first payment at the feast of St. Andrew after two years. G.: four capons.

1148 THERFIELD John Waryn and his wife, Agnes: one cotland with all demesne land recently held by John Peres Sr., for life, rendering annually in all things as did John Peres, with the first payment at the feast of the Nativity of John the Baptist. G.: two capons.

1149 BROUGHTON (January) John Corby and his wife, Margaret: one messuage and a half-virgate of land once held by Ivetta Schepperd, in *major censum* for life, rendering annually as do others in *major censum*, except that he will not be akirman, with the first payment at the feast of St. Andrew. He will repair and maintain the property at his own expense, except that the lord is responsible for carpentry, and John and Margaret will have rushes and herbage in Holywell fen, for their mowing and carrying. G.: excused, because of repairs.

1150 HOLYWELL Nicholas Baroun: a half-virgate of land with all appurtenant demesne land once held by John Palmer, for life, rendering annually in all things as did John. He will restore the crop of demesne at the end of the term according to the custom of the vill, and he will mow five acres in Holywell Fen, as *gersuma*. Pledge for keeping all agreements: John Palmer.

1151 WARBOYS John Schakestaf: the capital messuage of one mondayland once held by Lambert and recently held by John Lache, alias Taillor, and one quarter of land once held by the same Taillor, for life, rendering annually 12d. for the mondayland and 4s. for the quarter, and one autumn *precaria*, the supplying of one mower with one stacker for one day, and customs of the vill. G.: six capons.

1152 CHATTERIS John Fynyon Jr: one tenement and all land once held by Edmund Cate, for life, rendering annually in all things as did Edmund. G.: 6s.8d.

1153 CHATTERIS John Sawt: one plot with four acres of land with adjacent meadow once held by Thomas Lawesson, for life, rendering annually in all things as did Thomas. G.: 6s.8d.

1154 CHATTERIS John Cade: one cote once held by Nicholas Thawer, for life, rendering annually in all things as did Nicholas. G.: 4s.

1155 CHATTERIS Agnes Peroun: the fishpond previously held by John Horsethe, for life, rendering annually in all things as did John, with the obligation to maintain the weirs there at her own expense and dismiss them at the end of her term. G.: 24s.4d.

1156 CHATTERIS John Ace: one cote once held by Alicia Cok, for life, rendering annually in all things as did Alicia. G.: 8d.

1157 BROUGHTON (December) William of the Wold: a half-virgate of land once held by William Ivet and once held by Crane, in *minor censum* for life, rendering annually 6s. at the customary times and all other services rendered by those in *minor censum*, with the first payment at the feast of St. Andrew. G.: two capons.

1158   WARBOYS Thomas Eyre pays 5s. for license to marry Alicia, his daughter and naif of the lord by blood, to John Abbot of Ramsey.

1159   HOLYWELL William Hunne: one cotland and all appurtenant demesne land once held by Roger Cachesely, in bondage for life, rendering annually in all things as did Roger. G.: 2s.

1160   ELLINGTON William Taillor: one plot with a half-virgate of land in Cotont once held by Thomas Gymbyr, for life, rendering annually all services and customs owed therein. G.: 4s.

1161   THERFIELD Thomas Gamele: all lands and tenements with Burylond once held by Beatrix Symond, for life, rendering annually in all things as did Beatrix. G.: 10s.

1162   THERFIELD William Stonghton: all lands and tenement with Burylond once held by John Stonghton, for life, rendering annually in all things as did John. G.: 3s.4d.

1163   UPWOOD John Jerkyn pays 3s.4d. for license to marry Johanna Alcok, alias Heryng, naif of the lord by blood, and for entry into all lands and tenements once held by Johanna Heryng, for life, rendering annually in all things as did Johanna, with the condition that he fix his dwelling where Johanna now lives, and that a half-virgate now held by Johanna *ad opus* be held in *novum censum* as soon as other tenants are put at *novum censum*. G.: 3s.4d.

1164   ST. IVES Thomas Freman and his wife, Margaret: half of one row once held by Loretta Forister, for life, rendering annually 14s. in equal portions at the customary times, with the obligation to repair and maintain the property. *Et non licebit*, etc. G.: excused.

1165   ST. IVES Thomas Freman and his wife, Margaret: one shop between the property of Makeseye and Chesteyn, for life, rendering annually 20s. in equal portions at the customary times, with the obligation to repair and maintain the property. *Et non licebit*, etc. G.: excused because of repairs.

1166   ST. IVES John Barker and his wife, Johanna: a half-row once held by William Prentys, for life, rendering annually 12s. in equal portions at the customary times, with the obligation to repair and maintain the property. *Et non licebit*, etc. G.: 3s.4d.

1167   ST. IVES William Fitz Johanna and his wife, Isabella: one row once held by Walter Wodeward, for life, rendering annually 13s.4d. in equal portions at the customary times, with the obligation to repair and maintain the property. *Et non licebit*, etc. G.: 10s.

1168   ST. IVES William Smyth and his wife, Margaret: a half-row once held by Thomas Baa and recently held by John de Borugh, for life, rendering annually 10s. in equal portions at the customary times, with the obligation to repair and maintain the property. *Et non licebit*, etc. G.: 10s.

1169   WISTOW John Aspelond: three quarters of land once held by Walter Schepperd, for life, rendering annually 14s. at the customary times and all customs of the vill. G.: six capons.

1170   RAMSEY (August) Thomas Godfrey: from Brother Robert Moordon, subcellarer, nine acres of herbage in Hydiche reserved outside the property of John Scherwode, *firmarius*, for 20 years, rendering annually 5s. at the feast of the Nativity of Blessed Mary, with the first payment after one year. G.: one capon.

18 THOMAS BUTTERWYK (1413-1414)

87r   **1171** Burwell Robert Chapman: surrender of one tenement of 15 acres once held by William Swynedd, to the use of John Rolf Jr., for 30 years, rendering annually 23s. at the customary times and all other services and customs owed therein. G.: excused because of a rent increase.

1172 Hemingford Abbots Emma Newman, naif of the lord, pays one capon for license to marry, this time.

1173 Shillington Robert Grene pays 5s. for license to have the goods and chattels found in the court roll for 18 Thomas.

1174 Shillington Peter Breton: 40 acres of demesne land at Stokkyng recently held by the customaries of Hanscomb, for life, rendering annually 26s.8d. at the customary times, three acres of demesne land at Chyrchehill once held by Adam Messanger, for life, saving the right of anyone, rendering annually 2s. at the customary times. G. 3s.4d.

1175 Shillington Johanna, daughter of Thomas West and naif of the lord, pays 6s.8d. for license to marry, the first time.

1176 Barton (court) Edmund Roger: one toft and one croft called Kytcroft recently held by Robert del Downe, for life. G.: 3s.4d.

1177 Barton Richard Lyly Jr.: one messuage and one cotland recently held by Peter Benis, for life, rendering annually in all things as did Peter. G.: 5s.

1178 Cranfield (leet) Stephen French, alias Willyam, pays 3s.4d. for license to marry Agnes, widow of William Borell, and for entry into all land recently held by William Borell, for the lifetime of Agnes, rendering annually in all things as did William.

1179 Cranfield William of the Grene: one messuage and 14 acres of land once held by Thomas de Capellano *per copiam*, for life, rendering annually 7s. at the customary times; two acres of demesne land at Stalipras, and four acres, one rod of land from the tenement of Renge, for life, rendering annually 4s.3d. at the customary times. G.: 40s. and two capons.

1180 Cranfield Galfridus Taillor: one cote once held by Cristina Bailly, and three acres of demesne, of which one acre lies at Burysouthwode, one at Clerkeslond and one at Perydole, for life, rendering annually in all things as did Cristina. G.: 13s.4d.

1181 Ellington (leet) William Fowler: one messuage and one quarter of land in West Sibthorp recently held by William Holsoun, for life. G.: four capons.

1182 Weston (leet) Simon Selby: one messuage and a half-virgate of land once held by John Selby with demesne land pertaining to the half-virgate, for life.

1183 Elton (leet) Nicholas Grygge: one messuage and one virgate of land once held by William Fretter, for life. G.: 2s.

1184 Elton William Fretter: one cote recently held by Agnes Burnet, for life. G.: 12d.

87v   **1185** Elton William Keynes: one messuage and a half-virgate of land recently held by John Cante, for life. G.: 2s.

1186 Elton William Kent Sr.: one messuage and four acres and one quarter of land once held by William Kent Jr., for life. G.: 12d.

1187 Elton William Nicol: one messuage and one virgate of land recently held by John Burnet, for life. G.: one capon.

1188 Elton William Deche: one quarter of land recently held by William Martyn, for life. G.: one capon.

1189 Elsworth John Herry: one toft and one quarter in le Grave recently held by Simon Herry, for life, rendering annually in all things as did Simon. G.: two capons.

1190 Houghton Robert Mason: surrender of half of one virgate once held by John Gate, to the use of Thomas Tylly, for life, rendering annually 7s. at the customary times and all other services and customs owed therein. G.: three capons.

1191 Houghton (October) John Hornchyld and his wife, Alicia: one messuage with a half-virgate of land once held by William Aleyn, for life, rendering annually 6s., with the first payment due at the feast of St. Andrew after one year, and with the obligation to build one house on the property within two years. G.: 3s.

1192 Broughton William Everard: one quarter of land once held by John Hampson, alias Ropere, in *minor censum* for life, rendering annually hay-raising, without food from the lord, for two days, supplying one laborer in autumn for two days, without food and beer, and customs of the vill. G.: one capon.

1193 Broughton William Smyth: a half-virgate of land once held by William Everard, in *minor censum* for life, rendering annually for one day in the lord's meadow, without food, supplying one mower with one stacker in the barley, one mower with one stacker in the peas, for food and beer, and customs of the vill. Also: one quarter of land once held by Cleryvaux, for life, rendering annually 4s. and supplying one mower in Reseford, without food, one mower in the barley, with food from the lord. G.: two capons.

1194 Broughton John Ellesworth: one quarter of land from the Cleryvaux property, for life, rendering annually 3s.4d. while he serves the lord, and 5s. thereafter at the customary times, with the obligation to procure one laborer in mowing hay, without food, and one laborer in the barley, with food from the lord. G.: excused, because of his service to the lord.

1195 Warboys Thomas Eyr: one virgate of land in Caldecote previously held by him, in *arentatio* for life, rendering annually 12s. at the customary times, with the obligation to procure one mower with one stacker in autumn. G.: one capon.

1196 Warboys Richard Nunne: two cotes of a tenement once held by Roger Hirst next to the cotland of John Brynnewater, and one half-virgate in the fields of Caldecote once held by his father, in *arentatio* for life, rendering annually 8s., with the obligation to procure one mower for the fen, and one mower with one stacker in autumn. G.: two capons.

1197 Therfield John Jankyn: all lands and messuages at Fynehowsis recently held by him without copy, *per copiam* for life, rendering annually as did John ate (*cut off*). G.: two capons.

1198 Therfield Richard Gorneye: three small houses inside the manor with adjacent curtilage once held by John Waryn and those acres from the tenement of Peter Branncestre previously held by Richard himself, for life, rendering annually in all things as did John and Richard himself. G.: two capons.

1199 Elton John Colyn Jr.: one plot with a half-virgate of land once held by Laurence Pokebrook, for life, rendering annually all services and customs owed therein. G. : two capons.

1200 Elton John Dalton: one plot with a croft once held by Thomas Baker, for life, rendering annually in all things as did Thomas. G.: one capon.

1201 Elton (December) John Waryn: one quarter of one virgate of land called Bondes, for life, rendering all services and customs owed therein, with the first payment at the feast of St. Andrew. G.: 2s.

1202 Elton John Person: one cote with adjacent demesne land once held by Henry Carleton, for life, rendering annually 4s. at the customary times. G.: 6s.8d.

88r

1203 Elton John, son of Henry Hobbesson: one cotland, previously rendering 6s. and once held by John Cook, one toft of a cotland *ad opus* next to the gate of the manor once held by John Hikkes for 4d., and a half-virgate without a plot, in *arentatio* for life, rendering annually 10s. at the customary times. Also : three acres of akirmanland, rendering annually 16d. G.: two capons.

1204 Hurst Roger Cachesoly and his wife, Agnes: one and a half virgates of land once held by William Pylgrym, for life, rendering annually in all things as did William, respecting always his agreements with William. G.: 2s.

1205 Slepe Thomas Cut and his wife, Emma: one plot with one virgate of land once held by Thomas Bene, for life, rendering annually in all things as did Thomas Bene. G.: one capon.

1206 Houghton John Lye: a half-virgate of land once held by Robert atte Pool and one cotland once held by John Andrew, for life, rendering annually 10s. at the customary times. G.: one capon.

1207 Holywell Agnes Sewale: one cotland with garden recently held by William Porter and once held by William Goodsowle, for life, rendering annually in all things as did William. G.: 6s.8d.

1208 Elsworth John Elyot pays 6s.8d. for license to marry Alicia, his daughter and naif of the lord, to John Herry, son of Thomas Herry.

1209 Shillington John West and his wife, Alicia: surrender of one messuage and one virgate to the use of John Warde, for life, rendering annually in all things as did John and Alicia, and respecting always the rights in that property held by Johanna, widow of John atte Wode, as in the time of John West. G.: 6s.8d.

1210 Shillington John Warde: surrender of one plot with one virgate to the use of John West, and his wife, Alicia, for life, rendering annually in all things as did John Warde. G.: 6s.8d.

88v **1211** Wistow (January) Richard Dentan and his wife, Agnes: three quarter of land once held by Walter Schepperd, in *arentatio* for life, rendering annually 14s. at the customary times and works of the vill, with the first payment at the feast of St. Andrew. G.: three capons.

1212 Barton Hugo Gregory: surrender of one virgate with forland to the use of Walter, son of Richard Bennesson, for life, rendering annually in all things as did Hugo. G.: 13s.4d.

1213 Wistow Richard Barker pays 5s. for license to marry Isabella, daughter of John Freman and naif of the lord by blood, and for license to hold one half-virgate and one and a half cotlands recently held by William Barker, for life, rendering annually 16s. at the customary times, one ploughing *precaria*, one autumn *precaria*, all customs called "Town customs", supplying one mower for the fen, and one mower with one stacker for the barley. G.: 5s.

1214 Wistow John Owty Jr. and his wife, Agnes: one messuage with one virgate of land once held by Stephen de Ely, for life, rendering annually 10s. at the customary times, customs of the vill, supplying one mower for one day in the meadow, and one mower with one stacker for the barley and peas. The first payment is due at the feast of St. Andrew. G: six capons.

1215 Wistow John Owty, son of John Owty Sr.: one quarter and one cotland once held by Edmund Capellanus, for life, rendering annually in all things as did Edmund, with the first payment at the feast of St. Andrew. G.: two capons.

1216 Warboys William Smart: a half-virgate of land recently held by William Hoberd lying next to the land of John Benesson, for life, rendering annually 5s. at the customary times, customs of the vill, supplying one mower with one stacker for one day in the barley, at the lord's food, if he has a wife or servant with him. The first payment will be at the feast of St. Andrew. G.: excused.

1217 HEMINGFORD ABBOTS Walter Morry pays 13s.4d. for license to marry Alicia Yngel, naif of the lord by blood, and for license to hold two virgates and one plot of land once held by William Yngel, for life, rendering annually in all things as did William.

1218 WARBOYS John Hy of Woldwere and his wife, Katerina: one plot, previously rendering 9d., two houses of a dichmanland and one mondayland once held by John Brownote for 3s.4d., 12 acres of Alsonslond, previously rendering 12s., and six acres of land at Stokkyng once held by John atte Wode for 6s., in *arentatio* for life, rendering annually 17s. at the customary times. G.: two capons.

1219 RAMSEY (February) Henry Coupere: from Brother Robert Moordon, subcellarer, all shrubs, reeds and all herbage from Schimerlake to Ferthyng, for 20 years, rendering annually 6s.8d. in equal portions at the feasts of the Annunciation and Nativity of Blessed Mary. He is permitted to cut down willows and shrubs when it pleases him and to plant willows. *Et si predictus redditus*, etc. (arrears of 15 days). G.: one capon.

1220 HOLYWELL Thomas Grantham, alias Baker, and his wife, Alicia: one virgate with adjacent demesne land and one acre at Nethbrerecroft, one acre at Middilfurlong and one selion of meadow in Salmede, for life, rendering annually in all things as did John Baker. G.: 26s.8d.

1221 BROUGHTON John Brabon: one messuage and a half-virgate of land recently held by Roger Grymmesby, in *arentatio* for life, rendering annually 6s.8d. at the customary times, one autumn *precaria*, and all customs of the vill, except the office of akirman, relaxed for him by the lord. He will repair and maintain the property, for which he will receive at the beginning 6s.8d. from the seneschal. G.: two capons.

1222 RAVELEY John Owty, Richard Aspelond, John Hiche and Richard Willesson of Raveley: four virgates recently held by them *ad opus*, for life, rendering annually 13s.4d. per virgate in equal portions at the feasts of All Saints and the Nativity of John the Baptist, and the following customary obligations: payment of tallage for their cattle, common fine in the leet, recognition, when it occurs, and carrying of hay to Ramsey. Further, whoever holds a virgate will come to all plough *precariae*, receiving meat or fish and two measures of ale for food without any other reward, and bread, ale, cheese or herring for breakfast, depending on the number of days. Whoever holds a virgate will plough as on his own land and render two other ploughing *precariae* at the discretion of the bailiff, so that the bailiff can take their ploughs, the tenants receiving for the first three *precariae* as above, *pro rata*. A virgater will render sheep-shearing, and work for one full day with two men at the sowing of peas, at the will of the bailiff, with no further reward from the lord. He will supply one laborer for two full days in hoeing the demesne grain, with no reward; he will supply one mower with one laborer for one day in autumn, in any grain assigned to him, with bread, ale and a reasonable meal, and he will supply in autumn one laborer for one day for any work, with meal. For each semi-virgate, the tenant will mow in Thornbriggemede, but with no allowances for old works, but with 7d. among them, as with the customaries of Wistow. Whoever comes to all autumn *precariae* shall receive breakfast of bread, ale, cheese ; at lunch (*prandium*), sufficient food; and after *None*, one drink and no more. He will carry peas in autumn outside the field to the manor at the will of the bailiff, with two wagons, with no further reward, except ale. They will also do ploughing and carrying in their own bags from the granary of the manor to the granary of Ramsey, namely: five quarters of malt at the summons of the bailiff, with no reward. If any one of the customaries is impeded in doing the above, whether by rain or by other reasonable cause, so that no day work or task can be done, he will fulfil it another day, by a reasonable summons, *pro rata*. Finally, each will pay *gersuma*, heriot, *leyrwyte*, with liability to be reeve and beadle, and to perform all customs of the vill.

1223 SLEPE John Erethe and his wife, Cristina: a certain parcel of the horsepond of the lord now annexed to the garden in which the lord's dovecote is situated, for life, quit, because of new repairs. G.: one capon.

89v **1224** WISTOW (February) Thomas Breselaunce: the windmill there, for life, rendering annually 8s. in equal portions at the feasts of the Annunciation and Nativity of Blessed Mary, with the obligation to maintain the mill with all its appurtenances, both within and without, at his own expense, expect for timber and its transport from the lord. At the end of his term, he will leave two suitable mill stones for the following year, and because of repairs, he will pay nothing until the next Michaelmas. G.: two capons.

1225 BRINGTON William Betonsson: one messuage with a half-virgate and all land once held by William Facous, for life, rendering annually all services and customs owed therein, with the payment for this year waived. G.: 10s. and six capons.

1226 BRINGTON (April) William Smyt and his wife, Isabella: a quarter-virgate and half of the demesne land recently held by Walter Lucas, with two pieces of old demesne reserved to the lord, for life, rendering annually all services and customs owed therein, with the first payment at the feast of St. Andrew. G.: six capons.

1227 BRINGTON Gilbert Bartholomew and his wife, Emma: a half-virgate, one quarter, two butts pertaining to the half-virgate and messuage, and half of all the demesne land once held by Walter Lucas, with four acres in two pieces of old demesne being reserved to the lord, for life, with the obligation to repair the property at their own expense within two years, with 24 trees in the wood of Ellington ceded to them for that purpose by the lord in the preceding year. Pledge for repairs: Thomas Gandir. If Gilbert and Emma default, the lord shall retake the land and all the chattels there and dispose of them as he wishes. G.: two capons.

1228 BRINGTON Thomas Gandir: four acres in two pieces once held by Walter Lucas, reserved outside the conventions with William Smyt and Gilbert Bartholomew, for life, with the obligation to repair and maintain the property. If Gilbert Bartholomew does not maintain his tenement or if he relinquishes it, Thomas' term will end, and the land will be vacant, unless Thomas wishes to assume Gilbert's agreements. G.: two capons.

1229 BURWELL John Poket: all lands and tenements recently held by John Plumbe, from Michaelmas for 18 years, rendering annually as did John Plumbe, with a rent increase this year of 12d., and common fine, the reaping of one acre of wheat and one acre of barley, and the carrying of that grain. He will repair and maintain the property at his own expense. Pledges: William Poket and William Jay. G.: six capons.

1230 BURWELL Thomas Rower: the capital messuage of one tenement of 15 acres once held by John Kent, for 20 years, rendering annually as did John. G.: six capons.

1231 BURWELL Laurence Skenale: the capital messuage of one tenement of 20 acres recently held by Simon Calvysbane and held now by William Gell, and one tenement of eight acres, for 20 years, rendering annually for the capital messuage 2s. and for the eight acres, 8s., with 2d. as common fine and with the obligation to rebuild the *insathous* on that messuage within the next two years, under penalty of forfeit. G.: six good pullets.

1232 HURST Stephen Canne and his wife, Margaret: one virgate and a half-virgate once held by Cristina Canne, for life, rendering annually in all things as did Cristina. G.: 3s.4d.

1233 Hurst William Warener: a half-virgate of land once held by Cristina Canne, for life, rendering annually in all things as did Cristina. G.: 20d.

1234 Ripton William Marham and his wife, Juliana: one cote, called a messuage, next to the bridge opposite Stukeley and once held by John Swon, for life, rendering annually 12d., which property used to render 12s., one hen and 20 eggs. G.: excused, because he is an official of the lord.

90r   **1235** Warboys John Brynwater: one and a half acres recently held by John Chapman and one acre recently held by Robert Oliver at Lowefurlong, for life, rendering annually 15d. at the customary times. G.: two capons.

1236 Warboys William Smyth: half of one tenement once held by Robert Ravene and recently held by Robert Wright for 15s., four and a half acres at Calnhill previously rendering 2s.11d., one mondayland previously rendering 5s., a half-mondayland recently held by John Chapman, and a half-akirmanland once held by Robert Systerne for 6s.8d., in *arentatio* for life, rendering annually 25s., with 4d. as Scharsilver. G.: two capons.

1237 Warboys John Flemyng: those lands once held by Tennysford, one quarter of land once held by William Thorp and a half-virgate of land in Caldecote once held by John Alot, in *arentatio* for life, rendering annually 12s. at the customary times, four ploughing *precariae*, two autumn *precariae,* supplying one mower with one laborer for the fen for one day, mowing of barley, and customs of the vill. G.: two capons.

1238 Warboys Thomas Benet, alias Herde, and his wife, Johanna: one mondayland once held by William Squyer, and a half-virgate of land in Caldecote once held by Richard Hy, in *arentatio* for life, rendering annually 8s. at the customary times, autumn *precariae*, customs of the vill, supplying of one mower with one laborer in mowing barley and hay, and ploughing *precariae*, with the first payment at the feast of St. Andrew. G.: two capons.

1239 Warboys John Dally Jr. and his wife, Emma: one mondayland and a half-virgate in Caldecote previously held by himself, with another half-virgate in Caldecote once held by William Flemyng, in *arentatio* for life, rendering 10s. this year and 15s. next year at the customary times, with one bederepe for the mondayland, supplying one mower with one laborer in mowing barley, and customs of the vill. G.: one capon.

1240 Warboys Henry Norborough: a half-virgate in Caldecote once held by John Edward, for life, rendering annually 4s.6d. at the customary times. G.: excused.

1241 Warboys Galfridus Broun: three cotlands of a tenement once held by Roger de Hirst, in *arentatio* for life, rendering as did Roger for two cotlands, and 8d. for the third, which previously rendered 2s.6d., and supplying one laborer in raising hay for one day for the cotland. He will not relinquish the demesne land he holds from the lord. G.: three woodcocks.

1242 Warboys Roger Sisterne: six acres of Alsonslond, of which John Ravele recently held three acres, in *arentatio* for life, rendering annually 9d. per acre. G.: excused.

1243 Upwood John Milis Jr. and his wife, Agnes: one virgate of land once held by John Robyn and before that by William Alkos, in *arentatio* for life, rendering annually 16s., supplying one mower for the fen, one laborer with one stacker in mowing barley, one mower with one stacker in mowing peas, all customs of the vill, and ploughing and autumn *precariae*, with the first payment at the feast of St. Andrew. He is allowed to hold the *insathous* and the kiln in Upwood. G.: he will make 30 locks for a fold.

1244 Upwood William Aubys and his wife, Agnes: three quarters of land with one "land" of demesne and common once held by John Galopyn, for life, rendering annually 18s. at the customary times, carrying malt to Ramsey once a year with their own wagon, mowing, at the will of the bailiff, for one day in the meadow, one ploughing *precaria*, all customs of the vill, and sheep-shearing. For their ploughing *precaria*, they will receive what certain other customaries now receive. G.: one capon.

1245 WESTON Alicia, daughter of John Flesher and naif of the lord, pays 6s.8d. to marry John Ravene of Graveley, this time. Pledge: Simon Hacoun.

90v **1246** WESTON John Kyng: a half-virgate of land recently held by Walter Bythorne and once held by John Hochun, with all demesne land pertaining to it with three rods and a half of Burylond once held by the same Walter, and one acre of Hotoftis recently held by John Selby, for life, rendering annually for the half-virgate as do others who hold in like manner, and for the rest as did Bythorne and Selby. G.: one capon.

1247 WESTON Simon Hacoun: three pieces of land of ancient Burylond once held by John Selby, in *arentatio* for life, rendering annually in all things as did John. G.: one capon.

1248 WESTON Walter Flesshewer and his wife, Beatrix: one quarter of land with all pertaining demesne land once held by John Betoun, for life, rendering annually all services and customs owed therein. G.: one capon.

1249 HOUGHTON John Qwaplod: one virgate called Popeslond, for 10 years, rendering annually 8s. at the customary times, with the condition that if he dies within the aforesaid term, the term will end at the Michaelmas following his death. G.: two capons.

1250 SLEPE (February) Thomas Deraunt: a half-virgate once held by William Cut, for eight years, rendering annually 8s. at the customary times, with the first payment at the feast of St. Andrew after two years. If he dies within the term, the term will end at the Michaelmas following his death. G.: one capon.

1251 RIPTON (February) Robert Hendesson: half of a built up messuage once held by John West, alias Bondes, for life, rendering annually 8s. at the customary times, supplying one mower for the fen at the will of the bailiff, one mower and one laborer for one day in mowing barley, and common fine, with the first payment at the next feast of All Saints. G.: one capon.

1252 RIPTON Richard Hoberd: one quarter of land of four virgates once held by John Bailly and before that by Alicia Cartere, in *arentatio* for life, rendering annually 3s.4d., with the first payment at the feast of All Saints next year. G.: excused.

1253 RIPTON Thomas Wattes: one plot with one semi-virgate once held by Simon Smygt, in *secunda arentatio*, rendering annually 8s. and all other services and customs rendered by those in *secunda arentatio*, with the first payment at the feast of All Saints next year. G.: excused.

1254 RIPTON William Webstere: one messuage and one virgate, two acres, one rod in Calncroft, one lot in Langelond recently held by him, and three acres in Middeldole once held by John Webstere, in *arentatio* for life, rendering annually 20s. for the virgate, 3d. for the land at Calncroft, and 2s.3d. for Middeldole. G.: excused.

1255 RIPTON John London Jr.: two cotlands once held by John Baily, one lot in Langelond, three acres at Middeldole, one semi-virgate once held by Nicholas of the Hill, and two quarters of land from four virgates next to the church, for life, rendering annually 18s.7d., customs of the vill, ploughing for one day at the will of the bailiff, supplying one mower for the fen, and one mower with one stacker in mowing barley. G.: excused.

1256 RIPTON Thomas Buk and his wife, Alicia: two built up messuages at the corner of Burylake, with two semi-virgates and one messuage with one semi-virgate, two selions at Angerlond, half of one plot and one quarter once held by John atte Lane, for life, rendering annually 39s.2d. at the customary times, three ploughing *precariae*, ploughing for one day at the will of the bailiff with reward from the lord, and supplying one mower with one stacker for one day in autumn at the bailiff's summons at the lord's food, except supper. G.: excused.

1257 Ripton (February) William White: one plot with one virgate of land once held by John Robbys, one empty plot with a half-virgate recently held by the same John and once held by Bondes, for life, rendering annually 26s.8d. at the customary times, payments beginning at the feast of All Saints after two years, and for which relaxation of rent he will repair the aforesaid messuage within the next three years, with timber supplied by the lord, and provided that he not be burdened with two acres at Catteshegge and two selions at Depslade, because he does not hold them by this convention. G.: three capons.

91r **1258** Warboys William Scharp of Warboys and his wife, Agnes: one mondayland containing a half-virgate once held by Robert Oliver, for life, rendering annually 5s. at the customary times, three ploughing *precariae*, one autumn *precaria*, customs of the vill, and "mare silver", and provided that he not relinquish any part of the lands and tenements contained in this copy. Also: a parcel of a tenement recently held by Alicia Noreys and once held by Robert Oliver for 9s., for life rendering annually 8s. at the customary times; three acres at Calwelhill and one acre at Lowefurlong once held by the same Robert, for 3s., to be held by him for 2s. annually at the customary times. G.: 2s.

1259 Holywell (June) William Prykke: the windmill there, from the previous Michaelmas for 10 years, rendering annually 13s.4d. at the feast of the Translation of St. Benedict, with the obligation to maintain the windmill, both within and without, in good condition at his own expense, in stones, iron works and boards, except for timber in the woods and its transport from the lord, with its cutting and storing by William. At the end of his term he will dismiss the mill with stones and all things suitable for the following year. G.: excused, because of repairs.

1260 Brington John Botiller, alias Hacoun: surrender of all lands, tenements and demesne land that he holds from the lord in Weston and Brington, to the use of John Est Jr., and his wife, Helena, for life, rendering annually in all things as did Botiller. G.: 10s.

1261 Elsworth John Porter of Hinton and his wife, Johanna: one plot with one semi-virgate and one cotland once held by Thomas Cheneyn and recently held by William Grigge, from Michaelmas for life, rendering annually 14s. and all other services and customs rendered by William, with the obligation to repair one grange within one year at their own expense, the lord granting timber, its cutting and transport, and an allowance of rents for the first two years, with 7s. in pennies from the bailiff. Pledge: Thomas Peek. G.: 12d.

1262 Elsworth John Hardyng: one cotland with appurtenant croft, six selions of land and the sixth part of one virgate of St. Luke's land once held by John Sewyn, for life, rendering annually 11s. and all other services and customs rendered by Sewyn. G.: two fetlocks.

1263 Shillington (6 August) John Whitefelowe: surrender of all his status in all lands, meadows, pastures and demesne lands and all properties pertaining to the manor of Pegsdon once held by his father, Roger Whitefelowe, to the use of Richard Whitefelowe, and his wife, Rosa, for life, rendering in all things as did his father with the understanding that if he does anything against the customs of the manor he shall be expelled from the property, this *gersuma* not withstanding. G.: 40s.

1264 Ramsey William Marham: from Brother Richard Moordon, sub-cellarer, 26 selions lying at "longe Flewfeld", for life, rendering annually 2s. in equal portions at the feasts of the Annunciation and Nativity of Blessed Mary, with permission to dismiss those selions *ad firmam* as he wishes, all the above agreements reserved to the subcellarer. *Et si predictus redditus*, etc. (arrears of one month). G.: one capon.

91v 1265 CHATTERIS Simon Tomson, alias Spencer: one cotland with croft once held by Margaret Massely, for life, with the chief house on the property, half of one cote and croft reserved to the aforesaid Margaret, for life, and half of one tenement and eight acres once held by Peter Awbray, alias Chapman, for life, rendering annually in all things as did Peter. G.: 20s.

1266 CHATTERIS John Carsey: the fifth part of one messuage once held by Simon Carseye, for life, rendering annually in all things as did Simon. G.: 16s.

1267 CHATTERIS William Rede: half of one tenement of eight acres once held by John Lache Jr., for life, rendering annually in all things as did John. G.: 4s.

1268 CHATTERIS Simon Peroun: one cotland once held by Thomas Sempole, for life, rendering annually in all things as did Thomas. G.: one half-mark.

1269 CHATTERIS William Rede: surrender of one messuage lying between the messuage of Thomas Rede and that of John Mason, to the use of John, son of Andrew Clement, for life. G.: 6d.

1270 CHATTERIS Andrew Miller: one cotland recently held by Edmund Rede, for life, rendering annually in all things as did Edmund. G.: two capons.

1271 CHATTERIS John Pykerell: one tenement of eight acres and a parcel of one meadow recently held by Stephen atte Brigge, for life, rendering annually in all things as did Stephen. G.: nothing, because the land has lain fallow in the lord's hands.

1272 CHATTERIS John Bele: one parcel of the demesne pasture called Owsemore recently held by William Lassels, for life, rendering annually 10s. at the customary times. G.: two capons.

1273 RAMSEY John Cator Baxtere: from the sub-cellarer, two acres of land lying in Longe Newfeld, more or less, for life, rendering annually 2s. at the feasts of the Annunciation and Nativity of Blessed Mary, in equal portions. G.: one capon.

1274 ST. IVES (June) John Clerk and his wife, Margeria: two half-rows in Briggestrete previously held by Richard Cartbright, and one half-row previously held by Henry Hunte and his wife, Alicia, for life, rendering annually 26s.8d. at the customary times, with the obligation to repair and maintain the properties. *Et non licebit*, etc. G.: 13s.4d. — excused, because of repairs.

19 THOMAS BUTTERWYK (1414-1415)

92r 1275 ELSWORTH John Newman: one virgate once held by Howlet and the sixth part of one virgate of St. Luke's land, for life, rendering annually 13s.6d. for a half-virgate, for a total of 20s., and all other services and customs owed therein. Pledges: John Howesson, Walter Bele and John Howlet. G.: one capon.

1276 KNAPWELL Roger, son of William Joye, and John Pykerell: one semi-virgate without messuage once held by John himself, in *arentatio* from Michaelmas for life, rendering 8s. this year and 10s. each year thereafter. G.: two capons.

1277 UPWOOD John of the Wold and his wife, Agnes: one built up messuage with a forland once held by Richard Gouler, for life, rendering annually in all things as did Richard, and three ploughing *precariae*. G.: 6s.8d.

1278 CRANFIELD (leet) Robert Warner: two acres of land recently held by William Marshall at Puryhill, for life, rendering annually 2s. G.: 12d.

1279 CRANFIELD John Aleyn of Wode ende: six acres of land and meadow from the demesne and one acre and one gore at Longsouthwode, for life, rendering annually 6s. for the six acres, and 7d. for the land at Longsouthwode. G.: 4s.

1280 CRANFIELD Thomas Frost, naif of the lord, pays 10s. for license to marry Maria, his daughter, to Nicholas atte Strate, this time, and also to cover the fine for leyrwyte.

1281 CRANFIELD William del Pury: one toft and a half-virgate of land recently held by William Daylly, for life. G.: 5s.

1282 HOUGHTON (court) Anna, daughter of William Atkyn and naif of the lord, pays 40d. for license to marry Robert Morell, this first time. Pledge: William Atkyn.

1283 HOUGHTON Richard Smygt: one cotland recently held by Simon White, for life. G.: three capons.

1284 SHILLINGTON John Multon: one messuage and one and a half-virgates recently held by John Multon, and eight acres of demesne land and one parcel of meadow once held by the same John, for life, rendering annually in all things as did John. G.: 6s.8d.

1285 SHILLINGTON Alicia, daughter of John atte Wode and naif of the lord, pays 6s.8d. for license to marry whomever she wishes.

1286 SHILLINGTON John Gayton: one messuage and one virgate of land recently held by Robert Carter, for life, rendering annually in all things as did Robert. G.: 13s.4d.

1287 SHILLINGTON Johanna, widow of Adam Smygt: one messuage and three acres recently held by the same Adam, for life, rendering annually in all things as did Adam. G.: 12d.

1288 BARTON Emma, daughter of John Stonele and naif of the lord, pays 2s. for license to marry John Haus, this first time. Pledges: Edmund Roger and Walter Wodeward.

1289 WISTOW John Elmesley and his wife, Margaret: one built up messuage and three quarters of land once held by Hugo Lowthe, for life, rendering annually 15s. at the customary times, customs of the vill and the great *precaria*, with the first payment at the feast of St. Andrew after one year. They will repair the messuage, in consideration for which the lord grants them the crop sown on the property by Hugo, with all the hay reserved to the lord this year, the full farm of all acres dismissed by Hugo this year. G.: six capons.

1290 WISTOW Robert Nottyng and his wife, Alicia: three cotlands with one acre at Bombrigge, one acre at Stacroft, one acre at Chessefurlong, a half-acre at Langerhoo, and one acre at Lowefeld with the "fen pithel" once held by his father, for life, rendering annually in all things as did his father. Also: one cotland with adjacent croft recently held by William Wodeward, for life, rendering annually 2s. at the customary times and customs of the vill. G.: excused.

1291 WISTOW Robert Barker and his wife, Alicia: one quarter of land once held by John Owty, for life, rendering annually 6d. and all other services rendered by those *ad censum*. G.: three wagons of reeds in the marsh.

92v **1292** UPWOOD Richard Heryng pays 10s. for license to marry Agnes, his daughter and naif of the lord by blood, to John Forgon, freeman.

1293 HOUGHTON John Pertenhale: one messuage and one virgate recently held by Richard Smygt, for life, rendering annually in all things as did Richard. G.: two capons.

1294 ELTON John Hitche: five acres of land called akirmanland recently held by Thomas Herford, for life, rendering annually in all things as did Thomas. G.: 6d.

1295 ELTON William atte Gate: one messuage and a half-virgate of land recently held by John Hichebatte, for life, rendering annually in all things as did John. G.: 2s.

1296 ELTON William de Kent Jr.: one messuage and a half-virgate of land recently held by John Colyn, for life, rendering annually in all things as did John. G.: 12d.

1297 ELTON John Burnet Jr.: one quarter of land recently held by William Nicol, for life, rendering annually in all things as did William. G.: 6d.

1298 ELTON Richard Wodeward: one quarter of land recently held by John Philip, for life, rendering annually in all things as did John. G.: 12d.

1299 ELTON John Blatchall: one messuage and one parcel of land and meadow recently held by Richard Best, for life, rendering annually 10s. G.: 20d.

1300 ELTON John de Bythorne: one quarter of land recently held by John Hitchebatte, for life, rendering annually in all things as did John Hichebatte. G.: nothing, because the land is fallow.

1301 ELSWORTH John Smygt: one cotland once held by John Lundon and one quarter of land recently held by John Andrew, for life, rendering annually 7s. 4d. G.: two capons.

1302 WARBOYS Richard Wardon, alias Revesson: one plot with building with one acre in a croft, three quarters of land in the fields of Caldecote, for life, rendering annually 12s. and other services and customs, including work for one day with one mower in autumn in place of a half-day's work in autumn previously rendered by his father. G.: six wood cocks.

1303 WARBOYS William Altheworld and his wife, Alicia: one mondayland recently held by Thomas Child, for life, rendering annually in all things as did Thomas. G.: two capons, and no more because he is a servant of the manor.

1304 WISTOW John Wrighte and his wife, Johanna: one plot with one quarter of land once held by Thomas Owty, in *arentatio* for life, rendering annually 5s. at the customary times and customs of the vill. G.: making one new wagon from timber supplied by the lord.

1305 BRINGTON Katerina Howesson, naif of the lord by blood and daughter of Richard Howesson, pays 13s.4d. for license to marry John Warde of Papley. Pledge: Roger Eyr.

1306 ELLINGTON Thomas Fote pays 40s. for license to marry Agnes, his daughter and naif of the lord by blood, to whomever she wishes, this first time.

1307 SHILLINGTON Alicia, daughter of John atte Wode and naif of the lord by blood, pays 6s.8d. for license to marry, this first time.

1308 BARTON William Eynesham and his wife, Agnes: one messuage with one virgate of land once held by John Adam, for life, rendering annually in all things as did John. G.: 6s.8d.

93r **1309** BARTON John Geffrey: surrender of one messuage with one virgate and forland once held by William Geffrey to the use of John Bonde and his wife, Alicia, for life, rendering annually in all things as did John Geffrey. G.: 10s.

1310 SLEPE William Harrof and his wife, Juliana: one cote, two rods of land and one rod of meadow once held by John Roger, for life, rendering annually 2s. and all other services and customs rendered by John. G.: one capon.

1311 SLEPE (January) William Dryver: a half-virgate of land once held by William Bernewell, for life, rendering annually 7s. at the customary times and all other services rendered by those in *arentatio*, with the first payment at the feast of St. Andrew. G.: two capons.

1312 HOLYWELL Roger Sewale and his wife, Helena: one cotland with adjacent demesne land and one croft once held by William Reve, and one acre at Buryhegge at the end of the village, for life, rendering annually in all things as did Thomas Porter. And he will dwell on that cotland. G.: 2s.

1313 CRANFIELD Alexander Dunwode: a half-virgate of land once held by Elias Smygt, in bondage for life, rendering annually in all things as did Thomas Catelyn. G.: 3s.4d.

1314   CRANFIELD William Denton: two cotlands recently held by William of the Hirst, in bondage for life, rendering annually in all things as did William of the Hirst. G.: 2s.

1315   WISTOW John Owty: surrender of two cotlands in Raveley, to the use of Thomas Breselaunce and his wife, Johanna, in bondage for life, rendering annually in all things as did John. G.: 12d.

1316   WISTOW John Owty: surrender of one quarter of land in Raveley to the use of Richard Brunne, for life, rendering annually in all things as did John. G.: 12d.

1317   HURST Thomas Cok: one virgate and a half-virgate of land with all other lands recently held by William Cok, in bondage for life, rendering annually in all things as did William. G.: 3s.4d.

1318   HOUGHTON Stephen Marchal and his wife, Emma; one virgate of land once held by John Abbot, for life, rendering annually 12s. in *arentatio*. G.: two capons.

1319   HOUGHTON Simon Wyth and his wife, Cristina: a half-virgate of land once held by John Lye, for life, rendering annually in all things as did John. G.: four capons.

1320   RIPTON John Webstere and his wife, Agnes: one cotland with four butts of land in a croft and two butts in Lounde, one acre in Middildole, for life, rendering annually 4s.3d. for the cotland, 9d. for the acre, and one laborer for mowing wheat. G.: two capons.

1321   ELSWORTH Thomas Peek: one plot with one semi-virgate and one cotland once held by Thomas Cheneyn and William Grigge and recently held by John Porter, for life, rendering annually 14s. and all services and customs rendered by John, with the obligation to fulfil all the conventions made by Porter and contained in the Gersuma Book for last year. G.: two capons, and no more because Thomas was the pledge of John Porter.

1322   ELSWORTH John Beseworth, alias Peek, and his wife, Johanna: all lands and tenements once held by Thomas Peek, for life, rendering annually in all things as did Thomas. At the end of his term he will return the lands to the lord with stock. G.: 12d.

1323   ELSWORTH John Lucas and his wife, Isabella: a half-virgate of land once held by William White, for life, rendering annually as did William Willyham. G.: three capons.

1324   ELSWORTH John Howlet: a half-virgate of land once held by John Newman, one built up and enclosed cotland, and one semi-virgate of Gravelond, of which one quarter is held by John Newman and another quarter has been in the lord's hands for 20 years, from Michaelmas for life, rendering annually 11s. at the customary times and all services and customs owed therein for the half-virgate and cotland: and for the semi-virgate, 3s. for the next two years and 5s. each year thereafter. G.: one capon.

93v   **1325**   ST. IVES John Fyssher of St. Neots: one shop with a solar, which solar was once occupied by Maddyngle, for life, rendering annually 20s. at the customary times, with the obligation to repair and maintain the property. *Et non licebit*, etc. G.: 3s.4d.

1326   ST. IVES Walter Legge and his wife, Johanna: one shop with a solar which he recently held without copy, for life, rendering annually 16s. at the customary times, with the obligation to repair and maintain the property. *Et non licebit*, etc. G.: 3s.4d.

1327   ST. IVES John Mart and his wife, Margaret: one shop abutting High Street next to the corner, for life, rendering annually 10s. at the customary times, with the obligation to repair and maintain the property. *Et non licebit*, etc. G.: 20s.

1328   ST. IVES Hugo Arthorngh Lystere and his wife, Johanna: a half-row once held by Margaret Baxtere and recently held by himself, for life, rendering annually 16s. in equal portions at the customary times, with the obligation to repair and maintain the property.

1329 Sᴛ. Iᴠᴇs Richard Wrighte and his wife, Alicia: a half-row once held by Katerina Fissher, for life, rendering annually 13s.4d. in equal portions at the customary times, with the obligation to repair and maintain the property. *Et non licebit*, etc. G.: two capons.

1330 Sᴛ. Iᴠᴇs John Lystere and his wife, Margaret: a half-row once held by Richard Nicol, for life, rendering annually 20s. at the customary times, with the obigation to repair and maintain the property. *Et non licebit*, etc. G.: 20d.

1331 Sᴛ. Iᴠᴇs John Meyke: surrender of one row once held by Stephen Yremonger and recently held by Richard Baker and lying next to the row held by William Botheby, to the use of John Belleman, for life, rendering annually 15s. at the customary times, with the obligation to repair and maintain the property. *Et non licebit*, etc. G.: 10s.

1332 Sᴛ. Iᴠᴇs John Belleman: surrender of one row once held by John Meyke and lying next to that of William Botheby, to the use of John Caltrun, and his wife, Margaret, for life, rendering annually 15s. at the customary times, with the obligation to repair and maintain the property. *Et non licebit* etc. G.: 6s.8d.

1333 Sᴛ. Iᴠᴇs John Lystere: surrender of a half-row once held by Richard Nicol, to the use of John Sutton, and his wife, Margaret, for life, rendering annually 20s. at the customary times, with the obligation to repair and maintain the property. *Et non licebit*, etc. G.: one capon.

1334 Sᴛ. Iᴠᴇs Thomas Clerke Glovere and his wife, Anna: a half-row once held by John Belleman, annually 8s. at the customary times, with the obligation to repair and maintain the property. *Et non licebit*, etc. G.: excused because of repairs.

1335 Sᴛ. Iᴠᴇs William Gardyner: a half-row once held by John Bowes, for life, rendering annually 10s. at the customary times, and one *precaria* (i.e. a half-day in the fen, a half-day in autumn), with the obligation to repair the property within two years. *Et non licebit*, etc. G.: excused, because of repairs.

94r **1336** Wᴀʀʙᴏʏs Simon Hy Jr: one dichmanland recently held by John Edward and one dichmanland with nine rods of land recently held by his father, with 11 acres of land from the property once held by Roger de Hirst and two acres at Stokkyng, for life, rendering annually as did Edward for the first dichmanland, and as his father for the rest. G.: 40d.

1337 Wᴀʀʙᴏʏs John Ordemar and his wife, Johanna: one mondayland with two acres of land at Brenfurlong and three butts as Bascroft recently held by John Pappeworthe, for life, rendering for the mondayland as did John Pappeworthe, 2s. annually for the two acres at Brenfurlong and 12d. for the three butts. G.: excused.

1338 Rɪᴘᴛᴏɴ John Hitche: two virgates and a half-virgate with a half-acre at Depslade, with meadow called Monnemede and three selions of land at Angerlond once held by his father, from the previous Michaelmas in *arentatio* for life, rendering annually 35s. at the customary times, customs of the vill, three ancient ploughing *precariae*, and one autumn *precaria* with one man. G.: two capons.

1339 Bʀɪɴɢᴛᴏɴ John Cartere pays 6s.8d. for license to marry Margaret, daughter of Richard Howesson, this time.

94v *Blank*

20 THOMAS BUTTERWYK (1415-1416)

95r **1340** Eʟᴛᴏɴ John Waryn Jr.: one toft and a half-virgate of land recently held by Grege, for life, rendering annually in all things as did Grege. G.: one capon.

1341 Sʜɪʟʟɪɴɢᴛᴏɴ Richard Whitefelowe and his wife, Rosa: surrender of one messuage, one virgate recently held by John atte Hill Sr. in Pegsdon and the sixth part of the demesne land there, to the use of John atte Hill Jr., for life, rendering annually as did Richard. G.: 30s.

1342 SHILLINGTON John Goodmar: one messuage and a half-virgate of land, four acres of land at Essyngwell, and six acres of land at Tynehill recently held by Thomas Goodmar, for life, rendering annually in all things as did Thomas. G.: 9s.

1343 SHILLINGTON John Warde: four acres at Leecroft and four acres of land at Windmill Hill recently held by Nicholas Bredwan, for life, rendering annually in all things as did Nicholas. G.: 8s.

1344 SHILLINGTON John, son of William Couche: one messuage with four houses and one virgate of land recently held by William Couche, for life, rendering annually in all things as did William. G.: nothing.

1345 SHILLINGTON Richard Peres: surrender through the hands of John Beston, bailiff, of one messuage and a half-virgate of land recently held by Nicholas Peres, to the use of Thomas Smygt, for life, rendering annually in all things as did Richard. G.: 26s.8d.

1346 BURWELL Simon Styward pays 40d. for license to marry Agnes, his daughter, to John Fuller of Milford in Suffolk, the second time.

1347 BURWELL Thomas Rolf Jr: half of one tenement of 20 acres and half of one tenement of 15 acres, for 20 years, rendering annually as did Thomas (*cut off*). G.: three capons.

1348 BURWELL Robert Wylkyn: one tenement of eight acres recently held by Radulph Calvesbane, for 20 years, rendering annually in all things as did Radulph. G.: three capons.

1349 BURWELL Radulph Lyne and his wife, Margaret: half of one tenement of 15 acres *ad censum* and half of one tenement of eight acres once held by William Ideyne, *ad censum* for 20 years, rendering in all things as did William, in the time when the manor is in the lord's hands. G.: 5s.

1350 BURWELL William Taillor, alias Poket, and his wife, Margaret: one tenement of 15 acres in *arentatio* once held by Thomas Lyne, and one tenement of 24 acres in *arentatio* once held by Walter Ermyn, for 20 years, rendering annually 40s. and all other services and customs rendered by Thomas and Walter. G.: 3s.4d., and two capons.

1351 BURWELL William Ideyne and his wife, Agnes: one cotland with croft and one acre of land *ad censa* half of one tenement of 15 acres *ad censum*, with half of one tenement of eight acres *ad censum* and one pithel called Cheselenspightill, for life, rendering all services and customs previously rendered, in the time when the manor is in the lord's hands. G.: two capons.

1352 HOUGHTON Richard Cartere and his wife, Agnes: one virgate of land once held by John Roger, for life, rendering annually in all things as did John. G.: three capons.

1353 ELLINGTON George Carter: one messuage and one quarter of land recently held by William Burgeys, for life, rendering annually in all things as did William. G.: nothing.

1354 ELLINGTON Thomas Ponder: one messuage in Sibthorp and one quarter of land in the fields of Ellington recently held by John Ponder, for life, rendering annually in all things as did John. G.: 5s.

1355 WESTON John Felice: surrender of one quarter of land with adjacent demesne land, to the use of Robert Snayth, for life, rendering annually in all things as did John. G.: excused.

95v **1356** RIPTON Richard Ropere, alias Cartere, and his wife, Johanna: one built up cotland at Grene with one *camera* next to the warren, one semi-virgate opposite, one plot, one virgate at Estgrene by the cross, and one selion at Angerlond once held by John Fabian, for life, rendering annually 19s., with the supplying of one worker for the lord for one day's mowing of wheat. He will repair the property, with the lord supplying timber and one wagon of reeds and granting an allowance of all his rents this year. G.: three capons.

1357 SLEPE John Barton and his wife, Agnes: one cotland with one semi-virgate of land, one semi-virgate of land once held by John Esex, a half-virgate of land once held by John Goderich, and a half-acre at Longacre next to le Howe, for life, rendering annually 30s. for the cotland, semi-virgate and half-virgate, 6d. for the half-acre, at the customary times, one ploughing *precaria*, and supplying one man for the autumn *precaria*. The first payment will be at the feast of St. Andrew after one year. G.: four capons.

1358 CHATTERIS John, son of Richard Collesson: two parts of one messuage once held by John Cut Taillor, for life, rendering annually in all things as did John Cut. G.: 6s.8d.

1359 CHATTERIS Richard Meyk: one tenement of eight acres once held by John Mathew Sr., for life, rendering annually in all things as did John. G.: 6s.8d.

1360 CHATTERIS John Mathew: four acres of land parcelled out of one tenement of eight acres once held by Simon Bray, for life, rendering annually in all things as did Simon, and with the provision that the land not be altered. G.: 2s.

1361 CHATTERIS Thomas Fissher: one cotland at Pakerelldole once held by John Bele, for life, rendering annually in all things as did John. G.: 3s.4d.

1362 CHATTERIS John Wysebech: one cotland once held by Edmund Cade, for life, rendering annually in all things as did Edmund, with the obligation to maintain the property under penalty of a fine of 20s. G.: 2s.

1363 CHATTERIS Adam Cook: one messuage once held by John Trumpor, for life, with the obligation to maintain the property under penalty of a fine of 20s. G.: 12d.

1364 HURST Stephan Twyforde: one plot with half of the land once held by Lord de Wolle and recently held by William of the Hill, for life, rendering annually in all things as did William. G.: two capons.

1365 HOLYWELL Nicholas Baroun and his wife, Helena: one virgate of land once held by Nicholas Godfrey, with all adjacent demesne land and one selion of meadow in Salmede and one-half of Benehill, for life, rendering annually 10d. for Benehill and for the rest as did Godfrey. G.: 2s.

1366 BARTON Emma, daughter of John atte Chirche: one messuage with a half-virgate of land once held by John atte Chirche, for life, rendering annually all services and customs owed therein. G.: 6s.8d.

1367 BARTON Margaret atte Wode: surrender of one built up cotland with adjacent croft once held by Galfridus atte Wode, to the use of William, son of Edmund Child, for life, rendering annually all services and customs owed therein. G.: 40d.

1368 HOUGHTON John Andrew pays 6s.8d. for license to marry Agnes, his daughter, to Thomas Miller, this time.

1369 ELSWORTH William Hobbesson and his wife, Anna: one semi-virgate and one quarter of land once held by John Cristemasse, for life, rendering annually 15s. at the customary times, 2s. for works, and customs of the vill, with the provision that he continue to hold as before that semi-virgate he took from the lord previously. G.: two capons.

1370 WESTON Thomas Smygt: a half-virgate once held by his father, for life, rendering annually in all things as did his father. G.: two capons.

1371 BRINGTON William Hikkesson: a half-virgate of land once held by Simon Beverich, for life, rendering annually in all things as did Simon. G.: 6d.

1372 Upwood John Aleyn: a half-virgate of land surrendered back into the lord's hands by John and William Aleyn and once held by Pykeler, for life, rendering annually in all things as he and William previously rendered, with the provision that the capital messuage with croft will always be reserved to the lord. G.: making two fences as assigned to him.

1373 Upwood Nicholas Hendesson and his wife, Johanna: a half-virgate of land with one empty plot in Great Raveley once held by Peter Bray and recently held by William Purquoy, in *arentatio* for life, rendering annually 10s. at the customary times, and 7d. for the forland, and all other services and customs rendered by William. G.: two capons.

1374 Therfield (February) John Stoghton: all lands and tenements once held by William Qwas, alias Waryn, for life, rendering annually in all things as did William, with the first payment at the feast of St. Andrew after one year. Also: an allowance for life of 2s. from his rents from the seneschal, and all the *bulimong* (mixed crop) and wheat in the said plot, two quarters of barley, and timber sufficient for new repairs to the grange to be built within two years. He is allowed to let his land lie fallow this year. G.: two capons.

1375 Barton Thomas Child: surrender of all his lands and tenements, to the use of Richard Wylymot, son of Thomas Wylymot, for life, rendering annually in all things as did Thomas, and a payment annually of 3s.1d.ob. for timber. G.: 6s.8d.

1376 Warboys (March) Hugo Fordyngton: one tenement called maltmanland and one mondayland once held by John, son of Richard Plumbe, in *arentatio* for life, rendering annually 12s. at the customary times and all other customs rendered by those in *arentatio*. G.: excused.

1377 Holywell John Beaumeys and his wife, Katerina: one cotland with all appurtenant demesne land recently held by William Hunne and once held by Roger Cachesoly, for life, rendering annually in all things as did William. G.: 2s.

1378 Ripton (February) William Amery and his wife, Katerina: two semi-virgates of land once held by John West of Wennington, for life, rendering annually 20s. at the customary times, with the first payment at the feast of All Saints after one year. He will supply one mower for the meadow, and one mower with one laborer in autumn at the summons of the bailiff. G.: two capons.

1379 Warboys (February) Richard Horwode: one tenement called akirmanland once held by John Plumbe, for life, rendering annually 8s. at the customary times, with the first payment at the feast of All Saints. He will plough and supply one mower with one laborer in autumn for a full day. G.: two capons.

1380 Warboys Robert Ravele and his wife, Agnes: one and a half acres of demesne land in Lowefurlong, one dichmanland in *arentatio* once held by Robert Gildesowe, for life, rendering annually 15d. for the demesne land, and 12d., one hen and three eggs for the dichmanland. G.: two capons.

1281 Warboys Galfridus Broun and his wife, Agnes: one quarter of land in Caldecote, in *arentatio* for life, rendering annually 2s.6d., with the first payment due a year from now, and with the condition that they relinquish next year two and a half acres of demesne at Lowefurlong to the lord. G.: one capon.

1382 Warboys John Levot: one quarter of land in Caldecote recently held by John Wylkys, in *arentatio* for life, rendering annually 2s.6d., under the condition that he relinquish three acres in Lowefurlong to the lord. G.: one capon.

1383 Warboys Nicholas Bennesson: one built up tenement with one virgate of land in Caldecote once held by John Plumbe, in *arentatio* for life, rendering annually 12s. at the customary times, with the first payment at the feast of St. Andrew after one year.

He will render one ploughing *precaria* and come to the Great *Precaria* of autumn with one man, and he will repair the widows and doors on his property at his own expense. G.: excused.

1384 WARBOYS John Caton Jr.: a half-virgate of land once held by William Smart in Caldecote, in *arentatio* for life, rendering annually in all things as did William. G.: two capons.

96v **1385** RIPTON John Boreman and his wife, Agnes: one cotland, four butts in a croft and four butts in the field recently held by Thomson, one quarter of land recently held by Gilbert de Hirst, in *arentatio* for life, rendering annually for the cotland and appurtenances as did Thomson, and 3s.4d. for the quarter, with the first payment at the next feast of All Saints. He will supply one mower for the meadow for a full day in a place assigned by the bailiff, and one mower with one laborer for one day in autumn. G.: two capons.

1386 RIPTON Roger Gardiner and his wife, Cecilia: a half-virgate in Upende once held by John Colle, with the capital messuage reserved to the lord, for life, rendering annually 8s. at the customary times, with the first payment at the feast of All Saints after one year. He will supply one mower for the meadow at the summons of the bailiff, and one mower with one laborer in autumn. G.: excused.

1387 GRAVELEY John Drew: a half-virgate of land once held by William atte Slow, for life, rendering annually in all things as did William. G.: two capons.

1388 WISTOW Galfridus Hunne and his wife, Cristina: one quarter of land once held by John Symme, in *arentatio* for life, rendering annually 5s. at the customary times, with the first payment at the feast of St. Andrew next year. G.: two capons.

1389 WISTOW John Schepperd and his wife, Cristina: one quarter of land once held by John Waryn, in *arentatio* for life, rendering annually 5s. at the customary times. G.: two capons.

1390 WISTOW Same John Schepperd and Cristina: from the lord one hidemanland recently held by Juliana Taillor, in *arentatio* for life, rendering annually 12s. at the customary times. G.: two capons.

1391 WISTOW John Bakelond and his wife, Alicia: one virgate and half of one quarter of land with one acre of demesne land in Lowefeld once held by Thomas Randolf, for life, rendering annually in all things as did Thomas. G.: 6s.8d.

1392 WISTOW Thomas Breselaunce and his wife, Johanna: a half-virgate of land once held by John Owty and a half-virgate of land once held by Cleryvaux, in *arentatio* for life, rendering annually 14s. at the customary times, customs of the vill, all ploughing *precariae*, and the ancient autumn *precaria*. G.: six capons.

1393 ELSWORTH (May) Alexander Hobbesson: a half-virgate of land once held by Richard Owty and recently held by Henry Rolf, for life, rendering annually 12s. at the customary times, with the first payment at the next feast of St. Andrew. G.: two capons.

1394 ELSWORTH William Crisp: one cotland once held by John Clerk, for life, rendering annually 3s.4d. and all other services and customs owed therein. G.: 2s.

1395 ELSWORTH Robert Braughyng: a half-virgate of land once held by William Towselond and surrendered back into the lord's hands by William Fermer, for life, rendering annually 12s. at the customary times and all other services and customs rendered by Fermer. G.: two capons.

1396 ST. IVES (July) John Fuller and his wife, Katerina: one row once held by Stephen Yremonger and recently held by Robert Elyngham, for life, rendering annually 16s. in equal portions at the customary times, with the obligation to repair and maintain the property at their own expense. *Et non licebit*, etc. G.: 6s.8d.

1397 St. Ives Thomas Grygge Webstere and his wife, Beatrix: a half-row once held by Walter Pope Miller and adjoining the manor's pig sty, for life, rendering annually 8s. in equal portions at the customary times, with the obligation to repair and maintain the property. *Et non licebit*, etc. G.: 6s.8d.

1398 Holywell Margaret Hunne, daughter of John Hunne, pays 6s.8d. for license to marry Thomas Wylkyn, this time.

97r **1399** Holywell John Bate and his wife, Johanna: one toft once held by Thomas Hemyngton, for life, rendering annually in all things as did Thomas, with the obligation to rebuild one house called the Dayhous within the manor within one year at their own expense. G.: two capons.

1400 Holywell Richard Skot pays 6s.8d. for license to marry Agnes, his daughter and naif of the lord, to William Lanender, this time.

1401 Cranfield (20 July) John Curteys: one messuage and a half-virgate of land and one quarter of land recently held by Walter atte Milne, for life, rendering annually in all things as did Walter. G.: 13s.4d.

1402 Cranfield John Joy: surrender of three acres of demesne land recently held by Thomas Joye to the use of John Wodehill, for life, rendering annually in all things as did John. G.: 3s.4d.

1403 Cranfield Thomas Curteys: one cotland with another cotland recently held by Robert Curteys, his father, for life, rendering annually in all things as did Robert. G.: 6s.8d.

1404 Cranfield Johanna Seintjon: surrender of one messuage, a half-virgate, two cotes and one croft containing two acres recently held by Hugo Seintjon, to the use of Thomas Seintjon, for life, rendering annually in all things as did Johanna. G.: 6s.8d.

1405 Cranfield John Godewyn and his wife, Agnes, daughter of Cristiana Hayme: one messuage and a half-virgate recently held by Cristiana, for life. G.: 26s.8d.

1406 Cranfield John Kyng: one messuage and a half-virgate of land recently held by William Kyng, his father, for life, rendering annually in all things as did William. G.: 5s.

1407 Cranfield Matilda, Rydeler, naif of the lord, pays 5s. for license to marry, this time.

1408 Warboys John Berenger Sr. pays 3s.4d. for license to marry Emma, his daughter and naif of the lord by blood, to Hugo Fordyngton, this time.

1409 Woodhurst (September) John of the Forthe: one virgate of land once held by Roger White, for life, rendering annually in all things as did Roger, with the first payment at the next feast of the Translation of St. Benedict. G.: two capons.

1410 Ramsey William Bernewell: from Brother Robert Moordon, sub-cellarer, the "Welewrow" with "Couhousmede" with all fishponds, in ditches on either side, except for the fishpond dismissed to John Borell, for 10 years, rendering annually 4s. in equal portions at the feasts of the Annunciation and the Nativity of Blessed Mary, with permission to cut down and plant the trees and willows growing in Welewrow, and with the obligation to maintain all the ditches. Also: one meadow called "Ferthyng", for 10 years, rendering 16d. annually. G.: two capons.

1411 Ramsey Thomas Bysshop and his wife, Amicia: from Brother Robert Moordon, sub-cellarer, one plot with building lying in Briggestrete and built by Thomas de Celario, for life, rendering annually 10s. in equal portions at the feasts of the Annunciation and Nativity of the Blessed Mary, with the sub-cellarer obligated to maintain the property, except for plastering and supplying and transporting undergrowth for the enclosure. *Et si predictus redditus* (arrears for one month). G.: three capons.

97v *Blank*

21 THOMAS BUTTERWYK (1416-1417)

98r **1412** WARBOYS (5 October) Robert Honyter and his wife, Agnes: half of the lands and tenements once held by John atte Hill and recently held by John Heryng, for life, rendering annually in all things as did John, with the obligation to repair the property this year, the lord granting timber and an allowance of this year's rent. G.: four capons.

1413 WARBOYS John Waleys and his wife, Agnes: one plot and half of 22 acres of land once held by Roger de Hirst and recently held by John Boys, and a half-virgate of land in Caldecote recently held by Matilda Bennesson, for life, in *arentatio*, rendering annually 10s. for the plot and 6s. for the half-virgate. Also: one cote at Hoggeskynsrowe, which previously rendered 2s. annually. G.: excused.

1414 WARBOYS Richard Berenger: a half-virgate of land once held by Richard Smyth, in bondage for life, rendering annually 6s., customs of the vill, and supplying one mower with one laborer for one day in the barley. He will repair and maintain the property, except that the lord will supply timber, and the first payment will be due at the feast of St. Andrew this year. G.: two capons.

1415 WARBOYS William Berenger: one plot with one virgate of land recently held by John Hervy, for life, rendering annually 10s. at the customary times, with the first payment at the feast of St. Andrew after two years. He will not relinquish any other lands he holds, under penalty of expulsion. G.: two capons.

1416 WARBOYS Thomas Newman: one virgate once held by Richard Smyth in Caldecote, for life, rendering annually 10s. at the customary times, with the first payment at the feast of St. Andrew next year. G.: excused.

1417 WARBOYS John Berenger Sr: one quarter of land once held by John Plumbe, one selion of land called Longhanedoleland next to Ramseyeweye, and one butt of land once held by John Flemyng, for life, rendering annually 3s.4d. for the quarter, 4d. for the selion and 5d. for the butt, at the customary times. G.: one capon.

1418 WARBOYS Rober Schepperd: three acres of land in Aloneslond once held by Thomas Benet, for life, rendering annually 10d. per acre at the customary times. G.: one capon.

1419 WARBOYS William Sande pays two capons and two wood cocks for license to marry Emma, his daughter and naif of the lord, to John Schepperd of Holywell.

1420 WARBOYS Roger Smyth and John Flemyng: one toft with one virgate of land once held by Thomas Eyr, for life, rendering 8s. this year, and each year thereafter as did Thomas. G.: six capons.

1421 BURWELL (12 October: leet) John atte Hill: surrender of one vacant tenement of 20 acres once held by Thomas Trappe, to the use of William Taillor and his wife, Isabella, for 30 years, rendering annually in all things as did John, with common fine and suit to leet and court. Pledge: John atte Hill. G.: 20d.

1422 BURWELL (same leet) Richard Barker and his wife, Alicia: one tenement of eight acres once held by Andrew Kyrkeby, in *arentatio* for 10 years, rendering annually 11s.6d. and suit to leet and court. G.: two capons.

1423 HEMINGFORD ABBOTS (29 October: court) John Lee: one messuage and a half-virgate of land recently held by William Sly, for life, rendering annually in all things as did William. G.: 12d.

1424 HOLYWELL Thomas Scot, naif of the lord, pays 5s. for license to marry Margaret, his daughter, to Thomas Valentine, servant of John Pulter, this time.

98v **1425** HOUGHTON William Coles and his wife, Isabella: two virgates of land and one piece of meadow called Honymedes once held by William Bokyngham, cleric, in *aren-*

tatio for life, rendering annually 24s. and all other services rendered by those in *aren-tatio*. He will rebuild a building recently held by Robert Dylemaker within the next two years and maintain it thereafter at his own expense, and if he vexes or impedes any tenant for an old trespass or by trespassing on one selion at the end of the vill of Wyton pertaining to the lord, this conveyance will be void. G.: two capons.

1426 HOUGHTON John Marchall Jr.: half of the land once held by Gilbert Houghton, the other half of which is now held by John By the Re, for life, rendering annually 5s. in equal portions at the customary times, payments to begin next year. G.: one capon.

1427 HOUGHTON John By the Re: one plot with building with one virgate of land once held by Pertenhale for life, rendering annually 10s. at the customary times, with payments to begin next year. G.: 5s.

1428 HOUGHTON Richard Smyth and his wife, Johanna: one virgate of land once held by Whaplode, the other half of which is now held by William Smyth, for life, rendering annually 4s. at the customary times, with the first payment due next year. G.: two capons.

1429 HOUGHTON John Smyth: one virgate of land once held by John Cook, for life, rendering annually 12s. at the customary times, with the first payment due next year. He will have two trees for repairing one house within the next two years. G.: excused.

1430 HOUGHTON John Upton: one cotland once held by John Pool, for life, rendering annually 6s. at the customary times, with payments to begin this year. G.: excused.

1431 HOUGHTON Adam Fuller: surrender of one cote and one cotland, to the use of William Fuller and his wife, Johanna, for life, rendering annually 6s.8d. at the customary times. G.: 40d.

1432 HOUGHTON William Somersham: one built up messuage with one virgate of land once held by John Saundre, for life, rendering annually 8s. at the customary times, with the obligation to maintain the grange and *insathous* at his own expense, except for timber from the lord. G.: two capons.

1433 HOUGHTON Matilda Siward: one cote once held by Agnes Saundre, for life, rendering annually 3s. at the customary times. G.: one capon.

1434 HOUGHTON William Andrew and his wife, Margaret: one plot with building and one virgate, a half-toft and a half-virgate once held by William Dalby, for life, rendering annually in all things as did Dalby. G.: 12d.

1435 HOUGHTON William Prykke and his wife, Agnes: a plot with one quarter of land, and all crofts recently held by Thomas Styward, for life, rendering annually in all things as did Thomas. G.: 3s.4d.

1436 HOUGHTON Thomas Foster and his wife, Margaret: one cotland recently held by John Wyth, for life, rendering nothing this year and 6s. each year thereafter. G.: 40d.

1437 HOUGHTON William Saman, alias Fuller, and his wife, Johanna: four crofts recently held by William Dalby, Galfridus Smyth and John Cook, for life, rendering annually 6s. at the customary times, with an allowance of the rent for this year. G.: one capon.

1438 HOUGHTON John Personsman, alias Smyth, and his wife, Alicia: a half-messuage with a half-virgate of land once held by Thomas Tylly, for life, rendering annually 7s. G.: one capon.

1439 HOUGHTON John Pope, three selions of land at Berywelenys once held by John Cook, for life, rendering annually in all things as did Cook. G.: three capons.

1440 HOUGHTON Thomas Pulter and his wife, Agnes: one messuage with a half-virgate of land once held by John de Lye, for life, rendering annually in all things as did John. G.: 3s.4d.

1441 WISTOW Thomas Owty, son of John Owty of Raveley and naif of the lord by blood, pays 12d. for license to work as a blacksmith for as long as it pleases the lord. He will live within the lord's domain.

99r **1442** GRAVELEY William Robet and his wife, Alicia: a half-virgate of land once held by John Flote, for life, rendering annually in all things as did John. G.: two capons.

1443 GRAVELEY John Mannyng and his wife, Alicia: one messuage and one virgate of land recently held by Robert Newman, for life, rendering annually in all things as did Robert. G.: 12d.

1444 GRAVELEY Nicholas Conyene: a half-virgate of land once held by John Clerk, for life, rendering annually in all things as did John. G.: 12d.

1445 BROUGHTON Robert Crouch: surrender of all his lands and messuages to the use of Thomas Crouch and his wife, Matilda, for life, rendering annually in all things as did Robert. G.: four capons.

1446 CRANFIELD Thomas Terry: one cotland once held by William Sawtr and once held by John Cros and recently surrendered back into the lord's hands by the said William, for life, with permission to move the *insathous* to his property. G. and heriot: 13s.4d.

1447 CRANFIELD Richard Archer: one messuage and one quarter, one cote and two acres of land recently held by Robert Coupere, for life, rendering annually in all things as did Robert. G.: 4s.

1448 CRANFIELD John Whyteborow: one messuage and a half-virgate of land recently held by John Frost, for life, rendering annually in all things as did Frost. G.: 20d.

1449 CRANFIELD John Dunwode: one messuage and 12 acres of land recently held by William Catelyn, for life, rendering annually in all things as did William. G.: 6d.

1450 CRANFIELD Roger Donteson, one cotland once held by Margeria Catelyn, for life, rendering annually in all things as did Margeria. G.: 40d.

1451 CRANFIELD Thomas Wodehill: surrender of one virgate once held by his father and ond toft once held by Margaret, daughter of Robert atte Pyrye, to the use of John Wodehill, for life, rendering annually in all things as did Thomas. G.: 40s.

1452 ELLINGTON John Cok of Alconbury pays 2s. for license to marry Johanna, daughter of Nicholas Fot, alias Coupere, naif of the lord by blood.

1453 ELLINGTON William Fowler: surrender of one messuage and one quarter of land in Sibthorp recently held by William Hekkesson, to the use of Richard Freman, for life. G.: 12d.

1454 ELLINGTON John Thakker: one plot with building and a half-virgate once held by William Bedell, for life, rendering annually in all things as did William. G.: 5s.

1455 ELLINGTON William Fowler: one built up messuage and three quarters of land once held by John Hethe, for life, rendering annually in all things as did John. G.: 16d.

1456 ELLINGTON John Bate and William Bate: one plot with three quarters of land in Cotene once held by John atte Wode, for life, except for 5s. from each virgate in Cotene excused by the lord this year, of which John and William receive a *pro rata* allowance. The first payment will be due at the feast of St. Andrew. G.: two capons.

1457 ELLINGTON (February) John Hykkesson Jr.: one plot with one virgate and a half-virgate once held by William Coupere, for life, rendering annually in all things as did William, except for 5s. from each virgate in Cotene excused by the lord this year, of which John receives a *pro rata* allowance. G.: one capon.

1458 BARTON Emma Roger: one cotland containing one acre once held by Richard Roger, for life, rendering annually in all things as did Richard. G.: 12d.

1459 BARTON Walter Wylymot: one empty ploy with a half-virgate and pertaining forland once held by Richard Wylymot, for life, rendering annually in all things as did Richard. G.: 5s.

1460 BARTON Thomas Wylymot pays 5s. for license to marry Agnes, his daughter, to John Godmar of Shillington.

1461 BARTON (July) John Prior, son of John Prior Jr. and his wife, Agnes: one plot with one virgate once held by his father, for life, rendering annually in all things as did his father. G.: 13s.4d.

1462 BARTON John Broun and his wife, Agnes: one plot with a half-virgate of land once held by Thomas Broun, for life, rendering annually in all things as did Thomas. G.: 13s.4d.

1463 HURST Thomas Porter: one butt of land once held by Adam Brounfeld, for life, rendering annually 2d. at the customary times. G.: one capon.

99v **1464** BRINGTON (December: leet) William Deche: one toft and one quarter of land in Overton recently held by John Robery, for life, rendering 2s.6d. this year and 5s. each year thereafter. G.: nothing.

1465 BRINGTON Thomas Cubator: one plot called Heremitesplace and a half-virgate of land recently held by John Elyot, for life.

1466 BRINGTON (leet) John Cartere: two messuages and all lands and tenements recently held in Brington by Richard Howeson, for life, rendering annually in all things as did Richard. G.: 40d.

1467 BRINGTON William Pykkyng Jr: one messuage and a half-virgate of land recently held by John Revesson, for life, rendering annually in all things as did John, with the obligation to rebuild the *insathous* and the grange at his own expense, and to maintain one *camera* and bake house within the messuage under penalty of loss of his status in the tenement.

1468 BRINGTON William Smyth of Buckworth: surrender of one messuage and a half-virgate of land to the use of William Fre Smyth, for life. He will return the land at the end of his term in as good — or better — condition as when he received it. G.: two capons.

1469 BYTHORNE John Inglys: one cotland with adjacent garden recently held by John Smyth, for life. G.: 6d.

1470 BYTHORNE Roger Baroun: surrender of a half-virgate of land with adjacent demesne land, to the use of Robert Covington and his wife, Lucia, for life, rendering annually in all things as did Roger. G.: two capons.

1471 WESTON John Buncy: one cote with a garden and two acres in Weston recently held by John Buncy, his father, for life, rendering annually in all things as did his father. G.: two capons.

1472 WESTON (31 October) Roger Grymbold and his wife, Johanna: one quarter and one virgate of land with adjacent new demesne land and one and a half acres of Burylond, two acres, three rods of Hotoftys and two acres at le Brach and Langlond once held by Simon Hacoun, for life, rendering annually in all things as did Simon. G. and fine for marrying Johanna, naif of the lord: 6s.8d. and six capons.

1473 ELSWORTH Henry Smyth pays 2s. for license to marry Agnes Flessewer, naif of the lord.

1474 ELSWORTH Richard Broghyng: surrender of one messuage and a half-virgate of land, to the use of Alexander Hobbesson and his wife, Katerina, for life, rendering annually in all things as did Richard. G.: 2s.

1475 ELSWORTH William Herry: one toft and one quarter of land in Grave recently held by John Aldyrman, for life, rendering annually 3s.4d. at the customary times. G.: two capons.

1476 ELSWORTH Thomas Coo: a half-virgate of land recently held by Thomas Payn in Elsworth, for life, rendering annually in all things as did Payn. G.: 6d.

1477 ELSWORTH John Newman: one messuage and one virgate of land recently held by John Howlet, for life, rendering annually in all things as did Howlet. G.: 6d.

1478 ELSWORTH Robert Milner and his wife, Margaret: one cote recently held by John Wymondes, for life, rendering annually in all things as did John. G.: two hens.

1479 ELSWORTH John Beseworthe and his wife, Johanna: one toft with a half-virgate of land once held by John Chircheman and recently held by John Cok, for life, rendering annually 10s. at the customary times and all other services and customs owed therein, with the first payment at the feast of St. Andrew next year. G.: two capons.

1480 ABBOTS RIPTON John Walesby: one lot of two acres recently held by John Person, for life, rendering annually at the customary times. G.: one capon.

1481 ABBOTS RIPTON Richard Ropere, alias Cartere: surrender of one cote with a *camera* built on it next to the warren, one path opposite the tenement, one semi-virgate at Estgrene at the cross, and one selion at Angerlond once held by John Fabian, to the use of Richard Weston and his wife, Johanna, for life, rendering annually 19s. at the customary times, with the obligation to repair the property, the lord granting an allowance of the full rents for this year. He will supply one laborer for one day in mowing the wheat. G.: two hens.

100r **1482** SHILLINGTON (leet) Margaret Lambard: surrender of one built up messuage with two virgates recently held by John Lambard to the use of Nicholas Lambard, for life, rendering annually in all things as did Margaret. G. and heriot: 23s.4d.

1483 SHILLINGTON William Smyth: one built up cote once held by John Wyldefowle, for life, rendering annually in all things as did John, with the obligation to repair the property within two years at his own expense. G.: 5s.

1484 SHILLINGTON Isabella Smyth: surrender of one messuage with a half-virgate of Wodehallond to the use of Alicia Smyth, for life, rendering annually in all things as did Isabella. G.: 40d.

1485 SHILLINGTON Thomas Swayne: surrender of one long, tiled cattle shed within the manor, one adjacent curtilage as meted and bounded, and one lot of demesne land, to the use of John Hamond and his wife, Margeria, for life, rendering annually 2s.6d. for the cattle shed, 7s.6d. for the lot, with the obligation to repair other buildings there at their own expense. G.: 13s.4d.

1486 PEGSDON (21 May: court) William atte Hill by a judgment of the court, recovers his right in a half-virgate of land and a half-lot in Pekesdon from John Ede, for life, rendering annually all services and customs owed therein. G.: 40s.

1487 PEGSDON John Coche, son of John Coche Taillor: one messuage and a half-virgate of Wodehallond, for life, rendering annually all services and customs owed therein. G.: 40d.

1488 PEGSDON William Sperwe: surrender of one messuage and a half-virgate once held by Roger of the Hill and one lot of demesne land, which he and his wife, Agnes, receive again from the lord, for life, rendering annually all services and customs owed therein. G. and heriot: 13s.4d.

1489 PEGSDON Adam Coupere: 16 acres of demesne land at Chirchehill and Stokkyng, for life, rendering annually all services and customs previously rendered. G.: 3s.4d.

1490 PEGSDON John Grene: 12 acres in Ecroft and Estfeld for life, rendering annually as did Thomas Sweyn. G.: 3s.4d.

1491 PEGSDON John Lewyn, alias Coche: surrender of one messuage with a half-virgate previously held by Henry Lewyn and in the lord's hands for two years after

Henry's death in 18 Thomas because of default of heirs, to the use of Nicholas Coche, his son, for life, rendering annually in all things as did John. G.: 6s.8d.

1492 PEGSDON John Ede: a certain part of the manor of Shillington, namely: the hall with annexed *camera*, chapel, kitchen, bake house, kiln, abbot's bower, pig-sty, dovecote, adjacent garden, and a certain parcel of the garden lying for pasture as meted and bounded, with the hall, *camera*, principal chapel, kitchen and stables reserved to the lord, his seneschal and other *famuli* when they come; for life, rendering annually 6s.8d. Also: a granary and the large grange with a parcel of one garden and two lots of demesne once held by John Waryn and Thomas Hamond, for life, rendering annually 18s. at the customary times. Also: two lots once held by William Coche, one lot, three half-virgates once held by William Coche, and certain acres of demesne land once held by the same William, for life, rendering annually 15s. for the two lots, 9s. for the one lot, and all services and customs rendered by William for the three half-virgates and demesne land, with the obligation to repair all the houses in carpentry, roofing, enclosures and all other necessities at his own expense, except for timber, splints and poles from the lord. He will have *housbote, haybote* and *ferbote* whenever and as much as necessary, and he will support all the obligations as do others holding lots in the vill. Nor will he dismiss any part of the property without the license of the lord, nor place himself under the protection of any lord in prejudice of the abbot or to the harm of his neighbors, under penalty of forfeit. G.: 20s.

100v

1493 PEGSDON (same court, i.e., 21 May) William Smyth, John AtteMede, Henry Hamond, John Grene, John atte Grene, Robert Grene and John Goodmar: seven lots of demesne lands and meadows from the manor, to be held with all pastures and fishponds and all rents and services from tenants — both free and villein — together with one mill called Watewalemylne, and with all appurtenances for life, with the following reserved to the lord: Schepecotewyk, Colbynesgrene, all trees and hedges growing in the above demesne, Millemade, and pasture when the lord, seneschal of the court and clerics come. They will render annually for each lot, 9s. at the customary times, and for the mill all services and customs owed therein, with the obligation to support all the burdens and services and rents owed and accustomed. They will maintain the mill and all bridges pertaining to the manor at their own expense, except for large timber, splints and poles supplied by the lord, and they will dwell within the manor, under penalty of forfeit. Nor will they dismiss any part of the property to anyone without the lord's license, nor put themselves under the protection of any other lord to the prejudice of the abbot or damage to their neighbors. They may not cut down any hedges in the above demesne to the detriment of the enclosures, but they are to have all top branches growing within the ditches. They will also pay rents and *gersuma* under penalty of forfeit, and they will not overburden the pasture except with their own beasts and sheep. The bailiff is not to impound any of their animals seized at Colbynesgrene because of defects of enclosures attributable to the lord. And each ought to be collector at the will of the lord, receiving for that 13s.4d. annually, provided that after the death of any of them, the lord can appoint anyone to those lots, so that neither heirs nor executors can have a claim upon them, except that his widow will hold his lot while she remains a widow, at the special grace of the lord. G.: £7.

1494 PEGSDON Adam Coupere and Simon Goberd pay 40s. for two lots, to be held as above.

1495 THERFIELD (leet) John Jankyn Sr.: surrender, in the presence of the seneschal, of one virgate to the use of Robert Jankyn, for life, rendering annually 26s.8d. and all other services and customs rendered by John. G.: 40d.

1496 THERFIELD John Jankyn: one tenement of Payne with a portion of lands once held by John atte Wode, and Burylond, the fifth part of lands once held by John Waryn, the fifth part of Welmade, the fifth part of 40 acres, and half of five acres at Bedlond, for life, rendering annually 51s. at the customary times and all other services and customs rendered by other customaries. G.: three capons.

1497 THERFIELD John Rook: one virgate with one pithel and one quarter of land with Burylond once held by John Gerveys, for life, rendering annually 32s. for the virgate, 13s. for the quarter, and as Gerveys for Burylond. G.: six capons.

1498 THERFIELD Seizure from William Qwascher of all his lands and tenements because of his forfeits and failures to repair lands, as is more fully contained in the General Court. Conveyed to Henry Gerveys, for life, rendering annually 25s. for a virgate, 10s. for a cotland, and for demesne land as did William, except that he will render nothing for one acre at Berehill — which previously rendered 12d. — because he holds it in support of his virgate. G.: three capons.

1499 THERFIELD John Stonghton and his wife, Cecilia: all lands and tenements recently held by William de York and once held by William Wyngore, for life, rendering annually in all things as did William de York. Pledges: John Waryn and William Stonghton. G.: three capons.

101r **1500** CHATTERIS John Bate: one messuage with seven acres of land with meadow, for life, rendering annually as did Nicholas Schepperd. G.: 6s.8d.

1501 CHATTERIS Richard Michell: one messuage once held by John Webstere, for life, rendering annually in all things as did John. G.: 2s.

1502 CHATTERIS Richard Smyth: one messuage once held by John Trumpor, for life, rendering annually in all things as did John. G.: 12d.

1503 CHATTERIS Margaret Bele: surrender of one tenement of eight acres to the use of Robert Broun, for life, rendering annually in all things as did Margaret. G.: 20s.

1504 CHATTERIS John Therenesson: one cotland once held by William Taillor, for life, rendering annually in all things as did William. G.: 40s.

1505 CHATTERIS John Sempool Jr.: one tenement of eight acres once held by John Pykerell, for life, rendering annually in all things as did John Pykerell. G.: 13s.4d.

1506 HOLYWELL John Sewale, chaplain: one built up croft once held by William Baroun and recently held by Nicholas Baroun, for life, and one croft and two butts in a croft next to Holywell Cross once held by Nicholas Hardy and recently held by John Schepperd, for life, rendering annually in all things as did Schepperd. G.: 3s.4d.

1507 HOLYWELL Thomas Daye: surrender of one cotland with all adjacent new demesne land and the crop of that land to the use of John Schepperd and his wife, Agnes, for life, rendering annually in all things as did Thomas. G.: 3s.4d.

1508 ST. IVES William Pyle and his wife, Iveta Catworth: a half-row next to the water once held by John Catworth, for life, rendering annually 15s. in equal portions at the customary times, with the obligation to repair and maintain the property at their own expense. *Et non licebit,* etc. G.: 6s.8d.

1509 ST. IVES John Tebbe and his wife, Margeria: a half-row once held by Roger Chekesonde, for life, rendering annually 13s.4d. in equal portions at the customary times, with the obligation to repair and maintain the property. *Et non licebit*, etc. G.: 6s.8d.

1510 ST. IVES John Lystere and his wife, Margaret: a half-row once held by Thomas Crowcher, for life, rendering annually 20s. in equal portions at the customary times, with the obligation to repair and maintain the property. *Et non licebit*, etc. G.: 3s.4d.

1511 ST. IVES William Page and his wife, Margeria: a certain part of a half-row once held by Hugo Deye, for life, rendering annually 10s.8d. in equal portions at the customary times, with the obligation to repair and maintain the property. *Et non licebit*, etc. G.: 5s.

1512 St. Ives Henry Barbor and his wife, Johanna: a certain part of a half-row once held by Hugo Deye, for life, rendering annually 5s.4d. in equal portions at the customary times, with the obligation to repair and maintain the property. *Et non licebit*, etc. G.: 2s.

1513 St. Ives John Lystere and his wife, Margaret: one toft next to the vicarage, for life, rendering annually 12d., with the obligation to repair and maintain the property. *Et non licebit*, etc. G.: two capons.

1514 Wistow Simon Thoday, alias Bryslaunse, pays 6s.8d. for license to marry Johanna, daughter of Thomas Owty and naif of the lord by blood. Pledge: Thomas Bryslaunse.

1515 Wistow John Newman and his wife, Alicia: one quarter of land once held by Richard Wodecok, in *secunda arentatio* for life, rendering annually in all things as did Richard and all other services and customs rendered by those in *secunda arentatio*. G.: four capons.

1516 Hurst Stephen Warener: a half-virgate once held by Cristina Canne and recently held by William Warener, for life, rendering annually in all things as did William, with the first payment at the feast of St. Andrew next year. G.: one capon.

1517 Slepe Nicholas Chekesond and his wife, Agnes: one toft called Lumbescroft and another toft next to the tenement once held by Hawler, for life, rendering annually 21d. at the customary times. G.: two capons.

101v **1518** Slepe Henry Payn: one cotland recently held by Thomas Grenehill, for life, rendering annually in all things as did Thomas. G.: 12d.

1519 Slepe Richard White and his wife, Margaret: one messuage next to the horsepond recently held by Matthew Holwell, for life, rendering annually 6s. at the customary times. G.: 2s.

1520 Slepe John Bedford and his wife, Margaret: one cote at the corner of Cowlane once held by Henry Webstere, for life, rendering annually in all things as did Henry. G.: 5s.

1521 Slepe Thomas Deraunt: a half-virgate of land once held by William Cut and before that by Ailmare, for life, rendering annually 7s. at the customary times, with the first payment at the feast of St. Andrew next year. G.: two capons.

1522 Ramsey Robert Rydman and his wife, Ivota: from Brother Robert Moordon, sub-cellarer, four acres and one selion, of which seven selions lie between the land of the said Robert and John Borth, and the last selion lies next to the land of Nicholas Nabyly, for life, rendering annually 5s.4d. at the feasts of the Annunciation and Nativity of Blessed Mary and customs at Upwood. G.: three capons.

1523 Ramsey (1 October) Johanna Banham and her executors: Brother Robert Moordon, sub-cellarer, one messuage with appurtenances in Bridge Street next to the land of John Chaumberleyn and once held by John Weston, from Michaelmas for 21 years, rendering annually 13s.4d. in equal portions at Michaelmas and Easter, with the obligation to repair and maintain all houses in timber, roofing and other necessities at her own expense, with free access to the water in the ponds of that property reserved for life to John Chaumberleyn and his wife, Gracia. If Johanna lives longer than the 21 years, she will then hold the property for life, rendering 14s. annually at the customary times. G.: 6s.8d.

1524 Ramsey John Wayte and his wife, Emma: from Brother Robert Moordon, sub-cellarer, one messuage of nine messuages and one cote within Michgate, lying next to the chapel of the vill, for life, rendering annually 13s.4d. in equal portions at the feasts of the Annunciation and Nativity of Blessed Mary, with the sub-cellarer responsible for repairing and maintaining the houses, except that John and Emma will maintain the walls and enclosures, with splints, poles and undergrowth supplied by the sub-cellarer. G.: six capons.

1525 RAMSEY Thomas Chircheward and his wife, Margaret: from Brother Robert Moordon, sub-cellarer, one messuage next to Michegate by Cartesbrigge, for life, rendering annually 8s. in equal portions at the feasts of the Annunciation and Nativity of Blessed Mary. Also: one empty, enclosed plot opposite the above messuage, for life, rendering annually 12d. at the customary times, unless another's heir makes a claim and wins it. He will repair all enclosures and the messuage, toft, ditches and hedges at his own expense, with undergrowth, stakes, their cutting and carrying supplied by the sub-cellarer, who will be responsible for all other repairs. *Et si predictus redditus*, etc. (arrears of two months). G.: two capons.

1526 RAMSEY John Ryvenale and his wife, Alicia: from Brother Robert Moordon, sub-cellarer, one messuage at Grene next to the messuage of John Wayte and once held by John Berner, for life, rendering annually 6s.8d. in equal portions at the feasts of the Annunciation and Nativity of Blessed Mary, with the sub-cellarer responsible for maintaining the enclosures. *Et si predictus redditus*, etc. (arrears of one month). G.: two capons.

1527 RAMSEY Thomas Borugh and his wife, Agnes: from Brother Robert Moordon, sub-cellarer, one messuage next to the messuage held by John Meyke, for life, rendering annually 6s.8d. in equal portions at the feasts of the Annunciation and the Nativity of Blessed Mary, with the obligation to maintain all ditches and enclosures at their own expense, except for undergrowth, stakes and poles supplied by the sub-cellarer, together with their cutting and carting. The sub-cellarer will make all other repairs and be responsible for other maintenance. *Et si predictus redditus*, etc. (arrears for one month). G.: two capons.

1528 RAMSEY John Plomer of Cornwall (Cornuvea): from Brother Robert Moordon, sub-cellarer, one messuage next to that of Simon Sege at Grene, for life, rendering annually 5s. in equal portions at the feasts of the Annunciation and Nativity of Blessed Mary, with the obligation to maintain all ditches and hedges at his own expense, except for undergrowth, stakes, poles, their cutting and carrying supplied by the sub-cellarer, who will be responsible for all other maintenance. *Et si predictus redditus*, etc. (arrears of one month). G.: one capon.

22 THOMAS BUTTERWYK (1417-1418)

102r **1529** BURWELL (leet) John Clerk, alias Blaunteyn: one tenement of 20 acres once held by John Wyot and before that by Swynley, with the capital messuage reserved to the lord, for 20 years, rendering annually 16s., suit to court and leet and all other services and customs rendered by Wyot. G.: 2s.

1530 BURWELL John Rolf Jr. and his wife, Alicia: one tenement of 15 acres once held by Simon Calvesbane, with the capital toft reserved to the lord, for 20 years, rendering annually 15s.8d., suit to court and leet, and all other services and customs rendered by Simon. G.: 2s.

1531 BURWELL George Hervy Bocher and his wife, Katerina: half of one tenement of 24 acres once held by Simon Calvesbane, for 20 years, rendering annually 12s., suit to court and leet, and all other services and customs rendered by Simon. G.: 2s.

1532 BURWELL Johanna, widow of Robert Barow: one tenement of 15 acres once held by Wakelyn, and another tenement of 15 acres once held by John Barow, one cote once held by Helywys, with the croft reserved to the lord, two crofts at the lane of the rector, four acres of demesne land, and one cotland at Nesse called Longcroft, for

20 years, rendering annually 43s., ploughing, suit to court and leet and all other services and customs rendered by John. For the four acres of demesne she will render as agreed with the *firmarius*. G.: 6s.8d.

1533 BURWELL Thomas Webstere, alias Arnold, and his wife, Oliva: one cotland once held by Alexander Sperwe, a half-croft reserved to the lord, for 30 years, rendering annually 5s., suit to court and leet and all other services and customs rendered by Alexander. G.: 12d.

1534 BURWELL William Crabbe and his wife, Alicia: half of one tenement of 24 acres once held by Thomas Calvesbane, for 20 years, rendering annually 13s., suit to court and leet and all other services and customs rendered by Thomas. G.: 2s.

1535 BURWELL John Benet, *firmarius*, and his wife, Agnes: half of one croft once held by John Sadde and one pithel at Reche once held by Baroun, one croft once held by Swynley in Burwell, a half-croft once held by John Sperwe next to the gate of the manor, and seven acres once held by. John Jemes, for the life of whomever lives longer, rendering annually all services and customs owed therein. G.: three capons.

1536 THERFIELD (leet) William Frere: surrender of one messuage and one quarter of land recently held by Robert Steven and one toft and 10 acres recently held by Gilbert, to the use of his son, John Frere, for life, rendering annually in all things as did William. G.: six capons.

1537 SHILLINGTON (leet) John Colyn Jr.: seven acres of demesne land, of which three acres were recently held by Galfridus Fawkeswell and four acres were held by John Colyn, his father, for life, rendering annually in all things as did Gilbert and John Sr. G.: 2s.

1538 SHILLINGTON (*blank*) Martyn pays 12d. to marry Alicia, widow of Richard Smyth.

1539 SHILLINGTON Lucia West and her son, John West: one messuage and a half-virgate of land once held by Thomas West, her husband, for life, rendering annually in all things as did Thomas. G.: 6s.8d. And both will pay heriot.

1540 SHILLINGTON John West: one and a half acres of demesne land at Leecroft recently held by John atte Wode, for life. G.: one capon.

1541 SHILLINGTON John Lewyn and his wife, Margeria: surrender, through the hands of John Beston, bailiff, of one messuage and one virgate of land once held by Adam Lewyn, to the use of Nicholas Lewyn, for life, rendering annually in all things as did John. G.: 26s.8d. Heriot (of Margeria): 6s.8d.

1542 SHILLINGTON (January) The lord grants to all tenants and customaries holding demesne land at Chirchehill the right to plough and sow all that land up to three selions at their own will, rendering as they are accustomed to render. G.: six capons.

1543 BARTON (court) Thomas Stonley: one built up messuage and one toft, two virgates of land and one croftland once held by his father, Richard Stonley, for life, rendering annually in all things as did Richard. G.: 16s.8d.

1544 BARTON John Roger and his wife, Emma: one messuage and a half-virgate of land recently held by Richard atte Chirche, for life, rendering annually in all things as did the aforesaid Emma. G.: 6s.8d.

1545 BARTON John Prior Jr. and his wife, Agnes: one croftland once held by Agnes Adam, for life, rendering annually in all things as did Agnes Adam. G.: 20d.

1546 ELLINGTON (leet) William Milner: one quarter of land recently held by Richard Margeryson in Coton, for life, rendering annually in all things as did Richard. G.: 12d.

102v　**1547** CRANFIELD (leet) William Vauce: one messuage and a half-virgate of land recently held by Margaret Marshall, for life, rendering annually in all things as did Margaret. G.: 40d.

1548 CRANFIELD Thomas Wodehill Jr.: one messuage and a half-virgate recently held by William del Grene, for life, rendering annually in all things as did William. G.: 10s.

1549 CHATTERIS Thomas Cut: one piece of meadow called Ouse, or Ousemoor, for life, rendering annually 10s. at the customary times. G.: 20s.

1550 CHATTERIS John Sempool of Hithe: one messuage with one croft opposite, once held by John Trumpor, for life, rendering annually in all things as did Trumpor. G.: 40d.

1551 CHATTERIS John Hamond and his wife, Alicia: one cotland with four butts of land in Modmen containing one acre, with one acre next to the ditch once held by Alicia Cook, for life, rendering annually in all things as did Cook. G.: 2s.

1552 CHATTERIS William Newman and his wife, Johanna: half of one tenement of eight acres with another parcel, as found in the Rental, for life, rendering annually as is specified in the Rental. G.: 2s.

1553 CHATTERIS Alicia Peyte: all lands and tenements once held by her father, Stephen Peyte, for life, rendering annually in all things as did her father. G.: 5s.

1554 CHATTERIS John Balle and his wife, Margeria: one cotland with other parcels listed in the Rental and once held by John Newman, for life, rendering annually in all things as did John. G.: four capons.

1555 CHATTERIS John Ryvenale, half of one tenement of eight acres recently held by John Wynewyk, with adjacent pastures and fishponds, for life, rendering annually in all things as did Wynewyk. G.: 13s.4d.

1556 HEMINGFORD ABBOTS William Martyn, naif of the lord, pays 40d. for license to marry Cristiana, his daughter, to John Joyner, the first time.

1557 ST. IVES (leet) Agnes, widow of Richard Nicoll: surrender of one row to the use of William Fawne and his wife, Elena, for life, rendering annually 10s. in equal portions at the customary times, with the obligation to repair and maintain the property at their own expense. *Et non licebit*, etc. G.: (*blank*).

1558 ELTON Katerina Robery: one messuage and one quarter recently held by John Hobbesson, for life, rendering annually 5s. and all other services and customs rendered by John. G.: 6d.

1559 ELTON (October) Richard Bokelond: one toft and one quarter of land once held by Stephen Rodebode, for life, rendering annually in all things as did Stephen. G.: 6d.

1560 ELTON John Mond: one toft and one quarter recently held by Matilda Bate, for life, rendering annually in all things as did Matilda. G.: 6d.

1561 ELTON Reginald Cook: one messuage and one virgate recently held by Nicholas Gregge, for life, rendering annually in all things as did Nicholas. G.: 2s.

1562 ELTON John Bryan: one built up messuage and a half-virgate of land recently held by Hugo Hobard, for life, rendering annually in all things as did Hugo. G.: 12d.

1563 ELTON John Clerk: one toft and one quarter of land once held by John Hichebate, for life, rendering annually in all things as did John Hichebate. G.: 6d.

1564 ELTON John Hobson: one messuage and a half-virgate recently held by Reginald Cook, for life, rendering annually in all things as did Reginald. G.: 12d.

1565 ELTON John Brampton: one messuage and one quarter once held by John Jarwell, for life, rendering annually in all things as did Jarwell. G.: 6d.

1566 ELTON Thomas Robery: one messuage and a half-virgate once held by John Jarwell, for life. John Jarwell will have the tenement for two years after this court and give 8s. for repairs. G.: (*blank*).

1567　Elton John Cole: one messuage and three quarters of land recently held by William Herper, for life, rendering annually in all things as did William. G.: 6d.

1568　Elton John Bythorne and Henry atte Gate: one plot and one virgate and one quarter of land once held by Richard Bate, for life, rendering annually 25s. at the customary times. G.: four capons.

1569　Elton Henry Carleton: one cotland once held by John Page, and one quarter of land once held by John Bryan, for life, rendering annually 7s. at the customary times. G.: two capons.

1570　Elton William Harper: one messuage and certain lands containing approximately a half-virgate of land called Heremytes and recently held by Thomas de Lys, for life, rendering annually 8s. at the customary times, paying one-half of the rent this year. G.: one capon.

1571　Elton Henry atte Gate and his wife, Agnes: one toft once held by John Blakman of Oldmol, rendering annually 6d. at the customary times. G.: one capon.

1572　Brington John Benesson: one cotland and a half-acre of land recently held by John Betonson, for life, rendering annually in all things as did Betonson. G.: excused.

1573　Warboys Alicia Freman, naif of the lord by blood and widow of William Kyngesdolf, pays two capons for license to marry John Wernyngton, freeman.

103r　**1574**　Weston (leet) John Kyng Jr.: one toft and one quarter of land recently held by Walter Jekes, for life, rendering annually in all things as did Walter. G.: two capons.

1575　Weston Matilda, daughter of John Berton and naif of the lord by blood, pays 40d. for license to marry William Hikkesson of Brington.

1576　Weston John Jekesson, alias Buncy, and his wife, Agnes: one plot and certain lands once held by Richard Buncy, for life, rendering annually in all things as did Richard. G.: two capons.

1577　Weston John Hacoun Sr.: surrender of one cotland from Hotoft's tenement, half of one quarter once held by William Jekesson, one quarter of land parcelled out of one virgate recently held by Roger Cartere, a half-virgate once held by William Jekes, a half-virgate once held by William Miller, one quarter parcelled out of one virgate recently held by Roger Milner, two acres of Burylond, one acre of Hotoft's, demesne land recently dismissed, one acre of meadow of Hotoft's, one quarter once held by William Milner, and a parcel of one cotland once held by the same William, to the use of Simon Hacoun, for life, rendering annually in all things as did John. Regarding the enclosures, it appears in the following year *per copiam*. G.: six capons.

1578　Knapwell John Smyth: surrender of one toft and one quarter recently held by William Marchand, to the use of John Hote, for life, rendering annually in all things as did Smyth. G.: 8d.

1579　Knapwell John Creek: surrender of one toft and one quarter recently held by Roger Joye, to the use of John Sampson Schepperd, for life, rendering annually in all things as did Creek. G.: 8d.

1580　Knapwell Johanna Bet: one toft and 20 acres of land once held by John Bet, for life, rendering annually in all things as did John. G.: 6d.

1581　Holywell Thomas Baroun: one croft once held by his father, William Baroun, for life, rendering annually in all things as did William. G.: 3s.4d.

1582　Holywell Agnes Hunne, naif of the lord, pays 6s.8d. for license to marry.

1583　Holywell Alicia Sande, naif of the lord, pays 6s.8d. for license to marry.

1584　Abbots Ripton Walter Schepperd, alias Savage, and Thomas Michell: three semi-virgates with 10 acres at Cateshegge, once held by John Ivell, in *arentatio*, rendering annually 32s. at the customary times. One or both of them will come to sheepshearing and one *precaria*, receiving as do other customaries, and they will not be akirmen, but they will pay common fine and hundred geld. G.: four capons.

1585 ABBOTS RIPTON Elizabet, daughter of John Nicoll and naif of the lord by blood, pays 3s.4d. for license to marry Thomas Buntyng of Buryhatle.

1586 ABBOTS RIPTON (February) William Amery: surrender of two semi-virgates once held by John West of Wenyngton, to the use of Richard Savage and his wife, Johanna, in *arentatio* for life, rendering annually 20s. at the customary times, supplying one mower for the meadow, and one mower with one laborer in autumn at the summons of the bailiff. G.: 3s.4d.

1587 WISTOW John atte Gate Jr. and his wife, Johanna: one plot with building and a half-virgate, one toft and a half-virgate of land once held by John Randolf, for life, rendering annually as did John Randolf. G.: 20s.

1588 WISTOW John Owty Jr. and his wife, Agnes: one toft with a half-virgate once held by Cleryvaux and recently held by Thomas Bryselaunce, for life, rendering annually in all things as did Thomas. G.: six capons.

1589 WISTOW William Galopyn: one quarter of land once held by Thomas Bruselaunce, for life, rendering annually in all things as did Thomas. Pledge for maintenance: Thomas Bryselaunce. G.: two capons.

1590 WISTOW (January) John Wrighte: seven acres of land at le Brach once held by John Leighton, for life, rendering annually 5s.3d. in equal portions at the feasts of the Annunciation and Nativity of Blessed Mary. G.: one capon.

1591 WISTOW The rector of Wistow: a half-virgate of land of akirmanland once held by Hugo Lowthe, four acres of demesne land called Neyntene, and one acre at Toftdole with three acres called Godfreyslond. G.: two capons.

1592 WISTOW John Owty Jr., son of John Owty Sr.: one plot with three quarters of land once held by Richard Wyllesson, for life, rendering annually in all things as did Richard for the half-virgate, and 4s.6d. in *arentatio* for the quarter. G.: 2s.

1593 WISTOW John Elmesle: surrender of one messuage and three quarters of land, to the use of John Wryghte and his wife, Johanna, for life, rendering annually 15s. at the customary times, customs of the vill, one autumn *precaria*, with the obligation to repair and maintain all the buildings on the property under penalty of a fine of 40s. If he has hay at the end of his term, he will dismiss all the land fallow. G.: 3s.4d.

1594 WOODHURST Hugo Laurence and his wife, Alicia: one toft with a half-virgate of land once held by William Boner Jr., for life, rendering annually in all things as did William. G.: two capons.

1595 WOODHURST John Lawe: a half-virgate of land once held by his father, John Lawe, for life, rendering annually in all things as did his father. G.: two capons.

1596 WOODHURST Benedict Boner and his wife, Isabella: a half-virgate of land once held by John Lawe Sr., for life, rendering annually in all things as did John. G.: two capons.

1597 ELSWORTH John Herry and his wife, Alicia: one messuage and one quarter of land recently held by John Yntte and once held by John Philyp, in *arentatio* for life, rendering annually 6s., and 12d. to the lord or *firmarius* for works, and he will render other works as do those customaries in *arentatio*. G.: 2s.

103v **1598** BROUGHTON (December) Thomas Smyth: one virgate once held by Thomas Botiller, for life, rendering annually 12s. at the customary times, customs of the vill, three ancient ploughing *precariae*, one autumn *precaria*, mowing the fen for one day, and mowing of barley for one day with one laborer, with the first payment at the feast of St. Andrew. G.: two capons.

1599 BROUGHTON John Cabe Jr.: one quarter of land once held by John Ellesworth, for life, rendering annually 3s.4d. at the customary times, mowing of the fen for one day, and mowing of barley for one day with one laborer. Also: all lands held by Robert Balde, for life, rendering annually in all things as did Robert. G.: three capons.

1600   UPWOOD Nicholas Wyse and his wife, Cristina: one cotland and one quarter of land once held by Thomas Michell, for life, rendering annually in all things as did Thomas, customs of the vill, winnowing peas for one day with one man, at the lord's food, or another work similar to this. Nor may he dismiss the property without the lord's license, nor will the land stand vacant, under penalty of forfeit. G.: two capons.

1601   UPWOOD (Aril) John Kyng of Raveley and his wife, Johanna: one virgate and one quarter with a forland in Capewell and Wodepightill once held by Richard Newman, for life, rendering annually 27s.1d.ob. at the customary times, with the first payment at the feast of the Nativity of John the Baptist. He will enter into the property this year before the feast of St. George, as agreed with Richard, and he will repair the *insathous*, the grange and one bake house within three years, and maintain it thereafter; and he will render one ploughing *precaria,* as he ploughs on his own land, one autumn *precaria* with one man at the summons of the bailiff, carrying of malt once a year to Ramsey with his own wagon, and *capitagium.* G.: 3s.4d.

1602   GRAVELEY John Walis pays 3s.4d. for license to marry Margaret Swan, widow of John Swan and naif of the lord, and for entry into one plot and one virgate of land once held by John Swan, for the lifetime of the said Margaret, rendering annually in all things as did Swan. G.: 3s.4d.

1603   RAMSEY Thomas Brigge and his wife, Agnes: from Brother Richard Kymbolton, sub-cellarer, one plot in Briggestrete once held by John de Dam, for life, rendering annually 13s.4d. in equal portions at the feasts of the Annunciation and the Nativity of Blessed Mary, with the sub-cellarer responsible for repairing and maintaining the property. G.: 3s.4d.

1604   RAMSEY Laurence Derby Bocher and his wife, Johanna: from Brother Richard Kymbolton, sub-cellarer, one plot, in which he lives, next to the tenement once held by Thomas Wodeward, for life, rendering annually 12s. in equal portions at the feast of the Nativity of Blessed Mary and Easter, with the obligation to erect a *camera* the length of the plot within one year at his own expense. *Et si predictus redditus,* etc. G.: 20d.

1605   RAMSEY John Wernyngton alias John de Celar, and his wife, Alicia: from Brother Richard Kymbolton, sub-cellarer, one plot in le Wyght once held by William Kyngesdolf, for life, rendering annually 7s. in equal portions at the feasts of the Annunciation and Nativity of Blessed Mary. The sub-cellarer will maintain all the buildings with their appurtenances, but if John and Alicia damage any part of the plot with their beasts, they will make repairs at their own expense. G.: two capons.

1606   HOUGHTON Alicia, daughter of John Roger and naif of the lord by blood, pays 5s. for license to marry John, son of William Bocher of Ramsey.

1607   HOUGHTON (May) John Smyth and his wife, Margeria: one and a half-virgates once held by John Cook, for life, rendering 17s. annually at the customary times, with the obligation to repair one house on the property before next Easter at his own expense, except for two trees from the lord, and a reduction of this year's rent to 12s. G.: making all iron works for the draw-well in the manor.

1608   SLEPE (Pentecost Week) Richard Jonesson and his wife, Agnes: one plot with building, one grange and one virgate of land once held by Simon in the Slow, in *arentatio* for life, rendering annually 13s.4d. and all other services rendered by those in *arentatio.* G.: one capon.

23 THOMAS BUTTERWYK (1418-1419)

104r   **1609**   THERFIELD John Adam and his wife, Margaret: one pithel once held by Janyn Gurneye, for life, rendering annually in all things as did Janyn. G.: two capons.

1610   CRANFIELD Nicholas Wyngod: surrender of one cote next to the messuage of Agnes Brerele to the use of Thomas Brerele, for life. G.: 40d.

1611   CRANFIELD Galfridus Taillor: surrender of one cotland and three acres of land recently held by William Joye, to the use of Henry Cook, for life, rendering annually in all things as did Galfridus. G.: 10s.

1612   BARTON (court) William Schepperd: one parcel of waste next to the tenement once held by William Milward, containing 20 rods in length and 14 rods in width, for life, rendering annually 3d. G.: two capons, and no more because he will rebuild the property.

1613   BARTON William Broun: one cotland containing one acre and one cotland without buildings recently held by John Bocher, for life, rendering annually in all things as did John. G.: 40d.

1614   BARTON John Marchaund: one private pasture called Leede, containing approximately four acres, for life, rendering annually 2s. G.: 12d.

1615   BARTON John Felmesham: one built up cotland containing one acre recently held by John Cook, for life, rendering annually in all things as did John Felmesham. G.: 6d.

1616   SHILLINGTON John Barfot, naif of the lord, pays 3s.4d. for license to marry Cristiana, his daughter and naif of the lord by blood, to anyone.

1617   SHILLINGTON Thomas atte Well: one messuage and one virgate of land in Pegsdon recently held by John atte Well, for life, rendering annually in all things as did John. G.: 10s.

1618   SHILLINGTON John Hamond and his wife, Margeria: eight acres of demesne land in Shillington recently held by Johanna atte Wode, namely: 5 acres in Le Croft and three acres in Emondlond, for life, rendering annually in all things as did Johanna. G.: 5s.

1619   SHILLINGTON John Warde and his wife, Margaret: the reversion of one messuage and a half-virgate of land once held by Thomas Bonker and now held by Alicia Bonker, for life, rendering annually in all things as Alicia, saving always Alicia's heriot. G.: 3s.4d.

1620   SHILLINGTON John Brenham: one messuage and two semi-virgates of land once held by Thomas Hamond, for life, rendering annually in all things as did Thomas. G.: 13s.4d.

1621   SHILLINGTON (7 May) John Smyth: surrender through the hands of John Beston, bailiff, of one messuage in Wode ende and one virgate of land recently held by Henry atte Style, to the use of John At Abbey, for life, rendering annually in all things as did Smyth, with the provision that John Smyth will hold one *camera* called Schepenende and one garden called Bernewyke, without rents, for life, with the obligation of repairing it at his own expense. G.: 20s.

1622   SHILLINGTON John Wymyngham: surrender, through the hands of John Beston, bailiff, of one messuage and two virgates of land in Hanscombe, to the use of William West, for life, rendering annually in all things as did John. G.: 53s.4d.

1623   BURWELL Richard Wrighte and his wife, Alicia: one tenement of eight acres once held by John Bury, for 20 years, rendering annually 11s. at the customary times, common fine, suit to court and leet, and love boon, except that the lord or *firmarius* will have his croft in payment, or Richard will have an allowance of 8d. in any year. G.: 12d. and one crane.

1624 Burwell John Purt and his wife, Margaret: all lands and tenements once held by John Poket, for 20 years, rendering annually in all things as did Poket. G.: 40d.

1625 Burwell John Pryk Jr. and his wife, Johanna: all lands and tenements that Johanna, widow of Robert Barow, took up from the lord in 22 Thomas, for 20 years, rendering annually in all things as did Johanna. G.: one goose and two capons.

1626 Burwell John Rolf and his wife, Katerina: one tenement of 15 acres with one croft once held by Robert Wyet, from the previous Michaelmas for 22 years, rendering annually 15s, in *arentatio*. G.: two capons.

1627 Burwell Richard Spencer Sr. and his wife, Alicia: one tenement of 12 acres with a cotland and one and a half acres in a croft and three acres in the fields recently held by Radulph Calvesbane, for 20 years, rendering annually in all things as did Radulph, common fine, suit to court and leet and one love boon. G.: 6s. and two capons.

1628 Burwell Thomas Pury and his wife, Etheldreda: one tenement of 24 acres recently held by Simon Calvesbane, for 20 years, rendering annually in all things as did Simon and suit to court and leet. Pledges for rent and *gersuma*: William Taillor and John Pury. G.: 40d.

1629 Burwell Radulph Rower: one tenement of 15 acres and one cotland called Pellams recently held by Margaret Rower, for 20 years, rendering annually in all things as did Margaret, and suit to court and leet. G.: six capons.

1630 Burwell William Jay and his wife, Isabella: 24 acres with one plot once held by William Houghton, for 30 years, rendering annually 28s., customs of the vill and suit to court and leet, with the obligation to repair and maintain the property at their own expense. G.: two capons.

1631 Burwell John Payntor and his wife, Agnes: one tenement of 15 acres and one cote recently held by himself, for 22 years, rendering annually in all things as he did previously, and suit to court and leet, love boon and common fine. G.: 40d. and two capons.

1632 Graveley Robert Newman, naif of the lord, pays 3s.4d. for license to marry Custancia, his daughter and naif of the lord by blood, to John atte Slow, this time.

1633 Graveley John atte Slow and his wife, Custancia: one plot with building and two virgates of land once held by his father, Walter atte Slow, for life, rendering annually in all things as did Walter. G.: 3s.4d.

104v **1634** St. Ives John Sutton: surrender of a half-row recently held by John Lystere, to the use of Henry Bocher, alias Beerde, and his wife, Dionisia, for life, rendering annually 20s. in equal portions at the customary times, with the obligation to repair and maintain the property. *Et non licebit*, etc. G.: 10s.

1635 St. Ives Richard Baker: surrender of a half-row once held by John Boys, to the use of John Hamond and his wife, Agnes, for life, rendering annually 20s. in equal portions at the customary times, with the obligation to repair and maintain the property. *Et non licebit*, etc. G.: 20s.

1636 St. Ives Robert Chaumberleyn and his wife, Agnes: one row once held by John Clerk Fuller, for life, rendering annually 13s.4d. in equal portions at the customary times, with the obligation to repair and maintain the property. *Et non licebit*, etc. G.: 20s.

1637 St. Ives William French and his wife, Agnes: one row once held by John Gawtroun and recently held by John Meyke, for life, rendering annually 14s. in equal portions at the customary times, with the obligation to repair and maintain the property. *Et non licebit*. etc. G.: 6s.8d.

1638 St. Ives Henry Barbor and his wife, Johanna: three half-rows once held by John Clerke, rendering annually 26s.8d. in equal portions at the customary times, with the obligation to repair and maintain the property. *Et non licebit.* etc. G.: 6s.8d.

1639 St. Ives John Peek and his wife, Cecilia: a half-row recently held by John Tebbe and once held by Roger Chekesonde, for life, rendering annually 13s.4d. in equal portions at the customary times with the obligation to repair and maintain the property. *Et non licebit,* etc. G.: 6s.8d.

1640 St. Ives (May) Thomas Grigge and his wife, Beatrix: two half-rows once held by Robert Takil and recently held by Richard Fuller, for life, rendering annually 10s. in equal portions at the customary times, with the obligation to repair and maintain the property. *Et non licebit,* etc. G.: two capons.

1641 St. Ives John atte Wode and his wife, Margaret: a half-row once held by John Ryvenale, for life, rendering annually 24s. in equal portions at the customary times, with the obligation to repair and maintain the property. *Et non licebit,* etc. G.: 6s.8d.

1642 St. Ives John Cartere, alias Wale Smyth, and his wife, Helena: a half-row recently held by John Ravene and once held by John Hunne, for life, rendering annually 4d. in equal portions at the customary times, with the obligation to repair and maintain the property. *Et non licebit,* etc. G.: 6s.8d.

1643 St. Ives William Pope and his wife, Matilda: two half-rows next to Burylane recently held by John Fyllyngle and once held by John Peyntor, for life, rendering annually 9s. in equal portions at the customary times, with the obligation to repair and maintain the property. *Et non licebit,* etc. G.: one capon.

1644 St. Ives John Cartere, alias Wale Flecher, and his wife, Margaret: a half-row once held by John Baxtere and recently held by Roger Bumborough, for life, rendering annually 12s. in equal portions at the customary times, with the obligation to repair and maintain the property. *Et non licebit,* etc. G.: 5s.

1645 St. Ives Henry Goodman and his wife, Johanna: one row once held by William Couper and recently held by John Stodle, for life, rendering annually 13s.4d. in equal portions at the customary times, with the obligation to repair and maintain the property. *Et non licebit,* etc. G.: 5s.

1646 St. Ives John Tebbe and his wife, Margeria: a half-row once held by John Wylymot, for life, rendering annually 10s. in equal portions at the customary times, with the obligation to repair and maintain the property. *Et non licebit,* etc. G.: 10s.

1647 St. Ives Richard Baker and his wife, Margaret: a half-row once held by Richard Dewtre, for life, rendering to the lord annually 20s. in equal portions at the customary times, with the obligation to repair and maintain the property. *Et non licebit,* etc. G.: two capons.

1648 St. Ives William Judde and his wife, Emma: one shop with a solar, for life, rendering annually 16s. in equal portions at the customary times, with the obligation to repair and maintain the property. *Et non licebit,* etc. G.: two capons.

1649 St. Ives Walter Galopyn: surrender of one row, in which he lives, and one row once held by John Began, to the use of Robert Salesbury and his wife, Isabella, for life, rendering annually 15s.10d. during the lifetime of Walter, and 26s.8d. annually after his death, at the customary times, with the obligation to repair and maintain the property. *Et non licebit,* etc. G.: 26s.8d.

1650 St. Ives John Draper, recent servant of John Pulter, and his wife, Margaret: a half-row opposite the cross and one curtilage at the end of its garden once held by Thomas Caiso, for life, rendering annually in all things as did Thomas, with the obligation to repair and maintain the property. *Et non licebit,* etc. G.: 10s.

1651 St. Ives John Martyn and his wife, Katerina: one shop, rendering 6s.8d., at the river bank once held by John Bailly, with one shop with a solar on Bridge Street rendering 8s., and recently occupied by John Maddyngle, with another plot called "le Garith" built on the two shops, and a shop with a solar, the former rendering 12s., the latter rendering 20s., for life, rendering 36s.8d. in equal portions at the customary times, with the obligation to repair and maintain the property. *Et non licebit*, etc. G.: excused, because of repairs.

1652 WESTON John Wright pays 4s. for license to marry Margaret, his daughter and naif of the lord by blood, to Richard Decon of Barnwell, this time.

1653 WESTON Simon Selby and his wife, Johanna: one quarter of land once held by Longjonys and recently held by John Selby, with adjacent demesne land, for life, rendering annually in all things as did John. G.: three capons.

1654 WESTON Simon Hacoun: all the enclosure of the manor called Byggyng, for life, rendering annually 20s. at the customary times, with the obligation to repair and maintain the property, and with the condition that if Simon relinquishes or surrenders the property to the lord, the land that Simon received from his father, John Hacoun, without copy in 22 Thomas will he held null. G.: 20s.

1655 WESTON Richard Hacoun: one cotland with nine rods of land of the tenement of Hotoft's once held by William Wylby, for life, rendering annually 2s.6d. at the customary times. G.: excused because of repairs.

1656 ST. IVES The Prior of St. Ives: a certain parcel of a house situated at the western end of a plot held by Simon Tyler from the Prior next to the lane called Fresh Fish Lane, for life, rendering annually 6d. in equal portions at Michaelmas and Easter. Also: a certain waste lying between the above tenement and the common bank, which Simon occupied, with a pig-sty, reeds, thistles and other things dismissed to those coming to market, for life, rendering annually 12d., save that the road next to the plot up to the lane will be kept in the same condition as it was before this conveyance. He will repair and keep all the edge of the waste, and keep the lord abbot free from blame. G.: excused, because of repairs.

1657 RAMSEY John Sewer: from Brother William Bernewell, sub-cellarer, one parcel of meadow in Newmade called Ravenescorner, and five acres of land lying in Short-newfeld pertaining to the manor of Bigging, for life, rendering 9s. annually in equal portions at the feasts of the Annunciation and Nativity of Blessed Mary. *Et si predictus redditus*, etc. (arrears of one month). G.: 40d.

1658 BROUGHTON John Bone: surrender of one plot with a half-virgate of land once held by his father to the use of Simon Stoday and his wife, Johanna, in *major censum* for life, rendering annually 7s.4d. and all other customs rendered by those in *major censum*. G.: excused.

1659 BROUGHTON John Bone and his wife, Emma: one plot with a half-virgate of land once held by Corbie, *ad opus* for life, rendering annually as do other customaries *ad opus*. G.: two capons.

1660 BROUGHTON Thomas Styvecle: surrender of one built up messuage with two tofts and three semi-virgates to the use of his son, John Styvecle, for life, rendering annually in all things as did his father. G.: four capons.

1661 BROUGHTON William Smart and his wife, Agnes: one plot with a half-virgate of land and one pithel on the other side of the water, for life, rendering annually 7s.6d. in *major censum*, and all other customs rendered by those in *major censum*. G.: one capon.

1662 ELSWORTH John Brigges: one quarter of land recently held by John Howesson and once held by Roger Yntte, for life, rendering 3s.4d. annually at the customary times, with the first payment at the feast of St. Andrew next year. G.: 6d.

1663 ELSWORTH Thomas Aleyn: half of one quarter of Gravelond once held by Thomas Miller, and one quarter of land parcelled out of one virgate of Gravelond once held by William White and before that by Walter atte Wode, for life, rendering annually, for the quarter 3s.4d., and for the half-quarter, both as rent and tallage, 2s., in equal portions at the customary times. G.: 6d.

1664 ELSWORTH Thomas Lucas: the sixth part of the land of St. Luke once held by Walter Palfreyman and recently held by John Brok, for life, rendering annually 3s.4d. at the customary times. G.: 6d.

1665 ELSWORTH John Hardyng Jr: one quarter of the tenement of Alrehis once held by John Cook, and one quarter of land once held by John Clerk, for life, rendering annually 8s. at the customary times. G.: 6d.

1666 ELSWORTH William Athelstoun and his wife, Avis: one cotland and one croft recently held by William Thatcher and one croft recently held by William Thatcher and one toft with a croft recently held by John Hodest, for life, rendering annually in all things as did Thatcher and Hodest. G.: 14d.

1667 ELSWORTH William Wymond: one cotland recently held by Robert Miller, for life, rendering annually in all things as did Robert. G.: 14d.

1668 KNAPWELL John Pycot: one toft and a half-virgate recently held by William Bett, for life, rendering annually in all things as did William. G.: 12d.

1669 BYTHORNE William Godeselow: one quarter of land recently held by John Godeselow, and one cotland once held by Richard Evesham, for life, rendering annually in all things as did John and Richard. G.: three capons.

1670 BYTHORNE John Pumbray and his wife, Petronilla: a half-virgate of land with adjacent demesne land and one croft once held by Thomas Bole, for life, rendering annually in all things as did Thomas. G.: four capons.

1671 ELTON John Philip and his wife, Johanna: one virgate of land once held by John Colyn, for life, rendering annually in all things as did Colyn, and he will hold the property quit for the first four years because of repairs. Pledge for maintenance: John Waryn Sr. G.: three capons.

1672 ELTON John Bythorne and his wife, Agnes: one quarter of land once held by John Wrighte, for life, rendering annually in all things as did Wrighte, with the obligation to repair and maintain the property. G.: two capons.

1673 ELTON Same John Bythorne and Agnes: two cotlands in Oldmol once held by Radulph Baker and recently held by John Wrighte, for life, rendering annually in all things as did Wrighte. G.: excused by the seneschal.

1674 HOLYWELL Richard Smyth and his wife, Margaret: one plot with a half-virgate recently held by Thomas Edward, with all demesne land and its crop attached to it, for life, rendering annually in all things as did Thomas. G.: one goose and one capon.

1675 HEMINGFORD ABBOTS Robert White pays 6s.8d. for license to marry Agnes, daughter of William Heyne, naif of the lord.

105v **1676** HOUGHTON John Wyth Plowryte and his wife, Emma: three butts in Saltreweye next to Wodeweye, with one lot there once held by Galfridus Smyth, for life, rendering annually 8d. at the customary times. Also: one empty plot of one virgate with meadow called Bedelleslond until anyone else comes who wants to hold it, rendering annually 4s. at the customary times. G.: one capon.

1677 HOUGHTON John Wyth: one plot of one virgate once held by Nicholas Cristeyn and recently held by William Sleyn, until anyone else comes who wants to hold it, rendering annually 8d. at the customary times. G.: one capon.

1678 HOUGHTON John Bedell, alias Sandesson: one half-virgate of land once held by the rector, in *arentatio* for life, rendering annually 6s. at the customary times, with the condition that he will not relinquish any of that land to anyone. G.: one capon.

1679 HOUGHTON William Brampton and his wife, Agnes: one virgate of land once held by John By the Re and recently held by Stephen Marchall, for life, rendering 4s. this year and 9s. each year thereafter at the customary times. G.: excused.

1680 HOUGHTON John Cotene and his wife, Matilda: a half-virgate of land called Bellislond once held by Robert Upton, for life, rendering annually 6s. at the customary times. G.: excused, because he is a servant of the manor.

1681 HOUGHTON John Pope: one cotland once held by the rector, for life, rendering annually 6s. at the customary times, G.: ploughing for two days with his own plough, threshing for one day and winnowing for one day this year.

1682 HOUGHTON John Maddyngle and his wife, Cristina: a certain parcel of meadow in Wittonmede called Huddepool, for life, rendering annually 12s. at the feast of the Nativity of John the Baptist. G.: excused.

1683 WISTOW Richard Broun: one virgate of land once held by Nicholas Broun, in *arentatio* for life, rendering annually customs of the vill, three ancient ploughing *precariae* and one autumn *precaria*. Also: the reversion of one quarter of land now held by the same Nicholas, in *arentatio* for life, rendering annually in all things as Nicholas. G.: nine geese.

1684 WISTOW John Frere and his wife, Margaret: a half-virgate *ad opus*, a half-virgate in *secunda arentatio*, and one quarter of land in *arentatio* once held by Robert Waryn, for life, rendering annually in all things as did Robert. G.: 6s.8d.

1685 WISTOW John Aspelond: three quarters of land with a messuage once held by Walter Schepperd, for life, rendering annually 10s. at the customary times, customs of the vill, with the first payment at the feast of St. Andrew next year. G.: excused because of repairs.

1686 WISTOW Robert Nottyng pays one capon for license to marry Matilda, daughter of (*blank*) of Houghton, and no more because he surrendered one messuage next to the forge.

1687 WISTOW John Schepperd, alias Catelyn: surrender of one quarter of land *ad opus*, one quarter of land in *arentatio* and one acre of demesne in Lowefeld, to the use of William Warener Thakker and his wife, Mariota, for life, rendering annually 10s. for the two quarters, with customs of the vill, three ancient ploughing *precariae*, ploughing as he does on his own land, the Great *Precaria* of autumn, common fine in the leet, and 12d. for the acre of demesne, at the customary times. G.: excused because of repairs.

1688 WISTOW Reginald Grym Taillor and his wife, Agnes: one cotland with all adjacent land once held by John West, for life, rendering annually in all things as did John. G.: 40d.

1689 SLEPE Robert Chaumberleyn and his wife, Agnes: all parcels of the Outhousyerd recently held by John Clerk Fuller, for life, rendering annually 4s. at the customary times. G.: excused.

1690 WARBOYS Richard Sesterne and his wife, Beatrix: one dichmanland *ad opus*, two half-acres in Stokkyng, and three acres of Alsonslond recently held by his father, Roger Sesterne, for life, rendering annually in all things as did Roger. G.: 40d.

1691 ELLINGTON William Fowler: surrender of one plot with a half-virgate of land to the use of John Goodsped, for life, rendering annually in all things as did William. G.: 16d.

1692 CHATTERIS John Ingram: one messuage recently held by Adam Baxtere, for life, rendering annually in all things as did Adam. G.: 12d.

1693 CHATTERIS Nicholas Hamond: a parcel of one built up messuage with one cotland once held by John Clement, for life, rendering annually in all things as did John. G.: 12d.

1694 CHATTERIS John Cade: four acres and half of the meadow of one tenement of eight acres once held by Andrew Clement, for life, rendering annually in all things as did Andrew. G.: 40d.

1695 CHATTERIS John Therenesson: surrender of one cotland once held by William Taillor to the use of Hugo Chapman, for life, rendering annually in all things as did John. G.: 10s.

****

1 JOHN TYCHEMERSCH (1419-1420)

106r **1696** BURWELL Nicholas Lyne: one tenement of 20 acres recently held by Thomas Payer, for 30 years, rendering annually in all things as did Thomas, suit to court and leet, and one love boon. G.: two capons.

1697 BURWELL Thomas Payn: surrender of one plot once held by Simon Scot, to the use of John Benet and his wife, Margaret, for life, rendering annually in all things as did Thomas. G.: excused because of repairs.

1698 BURWELL Elisabeth Styward, naif of the lord by blood, pays 6s.8d. for license to marry.

1699 BURWELL Alicia Law: two cotes in Reche Assensum once held by Hugo Lawe, for six years, rendering annually in all things as did Hugo. G.: three capons.

1700 BURWELL John Saxtoun and his wife, Johanna: one cotland with adjacent croft once held by John Pury, for 22 years, rendering annually all services and customs owed therein. G.: two capons.

1701 BURWELL John Wylkyn and his wife, Oliva: one toft with adjacent croft, a parcel of one tenement of eight acres once held by Richard Berker, for 40 years, rendering annually 14d. at the customary times, with the obligation to build a grange on the toft within the next two years. Pledge: William Jay. G.: two capons.

1702 BURWELL Robert Wylkyn and John Wylkyn: one tenement of 24 acres once held by John Wyott, for 30 years, rendering annually 26s. at the customary times, common fine, holmsilver, when it occurs, raising or stacking hay for one day, one ploughing *precaria*, and all other services and customs rendered by Wyott, with no allowance granted for a mowed furlong on their land. G.: 3s.4d.

1703 ELSWORTH William Herry: one toft in Crane and one quarter of land once held by John Herry, for life, rendering annually 4s. and all other services and customs rendered by John. G.: 12d.

1704 ELSWORTH John Herry: a half-virgate once held by John Pycot with the capital messuage and a half-virgate once held by William Touselond, and one quarter of Cranelond with one cotland once held by Richard Schepperd and recently held by John Pycot, for life, rendering annually in all things as did Pycot. G.: 2s.

1705 ELSWORTH John Hardyng Smyth: one quarter once held by Alrede and recently held by Robert Broghyng, for life, rendering annually in all things as did Robert. G.: 12d.

1706 ELSWORTH John Waryn Jr.: one virgate once held by John Lucas and recently held by John, son of John West, for life, rendering annually in all things as did West. G.: 4s.

1707 ELSWORTH John Cristymesse: one cotland with a croft and six selions of land once held by John Dawys and recently held by John Hardyng, and two quarters of land once held by Walter atte Wode and recently held by John Cristemesse, for life, rendering annually 12s.8d. and all other services and customs owed therein. G.: two capons.

1708 ELSWORTH Thomas Connyng: one cotland called mondayland once held by Thomas atte Lane, and one quarter of land once held by John Howesson, for life, rendering annually 6s.4d. at the customary times. G.: two capons.

1709 HEMINGFORD ABBOTS Robert White: two messuages and two virgates recently held by John Selde, for life, rendering annually in all things as did John. G.: 10s.

1710 CHATTERIS John Beder: one tenement of eight acres once held by John Bele, for life, rendering annually in all things as did Bele, with the use of one long *camera* with annexed stable, the brew house, one eastern selion in a croft with a lodge, half of the fruit in the garden with free entry and exit, three selions of land — namely, one rod in any field — reserved for life to Margaret, widow of John Bele. He will repair and maintain the property at his own expense. G.: 33s.4d.

1711 CHATTERIS John Wedon: one tenement of eight acres with half of the meadow and fishponds once held by Robert Mathew, in bondage for life, rendering annually in all things as did Robert. G.: 6s.8d.

1712 CHATTERIS Richard Cokerell, one cotland with meadow in Oldhalow and a forland once held by John Cut of le Hythe, in bondage for life, rendering annually 3s.5d., as did John. G.: 6s.8d.

1713 BROUGHTON John Crowche and his wife, Johanna: one plot once held by Thomas Botiller next to the end of the village, and six quarters of land, for life, rendering annually in all things as did Thomas, with a relaxation of 20d. of rents any year. G.: six capons.

1714 WOODHURST William Trover and his wife, Isabella: one messuage and one virgate of land recently held by William Foster and once held by Nicholas Oky, for life, rendering 8s. this year, and each year thereafter as did Foster. G.: six capons.

1715 WOODHURST William Walton: surrender of one virgate to the use of Roger Laweman and his wife, Margaret, for life, rendering annually in all things as did William. G.: two capons.

1716 WOODHURST William Walton, alias Pope, and his wife, Margaret: 2 half-virgates of land once held by Trover, for life, rendering 4s.6d. this year and 9s. each year thereafter, at the customary times. G.: two capons.

1717 WOODHURST Robert Wryghte: surrender of one messuage and one virgate of land to the use of his son, John Wryghte and his wife, Alicia, for life, rendering annually in all things as did Robert. G.: cut down eight wagonloads of undergrowth, and collect two additional wagonloads of brush for the manor of Houghton.

106v **1718** SHILLINGTON CUM PEGSDON[38] John Schepperd and his wife, Agnes: one messuage and a half-virgate of land once held by Roger of the Hill and recently held by William Sperwe, and one lot of demesne land in Pegsdon, for life, saving the right of anyone, rendering annually all services and customs owed therein. G. and heriot: 20s.

1719 SHILLINGTON CUM PEGSDON John Laurence: surrender of one messuage and one virgate in Stondon, to the use of John Waryn, for life, rendering annually in all things as did John Laurence. G. and heriot: 13s.4d.

1720 SHILLINGTON CUM PEGSDON Robert Waleys and his wife, Margaret: one cotland with one acre of land once held by Robert Lewyn, for life, rendering annually in all things as did Lewyn. G.: 12d.

1721 SHILLINGTON CUM PEGSDON Richard Martyn: surrender of one parcel of land at Honythorn containing six acres, to the use of Nicholas Lambherd and Richard Colman, for life, rendering annually in all things as did Martyn. G.: 6s.

1722 SHILLINGTON CUM PEGSDON John Kychener: three acres in le Croft recently

[38] See PRO 179/56 for notice of William Sparwe's death.

held by himself, for life, rendering annually all services and customs owed therein. G.: 2s.6d.

1723 SHILLINGTON CUM PEGSDON John Grene: a half-virgate once held by his father, Richard Grene, and claimed by Adam Yonge, which claim failed when Adam was unable to find witnesses to the alleged surrender of the property to him by Richard; for life, rendering annually in all things as did Richard. G.: (*blank*).

1724 SHILLINGTON CUM PEGSDON John AtteWode: surrender of eight acres of land once claimed by John Kychener and John Grene, who alleged John AtteWode had surrendered the property to them outside the court, but which the said John denied, to the use of John Hamond and his wife, Margeria, for life, rendering annually in all things as did AtteWode. G.: 20d.

1725 SHILLINGTON CUM PEGSDON John atte Abbey pays 5s. for license to marry Helena, daughter of Henry Hamond and naif of the lord.

1726 CRANFIELD Agnes, daughter of Walter Rydeler and naif of the lord, pays 6s.8d. for license to marry, this first time, and for license to live off the manor until married.

1727 CRANFIELD John of the Hill pays 5s. for license to marry Margaret, his daughter and naif of the lord, to Thomas Rede, this time.

1728 CRANFIELD Thomas Catelyn Jr.: half of one virgate once held by Elias Smyth, in *arentatio* for life, rendering annually 10s. at the customary times. G.: 3s.4d., and no more because of 2s. paid for timber.

1729 CRANFIELD John Frayfeld: two acres of ancient demesne land once held by John Aleyn, for life, rendering annually 2s. at the customary times. G.: 8d.

1730 CRANFIELD Alicia, widow of Richard atte Wode: surrender of three quarters of land, to the use of William Warde, for life, rendering annually in all things as did Alicia, with one quarter of wheat and one quarter of barley reserved to Alicia annually for life. G.: 6s.8d.

1731 CRANFIELD William Aleyn: a half-virgate once held by John Aleyn, for life, rendering annually in all things as did John. G.: 2s.

1732 CRANFIELD William Wodill: one cotland with one acre of land and three and a half-acres of ancient demesne land once held by Payn and also once held by Johanna Bumbery, for life, rendering annually in all things as did Johanna. G.: 5s.

1733 CRANFIELD Thomas Milbroke: one cotland recently held *ad opus* and once held by Beatrix Scherman, for life, rendering annually in all things as did Beatrix. G.: 7s.

1734 CRANFIELD Thomas Aleyn: a half-virgate of land once held by John Aleyn and before that by Broghton, for life, rendering annually in all things as did John. G.: 40d.

1735 BARTON Simon Fraunces: surrender of one messuage and a half-virgate of land once held by John Fraunces, to the use of Walter Wylymot, for life, rendering annually in all things as did Simon. G. and heriot: 13s.4d.

1736 BARTON Richard Lorde: surrender of one cotland recently held by Thomas Carpenter to the use of Thomas Child, for life, rendering annually in all things as did Richard. G. and heriot: 2s.

1737 BARTON Thomas Martyn: one cotland once held by John Martyn, for life, rendering annually in all things as did John. G.: 3s.4d.

1738 BARTON Walter Wodeward pays 13s.4d. for license to marry Johanna, his daughter and naif of the lord, to Edmund Sampson, freeman.

1739 SLEPE John Bailly: one cotland next to Gravepitel once held by Nicholas Beaubras, for life, with tribute of sand sufficient for repairing the bridge of St. Ives reserved to the lord, and rendering annually 12d. at the customary times. In addition, he will pay William Herrof 7s. of the rents of his cotland in arrears. G.: excused.

1740 HOLYWELL Thomas Merton and his wife, Alicia: one plot with a half-virgate of land once held by Nicholas Godfrey, with all demesne land adjoining it, for life, rendering annually in all things as did Nicholas. G.: six capons.

1741 GRAVELEY Walter Newman pays 5s. for license to marry Agnes, daughter of Robert Newman and naif of the lord by blood, to Henry Wattes of Hardwick.

1742 GRAVELEY Robert Danyell: surrender of one messuage and a half-virgate of land once held by John Benet, to the use of William Smyth, for life, rendering annually in all things as did Robert. G.: 20d.

1743 WISTOW John Hyche Jr.: a half-virgate recently held by Thomas Breselaunce, with two cotlands and a half-virgate of land once held by Peter Waker, for life, rendering annually in all things as did Thomas and Peter. G.: 40d.

1744 UPWOOD Robert Wylde: surrender of one quarter of land, to the use of John Hurrd, and his wife, Agnes, for life, rendering annually in all things as did Robert. G.: two capons.

107r **1745** ST. IVES Thomas Ravene and his wife, Elizabeth: one row recently held by John Bocher, for life, rendering annually in all things as did John, with the obligation to repair and maintain the property. *Et non licebit,* etc. G.: 13s.4d.

1746 RAMSEY Richard Dewtre and his wife, Alicia: from Brother John Lavenham, sub-cellarer, one plot in le Wyght recently held by John Berdewell Sr., for life, rendering 8s. at the customary times. The sub-cellarer shall repair and maintain the property in all things the first time, and after that Richard and Alicia will repair and maintain it, and if they default in repairs, the sub-cellarer will retake the plot and retain it in perpetuity, without any contradiction. G.: 40d.

1747 CHATTERIS (25 March) John Sempool, alias Revessoun: the entire pasture of Hollode, with undergrowth, Newmade and "le pyngil" reserved to the lord, for 10 years, rendering annually £9 in equal portions at the feasts of St. Andrew and Michaelmas, with the obligation to maintain all the ditches. Nor may he cut down undergrowth, except at a reasonable time, nor make waste. If he dies within the term, the tenure will end and be null. G.: six capons.

1748 CHATTERIS (2 February) John Robyn of Bluntisham: the Newmade with one pyngil, for (*blank*) years, rendering to the lord annually £8., in equal portions.

1749 CHATTERIS John Wythed and his wife, Margaret: all lands and tenements once held by John Sempool Atte Chirche, for life, rendering annually in all things as did Sempool. G.: 40s.

1750 CHATTERIS John Kyng: one cotland once held by John Revenale and half of one tenement of eight acres once held by the same John, for life, rendering annually in all things as did Revenale. G.: 2s.

1751 GRAVELEY Thomas Robet, alias Ladde, and his wife, Agnes: one virgate and a half of land recently held by his mother, rendering annually in all things as did his mother. G.: 3s.4d.

1752 GRAVELEY William Robet pays 3s.4d. for license to marry Helena, his daughter, to Radulph of St. Neots.

1753 GRAVELEY Thomas Edward and his wife, Margaret: all lands and tenements recently held by William Smyth, for life, rendering annually in all things as did William. G.: 20d., and no more because of repairs.

107v **1754** ELLINGTON Thomas Burgeys pays 6s.8d. for license to marry Katerina, his daughter, to William Miller.

1755 UPWOOD (April) John Hikkysson: surrender of all the lands and tenements that he holds to the use of John Culpon, from Michaelmas for life, rendering annually in all things as did Hikkysson. G.: six capons.

1756 UPWOOD Richard Payn pays six capons for license to marry Alicia, daughter of William Howe and naif of the lord of Ripton, widow of William Justice of Broughton.

1757 BARTON John Grene and his wife, Katerina: one plot with one virgate of land once held by his father, for life, rendering annually in all things as did his father, Henry Grene. G. and heriot: 13s.4d.

1758 BARTON Reginald Pynchebek and his wife, Matilda: one cotland once held *ad opus* and held by John Richard and recently held by William Broun, for life, rendering annually in all things as did William. G.: and heriot: 13s.4d.

1759 HOUGHTON Robert Roger and his wife, Matilda: one toft and one virgate recently held by William Adekyn, for life, rendering annually 9s. at the customary times, with the first payment at the feast of St. Andrew next year. G.: ploughing for two days with his plough.

1760 HOUGHTON John Preston: one plot with a half-virgate of land once held by John Cartere, half of one plot with a half-virgate once held by William Aleyn, and one cotland containing a half-virgate once held by Alan Ede, for life, rendering annually 16s. and three ploughing *precariae*, ploughing as he does his own land, with the first payment at the feast of St. Andrew next year. G.: one capon.

1761 SLEPE Robert Wrighte and his wife, Agnes: one plot with a half-virgate of land once held by Marchaune and recently held by Botheby, and one empty plot with a half-virgate of land recently held by William Botheby and one cotland containing a half-virgate of land once held by the same William, for life, rendering annually for the cotland 8s., and for the two half-virgates in all things as did William, with the first payment at the feast of St. Andrew after one year. Also: the "Fynkilyerd" recently held by the same William, for life, rendering annually 5s. G.: one capon.

1762 HURST Stephen Warener, alias Cabe: surrender of one plot with two virgates once held by Reginald Canne, to the use of John Warde, and his wife, Agnes, for life, rendering annually in all things as did Stephen. G.: 6s.8d. and six capons.

1763 BROUGHTON Roger Aspelond and his wife, Margaret: one virgate with one pithel once held by Roger Aspelond, for life, rendering in all things as did Roger. G.: four capons.

1764 BROUGHTON William Justyce and his wife, Emma: all lands and tenements once held by his father, for life, with one plot and a half-virgate once held by Gerold reserved to the lord, and rendering to the lord annually in all things as did John Justyce. G.: four capons.

108r **1765** SHILLINGTON Johanna Burgeys: surrender of one messuage with one toft and two virgates with a forland to the use of John Clerk and his wife, Agnes, for life, rendering annually in all things as did Johanna. G. and heriot: 46s.8d.

1766 WESTON John Randolf pays 5s. for license to marry Margeria, his daughter, to John Detke, this time.

1767 BRINGTON (court) William Eston: one plot and one virgate recently held by Robert Asty, for life, rendering annually in all things as did Robert. G.: six capons.

1768 WARBOYS John Benet, naif of the lord, pays four capons for license to marry Anna, widow of Robert Morell of Houghton and daughter of William Adekyn of Houghton, naif of the lord.

1769 RIPTON Thomas Hawlond: the capital messuage of a half-virgate of land held by Roger Gardiner, for life, rendering annually 2s., with the obligation to repair and maintain the property. G.: three capons.

1770 HOLYWELL Simon Nicholas and his wife, Sarra: one virgate with adjacent new demesne land and one selion in Salmede once held by Thomas Nycholas, for life, rendering annually in all things as did Thomas. G.: 2s.

1771 HOLYWELL William Peek: one croft once held by Nicholas Baroun and one croft and two butts in a croft once held by John Schepperd, for life, rendering annually in all things as did John. G.: 2s. and two capons.

2 JOHN TYCHEMERSCH (1420-1421)

108v **1772** HOLYWELL John Sande and his wife, Margaret: a half-virgate with adjacent demesne land once held by Nicholas Baroun, for life, rendering annually in all things as did Nicholas. G.: 2s. and two capons.

1773 ST. IVES Thomas Barbor and his wife, Johanna: a half-row in le Schekker once held by William Moor, for life, rendering annually 8s. in equal portions at the customary times, with the obligation to repair and maintain the property. *Et non licebit*, etc. G.: 10s.

1774 ST. IVES Nicholas Bysschop: one row once held by Bellemen, for life, rendering annually 14s. in equal portions at the customary times, with the obligation to repair and maintain the property. *Et non licebit*, etc. G.: 10s.

1775 WARBOYS William London pays 6s.8d. for license to marry Agnes, daughter of John Berenger and naif of the lord, and for entry into one messuage and a half-virgate recently held by the same John, for life, rendering annually in all things as did John.

1776 CHATTERIS John Kyng. G.: 2s.

1777 BURWELL John Koole Jr.: one tenement of 15 acres recently held by his father, for life, rendering annually in all things as did his father, and suit to court and leet. G.: 3s.4d.

1778 SHILLINGTON CUM PEGSDON (27 September) Gilbert atte Hill and his wife, Margaret: the reversion of one plot with two virgates and adjacent demesne land, with one cotland and five acres of servile land, now held by his father, William Atte Hill, for life, rendering annually in all things as did William, saving always the heriot due to the lord after William's death. G.: 53s.4d.

1779 SHILLINGTON (September: at Broughton) William Atte Hill Jr.: the reversion of one plot with one virgate of land now held by his father, William Atte Hill, for life, rendering annually in all things as did his father. G.: 13s.4d.

109r **1780** GRAVELEY William Robat and his wife, Alicia: one plot with one virgate of land once held by Robert Denyell, for life, rendering annually in all things as did Robert. G.: four capons.

1781 ST. IVES Robert Wryghte and his wife, Agnes: a half-row lying opposite the booth recently held by William Botheby, for life, with the obligation to repair and maintain the property. *Et non licebit*, etc. G.: 13s.4d.

1782 CRANFIELD William Sowthwode, servant of Thomas Sowthwode: the reversion of a half-virgate of land with demesne land once held by the aforesaid Thomas, for life, rendering annually in all things as did Thomas, saving the heriot due to the lord at Thomas' death. G.: (*blank*).

1783 SHILLINGTON John Borugh, (at Ramsey): one messuage with a half-virgate of land once held by John Bernard, for life, rendering annually in all things as did John Bernard. G.: 3s.4d., and no more because the land has been in the lord's hands for a year.

1784 RAMSEY John Harhed and his wife, Johanna: one plot at Grene next to the plot of William Burton, for life, rendering annually 8s. in equal portions at the feast of the Annunciation and Nativity of Blessed Mary. Also: one plot with building at Grene recently held by Alicia Cartere, for life, rendering annually 5s.4d. at the terms above, with the sub-cellarer responsible for maintaining the property in all things except carpentry, roofing, wages and food for laborers. Further, John and Johanna may dismiss the property to anyone during their term, but if they are rebellious to the sub-cellarer in anything, he may expel them. G.: 3s.4d.

1785 RAMSEY William Borugh and his wife, Agnes: one plot at Grene next to the plot of John Wayte, for life, rendering annually 8s. in equal portions at the feasts of the Annunciation and Nativity of Blessed Mary, with the sub-cellarer responsible for maintaining the property. G.: 20d.

1786 RAMSEY John Barbor Jr. and his wife, Agnes: one plot at Grene next to that of Thomas Harpor, for life, rendering annually 8s. in equal portions at the feasts of the Annunciation and Nativity of Blessed Mary, with the sub-cellarer responsible for maintaining the property. G.: 20d.

1787 RAMSEY John Berdewell Jr. and his wife, Johanna: one plot in le Wyghte next to the plot of Richard Deutre, for life, rendering annually in all things 8s. in equal portions at the customary times. They may dismiss the property to anyone during the term, but if they are rebellious to the sub-cellarer in anything, he may expel them. G.: 20d.

1788 CRANFIELD John Robyn: half of one virgate once held by Thomas Catelyn Jr., for life, rendering annually in all things as did Thomas. G.: 3s.4d.

1789 CRANFIELD John Sare pays 3s.4d. for license to marry Isabella, his decrepit daughter, to John le Roodis, this time.

1790 BARTON (General Court: 24 October) William Revesson: one plot with one virgate once held by Agnes Falle, for life, rendering annually in all things as did Agnes. G. and heriot: 10s.

1791 BARTON (same court) William Revysson pays 13s.4d. for license to marry Isabella, his daughter, to Thomas Fenore of Dunstable.

1792 BARTON (same court) Jacob Child and his wife, Alicia: one plot with one virgate of land once held by his father, Richard Child, for life, rendering annually in all things as did his father. G. and heriot: 13s.4d.

1793 THERFIELD (leet) John Wynmer: surrender of one plot with one virgate, demesne land and other lands and tenements, to the use of his son, William Wynmer, and his wife, Felicia, for life, rendering annually in all things as did John. G.: six capons.

1794 THERFIELD Thomas Colle and his wife, Agnes: one plot with one virgate, demesne land and other lands and meadow lands recently held by his father, for life, rendering annually in all things as did his father. G.: six capons.

1795 BURWELL (leet) Thomas Goodynche and his wife, Cristina: one tenement of eight acres once held by John Purye and recently held by John Jay, for 30 years, rendering annually in all things as did John Jay. G.: 3s.4d.

1796 BURWELL (same leet) Robert Wyot and his wife, Margaret: one tenement of 20 acres once held by John Wyot Midwyf, his father, for 30 years, rendering annually in all things as did John. G.: 3s.4d.

1797 BURWELL (same leet) Thomas Rower pays 3s.4d. for license to marry Alicia, his daughter and naif of the lord by blood, to William Hurton, this time.

1798 BURWELL Nicholas AtteHiil and his wife, Cecilia: one tenement of 20 acres that he previously held, for 20 years, rendering annually in all things as he did previously. G.: 3s.4d.

1799 BURWELL (court) John Lyne Jr. and his wife, Agnes: one tenement of 20 acres *ad opus* recently held by Thomas Peyer, for life, rendering annually in all things as did Thomas, and suit to court and leet. G.: two capons.

1800 ELSWORTH (leet) William Michell and his wife, Margaret: one plot with a half-virgate of land once held by Roger Yntte, for life, rendering annually 10s. and all other services and customs owed therein. G.: 2s.

1801 ELSWORTH (same leet) William Athirston: from the lord one cotland with one quarter of land and two tofts once held by Janyn Frenchman, for life, rendering annually in all things as did Janyn. G.: 2s.

110r **1802** ELSWORTH (leet) John Beysworth and his wife, Johanna: a half-virgate of land once held by John in the Hirne, of Gravelond, for life, rendering annually 6s.8d. at the customary times, with the first payment at the feast of St. Andrew next year. G.: 6s.8d.
1803 ELSWORTH (same leet) John Brook and his wife, Margaret: a half-virgate of land of Graveland recently held by John Wymond, for life, rendering 6s.8d. at the customary times, with the first payment at the feast of St. Andrew next year. G.: 12d.
1804 ELSWORTH (same leet) Richard Braughyng: surrender of one cotland with one quarter of land once held by John Bette, and one quarter with a third part of one quarter of Gravelond once held by John Cowherde, to the use of John Wrighte and his wife, Johanna, for life, rendering annually in all things as did Richard. G.: 10s.
1805 RAMSEY (November) John Broun: one vaccary called Newstede, from the previous Michaelmas by copy for three years, rendering annually as he was accustomed to render by one copy previously made, namely 3s.4d. to the sub-cellarer. G.: 6s.8d. with which the sub-cellarer burdens himself for this year.
1806 ELLINGTON John Thacker: one messuage with a half-virgate of land in Sibthorp once held by William Fowler, for life, rendering annually in all things as did William. G.: 20d.
1807 UPWOOD (Christmas Week) William Edward Jr.: one plot with a half-virgate of land once held by Thomas Wardebusk and recently held by John Milis, in *arentatio* for life, rendering annually 8s. at the customary times, with the first payment at the next feast of St. Andrew, and with the obligation to repair and maintain the property at his own expense, except for timber sufficient for the first repairs of the plot. G.: two capons.
1808 HEMINGFORD ABBOTS John Smyth and his wife, Margaret: one plot and one and a half virgates once held by John Jurdon, for life, rendering annually in all things as did John Jurdon. G.: 6s.8d.
1809 UPWOOD John Milis and his wife, Agnes: one plot with five quarters of land recently held by Andrew Balle, for life, rendering annually in all things as did Andrew. G.: works.
1810 WARBOYS Agnes Margrete, daughter of Richard Margrete and naif of the lord by blood, pays 20s. for license to marry Richard Ferror of Earith.
1811 BRINGTON John Purye pays six capons for license to marry Alicia, his daughter, to William Galyoun.
110v **1812** RAMSEY John Wayneman and his wife, Margaret: from the subcellarer, Brother John Lavenham, one plot with building in Grene, rendering annually 6s.8d. in equal portions at the feasts of the Annunciation and Nativity of Blessed Mary. They will repair and maintain the building and pay wages for carpenters, roofers and laborers, with the sub-cellarer supplying timber, thatch, brush, undergrowth and clay for the walls, its transport, and bread and ale for the carpenters, etc. repairing the building. G.: 20d.
1813 BROUGHTON (April) John Clerk and his wife, Agnes: one cotland (or mondayland) recently held by William Everard with three selions of land and one selion of land at Olddole, for life, rendering annually 3s. for the cotland, which used to render 3s.2d., 12d. for the three selions, and 6d. for the selion in Olddole, with the first payment at the next feast of St. Andrew. G.: excused because of repairs.
1814 ST. IVES (April) William Smyth Barker and his wife, Margaret: two rows once held by John Meelton, for life, rendering annually 12s. in equal portions at the customary times, with the obligation to repair and maintain the property. *Et non licebit*, etc. G.: 13s.4d.

1815   ST. IVES John Elys and his wife, Margaret: a half-row in which Wylymot once lived, for life, rendering annually 12s. in equal portions at the customary times, with the obligation to repair and maintain the property. *Et non licebit*, etc. G.: 10s.

1816   ST. IVES Robert Pappeworth and his wife, Emma: a half-row recently held by John Wylymot, for life, rendering annually 10s. in equal portions at the customary times, with the obligation to repair and maintain the property. *Et non licebit*, etc. G.: 10s.

1817   ST. IVES John Chasteyn, alias Fyscher, and his wife, Alicia: a half-row once held by Alicia Fother and recently held by John Asplond, for life, rendering annually 13s.4d. in equal portions at the customary times, with the obligation to repair and maintain the property. *Et non licebit*, etc. G.: 13s.4d.

1818   ST. IVES Peter Cut and his wife, Emma: a half-row once held by Simon Legge, for life, rendering annually 13s.4d. in equal portions at the customary times, with the obligation to repair and maintain the property. *Et non licebit*, etc. G.: 13s.4d.

111r   **1819**   ST. IVES William in the Herne, alias Sadiller, and his wife, Agnes: a half-row once held by Thomas Belleman, for life, rendering annually 15s. in equal portions at the customary times, with the obligation to repair and maintain the property. *Et non licebit*, etc. G.: two capons.

1820   ST. IVES John Cooke and his wife, Margaret: a half-row abutting the pig-sty of the manor and once held by Robert Trym, for life, rendering annually 8s. in equal portions at the customary times, with the obligation to repair and maintain the property. *Et non licebit*, etc. G.: 20d.

1821   ST. IVES Thomas Gritton and his wife: two half-rows once held by Robert Takill, for life, rendering annually 10s. in equal portions at the customary times, with the obligation to repair and maintain the property. *Et non licebit*, etc. G.: 3s.4d.

1822   ST. IVES William Knotte, alias Nichool, and his wife, Johanna: a half-row once held by Simon Legge and recently held by William Faun, for life, rendering annually 13s.4d. in equal portions at the customary times, with the obligation to repair and maintain the property. *Et non licebit*, etc. G.: 6s.8d.

1823   SLEPE Richard Eyr and his wife, Alicia: one plot once held by Margeria Dene with one lane recently held by John Marcheaunt, for life, rendering annually 4s.4d. at the customary times. G.: 12d.

1824   SHILLINGTON John Grene and his wife, Isabella: one plot with one virgate of land once held by his father, Robert Grene, for life, rendering annually in all things as did Robert, with the condition that if John and Isabella do not live there, they will find a proper tenant to live there; otherwise this conveyance will be null. G.: 13s.4d.

1825   UPWOOD Agreement that Richard AtteWell will hold a cotland in Wodestrete that he now holds and one virgate once held by William Alcok, for life, rendering for this year and the next, 7s.6d. for the virgate and for the cotland as he is accustomed to render, and for all properties 18s. each years thereafter, namely: 15s. for the virgate and 3s. for the cotland, with no capons or hens, and no *gersuma*.

1826   HOLYWELL John Lanender and his wife, Agnes: one plot with one virgate and all other demesne land once held by Richard Scot, for life, rendering annually in all things as did Richard. G.: 13s.4d.

1827   RAMSEY William Lystere and his wife, Johanna: from Brother John Lavenham, sub-cellarer, one plot with building recently held by William Cook, for life, rendering annually 12s. at the feasts of the Annunciation and Nativity of Blessed Mary, with the sub-cellarer responsible for maintaining the property. G.: 3s.4d.

111v   **1828**   RIPTON (July) William Amery and his wife, Katerina: one messuage with a half-virgate recently held by John Buk and once held by Gilbert de Hirst, for life, rendering annually in all things as did John, with the obligation to repair the property within the next two years, the lord granting timber, all the goods of John Brook found this day in the manor, and an allowance of rents until Michaelmas next year. William will find a pledge for holding to these conditions. G.: three capons.

1829   CHATTERIS (27 June: court) John Tyd and his wife, Agnes: one cotland recently held by Simon Peroun and once held by Cartere, for life, rendering annually in all things as did Simon. G.: 3s.4d.

1830   CHATTERIS (same court) John Hertford Jr., alias Jongeioun: one cotland once held by Bettyssoun, for life, rendering annually in all things as did Bettyssoun. G.: 6s.8d.

1831   CHATTERIS (same court) Thomas Bronne and his wife, Margaret: one cotland at Pekkysland recently held by Agnes Seempool, for life, rendering annually in all things as did Agnes. G.: 12d.

1832   CHATTERIS (same court) Thomas Lytholf Jr. and his wife, Alicia: half of one tenement of eight acres recently held by John Somersham, for life, rendering annually in all things as did John. G.: excused because of repairs.

1833   CHATTERIS (same court) Thomas Page and his wife, Alicia: all lands and tenements once held by Stephen Peyte, for life, rendering annually in all things as did Stephen. G.: 8d.

1834   CHATTERIS (same court) Robert Enyfeld: all lands and tenements once held by Agnes Enyfeld, for life, rendering annually in all things as did Agnes. G.: 6s.8d.

1835   CHATTERIS (same court) John Massely Jr. and his wife, Margaret: one tenement of eight acres once held by Thomas Poppe, and one cotland and four acres recently held by his father, for life, rendering annually in all things as did his father. G.: 10s.

1836   CHATTERIS (same court) Robert Clerk pays 6d. for license to marry Margaret, widow of John Byller, and for entry into one messuage and three rods of land once held by John.

1837   CHATTERIS (same court) John Pykerell: one cotland once held by Richard Pyper, for life, rendering annually in all things as did Richard. G.: three capons.

1838   BYTHORNE (court) Robert Brewys: one cotland recently held by John Inglysch, for life, rendering annually in all things as did John. G.: three capons.

1839   BRINGTON (same court) Richard Wrighte pays 20d. for license to marry Matilda, widow of William Gander, and for entry into William's tenement.

1840   KNAPWELL (court) John Reignald: one quarter of land once held by John Russell, for life, rendering annually in all things as did Russell. G.: 16d.

1841   SLEPE John Frary pays 6s.8d. for license to marry Alicia, daughter of Simon Herrof and naif of the lord by blood, widow of William Thressher.

1842   SLEPE John Frary and his wife, Alicia: all lands and tenements recently held by William Thressher the day he died, for life, rendering annually in all things as did William. G.: 3s.4d.

112r   **1843**   ELTON (leet: 30 December) Thomas Fauconer: one cotland with garden recently held by Richard Hobard, for life, rendering annually in all things as did Richard. G.: one capon.

1844   ELTON (same leet) John Bryan: one messuage with a half-virgate of land once held by John Newman, for life, rendering annually in all things as did Newman, with the first payment at the next feast of St. Andrew. G.: four capons.

1845   ELTON (same leet) Edward Tayllor: one messuage and one quarter recently held by Richard Abbot, for life, rendering annually in all things as did Richard. G.: three capons.

1846 WYTON (20 November: leet) John Newman: one messuage and a half-virgate of land recently held by John Kebbe, one messuage with a half-virgate of land recently held by Henry Lawe, and one cotland recently held by the same Henry, for life, rendering annually 15s., three ploughing *precariae* with the lord's plough, mowing for one day in the meadow, making hay for one day, and mowing in autumn for one day, with one laborer. G.: 12d.

1847 WYTON (same leet) John Upton: one messuage with one virgate of land once held by Nicholas Marshall and a half-virgate recently held by Robert Upton, for life, rendering annually in all things as did Robert. G.: three capons.

1848 WYTON (same leet) John Bedyll: surrender of one messuage and one and a half virgates to the use of John Mayhew, for life, rendering annually in all things as did Bedyll. G.: 12d.

1849 HOUGHTON (same leet) John Wyth: one cotland with garden recently held by John Gerard, for life, rendering annually 2s. at the customary times. G.: excused, because he is a carpenter of ploughs in the manor.

1850 WYTON (same leet) Thomas Crane and his wife, Margaret: one messuage with one virgate of land once held by John Bonde and a half-virgate called Holderneslond recently held by Robert (Upton), for life, rendering annually in all things as did John. G.: 2s.

1851 WARBOYS (leet) John Heryng: one tenement called mondayland recently held by Thomas Bere and one toft with one quarter of land once held by the same Thomas in Caldecote, for life, rendering annually in all things as did Thomas. G.: two capons.

1852 RIPTON (leet) Richard Smyth and his wife, Johanna: one toft and a half-virgate recently held by Haywarde and one toft with a half-virgate recently held by Neve and once held by William Smyth, and three acres of Penylond, for life, rendering annually in all things as did William. G.: 5s.

1853 RIPTON (same leet) William Fuller: one croft called Cranescroft, next to Haywardes, for life, rendering annually 2s. at the customary times. G.: 12d.

1854 NEEDINGWORTH (leet) John Porter: one cotland with two acres of land, of which one lies in Stonydole and the other in Smethes, for life, rendering annually 16d. for the cotland, 12d. for Stonydole and 16d. for Smethes, with the obligation to repair and maintain the property. G.: 12d.

1855 WOODHURST William Waryn: surrender of a certain parcel of one virgate of land recently held by Thomas Wyngore, to the use of John Lawe, for life, rendering annually 8d., with the obligation to repair and maintain the property, for which repairs the lord will relax the 8d. rent. G.: 6s.8d.

1856 BARTON John Roger: surrender of the capital messuage of a half-virgate recently held by William Atte Chirche, to the use of John Davitt, and his wife, Emma, for life, rendering annually all services and customs owed therein, and another rent to the tenant of the half-virgate. G.: 12d.

112v **1857** RAMSEY William Botiller and his wife, Johanna: from Brother John Lavenham, sub-cellarer, the fishpond around Newmade, Swonhousmede, Brentymede, both within and without, outside the fishpond next to that parcel of meadow in Swonhousmede held now by Thomas Brewster, recently held by John Boorwell, for 20 years, rendering annually 2s. in equal portions at the feasts of the Annunciation and Nativity of Blessed Mary, with the sub-cellarer responsible for repairing and maintaining the ditches. Further, he may not relinquish the property without the lord's license. *Et si predictus redditus,* etc. G.: 20d.

1858 WARBOYS Margaret, daughter of Thomas Molt, pays 3s.4d. for license to marry John Skynner of Huntingdon. Alicia, daughter of the same Thomas, pays the fine for license to marry Thomas Scot of Godmanchester.

1859 SHILLINGTON Adam Jonge and his wife, Margaret: one long stable with two new buildings set up by John Hamond, a parcel of a garden, and one lot and eight acres of demesne land recently held by John Hamond, for life, rendering annually in all things as did John. G.: 13s.4d.

3 JOHN TYCHEMERSCH (1421-1422)

1860 KNAPWELL (leet: 29 September) John Pycot: one messuage with croft and one quarter of land recently held by John Pykerell, for life, rendering annually in all things as did John Pykerell. G.: two capons.

1861 WOODHURST (leet) Thomas Del Hill: one messuage and a half-virgate of land recently held by Thomas Trover and William Whalton, for life, rendering annually in all things as did Thomas and William. G.: two capons.

1862 RIPTON (leet) John Margerisson: one cotland and a half-virgate of land recently held by Adam Clerk, for life, rendering annually in all things as did Adam. G.: two capons.

1863 NEEDINGWORTH (leet) Roger Hunne: one messuage with one virgate and two acres of Penylond recently held by Thomas Grandoun, for life, rendering annually in all things as did Thomas. G.: 20s.

1864 SHILLINGTON John Clerk and his wife, Agnes: a half of one culture of demesne land at Hanscombe recently held by Gilbert atte Chirche, for life, rendering annually in all things as did Gilbert. G.: six larks.

1865 THERFIELD John Wenham pays 3s.4d. for license to marry Emma, daughter of John Colle and naif of the lord by blood, this time.

1866 THERFIELD (18 December: leet) John Colle Jr.: one messuage and one quarter of land recently held by John Frere, for life, rendering annually in all things as did Frere. G.: three capons.

1867 THERFIELD (same leet) John Ryflee: surrender of four acres of land at Buryhill recently held by William Wyngor, to the use of Robert Caldewell, for life, rendering annually 2s. G.: one capon.

1868 BURWELL (leet) Matilda Hals: surrender of one tenement of 15 acres recently held by Nicholas Hals, to the use of Thomas Hals, for 30 years, rendering annually in all things as did Matilda. G.: 16s. and two capons.

1869 BURWELL (same leet) Hugo Sayer: one cotland recently held by Thomas Sayer, his father, for life, rendering annually 2d. G.: three capons.

1870 WISTOW John Newman: surrender of a half-virgate in *arentatio* and one quarter of land in *secunda arentatio*, to the use of Richard Randolf, for life, rendering annually 12s. and all other services and customs rendered by John. G.: three capons.

1871 WISTOW Richard Wyllysson: one cotland in *arentatio* and one toft once held by Anna Gette by ancient customs and recently held by Anota Baroun, in bondage for life, rendering annually in all things as did Anota. G.: three capons.

1872 WISTOW John Asplond: two quarters of land once held by Anota Baroun and Richard Baroun, in bondage for life, rendering annually in all things as did Anota and Richard, with the obligation to build an *insathous* of six binding-posts on the tenement once held by Walter Shepperd before the next Michaelmas, otherwise this conveyance will be null. G.: 3s.4d. and 12 capons.

1873 WISTOW John Plumbe and his wife, Johanna: three quarters of land once held by Walter Schepperd and a half-virgate of land once held by John Owty Thakker and once held, also, by Henry Hych, in bondage for life, rendering annually 7s. for the half-virgate and for the rest as did Walter Schepperd. G.: six capons.

113r

1874 Wistow John Asplond: a half-virgate once held by Richard Baroun, in bondage for life, rendering annually 8s. and all other services and customs rendered by Richard, with the first payment at the feast of St. Andrew next year, because the land is fallow. G.: six capons.

1875 Wistow William Derworth and his wife, Johanna: a half-virgate in *arentatio* once held by Robert Wodecok and one messuage without a building next to the forge once held by John Schepperd, in bondage for life, rendering annually 8s., customs of the vill for the virgate, and 3s. for the messuage. G.: one capon.

1876 Wistow Richard Benet and his wife, Alicia: one virgate of land and a half-quarter of land *ad opus*, one acre at Lowefurlong once held by John Bokelond, and one-quarter of land in *secunda arentatio* once held by Robert Wrighte, in bondage for life, rendering annually all services and customs owed therein. G.: 6s.8d.

1877 Wistow John Owty and his wife, Alicia: one virgate of land *arentatio* once held by William Derworth, in bondage for life, rendering annually in all things as did William. G.: 12 capons.

1878 Wistow Richard Wrighte: one quarter of land in *arentatio* once held by himself, in bondage for life, rendering annually as he previously did. G.: one capon.

113v   **1879** Wistow Richard Aylmar and his wife, Johanna: one and a half quarters of land in *arentatio*, one hidemanland in *arentatio*, three rods of land at Litilhill and a half-acre of demesne land at Lowfurlong once held by John Love, for life, rendering annually in all things as did John. G.: six capons.

1880 Wistow Thomas Fraunce: one quarter of land once held by Richard Wrighte and once held also by John Wrighte, in *arentatio* for life, rendering annually in all things as did Richard. Thomas will pay half of the rents this year, with Richard Wrighte paying the other half. G.: one capon.

1881 Wistow (leet) John Helmesle: one acre lying at Wysweel and one acre at Nomanstond, rendering 16d., one acre at Waterlond, rendering 16d., and one acre called Gillecroft rendering 12d., for life, rendering annually 3s.8d. G.: three capons.

1882 Wistow William Wyllyam and his wife, Alicia: a certain part of a hydemanland with all land recently held by Thomas Botyller, for life, rendering annually 4s. at the customary times. G.: one capon, and no more because of a rent increase.

1883 Wistow John Wrighte pays one capon for license to marry Margaret, daughter of Robert Atte Gate (Yate), naif of the lord by blood.

1884 Weston (leet) Walter Barton: one messuage and a half-virgate of land once held by Roger Wattesson, with all demesne land and hotofts adjoining it, for life, rendering annually in all things as did Roger. G.: three capons.

1885 Weston Roger Man pays 40d. for license to marry Margaret, his daughter and naif of the lord by blood, to anyone, this time.

1886 Elton John Munde: all lands and tenements once held by Thomas del Le, for life, rendering all services and customs owed therein, with the first payment at the next feast of St. Andrew. G.: three capons.

1887 Elton John Philip Sr.: one messuage and one virgate of land once held by Reginald Coop, for life, rendering annually all services and customs owed therein. G.: 12d.

1888 Barton (leet) Nicholas Child: one croftland containing three acres of land once held by his father, Edmund Child, for life, rendering annually in all things as did Edmund. G.: 2s.

1889 Barton (same leet) John Chaloner: one cotland and one croftland recently held by John Smyth, for life, rendering annually in all things as did John Smyth. G.: 12d.

1890 BARTON (same leet) Richard Roger: one rod of meadow called Eylote once held by William Roger, for life, rendering annually in all things as did William. G.: one capon.

1891 BARTON (same leet) Thomas Wodeward: one croft once held by John Colman, for life, rendering annually   in all things as did John. G.: 20d.

1892 BARTON (same leet) Maria Lyly pays 15d. for having entry into one messuage and one cotland recently held by her husband, Richard Lyly.

114r **1893** BARTON (same leet) Emma, widow of John Alyn and tenant of one cote with one acre recently held by her (late) husband, marries. Heriot: 2s.

1894 HOLYWELL Thomas Nycholas pays three capons for license to marry Agnes, his daughter, to John Warde, this time.

1895 SHILLINGTON (leet) John Grene: a half-virgate recently held by John Ede, for life, rendering annually in all things as did Ede. G.: 10s.

1896 SHILLINGTON (same leet) John Warde: one croft called Murellcroft, once held by John Murell, for life, rendering annually in all things as did Murell. G.: 10s.

1897 SHILLINGTON (same leet) Henry Hamond: three acres lying in Stokkyng recently held by Adam Smyth, for life, rendering annually in all things as did Adam. G.: 12d.

1898 SHILLINGTON (same leet) John Grene of Wode ende: a half-virgate of land once held by John Ede, for life, rendering annually in all things as did Ede. G.: 5s.

1899 SHILLINGTON (same leet) Thomas Stonle: a half-virgate of land called Stokwellond once held by John Ede, for life, rendering annually in all things as did John. G.: 40d.

1900 SHILLINGTON (same leet) William AtteHill of Pegsdon pays 5s. for license to marry Maria, his daughter and naif of the lord by blood, to John Sampson, this time.

1901 SHILLINGTON (same leet) John Coke: one messuage and a half-virgate of Wodehallond recently held by Isabella Howson, for life, rendering annually in all things as did Isabella. G.: 2s.

1902 SHILLINGTON John Borugh pays 2s. for license to enter into one plot with one virgate of land once held by Robert atte Grene and recently held by William Lewyn, belonging by right to his wife, Margaret, daughter of the aforesaid William Lewyn, for life, rendering annually in all things as did William, with the obligation to rebuild the messuage — burned this year — within the next seven years at their own expense. Further, John is granted two oak trees and certain of the chattels and goods of William for 20s., with one multon, a nursing ewe, and a nursing lamb reserved to the lord as the heriot of William and his wife.

1903 WARBOYS (leet) John Waleys: one messuage and one mondayland recently held by John Swyer, and one messuage and one mondayland recently held by William Altheworld, for life, rendering annually 6s. and all other services and customs owed therein. G.: six partridges.

1904 WARBOYS (same leet) Richard Smyth: one messuage and a half-virgate recently held by Richard Eyr, for life, rendering 6s. the first year and thereafter as did Richard Eyr. G.: two capons.

1905 WARBOYS (same leet) John Hy Sr. and his wife, Katerina: one cotland with adjacent croft and two acres at the end of the croft, for life, rendering annually 3s. G. excused by the seneschal.

1906 UPWOOD John Fox and Thomas Smyth: a half-virgate of land once held by John Of the World and recently held by John Vernoun, and half of Stubbydole and Bennydole, for life, rendering for the half-virgate 4s. this year, and 8s. each year thereafter, and 5s. for the two parcels, at the customary times. G.: two capons.

114v **1907** SLEPE (court) Robert Wrighte: surrender of one messuage and a half-virgate recently held by William Botheby, to the use of Thomas Hemyngford and his wife, Margaret, for life, rendering annually in all things as did Robert. G.: 40d.

1908 SLEPE (same court) John Pulter: surrender of one croft with one dovecote called Haulercroft once held by John Roger, to the use of Thomas Buk, for life, rendering annually in all things as did John. G.: 40d.

1909 HURST (19 October) Thomas Warde: one messuage, one cote, one virgate, one toft and a half-virgate in Woodhurst recently held by Thomas Cok, for life, rendering annually in all things as did Cok. G.: 40s.

1910 WESTON William Wrighte of Swavessey pays 26s.8d. for license to marry Agnes Hacoun, daughter of John Hacoun and naif of the lord by blood.

1911 CHATTERIS (court) Thomas Russell: one tenement of eight acres recently held by Walter Russell, for life, rendering annually in all things as did Walter. G.: 40d.

1912 CHATTERIS (same court) John, son of John Kokerell: one cotland recently held by John Cokerell Sr., for life, rendering annually in all things as did John Sr. G.: 3s.4d.

1913 CHATTERIS (same court) Robert Clerk: one cotland recently held by John Byller, for life, rendering annually in all things as did John. G.: 8d.

1914 CHATTERIS (same court) John Ingram: one cotland once held by John Lawe and one acre of land at Pakerelldole, for life, rendering annually all services and customs owed therein. G.: 20d.

1915 CHATTERIS (same court) John Sempool: one tenement of eight acres with meadow in Eldhalf and a forland with one selion at "long grane" once held by John Berle, for life, rendering annually in all things as did Berle. G.: 10s.

1916 CHATTERIS (same court) John Brabon Webstere: one cotland once held by Thomas Fyshher, for life, rendering annually in all things as did Thomas. G.: 40d.

1917 CHATTERIS (same court) John Smyth: one tenement of eight acres with meadow in Crowlode once held by John Chounesson, for life, rendering annually in all things as did Chounesson. G.: three capons.

1918 CHATTERIS (same court) John, son of John Lytholf: one tenement of eight acres with meadow in Heldhalf, with a fishpond called Thommysdam Pakerell, with cotland once held by Thomas Reede, for life, rendering annually in all things as did Thomas. G.: three capons.

1919 CHATTERIS (same court) John Cade: one cotland with one adjacent butt once held by Nicholas Thakker, for life, rendering annually in all things as did Nicholas. G.: 2s.

1920 CHATTERIS (same court) Agnes, widow of John Pyroun: surrender of half of one cotland and half of the fishpond of Woolverwer, the fourth part of Achynwer and the fourth part of Redestachwer once held by John Pyroun, to the use of William Wodereve, alias William Pyroun, for life, rendering annually in all things as did John. G.: 6s.8d.

115r **1921** CRANFIELD (leet) Thomas Pury: one croft containing six acres of land called Hokeslond once held by John atte Cros, for life, rendering annually 6s.8d. and suit to court. G.: 10s.

1922 CRANFIELD (same leet) William Curteys: a half-virgate of land and one cotland recently held by Robert Alyn, for life, rendering annually in all things as did Robert. G.: 40d.

1923 CRANFIELD (same leet) Thomas Sowthwode: surrender of one messuage and a half-virgate of land to the use of William Gosvill, for life, rendering annually in all things as did Thomas, provided that William will supply Thomas and his wife, Johanna, with food and clothing for life. G.: 13s.4d.

1924 Cranfield (same leet) William Grene: three acres and three rods and one croft called Chapell Croft and three and a half acres of demesne land once held by William Grene, his father, for life, rendering annually in all things as did William. G.: 5s.
1925 Cranfield (same leet) Thomas Hayne: surrender of one cotland and a half-acre of land to the use of John Aleyn Smyth, for life, rendering annually in all things as did Thomas. G.: 12d.
1926 Cranfield (same leet) William Pury: one cotland with buttland once held by Emma Stokker, for life, rendering annually in all things as did Emma. G.: 12d.
1927 Cranfield (same leet) Roger Dowesson: one cotland and six acres of demesne land at Puryhill and two acres at Staliplace and two acres at Burysouth Woode recently held by Richard Catelyn, for life, rendering annually in all things as did Richard. G.: 5s.

115v **1928** Ramsey John Deneys: from Brother John Lavenham, sub-cellarer, one piece of land in Birdecroft once held by John Morton, for life, rendering annually 5s. in equal portions at the feasts of the Annunciation and the Nativity of Blessed Mary. Also: two acres of meadow in Newmede next to Ravenes Corner, the length of one corner in the north to the other corner, for life, rendering annually 5s.8d. at the customary times. G.: three capons.
1929 Ramsey John Braban and his wife, Alicia: from the sub-cellarer one messuage next to the tenement held by John Chamberleyn, for life, rendering annually 12s. in equal portions at the feasts of the Annunciation and Nativity of Blessed Mary, with the sub-cellarer responsible for maintaining the property. G.: 3s.4d.
1930 Ramsey John Hotwode and his wife, Margaret: one messuage once held by Thomas Brigge, for life, rendering annually 8s. at the customary times, with the sub-cellarer responsible for maintaining the property. G.: three capons.
1931 Ramsey John Fyscher: one meadow called Hidele recently held by John Schirwode, for life, with all profits and appurtenances, according to the terms set down in his copy, rendering to the lord annually 26s.8d. at the feasts of the Annunciation and Nativity of Blessed Mary, with the exception that three acres reserved to Henry Parker, who pays the aforesaid John 3s. annually, in aid of his farm. G.: 6s.8d.
1932 Ramsey Thomas Brigge: one perch of meadow with fishpond and willows in Swonhousmede in the northern part, for life, rendering annually 6s.8d. in equal portions at the customary times, with the obligation to maintain all the ditches, with Welwrowe, around that perch. G.: three capons.
1933 Bigging (September) John Hurre, of Upwood: in the time of Brother John Lavenham, sub-cellarer, 18 heads of meadow next to Nesthallepyghtill in the fields of Upwood, for life, rendering 2s.4d. in equal portions at Michaelmas and Easter; and he will not relinquish the property without the lord's license. *Et si predictus redditus*, etc. (arrears of one month). G.: six pullets.

4 JOHN TYCHEMERSCH (1422-1423)

116r **1934** Warboys (leet) Johanna Bowde: surrender of one quarter of land *ad opus* in Caldecote, half of one plot and a half-virgate *ad opus* in Caldecote, one dichmanland *ad opus* in Warboys once held by Simon Hy, with three rods of land in Stokkyng and one acre of demesne land at Barfurlong and one and a half-acres of demesne land at Bascroft, to the use of William Oundill and his wife, Cristina, for life, rendering annually 9s.1d. and all other services and customs rendered by Johanna, provided that William cede to Johanna one *camera* at the back of the bake house, one *camera* at the back of the grange, and one selion in a garden at the eastern end abutting the marsh, and one shed next to the above for impounding animals, with access to the bake house for brewing, access to the great gate, and one plot for supplying fuel, which Johanna will repair and maintain and for which she will supply one laborer in autumn for two days in reaping or tying grains. G.: one capon.

1935 WARBOYS (same leet) Richard Covyngton and his wife, Mariota: one mondayland once held by John Dally Sr., in *arentatio* for life, rendering annually 3s. at the customary times, and customs of the vill, with the obligation to repair and maintain the property. G.: three capons.

1936 WARBOYS (same leet) Thomas Berenger: one built up dichmanland with houses once held by John Hy Sr. in *arentatio* and one mondayland once held by John Brownote, with 12 acres of Alsonyslond, four acres and one rod of demesne land Galinghill and two acres in Holland, for life, rendering annually 13s.4d. at the customary times, customs of the vill, including three autumn *precariae* commuted to 4d. G.: 20d.

1937 WARBOYS (29 September) John (?) Covyngton: the windmill there, from the previous Michaelmas for 10 years, rendering annually 40s. at four customary times, with the obligation to maintain the mill after its repair by the lord, within and without, including the mill cote, with the lord repairing the axel and wheel and supplying timber, its transport, boards, stones, iron works, one bushel and one toll-dish provided that if the mills falls into disrepair in any of the above, the lord will grant the mill to another *firmarius*. In addition, John obligates himself to the lord for £20. G.: six capons.

1938 WARBOYS Thomas Baroun and his wife, Agnes: one quarter of land in *arentatio* and a half-virgate of land *ad opus* once held by John Herryesson, and a half-tenement of akirmanland in *arentatio* with meadow called Wodecokysmede recently held by William Baroun, his father, for life, rendering annually in all things as did William. G.: six capons.

1939 WARBOYS Richard Hervy: one tenement with one virgate of land in Caldecote in *arentatio* once held by his father, John Hervy, for life, rendering annually 8s. at the customary times, with the obligation to rebuild the *insathous* within two years at his own expense, except for timber from the lord. Also: one grange on the property of his brother, John Hervy, with the obligation to repair and maintain it, with the first payment at the feast of St. Andrew after two years. G.: three capons.

1940 WARBOYS John Hervy Jr.: one built up tenement with one virgate of land in *arentatio* once held by Richard Nonne and recently held by William Benson, with one grange reserved for the lord, for life, rendering annually 12s. in equal portions at the customary times, with the obligation to repair and maintain the property, with timber supplied by the lord. G.: three capons.

1941 BROUGHTON (leet) John Broun Smyth: one capital messuage of a half-virgate of land recently held by Thomas Pecher, alias Couper, with three lots of a tenement recently held by John de Dam, of which two were once held by Pynchebek and one was held by William Asplond, for life, rendering annually 5s. at the customary times, customs of the vill and one autumn *precaria*. G.: one capon.

1942 BROUGHTON (same leet) John Cabe: surrender of one virgate, one quarter and one messuage, to the use of William Cabe, for life, rendering annually in all things as did John. Further, John will have three acres and half of one solar next to one acre, one *meghstede* in the acres and eastern part of the garden, easement in the bake house and entry and exit with his wagon, fine for one pig sty, and easement in one house for two years. G.: six capons.

1943 BROUGHTON (same leet) Thomas Pulter: one messuage with a half-virgate of land once held by John Couper, one messuage and one quarter of land once held by Simon Dam and one empty plot with a half-virgate of land once held by John Grymesby, for life, rendering annually as did John Bygge. G.: 10s.

1944 BROUGHTON (same leet) Roger Castre: a half-virgate of land, three quarters, one lot of Damslond and the capital messuage of that land once held by Thomas Neel, for life, rendering annually in all things as did Thomas. G.: 10s.

1945 BROUGHTON (same leet) Edward Justyce: one messuage and a half-virgate of land *ad opus* once held by Thomas Broughton, a half-virgate in *minor censum* once held by the same Thomas, and a half-virgate in *major censum* once held by Alicia Justyce, for life, rendering annually in all things as did Thomas, together with receiving one lot once held by Thomas, with the condition that he maintain all the buildings on that property.

1946 BROUGHTON John Clerk and his wife, Agnes: one cotland or mondayland recently held by William Everard, with three selions of land at Oldole, for life, rendering annually 3s. for the cotland, 12d. for each selion, with one selion excused payment, with payments to begin at the next feast of St. Andrew. G.: excused because of repairs.

1947 BROUGHTON (December) John Fylhous: a half-virgate of land once held by William Oftheworld, for life, rendering annually in all things as did William, with the first payment at the next feast of St. Andrew. G.: two capons.

1948 BROUGHTON William Clerk pays six capons for license to marry Johanna, daughter of William Justice and naif of the lord by blood, this time.

1949 RIPTON (leet) John Lyndesey: one empty toft and a half-virgate of land recently held by John London and once held by Nicholas AttHill, in *secunda arentatio* for life, rendering annually in all things as did London. G.: two capons.

1950 RIPTON (same leet) William Halsham: one messuage once held by John Wake, for life, rendering annually in all things as did John, with the first payment at the feast of the Discovery of the Holy Cross. G.: excused because of repairs.

1951 RIPTON (13 December) William Savage: a parcel of land recently held by John Decon in Stokkyng, from the previous Michaelmas for seven years. William is allowed to cut down all the saplings that Adam le Dene once held, and to cut down undergrowth when he pleases. He will repair all hedges and enclosures around Brynde and Stokkyng, and maintain them at his own expense, dismissing those hedges and enclosures at the end of the seven years sufficient for one more year. In addition, the lord will supply one wagon, this year, for four days for carrying the undergrowth, and William will sustain all those parcels at his own expense, together with the entire coppice and spring around the saplings. Further, William will receive 6s.8d. for repairs at the beginning, and afterwards he will receive 6s.8d. from the lord from the sale of the saplings. And for greater secutiry, he obligates himself to the lord for £10. G.: excused by the lord.

1952 HOUGHTON (leet) William Atkyn: surrender of one messuage and one virgate of land *ad opus,* one virgate of land in *arentatio* and one croft in *arentatio,* to the use of his son, Richard, for life, rendering annually in all things as did William, with one *camera* in the garden and three rods in the fields reserved to William for life. G.: two capons.

1953 HOUGHTON Thomas Elyot: one messuage with a half-virgate of land once held by Robert Morell, for life, rendering annually 6s.8d. in equal portions at the customary times. G.: two capons.

1954 HOUGHTON Thomas Andrew: a half-virgate of land once held by his father, in *arentatio* for life, rendering annually 6s. in equal portions at the customary times, with

117r

the condition that his father, Peter Andrew, will rebuild the *insathous* of six binding-posts. Pledges: Thomas Andrew and William Andrew. G.: 6d.

1955 HOUGHTON John Somersham, alias Gerard: one cotland in *arentatio* and one and a half-virgates in *arentatio* called Grymeslond, for life, rendering annually 16s. in equal portions at the customary times and one ploughing *precaria*, as he ploughs on his own land. In addition, he will rebuild the cotland within three years, for which repairs he will have an allowance of half of this year's rent. Pledge: his father. G.: two capons.

1956 HOUGHTON William Prikke and his wife, Agnes: one virgate of land once held by Gilbert de Houghton and recently held by Galfridus Smyth, for life, rendering annually 7s. in equal portions at the customary times. G.: six capons.

1957 HOUGHTON John Marchall: one vacant plot with one virgate of land and one parcel of meadow of Honymede recently held by the rector, *ad opus* for life.

1958 HOUGHTON (January) John Symond: one messuage and a half-virgate of land recently held by Preston and once held by William Aleyn, in bondage for life, rendering annually 5s.4d. at the customary times, with the first payment at the next feast of St. Andrew. In addition, he will render one ploughing *precaria* and one autumn *precaria* annually. G.: one goose and one capon.

1959 HOUGHTON Thomas Foster and his wife, Margaret: the full messuage with a half-virgate recently held by Robert Morell, for life, rendering annually 5s. at the customary times, with the first payment at the next feast of St. Andrew, and one ploughing *precaria* and one autumn *precaria*, with the obligation to repair and maintain the property. G.: one capon.

1960 HOUGHTON William Andrew and his wife, Margaret: half of one toft with a half-virgate of land called Lonyslond, for life, rendering annually 5s. In addition, both for this half-virgate and another half-virgate called Palmerys that he holds, he will render all works and customs as do those who hold one virgate *ad opus*. G.: two capons.

1961 HOUGHTON (May) John Newman and his wife, Johanna: one messuage with a half-virgate of land once held by John Cros and one empty plot with a half-virgate of land once held by William Wrighte, for life, rendering annually 10s. and all other customs rendered by those *ad opus*, with the first payment at the next feast of St. Andrew. He will repair the *insathous* and all other buildings within three years, with timber supplied by the lord, and if he fails to make repairs, his annual rent will be 14s. G.: three capons.

1962 HOUGHTON Robert Mason and his wife, Isabella: a half-virgate of land once held by John Cook, for life, rendering annually 4s. at the customary times, with the first payment at the next feast of St. Andrew. G.: two capons.

1963 HOUGHTON Thomas Grave: one virgate of land once held by Robert Betoun and recently held by John Cross, for life, rendering annually 10s. at the customary times, with the first payment at the next feast of St. Andrew, and with the obligation to repair and maintain the property. G.: two capons.

1964 HOUGHTON John Upton and his wife, Margaret: one toft and one virgate of land once held by his father, for life, rendering annually 10s. and all other works and customs rendered by other customaries. In addition, he will repair a bake house on the property this year, for which he pays only 5s. in rent this year. G.: two capons and ploughing for one day.

1965 HOUGHTON John Marchall Jr.: one toft and one virgate of land called Dylemaker, with one acre of meadow called Honymede once held by Bokyngham, for life, rendering for the acre of meadow 2s. this year, and 10s. each year thereafter, at

117v

the customary times, as well as ploughing two acres of land, mowing in the meadow
for one day, and mowing for one day in autumn. In addition, the first payment will be
at the next feast of St. Andrew. G.: excused.

1966   ST. IVES John Denyas and his wife, Custancia: one cotland in the lane with
four acres of land in the fields, for life, rendering annually 10s. in equal portions at the
customary times, with the obligation to maintain the property. *Et non licebit*, etc. G.:
three capons.

1967   ST. IVES John Lystere and his wife, Margaret: one parcel of one cotland in the
lane now held by John Denyas, and the reversion of another cotland and four acres of
land after the death of John Denyas and his wife, Custancia, for life, rendering annually 2s.4d., and after the reversion, 10s., at the customary times. G.: 3s.4d.

1968   ST. IVES (November) John Martyn and his wife, Katerina: one shop now filled
with stones, at the river bank, recently held by John Chesteyn, for life, rendering annually 16s. in equal portions at the customary times, with the obligation to repair and
maintain the property. *Et non licebit*, etc. G.: excused, because of repairs.

1969   ST. IVES (November) John Martyn and his wife, Katerina: all easements at
Eebryngke, against all tenements and shops they hold from the lord, for supplying
both charcoal and reeds for fuel, saving always the reasonable use for diverse things
by merchants and the community, and saving always the lord's amercements in his
court according to the custom of the vill.

118r   **1970**   ST. IVES Frederick Skynnere and his wife, Agnes: a half-row recently built up
and once held by John Redere, for life, rendering annually 3s.4d. at the customary
times, with the obligation to repair and maintain the property. *Et non licebit*, etc. G.:
two capons.

1971   ST. IVES Same Frederick Skynnere and Agnes: a half-row in Bridge Street
previously held by himself, for life, rendering annually 24s. in equal portions at the
customary times, with the obligation to repair and maintain the property. *Et non
licebit*, etc. G.: two capons.

1972   ST. IVES (February) John Maboun and his wife, Margaret: a half-row recently
held by Adam Smyth, for life, rendering annually 10s. at the customary times, with the
obligation to repair and maintain the property. *Et non licebit*, etc. G.: three capons.

1973   ST. IVES John Denyas and his wife, Constancia: one cotland in the lane with
four acres of land, for life, rendering annually 2s.4d. in equal portions at the
customary times, with the obligation to repair and maintain the property. *Et non
licebit*, etc.

1974   BURWELL (19 October: leet). Thomas Koole: one tenement of 20 acres once
held by John At Hill, in *arentatio* for 20 years, rendering annually in all things as did
John, and suit to court and leet. G.: 2s.

1975   BURWELL (same leet) John Rolf Jr.: one tenement of 15 acres once held by
John Fraas, in *arentatio* for 30 years, rendering annually in all things as did Fraas. G.:
3s.4d.

1976   BURWELL (same leet) John Dene: one tenement of 20 acres recently held by
Thomas Pury, excluding the messuage and croft, for 20 years, rendering annually
13s.4d. and all other services and customs rendered by Thomas, including suit to
court. G.: 20d.

1977   BURWELL (same leet) William Taillor: half of one tenement of 24 acres once
held by William Crabbe, for 20 years, rendering annually in all things as did William
Crabbe, and suit to court. G.: four bushels of wheat.

1978   SHILLINGTON (16 October: leet) Thomas Iselham Jr.: one croft with one acre
of land once held by John Howson, for life, rendering annually in all things as did
John. G.: 12d.

118v **1979** BARTON (17 October: court) Henry Burrich: surrender of one messuage and one adjacent virgate of land recently held by Adam Taillor, to the use of Thomas Colman, for life, rendering annually in all things as did Henry. G. and heriot: 6s.8d.

1980 BARTON (same court) Henry Cademan: surrender of one messuage and one virgate of land, to the use of Isabella, wife of Thomas Wylymot, for life, rendering annually in all things as did Henry. G. and heriot: 4s.

1981 BARTON (same court) John Broun: one messuage and one virgate of land once held by Thomas Broun, for life, rendering annually in all things as did Thomas. G.: 12d., and no more, because he previously payed 13s.4d. for the lands of Fally and lost his copy.

1982 BARTON (same court) John Baroun: surrender of a half-virgate of land, to the use of Thomas Swayne, for life, rendering annually in all things as did John. G.: 3s.4d., and no more because the land is fallow.

1983 BARTON (same court) Agnes Fally: surrender of one messuage and one virgate of land recently held by William Fally, to the use of Edmund Sampson, for life, rendering annually in all things as did Agnes. G. and heriot: 12s.

1984 BARTON (same court) John Prior Sr.: one messuage and one virgate once held by John Prior, his father, for life, rendering annually in all things as did his father. G.: 6s.8d.

1985 BARTON (same court) Simon Fraunceys: one messuage and one virgate of land once held by John Geffrey, for life, rendering annually in all things as did John. G.: 12s.

1986 BARTON (same court) Richard Lord: surrender of one cotland once held by Thomas Carpenter, to the use of Thomas Pope, for life, rendering annually in all things as did Richard. G. and heriot: 3s.4d.

1987 ELSWORTH (14 October: leet) Maria Chircheman: two cotes recently held by John Chircheman, for life, rendering annually in all things as did John. G.: two capons.

1988 ELSWORTH (same leet) Thomas Sonnyng: one cotland, one quarter and one croft once held by William Brige, for life, rendering annually in all things as did William. G.: 12d.

1989 CRANFIELD (leet) John Wodhill: two acres of land in Litelhaus once held by John Donwode, for life, rendering annually in all things as did John Donwode. G.: 2s.

1990 CRANFIELD (same leet) John Joye: one cotland with adjacent garden recently held by Alexander Joy, chaplain, for rendering annually in all things as did Alexander. G.: 12d.

1991 CRANFIELD (court) Johanna, widow of William Wassyngle: one toft with a half-virgate of servile land recently held by William and once held by John of the Mede, for life, rendering annually 13s.6d., *capitagium* of 2d., and all other services and customs owed therein. In addition, she will not dig *gabulum*, but she will cut timber within the vill to rebuild the toft and pay 10s. heriot when it occurs. Also: seven acres of land at Bretyndenbush, for life, rendering annually 7s. at the customary times. Nor will she dismiss her status in that land to anyone, under pain of forfeit, and she will not enter into that land before next Michaelmas. G.: 6s.8d.

119r **1992** WESTON (leet) Simon Selby: one messuage and a half-virgate of land once held by William Wilby and Adam Cartere, for life, rendering annually in all things as did William and Adam, with the first payment at the feast of the Nativity of John the Baptist. G.: three capons.

1993 WESTON (31 May: court) William Fleshewer: half of one cotland and half of one quarter of land with appurtenant demesne land and Burylond recently held by

Henry Possewyk, for life, rendering annually 5s.11d.ob. and all other services and customs rendered by Henry. G.: two capons.

1994   WESTON (same court) John Kyng Jr.: one quarter of land with adjacent demesne land recently held by Simon Selby, for life, rendering annually in all things as did Simon. G.: two capons.

1995   ELTON (leet) Robert Dalton: one cotland with adjacent croft once held by Thomas Fauconer and one curtilage recently held by John Hiche, for life, rendering annually in all things as did John. G.: one capon.

1996   ELTON (same leet) Richard AtteWode: one toft and one quarter of land once held by John Munde, for life, rendering annually in all things as did John. G.: two capons.

1997   ELTON (same leet) William AtteGate: three acres of land recently held by Henry Atte Gate Schepperd, his father, for life, rendering annually in all things as did Henry. G.: two capons.

1998   ELTON (same leet) John Bythorne: two acres of land lying at Tollowes recently held by John Wright, for life, rendering annually 12d. Also: one messuage and a half-virgate once held by John Bryan, for life, rendering annually in all things as did Bryan. G.: one capon.

1999   ELTON Thomas Rede: one messuage and one virgate in Overton once held by William Taillor, for life, rendering annually 18s. and all other services and customs owed therein, with payments for the first four years excused because of repairs. Further, if he fails to make repairs, the land will be seized.

2000   ELTON John West: a half-virgate of land once held by his father, John West, for life, rendering annually in all things as did his father. G.: 3s.4d.

2001   ELTON Thomas Mokke: a half-virgate of land recently held by Thomas Gymbir in Cotoun, for life, rendering annually 10s. and all other services and customs owed therein. G.: (*blank*).

2002   BRINGTON John Dalby pays 10s. for license to marry Agnes, daughter of John Beverich and naif of the lord by blood, this time.

2003   BRINGTON (11 January) Thomas Sandir: surrender of three messuages and three quarters of land and ancient and new demesne land with Brokelond, to the use of John Dalby and his wife, Agnes, for life, rendering annually in all things as did Thomas. G.: three capons.

2004   BRINGTON (court) Simon Hunte: one quarter of land once held by William Bryngton, excluding a cotland and meadow called Burymede, for life, rendering annually in all things as did William. G.: 40d.

2005   BRINGTON John Bacheler and his wife, Johanna: a half-virgate of land with the land of Holwell and ancient and new demesne land once held by William Betonsone, for life, rendering annually in all things as did William. G. excused because of repairs.

2006   BRINGTON William Bacheler and his wife, Helena: three quarters of land with ancient and new demesne land recently held by his father, John Bacheler, for life, rendering annually in all things as did John. G.: 20s., assigned to John Bacheler for repairs to his tenement.

119v   **2007**   *Novus Locus* John Broun: one vaccary called Newstede, from the next Michaelmas for five years rendering to the sub-cellarer as he used to render according to his copy, and further, in the name of victuals (?), which the sub-cellarer is accustomed to receive, 3s.4d. G.: 5s.

2008   HEMINGFORD ABBOTS Thomas Awyngewyn and his wife, Johanna: all lands and tenements recently held by Robert Brendhous, excluding one cotland and a half-virgate now held by John Brendhous, for life, rendering annually in all things as did Robert. G.: 20s.

2009 CHATTERIS (court) John Skakedale: surrender of one cotland recently held by Richard Sempool to the use of Nicholas Dagworth, for life, rendering annually in all things as did John. G.: 12d.

2010 CHATTERIS (same court) Robert Clerk: surrender of one cotland once held by John Biller to the use of Edmund Lytholf, for life, rendering annually in all things as did Robert. G.: 12d.

2011 CHATTERIS John Hobkyn and his wife, Margaret: all lands and tenements previously held by him, for life, rendering as he previously rendered, with the provision that half a tenement of eight acres held by Margaret Mathew stand in the lord's hands because of default. (*Note added*: Now he will hold that half-tenement, or supply a proper tenant, under penalty of loss of meadow he holds in Crowlode). G.: 6s.8d.

2012 CHATTERIS John Smyth Jr. and his wife, Alicia: in place of John Revenhale, half of one tenement of eight acres previously held by John Kyng, with all other parcels specified in the Rental for this year, for life, rendering annually in all things as did Kyng. G.: 6s.8d.

2013 CHATTERIS (court: June) Margaret Dobyn: one cotland recently held by John Ingram, for life, rendering annually as did John, namely: 15d. G.: 4d.

2014 CHATTERIS (same court) John Thomson: one messuage in which Robert Clerk lives, and three rods of land in Elmen once held by John Byller, for life, rendering annually 3d. for the messuage and 9d. for the three rods. G.: one capon.

2015 CHATTERIS (March) Andrew Clement and John Clement: the manor of Hunneye, with all pastures, fishponds and appurtenances, from the previous feast of the Purification for 10 years, rendering annually 66s.8d. in equal portions at the feasts of St. Peter in Chains and the Nativity of Blessed Mary. They will repair the vaccary and maintain it thereafter in carpentry, roofing, walls, plastering, if it pleases the lord to give them sufficient timber and its transport to the manor. But they will carry the timber from the manor of Chatteris to the manor of Hunneye at their own expense. In addition, they may cut down all the undergrowth they want both in Hunneye and its appurtenant marsh at an appropriate time, and for the repair of the building, they may cut down all willows at will and reasonably plant new willows in their place. Further, they will repair and maintain all ditches of the manor and its appurtenant marsh, and keep the manor with all pastures and fishponds in their private use and liberty. The lord grant them an allowance of two marks, namely: one mark from each term until Andrew Clement is reimbursed for all his expenses as owed by the abbot, provided always that the said *firmarius* concede to John Colles of Huntingdon the right to have pasture in the first year, for which John will pay the lord half the farm. G.: two capons, two cranes, two bitterns.

120r **2016** SLEPE Frederick Skynnere and his wife, Agnes: one quarter of land and one cotland once held by Thomas Wrighte, for life, rendering annually 18s. for works and rents, at the customary times, common fine, and all other royal services. G.: excused.

2017 SLEPE Same Frederick Skynner and Agnes: one lot of the tenement of Bastler previously held by Frederick himself, for life, rendering annually 10d. per acre, with the first payment at the feast of St. Andrew nex year. G.: excused.

2018 SLEPE Alicia, daughter of Thomas Cut and naif of the lord by blood, pays 3s.4d. for license to marry John Fyscher of St. Ives, this time.

2019 GRAVELEY Elena, daughter of Walter Newman and naif of the lord by blood, pays 20d. for license to marry John Warwik, who is held to maintain and repair his tenement or find a tenant for the land who will do so, should he go away, or to pay 20s. when leaving.

2020 GRAVELEY Richard Dyke: one messuage and a half-virgate of land once held by William Smyth, for life, rendering annually in all things as did William. G.: 16d.

2021 GRAVELEY William Bukby pays 6s.8d. for license to marry Alicia, daughter of John (*blank*) and naif of the lord by blood, to John Denysforthe of Yaxley, carpenter.

2022 KNAPWELL Henry Prest and his wife, Johanna: a half-virgate of land *ad opus* recently held by John Smyth, for life, rendering annually all services and customs owed therein. Also: a quarter of land, for life, rendering annually 11s.8d. at the customary times. G.: 2s.

2023 KNAPWELL (February) John Joye and his wife, Johanna: a half-virgate of land recently held by William Bette, for life, rendering annually 11s.8d. at the customary times, with the first payment at the next feast of St. Andrew. G.: 12d.

2024 THERFIELD John Attenok Sr., of Sandon, pays the lord 13s.4d. for license to marry Agnes, daughter of William Waryn and naif of the lord by blood, the first time, and John will pay 12d. annually for chevage and license to have the said Agnes in his service until married.

2025 THERFIELD John Attenok Jr. pays 13s.4d. for license to marry Edith, daughter of William Waryn and naif of the lord by blood, the first time, and he will pay 12d. annually at Easter for chevage and license to have Edith in his service until married.

1026 THERFIELD William Waryn, naif of the lord, by blood, will pay the lord 2s. annually at Easter for license to live at Sandon for as long as it pleases the lord, remaining a naif as before, and coming annually to the leet.

2027 THERFIELD Simon Attenok of Sandon pays 16s.8d. for license to marry Margaret, daughter of William Waryn and naif of the lord by blood, the first time, and he will pay 12d. annually at Easter for chevage and license to have Margaret in his service until married.

2028 THERFIELD John Kook: one virgate of land with one pithel and one quarter of land, 18 acres of new demesne land, and one meadow called Nestmede, for life, rendering annually as he previously rendered.

2029 THERFIELD Same John Kook: one enclosed meadow called Cotecroft, in support of the aforesaid meadow, for life, rendering annually 10s., which meadow previously rendered 13s.4d. G.: two capons.

2030 THERFIELD Adam Taillor: one meadow called Wattesmede, for life, rendering annually 10s. at the customary times, provided that the lord can seize the said meadow and dismiss it to anyone after advising Adam of this at the leet before Michaelmas, except that Adam will be preferred over all others if he wishes to give for it as much as another. G.: one capon.

2031 HOLYWELL Johanna, daughter of Thomas Edward and naif of the lord by blood, of Needingworth, pays six capons for license to marry William Alenger, servant of Thomas Newman of Warboys, this time.

120v **2032** SHILLINGTON (1 November) Thomas Bradyfan and his wife, Alicia: a certain part of the manor there, namely: the hall with annexed camera, chapel, kitchen, bake house, kiln, abbot's bower, pig-sty, new stable with dovecote, the adjacent garden, and certain parcels of garden lying for pasture as meted and bounded, for life, rendering annually 6s.8d., with all the above buildings reserved to the lord or his *familia* when they come. Also: a large grange and granary, a parcel of a garden, and two lots of demesne land once held by John Waryn and Thomas Hamond, for life, rendering annually 3s. for the granary, grange and parcel of garden, and 15s. for the two lots, at the customary times. Also: two lots recently held by William Coche, for life, rendering annually 15s., with the obligation to repair and maintain all the buildings with the two parcels of the manor, at his own expense, except for timber, splints, and poles from the lord as determined by the seneschal or his deputy. In addition, Thomas will reasonably receive *housbote, haybote, fyrbote,* as much as and whenever obtained, at the judgment of the above, and he will support all the lands and plots and all burdens which other tenants of lots support, nor may he give away any of the property to anyone without the lord's license, except that he may grant all the above to his son, Robert, for fixing a dwelling there for life. Nor may he put himself under the protection of any other lord to the prejudice of the lord or damage to his neighbors, under pain of forfeit. And he will provide for the lord's *familia* and their horses, receiving the usual allowance. G.: 20s.

2033 SHILLINGTON John Wildefowll and his wife, Johanna: one messuage and one virgate of land once held by Thomas Olys and recently held by Gilbert Brook, for life, with the obligation to repair and maintain the property. If he defaults in making payments, the lord shall seize the property, with all its chattels and goods, without any contradiction. G.: excused.

2034 THERFIELD Thomas Angetill and his wife, Elena: the kitchen of the manor with one cotland once held by Andrew Fayrman, with six acres of land from the tenement of Peter Branncaster previously held by the same Thomas, 13 and a half-acres of the same tenement recently held by the rector, and six acres of the same tenement recently held by Thomas Gamyn, for life, rendering annually in all things as did the previous tenants. G.: (*blank*).

5 JOHN TYCHEMERSCH (1423-1424)

121r **2035** HOUGHTON Robert Bocher: one messuage and one virgate of land *ad opus*, two half-virgates of land in *arentatio*, one cotland in *arentatio*, and three selions of land at Burywell once held by John Pope and recently held by John Gowler, for life, rendering annually 32s. in equal portions at the customary times, with the obligation to repair and maintain the property. Also: in the messuage, one querne, one wagon, all the hay from two acres of meadow, and 13s.4d. in silver, to be restored at the end of his term. G.: two capons.

2036 HOUGHTON (leet) John Marschall: a half-virgate of land without a croft once held by John Sandir and called Pollyslond, for life, rendering annually 4s. at the customary times, with the first payment at the feast of St. Andrew after one year. G.: excused.

2037 HOUGHTON (same leet) John Whaplode Jr.: one toft and one virgate of land once held by John atte Pool and afterwards by John Whaplode Sr., for 10 years, rendering annually 8s. at the customary times. G.: excused.

2038 HOUGHTON John Elyot pays 6s.8d. for license to marry off his daughter, Alicia, naif of the lord by blood, this time.

2039 BURWELL (8 October) John Catelyn, chaplain, and John Ideyne, alias Rolf, will pay 2s. annually for license to have a fold, at the will of the lord, within the domain on both villein and demesne land, for as long as it pleases the lord. Fine: excused.

2040 BURWELL (leet) Thomas Notewyn and his wife, Maria: the capital messuage with croft and three rods of land of one tenement of eight acres held by Robert Edrich *ad opus* and once held by Richard Fabbe, and five and a half acres of demesne land, of which two acres lie in Dichefeld, two acres in Estfeld, and one and a half acres in Bradweye, for 40 years, rendering annually 2s.6d. for the capital messuage, and to the *firmarius* 5s.6d. for the five and a half acres, at the customary times, as well as suit to court. After their deaths, the *firmarius* will pay the rent of 5s.6d. for the demesne land. G.: two capons.

2041 BURWELL (same leet) Thomas Godale and his wife, Elena: one tenement of eight acres *ad censum* once held by Margaret Plumbe, for 15 years, rendering annually in all things as did Margaret, and suit to court and leet. G.: 12d.

2042 BURWELL (same leet) John Floure and his wife, Matilda: one tenement of 15 acres next to Tytheshithe once held by William Ideyne, and one tenement of eight acres next to Fysshestrete, for 20 years, rendering annually in all things as did William. G.: 12d.

2043 BURWELL (same leet) John Sayton: one tenement of 15 acres once held by Andrew Moryce, in *arentatio* for 20 years, rendering annually in all things as did Andrew. G.: 12d.

2044 BURWELL (same leet) Thomas Puryse and his wife, Etheldreda: one tenement of eight acres without adjacent land next to the common heath and once held by Laurence Skynner, for 20 years, rendering annually in all things as did Laurence. G.: 20d.

2045 ELSWORTH (leet) John Fuller: one messuage and three butts of land and one quarter of land once held by John Sonnyng, for life, rendering annually in all things as did Sonnyng. G.: two capons.

2046 ELSWORTH (same leet) Thomas Peek: two cotes with two tofts once held by William Adirfoon, for life, rendering annually 4s., with the condition that he will hold the aforesaid cotes free of rents for two years from next Easter. G.: "etc."

2047 ELSWORTH John Hewysson pays 6s.8d. for license to marry Alicia, daughter of John West and naif of the lord by blood, and also for license for her to live off the fief of the lord.

2048 KNAPWELL (May) John Yntte and his wife, Katerina: one cotland recently held by John Arnold, for life, rendering annually 3s.4d. at the customary times, with the first payment at the feast of St. Andrew after one year. In addition, he will repair the *insathous* before the feast of All Saints. G.: two capons.

121v **2049** WARBOYS (leet) Thomas Buntyng: one messuage and a half-virgate of land once held by William Smert and afterwards held by John Benson, for life, rendering annually in all things as did William, with the first payment at next Easter. G.: three capons.

2050 WARBOYS (same leet) John Sande: one mondayland *ad opus*, half of the land one held by Robert Athill, and five rods of land at Cleynehill, and two acres of demesne at Bascroft and meadow called Puttokmedow next to Humberdale recently held by his father, for life, rendering annually 10s. and services, namely: for the mondayland, finding one man in raising hay in Orcherdyerdslade, one laborer for one day in autumn at the lord's food, common fine, and customs of the vill. In addition, he will rebuild the *insathous* at his own expense, with timber supplied by the lord for that house and other houses, should he wish to rebuild them. G.: excused because of repairs.

2051 WARBOYS (December) Thomas Newman and his wife, Emma: half the lands and tenements once held by Robert Raven and recently held by William Smyth, rendering annually 10s. in equal portions at the customary times, with the obligation to repair one bake house and one forge on the property before Michaelmas, and to repair and maintain all houses and closes on the property, timber being supplied by the lord. The first payment will be at the next feast of St. Andrew. G.: three wood cocks.

2052 WARBOYS William Bonde and his wife, Johanna: one quarter of land *ad opus* once held by Matilda Bensson, for life, rendering annually in all things as did Matilda, with the obligation to repair one *insathous* of six posts before Michaelmas at this own expense, timber being supplied by the lord. G.: three wood cocks.

2053 WARBOYS John Plombe Sr., son of John Plumbe Bocher, pays 8d. annually for license to live off the fief at Whittlesey, for as long as it pleases the lord, remaining a naif as before. Pledges: John Warde and John Hayward of Whittlesey.

2054 RAMSEY John Draper and his wife, Margaret: from Brother Henry Tychemersh, sub-cellarer, one meadow in Wegenhale called Fannersmede once held by John Couper of Heighmongrove, for the life of whoever lives longer, rendering annually 6s.8d. at the feast of the Nativity of Blessed Mary. *Et si predictus redditus*, etc. (one month). G.: three capons.

2055 ABBOTS RIPTON Adam Decon: one plot with building aside the smithy with a semi-virgate of land once held by John Ivell, and one empty plot with a half-virgate of land once held by the same John, with one plot with building and a semi-virgate in the lane once held by Richard Martyn in *arentatio* and recently held by Thomas Mychell, with 10 acres of land at Cattesheg recently held by the same Thomas, for life, rendering annually 28s. and all other services and customs rendered by Thomas. G.: three capons.

2056 ABBOTS RIPTON (December) John Boner and his wife, Agnes: one virgate of land and a half-virgate, one quarter of land and demesne land once held by William Alson, for life, rendering annually 28s., with the obligation to repair and maintain the property. Also: through the hands of Reginald Pipwell, four bushels of wheat, three quarters of barley, three quarters of peas, one horse valued at 3s.4d., one wagon with plain wheels, one coulter with one ploughshare, one bee-hive, all waste land, manure with one wagon, one querne for milling malt, with two stones, all of which will be returned at his exit from the tenement. And he will supply one mower for one day in the meadow, without food. G.: six capons.

2057 ABBOTS RIPTON John Permanter pays 10s. for license to marry Alicia, daughter of Robert Jurdon and naif of the lord by blood, this time.

2058 ABBOTS RIPTON William Amery and his wife, Katerina: one messuage, one semi-virgate of land *ad censum* and two lots in Langlond once held by John Decon, for life, rendering annually 12s.5d.ob.q., and all other services and customs rendered by John, with the obligation to repair all the buildings on the property within two years and maintain them thereafter, timber being supplied by the lord. G.: three capons.

2059 ABBOTS RIPTON John Gosse of Little Stukeley, naif of the lord by blood, pays six capons for license to marry Margaret, daughter of John Robbys and naif of the lord by blood.

2060 HOLYWELL Thomas Mephale: surrender of one plot, one virgate with Burylond, and one appurtenant pithel, to the use of John Nycholas Jr. and his wife, Emma, for life, rendering annually in all things as did Thomas. G.: 20d.

2061 HOLYWELL (leet) Thomas Arnold and his wife, Petronilla: one cotland with adjacent croft recently held by Thomas Brayn, for life, rendering annually in all things as did Brayn. G.: three geese.

2062 HOLYWELL (April) John Asplond: one croft recently held by Thomas Baron, for life, rendering annually in all things as did Thomas. G.: 3s.4d.

122r **2063** HOLYWELL William Palfreyman: surrender of a half-virgate of land and all new demesne land adjoining it, with the yield of that demesne land, to the use of John AtWell and his wife, Margaret, for life, rendering annually in all things as did William. G.: 2s.

2064 HOLYWELL Roger Baker: surrender of one virgate with demesne land and a half-acre of Malwode, to the use of John Godfrey and his wife, Emma, for life, rendering annually in all things as did Roger. G.: 13s.4d.

2065 St. Ives Richard Machyng and his wife, Alicia: two half-rows recently held by John Wylymot, for life, rendering annually 10s. in equal portions at the customary times, with the obligation to repair and maintain the property. *Et non licebit*, etc. G.: 40s.

2066 St. Ives John Bedford and his wife, Margaret: one row recently held by John Fuller, for life, rendering annually 16s., with the obligation to repair and maintain the property. *Et non licebit*, etc. G.: 20s.

2067 St. Ives William Sabbe and his wife, Rosa: one row recently held by Nicholas Bysshop, for life, rendering annually 14s., with the obligation to repair and maintain the property. *Et non licebit*, etc. G.: 6s.8d.

2068 St. Ives William Charite and his wife, Isabella: a half-row previously held by him and seized by the lord for disobedience to the bailiff, for life, rendering annually 10s., with the obligation to repair and maintain the property. *Et non licebit.* etc. G.: excused.

2069 St. Ives John Burle and his wife, Custancia: a half-row recently held by William French, for life, rendering annually 6s.8d., with the obligation to repair the property. *Et non licebit*, etc. Pledge for repairs: Robert Chamberleyn. G.: 5s.

2070 St. Ives Thomas Judde, chaplain: a half-row in le Cheker recently held by Cristina Chaundeler, for life, rendering annually 13s.4d., with the obligation to repair and maintain the property. *Et non licebit*, etc. G.: 12s.

2071 St. Ives William Judde and his wife, Emma: one shop once held by John Chesteyn and recently held by Thomas Freman, for life, rendering annually 13s.4d., with the obligation to repair and maintain the property. *Et non licebit*, etc. G.: excused.

2072 Woodhurst (leet) John Smyth: one plot called Hervyesplace with adjacent land recently held by his father, and one quarter of land recently held by his father, for life, rendering annually 10s. for the plot, which previously rendered 11s., and 4s. for the quarter, and all other services and customs rendered by his father. G.: three capons.

2073 Woodhurst Reginald Lawe: one virgate and one quarter of land recently held by William Pope, for life, rendering annually 18s. in equal portions at the customary times. G.: one capon.

2074 Woodhurst (December) John Ropere and his wife, Lucia: one cotland once held by Jacob Saweyer and recently held by John himself from the tenement of the Lord de Wolle, for life, rendering annually 3s., which property previously rendered 5s. They will repair the property before Michaelmas at their own expense, and maintain it thereafter. G.: one capon.

2075 Woodhurst (August) William Wylymot: surrender of one toft with a half-virgate of land recently held by Hugo Taillor, to the use of William Trover and his wife, Isabella, for life, rendering annually in all things as did Wylymot. G.: two capons.

2076 Woodhurst William Trover: surrender of one messuage with one virgate of land recently held by William Foster, to the use of William Wylymot, for life, rendering annually in all things as did Trover. G.: two capons.

122v **2077** Slepe (leet) William Moor: one lot of the tenement of Bustler recently held by Simon Love, for life, rendering annually 10d. per acre in equal portions at the feasts of the Annunciation and Nativity of Blessed Mary. G.: one capon.

2078 Slepe William Lokwode: one lot from the tenement of Bustler recently held by John Slough Jr., and another lot recently held by Richard Wayte, for life, rendering annually 10d. per acre at the terms above. G.: one capon.

2079 Slepe John Frary: one lot from the same tenement recently held by William Martyn, for life, rendering annually 10d. per acre at the terms above. G.: one capon.

2080 SLEPE John Wale: one lot from the same tenement recently held by Simon Cartere, for life, rendering annually 10d. per acre at the customary times. G.: one capon.

2081 SLEPE Thomas Whaplode and William Nycholl: one lot from the same tenement recently held by Roger Carter, for life, rendering annually 10d. per acre at the customary times. G.: one capon.

2082 SLEPE John Sutton: one lot from the same tenement recently held by John Slough Sr., for life, rendering annually 10d. per acre at the customary times. G.: one capon.

2083 SLEPE (December) John Whilton and his wife, Katerina: two messuages and two virgates of land once held by William Roger in *arentatio*, for life, rendering annually 28s. in equal portions at the customary times, with the obligation to repair the property at their own expense, timber being supplied by the lord, and with the first payment at the feast of St. Andrew after one year. G.: six capons.

2084 SLEPE Thomas Cut: one lot recently held by himself and his father, William Cut, for life, rendering annually 10d. per acre at the customary times. G.: one capon.

2085 BROUGHTON John Cabe Sr. and his wife, Margaret: a half-virgate of land in *arentatio* once held by John Webster Brabon, for life, rendering annually 6s. and all other services and customs rendered by Webster. G.: two capons.

2086 BROUGHTON (leet) Robert Corner: one cotland and two selions of land recently held by John Bernewell, for life, rendering annually 3s.8d. at the customary times. G.: three capons.

2087 BROUGHTON Reginald Webster: one quarter of land recently held by John Wright, for life, rendering annually in all things as did John. G.: two capons.

2088 CHATTERIS John Say: surrender of one tenement of eight acres with meadow in Crowlode, two acres at Watergate in four selions, with five selions containing two acres in Stokkyng, and one gore, to the use of John Balle, for life, rendering annually 12s.6d.ob., and all other services and customs rendered by John Say. G.: 5s.

2089 CHATTERIS John Kyng and his wife, Alicia: one cotland once held by Andrew Miller, with three cotlands containing one large acre in Stokkyng and four cotlands containing two acres once held by John Say, for life, rendering annually 4s. at the customary times. G.: two capons.

2090 CHATTERIS (court) William Hunte: half of one tenement of eight acres, one acre opposite Schiphirnesen, and a half-acre in Ellemen recently held by William Rede, for life, rendering annually in all things as did Rede. G.: 3s.4d.

2091 CHATTERIS (same court) John Clerk: one built up cotland recently held by Richard Michell, alias Webster, for life, rendering annually 6s. and suit to court. G.: 20d.

2092 CHATTERIS (same court) William Poppe: one built up cotland and a half-acre of land of the forland in Oldbrich, and a half-acre of land at Horslade recently held by John Poppe, for life, rendering annually 2s.8d.ob. and suit to court. G.: 20d.

2093 CHATTERIS (same court) John Lyster: half of one tenement of eight acres recently held by Andrew Meyke and one acre of land at Pakereldole recently held by John Biller, and one acre at Schiphirnesen recently held by Andrew Meyke, for life, rendering annually 5s.7d.q. G.: 40d.

2094 CHATTERIS (same court) John Mathew Jr.: half of one tenement of eight acres recently held by Margaret Mathew, and half of one fishpond called le Dam at Horslade, for life, rendering annually in all things as did Margaret. G.: 20d.

2095 CHATTERIS (same court) John Herforth: half of one tenement of eight acres and five selions recently held by John Poppe, for life, rendering annually in all things as did Poppe. G.: 4s.

2096 CHATTERIS (same court) William Carter: one long butt at Derehadlond containing a half-acre and 20 perches recently held by John Poppe, for life, rendering annually 5d. G.: 6d.

2097 CHATTERIS (same court) John Massely: one tenement of eight acres recently held by Alicia Massely, and one fishpond called Massely Dam, with forland, for life, rendering annually in all things as did Alicia. G.: 13s.4d.

2098 CHATTERIS (same court) John Revesson: half of a certain meadow in Oldhalf recently held by John Newman, on the north, the other half of which is now held by William Carter, for life, rendering annually in all things as did Newman. G.: 12d.

2099 CHATTERIS (same court) Richard Smyth: one messuage, two acres of land with toll ferry, six selions at Stokkyng, one selion with a forland there, six selions and four selions and one selion with one gore containing one acre, and three selions in Stokkyng containing one acre, once held by John Smyth, for life, rendering annually in all things as did John, with the condition that he take nothing from the lord or his servants in ferry toll. G.: 10s.

2100 CHATTERIS (same court) John Lawe: half of one tenement of eight acres recently held by Richard Enefeld, for life, rendering annually in all things as did Richard. G.: 5s.

2101 ELLINGTON (leet) William Burgeys, naif of the lord, pays 20d. for license to marry Margaret, his daughter, to John Scotland, this time.

2102 ELLINGTON (same leet) William Burgeys pays 20d. for license to marry Emma, his daughter and naif of the lord, to John Schepperd, this time.

2103 ELTON (leet) Henry atte Gate: surrender of one messuage with one virgate of land recently held by Richard Bate, one messuage with one quarter of land recently held by the same Richard, and one messuage and one quarter of land recently held by Richard Wodeward, to the use of William atte Gate, and his wife, Isabella, for life, rendering annually 27s. at the customary times and all other works and services owed therein. G.: 2s.

2104 ELTON (same leet) John Philip Sr.: one messuage and one quarter recently held by Roger Miller, for life, rendering annually 4s.6d., with the first payment at the next feast of St. Andrew. G.: one capon.

2105 ELTON (same leet) John Bytherne: one acre of meadow called Goryacre, for life, rendering annually 2s. at the customary times. G.: one capon.

2106 ELTON (same leet) John Burnet: one tenement once held by John Nold and a half-virgate of land once held by Richard Cowherde, for life, rendering annually 12s. at the customary times, with the obligation to repair and maintain the property, with beams supplied by the lord. G.: three capons.

2107 ELTON (June) John Caldecote, alias Smyth, and his wife, Johanna: one virgate of land once held by Trowny, one quarter of land of Wedweslon, one virgate of land called Bowebrook, a half-virgate of land once held by Alota Atte Greene, and three quarters of land once held by Maynarde, for life, rendering annually 40s. in equal portions at the customary times, with the obligation to repair and maintain the property, beams being supplied by the lord, and with the first payment at the next feast of St. Andrew. G.: six capons.

2108 THERFIELD (leet) John Sparver, naif of the lord, pays 3s.4d. for license to marry Agnes, his daughter, to Thomas Fayreman of Steeple Morden, this time.

2109 THERFIELD (same leet). John Sparver: surrender of one messuage and one virgate of land once held by John Sparver Sr. and one cotland and one quarter of land once held by Jankyn, to the use of John Martyn, for life, rendering annually in all things as did Sparver. G.: (*blank*).

2110 THERFIELD (same leet) Richard, son of John Waryn: 18 acres of demesne land recently held by William Waryn, for life, rendering annually 12s.9d. at the customary times. G.: 3s.4d.

2111 RAVELEY Thomas Owty and his wife, Anna: one quarter of land in *arentatio* recently held by John Owty Thakker, for life, rendering annually 4s. at the customary times. G.: 12d.

2112 ABBOTS RIPTON (July) William Halsam and his wife, Agnes: one semi-virgate of land recently held by John Lyndesey in *secunda arentatio* and one messuage once held by John Wale and recently held by William Feldew, for life, rendering annually 8s. for the semi-virgate and 2s. for the messuage, with the first payment at the next feast of St. Andrew. G.: three capons.

2113 BRINGTON (August) Elena Pykkyng: surrender of one messuage, a half-virgate and adjacent demesne land, to the use of William Eston and his wife, Johanna, for life, rendering annually in all things as did Elena. Also: a half-virgate of land with fallow and reploughed demesne land and one acre and one rod of manured land. G.: 6s.8d.

2114 WESTON Richard Deppis of Little Stukeley pays 10s. for license to marry Johanna, daughter of Walter Fleschewer, naif of the lord by blood, this time.

123v **2115** SHILLINGTON (1 August: court) William Chybbele pays 40d. for license to marry Lucia, his daughter, to John Shelle, this time.

2116 SHILLINGTON (same court) John Wenyngham: one messuage and one virgate of land with appurtenant demesne land once held by John Warde, for life, rendering annually in all things as did Warde. G.: 40d.

2117 BARTON (2 August: court) Isabella Felmesham, daughter of Agnes Fally: one cotland with curtilage containing one acre recently held by Agnes, for life, rendering annually in all things as did Agnes. G.: 6d.

2118 BARTON (same court) John AtWode and his wife, Edith, daughter and heiress of William Fally: one cotland with croft called Kokyscroft containing two acres recently held by William, for life, rendering annually in all things as did William. G.: 6s.8d.

2119 BARTON (same court) William Roger: one virgate of land once held by William Roger, his father, for life, rendering annually in all things as did his father. G.: 8s.4d.

2120 BARTON (same court) Walter Wodeward: one cotland recently held by Richard Lyllye, for life, rendering annually in all things as did Richard, with the obligation to repair and maintain the property. G.: 40d.

2121 BARTON (same court) John Burnard: one cotland and one croft recently held by his father, Edmund Burnard, for life, rendering annually in all things as did Edmund. G.: 13s.4d.

2122 BARTON (same court) Walter Wylymot: surrender of a half-virgate of land with appurtenant forland, to the use of John Colman, alias Mathew and his wife, Isabella, for life, rendering annually in all things as did Walter. G.: 40d.

2123 BARTON (same court) Edmund Roger pays 10s. for license to marry Alicia, his daughter and naif of the lord by blood, to John Noreys, freeman, this time.

2124 RAMSEY John Warde and his wife, Agnes: from Brother Henry Tychemarsch, sub-cellarer, one tenement recently held by John Horwode and once held by Thomas Brigge, from next Michaelmas for life, rendering annually 8s. in equal portions at Michaelmas and Easter. The sub-cellarer will repair and maintain the property in all things, and he will supply John and Agnes with undergrowth, enclosures and stakes for the banks, at his own transport. *Et si predictus redditus*, etc. (arrears of one month, with property to be seized until satisfaction is made). In addition, John and Agnes may dismiss the property to anyone, saving always the rents owed to the sub-cellarer. Note that John paid 4s. rent for the Michaelmas term when he first came. G.: 20s.

6 JOHN TYCHEMERSCH (1424-1425)

124r   **2125** BURWELL (2 October: leet) John Moleman and his wife, Emma: two cotlands *ad censa* and three acres of land once held by Hugo Lawe, for 20 years, rendering annually in all things as did Hugo. G.: two capons.

2126 BURWELL Agnes Role: one tenement of 15 acres in *arentatio* recently held by her husband, John Role, for 20 years, rendering annually in all things as did John and suit to court and leet, with a half-croft next to the manor gate reserved to the lord. G.: two capons.

2127 KNAPWELL (3 October) Andrew Boykyn, naif of the lord, pays 10s. for license to marry off his daughter, Rosa, the first time. Rosa will pay 6d. annually at Michaelmas until she is married, payments to cease when she marries.

2128 HEMINGFORD ABBOTS (leet) Robert Wrighte: one messuage with one virgate of land recently held by John Osemund, for life, rendering annually in all things as did John. G.: six capons.

2129 HEMINGFORD ABBOTS (same leet) Alan Ver and his wife. Petronilla: one messuage and a half-virgate of land recently held by John Feld, for life, rendering annually in all things as did John. G.: three capons.

2130 HEMINGFORD ABBOTS Thomas Typtet pays six capons for license to marry Margeria, daughter of John Heyne and naif of the lord by blood, this time.

2131 HOUGHTON (leet) William Smyth and his wife, Johanna: a half-virgate of land in *arentatio*, one quarter in *arentatio*, one croft called Withjonesyerd, one croft called Geryldesyerd, "le Beauraper", one alder-ground called Gesholm, one alder-ground called Ankersholm, six selions at Temisfurlong, one croft, which renders 8d. as common finc, one forge at Hougtoncros with a parcel of a croft called Bedellysyerd recently assigned to that forge, one "leightonplace" at Bedellysyerd, three crofts in *arentatio* and another croft recently held by John Prikke, for life, rendering annually 21s.4d. and all works and services owed therein, with the obligation to rebuild one house at Beauraper within two years at their own expense. G.: three capons.

2132 HOUGHTON (same leet) William Deche Wythe: one messuage and one virgate of land once held by John Gerard and recently held by Robert Nycoll, for life, rendering annually in all things as did Robert. G.: four capons.

2133 HOUGHTON (October) Robert Barker: one plot called Grymes, alias Grenes, with two semi-virgates of land once held by John Pope and recently held by John Gouler, in *arentatio* for life, rendering annually 14s. and all services and customs owed therein, with the obligation to build one *insathous* with a solar of eight binding-posts on that plot of the half-virgate next to the plot of Richard Carter in Wyton within two years, at his own expense. The first payment will be at the next feast of St. Andrew. Pledge: John Whaplode. G.: four capons.

2134 HOUGHTON (December) John Smyth, alias Knap, and his wife, Alicia: one messuage with a half-virgate of land *ad opus* and one cotland in *arentatio* with three selions at Burywelnes once held by John Pope and recently held by John Gowler, for life, rendering annually 20s., which property previously rendered 22s. He will repair and maintain the property, and he will have a right to all the hay coming from the aforesaid messuage, and one querne, to be restored at the end of his term. The first payment will be at the next feast of St. Andrew. G.: 3s.4d., with 12d. for one wagon.

2135 HOUGHTON John Whaplode: one cotland once held by John Prikke, the other half of which is now held by Richard Cartere, one croft called Sampsons, and a croft at the end of the village, for life, rendering annually 6s.8d. at the customary times. G.: two capons.

2136 HOUGHTON Robert Roger Sr.: surrender of one cotland in *arentatio*, to the use of Robert Atte Forle, and his wife, Margaret, for life, rendering annually in all things as did Robert Roger. And he will have the other half of his rent. G.: three capons.

2137 HOUGHTON (June) Richard Wilkis: one messuage and one virgate of land *ad opus* and one cotland in *arentatio* once held by John Pope and recently held by John Gowler, for life, rendering annually 18s. at the customary times, (first payment at the next feast of St. Andrew) with the obligation to repair and maintain the property. Also, this year he receives one wagon of hay, to be restored at the end of his term.

2138 HOUGHTON (April) John Spycer and his wife, Petronilla: one toft and a half-virgate in *arentatio* once held by William Roger, and one cotland in *arentatio* recently held by the same William, for life, rendering annually 13s.4d., with the first payment at the next feast of the Annunciation, because of repairs and maintenance, except for staves. G.: three capons.

124v **2139** HOUGHTON John Coton and his wife, Matilda: one cotland once held by Matilda Styward, for life, rendering annually in all things as did Matilda, with the obligation to repair and maintain the property. G.: six capons.

2140 HOUGHTON (April) John Whaplode Jr. and his wife, Alicia: half of one virgate once held by Cook and recently held by John Smyth, and three selions of land at Burywelnys recently held by John Gowler, for life, rendering annually 5s. for the half-virgate and 2s. for the three selions, with the first payment at the next feast of St. Andrew. G.: three capons.

2141 HOUGHTON John Hill and his wife, Elena: the other half of that virgate once held by Cook, for life, rendering annually 5s., with the first payment at the next feast of St. Andrew. G.: three capons.

2142 HURST Thomas Trover: surrender of one messuage and one virgate of land to the use of his son, John Trover, for life, rendering annually in all things as did Thomas. G.: 3s.4d., one capon.

2143 SLEPE (1 October) Thomas Trover and his wife, Emma: one cotland with a half-virgate of land once held by Thomas Hemyngton and seized by the bailiff for default of repairs and rents, for life, rendering annually 10s. at the customary times, with the obligation to repair and maintain the property. G.: two capons.

2144 SLEPE John Hogge: surrender of one messuage, one virgate of land at the end of the village recently *ad opus*, one cotland containing a half-virgate of land recently *ad opus*, one plot and one virgate of land inside le Barres in *arentatio* and one lot of Bustelers land containing five acres and a half, to the use of John Sewyn, for life, rendering annually 44s. in equal portions at the customary times, one ploughing *precaria*, and supplying one man for the autumn *precaria* for a full day. In addition, he will repair and maintain the property at his own expense. G.: six capons.

2145 HOLYWELL John Bryan: surrender of two cotlands with adjacent demesne land and two rods of meadow in Salmade, to the use of Richard Cristemesse and his wife, Margaret, for life, rendering annually in all things as did John. G.: 6s.8d.

2146 HOLYWELL Thomas Scot: surrender of one cotland with adjacent demesne land, to the use of Thomas Valentyn and his wife, Margaret, for life, rendering annually in all things as did Scot. G.: 3s.4d.

2147 HOLYWELL Roger Godfrey and his wife, Agnes: one cotland and one selion of land and meadow with one acre of land in Stonydole for life, rendering annually 22d. at the customary times, with the obligation to repair and maintain the property. G.: 3s.4d.

2148 HOLYWELL John Seberne and his wife, Agnes: one plot and one virgate of land and demesne land once held by John Tayllor, rendering annually in all things as did Tayllor, except for the crop of that demesne land. He will repair and maintain the property, and he will have one acre of meadow in Holywell Fen with two furlongs called Dichfurlong every year, and for repairs he will receive the rent of this year from the tenants, and the rent of next year from the lord. G.: three capons.

2149 HOLYWELL Alicia, daughter of Richard Scot and naif of the lord by blood, pays 6s.8d. for license to marry anyone she wishes this time, and to be in service to John Nicholas until married. Pledge: John Nicholas.

2150 ST. IVES (October) John Peek and his wife, Cecilia: two cotlands of Dysthalle recently held by Thomas Baker, for life, rendering annually 4s., with the first payment at Easter after two years, and with the obligation to repair and maintain the property within two years. *Et non licebit*, etc. G.: excused because of repairs.

2151 ST. IVES John Grene and his wife, Cecilia: a half-row once held by Matilda Fuller and recently held by Richard Fuller, for life, rendering annually 10s. at the customary times, with the first payment at Michaelmas after one year, and with the obligation to repair and maintain the property. *Et non licebit,* etc. G.: three capons.

2152 ST. IVES William Smyth: surrender of one half-row once held by John Edenham, chaplain, and recently held by John Sutton, to the use of John Herrof and his wife, Agnes, for life, rendering annually 10s., with the obligation to repair and maintain the property. *Et non licebit*, etc. G.: 6s.8d.

125r **2153** WARBOYS Robert London: one tenement called Akirmanland once held by John Plombe and recently held by Richard Horwode, for life, rendering 4s. this year, because the land is uncultivated, and 10s. each year thereafter, at the customary times, and customs of the vill. G.: two capons.

2154 WARBOYS Robert Honyter: three acres of land in Bascroft parcelled out of eight acres previously held by John Schepperd and once held by John Wrighte, one and a half acres recently held by John Wrighte, and one acre at Lowefurlong recently held by Robert Olyver, for life, rendering annually to the lord 2s. for the three acres in Bascroft and 16d. for the rest, at the customary times. G.: one capon.

2155 WARBOYS (January) John Berford: a half-virgate of land in *arentatio* recently held by William Olyver and once held by Henry Prestiscosyn, and half of one tenement of akirmanland previously held by him and once held by Margeria Catoun, for life, rendering annually 12s. at the customary times. G.: nothing.

2156 WARBOYS William Bethewater and his wife, Katerina: one mondayland in *arentatio* once held by Richard Taillor, for life, rendering annually in all things as did Richard. G.: three capons.

2157 WARBOYS John Thakker and his wife, Alicia: one plot of Ravene's tenement recently held by Hamond Carpenter, for life, rendering annually 3s. in equal portions at the customary times. G.: 3s.4d.

2158 WARBOYS William Berenger Jr.: one mondayland once held by John Swyer in *arentatio,* one mondayland in *arentatio* once held by William Altheworld, and a half-virgate of land in Caldecote in *arentatio* recently held by his father, for life, rendering annually 13s.4d. at the customary times, with the obligation to repair and maintain the property and to repair one grange in all things except timber, for which repairs he receives a reduction of rent of 4s. this year. G.: six capons.

2159 WARBOYS (January) John Cobbe and his wife, Emma: one cotland of Hochekynsrowe and one cotland once held by Papworth with three selions of land at Wodefurlong once held by John Brenwater, 22 acres of land from the tenement of Roger de Hirst, one cotland at the end of the village next to Haweyattegat at the beginning of Hochekynsrowe, and a half-virgate of land in Caldecote once held by Matilda Benson, for life, rendering annually 24s. in equal portions at the customary times, with the obligation to repair and maintain the property, timber being supplied by the lord. Further, the first payment will be at the feast of St. Andrew after one year. G.: six capons.

2160 WARBOYS John Berenger Sr. and his wife, Juliana: a half-virgate of land *ad opus* once held by John Mold, for life, rendering annually in all things as did Mold, with the obligation to maintain one *camera* and one grange at his own expense, for which he receives a reduction of half of the rent of this year, namely: 3s. G.: three capons.

2161 WARBOYS (leet) William Ravele: one messuage and a half-virgate of land *ad opus* recently held by Robert Benet, for life, rendering annually 6s. and customs of the vill. G.: excused.

2162 WARBOYS (same leet) Thomas Bene: one cotland in Hogekynsrowe recently held by John Caton, for life, rendering annually 4s. at the customary times, with the first payment at the next feast of St. Andrew. G.: excused.

2163 WARBOYS William Strugge and his wife, Margaret: one mondayland in *arentatio* once held by Alicia Wytleseye, for life, rendering annually 4s., sheep-shearing, autumn *precaeiae*, raising of hay in Chevereth, common fine and customs of the vill. G.: three capons.

2164 BROUGHTON John Cabe Jr.: surrender of a half-virgate of land in *major censum* and one quarter of land in *minor censum* and one lot of Dammeslond recently held by himself to the use of William Cabe and his wife, Cristina, for life, rendering annually in all things as did John. G.: 3s.4d.

2165 BROUGHTON John Cabe Jr.: surrender of one quarter of land in *minor censum* once held by Robert Balde, to the use of William Neell, for life, rendering annually in all things as did John. G.: excused.

2166 BROUGHTON William Cabe: surrender of one virgate of land in *minor censum*, one quarter of land in *major censum*, one quarter of Cleryvaux land, to the use of John Cabe Jr. and his wife, Johanna, for life, rendering annually in all things as did William and supplying one mower in mowing barley. G.: 3s.4d.

2167 BROUGHTON Thomas Crowche: surrender of a half-virgate of land *ad opus* and a half-virgate of land in *minor censum*, one quarter of land in *major censum*, to the use of John Pool and his wife, Alicia, for life, rendering annually in all things as did Thomas. G.: three capons.

2168 BROUGHTON John Pool: license from the lord to marry Alicia, daughter of John Justyce, naif of the lord by blood, this time. Payment excused because he is a servant of the lord.

125v   **2169** BROUGHTON John Crowch: surrender of a half-virgate of land *ad opus*, a half-virgate of land recently held by Thomas Boteler in *major censum*, one quarter of land in *minor censum*, one quarter of Cleryvaux land, and one lot of Dammeslond, to the use of Thomas Crowch and his wife, Matilda, for life, rendering annually in all things as did John. G.: 12 capons.

2170 BROUGHTON John Schepperd: surrender of a half-virgate of land *ad opus*, a half-virgate of land in *minor censum*, with two lots of Dammeslond, to the use of John Crowche and his wife, Margaret, for life, rendering annually in all things as did John Schepperd, with the provision that both men will rebuild one *camera* in which John Schepperd lives, and Schepperd will have rights in one and a half-acres, two lots in Dammeslond, a half-mowestede in the grange, a parcel of the garden between the bake house and the grange, and easement in the hall and stable for his needs. G.: 12 capons.

2171 BROUGHTON John Schepperd: surrender of one quarter of land in *minor censum*, to the use of Robert Turnor, for life, rendering annually in all things as did John. G.: six capons.

2172   BROUGHTON (June) John Pooll and his wife, Alicia: one virgate of land without messuage in *minor censum* once held by Thomas Fycher, for life, rendering annually 10s. at the customary times, with the first payment at the feast of St. Andrew after one year. G.: three capons.

2173   BROUGHTON John Broun Faber and his wife, Agnes: one quarter of land in *major censum* once held by John Bernewell, for life, rendering annually 3s.4d., with the first payment at the feast of St. Andrew. G.: two capons.

2174   BROUGHTON Thomas Typtot: a half-virgate of land in *minor censum* and one quarter of land from Cleryvaux land once held by William Smyth, for life, rendering annually in all things as did William, with the obligation to repair and maintain the property in all things, timber supplied by the lord. G.: two capons.

2175   BROUGHTON (June) William Neell Sr.: a half-virgate of land once held by Simon Thoday, alias Breselaunce, in *minor censum* for life, rendering annually as do others in *minor censum*. G.: two capons.

2176   BROUGHTON Thomas Clerk: one quarter of land once held by Balde and recently held by Pynchebekk in *arentatio* and one quarter of land once held by Thomas Gernon next to Baldesplace, for life, rendering annually 6s.8d. and customs of the vill, with the obligation to repair and maintain the property at his own expense, except for timber supplied by the lord. G.: two capons.

2177   BROUGHTON (April) Walter Miller and his wife, Alicia: a half-virgate of land *ad opus* and a half-virgate of land in *minor censum* recently held by William Wold, for life, rendering annually 3s. for the half-virgate *ad opus* and 6s. for the half-virgate in *minor censum*, with the first payment at the feast of the Translation of St. Benedict after one year. Further, he will repair and maintain the property at his own expense, with timber supplied by the lord. G.: two capons.

2178   WISTOW CUM RAVELEY Stephen Atte Gate: a half-virgate of land from akirmanland and a half-virgate of land surrendered into his hands by Robert Atte Gate, *ad opus* (one half-virgate) and in *arentatio* (one half-virgate), rendering annually 15s. at the feasts of St. Andrew, the Annunciation, the Nativity of John the Baptist and the Nativity of Blessed Mary. Further, he and Robert will build a *camera* on the half-virgate of akirmanland in which Robert may live, if he should wish it. G.: three capons.

2179   WISTOW CUM RAVELEY (June) Simon Thoday and his wife, Johanna: one quarter of land once held by Nicholas Martyn, alias Broune, for life, rendering annually in all things as did Nicholas, with the first payment at the feast of the Annunciation. G.: three capons.

2180   WISTOW CUM RAVELEY John Whyte and his wife, Margaret: one messuage with six acres of demesne land and a half-acre at Bysshoppisweng recently held by Stephen Ailmar, for life, rendering annually in all things as did Stephen, with the obligation to repair and maintain the property. He receives at the beginning three rods of wheat, two acres of barley, one acre of peas, all valued at 31s., and reeds and timber (i.e. two staves 20 feet long, hemp canvas valued at 8d.), to be restored at the end of the term. G.: 3s.4d.

2181   UPWOOD William Baker: surrender of a half-virgate of land of akirmanland now *ad opus*, and a parcel of one close of a certain cotland of two acres, the remainder of which is now held by Peter Bray, and a half-acre of land between the butts at Asplonddole, to the use of John Freston, for life, rendering annually in all things as did William, with the obligation to repair and maintain the property at his own expense, with timber supplied by the lord. G.: four capons.

2182   UPWOOD John Freeston: a half-virgate of land of akirmanland now *ad opus* with a parcel of a close of one cotland of two acres, and a half-acre next to the butts at

Asplondole once held by William Baker, for life, rendering annually in all things as did William, with the obligation to repair and maintain the property. Further, he will receive from the *receptor* as seen in the account for this year, namely: 6s.8d., and the rent of this year. Also: nine butts of land next to Asplondole once held by Thomas Wardebusk and Thomas Peny, for life, rendering annually 12d. at the customary times. G.: four capons.

2183 UPWOOD John Boner: two pieces of fallow land next to Raveley once held by Richard Wyllesson and recently held by the customaries there, for life, rendering annually 5s. at the customary times. G.: 12d.

126r **2184** ABBOTS RIPTON John Prikke Jr.: one messuage and one semi-virgate of land in Holle ende once held by Andrew Reve *ad opus*, one empty plot in Millende with one semi-virgate next to the mill in *secunda arentatio*, and one selion at Angerlond recently held by John Sachell, from the previous Michaelmas for life, rendering annually in all things as did Sachell. G.: 40d.

2185 ABBOTS RIPTON (February) Thomas Smyth of Shillington: one messuage and a half-virgate once held by Roger Gardener and recently held by John Martyn, from the previous Michaelmas for life, rendering annually 10s. and all other services and customs rendered by John, with the first payment at the next feast of All Saints. G.: two capons.

2186 ABBOTS RIPTON (March) William Wattes and his wife, Margaret: two messuages with two semi-virgates of land once held by William Savage, and two acres of land at Cattesheg once held by John Bele, for life, rendering annually 21s. in equal portions at the customary times, with the first payment at the next feast of St. Andrew. Also: one plot and one semi-virgate of land once held by John Saly and recently held by himself, for life, rendering annually 8s., with the obligation to repair and maintain the property. G.: six capons.

2187 ABBOTS RIPTON (leet) William del Wode and his wife, Johanna: one messuage and a half-virgate of land recently held by John Lavyn, for life, rendering annually in all things as did John. G.: 6s.8d.

2188 ABBOTS RIPTON William Kelsey and his wife, Agnes: one messuage and one semi-virgate of land at the corner of Burlane, one messuage and one semi-virgate, another messuage and semi-virgate, and one plot and a half-virgate opposite Burylane once held by John Northerneman, alias Wattysson, for life, rendering annually 26s.8d. at the customary times, two ploughing *precariae,* one autumn *precaria*, with the first payment at the next feast of All Saints. He will repair and maintain the property at his own expense, with timber supplied by the lord, and he will receive all the hay of this year for fallowing the land. G.: six capons.

2189 SHILLINGTON (7 November: leet) John Smyth and his son, Thomas: one messuage and one virgate of land called Symondeslond previously held by the same John and surrendered by him, for the life of whomever lives longer, rendering annually all services and customs owed therein, with either being obligated to pay the heriot at the death of the other. G.: 40d.

2190 SHILLINGTON (same leet) Thomas Stonle: six acres of demesne land recently held by John Grene, three and a half acres of land recently held by John Kychener, and one acre of land recently held by William Porter, for life, rendering annually 5s.3d. G.: 12d.

2191 SHILLINGTON (same leet) John Grene: surrender of one cotland with a small adjacent garden lying opposite the eastern part of the tenement recently held by William Lewyn, to the use of John Burgir, for life, rendering annually 8d. G.: 8d.

2192 SHILLINGTON (same leet) Henry Hamond, naif of the lord, pays 5s. for license to marry Johanna, his daughter and naif of the lord, to William Berford, this time.

2193 WESTON (leet) Richard Chycheby: one built up cotland recently held by John Hacon, and one cotland with garden and nine acres of land once held by William Wilby, for life, rendering annually 2s.6d. G.: three capons.

2194 WESTON (same leet) Thomas Curteys: one messuage and one quarter of land once held by Adam Carter, for life, rendering annually 8s.9d. and all other services and customs rendered by Adam. He also receives permission to rebuild an old solar on the property once belonging to William Lewyn. G.: two capons.

2195 BARTON (court) Walter Wylymot: one cotland with adjacent three butts once held by William Wylymote, for life, rendering annually 3s. and suit to court, with the obligation to repair and maintain the property. G.: 12d.

2196 BARTON (same court) John Carpenter: one cotland and adjacent croft recently held by John Baron, for life, rendering annually in all things as did Baron. G.: 6d.

2197 HOUGHTON Richard Carter: surrender of one plot and a half-virgate of land in *arentatio* once held by his father, Robert Dylemaker, alias Carter, to the use of Richard Wylkys, in *arentatio* for life, rendering annually in all things as did Carter, and three old ploughing *precariae*. G.: 40d.

2198 LITTLE STUKELEY (23 April) Thomas Gosse and his wife Margaret: one messuage and a half-virgate of land recently held by John Whytyng and afterwards held by Richard Desburgh from the land pertaining to the *camera* of the lord, for life, rendering annually 4s.5d. at the customary times, with the obligation to repair and maintain the property at their own expense. G.: 6s.8d.

2199 ELTON (court) John Kent, alias Sutbury: one messuage and one virgate of land once held by Hugo Hoberd, for life, rendering annually 18s. and all other services and customs owed therein, with the obligation to repair and maintain the property at his own expense, and with the first payment will be at next Christmas. G.: two capons.

126v **2200** CRANFIELD (26 April: leet) John, son of Thomas Terry: one plot in Horle, rendering 7s.3d., one tenement once held by Richard Aleyn, rendering 5s., one tenement once held by Robert Hert, rendering 5s.11d., one tenement once held by Pentrich Wodecok, rendering 22d., one plot once held by Sabba Wodecok, rendering 12d., Bryndecroft and Smethecroft, rendering 12d., two tofts called Gardener's pithel, rendering 15d., and three and a half-acres recently held by Staliprate, rendering 21d., for life. G.: 20s.

2201 CRANFIELD (same leet) Thomas Eyr: a half-virgate of land once held by Burgolon and six acres of land next to Thikke in the Way recently held by John DunWode, for life, rendering annually in all things as did John. G.: 2s.

2202 CRANFIELD (same leet) William Coke: three acres of old demesne land lying at Puryhill recently held by Thomas Coke, for life, rendering annually in all things as did Thomas. G.: 12d.

2203 CRANFIELD (same leet) William Melbroke: one cotland with one pithel once held by Simon Milbrok and one cotland once held by John Sherman, and afterwards held by Thomas Milbrok, for life, rendering annually in all things as did Thomas. G.: 6s.8d.

2204 CRANFIELD (same leet) John Borell: half of one virgate of land once held by William Godewyn, three and a half acres and a half-rod of land in Overhorscroft, six and a half acres and a half-rod of land at Stalyprate and one acre, and one and a half rods at Netherhors, for life, rendering annually in all things as did William. G.: 16d.

2205 CRANFIELD (same leet) Thomas Catelyn, naif of the lord, pays 5s. for license to marry Alicia, his daughter and naif of the lord, to John Aleyn, this time.

2206 CRANFIELD (same leet) William Joye, naif of the lord, pays 6s.8d. for license to marry Agnes, his daughter, to John Lovell.

2207 CRANFIELD (same leet) Anna Aleyn, naif of the lord, pays 5s. for license to marry whomever she wishes, this first time.

2208 CRANFIELD (same leet) Thomas Aleyn, naif of the lord, pays 13s.4d. for license to marry Christiana, his daughter and naif of the lord, to John Ladde of Millbrook, and for license to marry Alicia, his daughter and naif of the lord, to Roger Heyne of Mentmore, this time.

2209 CHATTERIS John Bate: all lands and tenements and cotes previously held by Richard Smyth of Horsheath, for life, rendering annually in all things as did Richard. G.: 13s.4d.

2210 CHATTERIS John Revysson, son of John Revysson: half of one tenement of eight acres and half of the meadow of Oldhalf with the fishpond at Alyotesmer, with three selions at Watergate and two selions at Wodegate, with herbage once held by Andrew Clement, for life, rendering annually in all things as did Andrew. G.: 6s.8d.

2211 CHATTERIS John Revysson: all lands and tenements previously held by Agnes Mathew, for life, rendering annually in all things as did Agnes. G.: 6s.8d.

2212 RAMSEY Richard Cook and his wife, Agnes: one plot called Bramptonsplace, for life, rendering annually 8s. in equal portions at the feasts of the Annunciation and Nativity of Blessed Mary. G.: excused.

2213 RAMSEY John In the Herne, alias Sadeler, and his wife, Katerina: from the sub-cellarer, Brother John Styvecle, one plot once held by William Hulle and recently held by Thomas Smyth, rendering annually 13s.4d. at the feasts of the Annunciation and Nativity of Blessed Mary, with the obligation to repair the property at their own expense. *Et si predictus redditus*, etc (arrears of one month). G.: 3s.4d.

2214 RAMSEY Thomas Smyth, alias Wayte, and his wife, Margeria: from the sub-cellarer, one plot once held by Thomas Leche, for life, rendering annually 8s. in equal portions at the customary times, with the obligation to repair and maintain the property at their own expense, timber being supplied by the lord. *Et si predictus redditus*, etc. (arrears of one month). G.: 3s.4d.

2215 THERFIELD (leet) John Martyn: one messuage and one virgate of land recently held by John Sparver, one quarter of land once held by John Jankyn and recently held by Sparver, and nine acres of demesne land recently held by the same Sparver, for life, rendering annually in all things as did Sparver. G.: 20s.

2216 THERFIELD (same leet) William Frere, naif of the lord, pays 10s. for license to marry Katerina, his daughter, to William Tebbe of Buckland.

2217 THERFIELD (same leet) John Evadet Jr. and his wife, Johanna: one messuage and one virgate of land recently held by John Colyn, and 18 acres of new demesne land and one meadow called Hunwellesmade recently held by John Colyn and seized by the lord because of disrepair, for life, rendering annually in all things as did Colyn. G.: three capons.

2218 ELLINGTON (court) John Skynner, alias Wright, his heirs and assigns: one messuage and one quarter of land in Sibthorp recently held by John Gymber, rendering annually in all things as did Gymber. G.: 12d.

127r **2219** GRAVELEY (leet) William Bukby, his wife, Agnes and son, John: one messuage and two virgates of land recently held by John Chirche, with grain growing in the land valued at four marks, for life, rendering annually in all things as did John. Note that the land was originally fallow and that William receives 40 cart loads of hay, to be restored at the end of the term, as well as 40s. of the aforesaid four marks. G.: three capons.

2220 GRAVELEY (same leet) William Bukby: surrender of one messuage, one virgate and two quarters of land, to the use of John Waltham and his wife, Alicia, for life.

Note that it was agreed between William and John that William will pay the latter 13s.4d. of the four marks (above), and that this shall be returned to the lord at the end of the term. Further, he will receive all the fallow and reploughed land, four acres of manured land, with a wagon, which he will restore at the end of the term. G.: three capons.

2221 BRINGTON William Eston and his wife, Katerina: one cotland from the tenement of Bowyerys with three butts of land at le Marsch once held by John Revysson, for life, rendering annually in all things as did John, with the obligation to repair and maintain the property. G.: 10s.

7 JOHN TYCHEMERSCH (1425-1426)

127v   **2222** CRANFIELD (1 October: leet) John Baldeswell and his wife, Isabella: two half-virgates of land once held by Elias Smyth, one messuage and one croft recently held by the same Elias, for the life of Isabella, rendering annually 27s.6d. and all other services and customs owed therein. G.: 2s.

2223 CRANFIELD (same leet) Galfridus Webbe: permission to marry Agnes, widow of Henry Cook, and to enter into one cotland and three acres of land recently held by Henry, for the life of Agnes, rendering annually all services and customs owed therein. G.: 8d.

2224 CRANFIELD (same leet) Thomas Burgolon: a half-virgate of land recently *ad opus* and one croft lying beneath DoleWode, three acres of land lying at Stalipras, and one cotland once held by Robert Couper and recently held by Galfridus Burgolon, his father, for life, rendering annually in all things as did Galfridus. G.: 4s.

2225 CRANFIELD (same leet) John del Hirst: two cotlands recently held by William Curteys and once held by his father, Willlam del Hirst, for life, rendering annually in all things as did William. G.: 20d.

2226 BARTON (3 October: court) Isabella, wife of William Vale, claims that she is the closest heir of Emma Gregory for one messuage and one virgate of land with forland recently held by Simon Gregory, and she requests that her claim be justified through in inquest of the court. Concerning this, jurors are elected, and they say that she is right. Afterwards, the said Isabella and her husband, William, come and surrender the said property to Walter Revysson Jr., for life, rendering annually in all things as did Simon. G. and heriot: 40d., and no more because he had previously paid 13s.4d. as *gersuma*.

2227 BARTON (same court) Nicholas Chyld: a half-virgate of land recently held by John Colman, for life, rendering annually in all things as did John. G.: 2s.

2228 BARTON (same court) William Colman: surrender of one messuage, one virgate of land, one toft with adjacent croft called Mathew Croft and one cote with adjacent croft called Brigendecroft, to the use of his son, John Colman, for life, with the provision that William will take the yield of Brigendecroft during his lifetime, as well as being supplied with adequate food by John, together with one quarter of barley at Martinmas and Christmas. Further, he will have a house at the eastern end of the said messuage for life, without any contradiction or impediment by John. G.: 6s.8d.

2229 SHILLINGTON (4 October: leet) Nicholas Laurence: surrender of two messuages and two virgates of servile land (one built up, the other vacant), with all demesne land once held by Thomas Atte Made, except for nine acre at Newmandlond, to the use of his son, John Laurence, in bondage, rendering annually in all things as did Nicholas. G.: 6s.8d.

2230 SHILLINGTON (same leet) John Brouham: surrender of one messuage and two semi-virgates of land once held by Thomas Hamond, to the use of John Warde, for life, rendering annually in all things as did Brouham. G.: 40d.

2231 SHILLINGTON (same leet) John Colyn Sr.: surrender of one messuage and two semi-virgates of land to the use of his son, John Colyn, for life, rendering annually in all things as did John Sr. G.: 6s.8d.

2232 SHILLINGTON (same leet) Adam Sparwe: one cotland with one acre of land recently held by Thomas Fyncham, for life, rendering annually in all things as did Thomas, with the obligation to repair and maintain the property at his own expense. G.: 12d.

2233 SHILLINGTON (same leet) Nicholas Grave: surrender of one messuage and one virgate of land once held by Henry del Abbey and one half-virgate of land once held by Robert Grave, to the use of John Grave, for life, with the provision that Nicholas will have easement of living in that messuage for life, and he will also have grain from the half-virgate. G.: 13s.4d. Heriot: 20d.

2234 WOODHURST John White: one quarter of land once held by John Colle, for life, rendering annually in all things as did Colle. G.: three capons.

128r **2235** BURWELL (8 October: leet) John Payer: one cotland with adjacent curtilage previously held by his father, by the rod, for life, rendering annually in all things as did his father, suit to court, and reaping of a half-acre of wheat. G.: 6d.

2236 BURWELL (same leet) George Bocher and his wife, Elena: half of one tenement of 24 acres in *arentatio* recently held by John Wright, and half of one croft at le Nesse recently held by John Fraas in support of the above tenement, for life, rendering annually in all things as did Wright, and suit to court, common fine and holmsilver. G.: 2s.

2237 BURWELL (same leet) Maria Alot: one cotland with one croft containing one acre, and one acre of land recently held by Adam Alot, for 20 years, rendering annually in all things as did Adam, and suit to court. G.: 12d.

2238 BURWELL (same leet) John Payntor: one tenement of eight acres in Wodelane once held by John Peryng, for 30 years, rendering annually in all things as did John Peryng, common fine and suit to court. G.: 2s.

2239 HOUGHTON Thomas Andrew: a half-virgate of land once held by Robert Roger Atte Style and once held by Snowy, for life, rendering annually in all things as did Robert Roger. G.: two capons.

2240 HOUGHTON William Wyth and his wife, Juliana: one virgate of land once held by Thomas Elyot, for life, rendering annually 11s. at the customary times. G.: two capons.

2241 HOUGHTON Richard Atkyn receives from the lord one virgate of land in *arentatio* recently held by William Atkyn, for life, rendering annually 10s. and all other services formerly rendered by his father. G.: three capons.

2242 HOUGHTON (March) William Prikke and his wife, Agnes: half of one messuage with croft, 26 acres, one rod of land and meadow once held by Richard Twywell, alias Dykes, and recently held by Juliana Hardyng, for life, rendering annually 12s. at the customary times, with the first payment at the next feast of St. Andrew. G.: four capons.

2243 HOUGHTON (January) William Frank and his wife, Alicia: one plot with one virgate of land *ad opus* recently held by John Smyth, for life, rendering annually at the customary times and all other services rendered by tenants *ad opus*, with the first payment at the next feast of St. Andrew. Further, they will repair and maintain the property at their own expense. G.: three capons.

2244 WARBOYS Robert Ravene and his wife, Emma: a half-virgate of land once held by Thomas Newman and once also by William Harsene, for life, rendering annually 6s. at the customary times and all other services and customs rendered by Thomas, including carting services to Ramsey. G.: three capons.

2245 WARBOYS Robert Honyter and his wife, Agnes: the third part of one dichemanland recently held by Maria Wene, for life, rendering annually in all things as did Maria. G.: 20d.

2246 WARBOYS John Schakestaf: one acre of land at Brenfurlong once held by John Miller and two acres there recently held by John Edward and one acre there recently held by Richard Revesson with a half-acre of land in a *forera*, for life, rendering annually 3s., which property formerly rendered 3s.4d. G.: three capons.

2247 WARBOYS John Ode and his wife, Anna: one mondayland once held by John Dalby Sr., and two acres at Brenfurlong once held by John Ordmar, for life, rendering annually 4s.8d. at the customary times, and customs of the vill, with the obligation to repair and maintain the property at their own expense. G.: six capons.

2248 WARBOYS William Berenger Sr. and his wife, Johanna: one plot with a half-virgate of land in *arentatio*, two acres of land parcelled out of eight acres at Bascroft, one acre of land at Bascroft and one selion of demesne land at Stocroft once held by John Brampton, for life, rendering annually in all things as did John, with the obligation to repair and maintain the property, timber being supplied by the lord. G.: 40s.

2249 ELTON Richard Wodeward and John Bythorne: one plot with building with an oven in Netherton recently held by John Pylketon, for life, rendering annually 6s.8d., with the obligation to repair and maintain the house and oven. Pledge for repairs: Thomas Aloun. G.: six capons.

2250 ELTON (leet) Richard Wodeward: one toft and one quarter of land recently held by William Saunde, for life, rendering annually in all things as did William. G.: 6d.

2251 ELTON (same leet) Richard Ryde: one messuage and one quarter of land recently held by Roger Miller, for life, rendering annually in all things as did Roger. G.: 6d.

2252 ELTON (same leet) Henry Spencer: one messuage and one quarter of land once held by Henry Atte Gate, for life, rendering annually in all things as did Henry. G.: 6d.

2253 ELTON (same leet) Richard Fuller: one messuage and three acres and a half of land recently held by William Kent, for life, rendering annually 5s. at the customary times. G.: two capons.

2254 ELTON (same leet) John Welles: four acres and three rods of land once held by John Hobbysson, for life, rendering annually 2s.8d. G.: three capons.

128v **2255** ELTON (same leet) John Phylip Jr.: one messuage and one quarter of land once held by Richard Ryde, for 10 years, rendering annually in all things as did Richard. G.: 6d.

2256 ELTON (same leet) Edward Tayllor: one quarter of land once held by Richard Bokeland, for life, rendering annually 4s.6d. and all other services and customs owed therein. G.: one capon.

2257 ELTON (same leet) John Moleyn: one cotland recently held by William Fretter and one quarter of land once held by Katerina Robury, for life, rendering annually 5s., with the first payment at the feast of St. Andrew after one year. G.: 6d.

2258 ELTON (same leet) John Hoberd and his son, Richard: one cotland with adjacent croft recently held by Robert Dalton, for life, rendering annually in all things as did Robert. G.: 6d.

2259 ELTON (same leet) John Colyn: one oven with bake house in Overton, for life, rendering annually 2s. G.: two capons.

2260 ELTON (same leet) John Blechalf: one cotland recently held by John Pilton for 6d., and one quarter of land recently held by John Colyn for 4s.6d., for life. G.: two capons.

2261 ELTON (October) John Whytyng: two mills in one house with seven appurtenant acres of land and meadow, from the next feast of All Saints for 10 years, rendering annually 10 marks in equal portions at the feasts of St. Andrew, the Annunciation, Nativity of John the Baptist, and Nativity of Blessed Mary. Further, he will repair the mills, the dam, all appurtenances, with the entrance-way, outside the water, and he will have willows at the dam, keeping the abbot and tenants free of blame regarding amercements in the court of Fotheringay. He will receive three new millstones and one old drainage channel, to be restored at the end of the term, and he is obligated to the lord for 20 marks, for keeping all the above.

2262 HOLYWELL John Peny: three and a quarter acres in le Brach and three acres in Schepenfurlong once held by William Schepperd, for life, rendering annually 2s. for le Brach, 3s.6d. for the rest, and all other services and customs rendered by William. G.: 2s.

2263 HOLYWELL John Nycholas Jr. and his wife, Emma: four and a half acres of land in Benehill recently held by William Carter, for life, rendering annually 4s.6d. at the customary times. G.: 20d.

2264 HOLYWELL John Edward Sr. and his wife, Margaret: a half-virgate of land with demesne land and one acre of land at Nethbrerecroft and one croft once held by John Hamond and recently held by William Carter, for life, rendering annually in all things as did William, with the obligation to repair and maintain the property at their own expense. G.: 13s.4d.

2265 KNAPWELL (leet) Margeria Crek: a half-virgate of land recently held by Richard Creek, for life, rendering annually in all things as did Richard. G.: 20d.

2266 SLEPE Thomas Cut pays 3s.4d. for license to marry Agnes, his daughter and naif of the lord by blood, to John Trover, this time.

2267 SLEPE John Baylly: surrender of one plot next to a solar, with a half-virgate of land at le Howe, a half-virgate and one cotland in *arentatio*, and a parcel of one cotland once held by Nicholas Bewbray next to the gravel pit, to the use of John Webster, and his wife, Margaret, for life, rendering annually in all things as did Baylly, with the obligation to repair and maintain the property at their own expense. G.: three capons.

2268 SLEPE John Freman and his wife, Katerina: one messuage and two virgates of land and one toft called Lombercroft recently held by Nicholas Chikesand, for life, rendering annually 38s., with the first payment at the next feast of the Annunciation. G.: two capons.

129r **2269** WISTOW William Syre pays 6s.8d. for license to marry Johanna Randolf, daughter of Robert Randolf and naif of the lord by blood, this time.

2270 WISTOW (December) Richard Wyllesson: one cotland with one cotland recently held by John Owty Sr., for life, rendering annually in all things as did John. G.: two capons.

2271 WISTOW Robert Rede and his wife, Alicia: one cotland in *arentatio* and one plot with adjacent land once held by Richard Pycard, for life, rendering annually 6s.8d. at the customary times, with the obligation to repair and maintain the property at their own expense. G.: two capons.

2272 WISTOW (May) Thomas Asplond, alias Plougwrighte, naif of the lord by blood, will pay 4d. annually for license to live at Sutton in Ely for as long as it pleases the lord, remaining a naif as before.

2273 WISTOW Thomas Asplond will pay 4d. annually for license for his son, Peter Asplond, to live at Sutton, for as long as it pleases the lord, remaining a naif as before.

2274 WISTOW Thomas Asplond will pay 4d. annually for license for his son, John Asplond, to live at Sutton, for as long as it pleases the lord, remaining a naif as before. Note: Thomas has a daughter, Anna, approximately a half-year old.

2275 WISTOW (April) Richard Pycard and his wife, Agnes: lord one plot with a half-virgate of land once held by John Atte Gate Sr., for life, rendering annually in all things as did John, with the obligation to repair and maintain the property, timber being supplied by the lord. Because of repairs they will receive the yield of John Atte Gate at the beginning of their term, together with one jar holding one gallon, and one querne, to be returned at the end of their term. Further, the first payment will be at the next feast of St. Andrew. G.: two capons.

2276 ELSWORTH Robert Yntte: one cotland once held by John Pygot at Brokyl-brigge, and one croft Gravelond once held by Henry Colet and recently held by Thomas Smert, for life, rendering annually in all things as did Thomas, with the obligation to repair and maintain the property. G.: two capons.

2277 ST. IVES John Welles, surrender of a half-row, to the use of Thomas Smyth and his wife, Juliana, for life, rendering annually in all things as did John, with the obligation to repair and maintain the property. *Et non licebit*, etc. G.: 6s.8d.

2278 ST. IVES John Esex Sr. and his wife, Margeria: two half-rows once held by Thomas Grigge, for life, rendering annually 8s. at the customary times, with the obligation to repair and maintain the property. *Et non licebit*, etc. G.: two capons.

2279 WESTON Walter Reignald: a half-virgate of land with new demesne land and one acre and one rod and a half of Burylond and one part of one cotland once held by Roger Miller, and a half-virgate of land once held by Cobeler, with new demesne land once held by John Smyth, for life, rendering annually in all things as did the previous tenants, with the obligation to repair and maintain the property, for which repairs he receives the full crop of Smyth. G.: two capons.

2280 WESTON William Fleschall and his wife, Emma: one forge called the Overforge once held by John Smyth, for life, rendering annually in all things as did John, with the obligation to repair and maintain the forge. G.: two capons.

2281 WESTON John Pury and his wife, Dionisia: all lands and tenements recently held by Roger Grymbold and once held by Simon Hacon, for life, rendering annually in all things as did Roger, with the obligation to repair the property, timber being supplied by the lord. Further, the first payment will be at the feast of St. Andrew after one year. G.: six capons.

2282 BROUGHTON (11 December: leet) William Clerk and his wife, Johanna: one messuage and a half-virgate of land once held by his father in *minor censum*, and one quarter of land once held by William Everard, for life, rendering annually 3s.8d. for the quarter, and for the half-virgate as did his father. G.: 20d.

2283 BROUGHTON (same leet) Robert Turnor: one tenement and one-quarter of land recently held by John Schepperd in *minor censum*, and one toft and one quarter of land once held by Thomas del Wold in *major censum*, for life, rendering annually for the tenement and quarter in *minor censum* 3s. and all services and customs rendered by John, and for the toft and quarter in *major censum*, 3s.8d. and customs of the vill. G.: eight capons.

2284 BROUGHTON (same leet) John Crouche and his wife, Margaret: one toft with a half-virgate of land recently held by William Pynchebek, in *minor censum* for life, rendering annually 6s., with the first payment at the next feast of St. Andrew. G.: three capons.

2285 BROUGHTON (same leet) William Smart and his wife, Agnes: one toft with one quarter of land recently held by John Webster in *minor censum*, for life, rendering annually 3s. at the customary times, with the first payment at the next feast of St. Andrew. G.: two capons.

2286 BROUGHTON (same leet) Edward Justyce and his wife: one toft and one quarter of land once held by Pelage and recently held by Thomas of the Wold, for life, rendering annually 3s.4d., with the first payment at the next feast of St. Andrew. G.: two capons.

2287 BROUGHTON (same leet) Nicholas Turnor: one messuage with a half-virgate of land recently held by William Pynchebek in *major censum*, for life, rendering annually 7s.4d. and all other services rendered by similar tenants, with the first payment at the next feast of St. Andrew. He will rebuild one *insathous* on the property at his own expense, timber being supplied by the lord. Also: one quarter of land recently held by him in *minor censum*, for life, rendering annually 3s. and suit to court, with the first payment at the next feast of St. Andrew. G.: two capons.

2288 BROUGHTON (same leet) Nicholas Bocher and his wife, Katerina: one toft with a half-virgate of land recently held by him, in *minor censum* for life, with the first payment at the next feast of St. Andrew. Also: one messuage and a half-virgate of land recently held by John Smyth, in *arentatio*, for life, rendering annually 6s.8d. G.: two capons.

2289 ABBOTS RIPTON (February) John Burton: one messuage and one semi-virgate of land in Hollende once held by Andrew Reve, one empty plot with one semi-virgate next to the mill, one selion of land at Angirlond once held by John Nicholl and recently held by John Prikke Jr., for life, rendering annually 16s. at the customary times and three *precariae*, with the obligation to repair and maintain the property. He will not relinquish any parcel of the above, and the first payment will be at the feast of All Saints. G.: three capons.

2290 ABBOTS RIPTON Thomas Hychecok and his wife, Matilda: one cotland in Esthorp once held by John Baskyn, for life, rendering annually in all things as did John, with the first payment at the feast of All Saints. He will repair and maintain the property at his own expense. G.: two capons.

2291 THERFIELD John Waryn and his son, William, one messuage and a half-virgate of land with demesne land once held by Thomas Wyngor and surrendered by the same John, for the life, of whomever lives longer, with the provision that whenever a new agreement of general dismissal is made in the manor, this conveyance will be void. Further, whenever the said John dies, William will pay the lord for entry as do other tenants in new conveyances. G.: excused because of repairs.

2292 HURST John Vycory: one messuage and a half-virgate of land recently held by Thomas Potter, for life, rendering annually 8s. at the customary times, with the obligation to repair and maintain the prooerty at his own expense, timber being supplied by the lord, together with an allowance of the rent of the preceding year. G.: two capons.

8 JOHN TYCHEMERSCH (1426-1427)

130r   **2293** HOUGHTON John Upton of Hemingford pays 6s.8d. for license to marry Alicia, daughter of Robert Upton and naif of the lord by blood, and for license to have her in his service until married, this time.

2294 KNAPWELL William Doraunt and his wife, Katerina: one messuage with one semi-virgate of land in *arentatio* recently held by John Hoot, for life, rendering annually in all things as did John, with the obligation to repair and maintain the property at their own expense. G.: 3s.4d.

2295 SHILLINGTON Alicia Longe: surrender of one messuage and one virgate of land once held by Roger AtteWelle, one messuage with one virgate of land once held by Roger Everard with three acres of demesne, to the use of John Warde and his wife, Margaret, for life, rendering annually in all things as did Alicia. G.: and heriot: 26s.8d.

2296 SHILLINGTON John Warde: surrender of one messuage and a half-virgate of land once held by Alicia Bunker, to the use of John Grenefeld, and his wife, Matilda, for life, rendering annually in all things as did Warde. G.: 6s.8d. Heriot (by John Warde): 6s.8d.

2297 WISTOW John Plombe and his wife, Johanna: a half-virgate of land recently held by Thomas Owty Sr. and once held by Richard Weston, for life, rendering annually 6s. and all other services and customs rendered by Thomas, with an allowance of this year's rent. G.: six capons.

2298 RIPTON John Burton: surrender of one messuage and a semi-virgate of land in Hollehende once held by Andrew and one empty plot with one semi-virgate next to the mill and one selion of land next to Angirlond once held by John Nycholl, to the use of William Kelsill, for life, rendering annually 16s. at the customary times, and three ploughing *precariae*, with the obligation to repair and maintain the property. G.: four capons.

2299 CHATTERIS (March) John Clement and John Robyn: the manor of Hunneye, with all pastures and fishponds pertaining to the manor, from the feast of the Purification for 20 years, rendering annually 66s.8d. at the feast of the Exaltation of the Holy Cross, with the obligation to repair one hall 20 feet long and the *camera* annexed to it under the supervision and with the consent of the seneschal. And they will maintain it in hedges and ditches, and repair the houses. They have permission to cut down and take all the undergrowth either in the manor or in the appurtenant marsh, as well as old willows, provided they replant other willows within the manor. They will maintain the manor in severalty during the period they hold it, and if they default in paying the farm, or if they are in arrears for 15 days, the lord shall take it back. Finally, John Robyn is obligated to the lord to £20 as a pledge that these conditions will be kept. G.: excused.

2300 HURST (March) John Herrod and his wife, Margaret: one quarter of land once held by John Smyth, for life, rendering annually 4s. and all other services and customs rendered by Smyth. Note that John receives one acre sown with wheat. G.: excused.

2301 HURST Thomas Cut and his wife, Emma: one plot with one virgate of land recently held by John Trover, for life, rendering annually in all things as did John. Further, he receives four acres and three rods sown with wheat. G.: two capons.

2302 HURST Roger Cachesoly and his wife, Agnes: one plot with one virgate of land recently held by John Wrighte, for life, with the obligation to repair that plot and another plot he already holds under penalty of forfeit. G.: six capons.

130v   **2303** CRANFIELD (28 October: leet) William Joye: one cote with garden once held by John Joye, for life, rendering annually 2s. and one capon. G.: 18d.

2304 CRANFIELD (same leet) William Berne pays 2s. for license to marry Agnes, widow of John Frayfelde, and to enter into one cote and one croft and two acres of land, for the life of Agnes.

2305 CRANFIELD (same leet) John Rede: the reversion of one messuage and one virgate of land *ad opus* recently held by Thomas Godwyn and now held by Margeria Godwyn, for life, rendering annually in all things as Margeria. G.: 20s.

2306 CRANFIELD (same leet) William Conquest: one messuage and one quarter and a half of land recently held by John Herton, for life, rendering annually in all things as did John. G.: 13s.4d.

2307 CRANFIELD (same leet) John Warde: surrender of one messuage and three quarters of land once held by William Warde, to the use of Thomas Grene Jr., for life, rendering annually in all things as did John. G.: 26s.8d.

2308 CRANFIELD (21 July: court) Thomas Brerele: one messuage and a half-virgate of land recently held by Agnes Brerele, for life, rendering annually in all things as did Agnes. G.: 5s.

2309 CRANFIELD (same court) John Aleyn of Wodende: one messuage and a half-virgate of land and one quarter of land recently held by his father, John Aleyn, and one messuage and one quarter and a half of land recently held by John Herton, for life, rendering annually in all things as did his father. G.: 20s.

2310 CRANFIELD (same court) William Colles: one messuage, a half-virgate and four acres of land recently held by his father, John Colles, for life, rendering annually in all things as did John. G.: 6s.8d.

2311 SHILLINGTON (24 October: leet) John Colyn: seven and a half-acres of land, of which four acres are next to Wyndmillehill and three and a half lie in Estfeld, recently held by Nicholas Laurence, for life, rendering annually in all things as did Nicholas. G.: 12d.

2312 SHILLINGTON (24 July: court) William Cecilly and his wife, Maria: one messuage with three houses and one virgate of land once held by John West in Chibbely, for life, rendering annually in all things as did John, with the obligation to repair and maintain the three houses. G.: 5s.

2313 BARTON (26 October: court) Thomas Broune and his wife, Emma: one messuage and one cotland recently held by Reginald Milward, for life, rendering annually in all things as did Reginald. G.: 40d.

2314 BARTON (same court) John Roger Jr.: one and a half virgates of land recently held by John Roger Sr., for life, rendering annually in all things as did John Sr. G. and heriot: one mark.

2315 BARTON (same court) Thomas Wylymot, naif of the lord, pays 4s. for license to marry Agnes, his daughter, to Jacob Pope, this time.

2316 BARTON Richard Roger pays 6s.8d. for license to marry Agnes, his daughter and naif of the lord, to John Martyn of Hexton, this time.

131r **2317** HOUGHTON (29 November: leet) John Plombe Jr.: one messuage and a half-virgate of land in Wyton recently held by John Symond, for life, rendering annually in all things as did Symond. G.: four capons.

2318 HOUGHTON (same leet) John Apirle: three quarters of land recently held by Robert Andrew, for life, rendering annually in all things as did Robert. G.: 20d.

2319 HOUGHTON William Fuller: surrender of one built up croft with five adjoining crofts and a half-virgate of land once held by John Hervy, to the use of John Fuller and his wife, Agnes, for life, rendering annually in all things as did William, with the obligation to repair and maintain the built up croft. G.: 3s.4d.

2320 HOUGHTON Margaret Andrew: one quarter of land parcelled out of one virgate of land once held by John Evot and recently held by John Andrew Smyth, for life, rendering annually 2s. and all services and customs rendered by John. G.: three capons.

2321 St. Ives (25 November: leet) Thomas Baker and his wife, Johanna: four shops in "Le Cheker" once held by Matilda Smyth, for life, rendering annually 9s., with the obligation to repair and maintain the property. *Et non licebit*, etc. G.: 3s.4d.

2322 St. Ives (same leet) John Chekesand and his wife, Alicia: a half-row once held by John Ellesworth, with a half-row next to it, for life, rendering annually 13s.4d. for one, and 10s. for the other, at the customary times, with the obligation to repair and maintain the property. *Et non licebit*, etc. G.: excused.

2323 St. Ives (same leet) John Berker: surrender of a half-row once held by William Prentys, to the use of Thomas Sowle and his wife, Margaret, for life, rendering annually 12s. at the customary times, with the obligation to repair and maintain the property. *Et non licebit*, etc. G.: two capons.

2324 St. Ives John Eston and his wife, Isabella, a half-row once held by Alan Cook and recently held by Agnes Foster, for life, rendering annually 14s. at the customary times, with the obligation to repair and maintain the property. *Et non licebit*, etc. G.: 40d.

2325 St. Ives John Bunte and his wife, Margaret: a half-row in Bridge Street next to Schaylleslane recently held by Frederick Skynnere, for life, rendering 26s.8d. at the customary times, with the obligation to repair and maintain the property. *Et non licebit*, etc. G.: 26s.8d.

2326 St. Ives Thomas Ravene: surrender of one row recently held by Thomas Freman, to the use of Laurence Barker and his wife, Alicia, for life, rendering annually 20s. in equal portions at the customary times, with the obligation to repair and maintain the property. *Et non licebit*, etc. G.: 10s.

2327 Slepe (same leet) Simon Herrof: surrender of one messuage, one virgate and one quarter of land, to the use of William Inger and his wife, Johanna, for life, rendering annually in all things as did Simon. G.: four capons.

2328 Slepe Agnes, daughter of Thomas Cut and naif of the lord by blood, pays 6s.8d. for license to marry John Feld Jr. of Hemingford Abbots, this time.

2329 Slepe Frederick Skynnere: surrender of one messuage with a half-virgate of land, to the use of John Bedford and his wife, Margaret, for life, rendering annually in all things as did Frederick. G.: 5s.

131v   **2330** Graveley (4 December: leet) Thomas Baron: one and a half virgates of land recently held by his father, John Baron, for life, rendering annually in all things as did John. G.: 3s.4d.

2331 Graveley (17 June: court) John Baron, naif of the lord, pays 6s.8d. for license to marry off Alicia, his daughter and naif of the lord, this first time.

2332 Burwell (9 January: leet) John, son of John Rolf Stameryng, his wife, Cecilia,and his son, John: one cotland in Northstrete recently held by William Grantham, for 30 years, rendering annually 4s. at the customary times, to court and leet and all other services and customs owed therein, with the obligation to repair the property. G.: 20d.

2333 Broughton (5 December: leet) Henry Thurberne: one messuage and four acres of land recently held by John Broun Smyth, and one quarter of land recently held by the same John Smyth, for life, rendering annually 5s. for the messuage and four acres, and 3s. for the quarter, at the customary times. G.: 12d.

2334 Broughton Johanna Wrighte, naif of the lord by blood, pays 10s. for license to marry Robert Moor of Ramsey, this time.

2335 WARBOYS (6 December: leet) Roger Smyth: surrender of one acre of demesne land lying in Bascroft, to the use of Robert Slough, for life, rendering annually 8d. at the customary times. G.: two capons.

2336 WARBOYS (same leet) John Horwode Jr.: one messuage, one quarter of land and one mondayland and three acres of Penylond recently held by William Smyth, for life, rendering annually in all things as did William. G.: 3s.4d.

2337 WARBOYS (5 May: court) William London: one toft and a half-virgate of land in Caldecote recently held by John Caton Jr., for life, rendering annually 4s.6d. at the customary times. G.: one capon.

2338 WARBOYS (same court) John Horwode: one toft and a half-virgate of land in Caldecote recently held by Thomas Hirde, alias Benet, for life, rendering annually 3s.4d. at the customary times. G.: two capons.

2339 CHATTERIS (25 January: court) Andrew Sempool: one tenement of eight acres with meadow in Oldhalf recently held by John Sempooll Sr., for life, rendering annually in all things as did John. G.: 6s.8d.

2340 CHATTERIS (same court) John Revesson: one meadow called Owse and Owsemor recently held by John Cut of Ely, for life, rendering annually 10s. G.: 5s.

2341 CHATTERIS (same court) John Smyth of Horseheath: one cotland recently held by John Newman, for life, rendering annually in all things as did John Newman, with the obligation to repair one barn on that cotland, and no more buildings. G.: three capons.

2342 CHATTERIS (same court) John Thomson Jr.: one cotland recently held by John Webstere, for life, rendering annually in all things as did Webstere. G.: 20d.

2343 CHATTERIS (same court) Thomas Cambrigge: one cotland recently held by Katerina Baxtere, for life, rendering annually in all things as did Katerina. G.: two capons.

2344 CHATTERIS (same court) Nicholas Tilney: one cotland with diverse parcels recently held by John Wartir, for life, rendering annually in all things as did John. G.: 2s.4d.

2345 CHATTERIS (same court) Thomas Everard: a half-cotland and four acres of land recently held by Agnes Mathew, for life, rendering annually in all things as did Agnes. G.: 10s.

132r **2346** CHATTERIS (18 September: court) Agnes Pyron: one cotland previously held by her, for life, rendering annually as she previously did. G.: two geese and two capons.

2347 CHATTERIS (same court) Agnes Pyron: surrender of one fishpond and one cotland with one rod of land recently held by John Pyron, to the use of William Pyron, for life, rendering annually in all things as did Agnes. G.: 40d.

2348 CHATTERIS (same court) Thomas Halle: one cotland with one rod of land once held by John Dryng, for life, rendering annually in all things as did John. G.: 5s.

2349 CHATTERIS (same court) Laurence Gilson: two cotlands recently held by Richard Smyth, for life, rendering annually in all things as did Richard. G.: eight geese.

2350 CHATTERIS (same court) John Skynner: one and a half-acres of land recently held by John Pilgryme, for life, rendering annually in all things as did Pilgryme. G.: two capons.

2351 CHATTERIS (same court) John Mathew: one cotland and four acres of land and four acres of meadow in Crowlode recently held by William Whithed, for life, rendering annually in all things as did William. G.: 6s.8d.

2352 CHATTERIS (same court) John Hikkesson Collesson: one cotland recently held by Juliana Bate, for life, rendering annually in all things as did Juliana. G.: 12s.

2353 UPWOOD Robert Miles of Raveley, naif of the lord by blood, pays 12 capons for license to live off the fief at King's Ripton, for as long as it pleases the lord, remaining a naif as before, and rendering two capons to the lord each year.

2354 UPWOOD Robert Miles: surrender of one messuage and a half-virgate of land *ad opus*, another half-virgate with forland in *arentatio*, and half of one virgate of land recently held by his father, with forland, and half of one pithel and one acre, to the use of John Porquoy and his wife, Agnes, for life, rendering annually in all things as did Robert, with the obligation to repair the messuage. Pledge for repairs: Robert Miles. G.: 20d.

2355 UPWOOD Robert Miles: half of one virgate of land once held by his father, with forland and half of one pithel, and three rods of land at Stokkyng once held by John Holy and recently held by himself, for life, rendering annually in all things as he and his father did. G.: 20d.

2356 UPWOOD John Culpon and his wife, Agnes: a half-virgate of land once held by John Hikson and recently *ad opus*, for life, rendering annually 10s. and all other services rendered by those in *arentatio*. G.: two capons.

2357 UPWOOD John Wold: surrender of one plot with a half-virgate of land with forland in *arentatio* once held by Richard Gowler, to the use of Thomas Gowler, for life, rendering annually in all things as did John, with the obligation to repair and maintain the property. G.: 2s.

2358 NEEDINGWORTH Richard Edward, naif of the lord by blood, pays 6s.8d. for license to marry Alicia, his daughter, to a certain freeman, this time.

2359 HURST Thomas Hill and his wife, Emma: the fourth part of one virgate with messuage once held by John Symme and recently held by John Oky, for life, rendering annually 4s. and all other services and customs rendered by John, with the obligation to repair the property at their own expense, timber being supplied by the lord. Further, if anyone comes to claim the whole virgate, Thomas will relinquish his property. G.: three capons.

132v **2360** BYTHORNE Elena, daughter of William Randolf and naif of the lord, pays 40d. for license to marry Roger Bruce, the first time.

2361 BYTHORNE John Baron pays 3s.4d. for license to marry Margaret, his daughter and naif of the lord, to John Randolf.

2362 HOLYWELL (6 May) Adam Sewale and his wife, Rosa: one croft with two butts recently held by Henry Kyng, for life, rendering annually 20d. at the customary times, with the obligation to repair one house on the croft at their own expense, with 40 staves being supplied by the lord. G.: six capons.

2363 HOLYWELL (16 July: court) John Merton: certain land called le Brache and three acres in Schepenfurlong once held by William Peres, for life, rendering annually in all things as did William. G.: 20d.

2364 HOLYWELL Alicia Merton: surrender of one messuage with three acres of land and adjacent demesne land recently held by Richard Merton, to the use of Roger Godfrey and his wife, Alicia, for life, rendering annually in all things as did Alicia. G.: 6s.8d.

2365 WESTON Richard Grymbald: a half-virgate of land with demesne land and burylond and three tofts once held by John Baron and recently held by John Felyce Sr., for life, rendering annually in all things as did John, with the first payment at the next feast of St. Andrew. G.: six capons.

2366 WISTOW Thomas Hyche: one virgate of land *ad opus* with two quarters of land in *arentatio* once held by his father, John Hyche, for life, rendering annually in all things as did John. G.: 6s.8d.

2367 WISTOW John Wyllesson and Thomas Wyllesson: one quarter of land in *aren-*

tatio recently held by Nicholas Broune, for life, rendering annually 4s. and all other services and customs rendered by Nicholas. G.: 2s.

2368 WISTOW (15 July: court) Robert Farewell: one messuage and one virgate of land and a half-virgate of land recently held by John Smyth, for life, rendering annually in all things as did John. G.: 12d.

2369 WISTOW (same court) Edmund Mariet: one messuage and a half-virgate of land recently held by William Martyn, for life, rendering annually in all things as did William. G.: 8d.

2370 WISTOW (same court) John Pope: one messuage and one and a half virgates of land recently held by Thomas Hirde, for life, rendering annually in all things as did Thomas. G.: 12d.

2371 ELSWORTH (18 June: court) Simon Bateman and his wife, Johanna: one cotland, one toft, one virgate and half of one quarter-virgate recently held by John Hobbes and a half-virgate recently held by Thomas Hervy and afterwards by John Michell, for life, rendering annually in all things as did Michell. G.: four capons.

2372 ELSWORTH (same court) Alexander Hobbesson and Henry Hobbesson: one messuage and one semi-virgate of land and a parcel of one virgate once held by Thomas Clerk, in *arentatio* for life, rendering annually 12s. and customs of the vill, with the obligation to repair the messuage. G.: 40d.

2373 ELSWORTH (same court) William Hervy: one messuage recently held by Robert Ynt and one quarter of land recently held by John Hardyng, for life, rendering annually in all things as did Robert and John. G.: 12d.

2374 ELSWORTH (same court) Robert Ynt: one toft and one quarter of land once held by John Herry, for life, rendering annually in all things as did John. G.: 12d.

2375 ELSWORTH (same court) Richard Braughyng: one virgate of land in Grave once held by John in the Hirne, and two parts of one virgate of land there once held by Simon Mathew, for life, rendering annually in all things as did John and Simon. G.: two capons.

133r **2376** ELLINGTON (17 July: court) William Kyng: surrender of one messuage and one quarter of land once held by William Foot to the use of John Kyng, for life, rendering annually in all things as did William. G.: 40d.

2377 KNAPWELL (court) John Ynt, naif of the lord, pays 5s. for license to marry off Katerina, his daughter, this time.

2378 KNAPWELL (same court) John in the Herne and his wife, Aiicia: one messuage and a half-virgate recently held by Thomas Danyell, for life, rendering annually in all things as did Thomas. G.: 12d.

9 JOHN TYCHEMERSCH (1427-1428)

2379 BURWELL (29 September: leet) Thomas Anabele Smyth: one tenement of eight acres once held by John Jay, for 40 years, rendering annually in all things as did John, with suit to court and payment of *capitagium*. G.: a half-mark.

2380 BURWELL (same leet) William Hurbe Taillour and his wife, Alicia: one capital messuage of 15 acres with one croft containing two acres of land once held by John Toyses, for 40 years, rendering annually in all things as did John, suit to court, payment of *capitagium* and holmsilver. G.: 40d.

2381 BURWELL (same leet) John Prikke Sr. and his wife, Margaret: two tenements of 20 acres recently held by Robert Wyot and William Pycot, for 20 years, rendering annually in all things as did Robert and William, with suit to court and payment of *capitagium* and holmsilver. G.: 6s.8d.

2382 WESTON John Possewyk: permission to marry Margaret, widow of Walter Barton, naif of the lord, and to enter into one messuage and a half-virgate of land.
2383 WESTON Walter Fleshewer and his wife, Elena: the capital messuage once held by Hotoft, three quarters of land and demesne land and Burylond once held by William Wattesson, for life, rendering annually in all things as did William. G.: 3s.4d.
2384 KNAPWELL (leet) John Lawe Jr. and his wife, Alicia: one built up messuage and a half-virgate of land recently held by Nicholas Dynyell, for life, rendering annually in all things as did Nicholas. G.: 12d.
2385 HEMINGFORD ABBOTS (leet) John Doraunt and his wife, Johanna: one messuage, one virgate of land, half of one croft recently held by John Bryndhous Jr., for life, rendering annually in all things as did Bryndhous. G.: 40d.
2386 HEMINGFORD ABBOTS (same leet) John Welles: a half-toft and a half-virgate of land once held by John Marschall, for life, rendering annually in all things as did Marschall. G.: two capons.
2387 HOUGHTON (leet) Richard Atkyn and his wife, Margeria: one toft and a half-virgate of land once held by John Andrew, for life, rendering annually in all things as did John. G.: four capons.
2388 HOUGHTON (same leet) William Sayer and his wife, Johanna: one messuage and one virgate of land recently held by John Almer, for life, rendering annually in all things as did John. G.: six capons.
2389 HOUGHTON Thomas Elyot: one croft and one virgate of land recently held by William Atkyn, for life, rendering annually in all things as did William. G.: six capons.
2390 CRANFIELD (leet) John, son of Thomas Grene: one well built up messuage and three quarters of land recently held by John Grene Sr., for life, rendering annually in all things as did John Sr. G.: 13s.4d.
2391 CRANFIELD (same leet) John Whitbrowne: one cotland, one toft and three rods of land recently held by John Hirst, for life, rendering annually in all things as did Hirst. G.: 16d., one capon.
2392 BARTON (court) Thomas Wylymote: surrender, through the hands of John Priour, bailiff, of a half-virgate of land recently held by Richard Wylymote, to the use of Jacob Pope and his wife, Johanna, for life, rendering annually in all things as did Thomas. G.: 40d.
2393 BARTON (same court) Thomas Wylymote pays 40d. for license to marry Margaret, his daughter and naif of the lord, to John Bedford of Schefford.
2394 BARTON (same court) John Bonde: surrender of one messuage and one virgate of land recently held by John Geffrey, to the use of Richard Martyn, for life, rendering annually in all things as did John. G. and heriot: 10s.
2395 BARTON (same court) Johanna Foster: two messuages and one virgate and a half of land recently held by John Hexton, for life, rendering annually in all things as did John. G.: 30s.
2396 BARTON (same court) Richard Revesson, naif of the lord, pays 3s.4d. for license to marry Margaret, his daughter and naif of the lord, to Thomas West of Hanscombe.
133v **2397** BARTON (same court) Richard Roger and his wife, Isabella: one messuage and one virgate of land with forland recently held by John Grene, for life, saving the right of anyone, rendering annually in all things as did John. Further, if any heir claims that land, he shall reimburse Richard for repairs effected by him. G.: 13s.4d.
2398 SHILLINGTON (leet) John Grene of Pegsdon: one messuage, one virgate, and the sixth part of demesne land recently held by his father, John Grene, for life, rendering annually in all things as did his father. G.: 13s.4d.
2399 SHILLINGTON (same leet) John Schepperd Sr.: one messuage and a half-virgate

of land recently held by Richard Schepperd, for life, rendering annually in all things as did Richard. G.: 6s.8d.

2400 SHILLINGTON John Porter and his wife, Petronilla: one messuage and one virgate of land once held by John Gayton, for life, rendering annually in all things as did Gayton. G.: 5s.

2401 SHILLINGTON (26 July: court) John Gobard: two messuages and the sixteenth part of Burylond with one garden, three acres of land in Wodemanende and one cotland with one acre of land once held by Simon Gobard, for life, rendering annually in all things as did Simon. G.: 8s.

2402 SHILLINGTON (same court) John Burgeys: 10 acres of land in Hanscomb once held by Gilbert Atbrook, for life, rendering annually 6s. at the customary times. G.: 12 capons.

2403 SHILLINGTON (same court) Margeria Ede: surrender of one messuage and one virgate of land recently held by John Ede, to the use of Robert Geyton, for life, rendering annually in all things as did Margeria. G.: 6s.8d., six capons.

2404 SHILLINGTON (same court) John Chekener: one messuage and one pithel called Dylly, with one parcel recently from the common and held by Adam Smyth for 14d., for life, rendering annually 20d. at the customary times. G.: three capons.

2405 SHILLINGTON (same court) John Cook: one messuage and a half-virgate of land in Grenende recently held by Sibilla Howson, for life, rendering annually in all things as did Sibilla. G.: six capons.

2406 SHILLINGTON (same court) John Clerk: one pithel called Borespightill containing approximately three rods of land, for life, rendering annually all services and customs owed therein. G.: six capons.

2407 SHILLINGTON (same court) Thomas West: one messuage and two virgates recently held by Alicia West, for life, rendering annually in all things as did Alicia. G.: 20s.

2408 UPWOOD Robert Preston: surrender of one messuage and a half-virgate of land *ad opus* from Akirmanland, with a forland, to the use of Robert Newman and his wife, Johanna, for life, rendering annually in all things as did Robert, with the obligation to repair and maintain the property. G.: eight capons.

2409 UPWOOD Robert Newman: surrender of a half-cotland of one acre once held by John Sywell and one cotland of one acre with another toft in one close at the end of the village next to Dufhousdale, with 4d., to the use of Robert Preston, and his wife, Cristina, for life, rendering annually in all things as did Robert, with the obligation to repair and maintain the property at their own expense. G.: two capons.

2410 ST. IVES (June) Thomas Judde and his wife, Alicia: a half-row recently held by Frederick Skynner and rebuilt by him, next to the free tenement once held by John Chesteyn, rendering annually 4s. in equal portions at the customary times, autumn *precariae*, mowing of the meadow, and four works, as other tenants render, and suit to the lord's mill. Further, they will repair and maintain the property. *Et non licebit*, etc. G.: 20s.

2411 ST. IVES John Elys and his wife, Elena: a half-row once held by Robert Papworth, for life, rendering annually 10s., with the first payment at Michaelmas after one year. Further, they will repair and maintain the property. *Et non licebit*, etc. G.: 6s.8d.

2412 ST. IVES William Smyth of Houghton: surrender of a half-row at le Barres once held by Alan Smyth, to the use of Laurence Boywell and his wife, Alicia, for life, rendering annually 10s. at the customary times, with the obligation to repair and maintain the property. *Et non licebit*, etc. G.: 6s.8d.

2413 HOLYWELL John Nycholas: surrender of one messuage and one virgate of land with demesne land and one pithel at the end of the garden once held by Thomas

Fycheler, to the use of William Smyth and his wife, Alicia, for life, rendering annually in all things as did John. G.: six capons.

2414 HOLYWELL Thomas Cadman of Hemingford pays 3s.4d. for license to marry Margeria, widow of Thomas Nycholas and naif of the lord by blood.

2415 ABBOTS RIPTON Thomas Hacon: surrender of two messuages with two semi-virgates of land once held by William Lawe and one empty plot with one virgate of land in *arentatio*, together with another parcel, to the use of John Reed and his wife, Agnes, for life, rendering annually in all things as did Thomas. G.: 3s.4d.

2416 ABBOTS RIPTON Richard Smyth and his wife, Johanna: one cotland once held by John Flecher, one messuage at the end of the village up to Stukeley, two cotlands lying in one close and six butts of land in a croft recently held by John Bailly, for life, rendering annually 4s. at the customary times, with the obligation to repair the cotland, timber being supplied by the lord. G.: eight capons.

2417 ABBOTS RIPTON John Hawlond and his wife, Johanna: one cotland in *arentatio*, with four butts in a croft and two butts in Lounde once held by John Webstere, rendering annually 4s., which property previously rendered 5s. Further, they will repair the cotland before the feast of St. John the Baptist. G.: two capons.

2418 WARBOYS John Wylkis: surrender of one messuage and a half-virgate of land *ad opus* once held by John Levot, to the use of Richard Wylkys, for life, rendering annually in all things as did John. G.: 2s.

2419 WARBOYS John Wylkys and his wife, Agnes: a half-virgate of land previously held by him, for life, rendering annually 8s. and all other services rendered by tenants in *arentatio*. G.: three capons.

2420 GRAVELEY (court) Thomas Newman: one messuage and one virgate of land once held by his father, Robert Newman, and recently held by William Mannyng, and two acres and a half sown with wheat, five and a half acres sown with barley, and nine acres sown with peas, four quarters of barley, four quarters of wheat in sheaves, and one quartet to be returned at the end of the term, for life, rendering annually in all things as did William. G.: 6s.8d.

2421 ELTON (leet) Thomas Waleys: one messuage and two half-virgates and one parcel of meadow once held by John Hobbysson, for life, with the first payment for the virgate at the next feast of St. Andrew. G.: 2s.

2422 ELTON (same leet) John Bate: one messuage and one quarter of land once held by William Kent, for life, rendering annually 5s. and all other services and customs owed therein. G.: 6d.

2423 ELTON (same leet) John Best: one virgate, one messuage and one quarter of land once held by John Philip Jr., for life, rendering annually in all things as did Philip. G.: 2s.

2424 ELTON (same leet) John Clement: a half-virgate of land recently held by Agnes Waryn, for life, rendering annually in all things as did Agnes. G.: 12d.

2425 ELTON (same leet) Richard Smyth: one empty garden recently held by Schathelok and Rombolde, and one quarter of land recently held by Robert Adam, for life, rendering annually 5s. at the customary times. G.: two capons.

2426 ELTON (same leet) John Herp: one tenement once held by Webster and recently held by Richard Schepperd for 4s., for life, rendering annually 12d. G.: six capons.

2427 ELTON Thomas Alom and his wife, Emma: all akirmanland recently in the lord's hands and not granted out to any tenant *per copiam* or dismissal, and previously held by Thomas himself, with the exception of five acres recently taken up by John Hobbesson and once reserved to the lord, three acres granted out quit to John Germyn, and three acres assigned to Carleton's tenement, for life, rendering annually 8s. at the customary times. G.: 20d.

2428 BROUGHTON (January) Thomas Pulter and his wife, Johanna: the lands and tenements once held by Simon Byggyng and recently held by John Wrighte, for life, rendering annually 5s. at the customary times, with the obligation to repair one *in-sathous* anew and maintain it thereafter, with the first payment at the next feast of St. Andrew. G.: two capons.

2429 BROUGHTON William Clerk and his wife, Johanna: one acre with four selions of land at Ramseyeweye once held by William Justyce, for life, rendering annually in all things as did William. G.: 5s.

2430 BROUGHTON Richard Cabe pays 6s.8d. for license to marry Alicia, his daughter and naif of the lord by blood, to John Couper of Ramsey, cooper.

2431 HURST Thomas Sewer and his wife, Margaret: one cotland once held by John Lawe, for life, rendering annually 2s., which property previously rendered 5s. Also: a half-virgate of land once held by John Lawe with one building on the virgate of William Waryn erected by John Lawe, for life, rendering annually in all things as did John, with the obligation to repair the property, timber being supplied by the lord. G.: excused.

2432 CHATTERIS John Herde and his wife, Anna: one empty plot at the end of the village next to the mill called Hogonsyerd once held by Robert Mathew, for life, rendering annually in all things as did Robert. G.: 12d.

2433 CHATTERIS (court) John Gere: one cotland with the ponds recently held by Peter Chapman, for life, rendering annually in all things as did Peter. Further, he will not put himself under the protection of any other lord, under pain of forfeit. G.: 3s.

2434 CHATTERIS (same court) Agnes Beche: one cotland recently held by Thomas Cambrigge, for life, rendering annually in all things as did Thomas. G.: three capons.

134v **2435** THERFIELD (8 April: leet) John Sparver pays 3s.4d. for license to marry Felicia, his daughter and naif of the lord, to William Sundiller, this time.

2436 THERFIELD (same leet) Thomas Amptill pays 3s.4d. for license to marry Alicia, daughter of William Frere and naif of the lord, to John Gurney, this time.

2437 THERFIELD (same leet) Isabella Wattes: surrender of five acres of new demesne land, to the use of William Smyth and his wife, Alicia, for life, rendering annually 3s.10d. and all other services and customs rendered by Isabella. G.: 8d., one capon.

2438 THERFIELD (same leet) John AtteWode and his wife, Elena: a half-virgate of land recently held by William Waryn, one tenement of Paynes recently held by the same William, the fifth part of land recently held by John Waryn and the fifth part of Wellemede and the fifth part of 40 acres of land with second crops of hay recently held by William Waryn, for life, rendering annually 40s.7d. at the customary times, and all other services and customs rendered by William. G.: three capons.

2439 HURST (February) Nicholas Lacy and his wife, Agnes: one messuage and two semi-virgates once held by Stephen Lytholf and John Smyth, for life, rendering annually in all things as did Stephen and John, with the first payment for the half-virgate at the next feast of St. Andrew, and for the second half-virgate at the feast of St. Andrew following. Further, they will repair and maintain one kiln on the tenement once held by John Smyth within one year, with 20 saplings supplied by the lord, and they receive wheat and barley, to be restored at the end of the term. G.: six capons.

10 JOHN TYCHEMERSCH (1428-1429)

2440 ELSWORTH (21 October: leet) Richard Parnell: one messuage and one quarter of land and a half-virgate in le Grave recently held by Robert Broghyng, for life, rendering annually in all things as did Robert. G.: 13s.4d.

2441 ELSWORTH (same leet) Thomas AtteWode, parson of the church: one cotland once held by John Smyth, for life, rendering annually 2s.6d. at the customary times, with payments beginning at the feast of St. Andrew after four years. Further, he will repair the property, timber being supplied by the lord. G.: one capon.

2442 ELSWORTH (same leet) Thomas Elyot: a half-virgate of land recently held by Robert Broghyng, for life, rendering annually in all things as did Robert. G.: 12d.

2443 ELSWORTH (same leet) John Hardyng Sr.: two cotlands without buildings, one recently held by Henry Leman, the other by Henry Tritche, and a half-virgate recently held by John Hardyng Jr. and called Alredeslond, for life, rendering annually in all things as did the previous tenants, with the obligation to repair one house at his own expense, timber being supplied by the lord sufficient for two sides. G.: 20s.

2444 UPWOOD (leet) Richard Whyte: one messuage and one quarter of land with forland recently held by John Albyn, for life, rendering annually in all things as did John. G.: one capon.

2445 LITTLE RAVELEY (same leet: at Wistow) John Walgate: surrender of one messuage and one virgate recently held by Richard Catelyn, to the use of John Owty, son of John Owty Jr., for life, rendering annually in all things as did Walgate. G.: two capons.

2446 LITTLE RAVELEY (same leet) John Walgate: surrender of his "*mensa*" for the coming year, with wheat to be sown on three and a half-acres of land, three quarters and six bushels of barley to be sown, and three horses, namely Bayard, Balle and Don, to the use of John Owty, son of John Owty Jr. In addition, after the end of a full year, he will grant John Owty one plough with apparatus for three horses and sustenance for three horses, in return for which John Owty concedes to John Walgate one *camera* at the gate and one carthous, and easement in the garden, the foryard, and one virgate of land.

2447 LITTLE RAVELEY (December) Richard Willesson and his sons, John and Thomas: all lands and tenements with meadows, pastures, the pasture of Raveley, and all works rendered by the customaries, *ad firmam* to be held by them, with the exception of court fines of *gersumae*, marriages, reliefs, escheats reserved to the lord, although they shall receive the amercements of brewers and tasters. Further, they will hold all the above from the previous Michaelmas for 15 years, rendering annually £10 in equal portions at the feasts of the Purification, the Nativity of John the Baptist, and St. Matthew, with the obligation to repair properties burned down there, namely: in the tenement of John Plombe, one grange of eight binding-posts, with wood supplied by the lord; everything in the tenement recently held by John Hyche Sr., including one *insathous* of eight binding-posts, one grange of eight binding-posts, and one bake house of six binding-posts, with timber and thatch being supplied by the lord; one *insathous* of eight binding-posts in the tenement of Richard Broune, and one grange of eight binding-posts and one bake house in six binding-posts. Further, they will repair and maintain all houses and buildings there at their own expense, and support all other royal burdens and tallages falling upon those lands and tenements, and, if they desire to rebuild any tenements, the lord will grant them sufficient timber, and they will have all the small and top branches of that timber for the houses. Finally, the first payment will be due at the feast of the Purification after one full year. G.: excused, because of repairs.

135r

2448· WISTOW (leet) Richard Rede: surrender of one messuage and three quarters of land recently held by John Gowler to the use of Richard Baker and his wife, Margaret, for life, rendering annually in all things as did Rede. G.: 40d., six capons.

2449 WISTOW (December) John Barker: three quarters of land once held by John Wrighte in *arentatio*, for life, rendering annually in all things as did Wrighte, with the first payment at the feast of St. Andrew.

2450 RIPTON (leet) Anna Bailly: one messuage and one quarter of land recently held by William Halsham in Wennington, for life, rendering annually in all things as did William. G.: one goose.

2451 BROUGHTON (leet) Henry Thurberne and his wife, Johanna: one messuage and one virgate of land recently held by William del Wold, for life, rendering annually in all things as did William, with payments beginning at the feast of St. Andrew after two years. Further, he will repair the property at his own expense, timber being supplied by the lord. G.: six capons.

2452 BROUGHTON (December) Thomas Crowche: one mondayland with a garden recently held by Robert Gorner, for life, rendering annually in all things as did Robert. G.: two capons.

2453 BROUGHTON (October) William Smyth and his wife, Katerina: one messuage and five quarters of land recently held by Roger Castre and one messuage and a half-virgate of land recently held by Nicholas Bocher, one messuage and a half-virgate of land once held by Robert Turnor and one garden recently held by John del Dam, and one acre of Damlond, for life, rendering annually in all things as did John. G.: 13s.4d.

2454 HOLYWELL (leet) Roger Cristemasse and his wife, Agnes: one messuage, a half-cotland and three acres of land recently held by Thomas Cademan, for life, rendering annually in all things as did Thomas. G.: 2s.

135v **2455** ST. IVES (leet) John Norton and his wife, Johanna: one row recently held by John Sutton, for life, rendering annually 13s.4d. at the customary times. They will rebuild the row at their own expense, except that the lord will supply 12 boards at Ekell for posts and spars, and they will pay no rent for four years. Pledges for repairs: Thomas Sowle and William Nycholl. G.: six capons.

2456 ST. IVES (same leet) Robert Bokenham and his wife, Cristiana: one row recently held by John Essex, for life, rendering annually 8s. at the customary times, with the first payment at next Michaelmas. G.: two capons.

2457 ST. IVES John Lyster: surrender of a half-row once held by Thomas Crowcher, to the use of William Fuller and his wife, Alicia, for life, rendering annually 20s. in equal portions at the customary times, with the obligation to repair and maintain the property at their own expense. *Et non licebit*, etc. G.: 13s.4d.

2458 ST. IVES John Lyster: surrender of one cotland with four acres of land once held by John Denyas, to the use of William Fuller and his wife, Alicia, for life, rendering annually 10s. in equal portions at the customary times, with the obligation to repair and maintain the property at their own expense. Further, they will mill at the mill of the prior. *Et non licebit*, etc. G.: 6s.8d.

2459 ST. IVES John Makesey: surrender of a half-row next to the pillory once held by William Tadlowe, to the use of Walter Bedford and his wife, Sibilla, for life, rendering annually 24s. in equal portions at the customary times, with the obligation to repair and maintain the property. *Et non licebit*, etc. G.: two capons.

2460 ST. IVES Robert Salusbury: surrender of a half-row next to the row in which he lives once held by John Begyn, to the use of John Moor and his wife, Johanna, for life, rendering annually 13s.4d. in equal portions at the customary times, with the obligation to repair and maintain the property. *Et non licebit*, etc. G.: 10s.

2461 ST. IVES William Sabbe and his wife, Rosa: surrender of one row recently held by Nicholas Byschop, to the use of Robert Goodman and his wife, Johanna, for life, rendering annually 14s. in equal portions at the customary times, with the obligation to repair and maintain the property. *Et non licebit*, etc. G.: 10s.

2462 ST. IVES John Balle: a half-row once held by William Gardener and recently held by William AtteHill, for life, rendering annually 10s. in equal portions at the customary times, with the obligation to repair and maintain the property. *Et non licebit*, etc. G.: 6s.8d.

2463 St. Ives (6 September) John Martyn, his wife, Katerina, his son, John, and daughters, Agnes and Emma: two shops with garret and one shop with a solar, and one shop against the bank once held by John Chesteyn, for life, rendering annually 52s.8d. in equal portions at the customary times, with the obligation to repair and maintain the property. *Et non licebit,* etc. G.: 40s.

2464 St. Ives (7 September) John Martyn, his wife, Katerina, their son, John, and their daughters, Agnes and Emma: a half-row once held by John Boys and recently held by John Hamond, for life, rendering annually 20s. in equal portions at the customary times, with the obligation to repair and maintain the property. *Et non licebit,* etc. G.: 20s.

2465 St. Ives (8 September) John Martyn, his wife, Katerina, their son, John, and their daughters, Agnes and Emma: a half-row once held by Richard Dewetre and recently held by Richard Baker, for life, rendering annually 8s. in equal portions at the customary times, with the obligation to repair and maintain the property. *Et non licebit,* etc. G.: 40s.

2466 Houghton (leet) William Heyne: one croft and a half-virgate of land called Laweslond once held by John Whaplode, for life, rendering annually in all things as did John. G.: four capons.

2467 Houghton (same leet) John Spycer Jr.: one croft and a half-virgate called Loveslond recently held by William Roger, for life, rendering annually 6s. in equal portions at the customary times. G.: four capons.

2468 Houghton (same leet) Robert Barker: one messuage and one virgate and a half-virgate of land recently held by John Andrew, for life, rendering annually in all things as did John. G.: six capons.

2469 Houghton John Whaplode Jr.: surrender of one virgate in *arentatio* once held by John Whaplode Sr., to the use of John Hill of Hartford, for life, rendering annually in all things as did John Jr. G.: 2s.

2470 Houghton (February) John Newman: surrender of one messuage and one virgate of land once held by Thomas Crane, to the use of John Plombe, for life, rendering annually in all things as did Newman, with the obligation to repair the messuage before the feast of St. John the Baptist, under penalty of a fine of 40s. G.: six capons.

2471 Houghton Richard Wilkis: surrender of one plot with a half-virgate of land once held by Richard Carter, to the use of John Gerard and his wife, Alicia, for life, rendering annually in all things as did Richard. G.: four capons.

2472 Houghton John Newman: surrender of one cotland *ad opus* once held by John Abbot, to the use of Simon Thoday and his wife, Johanna, for life, rendering annually 7s. and all other works rendered by those *ad opus*. G.: 3s.

2473 Houghton John Newman: one cotland and one croft in *arentatio* once held by Henry Lawe, for life, rendering annually in all things as did Henry. G.: (*blank*).

2474 Hemingford Abbots (leet) Walter Ingell Jr.: one messuage and one virgate of land recently held by Edmund Mariot, for life, rendering annually in all things as did Edmund. G.: one capon.

2475 Hemingford Abbots (same leet) John Kirkeby: one messuage and a half-virgate of land recently held by Edmund Mariot, for life, rendering annually in all things as did Edmund. G.: one capon.

2476 Shillington (leet) John Aylmer: one messuage and one and a half-virgates of land recently held by his father, John Aylmer, for life, rendering annually in all things as did John Sr. G. and heriot: 18s.4d.

2477 Shillington (same leet) John Ward: surrender of one messuage and one

136r

virgate of land recently held by John Burnham, to the use of William Kirkeby for life, rendering annually 20s.7d. and all other services and customs owed therein. G.: 2s.

2478 SHILLINGTON (same leet) Richard, son of John Grave, and his wife, Elizabeth: one parcel of the manor and one lot of demesne land recently held by Adam Couper, for life, rendering annually in all things as did Adam, with two acres reserved to Johanna Couper for life. G.: 6s.8d.

136v **2479** SHILLINGTON (same leet) John Davy: one messuage and a half-virgate of land recently held by John Bernet, for life, rendering annually in all things as did Bernet. G.: 20d.

2480 SHILLINGTON (same leet) William Smyth Jr., servant of William Bradyvan: with the consent of William Bradyvan, the reversion of one messuage and one virgate and one lot of demesne land now held by William Bradyvan and his wife, Matilda, for life, rendering annually 18s.10d.ob. for the messuage and virgate, and 9s.4d. for the demesne land, and all other services and customs rendered by William and Matilda. Fine for entry into the property after their deaths: 26s.8d.

2481 SHILLINGTON Master Richard Hethe, rector of the church: one pasture called Newstokkyng recently held by Peter Cook, for life, rendering annually 16s. at the customary times. G.: excused.

2482 THERFIELD (3 December: leet) Roger Hycheman pays the fine for license to marry Margaret, daughter of John Adam Sr. and naif of the lord by blood.

2483 RAMSEY Robert Toly, alias Of the Kechen, and his wife, Alicia: from Brother John Stucle, sub-cellarer, one plot at Grena once held by William Burton, for life, rendering annually 6s.8d. in equal portions at the customary times, with the sub-cellarer responsible for repairs and maintenance. G.: four capons.

2484 RAMSEY John West: from the sub-cellarer, one parcel of meadow with "le Welugrowe" next to Hemyngg called "Fayrsholle" recently held by John Borell, with the fishpond pertaining to it, for 21 years, rendering annually 3s.4d. at the feasts of the Annunciation and Nativity of Blessed Mary. Further, he will make one ditch between the parcel and another parcel held by William Claxton, at his own expense, with the right to cut down and replant the willows there. *Et si predictus redditus,* etc. G.: 6s.8d.

2485 CHATTERIS (court) John, son of Robert Gere: two acres of land previously held by John Massely Bocher, for life, rendering annually in all things as did Massely. G.: 8d.

2486 CHATTERIS (same court) John Sempooll of Briggesplace: one cotland recently held by John Cokerell in Wenney ende, for life, rendering annually in all things as did Cokerell. G.: 2s.7d.

2487 CHATTERIS (same court) John Clerk: one cotland with another parcel recently held by John Tylney, for life, rendering annually 19d. and all other services and customs owed therein. G.: 2s.4d.

2488 CHATTERIS (same court) Edmund Thommysson, one cotland with half the meadow in Oldhalf once held by John Chownesson, for life, rendering annually in all things as did John, with one *camera* and easement in the cotland ceded by Edmund to his mother, Anna, for life. G.: 20d.

2489 CHATTERIS (court) John Lawe Sr.: one messuage and four acres of land recently held by John Clerk, for life, rendering annually in all things as did Clerk. G.: 2s.

2490 CHATTERIS (same court) John Michell: one cotland recently held by John Hertford, for life, rendering annually in all things as did Hertford. G.: 2s.

137r **2491** UPWOOD CUM RAVELEY William Cufse and his wife, Johanna: three half-virgates of land with forland and one pithel once held by Robert Myles and recently held by John Purquoy, in *arentatio* for life, rendering annually 25s.4d. at the customary times, one ploughing *precaria*, supplying one man for the Great Autumn *Precaria*, customs of the vill, except the office of beadle. G.: two capons.

2492 HURST (April) William Bryngton: one messuage with half of one virgate of land once held by John Oky and recently held by William Foster, for life, rendering annually 8s. and all other services and customs rendered by Foster, with the first payment at the feast of St. Andrew after two years. Further, he will repair the property within one year, with boards and posts supplied by the seneschal of Ramsey. G.: six capons.

2493 GRAVELEY William West, naif of the lord by blood, pays 2s. for license to marry Agnes West, his daughter, to Henry Bokeleswade, this time.

2494 CRANFIELD (leet) John Webbe: surrender of three acres of demesne land up to Purybroke, to the use of William Wodhill, for life, rendering annually in all things as did John. G.: 12d.

2495 CRANFIELD (same leet) John Aleyn, naif of the lord, pays 6s.8d. for license to marry off Agnes, his daughter, this time.

2496 CRANFIELD (same leet) Margaret, daughter of Thomas Terry and naif of the lord, pays 6s.8d. for license to marry, this time. Pledge: Thomas Brereley.

2497 BRINGTON John Wrighte: surrender of one cotland from Bowyer's tenement with three butts of land at le Marsch once held by John Revysson, to the use of Hugo Goldyngton, for life, rendering annually in all things as did John. G.: 2s.

2498 WARBOYS Henry Norburgh: surrender of one plot with a half-virgate *ad opus* recently held by Richard Mold, to the use of John Bonde, for life, rendering annually in all things as did Henry. G.: 3s.4d.

2499 BURWELL (court) John Herpour and his assigns: one cotland recently held by Thomas Dryver and another cotland held by Katerina Fuller, previously rendering 2s.10d. and two works, for 60 years, rendering annually 2s. at the customary times and two suits to court, with the obligation to rebuild a house on the property at his own expense. G.: two capons.

2500 BURWELL (same court) William Jay: one cotland with one and a half acres of land lying at the northern end of the village once held by Margaret Rower, for life, rendering annually in all things as did Margaret.

11 JOHN TYCHEMERSCH (1429-1430)

137v **2501** WISTOW CUM RAVELEY (December) John Randolf: one messuage and three quarters of land once held by John Wrighte, with the fourth part of Wolney Made once held by John White and recently held by Stephen Aylmar, for life, rendering annually 19s. and all other services and customs rendered by Stephen, with the first payment for the three quarters at the feast of St. Andrew after one year. Further, he will repair the property. G.: three capons.

2502 WISTOW CUM RAVELEY (December) John Hych and his wife, Alicia: one empty plot and a half-virgate of land from akirmanland once held by John Randolf, for life, rendering annually 7s. at two terms, with the first payment at the feast of the Annunciation after one year. G.: six pullets.

2503 WISTOW CUM RAVELEY (leet) Radulph Wrighte: one messuage, one virgate and one quarter of land recently held by John Owty and John Hyche Jr., for life, rendering annually in all things as did John. G.: 2s.

2504 WISTOW CUM RAVELEY (same leet) John Walgate: one messuage and one quarter of land recently held by Thomas Owty, for life, rendering annually in all things as did Thomas. G.: three capons.

2505 WISTOW CUM RAVELEY John Aylmar, naif of the lord, and his wife, Alicia: a half-virgate of land *ad opus*, one messuage recently held by his father, and one quarter of land recently held by John Love, for life, rendering annually in all things as did Love. G. and fine for marrying Alicia, daughter of Richard Plumbe of Warboys and naif of the lord: 6s.8d.

2506 WISTOW CUM RAVELEY Robert Aylmar and his wife, Johanna: one quarter of land once held by Richard Holbech and one messuage and half of one quarter of land, one hydemanland, three rods of demesne land at Litilclayhill, and a half-acre of land at Lowefurlong once held by John Love, for life, rendering annually in all things as did John. G.: excused.

2507 WISTOW CUM RAVELEY Robert Rede: surrender of one cotland in *arentatio* and one plot with adjacent land once held by Richard Pycard, to the use of William Elys and his wife, Johanna, who also receive: one parcel of meadow called Redyng, one acre of demesne land called Burysevene, and six selions of land in Chesfurlong containing approximately one acre recently held by Robert Nottyng, in *arentatio* for life, rendering annually 8s. for rents and customs, at the customary times, with the obligation to repair and maintain the property. G.: four capons.

2508 BURWELL (leet) Thomas Goodale: one cotland and seven acres of land once held by Thomas Purye, for 32 years, rendering annually in all things as did Purye, and suit to court and leet. G.: 20d.

2509 BURWELL (court) William Jay and his wife, Isabella: one tenement of 15 acres recently held by John Powle, one built up cotland, and one adjacent croft recently held by Radulph Rower, for 30 years, rendering annually 16s. at the customary times, suit to court and leet and *capitagium* for the 15 acres, and 6s. and suit to court and leet for the cotland and croft. G.: 40d.

2510 BURWELL (same court) John Dene and his wife, Agnes: one tenement of 24 acres built up with one barn and recently held by Thomas Rolf, for 30 years, rendering annually in all things as did Thomas, and suit to court and leet and *capitagium*. G.: four capons.

2511 BROUGHTON (leet) Richard Webstere and his wife, Katerina: one messuage and a half-virgate of land once held by Nicholas Bocher Jr., for life, rendering annually in all things as did Nicholas, with the first payment at the feast of St. Andrew after one year. G.: four capons.

2512 BROUGHTON (same leet) John Clerk Jr.: one cotland and three quarters of land recently held by John Clerk Sr., for life, rendering annually in all things as did John Sr. G.: six capons.

2513 BROUGHTON (same leet) Thomas Botiller: surrender of one messuage, six quarters of land and one and a half acres of damlond, to the use of William del Wold, for life, rendering annually in all things as did Thomas. G.: 6s.8d.

2514 BROUGHTON (same leet) William Smert: one mondayland with four butts and a half-acre of land at Olddole recently held by William Ivell, for life, rendering annually 2s. at the customary times. G.: two capons.

138r **2515** HEMINGFORD ABBOTS (leet) William Martyn: surrender of one messuage, one virgate of land, a half-croft and a half-virgate of land, to the use of Thomas Ingill and his wife, Cecilia, for life, rendering annually in all things as did William. G.: 6s.8d.

2516 HEMINGFORD ABBOTS Thomas Aungewyn and his wife, Johanna: one empty plot, two rods of land and 22 feet of meadow recently held by John Weston, four selions of land next to Bosebalk, a half-acre of Long Ripton and two selions at Gormeschester Barre once held by Thomas Fuller, for life, rendering annually 20d. at the customary times. G.: four capons.

2517   HEMINGFORD ABBOTS (court) William Felde: one plot with croft and two virgates of land recently held by Galfridus Cadman, for life, rendering annually in all things as did Galfridus. G.: 3s.4d.

2518   HEMINGFORD ABBOTS Matilda Lincolne: one small parcel of land recently held by John Lincolne, for life, rendering annually in all things as did John. G.: one capon.

2519   WARBOYS (October) William Colvyle: one messuage and one virgate of land *ad opus* recently held by William Ravele, for life, rendering annually in all things as did William. G.: six capons.

2520   WARBOYS (March) William Berenger Jr.: one tenement from the tenement of Temesford with certain adjacent lands, and one quarter of land in *arentatio* once held by John Flemyng, for life, rendering annually in all things as did John, with the first payment at the next feast of St. Andrew. The lord agrees to repair the grange and all buildings in carpentry, with William obligated to effect remaining repairs, and William gives the lord this year, both for rent and repairs, 20s.

2521   STUKELEY Beatrix Foot, servant of Thomas Gosse and naif of the lord by blood, pays 6s.8d. for license to marry John Denyle, this time.

2522   ST. IVES (leet) John Goodman and his wife, Johanna: a half-row recently held by John Makesey lying next to the row of Thomas Markham and that of John Scharp, for life, rendering annually 17s. at the customary times, with the obligation to repair and maintain the property. *Et non licebit* etc. G.: two capons.

2523   ST. IVES (same leet) John Sutton and his wife, Margaret: a half-row recently held by William Pope, for life, rendering annually 4s. at the customary times, with the obligation to repair and maintain the property. *Et non licebit*, etc. G.: 3s.4d.

2524   ST. IVES (same leet) John Mildenhale and his wife, Johanna: a half-row next to the pillory recently held by William Bedford, rendering to the lord annually 24s. at the customary times, with the obligation to repair the property within three years. *Et non licebit*, etc. G.: (*blank*).

2525   ST. IVES (November) Thomas Barbor and his wife, Johanna: one row recently held by John Flecher and once held by Thomas Smyth, for life, rendering annually 3s.4d. in equal portions at the customary times, with the obligation to repair the property within three years. *Et non licebit*, etc. G.: 6s.8d.

2526   ST. IVES William Moor: surrender of one garden called Ballardisfoorthe, to the use of William Fychion, and his wife, Isabella, for life, rendering annually in all things as did William Moor and 8s. at the customary times, with the obligation to maintain and keep the garden in enclosures and spring at their own expense. G.: two capons.

138v   **2527**   ST. IVES Henry Spicer and his wife, Emma: one row in which he lives, for life, rendering annually 3s.4d. in equal portions at the customary times, with the obligation to repair and maintain the property. *Et non licebit*, etc. G.: excused.

2528   ST. IVES William Pynnok and his wife, Margaret: one row recently held by Robert Salisbury and once held by William Galapyn, for life, rendering annually 20s. at the customary times, with the obligation to repair and maintain the property. *Et non licebit*, etc.: 20s. Pledge: John Pynnok, chaplain.

2529   ST. IVES John Gonne and his wife, Margaret: a half-row once held by John Papworth and recently held by John Elys, for life, rendering annually 10s. in equal portions at the customary times, with the obligation to repair and maintain the property. *Et non licebit*, etc. G.: 2s.

2530   ST. IVES (1 September) Thomas Baker and his wife, Johanna: a half-row in "le Cheker" recently held by John Flecher, for life, rendering annually 12s. at the customary times, with the first payment at Michaelmas after three years. They will repair one house within one year, receiving one board, from the lord for beams. *Et non licebit*, etc. G.: two capons.

2531 ST. IVES John AtteWode and his wife, Margaret: one row once held by William Tadlowe and recently held by Thomas Raven, for life, rendering annually 2s.8d., with the obligation to repair and maintain the property. *Et non licebit*, etc. G.: 20d.

2532 CRANFIELD (leet) Johanna, daughter of Richard Aleyn and naif of the lord, pays 6s.8d. for license to marry whomever she wishes, this time.

2533 CRANFIELD (same leet) Alicia, daughter of Thomas DunWode, pays 6s.8d. for license to marry whomever she wishes, the first time.

2534 CRANFIELD (same leet) John Sare, naif of the lord, pays 6s.8d. for license to marry Christiana, his daughter and naif of the lord, to John Hare, this time.

2535 BARTON (court) William Roger: surrender, through the hands of his attorney, of one messuage and two half-virgates of land recently held by him, to the use of Thomas Child, for life, rendering annually in all things as did William. G.: 10s.

2536 BARTON (same court) William, son of Edmund Roger: one messuage and two virgates of land once held by John Hexton, for life, rendering annually in all things as did John. G.: one mark.

2537 BARTON (court) William Schepperd: surrender, through the hands of Jacob Child, of 12 acres recently held by William Messanger, to the use of Henry Burrch and his heirs, rendering annually in all things as did William, with three acres reserved to the said William Messanger for life for an annual payment of 2s. (i.e. 6d. at the feast of St. Andrew, 6d. at the feast of the Annunciation, 6d. at the feast of John the Baptist, 6d. at Michaelmas). Further, if William Messanger defaults in his payments, he will lose his status in the property; nor may he alienate this tenement to anyone under penalty of forfeit. G.: 6s.8d.

2538 BARTON (same court) William Child and his wife, Matilda: one messuage and one virgate of land recently held by Edmund Child, for life, provided that they — or whoever holds the tenement — will provide food and clothing and dwelling for the said Edmund for as long as he lives, under penalty of forfeit. G.: 6s.8d.

2539 BRINGTON (court) John Wright: one messuage and one quarter of land with appurtenances recently held by John Dalby and recently held by Thomas Gandir, for life, rendering annually in all things as did the previous tenants. G.: 20d.

139r **2540** SHILLINGTON (leet) John Webbe and his wife, Agnes: one messuage and one virgate of land once held by Walter Porter, for life, rendering annually in all things as did Walter. G.: 2s.

2541 SHILLINGTON (same leet) William Berford and his wife, Johanna: three acres of land at Tynehill with appurtenances once held by John Grene of Upenende, for life, rendering annually in all things as did John. G.: 12d.

2542 SHILLINGTON (same leet) John Maynard: two cotes and four acres recently held by Simon Gobard, for life, rendering annually 5s. at the customary times and all other services and customs rendered by Simon. G.: 12d.

2543 SHILLINGTON (court) Gilbert del Hill: one messuage and one virgate of land recently held by William del Hill, for life, rendering annually in all things as did William. G.: 2s.

2544 SHILLINGTON (same court) Richard Whitefelow, naif of the lord, pays 6s.8d. for license to marry Alicia and Margaret, his daughters, to whomever they wish, the first time.

2545 THERFIELD (leet) John Bekeswell: one built up cotland with a garden containing one acre of land recently held by John Hatle, for life, rendering annually in all things as did John Hatle.

2546 THERFIELD (same leet) John Tayllor: one close called Peterscroft recently held by John Gurney, for life, rendering annually 12s. in equal portions at Michaelmas and Easter. G.: one capon.

2547 THERFIELD (same leet) William Smyth and his wife, Alicia: one pithel once held by Mauritius Martyn, for life, rendering annually 3s. in equal portions at Michaelmas and Easter, with the obligation to rebuild one house there within two years under penalty of forfeit. G.: two capons.

2548 HURST (December) Simon Oldich, alias Romburgh, and John Arnewey: one messuage and half of one virgate of land recently held by Stephen Lytholf and once held by William atte Halle, for life, rendering annually 8s. and all other services and customs rendered by Stephen, with the first payment at the next feast of St. Andrew. G.: three capons.

2549 HURST (1 March) William Vycory: one messuage and one virgate of land once held by Thomas Porter, for life, rendering annually 13s.4d. and all other services and customs rendered by Thomas, with the obligation to repair the property, timber being supplied by the lord, and with the first payment at the feast of the Annunciation after four full years. G.: two capons.

2550 HURST (March) John Hall and his wife, Johanna: one messuage at the end of the village next to Haldeyerd, with certain lands in the fields once held by Amicia Ulf and recently held by John Laweman, for life, rendering annually 13s.4d., which property previously rendered 40s. Further, they will perform all other services and customs owed therein, with the first payment at the feast of St. Andrew after one year. G.: two capons.

2551 UPWOOD Richard Skynner and his wife, Olyva: one messuage and a half-virgate of land once held by John Hikkisson, one quarter of land once held by Galfridus Hawkyn with adjacent forland recently held by John Culpon, one quarter of land once held by Nicholas Alston with adjacent forland and land at Hymadeknoll and Coppidwell and recently held by the same Nicholas, and one half-virgate of land once held by Richard Payn, for life, rendering annually 21s.6d. at the customary times and other services rendered by those in *arentatio*. G.: three capons.

2552 GRAVELEY Richard Dekes: surrender of one messuage and one virgate of land to the use of John Rolf Jr. and his wife, Johanna, for life, rendering annually in all things as did Richard. G.: 40d.

139v **2553** KNAPWELL (leet) John Ilger: one messuage recently held by Richard Holm, with a half-virgate *ad opus*, for life, rendering annually in all things as did Richard. G.: 12d.

2554 KNAPWELL (same leet) William Aubry: one quarter of land recently held by William Joye, for life, rendering 3s.1d. the first year, and 6s.2d. each year thereafter, and all other services and customs rendered by William Joye. G.: 8d., one capon.

2555 ELSWORTH (same leet) John Cristemesse: one quarter of land recently held by William Herry, for life, rendering annually in all things as did William. G.: 6d.

2556 ELSWORTH John Herry and his wife, Alicia: one plot and a half-virgate of land and one croft once held by Thomas Peek, for life, rendering annually in all things as did Thomas. G.: 4s.

2557 ELSWORTH Richard Bene and his wife, Margaret: one plot with a half-virgate of land once held by William Pygot, for life, rendering annually in all things as did William. G.: 20d., two capons.

2558 ELSWORTH (court) John Swynford: one messuage and a half-virgate of land recently held by Simon Herry, for life, rendering annually in all things as did Simon. G.: 2s.

2559 HOUGHTON Richard Michell: surrender of one cotland once held by John Gowler to the use of John Mayhew and his wife, Margaret, for life, rendering annually in all things as did Richard. Further, John is the pledge for Richard that he will not relinquish the messuage and virgate that he now holds. G.: 2s.

2560 HOUGHTON John Deerson and his wife, Alicia: one empty messuage and a half-virgate of land once held by William Aleyn and recently held by John Coton and once held by Preston, for life, rendering annually in all things as did John Coton. G.: two capons.

2561 UPWOOD (March) John Miles: surrender of one messuage and a half-virgate of land in *arentatio*, a half-virgate *ad opus*, and one quarter called Snaplond recently held by Andrew Balle, to the use of John Fox, and his wife, Johanna, for life, rendering annually in all things as did John, with the obligation to repair and maintain the property at their own expense, and with the first payment at the feast of St. John the Baptist. Until then, John Miles will pay the rent. G.: three capons.

2562 UPWOOD (January) John Bole and his wife, Alicia: one cotland of two acres recently held by Richard Bucworth with five butts of land next to Longwong recently held by William Baker, for life, rendering annually 5s. at the customary times, with the obligation to repair the property, with timber supplied by the lord, and with the first payment at the next feast of the Annunciation. G.: three capons.

2563 HOLYWELL (court) Nicholas Oky and his wife, Margaret: one acre of land in Nethbrerecroft once held by Radulph Muryell, for life, rendering annually in all things as did Radulph. G.: two capons.

2564 HOLYWELL John Scot Sr.: surrender of one cotland with demesne land and croft, another parcel there, and half of Dryhurst, to the use of John Scot Jr. and his wife, Alicia, for life, rendering annually in all things as did John Sr. G.: six geese.

2565 ABBOTS RIPTON (court) William Laveyn: one messuage and a half-virgate of land, and half of one quarter of land recently held by William de Wold, for life, rendering annually in all things as did William. G.: 6s.8d.

2566 ABBOTS RIPTON (same court) John Hyche and his wife, Agnes: two buildings and one empty plot with one virgate of land, a half-virgate of land, and 10 acres of land at Catesheg once held by Adam Dycon, for life, rendering annually 28s. at the customary times. G.: four capons.

2567 ABBOTS RIPTON (same court) William del Wold: one messuage and a half-virgate of land recently held by William Lavyn, for life, rendering annually in all things as did William. G.: 20d.

2568 ABBOTS RIPTON (same court) Thomas Billyng: one plot at le Grene recently held by John Robbis, for life, rendering annually in all things as did John. G.: 12d.

2569 ABBOTS RIPTON[39] Note of an agreement between John Person and Thomas Chesterton Sr. to hold one messuage and one virgate recently held by John Cadman, for life, rendering annually in all things as did John, with the obligation to repair the property, timber being supplied by the lord, and with the first payment at Michaelmas after two years.

---

[39] B.L. Add. Roll. 39480. "Memorandum quod Johannes Person in presenti curia fecit convencionem cum senescallo ad tenendum unum messuagium et dimidiam virgatam terre nuper in tenura Johannis Cadman ad terminum vite ipsius Johannis Person ad voluntatem domini secundum consuetudinem manerii, reddendo et faciendo inde in omnibus sicut predictus Johannes Cademan nuper fecit. Et reparabit predictum messuagium competenter sumptibus suis propriis praeter quod habebit de domino meremium. Primo termino solucionis incipiente in festo sancti Michaelis proximo futuro post duos annos completos, etc. Set idem Johannes Person dicit quod non vult stare obligatus per istam scriptam."

140r **2570** CHATTERIS (July: court) Jacob Biller: one built up cote in le Hythe and four acres once held by Stephen Cokerell, for life, rendering annually in all things as did Stephen, with the obligation to repair the property. Pledge for repairs: John Wetyng. G.: four capons.

2571 CHATTERIS (same court) John Clerk: one tenement of eight acres recently held by Richard Meyke, for life, rendering annually in all things as did Richard. G.: 40d.

2572 CHATTERIS (same court) John Costyne: one cotland recently held by John Bate, for life, rendering annually in all things as did Bate. G.: 40d.

2573 CHATTERIS (same court) Edmund Lytholf: four acres of land recently held by William Whithed, for life, rendering annually in all things as did William. G.: two capons.

2574 CHATTERIS (same court) John Pyper: one cotland recently held by John Sempool, for life, rendering annually in all things as did Sempool. G.: three capons.

2575 ELLINGTON William Smyth of Keston pays 6s.8d. for entry into one tenement with a half-virgate recently held by Thomas Burgeys, and for license to marry Margaret, daughter of the said Thomas and naif of the lord.

2576 RAMSEY John Sutton and his wife, Johanna: one messuage in High Street next to the messuage in which William Hill lives and once held by Thomas Borugh and recently held by John Berenger, for life, rendering annually 6s.8d., with the obligation to repair and maintain the property, timber and thatch being supplied by the subcellarer. *Et si predictus redditus*, etc. (arrears of one month). G.: 2s.

12 JOHN TYCHEMERSCH (1430-1431)

140v **2577** ELSWORTH (leet) William Howlot: one cotland with croft recently held by Thomas Peek with three rods of land, for life, rendering annually 4s. at the customary times, provided that the lord may enter the tenement if it is not occupied by a tenant. G.: 12d.

2578 KNAPWELL (leet) Richard Lavell and his wife, Katerina: one messuage and a half-virgate of land with one quarter of land recently held by William Doraunt and one toft and a half-virgate of land recently held by William Merchaund, for life, rendering annually in all things as did the previous tenants. G.: 40d.

2579 KNAPWELL (same leet) John Reignald: one quarter of land recently held by John Joynor, for life, rendering annually in all things as did John. G.: 12d.

2580 BURWELL (leet) Thomas Arnald: surrender of one cotland with croft once held by Alexander Sparwe (half of the croft being reserved to himself), to the use of John Godale and his wife, Alicia, for life, rendering annually 5s., suit to court and leet, and all other services and customs owed therein. G.: 20d.

2581 BURWELL (same leet) Radulph Lyne and his wife, Margaret: one pithel recently held by William Ideyne, for life, rendering annually 2s. at the customary times, suit to court and leet, and all other services and customs owed therein. G.: 40d.

2582 BARTON (leet) John Wylymote: one messuage and one virgate of land recently held by John atte Fan, for life, rendering annually in all things as did John. G.: 4s.

2583 BARTON (same leet) John Milward: one plot with building recently held by Johanna Foster, for life, rendering annually in all things as did Johanna. G.: 2s.

2584 RIPTON (leet) William Fysscher: one toft and a half-virgate of land recently held by John Halom, for life, rendering annually 8s. at the customary times and all other services and customs rendered by John, with the obligation to build one house 24 feet long within two years at his own expnese, timber for beams being supplied by the lord. He will receive 8s. if he does not default in this matter, and if he does default, he will receive 4s. G.: two capons.

2585 St. Ives (leet) John Baylly and his wife, Alicia: a half-row once held by Ambrose Newyngton and recently held by the aforesaid John, for life, rendering annually 5s., with the obligation to repair and maintain the property. *Et non licebit,* etc. G.: 6s.8d.

2586 St. Ives (same leet) John Bernewell and his wife, Isabella: the western parcel of one tenement called Disthall next to the tenement of the Prior and recently held by William Pynnok, for life, rendering annually 2s. in equal portions at the customary times, with the obligation to repair and maintain the property. *Et non licebit,* etc. G.: two capons.

2587 Hemingford Abbots (leet) Edmund Mariot and his wife, Katerina: one messuage and one virgate of land recently held by Margaret Ibbot, for life, rendering annually in all things as did Margaret. G.: 5s.

141r **2588** Holywell (leet) John Smyth and his wife, Alicia: one plot and one virgate of land recently held by Thomas Edward, for life, rendering annually in all things as did Thomas. G.: eight capons.

2589 Holywell John Wodecok: one cotland and one parcel of a garden once held by William Spercoll and recently held by Thomas Edward, with one acre of land at le Smethe and two acres in Stonydole recently held by the same Thomas, for life, rendering annually in all things as did Thomas, with the obligation to repair and maintain the cotland. G.: 2s.

2590 Weston John Repon: surrender of half of one cotland with half of four acres of land and half of one quarter of land, a half-virgate and one quarter, and demesne land recently held by Adam Burgeys, to the use of Richard Miller, and his wife, Margaret, for life, rendering annually in all things as did Adam, with the obligation to repair the property. Pledges for repairs: Thomas Grym of Spaldwick, John Repon and Reginald Taillor. G.: six capons.

2591 Weston Thomas Dyngele and his wife, Johanna: one messuage with appurtenances recently held by Walter Kyng and once held by William Magetesson, for life, rendering annually in all things as did Walter. Thomas will have an allowance of half of this year's rents, he will leave the land fallow, and he receives four quarters of barley, to be repaid to the lord next year. G.: two capons.

2592 Weston John Possewik and his wife, Margaret: a half-virgate of land once held by John Felyce and recently held by John Sqwyer, for life, rendering nothing this year and 32s. each year thereafter — both for this property and for other property he holds. Further, he will repair one house on the property, and he receives one quarter of barley from the lord, to be returned next year. G.: four capons.

2593 Warboys (December) John Gylys and his wife, Agnes: one plot of Ravene's tenement once held by Hamond Carpenter and recently held by John Thakker, for life, rendering annually 4s. at the customary times. G.: 6s.8d.

2594 Warboys (January) Richard Wilkis: one virgate once held by John Brownote in Caldecote, for life, rendering annually 13s.4d., with the first payment at the next feast of St. Andrew. G.: excused.

2595 Warboys (January) Thomas Buntyng and his wife, Isabella: one messuage and a half-virgate of land recently held by William Smart and recently held by John Bennysson, and a half-virgate of land once held by John Hy Sr., and recently held by John Hy Miller in Caldecote, for life, rendering annually 11s. at the customary times, customs of the vill, and all other services rendered by those in *arentatio.* Further, he is granted an allowance of 6s. of the rent of this year. G.: threshing peas at Bigging for one day.

2596 Ellington (leet) Robert Mokke, naif of the lord, pays 20s. for license to marry Agnes, his daughter, to John Skynner of Little Stukeley.

2597   ELTON (January) John Clement: one messuage and one virgate of land once held by William Pokebrook, for life, rendering annually 16s. and all other services and customs rendered by William, with the first payment at the next feast of St. Andrew. G.: three capons.

141v   **2598**   HURST Thomas Pope and his wife, Margaret: one tenement of the tenement of Lord de Wolle, once held by John Roper, for life, rendering annually 12d. at the customary times, with the provision that he not relinquish any other parcels of land that he holds, under penalty of loss of the cotland. G.: 6d.

2599   HURST Roger Cachesoly and his wife, Agnes: one cotland with croft lying in Westende once held by Thomas Wyngod, for life, rendering annually 20d., which property previously rendered 3s. G.: one capon.

2600   HURST Thomas Pope and his wife, Margaret: a half-virgate of land once held by William Trover and one quarter of land once held by Roger Porter and recently held by William Pope, for life, rendering annually 13s.4d. at the customary times. G.: 6d.

2601   SHILLINGTON Laurence Chybbele, alias Atte Fan, naif of the lord by blood, pays 20d. for license to live off the manor, and he will pay 20d. annually at the leet of Shillington, with his own hands.

2602   SHILLINGTON William Kirkeby: surrender of one messuage and one virgate of land once held by John Burnham, to the use of Matthew Chambre, and his wife, Agnes, for life, rendering annually 20s.7d.ob. at the customary times, and all other services and customs owed therein, with the obligation to rebuild a hall and repair the grange within three years, and maintain it thereafter, at their own expense. G.: 3s.4d.

2603   BRINGTON John Stable Jr.: one cotland of Bowyer's tenement with three butts of land at le Marsch from the tenement recently held by John Wryghte and once held by Hugo Goldyngton, for life, rendering annually in all things as did John. G.: six capons.

2604   SLEPE (July) William Dryver and his wife, Agnes: a half-virgate of land in *arentatio* once held by William Yoman and recently held by Thomas Pope, for life, rendering annually 8s. and all other services and customs rendered by Thomas. G.: six capons.

2605   SLEPE (July) Richard Morgon and his wife, Alicia: a half-virgate of land in *arentatio* once held by John Cartere and recently held by Nicholas Mabon, for life, rendering annually 7s. and all other services and customs rendered by Nicholas, with the first payment at the next feast of St. Andrew. G.: 12d.

2606   SLEPE John Burdewys: one cotland called "cotar" with two rods of land and one rod of meadow and a half-acre of land at le Howe recently held by William Herrof, for life, rendering annually in all things as did William. G.: 5s.

2607   SLEPE (1 September) Nicholas Mabon: one messuage with one virgate of land once held by Nicholas Chekesand and recently held by John Freman, in *arentatio* for life, rendering annually 13s. at the customary times, with the first payment at the next feast of St. Andrew. Further, he will render certain other customs rendered by those in *arentatio*. G.: two capons.

2608   THERFIELD (20 September) John Curteys and his wife, Agnes: all lands and tenements with lands and tenements of Brauncestre once held by John Adam, for life, rendering annually in all things as did John. G.: 13s.4d.

2609   RAMSEY Nicholas Morell and his wife, Katerina: from Brother John Stucle, sub-cellarer, one messuage in High Street once held by Thomas Prat, for the life of whomever lives longer, rendering annually 10s. in equal portions at the feasts of the Annunciation and Nativity of Blessed Mary, with the sub-cellarer responsible for repairing and maintaining the property. Further, if Nicholas and Katerina make any further repairs, the sub-cellarer will grant them an allowance of rent from the term after the repairs. *Et si predictus redditus*, etc. (arrears of one month, with distraints until satisfaction made). G.: 13s.4d.

142r **2610** RAMSEY Leonard Wene and his wife, Elena: from the sub-cellarer, one messuage in Little Whyte recently held by John Barker, with one wine shop, for life, rendering annually 7s., with the obligation to repair the property, with timber, thatch, undergrowth, clay, splints, poles, piles and their transport, food and ale for workmen being supplied by the sub-cellarer. *Et si predictus redditus*, etc (arrears of one month, with distraints until satisfaction is made). G.: 40d.

2611 CHATTERIS Walter Toye: one parcel called Keyscroft recently held by John Bate, for life, rendering annually in all things as did John. G.: four capons.

13 JOHN TYCHEMERSCH (1431-1432)

142v **2612** CRANFIELD (18 October: leet) William, son of Thomas Wodhall: one messuage and a half-virgate of land once held by Thomas Bailly and recently held by William Pury, for life, rendering annually in all things as did William. G.: 20d.

2613 CRANFIELD (same leet) William Melbrook: surrender of one cote and one cotland and 10 acres of land recently held by Thomas Melbrook, to the use of John Tybbey and his wife, Agnes, for life, rendering annually in all things as did William. G.: 5s.

2614 CRANFIELD (same leet) William Vaux: surrender of one messuage and 20 acres of land recently held by Robert Waryner, to the use of John Woodhill, for life, rendering annually in all things as did William. G.: 5s. Heriot: one ox valued at 12s.

2615 CRANFIELD (same leet) Thomas Brerele: one messuage and one virgate of land recently held by William del Hill, for life, rendering annually in all things as did William. G.: 20d.

2616 CRANFIELD (same leet) John Terry: surrender of one messuage and a half-virgate of land once held by Hugo Terry, to the use of Thomas Archer, for life, rendering annually in all things as did John. G.: 5s.

2617 CRANFIELD (court) John Skynner: one messuage and a half-virgate of land recently held by Thomas Alyn, for life, rendering annually in all things as did Thomas. G.: 5s.

2618 CRANFIELD (same court) William Wodhill: three acres at Stalypras recently held by John Webbe, for life, rendering annually in all things as did John. G.: 12d.

2619 CRANFIELD (same court) John Goodwyn: one messuage and one virgate of land recently held by his father, John Goodwyn, for life, rendering annually in all things as did his father. G.: 21s.8d.

2620 BARTON Edmund Child pays 12d. for license to marry Matillis, widow of John Chaloner, and to enter into one cotland with croft recently held by John.

2621 BARTON (court) John Kyng: one messuage and one virgate of land recently held by John Atte Fan, for life, rendering annually in all things as did John. G.: 3s.4d.

2622 SHILLINGTON (leet) Peter de Wrangill and his wife, Matilda: one cotland with croft recently held by Adam Sparwe, for life, rendering annually in all things as did Adam. G.: 12d.

2623 SHILLINGTON (same leet) John Coche of Grenende: one built up cotland with one house, and one cotland with four acres called Goberd's recently held by Simon Goberd, for life, rendering annually in all things as did Simon. G.: 12d.

2624 SHILLINGTON (same leet) John Launden and his wife, Leticia: one cotland built up with two buildings recently held by John Smyth, for life, rendering annually in all things as did John. G.: 12d.

2625 SHILLINGTON (same leet) William Smyth: one messuage and a half-virgate of land of Wodehallelond recently held by John Cook, for life, rendering annually in all things as did John. G.: 20d.

143r **2626** SHILLINGTON (same leet) John Cook: one cotland and two acres of land recently held by William Smyth, for life, rendering annually in all things as did William, with the obligation to repair the cotland. Pledges: Thomas Stonle and John Grene. G.: 20d.

2627 SHILLINGTON (same leet) Henry Hamond: surrender of one messuage and one virgate of land, a half-virgate and one dole of demesne land, to the use of William Barfoot and his wife, Johanna: for life, rendering annually in all things as did Henry. G.: 26s.8d.

2628 SHILLINGTON (same leet) William del Chambre and his wife, Agnes: four acres of land recently held by Peter Cook, for life, rendering annually 2s. G.: 20d.

2629 SHILLINGTON (same leet) Johanna Coupere: surrender of 18 acres of land recently held by Adam Coupere, to the use of Richard Grave, for life, rendering annually in all things as did Johanna. G.: 5s.

2630 SHILLINGTON (same leet) John Barfoot, naif of the lord, pays 5s. for license to marry Margaret, his daughter, to John Body of Arlesey, this time.

2631 THERFIELD (leet) William Frere and his wife, Matillis: one pasture called Aftmade recently held by John Rook, for life, rendering annually 16s.8d. at the customary times. G.: one capon.

2632 BURWELL (leet) John Ballard: one messuage and two tenements of eight acres recently held by Radulph Rower, for 60 years, rendering as did Radulph, with suit to court and leet and payment of common fine.

2633 BURWELL (same leet) William Purye and his wife, Christiana: one cotland recently held by Richard Southman, for 50 years, rendering annually 2s., suit to court and leet, and payment of common fine. G.: one crane.

2634 ELSWORTH (leet) Thomas Cok: one cotland with two acres in a croft recently held by Roger Ynt, for life, rendering annually in all things as did Roger. G.: two capons.

2635 ELSWORTH (same leet) John Hardyng Jr.: one messuage and a half-virgate of land recently held by John Swynford, alias Broghton, for life, rendering annually in all things as did John. G.: 20d.

2636 ELSWORTH (same leet) Richard Broghyng: one cotland recently held by Robert Ynt, for life, rendering annually in all things as did Robert. G.: 20d.

2637 ELSWORTH (same leet) Robert Ynt and his wife, Alicia: one messuage and one virgate of land recently held by John Waryn, and one messuage with a croft and one quarter of land recently held by Thomas Sonnyng, for life, rendering annually in all things as did John and Thomas. G.: (*blank*).

2638 ELSWORTH (same leet) William Warde: one croft and one quarter of land recently held by Robert Ynt, for life, rendering annually in all things as did Robert. G.: 12d.

2639 ELSWORTH (same leet) Thomas AtteWode, parson of the church, and William Style: one messuage with a croft and four butts of land called Alredesplace, for life, rendering as do others for such land. G.: excused.

143v **2640** BROUGHTON William Clerk and his wife, Johanna: one virgate and a halfvirgate with forland and one lot of Dammyslond recently held by Thomas Botiller, in *minor censum*, for life, rendering annually as did Thomas, with repairs. G.: 6s.8d.

2641 BROUGHTON (leet) John Loot and his wife, Margeria: two messuages and one virgate of land, one quarter of land and one close called Dammysclose recently held by William Smyth, for life, rendering annually in all things as did William. G.: 2s.

2642 BROUGHTON (same leet) John Crowch and his wife, Margeria: one messuage and a half-virgate recently held by Richard Webster, for life, rendering annually in all things as did Richard, with the obligation to pay John Schepperd 12d. annually and plough and sow a half-acre of his land, with John's seed, each year for the duration of his life. G.: six capons.

2643 BROUGHTON (same leet) John Crowch: surrender of two messuages and two half-virgates of land recently held by John Schepperd, to the use of John Bone Jr., for life, rendering annually in all things as John, with the obligation to plough and sow a half-acre of John Schepperd's land with John's own seed for the lifetime of John. G.: excused.

2644 BROUGHTON (same leet) John Berly: one messuage and a half-virgate of land, and one quarter of land recently held by Thomas Typtot, for life, rendering annually in all things as did Thomas. G.: six capons.

2645 BROUGHTON William Fleschewer: one messuage and one acre and one rod of land, four selions at Ramseywere once held by William Gore and recently held by William Taillor, with one quarter of land once held by William Everard and recently held by William Clerk, for life, rendering annually in all things as did the previous tenants. G.: 6s.8d.

2646 BROUGHTON (March) Robert Turnor and his wife, Maria: half of one virgate of land recently held by John Pool, one quarter in *minor censum* once held by John Schepperd and one quarter of land in *major censum* once held by Thomas Wold, for life, rendering annually 6s. for the half-virgate and 6s.8d. for the two quarters, with the obligation to repair the property, and with the first payment at the next feast of St. Andrew. G.: four capons.

2647 BROUGHTON William Fleschewer: surrender of one messuage, one acre and one rod of land with four selions at Ramseyweye once held by William Taillor, and one quarter of land one held by William Clerk, to the use of Roger Castre, and his wife, Johanna, for life, rendering annually in all things as did William. G.: 6s.8d.

2648 HOUGHTON (court) William Brampton: one toft and one virgate of land once held by John Coton and called Bedelslond, for life, rendering annually in all things as did John. G.: two capons.

2649 HOUGHTON (same court) John Deresson: one messuage and one virgate and a half of land once held by John Andrew, for life, rendering annually in all things as did John. G.: 4d.

2650 HOUGHTON (January) John Fuller and his wife, Agnes: a half-virgate of land once held by John Abirle, for life, rendering annually 5s. at the customary times, and all other services and customs rendered by John, with the first payment at the next feast of St. Andrew. G.: excused.

2651 BRINGTON John Est and other customaries: one cotland with one acre of land in a croft recently held by William Cartere, except for four acres conceded to John Stabill, for life, rendering annually 20d. at the customary times. G.: two capons.

2652 BRINGTON William Burgeys, alias Carter: surrender of one messuage and a half-virgate of land and demesne land, both old and new, a half-virgate and one quarter of land once held by William Reignald, one quarter once held by Simon Beverich, a half-virgate once held by William Gandir, two acres parcelled out of eight acres at Broedholis and Westweye, four acres of land and meadow, and one cotland recently held by John Est, to the use of John Stabill and his wife, Margaret, for life, rendering annually 25s., which properties previously rendered 26s.5d. G.: 40d.

144r   **2653** ST. IVES (leet) Robert Wrighte: surrender of one row recently held by William

Botheby, to the use of his son, William Wrighte, and his wife, Margaret, for life, rendering annually 13s.4d. at the customary times, with the obligation to repair and maintain the property. *Et non licebit*, etc. G.: 6s.8d.

2654 St. Ives Richard Charite: a half-row once held by Robert Papworth and recently held by John Gonne, for life, rendering annually 12s. at the customary times, with the obligation to repair and maintain the property. *Et non licebit*, etc. G.: 2s.

2655 St. Ives John Arnewey and his wife, Alicia: one row once held by Robert Salusbury and recently held by John Moor, for life, rendering annually 13s.4d., with the obligation to repair and maintain the property. *Et non licebit*, etc. G.: 6s.8d.

2556 Slepe (same leet) William Wright and his wife, Margaret: a half-virgate of land opposite the vaccary in *arentatio* recently held by Robert Wright, for life, rendering annually in all things as did Robert. G.: three capons.

2657 Slepe John Frary and his wife, Alicia: one empty toft called Lombescroft recently held by John Gylot and once held by Nicholas Chiksand, for life, rendering annually 16d. at the customary times. G.: excused by the seneschal.

2658 Slepe Thomas Trover and his son, Robert: a half-virgate of land in *arentatio* once held by John Rotor and recently held by Thomas Pope, for life, rendering annually 8s. at the customary times. G.: three capons.

2659 Slepe Henry Payn and his wife, Rosa: one pithel next to that of the Prior, with one virgate of land recently held by John Gylot, in *arentatio* for life, rendering annually 14s. at the customary times, and all other services rendered by those in *arentatio*. G.: 40d.

2660 Slepe Thomas Buk and his wife, Agnes: two cotlands recently *ad opus* and once held by William Herrof and recently held by John Buk, for life, rendering annually 14s. at the customary times, and all other services rendered by those in *arentatio*. G.: excused.

2661 Abbots Ripton (leet) Richard Weston: one messuage and a half-virgate of land recently held by John Bonke, for life, rendering annually 6s.8d. and all other services and customs rendered by John. G.: three capons.

2662 Abbots Ripton (same leet) John Gardyner: one messuage and two virgates of land recently held by William Kelsell, for life, rendering annually in all things as did William, with the first payment at the feast of the Purification after one year. G.: six capons.

2663 Abbots Ripton John Gillyng, rector of the church: 12 lots of demesne land in Langlond recently held by the customaries, for as long as he holds his benefice, rendering annually 12s. at Easter, with prohibition against dismissing any of that land during the said period. Further, if he defaults in payments at any term, or in any other obligation, the lord shall retain and hold the property without any contradiction. G.: excused.

2664 Hemingford Abbots John Sutton and his wife, Johanna: one built up cotland once held by his son, John Grace, for life, rendering annually 18d. and all other services and customs owed therein, with the obligation to repair and maintain the property at their own expense. G.: two capons.

144v **2665** Holywell (leet) Launder and his wife, Agnes: one virgate of land recently held by Thomas Hunne, for life, rendering annually in all things as did Thomas. G.: three capons.

2666 Holywell (December) Simon Dallyng, rector of the church, and Richard Wattes: one plot with croft and seven acres of land and meadow once held by Thomas Gere and recently held by John Scot, and one cotland with garden once held by John Selde, recently held by William Porter, for life, rendering annually 15s., with permission granted to the attorney or executor of either Simon or Richard, to hold the property after their deaths for three years without any contradiction. G.: excused by the lord.

2667 HOLYWELL Helena Sewale and her son, Richard: one cotland with adjacent demesne land, one croft once held by William Reve, and one acre at Buryheg at the end of the village recently held by her husband, Roger Sewale, for life, rendering annually in all things as did Roger. Further, she will abide there. G.: 2s.

2668 HOLYWELL John Edward Jr. and his wife, Alicia: one virgate with new demesne land and one and a half-cotlands with demesne land and one acre in Stonydole, one acre and one rod in le Smethe, and a half-acre of meadow in Salmade recently held by Richard Edward, his father, for life, rendering annually in all things as did Richard. G.: 3s.4d.

2669 ELTON William Deche, naif of the lord by blood, pays six capons for license to marry Johanna, his daughter, to William Coyf Carpenter.

2670 WISTOW CUM RAVELEY (leet) John Rauceby: one messuage and one virgate of land and a half-virgate recently held by John Hyche Sr., for life, rendering annually in all things as did John. G.: two capons.

2671 WISTOW CUM RAVELEY (same leet) William Thurston: one messuage, one virgate and one quarter of land recently held by Richard Asplond, for life, rendering annually in all things as did Richard. G.: two capons.

2672 WISTOW CUM RAVELEY (February) John Frere and his wife, Margaret: one empty plot and a half-virgate of land in *arentatio* from the akirmanland, with three acres of demesne land called Nynetene, one acre of demesne land at Toftdole, a parcel of six acres at Lowfurlong, three acres of demesne land called Godfreyslond, with Loundhed and Langherhoo recently held by the rector, one parcel of meadow called Aldeburyslade, and three acres of demesne land next to the aforesaid meadow, for life, rendering annually 14s. in equal portions at the feasts of the Annunciation, Nativity, of John the Baptist, the Nativity of Blessed Mary, and the feast of St. Andrew, with the first payment at the next feast of St. Andrew. G.: six pullets.

2673 WISTOW CUM RAVELEY Thomas Botheby: a half-cotland recently held by Alicia Fraunce, for life, rendering annually 10d. at the customary times. G.: two hens.

2674 WISTOW CUM RAVELEY Richard Willesson pays 6s.8d. for license to marry Emma, his daughter and naif of the lord by blood, to a certain freeman, this time.

2675 UPWOOD (August) Richard Alyn and his wife, Alicia: one messuage and two semi-virgates of land once held by John Jerkyn and recently held by William Robyn, in *arentatio* for life, rendering annually 20s. and all other services and customs owed therein, with the obligation to repair the property, timber being supplied by the lord. G.: one capon.

2676 WESTON (May) John Foster and his wife, Johanna: one cotland from the tenement of Hotoft with three acres of adjacent land and three acres of demesne land, and a half-rod of land from the tenement of Hotoft recently held by Richard Chichele, one cotland from Hotoft's tenement and a half of one quarter recently held by John Hacon Sr., for life, rendering annually 8s.10d. and all other services and customs rendered by John, with the first payment at the next feast of the Annunciation. G.: two capons.

2677 WESTON John Buncy and his wife, Johanna: a half-virgate of land and a half-virgate with six acres of demesne land, two acres of the tenement of Hotoft, and one quarter of land recently held by William Miller, with other parcels, for life, rendering annually in all things as did William. G.: six capons.

145r **2678** HURST Thomas Whiston and his wife, Maria: one messuage and a half-virgate of land once held by Walter Smyth and recently held by John Lacy, for life, rendering annually in all things as did John, with the obligation to repair one *insathous* before Michaelmas. G.: four capons.

2679 RAMSEY (March) Radulph Stokkis and his wife, Johanna: from Brother John Stucle, sub-cellarer, the reversion of one plot recently held by Thomas Otewy which Agnes Otewy holds for life, rendering annually 8s. in equal portions at the feasts of the Annunciation and Nativity of Blessed Mary. Further, they will repair and maintain the property, timber, splints, poles, clay, stones, lime, nails and their transport for the first repairs supplied by the lord. After the initial repairs, they will effect repairs and maintenance at their own expense, except for timber supplied by the lord. *Et si predictus redditus*, etc. G.: excused by the lord.

2680 CHATTERIS (14 February: court) John, son of John Hertford: one tenement of eight acres recently held by John Dryngesman, and one parcel in Endhalf, for life, rendering annually in all things as did John. G.: 6s.8d.

2681 CHATTERIS John Hertford Baylly: one and a half-acres of new land in Medmen recently held by John Sempool of Mille Ende, for life, rendering annually in all things as did John. G.: two capons.

2682 CHATTERIS Thomas Horsythe: one acre at Pakerelldole recently held by John Ingram, for life, rendering annually in all things as did John. G.: 6d.

2683 CHATTERIS John Whyte: one cotland with croft with a parcel called Josepfen recently held by John Clerk, for life, rendering annually in all things as did John. G.: 20d.

2684 CHATTERIS John Symmesson: surrender of five acres of Newtakenlond, to the use of Laurence Hikson, for life, rendering annually in all things as did John. G.: 20d.

2685 CHATTERIS Thomas Russell: surrender of four acres and half of a meadow in Eldhalf, to the use of Edmund Chownesson, for life, rendering annually in all things as did Thomas. G.: 20d.

2686 CHATTERIS Edmund Lytholf: surrender of one cotland, to the use of John Reche, for life, rendering annually in all things as did Edmund. G.: 12d.

2687 CHATTERIS Katerina Lawe: surrender of one cotland to the use of Thomas Broune, who also receives four acres of land recently held by Edmund Lytholf, for life, rendering annually in all things as did Katerina and Edmund. G.: 2s.

2688 CHATTERIS Thomas Broune: surrender of one cotland in Slade ende to the use of John Hunte, for life, rendering annually in all things as did Thomas. G.: 12d.

2689 CHATTERIS Alicia Drynge: surrender of one tenement of eight acres recently held by John Drynge, to the use of John Revesson Jr., for life, rendering annually in all things as did Alicia. G.: 40d.

2690 CHATTERIS Agnes Hertford: half of one tenement of eight acres with meadow in Eldhalf and Wenneye recently held by John Revysson Jr., for life, rendering annually in all things as did John. G.: 40d.

2691 CHATTERIS John Cade: half the meadow in Wenneye recently held by Andrew Clement, for life, rendering annually in all things as did Andrew. G.: two capons.

2692 CHATTERIS John Heymes: one cotland with a meadow between Sutton Mede and Popilholt Mowth recently held by John Whithede, for life, rendering annually in all things as did John. G.: 12d.

145v **2693** CHATTERIS John Skybb: one cotland recently held by Richard Dobyn, for life, rendering annually in all things as did Richard, with the first payment at Michaelmas after two years. G.: two capons.

2694 CHATTERIS John Hopkyn of Mile Ende: half of one tenement of eight acres with meadow and fishpond, one cotland and a half-acre of land in Elmen once held by John Sempooll in Mille Ende, for life, rendering annually in all things as did John. G.: 40d.

2695 UPWOOD (May) Richard Baron of Dokeden and his wife, Agnes: one virgate of land in *arentatio* and a half-virgate *ad opus* with forland and one empty plot of one virgate once held by Richard Attehill and recently held by Thomas Carter, from the previous Michaelmas at the will of the lord for 12 years, rendering annually 24s.3d. and all other services and customs rendered by Thomas, except mowing in barley and peas, with the obligation to repair and maintain the property within one year, timber for beams and posts, two acres of wheat, five acres sown with barley, and the rent for this year and the next, up to Easter, granted by the lord. G.: two capons.

2696 RAMSEY Andrew Perkyn and his wife, Agnes: from the sub-cellarer, two parcels of meadow with appurtenances recently held by William Claxton, for life, rendering (*blank*) at the customary times. *Et si predictus redditus*, etc (arrears of one month). G.: (*blank*).

2697 RAMSEY Robert Godfrey his wife, Alicia, and John Wernyngton: from the sub-cellarer, one plot in which they live recently held by John Wernyngton, father of the aforesaid John, for life, rendering annually 7s. at the customary times, with the sub-cellarer responsible for repairs and maintenance. *Et si predictus redditus*, etc. (distraints to be made until satisfaction made). G.: 40d., which they pay.

2698 HURST (March) William Halle: one quarter of land once held by John Colle and recently held by John Foorthe, for life, rendering annually 4s. at the customary times. G.: two capons.

2699 WISTOW William Hyche: surrender of one quarter of land once held by Baron, to the use of Richard Pycard and his wife, Agnes, for life, rendering annually in all things as did William. G.: four capons.

2700 RAVELEY Thomas Wyllesson and his wife, Agnes: one messuage and one virgate of land once held by John Hych and one quarter of land once held by Richard Bronne, for life, rendering annually in all things as did John and Richard. G.: four capons.

2701 WARBOYS John Willesson of Raveley pays four capons for license to marry Emma, daughter of John Scut, naif of the lord by blood.

14 JOHN TYCHEMERSCH (1432-1433)

146r **2702** BURWELL (11 October: leet) William Tayllour and his wife, Elizabeth: one tenement of 15 acres recently held by his father, William Taillour, for 40 years, rendering annually in all things as did his father, and suit to court and leet. G.: 3s.4d.

2703 BURWELL (same leet) John Calvesbane and his wife, Margaret: one meadow next to the common heath and eight acres of land recently held by John Flour, for 40 years, rendering annually in all things as did John, and suit to court and leet. G.: excused.

2704 BURWELL (same leet) William Goodwyn and his wife, Olyva: one cote with garden recently held by John Goodwyn, rendering annually in all things as did John. G.: two capons.

2705 WOODHURST (leet) John Smyth: one messuage, one and a half virgates of land recently held by Thomas Warde, for life, rendering annually in all things as did Thomas . G.: 40d.

2706 WOODHURST (June) John Burton and his wife, Elena: one messuage at the end of the village next to Falleyerd with certain land adjoining once held by John Lawman and recently held by John Hill, for life, rendering annually 13s.4d. at the customary times, which property previously rendered 40s. Further, he will render all services and customs owed therein. G.: one capon.

2707 Holywell (leet) John Promyter: one messuage and one virgate of land once held by Thomas Hunne, for life, rendering annually in all things as did Thomas. G.: two capons.

2708 Holywell Nicholas Baron: surrender of one virgate of land recently held by Nicholas Godfrey and all adjacent demesne land, one selion of meadow in Salmade and half of Benehill, to the use of John Albry and his wife, Alicia, for life, rendering annually in all things as did Nicholas, with the obligation to repair one grange of eight posts within two years, and with the first payment at the feast of St. Andrew after one year. Pledge: William Albry. G.: three capons.

2709 Holywell John Blossoum Fuller: seven acres of land of Penylond recently held by John Merton, for life, rendering annually in all things as did John. G.: three capons.

2710 Holywell John Cristemasse and his wife, Agnes: one messuage with one virgate of land and demesne land, one butt in Salmade once held by Thomas Edward, for life, rendering annually in all things as did Thomas, with the obligation to repair and maintain the property, beams, posts and thatch supplied by the lord. Pledges: Roger Cristemasse and Richard Cristemasse. G.: six geese.

2711 Abbots Ripton (leet) Johanna Forster: one cotland once called a messuage, next to the bridge towards Stukeley once held by John Swone and recently held by William Marham, for life, rendering annually 12d., one hen and 20 eggs, with the obligation to repair the property under penalty of forfeit. Further, the lord remits the payments of hens and eggs for life. G.: excused.

146v **2712** Abbots Ripton (21 March) Master John Gyllyng, rector of the church: one piece of demesne land called Wranglond once held by Adam Knaresburgh, rector, from next Easter for as long as he enjoys his benefice, rendering annually 6s. at Easter. Further, if he defaults in payments or duties, the lord shall retain the property, this grant nor withstanding, with the first payment at Easter after one full year.

2713 Abbots Ripton William Wodeward and his wife, Alicia: 25 acres of demesne land once cultivated and called Freeland, next to Smalsen between two pieces of demesne land called Howlye and Wronglond, for life, rendering annually 6s.8d. at the customary times. G.: excused by the lord.

2714 Hemingford Abbots Thomas Aungewyn and his wife, Johanna: one plot and one virgate of land in which he lives, with one plot once held by Everard, one virgate, and one cotland called Clarell, for life, rendering annually in all things as did the previous tenant. G.: four capons.

2715 Hemingford Abbots same Thomas Aungewyn and Johanna: one croft once held by Walter Ivot, for life, rendering annually 12d. at the customary times. G.: four capons.

2716 Hemingford Abbots Robert Marchall, naif of the lord by blood, pays 20d. for license to live off the manor at Holywell with the rector of the church, for as long as it pleases the lord, remaining a naif as before.

2717 Ramsey John Berenger and his wife, Agnes: from Brother John Styvecle, sub-cellarer, one tenement in Bridge Street once held by Thomas Chircheward, for life, rendering annually 16s. in equal portions at the feasts of the Annunciation and Nativity of Blessed Mary, with the sub-cellarer responsible for repairs. G.: excused because of repairs to one grange.

2718 Ramsey Thomas Wayte Smyth and his wife, Margaret: from the sub-cellarer, one tenement in High Street recently held by Thomas Pykeryng, for life, rendering annually 8s. in equal portions at the feasts of the Annunciation and Nativity of Blessed Mary, with the sub-cellarer responsible for repairs. G.: three capons.

2719 RAMSEY (September) Robert Rede and his wife, Alicia: from Brother John
147r Styvecle, sub-cellarer, two acres in the fields of Ramsey lying in one furlong called
Trestiswell recently held by Elena Randolf, for life, rendering annually 2s. in equal
portions at the feasts of the Annunciation and Nativity of Blessed Mary, which
property previously rendered 2s.4d. *Et si predictus redditus,* etc. G.: two capons.
2720 CRANFIELD (28 October: leet) William Monce: one messuage and three quarters of land, one cote, and one acre of land at Purybrook from the demesne land recently held by Thomas Monce, for life, rendering annually in all things as did Thomas.
G.: 10s.
2721 SHILLINGTON (30 October: leet) Peter Wrangill: surrender, through the hands
of the bailiff, of one cote with adjacent croft, to the use of John Hokelyff and his wife,
Isabella, for life, rendering annually in all things as did Peter. G.: G.: 12d.
2722 BARTON (28 October: court) Jacob Pope: one messuage and one virgate of land
recently held by John Colman, for life, rendering annually in all things as did John.
G.: 5s.
2723 BARTON (same court) William Revesson: one messuage and one and a half
virgates of land recently held by Richard Revesson, for life, rendering annually in all
things as did Richard. G.: 10s.
2724 BARTON (same court) John Gregory: one messuage and a half-virgate of land
recently held by John Smyth, for life, rendering annually in all things as did John. G.:
20d.
2725 HOUGHTON Agnes Plombe and her son, Robert: two virgates of land and one
cotland recently held by her husband, John Plombe, for life, rendering annually 12s.
for the messuage and half-virgate in which they live, 6s. for a half-virgate in *arentatio,*
7s. for the cotland, and 5s. for the other half-virgate, all of which previously rendered
35s. Further, they will rebuild one *camera* of eight binding-posts within two years; nor
will they relinquish any parcel of the above. G.: six capons.
2726 HOUGHTON John Tyffyn and his wife, Alicia: one messuage and one virgate of
land recently *ad opus* and once held by John Pope and recently held by John Gowler,
in *arentatio,* for life, rendering annually 13s.4d. at the customary times, with the
obligation to repair and maintain the property at their own expense, except for beams
supplied by the lord. G.: 40d.
147v **2727** ELTON (4 November: leet) William Kent: one messuage and one quarter of
land recently held by John Brampton, for life, rendering annually in all things as did
John. G.: three capons.
2728 (same leet) Henry Wales: one messuage and a half-virgate of land recently held
by Stephen Rutland, for life, rendering annually in all things as did Stephen. G.: 10d.
2729 ELTON (same leet) John Sempere: one messuage and three quarters of land
recently held by John Moleyn, for life, rendering annually in all things as did John.
G.: 12d.
2730 WESTON (5 November: leet) John Bocher: one messuage and one quarter of
land recently held by John Reynold and one toft with adjacent land recently held by
Thomas Dyngley, for life, rendering annually in all things as did John and Thomas.
G.: three capons.
2731 KNAPWELL Johanna, daughter of Andrew Boykyn and naif of the lord by
blood, pays 2s. for license to marry Thomas Gray, this time.
2732 KNAPWELL Richard Laveyn: surrender of one messuage and one semi-virgate
of land *ad opus* and one messuage and one semi-virgate and a half-semi-virgate in
arentatio once held by John Hoot, to the use of Jacob Hopper and his wife, Johanna,
for life, rendering annually in all things as did Richard. G.: six capons.

2733 WISTOW Robert Hyche: surrender of one hidemanland *ad opus* recently held by John Atte Gate and one acre of land at BysshopsWong, and a half-acre of land at Lowefurlong, to the use of John Honyter, and his wife, Alicia, for life, rendering annually in all things as did Robert. G.: 2s.

2734 WISTOW Richard Brampton and his wife, Agnes: one quarter of land with a messuage once held by Richard Wrighte and recently held by John Wardeboys, for life, rendering annually 6s.8d. and all other services and customs rendered by John. Further, the lord will supply undergrowth for his enclosure. G.: work for two days in carpentry.

2735 UPWOOD (January) Walter Baldok: one messuage and two virgates of land and one quarter of land with forland once held by Richard Payn, in *arentatio* for 10 years, rendering annually 26s.8d. at the customary times, with the obligation to repair the hall with *camera* at the beginning, and afterwards to repair and maintain the property. Further, when the lord grants license to other tenants to enclose one meadow, then Walter will render 30s.4d. for the messuage and meadow. The first payment will be at the next feast of St. Andrew. G.: six capons.

2736 UPWOOD (August) William Skynner and his wife, Agnes: a half-virgate of land with forland recently held by John Kyng, for life, rendering annually 8s.7d. at the customary times, with the first payment at the feast of St. Andrew after one year. G.: four days' mowing at Bigging.

148r **2737** ELSWORTH (March) John Howysson Sr. and his son, John: the windmill there, from the previous Michaelmas for 20 years, rendering annually 8s. in equal portions at the feasts of the Annunciation and Nativity of Blessed Mary. They will repair and maintain the windmill, with the lord supplying timber, its transport, thatch, and two millstones and the wheel called Cogwhell from the mill at Holywell, and they will return the mill at the end of the term in good condition, both in carpentry and in millstones.

2738 THERFIELD (9 February: leet) William Frere, naif of the lord, pays 6s.8d. for license to marry Maria, his daughter, to John Hampton, the fine to be paid at the next account.

2739 THERFIELD (same leet) John Okes of Royston and his wife, Cristiana: 35 acres of fallow land recently held by John Paton, for 20 years, rendering annually 15s. at the feasts of Easter and the Exaltation of the Holy Cross. G.: nothing, because the land is fallow and in the lord's hands.

2740 THERFIELD (same leet) William Overton and his wife, Margeria: one messuage and a half-virgate of land recently held by Gervays and one pithel called Bernwyk, recently held by Thomas Coll, for life, rendering annually in all things as did Thomas. G.: four capons.

2741 CHATTERIS (4 August: court) William Poppe: four acres of land from land recently held by John Clerke, for life, rendering annually in all things as did John. G.: 2s.4d.

2742 CHATTERIS (same court) William Thakstede: one cotland recently held by Robert Enfeld with the marsh in Crowlodmore, and one parcel of meadow in Crowlodd lying next to the low meadow in Crowlode, for life, rendering annually 2s.10d. at the customary times, provided that one *camera* and one parcel of garden in the aforesaid cotland be reserved always to Alicia Hoberd, a married woman without a husband ("quaedam uxorata absque marito"). G.: two capons.

2743 CHATTERIS (same court) John, son of John Balle of Horsheath: one tenement of eight acres in Horsheath recently held by his father, for life, rendering annually in all things as did his father. G.: 2s.4d.

2744 CHATTERIS (same court) Agnes Payte: one cote recently held by Nicholas Hamond, for life, rendering annually in all things as did Nicholas. G.: 4d.

2745 CHATTERIS (same court) John Coke: license to marry Katerina, widow of John Fythion, and for entry into four acres of land with adjacent meadow and a parcel of one tenement of eight acres recently held by John Fythion, and one acre lying at Horsheath, for life, rendering annually in all things as did John. G.: 6s.8d., one capon.

148v **2746** CHATTERIS (same court) Thomas Gere: half of one tenement of eight acres and four acres of one toft with meadow in Wenney and a forland recently held by John Horlond, for life, rendering annually in all things as did John. G.: (*cut off*).

2747 CHATTERIS (same court) John Berley Jr: four acres and half the land of a forland and, three acres of 12 acres of Penylond, for life, rendering annually 6s.1d. G.: (*cut off*).

2748 CHATTERIS (same court) John Berley Sr.: a half-acre of land at Langrave and a half-acre of land in Elmen at Longdole and two rods in Elmen, for life, rendering annually 24d. q. G.: seven (*cut off*).

2749 CHATTERIS (court) John Whytehede: one acre of land of the forland lying at Horshethehoke against Shipherne Fen recently held by John Skynner, for life. G.: 6d.

2750 WISTOW John Helmesle and his wife, Margaret: one messuage and one quar-ter of land in *arentatio* once held by Robert Wryghte and recently held by John War-deboys, for life, rendering annually in all things as did John. G.: two capons.

2751 SLEPE John Whyte and his wife, Alicia: one cotland recently held by William Nicholl and once held by John Chekesand, for life, rendering annually 12s. at the customary times. Also: one messuage with one virgate of land, one plot next to the horsepond with certain lands and meadow as is found in the Rent Role and previously held by his father, Richard Whyte, for life, rendering annually 19s.4d. and all other services and customs rendered by Richard. G.: six capons.

2752 ELSWORTH Thomas Howysson and his wife, Agnes: one plot with one virgate of land recently held by John Alyn, for life, rendering annually 24s. for works and rents, and all other services and customs owed therein, with the obligation to rebuild one *insathous* within two years at their own expense. G.: 3s.4d.

2753 ST. IVES Robert Trover: a half-row in le Cheker once held by Cristina Chaun-deler and recently held by Robert Borncher, for life, rendering annually 6s.8d. at the customary times. G.: excused.

2754 ST. IVES (March) William Smyth Barker and his wife, Margaret: a half-row once held by Robert Papworth and recently held by John Elys, from next Michaelmas for life, rendering annually 8s. at the customary times, with the first payment at Michaelmas. They will repair and maintain the property. *Et non licebit*, etc. G.: ex-cused.

149r **2755** ST. IVES (September) Richard Charite and his wife: a half-row once held by Robert Papworth and recently held by William Smyth Barker, for life, rendering an-nually 8s. at the customary times, with the obligation to repair and maintain the property. *Et non licebit*, etc. G.: six capons.

2756 ST. IVES William Pynnok and his wife, Margaret: one row once held by Robert Salusbury and recently held by John Arnewey, for life, rendering annually 13s.4d. at the customary times, with the obligation to repair and maintain the property. *Et non licebit*, etc. G.: two capons.

2757 ELLINGTON Thomas Buk, naif of the lord by blood, pays 3s.4d. for license to marry Alicia, his daughter and naif of the lord, to anyone she wishes, this time.

15 JOHN TYCHEMERSCH (1433-1434)

149v   **2758** ELSWORTH (22 October: leet) John Reesham and his wife, Agnes: one tenement of 15 acres recently held by John Wilkyn, for 20 years, rendering annually 15s. at the customary times, and suit to court and leet and payment of common fine. G.: 40d.

2759 ELSWORTH (same leet) Radulph Lyne and his wife, Margaret: one pithel recently held by William Peyner and one fishpond called "le Nesse" with meadow and pond recently held by Thomas Rower, for 10 years, rendering annually 2s. for the pithel and 5s.6d. for the fishpond, and suit to court. Further, he will keep the lord blameless from any amercements against anyone involving the fishpond. G.: 2s.

2760 ELSWORTH (same leet) Thomas Berker: surrender of one tenement of 15 acres of land once held by Thomas Paule, to the use of Robert Edrych, and his son, Radulph, for 24 years, rendering annually 8s.6d., suit to court and leet, payment of common fine and holmsilver. G.: 4s.

2761 SHILLINGTON (26 October: leet) Laurence: surrender of one cotland with three acres of land recently held by Laurence Taillour, and one grove called Wodehall, to the use of Jacob Graunger and his wife, Agnes, for life, rendering annually in all things as did Laurence. They will repair and maintain the close around the grove, and the wood in the grove shall always be reserved to the lord. G. and heriot: 10s.

2762 SHILLINGTON (same leet) John Davy: surrender of one messuage and one half-virgate once held by John Bernet, to the use of John Wenyngham, for life, rendering annually in all things as did John. G.: 2s.

2763 BARTON (27 October: court) Alicia Lorde: surrender of one messuage and a half-virgate of land recently held by Richard Lorde, to the use of Richard Wodewarde Jr., for life, rendering annually in all things as did Alicia. G.: 3s. Heriot: one sheep.

2764 BARTON (same court) Agreement between Walter Wodeward and John Burnard, alias Hyllary, naif of the lord, that Walter will hold one lot of demesne land once held by Edmund Burnard, John's father, for three years, with John holding three acres of the said land, namely: one acre in le Combes, one acre in Wodemarsch near the land of Jacob Child, and one acre in Bergren next to the land of Jacob Child, rendering to the lord annually all services and customs owed therein. After the three years, the land will remain with the said John and his heirs, according to the custom of the manor.

2765 BARTON (29 October: leet) Thomas DunWode pays 10s. for license to marry Johanna, his daughter and naif of the lord, to Thomas Barbour of Turvey, this time.

2766 CRANFIELD Agnes del Made pays 8s. for license to marry, the first time.

2767 CRANFIELD (25 May: court) Alicia Terry: surrender, through her attorney, Thomas Catelyn, to William Rede of the reversion of one messuage and all other lands and tenements recently held by John Terry, for life, rendering annually in all things as does Alicia. G.: 10s.

2768 CRANFIELD Alicia Terry: license to grant to William Rede the messuages, lands and tenements mentioned above *ad firmam* during Alicia's lifetime, rendering to Alicia annually one quarter and one bushel of wheat, two quarters of barley, a half-quarter of peas, and one cart load of fuel. Further, he will render to the lord annually all services and customs owed therein.

2769 CRANFIELD (same court) John Rede: that parcel of demesne land in Lordesmade recently held by Thomas Eeyre, for life, rendering annually in all things as did Thomas. G.: 12d.

2770 CRANFIELD (same court) Thomas Rydeler: one messuage and three quarters of

150r   land recently held by William Rydeler, for life, fendering annually in all things as did William. G.: 5s.

2771   St. Ives John Marteyn, his wife, Katerina, and their daughter, Emma: a half-row once held by John Boys and recently held by John Hamund, for life, rendering annually 13s.4d. in equal portions at the customary times, with the obligation to repair and maintain the property. *Et non licebit,* etc. G.: excused.

2772   St. Ives John Martyn, his wife, Katerina, and their daughter, Emma: a half-row once held by Richard Dewtre and recently held by Richard Daker, for life, rendering annually 8s. at the customary times, with the obligation to repair and maintain the property. *Et non licebit,* etc. G.: excused by the lord.

2773   St. Ives John Martyn, his wife, Katerina, and their daughter, Emma: one shop once held by John Chesteyn, for life, rendering annually 13s.4d. at the customary times, which property previously rendered 20s. Further, they will repair and maintain the property. *Et non licebit,* etc. G.: excused by the lord.

2774   St. Ives John, Katerina and Emma Martyn: two shops with garret and one shop with a solar previously held by them, for life, rendering annually 26s.8d. at the customary times, with the obligation to repair and maintain the property. *Et non licebit,* etc. G.: excused.

2775   St. Ives John, Katerina and Emma Martyn: one shop alongside the bank once held by John Makesey, for life, rendering annually 13s.4d. at the customary times, with the obligation to repair and maintain the property. *Et non licebit,* etc. G.: excused.

2776   St. Ives John Pope Jr.: a half-row once held by William Frenche and recently held by John Burle, for life, rendering 6s.8d. at the customary times, with the obligation to repair and maintain the property. *Et non licebit,* etc. G.: 2s.

2777   St. Ives John White and his wife, Alicia: one row once held by William Galapyn and recently held by William Pynnok and seized by the lord for default in repairs, for life, rendering annually 20s. at the customary times, with the obligation to repair the property. *Et non licebit,* etc. G.: 3s.4d.

2778   Upwood John Myles and his wife, Agnes: one messuage and one virgate of land recently held by Peter Bray, for life, rendering annually 22s. at the customary times, and one ploughing *precaria* and customs of the vill. G.: six capons, and making one new plough.

2779   Wistow (November) Richard Pope and John Pegge Jr. of Somersham: the windmill there, from the previous Michaelmas for 13 years, rendering annually 13s.4d. at the customary times, with the obligation to repair and maintain the mill both within and without, timber and transport of posts being supplied by the lord, and with the

150v   first payment at the next Michaelmas. G.: excused because of repairs.

2780   Wistow (30 October: leet) Richard Derker: one garden and a half-virgate of land recently held by John Frere, for life, rendering annually 8s. at the customary times. G.: 3s.

2781   Wistow (August) Robert Rede and his wife, Alicia: one cotland and one plot with building in *arentatio* once held by Richard Pycard and recently held by William Elys with one parcel of meadow called Redyng and one acre of demesne land called Burysnene, six selions of land in Shefforlong containing approximately one acre, recently held by Robert Nottyng, in *arentatio* for life, rendering annually 8s. for rents and customs at the customary times, with the obligation to repair the property. G.: excused.

2782   Wistow (22 February: court) Andrew Tyler: one cote recently held by William Wylyam, for life, rendering annually in all things as did William. G.: 40d.

2783   Brington (January: leet) Henry Eston: surrender of one messuage and a half-virgate of land with demesne land and one croft called Speserscroft recently held by

John Dalby, to the use of John Eston Carpentar and his wife, Katerina, for life, rendering annually in all things as did Henry, with the obligation to repair and maintain the property at their own expense. Further, John obligates himself to the lord for payments and repairs to the amount of £20. G.: 3s.4d.

2784 BRINGTON (same leet) Henry Eston: one messuage, a half-virgate, demesne land and one croft called Speserscroft recently held by John Dalby, for life, rendering annually in all things as did John. G.: 12d.

2785 BRINGTON (same leet) William At Chirche: one cote and six acres of land recently held by John Dalby and once held by Spencer, for life, rendering annually in all things as did John. G.: 21d.

2786 HOLYWELL William Harrof of Hurst and his wife, Alicia: the first yield of one gore in Dichfurlong and one acre in Merlakfurlong and Holywell Fen and once held by John Wengoode, for life, rendering annually 20d. at the customary times. G.: two capons.

2787 HOLYWELL John Edward Sr. and Roger Cristemasse: the first yield of one gore in Middilfurlong in Holywell Fen, for life, rendering annually 16s.8d. at the customary times. G.: six capons.

2788 HOLYWELL John Blakwell and his wife, Alicia: one cotland and half of one cotland with new demesne land and one selion of meadow in Salmade recently held by Roger Godfrey and once held by Richard Merton, for life, rendering annually 16s.6d.q. and all other services and customs rendered by Roger, with the obligation to repair and maintain the property at their own expense. G.: 40d.

151r **2789** HOLYWELL (19 November: leet) John Peryngton: surrender of one messuage and one virgate of land with one acre at Middilfurlong, to the use of William Albry, for life, rendering annually in all things as did John, with the obligation to repair and maintain the property at his own expense, timber being supplied by the lord. G.: three capons.

2790 HOLYWELL (same leet) Nicholas Baron: three acres in Shepenfurlong, one acre in Nethbrerecroft and three acres in le Brache recently held by John Merton, for life, rendering annually in all things as did John. G.: three capons.

2791 HOLYWELL (same leet) John Bate and his son, John: 12 acres of meadow recently held by Thomas Hemyngton, for life, rendering annually in all things as did Thomas. G.: three capons.

2792 HOLYWELL John Seberne: surrender of one plot and one virgate of land with demesne land and one selion of meadow in Salmade once held by John Taylor, to the use of William Hunne and his wife, Alicia, for life, rendering annually 20s.4d.ob. in equal portions at the customary times, and all other services and customs rendered by John, with the obligation to repair and maintain the property at their own expense. G.: 3s.4d.

2793 CHATTERIS (court) Thomas Tylneye: one acre of demesne land in Schepenherne Fen, one acre of land in Medmen and a half-acre of land at Wodgatte previously held by him, for life, rendering annually as he previously did. G.: 14d.

2794 CHATTERIS (same court) John Bate Sr.: surrender of one cotland with adjacent demesne land in diverse parcels once held by John Horsethe, to the use of John Ball Jr., for life, rendering annually 7s.ob.q. and all other services and customs rendered by John. G.: 4s.6d.

2795 CHATTERIS (same court) John Hobkyn: two acres of demesne land in Dernehadlond, one acre and 20 perches in Grescroft, three acres in Elmen and two acres in Medmen previously held by him, and three acres in Elmen, for life, rendering annually in all things as he previously did. G.: 2s.4d.

2796 CHATTERIS (same court) John Tylney: two acres of land in Medmen, one acre of land in Sokkyng, a half-acre at Muslake and one "land" at Longgrave recently held by John Fythyon Sr., for life, rendering annually in all things as did John. G.: 20d.

2797 CHATTERIS (same court) Conveyance by the lord of six acres of land and meadow in Crowlondmede and one acre in Elmen. Recipient and previous tenants unnamed. Life tenure. G.: (*blank*).

151v **2798** CHATTERIS (same court) John Lytholf in Sladesende Prope: one acre and one rod and 20 perches of land at Muslak, one acre in Schereherne Fen and one acre in Elmen once held by John Wysebetche, for life, rendering annually in all things as did John. G.: 14d.

2799 CHATTERIS (same court) John Pypere: one acre of land next to Schipphyrne Fen and a half-acre in Elmen recently held by Thomas Bene, for life, rendering annually in all things as did Thomas. G.: two capons.

2800 CHATTERIS (same court) John Hykson Collesson: one messuage and two parts once held by John Cut, for life, rendering annually 8s.6d.q. and all other services and customs rendered by John. G.: 20d.

2801 CHATTERIS (same court) Thomas Horshethe: one acre of land in Stokkyng and two acres of land in six selions there recently held by him, for life, rendering annually in all things as he did previously. G.: 12d.

2802 CHATTERIS (same court) John Hopkyn Jr.: one selion in place of one cotland at Townesend next to the land of John Sempole, for life, rendering annually 12d. G.: 8d.

2803 CHATTERIS (same court) John Swetemylk: half of one tenement of eight acres with another parcel recently held by John Weddon, for life. G.: 6s.8d.

2804 CHATTERIS (same court) Richard Cokerell: one butt in Langgrave and one acre of land in Elmen once held by John Cokerell Sr., for life, G.: 6d.

2805 CHATTERIS (same court) John Lytholf Sr., son of Thomas Lytholf: one cotland and a half-cotland once held by Thomas Everard and recently held by Agnes Mathew, for life, rendering annually in all things as did Agnes. G.: 6s.8d.

2806 CHATTERIS (same court) John Lawe: surrender of three acres and one rod of land from a forland, to the use of Edmund Cate, for life, rendering annually in all things as did John. G.: 12d.

2807 CHATTERIS (same court) Thomas Masson: one tenement of eight acres and four acres of meadow in Crowlode recently held by John Masson, for life, with one *camera* at the eastern end of the hall next to the Carthous and a parcel of a garden, one rod in two butts in Elmen, a half-acre outside the gate of John Cade and one rod in Millefeld, with free entry and exit, reserved to Agnes, widow of John Masson, for life, quit of payments. Further, Thomas will render to the lord annually in all things as did John. G.: 2s.

2808 CHATTERIS (same court) Alicia, widow of John Collesson: one acre and a half recently held by John, for life. G.: 6d.

2809 CHATTERIS (same court) John Smyth: one acre in Horsheath and a half-acre of land in Medmen, for life, rendering annually all services and customs owed therein. G.: one capon.

2810 CHATTERIS (same court) John Wetyng: one cotland and all other lands and meadows recently held by John Mayke, for life, rendering annually in all things as did John. G.: 2s.

2811 CHATTERIS (same court) John Skyll: one cotland recently held by Agnes Pyron, for life, rendering annually in all things as did Agnes. G.: two capons.

152r **2812** CHATTERIS (same court) Galfridus Taillour: two cotes recently held by John Skyll, for life, rendering annually in all things as did John. G.: 12d.

2813 CHATTERIS (same court) Alicia Pop: a half-acre in Elmen and two acres of land in Crowlode, for life, rendering annually in all things as did the previous tenant. G.: one capon.

2814 CHATTERIS (same court) John Lytholf, the father of sons (pater filiorum): one tenement of eight acres and one acre in Medmen recently held by Stephen Lytholf, for life, rendering annually in all things as did Stephen. G.: 4d.

2815 CHATTERIS (same court) John Tomsone: one cotland and one and a half acres in Medmen, one acre of land in Pakereldole, a half-acre in Elmen, and three rods pertaining to the tenement recently held by Biller, for life, G.: 6d.

2816 CHATTERIS (same court) Thomas Lytholf Sr.: one tenement and one croft and five selions of land at the end of the said croft and two acres of land in Medmen, two acres of land next to the manor, one acre of meadow at Craveway and one parcel of meadow at the Rounds recently held by John Sewtes, for life, rendering annually in all things as did John. G.: 16d.

2817 CHATTERIS (same court) William Newman: the capital messuage of eight acres and four acres of land of the aforesaid eight acres, two acres of meadow in Crowlode and two acres of meadow in Oldhalf recently held by Thomas Collesson, and one acre of land in Elmen, for life, rendering annually in all things as did Thomas. G.: 4d.

2818 CHATTERIS (same court) Simon Reder: one tenement of eight acres and one acre of land in Elmen, one acre in Medmen and four acres of meadow in Oldhalf and four acres of meadow in Crowlode, for life. G.: 4d., and no more because he previously paid *borsuma* for four acres in Crowlode.

2819 CHATTERIS (same court) John Bate: two cotes and eight acres of land and four acres of meadow in Crowlode recently held by John Smyth, for life. G.: nothing, because he previously paid *gersuma* in the time of Richard Crowlond, seneschal.

2820 RIPTON John Person: surrender of one messuage and three semi-virgates of land once held by William White, to the use of Richard Grene, for life, rendering annually in all things as did John. G.: 4s.

2821 RIPTON John Person: one messuage and one semi-virgate of land once held by John Bele and recently held by John Cademan, and previously held by John Person himself, for life, rendering annually in all things as did John. G.: 20d.

2822 RIPTON Robert Wryghte of Huntingdon and his wife, Agnes: one messuage and one semi-virgate of land recently *ad opus* and recently held by John Weste, one empty plot with one semi-virgate of land once held by Stephen William and recently held by the same John, and one messuage with one semi-virgate of land once held by Stephen Prykke and recently held by the same John, in *arentatio* for life, rendering annually 26s., for rents and works, at the customary times. G.: 40d.

152v   **2823** ELSWORTH (1 December: leet) John Wright: surrender of one virgate and one quarter of land called Couhirdes, and the third part of one croft and one virgate in Grave called Mathewslond, to the use of Thomas Shaver and his wife, Margaret, for life, rendering annually in all things as did John. G.: 3s.

2824 ELSWORTH (court) John Hogon: one plot once held by John Underwode and one quarter of land once held by John Lucas, for life, rendering annually 7s. at the customary times, and all other services and customs rendered by his peers. G.: 20d.

2825 ELSWORTH (same court) Richard Swynford: surrender, through the hands of Alexander Hobson, bailiff, of one cotland with garden once held by Robert Ghutle, to the use of John Swynford Jr. and his wife, Johanna, for life, rendering annually in all things as did Richard. G.: 40d.

2826 BROUGHTON Richard Here Webster and his wife, Helena: a half-virgate of land in *minor censum* once held by John Cane Sr. and recently held by John Webster

Brabon, for life, rendering annually 6s. and all other services and customs rendered by John. G.: 12d.

2827 GRAVELEY John Waltham: surrender of one messuage, one virgate of land and one quarter of land once held by William Bukby, to the use of John Arnald, and his wife, Johanna, for life, rendering annually in all things as did John. G.: three capons.

2828 GRAVELEY William Garveys and his wife, Johanna: one messuage, one virgate and one quarter of land recently *ad opus* and held by William West, for life, rendering annually in all things as did William, with the provision that William shall hold the quarter-virgate for life. G.: three capons.

2829 GRAVELEY (17 July: court) Thomas Parys: surrender of one messuage and a half-virgate of land to the use of William Smyth, for life, rendering annually 6s.8d. at the customary times. G.: four capons.

2830 WARBOYS John Catelyn, alias Schepperd, and his wife, Johanna: one quarter of land once held by John Wryght, one mondayland once held by John Wodhill, one acre at Calnhill recently held by John Benet, and two acres and three rods of land in Lowfurlong once held by Richard Bron and Walter Wodeward in *arentatio*, for life, rendering annually 6s.8d. G.: two capons.

2831 WARBOYS Walter Catelyn, son of John Schepperd: one mondayland recently held by Thomas le Hird, and one acre of demesne land in Brenfurlong in *arentatio*, for life, rendering annually 8s. at the customary times, with the obligation to repair in mondayland at his own expense, timber being supplied by the lord. Further, the lord grants him an allowance of 4s. of this year's rent. G.: excused.

153r **2832** WESTON (10 November: leet) Thomas Forster: one messuage, one toft, three quarters of land and all other lands recently held by William Buncy, for life, rendering annually in all things as did William. G.: 40d.

2833 ELTON (9 November: leet) William Fawcon, his wife, Agnes, and Margeria, daughter of Agnes: one cote and three acres of land previously rendering 18d. and works, for life, rendering annually 40d. G.: nothing, because of the rent increase.

2834 ELTON (same leet) Richard Best: one messuage and one quarter of land recently held by John Smyth, for life, rendering annually 7s.10d. at the customary times, and works and customs. G.: 12d.

2835 ELTON (same leet) Henry At Ghate: one croft called Tydewell Croft once held by John de Bytherne, for life, rendering annually 6d. G.: 4d.

2836 GRAVELEY (25 November: leet) Robert Sloght: surrender of one messuage and one and a half-virgates of land, to the use of John Sloght and his wife, Alicia, for life, rendering annually in all things as did Robert. Pledges for repairs: John Baron and Robert Sloght. G.: 5s.

2837 HEMINGFORD ABBOTS (20 November: leet) Bartholomew Bowes and his wife, Margaret: one cote, one garden with adjacent croft once held by Thomas Carter, for life, rendering annually in all things as did Thomas. G.: 12d.

2838 HEMINGFORD ABBOTS (same leet) Thomas Whyn: one messuage and a half-virgate of land once held by Alan Veer, for life, rendering annually in all things as did Alan. G.: 12d.

2839 HEMINGFORD ABBOTS (same leet) John Upton: a half-virgate of land recently held by Robert Bythewater, for life, rendering annually in all things as did Robert. Further, John shall have the next croft falling into the lord's hands, without any *gersuma*. G.: 6d.

2840 HEMINGFORD ABBOTS (same leet) Edmund Maryot: one messuage and the third part of one virgate of land recently held by Robert Whyte, for life, rendering annually in all things as did Robert. G.: 4d.

2841 HOUGHTON (21 November: leet) Robert Mason and his wife, Isabella: one messuage, one virgate and one croft called Grenesyerde once held by Robert Parker of Huntingdon, for life, rendering annually in all things as did Robert, with the obligation to build one house of eight binding-posts at their own expense, with beams supplied by the lord. G.: 3s.

2842 HOUGHTON Simon Thoday and his wife, Johanna: one plot and one virgate of land recently held by Peter Andrew and once held by John Heyne, for life, rendering annually in all things as did Peter. G.: 2s.

2843 HOUGHTON Simon Thoday: surrender of one tenement and a half-virgate of land recently held by John Newman, to the use of John Theyn, for life, rendering annually 7s.6d. at the customary times, and three ploughing *precariae*. G.: 12d.

2844 HOUGHTON Robert Smyth and his wife, Johanna: one plot with one virgate of
153v land once held by John Bethe and recently held by Thomas Foster, for life, rendering annually 10s. for rent and 2s. for works. G.: 12d.

2845 HOUGHTON (July) William Tyffyn: one messuage and one virgate of land and half of one cotland recently held by Carle, in *arentatio* for life, rendering annually 13s.6d. for rent and 2s. for works, with the first payment at the next feast of the Nativity of John the Baptist. G.: 2s.

2846 HOUGHTON (court) Stephen Marschall: surrender of one plot with one virgate of land once held by Thomas Hervy, to the use of John Perstusmann, alias Mode, for life, rendering annually 14. for rent and 2s. for works, at the customary times. G.: 2s.

2847 HOUGHTON (same court) William Mylner: one built up cote and five selions of land in Ree Street called crofts, recently held by William Pryk, for life, rendering annually 5s. for the cote, at Michaelmas, and 5s.8d. for the selions, at the customary times, as did William. G.: 40d.

2848 SLEPE (24 November: leet) Thomas Buk: surrender of one messuage and one virgate of land recently held by William Herroff, to the use of William Pecok, and his wife, for life, rendering annually in all things as did Thomas. Pledge: Thomas Buk. G.: 2s.

2849 SLEPE (same leet) Thomas Buk: surrender of one quarter of land recently held by John Roger, to the use of Nicholas Mabon and his wife, Johanna, for life, rendering annually in all things as did Thomas. G.: 6d.

2850 SLEPE Robert Profit: surrender of one messuage, one virgate at the end of the village, one cotland containing a half-virgate of land, and one plot and one virgate called Popys once held by John Hogge, to the use of William Prik and his wife, Agnes,
154r for life, rendering annually 39s.5d. at the customary times, and all other services and customs rendered by those in *arentatio*, with the obligation to repair and maintain the plot and messuage. Further, he will find a pledge for payments and repairs. G.: 40d.

2851 HURST (same leet) Benedict Boner: one toft and one quarter of land recently held by John Lawe, for life, rendering annually 4s. at the customary times. G.: two capons.

2852 HURST (same leet) William Fylhous: one toft with a croft and a half-virgate of land and one *longe* (?) in Woodhurst recently held by John Wynngoode, for life, rendering annually 6s.8d. at the customary times. G.: four capons.

2853 HURST (July) John Say and his wife, Margaret: one empty plot with one virgate of land recently held by John Forthe, for life, rendering annually 13s.4d. at the customary times, and all other services and customs rendered by John, with the first payment at the feast of St. Andrew after one year. G.: three capons.

2854 BROUGHTON Thomas Burder of Buckworth and his wife, Alicia: one plot and three quarters of land in *major censum* recently held by John Woolde, for life, rendering annually 10s. at the customary times, which property previously rendered 11s. Further, they will render all other services rendered by John, except the office of beadle, and they will repair and maintain the property at their own expense. G.: 2s.

* * * * *

1 JOHN CROYLAND (1434-1435)

154v   **2855**   CHATTERIS (12 September) John Robyn of Bluntisham: the manor of Hunney, with all appurtenant fishponds and pastures, from the feast of St. Andrew for three years, rendering annually 66s.8d. at the feast of the Exaltation of the Holy Cross, with the obligation to repair and maintain one hall and annexed *camera*, and ditches and closes at his own expense. Further, he is granted permission to cut down the undergrowth both in the manor and in the appurtenant marsh for closes, and he may also cut down the willows, provided he plant new willows. He will keep the manor and its appurtenances in severalty, and if he defaults in either payments for a period of 15 days or in any of the above conditions, the lord shall take back the manor without any contradiction. G.: excused by the lord.

2856   CHATTERIS (29 December: court) John Brewster: one tenement of eight acres once held by Andrew Sempole and four acres of meadow in Oldhalf, for life, rendering annually in all things as did Andrew. G.: 6s.8d.

2857   CHATTERIS (same court) John Ingram: surrender of one cote to the use of John Brauncestre, for life, rendering annually in all things as did John. G.: 12d.

2858   CHATTERIS (same court) Thomas Barley: one cotland recently held by John Reche, for life, rendering annually in all things as did John. G.: 12d.

2859   CHATTERIS (same court) William Newman: one cote recently held by John Brewster, for life, rendering annually in all things as did John. G.: 12d.

2860   CHATTERIS (August) John Bray: one tenement of eight acres recently held by John Whithed and one acre of land from a forland, with meadow in Oldhalf, for life, rendering annually in all things as did John. G.: 5s.

155r   **2861**   CHATTERIS (23 November: court) Thomas Berle: two parts of one messuage with certain lands and meadows pertaining to it once held by John Cut and recently held by John Hikkesson, for life, rendering annually in all things as did John. G.: 2s.6d.

2862   CHATTERIS (same court) John Beche Mason: half of one tenement of eight acres with other appurtenances once held by Andrew Clement and recently held by John Dycon, for life, rendering annually in all things as did John. G.: 5s.

2863   CHATTERIS (same leet) Alan Rede: half of one tenement of eight acres with other parcels once held by John Meyke and recently held by John Wetyng, for life, rendering annually in all things as did John. G.: 2s.

2864   CHATTERIS (same court) Robert Gere: one cotland recently held by Simon Bray, for life, rendering annually in all things as did Simon. G.: 2s.

2865   CHATTERIS (same court) Galfridus Reynold: one cotland with appurtenances recently held by John Tyd, for life, rendering annually in all things as did John. G.: 2s.

2866   CHATTERIS (same court) John Meysent: one messuage once held by John Trinpor and recently held by John Ingram, for life, rendering annually 15d. and all other services and customs rendered by John. G.: one capon.

2867   THERFIELD (8 November: leet) John Colle, who lives next to Bury Gate, and his wife, Katerina: one messuage, one virgate with croft called Burywyke and 18 acres of demesne land recently held by his father, John Colle, for life. G.: 40d.

2868 THERFIELD (same leet) John Wenham Thakker and his wife, Emma: one messuage and a half-virgate of land and 18 acres of demesne land and two acres at Berehill recently held by William Waryn, for life, rendering annually in all things as did William. G.: three capons.

2869 THERFIELD (same leet) Richard Waryn and his wife, Agnes: one cote with one garden recently held by Isabella Wattes, for life, rendering annually in all things as did Isabella. G.: 6d.

2870 THERFIELD (same leet) John Frere and his wife, Elena: one messuage and a half-virgate of land once held by William Wynnere, for life, rendering annually in all things as did William. G.: 5s.

2871 THERFIELD (same leet) William Adam and his wife, Isabella: one messuage and a half-virgate of land and 18 acres of demesne land and one croft called Awbescroft once held by John Adam, for life, rendering annually in all things as did John. G.: 6s.8d.

155v **2872** THERFIELD (same leet) William Gervas and his wife, Agnes: one toft and 10 acres of land once held by Henry Gervas, for life, rendering annually in all things as did Henry. G.: six capons.

2873 THERFIELD (same leet) John Waryn Jr. pays 3s.4d. for license to marry Margaret, his daughter and naif of the lord, to whomever she wishes.

2874 THERFIELD (same leet) William Wenham and his wife, Alicia: one messuage, one virgate and one quarter of land recently held by John Sperver and one rod of demesne land once held by John Gurney, for life, rendering annually in all things as did John. G.: six capons.

2875 ELSWORTH (15 November: leet) Thomas Coupere: one and a half virgates of land in Elsworth and one croft and one quarter in Grave recently held by John Herry, for life, rendering annually in all things as did John. G.: 12d.

2876 ELSWORTH (same leet) William Ansley: one cote with one croft once held by Thomas Laurence, for life, rendering annually in all things as did Thomas. G.: 12d.

2877 ELSWORTH John Lucas: surrender of one messuage and a half-virgate of land once held by William White, to the use of Laurence Esex and his wife, Agnes, for life, rendering annually in all things as did John. G.: (*cut off*).

2878 ELSWORTH John AtteWood, naif of the lord by blood, pays 5s. for license to marry Agnes, his daughter, to Laurence Esex Carpentar, this time.

2879 ELSWORTH (15 November: leet) John Herry and his wife, Alicia: a half-virgate of land once held by Simon Bateman, for life, rendering annually in all things as did Simon. G.: two capons.

2880 ELSWORTH (June) John Swynford: one quarter of land recently held by Thomas Lucas, for life, rendering annually 40d. G.: two capons.

2881 ELSWORTH (June) Richard Raven and his wife, Isabella: one messuage and a half-virgate of land once held by William Pycot, for life, rendering annually in all things as did William. G.: 12d., two capons.

156r **2882** KNAPWELL (same leet) John Codlyng and his wife, Elena: one messuage and a half-virgate of land once held by John in the Herne, for life, rendering annually in all things as did John. G.: 12d.

2883 BURWELL (16 November: leet) William Jay and his wife, Cecilia: one cote and one croft once held by Thomas Rower, for 50 years, rendering annually 5s. at the customary times, and all customs pertaining to the land. G.: 20d.

2884 BURWELL (same leet) Radulph Calvesbane and his wife, Margaret: one messuage and 15 acres of land *ad opus* once held by William (*blank*), for 40 years, rendering annually in all things as did William. G.: 12d.

2885 Burwell (same leet) John Rolf Jr. his wife, Cecilia, and their son, John: one cotland with one croft and one acre of land once held by William Ideyne, for 50 years, rendering annually in all things as did William. G.: one capon.

2886 Burwell (same leet) Thomas Rower, his wife, Agnes, and Agnes Rower, "Bastard": one cote and one croft and one acre of land once held by George Tryver, for 40 years, rendering annually in all things as did George. G.: three capons.

2887 Burwell (same leet) William Taillour and his son, John: eight acres of land once held by Thomas Smyth, *ad opus*, for 30 years, rendering annually in all things as did Thomas. G.: 6s.8d.

2888 Burwell (same leet) George Burthen and his son, Thomas: 12 acres of land once held by Thomas John Lombe, for 40 years, rendering annually in all things as did Thomas. G.: 6s.8d.

2889 Burwell (25 July: court) Thomas Sparwe: one cote and two crofts in Reche recently held by John Mileman Jr., for life, rendering annually in all things as did John. G.: 12d.

2890 Burwell (same court) William Godewyn and his son, Thomas: one tenement of 15 acres recently held by John Koole Jr., for 24 years, rendering annually in all things as did John. G.: 40d.

2891 Shillington (29 November: leet) John Cook and his wife, Katerina: two messuages and two virgates of land once held by William Bally, and two acres of land at Windmill Hill, for life, rendering annually in all things as did William. G. and heriot: 24s.

156v **2892** Shillington (same leet) John West and his wife, Alicia: one toft and a half-virgate of land once held by John AtteWode, for life, rendering annually in all things as did John. G.: 3s.4d.

2893 Shillington (same leet) John Rokley and his wife, Agnes: one cotland with croft and two acres of land once held by John Cok, for life, rendering annually in all things as did John. G.: 20d.

2894 Shillington (same leet) John de Burgh and his wife, Margeria: one messuage and one virgate of land recently held by Henry Hamond, for life, rendering annually in all things as did Henry. G.: 13s.4d.

2895 Shillington (same leet) Thomas atte Bryge: one messuage and a half-virgate of land once held by Reginald atte Bryge, for life, rendering annually in all things as did Reginald. G.: 6s.8d.

2896 Barton (23 November: court) Thomas Colman: one toft with croft once held by Alan Mathewe, for life, rendering annually in all things as did Alan. G.: 3s.

2897 Barton (same court) John Mathewe and his wife, Isabella: one messuage and a half-virgate of land recently held by Thomas At Fan, for life, rendering annually in all things as did Thomas. G.: 40d.

2898 Barton John Grene pays 40d. for license to marry off Isabella, his daughter and naif of the lord, this time.

2899 Cranfield (25 November: leet) John Curtes will pay 5s. at Christmas for license to marry Johanna, his daughter and naif of the lord, to John Pegge of the parish of Bletchley.

2900 Cranfield William Coche, son of John Coche of Shillington, pays 6s.8d. for license to marry Margaret, daughter of William Alyn and naif of the lord by blood, this time.

2901 Hemingford Abbots (3 December: leet) Robert Bythewater and his wife, Agnes: one cote with one croft in Estende recently held by John Trappe, for life, rendering annually in all things as did John. G.: 3s.

2902   HEMI GFORD ABBOTS (same leet) John Hamond and his wife, Alicia: one messuage and two virgates of land recently held by John Marchall Sr., for life, rendering annually in all things as did John. G.: 20d.

157r   **2903**   HEMINGFORD ABBOTS ((May) John Lee, his wife, Beatrix, and their son: one messuage and a half-virgate of land recently held by William Sly, for life, rendering annually in all things as did William. G.: 12d.

2904   HEMINGFORD ABBOTS (May) Margeria Fanell and one of her children: one cote and two crofts recently held by Nicholas Fanell, for life, rendering annually in all things as did Nicholas. G.: 12d.

2905   HEMINGFORD ABBOTS (15 July: leet) John Upton: surrender of one half-virgate of land once held by Thomas Almer, to the use of Robert Lyncoln, for life, rendering annually in all things as did John. G.: 8s.

2906   HEMINGFORD ABBOTS (same leet) William del Hill: one toft and one quarter of land recently held by John Whyn, for life, rendering annually in all things as did John. G.: excused.

2907   HEMINGFORD ABBOTS (August) John Moton and his wife, Margaret: 16 acres of land called Fullerlond once held by Thomas Fuller, for life, rendering annually 6s. at the customary times, with the first payment at next Michaelmas. G.: two capons.

2908   HOUGHTON (4 December: leet) Richard Atkyn: one virgate of land called Gylon once held by William Pryk, for life, rendering annually in all things as did William. G.: 20d.

2909   HOUGHTON (same leet) Thomas Forster: one messuage and one virgate of land once held by Robert at Stile, for life, rendering annually in all things as did Robert. G.: 20d.

2910   HOUGHTON (same leet) John Whaplode Jr.: one messuage and a half-virgate of land recently held by John Upton, for life, rendering annually in all things as did John. G.: 10d.

2911   HOUGHTON (same leet) William Fraunk Jr.: one messuage and one virgate of land once held by John Smyth and recently held by William Fraunk Sr., for life, rendering annually 13s.4d. for all customs and services. G.: three capons.

2912   HOUGHTON Richard Menowr and his wife, Johanna: one cotland recently held by John Bythe, for life, rendering annually in all things as did John, with the obligation to rebuild one house of six binding-posts within three years at their own expense, with beams supplied by the lord. Further, they will maintain the property thereafter, and they will have an allowance for the house. G.: two capons.

2913   HOUGHTON John Whaplode Sr., his son, William, and William's wife, Agnes: one messuage and a half-virgate of land recently held by John Gerard, for life, rendering annually in all things as did John, with the obligation to rebuild the hall with *camera* at their own expense. G.: excused because of repairs.

157v   **2914**   RIPTON (11 December: leet) William, son of Thomas Wattes, and his wife, Anna: the reversion of one messuage and one quarter of land and one cote now held by Matilda, widow of John in the Hirne, and once held by the said John, for life, rendering annually in all things as does Matilda. G.: 3s.4d.

2915   RIPTON Thomas Gyddyng, alias Netherde, and his wife, Johanna: one plot with one virgate of land once held by John Robbys and recently held by William (*cut off*), for life, rendering annually 18s.6d. and all other services and customs rendered by William, with the obligation to repair the property. Pledge for repairs and payments: Robert Ivell. G.: one quarter of barley, two capons.

2916   ELLINGTON (9 December: leet) Alicia, daughter of Thomas Burges, and Agnes, daughter of the same Thomas, pay 3s.4d. for licenses to marry whomever they wish.

2917 WARBOYS (same leet) John Browne: one cotland, a toft and one quarter of land in Caldecote recently held by John Levet, for life, rendering annually in all things as did John. G.: 40d.

2918 WARBOYS Alicia Chapman: surrender of one tenement called Alsonslond and one maltmanland in *arentatio* with one acre and a half of demesne land at Bascroft and two acres of land from Temsefeld at Ryvelond recently held by her husband, John Chapman, to the use of her son, Simon Chapman and his wife, Katerina, for life, rendering annually in all things as did Alicia. G.: six capons.

2919 WARBOYS (March) William Birchere, alias Barbor, and his wife, Alicia: one plot and a half-virgate of land, previously rendering 6s. and recently *ad opus*, and three quarters of land in *arentatio* recently held by Richard Berenger, for life, rendering annually 16s., common fine, mowing in Cheverethe, with the first payment at the feast of St. Andrew after two years. Further, they will repair one grange on the said plot and two houses there within one year at their own expense, timber being supplied by the lord. G.: two capons.

2920 WARBOYS (March) William Scharp and his wife, Agnes: one mondayland once held by Nicholas Schepperd and a half-mondayland, one acre in a croft, and a half-virgate recently *ad opus* and recently held by Richard Smyth, in *arentatio* for life, rendering annually 10s. at the customary times and all other services and customs rendered by Richard, for the mondayland. Further, he will repair and maintain all the houses and one *camera* on the property at his own expense, with the first payment at the next feast of St. Andrew. G.: two capons.

2921 WARBOYS (May) Robert Russell: one parcel of land called Tocroft recently held by William de Hyche, for life, rendering annually in all things as did William. G.: one capon.

2922 WISTOW (18 December: leet) William Hyche and his wife, Alicia: one cotland once held by William Wylyam, for life, rendering annually in all things as did William. G.: 8d.

2923 WISTOW (same leet) John Rede and his wife, Agnes: one messuage and three quarters of land once held by William Hyche, for life, rendering annually in all things as did William. G.: 4s.

158r **2924** WESTON (16 December: leet) John Filice: half of one quarter of land recently held by Richard Dycon, for life, rendering annually in all things as did Richard. G.: 8d.

2925 BRINGTON (same leet) Richard Forster and his wife, Elyzabella: one messuage and three quarters of land once held by William Reynold, for life, rendering annually in all things as did William. G.: 20d.

2926 BRINGTON (same leet) Henry Eston and his wife, Katerina: one messuage and one quarter of land recently held by John Wright, for life, rendering annually in all things as did John. G.: 12d.

2927 BRINGTON William AtteChirche: surrender of one plot and a half-virgate of land with demesne land once held by his father, John Chirche, to the use of Thomas Evesham and his wife, Johanna, for life, rendering annually in all things as did William, with the obligation to repair and maintain the property at their own expense. G.: 20d., two capons.

2928 ELTON (7 February: leet) Robert Asshby and his wife, Margaret: one messuage and one virgate of land once held by Thomas Wales, for life, rendering annually in all things as did Thomas. G.: 2s.

2929 ELTON Robert Godwyff and his wife, Agnes: one messuage and one virgate of land recently held by John de Bytherne and one acre of meadow in the "in-meadow" and a half-rod in Stodehole and a half-rod in Atterdolme, and the reversion of one messuage and three quarters of land recently held by John and now held by Agnes de Bytherne, for life, rendering annually in all things as did John, with the obligation to repair and maintain the property. G.: excused, because of the ruined condition of the property.

2930 ELTON William Feryby and his wife, Alicia: one messuage and a half-virgate of land recently held by John de Bytherne, for life, rendering annually in all things as did John. G.: 12d.

2931 HURST William Bryngton and his wife, Margaret: one plot and a half-virgate of land once held by Oky and recently held by William Foster, for life, rendering annually 6s. at the customary times, with the obligation to repair and maintain the property at their own expense, timber being supplied by the lord, as well as an allowance of this year's rent. G.: two capons.

2932 HURST (May) Thomas Filhous: a half-virgate of land once held by William Wyngood, for life, rendering annually 6s. at the customary times, and all other services and customs rendered by William, with the first payment at the next feast of St. Andrew. G.: two capons.

2933 RAMSEY (August) Alicia Ramsey: from Brother William Bernewell, sub-cellarer, one messuage previously held by her husband, Thomas Ramesey, and previously held by Simon Sege, for life, rendering annually 5s. in equal portions at the feasts of the Annunciation and Nativity of Blessed Mary, with the sub-cellarer responsible for repairs. *Et si predictus redditus*, etc. G.: 6s.8d.

158v **2934** RAMSEY (March) John Cook and his wife, Alicia: from Brother William Bernewell, one messuage recently held by Richard Sande and once held by William Kyng, for 50 years from next Easter, rendering annually 12s. in equal portions at the feasts of the Annunciation and Nativity of Blessed Mary, with the sub-cellarer responsible for repairs. *Et si predictus redditus*, etc. (distraints after arrears of 15 days; seizure of property and chattels after arrears of one month).

2935 RAMSEY Agnes Prykke: from Brother William Bernewell, one messuage at Grene previously held by her and once held by William Burton, for life, rendering annually 6s.8d. in equal portions at the feasts of the Annunciation and Nativity of Blessed Mary, with the sub-cellarer responsible for repairs. *Et si predictus redditus*, etc. (arrears of one month). G.: 3s.4d.

2936 RAMSEY (August) John Warde and his wife, Agnes: from the sub-cellarer, one plot in Little Whyte recently built up by the sub-cellarer on a recently burned tenement previously held by the same John and Agnes, for life, rendering annually 10s. in equal portions at the feasts of the Annunciation and Nativity of Blessed Mary. The sub-cellarer will build one *camera* 24 feet long within one year and John and Agnes may relinquish that property, saving always the rents due to the sub-cellarer. *Et si predictus redditus*, etc. (distraints after arrears of one month). G.: two capons.

2937 RAMSEY Thomas Cok, alias Webster, and his wife: from the sub-cellarer, one plot recently held by Richard Baron and once held by William Cook, from next Michaelmas for 10 years, rendering annually 10s., with the sub-cellarer responsible for repairs. *Et si predictus redditus*, etc. (arrears of one month). G.: 3s.

2938 RAMSEY (August) John Kyng: from the sub-cellarer, eight acres of land recently held by John Denys, from next Michaelmas for life, rendering annually 8s. in equal portions at the feasts of the Annunciation and Nativity of Blessed Mary. *Et si predictus redditus*, etc. (arrears of one month). G.: 20d.

159r **2939** RAMSEY John Wayte and his wife, Emma: from Brother William Bernewell, one messuage at Grene recently held by William Burgh and located next to the messuage held by John Eyr, for life, rendering annually 14s. in equal portions at the feasts of the Annunciation and Nativity of Blessed Mary, with the sub-cellarer responsible for repairs. Further, they may relinquish the property at will. *Et si predictus redditus*, etc. (distraints after arrears of 15 days). G.: three capons.

2940 St. Ives William Fuller and his wife, Alicia: a half-row recently held by John Lister and once held by Richard Brabon, with one cote in the lane and four acres of land recently held by the same John, for life, rendering annually 26s.8d. at the customary times, which properties previously rendered 30s. Further, they will repair and maintain the property. *Et non licebit*, etc. G.: excused because of repairs, with the lord further granting them an allowance of 6s.8d. of this year's rents for repairs.

2941 Graveley (June) John Wale and his wife, Margaret: a half-virgate of land called Hallelond recently held by John Slough and once held by Walter Slough, for life, rendering annually 8s. and all other services and customs rendered by John, with the first payment at the feast of St. John the Baptist after one year. G.: two capons.

2942 Warboys (July) John Bonde and his wife, Alicia: four acres of demesne land at Bascroft recently held by Simon Hy Sr., for life, rendering annually 2s.6d. at the customary times, which property previously rendered 4s. Further, the first payment will be at the next feast of St. Andrew. G.: two capons.

2 JOHN CROYLAND (1435-1436)

159v **2943** Cranfield (3 October: leet) William Frost: one messuage and a half-virgate of land recently held by Thomas Frost, his father, for life, rendering annually in all things as did Thomas, with the first payment at Christmas. G.: 6s.8d.

2944 Cranfield (same leet) John Godwyn: one cote with one garden recently held by William Godwyn, for life, rendering annually in all things as did William. G.: 10s.

2945 Cranfield (same leet) William del Hill: one messuage and a half-virgate of land and one toft and one quarter of land recently held by Alicia del Hill, for life, rendering annually in all things as did Alicia. G.: 5s.

2946 Cranfield (same leet) William Houghton pays 20d. for license to marry Agnes Tybey and to enter into one cotland.

2947 Cranfield (same leet) William Wodhill: one messuage with two houses and a half-virgate of land recently held by Thomas del Made, with demesne land, for life, rendering annually in all things as did Thomas. G.: 12d.

2948 Cranfield (same leet) William Wodhill: one quarter of land recently held by Richard Archer, for life, rendering annually in all things as did Richard. G.: 2s.

2949 Barton (5 October: court) John Turnour: one cotland once held by Johanna Child, for life, rendering annually in all things as did Johanna. G.: 12d.

2950 Barton (same court) Etheldreda Grene pays 20d. for license to marry Isabella, her daughter and naif of the lord, to anyone, this time.

2951 Barton (same court) William Hale: one messuage and one virgate of land recently held by Stoneld, for life, rendering annually in all things as did Stoneld. G.: 40d.

2952 Barton (same court) William, son of Richard Martyn: one messuage and one virgate of land recently held by John At Fan, for life, rendering annually in all things as did John. G.: 12d.

2953 Ripton William Wodeward and Richard Smyth: one piece of land called Langland recently held by Master John Gyllyng and previously part of the lord's

demesne, for life, rendering annually 12s. in equal portions at the feasts of the Annunciation and Nativity of Blessed Mary. G.: three capons.

2954 RIPTON William Halsham and his wife, Agnes: one messuage opposite the gate
of the rector with a half-virgate of land and one messuage with a half-virgate of land
and appurtenances once held by John Carter and recently held by William Ivelle, for
life, rendering annually in all things as did William. G.: 40d.

2955 SHILLINGTON (6 October: leet) Gilbert del Hill his wife, Matillis, and Gilbert's
heirs: one messuage and one virgate of land in Pegsdon once held by Richard Lewyns,
for life, rendering annually in all things as did Richard. G.: 2s.

160r **2956** SHILLINGTON Gilbert del Hill, naif of the lord, pays the fine for license to
marry Justiniana, his daughter, to whomever she wishes.

2957 SHILLINGTON (same leet) John Wyseman Jr. and his wife, Agnes: one cote and
one croft recently held by John Messenger, for life, rendering annually in all things as
did John. G.: 40d.

2958 SHILLINGTON (same leet) Richard Bradyvan: one messuage and six acres of
land recently held by William Baven, for life, rendering annually in all things as did
William. G.: 2s.

2959 BURWELL (12 November: leet) Thomas Pury and his son, John Pury: one
tenement of eight acres once held by Thomas Plombe and recently held by Thomas
Goodeale, for 50 years, rendering annually 7s.1d. and all other services and customs
rendered by Thomas, with the obligation to repair the tenement before the next leet.
G.: 12d., two capons.

2960 BURWELL (same leet) John Payntour and his son, John: the capital messuage
of one tenement of 15 acres now held by John Toys, for 40 years, rendering annually
8s. at the customary times, and suit to court, with the obligation to repair and maintain the messuage. G.: 20d.

2961 ELSWORTH (14 November: leet) William Burbage and his wife, Isabella: one
messuage and a half-virgate of land recently held by Alexander Hobbesson and once
held by Braughyng, for life, rendering annually in all things as did Alexander. G.:
40d., two capons.

2962 ELSWORTH (14 November: leet) John Sonnyng and his wife, Johanna: one
messuage and one quarter of land once held by John Lucas and recently held by
Laurence Esex, for life, rendering annually in all things as did Laurence. G.: 20d.

2963 ELSWORTH (same leet) John Alderman and his wife, Rosa: one messuage and a
half-virgate of land recently held by John Couherd, for life, rendering annually in all
things as did John. G.: 6d.

2964 ELSWORTH (same leet) Alexander Hobson and his wife, Katerina: one toft and
one quarter of land recently held by William Burbage, for life, rendering annually in all
things as did William. G.: 6d.

2965 HOUGHTON (17 November: leet) William Heyn: one messuage and one virgate
of land recently held by Peter Andrew, for life, rendering annually in all things as did
Peter, with the obligation to repair the property within two years, timber for beams
being supplied by the lord. G.: two capons.

2966 HOUGHTON William Tyffyn and his wife, Matilda: one plot and two virgates
and a half of land recently held by Robert Roger Atte Stille, for life, rendering annually in all things as did Robert. G.: 20d., two capons.

2967 HOUGHTON John Dersson: surrender of one plot and one virgate and a half of
land recently held by John Andrew, to the use of Robert Barker and his wife, Alicia,
for life, rendering annually in all things as did John. G.: 2s.

160v **2968** HOUGHTON (May) William Tyffyn: surrender of one plot and one virgate and one quarter of land once held by Richard Carter, to the use of Thomas Elyot Jr., for life, rendering annually in all things as did Richard, with the first payment at the feast of the Nativity of St. John the Baptist after one year. Further, he will repair the property. G.: two capons.

2969 HOUGHTON Richard Pooll, naif of the lord by blood, pays 3s.4d. for license to marry Agnes, his daughter and naif of the lord, to a certain freeman, this time.

2970 HURST (1 November) William Halle and his wife, Emma: one toft and two half-virgates of land recently held by John Colle and John Boner, for life, rendering annually 13s.4d. and all other services and customs rendered by the previous tenants, with the first payments at the feast of St. Andrew aftter two years. G.: three capons.

2971 HURST William Filhous: surrender of one built up messuage with one house and one quarter of land once held by John Wyngood, to the use of William Herrof, and his wife, Alicia, for life, rendering annually in all things as did William, with the obligation to repair and maintain the property, timber for beams being supplied by the lord. G.: 12d., two capons.

2972 HURST (24 May: leet) William Boner: surrender of one messuage and one virgate once held by John Edenham, one quarter of land once held by Radulph Smyth, to the use of his son, William Boner, for life, rendering annually in all things as did his father, with the first payment at the next feast of the Annunciation, with the obligation to build one grange of eight binding-posts and rebuild other houses there at his own expense before Easter, timber being supplied by the lord. G.: five capons.

2973 WARBOYS John Cobbe: surrender of one cotland, previously rendering 2s. and located at the end of the village next to Halle Gate, with 22 acres of land from the tenement of Roger Hirst, previously rendering 22s., to the use of William Ravele Jr. and his wife, Johanna, for life, rendering annually 12s. at the customary times and all other services and customs rendered by John, with the obligation to repair and maintain the cotland. G.: 20d., two capons.

2974 WARBOYS (February) Hugo Botiller: one mondayland recently held by John Wode and a half-virgate of land in *arentatio* in Caldecote once held by John Femyng, for life, rendering annually 7s. at the customary times, with the first payment at next Michaelmas, and with the obligation to repair the property. G.: two capons.

2975 WARBOYS (March) John Benesson, alias Palfreyman, of Raveley, naif of the lord by blood, will pay 8d. at next Christmas for license for himself, his sons, Thomas and John, and his daughter, Florence, to live off the manor. Pledge for annual payments: John Warde, recently of Upton, now of Raveley.

2976 ELTON (21 November: leet) Andrew Coddyng and his wife, Alicia: one cotland recently held by John Burnet, for life, rendering annually in all things as did John. G.: 2s., two capons.

161r **2977** ELTON (same leet) John Saunder and his wife, Margaret: one messuage and one quarter of land recently held by Henry At Gate, for life, rendering annually in all things as did Henry, with the obligation to build one hall at their own expense. G.: two capons.

2978 WESTON (22 November: leet) John Possewyk and his wife, Margaret: one messuage, one quarter of land recently held by John Squyer, for life, rendering annually in all things as did John, with the obligation to repair the property before Pentecost. G.: 12d., two capons.

2979 WESTON (same leet) William Flesshewer: one pithel containing a half-rod recently held by John Reynold, for life, rendering annually in all things as did John. G.: one capon.

2980 SLEPE William Boys and his wife, Margaret: one plot next to the church with a half-virgate of land recently held by John Barker and one cotland recently held by the same John, with a parcel of one cotland next to "le Gravellpates" recently held by the same John with a half-acre at Longhower, for life, rendering annually 16s.6d. at the customary times, which property previously rendered 21s.6d. Further, they will repair the property within one year, timber being supplied by the lord, and maintain it thereafter. G.: 12d., two capons.

2981 SLEPE John Whilton, his son, John and Katerina, wife of John Sr.: one messuage and a half-virgate of land recently held by John Frary, for life, rendering annually in all things as did John. G.: 2s.

2982 GRAVELEY (January) Richard Smyth, naif of the lord by blood and son of William Smyth, pays 12d. for license to live off the manor at Hemingford Abbots with his cousin, Margaret Fanell, for as long as it pleases the lord, rendering annually two capons and suit to court at Graveley. Pledge: William Smyth, his father.

2983 RAVELEY John Owty: surrender of one messuage and one virgate and a half-virgate of land previously held by his father, to the use of his son, William Owty, for life, rendering annually in all things as did John, with the obligation to repair and maintain the property. G.: six capons.

2984 RAVELEY Richard Willesson and his wife, Agnes: one cote with a cotland once held by John Owty, for life, rendering annually in all things as did John. G.: two capons.

2985 ST. IVES (January) William AtteWode and his wife, Alicia: a half-row once held by John Sutton, for life, rendering annually in all things as did John, with the obligation to repair the roofing of the row to the value of 20d. before Easter. *Et non licebit*, etc. G.: 3s.4d.

2986 ST. IVES William Smyth Barker: surrender of two rows recently built up and once held by John Multon, to the use of Thomas Stok Barker, for life, rendering annually 12s. in equal portions at the customary times, with the obligation to repair and maintain the property. *Et non licebit*, etc. G.: 3s.4d.

*   *   *   *   *

1 JOHN STOWE (1436-1437)

161v **2987** HEMINGFORD ABBOTS (25 May: court) John Kestevyn and his heirs: one cote with adjacent garden recently held by William Smyth, rendering annually in all things as did William. G.: 12d.

2988 HEMINGFORD ABBOTS (26 July: court) Thomas Aungewyn, his wife, Johanna, and Thomas, son of Johanna: the capital messuage of one virgate of land once held by John Selde and recently held by Robert Whet, and a virgate and a croft at the eastern end of the village, for life, rendering annually 12d. for the messuage and 6s. for the virgate and croft at the customary times, with the first payment at the next feast of the Annunciation. Further, they will repair the property at their own expense, two gates and one door being supplied by the seneschal. G.: two capons.

2989 CHATTERIS (31 May: court) Radulph Tebalde: one cotland with adjacent croft recently held by John Skynner, for life, rendering annually in all things as did John. G.: 12d.

2990 CHATTERIS (same court) John South: one cotland once held by Nicholas Dagworth and one cotland once held by Richard Dobyn, for life, rendering annually in all things as did Nicholas and Richard. G.: 12d., two capons.

2991 CHATTERIS (same court) John Bray Jr.: half of one tenement of eight acres with meadow in Oldhalf and a half-acre in land in Elmen once held by Thomas Taillour, for life, rendering annually in all things as did Thomas. G.: 20d.

2992 CHATTERIS (same court) William Hunte: one cotland in Pekesland recently held by Thomas Brunne, for life, rendering annually in all things as did Thomas. G.: 10d.

2993 CHATTERIS (same court) John Dycon: half of one tenement of eight acres with half of the meadow in Oldhalf and the fishpond of Alictosmer, three selions at Water Gate, two selions at Wode Gate, with herbage in Wenney recently held by Andrew Clement, for life, rendering annually in all things as did Andrew. G.: 4s.

2994 CHATTERIS (same court) John Pop Jr.: one tenement of eight acres with half of the meadow in Cowlode recently held by his father, John Pop, for life, rendering annually in all things as did his father. G.: 20d. one capon.

2995 CHATTERIS (same court) John Lytholf: half of one tenement of eight acres recently held by William Whithede, for life, rendering annually in all things as did William. G.: 12d., one capon.

2996 SHILLINGTON (16 June: court) John Ede of Pegsdon: one messuage and one virgate of land recently held by Adam Sparwe, for life, rendering annually 16s.6d. G.: 20d.

2997 SHILLINGTON (same court) William AtteHill, his wife, Justina, and their son, Richard: one messuage and one virgate of land in Pegsdon with one lot of demesne land recently held by John del Hill, for life, rendering annually in all things as did John. G.: 6s.8d.

162r **2998** SHILLINGTON (court) William Herberd and his wife, Agnes: one messuage and one virgate and a half of land with one lot of demesne land recently held by his father, John Herberd, for life, rendering annually in all things as did his father. G.: 13s.4d. Heriot: 20d., for one sheep, to be paid before the feast of All Saints.

2999 SHILLINGTON (same court) John Grene of Wodemanende: one cote and adjacent garden recently held by Johanna Coupere, for life, rendering annually in all things as did Johanna, with the obligation to repair two houses before Christmas. Pledges: John Grene of Upponende and John Laurence. G.: 5s.

3000 SHILLINGTON (same court) John Ede Sr.: one messuage and one and a half-virgates of land recently held by Rosa Ede, for life, rendering annually in all things as did Rosa, and 24s.8d. G.: 6s.8d., two capons.

3001 SHILLINGTON John Grene, naif of the lord, pays 5s. and two capons for license to marry off Agnes, his daughter, the first time.

3002 SHILLINGTON (same court) John Ede Medius and his wife, Lucia: one messuage and a half-virgate of land in Pegsdon recently held by his father, Thomas Ede, for life, rendering annually in all things as did Thomas. G.: 2s.

3003 SHILLINGTON (same court) Richard Godard: one messuage, one and a half virgates, five and a half acres of demesne land and a parcel of meadow called Caldewelle Marsch once held by John At Wode, and one toft, and a half-virgate of land recently held by William Godard, for life, rendering annually 2s.10d. for the demesne land, and for the rest as did John and William. G.: 40s., to be paid in three installments, (i.e. 13s.4d at the next leet, 13s.4d. at Easter, and 13s.4d. at the feast of the Nativity of John the Baptist).

3004 BARTON (18 June: court) William Burrych: one toft with adjacent croft once held by William Childe, for life, rendering annually in all things as did William. G.: 40d.

3005 BARTON (same court) Alicia Lord and Agnes Wodeward: one cote with ad-

jacent croft recently held by John Holywode, her late husband, for life, rendering annually in all things as did John. G.: 40d.

3006 CRANFIELD (19 June: court) John Robyn: one messuage and a half-virgate
recently held by William del Pury, and two acres of demesne land, for life, rendering
annually in all things as did William. G.: 6s.8d.

3007 CRANFIELD (same court) Johanna, daughter of Thomas Frost and naif of the
lord, pays 6s.8d. for license to marry whomever she wishes.

3008 CRANFIELD (same court) John Lovel: one messuage and a half-virgate of land
with all other lands recently held by Thomas At Made in Horley, for life, rendering
annually in all things as did Thomas. G.: two capons.

162v **3009** CRANFIELD (same court) Thomas Catelyn: one messuage and a half-virgate of
land recently held by his father, Thomas Catelyn, for life, rendering annually in all
things as did his father. G.: 4s.

3010 BURWELL (9 July: court) John Jay and his wife, Sibilla: one cotland with adjacent croft recently held by Richard Rower, for 50 years, rendering annually 5s.ob.q.
at the customary times, and all other services and customs owed therein, with the
obligation to maintain three houses on the property at their own expense. G.: two
capons.

3011 BURWELL (same court) John Fabbe and his son, John: half of a messuage of
24 acres and half of a messuage of 15 acres recently held by Richard Fabbe, for 20
years, rendering annually 20s. at the customary times, and all other services and
customs owed therein. G.: 40d.

3012 BURWELL (9 October: leet) John Bury and his wife, Margaret: one tenement of
15 acres and one cotland once held by John Plombe and recently held by him, for 40
years, rendering annually 19s.4d. and all other services and customs rendered by John.
G.: 5s.

3013 BYTHORNE John Hill and his wife, Agnes: one plot with three houses and a
half-virgate of land recently held by William Wateson, for life, rendering annually 18s.
and all other services and customs rendered by William, with the obligation to repair
the three houses at their own expense.

3014 BYTHORNE John Bocher, naif of the lord by blood, pays 4s. for license to
marry Alicia, his daughter and naif of the lord, to Robert Brews, this time. Pledge:
John Beverech.

3015 ST. IVES Agnes Cook and her son, Thomas: one row recently held by
Etheldreda Prykke and once held by William Prykke, her husband, lying next to the
row now held by Robert Chamberleyn, for life, rendering annually in all things as did
Etheldreda, with the obligation to repair and maintain the property. *Et non licebit*, etc.
G.: 40d., two capons.

3016 ST. IVES William Goodman and his wife, Agnes: a half-row once held by
Baldwin Purchas and recently held by Thomas Glover, for life, rendering annually in
all things as did Baldwin, with the obligation to repair and maintain the property. *Et
non licebit*, etc. G.: two capons.

3017 RAMSEY Galfridus Dalby: from Brother John Stucle, sub-cellarer, one
messuage next to Baxter's Bridge once held by Richard Tyler, for life, rendering annually 7s. at the customary times, with the sub-cellarer responsible for repairs. Further, easement in water on that tenement is reserved to William Clerke, in return for
an annual payment of 4d. to Galfridus. *Et si predictus redditus*, etc. (arrears of one
month). G.: 2s.

3018 RAMSEY John Warde: surrender, through the hands of John Stucle, sub-
cellarer, to John Cator and his wife, Agnes Baxster of one messuage in Little Whyte

163r recently burned, for life, rendering annually 10s. in equal portions at the feasts of the Annunciation and Nativity of Blessed Mary, with the sub-cellarer responsible for repairs. *Et si predictus redditus*, etc. G.: two capons.

3019 RAMSEY John Revanale and Elena Mody: from John Stucle, sub-cellarer, one plot in Bridge Street recently held by Laurence Darby, for life, with John rendering annually 3s.4d. for a shop, and Elena rendering 7s.4d. in equal portions at the feasts of the Annunciation and Nativity of Blessed Mary. Further, the sub-cellarer will repair the property. *Et si predictus redditus*, etc. (arrears of one month). G.: two capons.

3020 WISTOW (26 July: court) John Aylmer, half of one messuage and one quarter recently held by Thomas Fraunce and afterwards held by Robert Cotty, for life, rendering annually in all things as did Robert. G.: 12d.

3021 WISTOW (same court) John Honyter: one messuage and three quarters of land once held by Thomas Fraunce and afterwards held by Robert Cotty, for life, rendering annually in all things as did Robert. G.: 20d., two capons.

3022 WISTOW Richard Brampton and his wife, Agnes: one hidemanland *ad opus*, one acre of land at Bysshoppis Wong, and a half-acre in Lowfeld recently held by Robert Hycher and once held by John Attegate, for life, rendering annually in all things as did Robert, with the obligation to repair the property at their own expense. G.: 2s.

3023 WISTOW John Tayllor and his wife, Alicia: one hidemanland, one acre of demesne land at Waterlond, one acre of demesne land at Wysewell recently held by John Catelyn and once held by John Helmeslse, for life, rendering annually 3s.4d. and all other services and customs rendered by John. G.: 12d.

3024 WISTOW Thomas Rede and his wife, Margaret: a half-cotland recently held by Thomas Botheby and once held by Alicia Randolf, and a half-acre of land at Bysshoppis Wong recently held by Stephen Ailmer, for life, rendering annually 12d. at the customary times, which property previously rendered 18d. Also: a half-virgate of land *ad opus* once held by John Randolf, for life, rendering annually in all things as did John. G.: three capons.

3025 UPWOOD Thomas Gowler, alias Love, and his wife: one quarter of land recently held by John Fox, for life, rendering annually in all things as did John. G.: three capons.

3026 KNAPWELL (11 October: leet) John Hot: one messuage and three quarters of land recently held by John Lawe, for life, rendering annually in all things as did John. G.: 2s.6d.

163v **3027** KNAPWELL (same leet) Margeria Joye: surrender of one messuage and one toft with three quarters of land recently held by John Joye Sr., to the use of her son, John Joye, for life, rendering annually in all things as did Margeria. G.: 2s.6d.

3028 KNAPWELL (same leet) Thomas Gray: surrender of half of one toft and one quarter of land once held by William Joye, to the use of John Bedlyng and his wife, Elena, for life, rendering annually in all things as did William. G.: 10s.

3029 ELSWORTH (same leet) John Newman and his wife, Johanna: one cotland with appurtenant land recently held by John Wright and once held by Thomas Atte Lane, for life, rendering annually in all things as did John, with the obligation to repair the property at their own expense. G.: 8d.

3030 ELSWORTH (same leet) Robert Yntte Carpenter and his wife, Alicia: one messuage and a half-virgate of land once held by John Cowherde and recently held by John Wrighte, for life, rendering annually in all things as did John. G.: excused, because of repairs to the kiln of the manor.

3031 SHILLINGTON (15 October: leet) Robert Geyton: surrender of one messuage and one virgate of land from Grene ende once held by John Cook, to the use of John Couche Jr. of Upponend and his wife, Alicia, for life, rendering annually in all things as did Robert. G.: 10s. Heriot: to be paid by Robert Geyton.

2 JOHN STOWE (1437-1438)

164r   **3032**   SHILLINGTON (15 October: leet) Adam Yonge: surrender of one inner site of the manor with one lot and two pieces of demesne land once held by John Hamond, to the use of William Grene, for life, rendering annually in all things as did Adam, with the obligation to repair the property at his own expense. G. and heriot: 20s. Pledge for payments and repairs: Simon Eynesham.

3033   SHILLINGTON (same leet) John Hill: one messuage and one virgate of land in Pegsdon and the sixth part of demesne land there recently held by John At Hill, for life, rendering annually in all things as did John. G.: 6s.8d.

3034   SHILLINGTON Richard Godard: surrender of one messuage and two virgates of land with appurtenances in Stondon, to the use of John Colman, and his wife, Johanna, for life, rendering annually in all things as did Richard. G.: and heriot: 23s.4d.

3035   SHILLINGTON (22 February: court) William Herford, naif of the lord, pays 3s.4d. for license to marry Justina, his daughter, to John Rede of Pulloxhill.

3036   BARTON (16 October: court) William Wylymote: one messuage and a half-virgate of land recently held by Thomas Wylymote, for life, rendering annually in all things as did Thomas. G.: 20d.

3037   BARTON (same court) William Bonde: one messuage and a half-virgate of land recently held by his father, John Bonde, for life, rendering annually in all things as did John. G.: 5s.

3038   BARTON (1 August: court) Margaret, daughter of John Grene and naif of the lord by blood, pays 3s.4d. for license to marry whomever she wishes, this time.

3039   CRANFIELD (18 October: leet) Thomas Mylbroke: the reversion of one messuage and three quarters of land recently held by John Milbroke and now held by Maria Milbroke, for life, rendering annually in all things as Maria. G.: 13s.4d. (6s.8d. at Christmas, 6s.8d. at the autumn court).

3040   CRANFIELD (same leet) Roger Berne: one cotland and three and a half acres of land once held by Frafeld, for life, rendering annually in all things as did Frafeld. G.: 3s.

3041   CRANFIELD (same leet) Emma, widow of William del Rood: surrender of one messuage and three quarters of land of Molelond and a half-virgate of land *ad opus* recently held by William del Rood, to the use of William Baker, for life, rendering annually in all things as did Emma. William will allow Emma the capital *camera* under the principal *camera*, with free entry and exit, and render to her annually 12 bushels of well-winnowed wheat, two quarters of malt of the best grain of the croft, one peck of oat flour, a third portion of better fat, two cart loads of wood for fuel, and sustenance for six nursing sheep. Further, if he defaults in any of these obligations, Emma will be allowed to re-enter the property, this alienation not withstanding. G.: 40s. Heriot: one cow.

3042   CRANFIELD (same leet) John Goodwyn: 11 acres of land of a forland recently held by his father, John Goodwyn, for life, rendering annually in all things as did his father. G.: 3s.4d.

164v   **3043**   CRANFIELD (same leet) Thomas Alyn Sr. and his wife, Margeria: a half-virgate of land recently held by John Alyn, his father, for life, rendering annually in all things as did John. G.: four partridges.

3044 CRANFIELD (31 July: court) John Har: one messuage and a half-virgate recently held by John Sare, for life, rendering annually in all things as did John. G.: 4s.

3045 CRANFIELD (same court) Agnes Hoghton: surrender of one cotland once held by Beatrix Shereman, to the use of Thomas Grene, for life, rendering annually in all things as did Agnes. G.: 2s.

3046 CRANFIELD (same court) Thomas Grene: six acres of demesne land, of which three are at Stalipras and recently held by John Webbe, and three are at Puryhill and recently held by William Cook, for life, rendering annually in all things as did John and William. G.: 20d.

3047 HOUGHTON (20 October: leet) Richard Soverayn: one messuage and a half-virgate of land recently held by Thomas Theyn, for life, rendering annually in all things as did Thomas. G.: 12d.

3048 HOUGHTON John Plombe and his wife, Margaret: a half-virgate of land recently held by John Marshall Jr., for life, rendering annually in all things as did John. G.: 12d., three capons.

3049 HOUGHTON Margaret Nottyng, daugher of Robert Herveys of Houghton and naif of the lord by blood, pays 5s. for license to marry whomever she wishes, this time. Pledge: John Frere.

3050 HOUGHTON (5 June: court) Robert Roger At Grene: surrender of one messuage and one and a half virgates of land, to the use of William Atkyn, for life, rendering annually in all things as did Robert, with a half-virgate and one *camera* and three rods of land reserved to Robert and his wife, Johanna, for life, for which William will pay the rents. G.: 20d.

3051 HOUGHTON (same court) William Dyke: one messuage and a half-virgate of land recently held by John Hill, for life, rendering annually in all things as did John. G.: 20d.

3052 HOUGHTON William Wither and his wife, Juliana: one quarter of land recently held by John Whaplode Sr. and once held by Richard Sampson, for life, rendering annually in all things as did John. G.: 3s.4d., which he paid the lord.

3053 HOUGHTON (1 July) Richard Meynor: surrender of one empty toft and a half-virgate of land once held by Simon Wyth, to the use of Robert Andrew, for life, rendering annually in all things as did Richard. Further, he will build one hall with a *camera* on the toft at his own expense before Michaelmas. G.: 2s.

165r **3054** ELTON (22 October: leet) Thomas Robury: one messuage and a half-virgate of land recently held by John Wodeward, for life, rendering annually in all things as did John. G.: 12d.

3055 ELTON (same leet) John Bate: one messuage, one virgate of land, one quarter and a half-acre of land at Stokwell recently held by John Herp, and one messuage recently held by Richard Schepperd, for life, rendering annually in all things as did John and Richard. G.: 12d.

3056 WARBOYS (23 October: leet) John Berenger Sr., his wife, Juliana, and his son, William: one plot recently built up by John, with a half-virgate of land previously held by him and once held by Flemyng, in *arentatio* for life, rendering annually 6s.8d. at the customary times, customs of the vill, one bederepe and one ploughing *precaria*. Also: one croft next to Fensyde called Boyscroft, for life, rendering annually 6s.8d. at the customary times. Further, John and William May have the undergrowth for the enclosure of the croft, as they were accustomed to have before. G.: 13s.4d.

3057 WARBOYS William Scut, son of John Scut and naif of the lord by blood, will pay annually at Easter 8d. for license to live off the manor for as long as it pleases the lord, remaining a naif as before. Pledges for payments: Richard Willesson and John Willesson, son of Richard.

3058 WARBOYS (January) Thomas Wilkes: one quarter of land in Caldecote recently held by Robert Honyter and once held by Richard Berenger, for life, rendering annually 3s.4d. and customs of the vill, with the first payment at the next feast of St. Andrew. G.: two capons.

3059 WARBOYS John Sande: surrender of half of the land once held by Robert At Hill, to the use of Robert Honyter, for life, rendering annually in all things as did John. G.: four capons.

3060 WARBOYS (May) Hugo Botiller: a half-virgate of land in *arentatio* recently held by John Dallyng, for life, rendering annually 5s. and all other services and customs rendered by John, with the first payment at the feast of St. Andrew. G.: 8d.

3061 WARBOYS (May) Hugo Fordyngton: one quarter of land once held by Thomas Newman and recently held by William Ravele, for life, rendering annually 2s.6d. at the customary times, with the first payment at the next feast of St. Andrew. G.: two geese, one capon.

3062 HOLYWELL Thomas Valentyn: surrender of one cotland with demesne land once held by Thomas Scot to the use of Richard Wattes, for life, rendering annually in all things as did Thomas. G.: 40d.

3063 HOLYWELL John Blacwell: surrender of one cotland and a half, with new demesne land and one selion of meadow in Salmade recently held by Roger Godfrey and once held by Richard Merton, to the use of Roger Cristmesse, his son, John, and Agnes, wife of John, for life, rendering annually 16s.6d.q. at the customary times, and all other services and customs rendered by John, with the obligation to repair the property, at the approval of the seneschal, under penalty of forfeit. G.: 5s.

165v   **3064** HEMINGFORD ABBOTS (7 November: leet) Roger Lessy and his wife, Matillis: the third part of one messuage and the third part of one virgate of land recently held by Edmund Mariet, for life, rendering annually in all things as did Edmund. G.: 12d.

3065 HEMINGFORD ABBOTS (same leet) John Barbour: one messuage and one virgate of land recently held by Thomas Whyn, for life, rendering annually all services and customs owed therein, with the obligation to repair one grange, and with the first payment at the next feast of the Annunciation. G.: 12d.

3066 GRAVELEY John Rabat, naif of the lord by blood, pays 8d. for license to serve anyone he wishes within the village of Graveley, rendering 8d. and suit to court and leet, for as long as it pleases the lord, remaining a naif as before. Pledges for payments and suit to court: John Seberne and John Baron.

3067 GRAVELEY John Arnald pays two capons for license to exchange one messuage once held by John Waltham for another messuage held by Richard Dyke and recently held by Robert Denyell, called Benottis.

3068 GRAVELEY John Arnald: surrender of one quarter of land recently held by William West, to the use of Nicholas Tonyng and his wife, Agnes, for life, rendering annually in all things as did John. G.: two capons.

3069 GRAVELEY (4 June: court) John Mordon: one messuage and a half-virgate of land recently held by Richard Dyke, for life, rendering annually in all things as did Richard. G.: 20d.

3070 HURST John Say and Margaret Say: one cotland once held by John Boner and recently held by Thomas Sower, for life, rendering annually 2s. at the customary times, which property previously rendered 5s. Also: a half-virgate of land once held by John Lawe with one house on one virgate of land held by William Waryn and built by John Lawe, and recently held by Thomas Sower, for life, rendering annually in all things as did Thomas, with the obligation to repair the property at their own expense, timber being supplied by the lord. G.: four capons.

3071 HURST (January) William Boner: one burned messuage, one virgate and a quarter of land recently held by his father, William Boner, for life, rendering annually in all things as did his father, with the obligation to rebuild one grange of 10 binding-posts and one bake house 30 feet long, and to repair all other houses in beams and posts before Easter a year from now, with timber supplied by the lord. He also receives an allowance of this year's rent and 24s. from the arrears of Halsham and 8d. from the arrrears of Cachsoly from the preceding year. G.: four capons.

166r **3072** HURST Reginald Lawman: surrender of one messuage, one virgate and one quarter of land, to the use of his son, Thomas, for life, rendering annually in all things as did Reginald, with the obligation to repair the property at his own expense, timber being supplied by the lord. G.: four capons.

3073 ST. IVES Margaret White: surrender of one row recently held by her husband, Richard White, to the use of William Bele and his wife, Isabella, for life, rendering annually in all things as did Margaret, with the obligation to repair and maintain the property. *Et non licebit*, etc. G.: 6s.8d.

3074 ST. IVES (January) John Clynt, his wife, Emma, and his son, Richard: a half-row in ruined condition recently held by William Charite, for life, rendering annually 8s. at the customary times, with the first payment at next Michaelmas, with the obligation to repair and maintain the property. Note that the property previously rendered 10s. *Et non licebit*, etc. Further, the lord will supply wood for repairing the front and other defective parts of the property. G.: 6d.

3075 ST. IVES Thomas Sowle, his wife, Margaret, and his son, William: one row recently held by William Moor, for life, rendering annually 13s.4d. at the customary times, with the obligation to repair and maintain the property. *Et non licebit*, etc. G.: 20d.

3076 ST. IVES William Goodman: surrender of a half-row once held by Baldewin Purchas and recently held by Thomas Glover, to the use of John Cossale and his wife, Johanna, for life, rendering annually in all things as did William, with the obligation to repair the front of the property. *Et non licebit*, etc. G.: two capons.

3077 ST. IVES John Awbry and his wife, Agnes: a half-row once held by John Fyssher and recently held by him, and a half-row near the pillory recently held by John Mildenale, for life, rendering annually 10s. for the first half-row and 13s.4d. for the other, at the customary times, with the first payment at Michaelmas. Further, they will repair and maintain the property. *Et non licebit*, etc. G.: two capons.

166v **3078** ST. IVES (January) Henry Barbour, his wife, Johanna, and their son: a half-row recently held by John Tebbe and once held by William Gardener, for life, rendering annually 4s. at the customary times, which property previously rendered 10s. Further, the first payment will be at Easter after one year, and they will repair and maintain the property. *Et non licebit*, etc. G.: two capons.

3079 CHATTERIS (court) The lord returns to John Cok all his tenements formerly seized because of John's many trespasses and rebelliousness against the lord and his neighbors, and which properties are restored after John's oath to refrain from such behavior. Fine: 6s.8d.

3080 CHATTERIS Alicia Collesson: surrender of one cotland with meadow in Oldhalf with fishpond and arable land, and certain acres of land once held by John Symmesson, to the use of Richard Hopkyn, for life, rendering annually in all things as did Alicia, with a fourth part of the meadow reserved to Alicia for life. G.: 2s.

3081 CHATTERIS Laurence Hikkesson: one tenement of eight acres with other appurtenances recently held by Anna Hikkesson, for life, rendering annually in all things as did Anna. G.: 2s.

3082 CHATTERIS Alicia Swetemelk: surrender of one cotland with forland and land with meadow in Crowlade once held by Galfridus Swetemelk, to the use of John Bonyard, for life, rendering annually in all things as did Alicia.

3083 CHATTERIS (8 July: court) John Hunt: one cote and one tenement of four acres recently held by Jacob Wetyng, for life, rendering annually in all things as did Jacob, with the obligation to repair and maintain the property at his own expense. G.: 12d.

3084 CHATTERIS (same court) John Poppe: one cotland recently held by Robert Gery and once held by Simon Bray, for life, rendering annually in all things as did Robert. G.: 2s.

3085 CHATTERIS (same court) John Piper: two acres of forland recently held by Roger Oriell, for life, rendering annually 20d. G.: 8d.

167r **3086** CHATTERIS (same court) John Kyng: surrender of three acres in Sokkyng recently held by John Balle to the use of John Smyth of Horsheath, for life, rendering annually 2s.1d. at the customary times. G.: three capons.

3087 ST. IVES (May) Thomas Kyngeston and his wife, Agnes: one row recently held by John Prikke and lying in the lane which leads to the manor, for life.

3088 CHATTERIS (January) John Bate: one messuage with two acres of land and certain selions of land in Stokkyng, half of the meadow pertaining to that messuage in CrowlodMede next to Parkhall recently held by John Smyth, and a certain toll-ferry at Swyneshedwer, for life, rendering annually 3s.4d. for the toll-ferry and all other services and customs rendered by John Smyth for the rest, with the obligation to maintain the property at his own expense, and to ferry the chattels of the abbot and his confreres, ministers and servants whenever required. G. and fine: 6s.8d.

3089 ELSWORTH (3 June) William Fermer, alias Hobbesson, and his wife, Anna: one toft called Balwenscrofte once held by Thomas Newman and recently held by Walter Boole, for life, rendering annually 6s. at the customary times, and all other services and customs rendered by Walter. G.: two capons.

3090 ELSWORTH (3 June: court) William Hawke: his wife, Johanna, and their heirs: one toft and a half-virgate of land in Grave recently held by William Herry, rendering annually in all things as did William. G.: 12d.

3091 ELSWORTH (same court) Richard Parnell and his wife, Isabella: one quarter of land recently held by John Collesson, for life, rendering annually in all things as did John. G.: three capons.

3092 ELSWORTH John Boole and his wife, Margeria: one toft called Baldewynscroft, one messuage and four acres, one quarter of land once held by Lucas, one croft called Typperislane, and one croft once a capital messuage containing a tenement recently
167v held by Walter Boole, for life, rendering annually 27s.8d. at the customary times, and all other services and customs rendered by Walter, with Baldewynscroft reserved to William Fermer and his wife for life, in return for an annual payment of 6d. G.: 3s.4d.

3093 ELSWORTH (same court) Thomas, son of John Newman: one quarter and a half of land recently held by William Wymond, for life, rendering annually in all things as did William. G.: 12d.

3094 ELSWORTH (same court) John Wright and his wife, Johanna: one messuage and one croft recently held by William Wymond, and half of one quarter recently held by Thomas Lucas, for life, rendering annually in all things as did William and Thomas. G.: four capons.

3095 BRINGTON John Goodeslow and his wife, Helena: one cotland and one acre of land in a croft recently held by William Carter, alias Burgeys, less four acres dismissed to John Stabull, for life, rendering annually 20d., with the obligation to repair the cotland under penalty of forfeit. G.: 12d.

3096 BRINGTON William Clepton Taillor and his wife, Johanna: one messuage and one quarter of land with appurtenances recently held by Richard Est (*cut off*) and once held by John Dalby, for life, rendering annually in all things as did Richard. G.: 12d., three capons.

3097 WESTON (January) Richard Dicon pays two capons for license for John Wrighte to live with him at Leighton for the length of John's life.

3098 WESTON (January) Richard Dycon: surrender of one messuage and the third part of land once held by John Myller and recently held by John Wryghte, and two half-virgates with demesne land, to the use of John Foster and his wife, Johanna, for life, rendering annually in all things as did Richard, with the obligation to repair and maintain the property at their own expense. Pledge for repairs and payments: Thomas Foster. G.: 5s.

3099 WESTON (January) John Forster: surrender of one cotland of Hotoft's tenement, three acres of adjacent land, four acres of Burylond, a half-rod of land from Hotoft's tenement once held by Richard Chichele, and half of one quarter of land once held by John Hacon, to the use of William German Tayllor and his wife, Johanna, for life, rendering annually 8s. and all other services and customs rendered by John. G.: four capons.

168r **3100** WESTON (March) Richard Graunt, rector of the church of Barnwell: two plots with all other lands and tenements in Barnwell pertaining to the manor of Weston, of which one plot was once held by John Tayllor, and another plot is called Masonsplace, for life, rendering to the *collector redditus* 3s.4d. annually, at the customary times, with the first payment at Easter after two years. Further, he will repair and maintain the property once held by John Tayllor — namely, the hall, *camera*, kitchen, grange, and all houses — at his own expense, and he will repair and maintain Masonsplace — namely, the hall, *camera* and solar. For these repairs he will receive all the trees growing on that plot. G.: excused.

3101 RIPTON (January) John Crosse of Barton of Northamptonshire and his wife, Alicia: one messuage, three half-virgates and demesne land recently held by William Colle and once held by John Hyche, for life, rendering annually as did William, with the first payment at the next feast of All Saints. Further, three quarters of barley will be supplied by the seneschal. G.: three capons.

3102 RIPTON John Smyth and his wife, Margaret: one messuage and two half-virgates of land recently held by William Kelsethe and previously held by John Nycoll, for life, rendering annually in all things as did William . G.: six capons.

3103 RIPTON Thomas Baron: one cotland in *arentatio* and two selions in a croft and three selions once held by William Gaunt and recently held by John Bamburgh, for life, rendering annually in all things as did John. G.: two capons.

3104 RIPTON John London: surrender of one plot and one semi-virgate *ad opus* once held by John Hawlond and one semi-virgate in *secunda arentatio* recently held by the same John, with one selion of land at Angerlond, to the use of Thomas Schitlyngdon, alias Smyth, and his wife, Margaret, for life, rendering annually in all things as did John. G.: 12d.

3105 RAMSEY (1 March) John Warde, his wife, Agnes, and their son, John: one pasture called Lytill lawnde and located next to the eleemosynary's orchard and pertaining to the office of the sub-cellarer, recently held by Thomas Claryvaux, from next Easter for life, rendering annually 2s. in equal portions at the customary times. They may cut down the willows, trees and ashes, and relinquish the property at will. *Et si predictus redditus,* etc. (distraints until satisfaction made). G.: (*illegible*).

168v **3106** RAMSEY (July) John Awbis: from Brother John Swasham, sub-cellarer, that parcel of meadow in Hilk reserved outside the farm of John Wetton and recently held by Thomas Godfrey, from the previous Michaelmas for life, rendering annually 5s.6d. in equal portions at the customary times and all other services and customs rendered by Thomas. *Et si predictus redditus*, etc. (arrears of one month). G.: 12d., two capons.

3107   RAMSEY (July) Thomas Botheby and his wife, Alicia: from the sub-cellarer, one messuage in the Whyte once held by John Randys and recently held by them, from the previous Michaelmas for life, rendering annually 5s. at the feasts of the Annunciation and Nativity of Blessed Mary, with the sub-cellarer responsible for repairs. *Et si predictus redditus*, etc. (distraints after arrears of 15 days; seizure after arrears of one month). G.: 12d., two capons.

3108   RAMSEY (August) Thomas Bangolf and his wife, Margaret: from the sub-cellarer, one parcel of the meadow of Swonhousmede with ditches and willows, recently held by Thomas Brigge, from the previous Michaelmas for 20 years, rendering annually 6s.8d. in equal portions at the feasts of the Annunciation and Nativity of Blessed Mary, with the obligation to repair the ditches and closes of the property. Further, they may cut down the willows growing there. *Et si predictus redditus*, etc. G.: 6s.8d.

3109   RAMSEY (August (?)) Thomas Bangolf and his wife: Margaret: from the sub-cellarer, one messuage in which they live recently held by Thomas Brigge and once held by John Chaumberleyn, for life, rendering annually 12s. in equal portions at the feasts of the Annunciation and Nativity of Blessed Mary. *Et si predictus redditus*, etc. (arrears of one month). G.: 6s.8d.

3110   RAMSEY (August (?)) William Stedman and his wife, Isabella: the sub-cellarer one messuage in Bridge Street recently held by Robert Mason and once held by John Banham, for life, rendering 16s. in equal portions at the feasts of the Annunciation and Nativity of Blessed Mary. Further, the sub-cellarer will build one *camera* there, and afterwards William will maintain it, with timber, carpentry, thatch, clay, undergrowth for enclosures and their transport and food for laborers supplied by the sub-cellarer. *Et si predictus redditus,* etc. (arrears of six weeks). G.: 11s.8d.

3111   RAMSEY Thomas Godfrey: from the sub-cellarer, one messuage in Little Whyte recently held by Alicia Wernyngton, for life, rendering annually 7s. at the customary times, with the sub-cellarer responsible for repairs. *Et si predictus redditus*, etc. (arrears of one month). G.: 3s.4d. *(crossed out)*.

3112   RAMSEY Thomas Filhous and his wife, Margaret: from the sub-cellarer, one messuage in which Thomas Baxter recently lived, for life, rendering annually 8s. in equal portions at the feasts of the Annunciation and Nativity of Blessed Mary. Further, if the land is dismissed to another, the sub-cellarer can reclaim it and dispose of it as he pleases. *Et si predictus redditus*, etc. (arrears of six weeks). G.: two capons.

3113   RAMSEY John Rasour and his wife, Agnes: from the sub-cellarer, one cote within Mechegates in which he lives, recently held by John Colles and once held by Walter Sporysor, for life, rendering annually 5s. in equal portions at the feasts of the Annunciation and Nativity of Blessed Mary, with the sub-cellarer responsible for repairs. *Et si predictus redditus,* etc. (arrears of one month). G.: 12d., two capons.

3114   RAMSEY William Ravele and his wife, Alicia: from the sub-cellarer, one messuage in Little Whyte, recently rebuilt, and previously held by Leonard Wyne, for life, rendering annually 10s. in equal portions at the feasts of the Annunciation and Nativity of Blessed Mary, with the sub-cellarer responsible for repairs. *Et si predictus redditus*, etc. (arrears of one month). G.: 3s.4d.

3115   RAMSEY John Fythyon and his wife, Elena: from the sub-cellarer, one rebuilt messuage in Little Whyte previously held by him, for life, rendering annually 10s. in equal portions at the feasts of the Annunciation and Nativity of Blessed Mary, with the sub-cellarer responsible for repairs. *Et si predictus redditus*, etc. (distraints after arrears of 15 days). G.: 6s.8d.

169v **3116** RAMSEY John Welles and his wife, Isabella: from the sub-cellarer, one rebuilt messuage in Little Whyte once held by Thomas Wedon, for life, rendering annually 8s. in equal portions at the feasts of the Annunciation and Nativity of Blessed Mary, with the sub-cellarer responsible for repairs. Further, they are not allowed to give away the property. *Et si predictus redditus,* etc. (arrears of one month). G.: 3s.4d.

3117 RAMSEY Richard Pycard and his wife, Alicia: from the sub-cellarer, one messuage in the Whyte next to the bridge called Baxter's Bridge, recently held by Galfridus Dalby, for life, rendering annually 7s. in equal portions at the feasts of the Annunciation and Nativity of Blessed Mary, with the obligation to repair and maintain the property, with timber, straw and clay supplied by the sub-cellarer. Further, they may not dismiss the property. *Et si predictus redditus*, etc. (distraints after arrears of 15 days). G.: 2s., four capons.

3118 RAMSEY John Newman: from the sub-cellarer, one empty toft at the end of the village lying between the free tenement held by the same John and the tenement of John Austyn, with three selions of land in a croft recently held by Robert Coupere Sr., for 20 years, rendering annually 20d. in equal portions in the feasts of the Annunciation and Nativity of lessed Mary. *Et si predictus redditus*, etc. (arrears of one month). G.: 12d., two capons.

3119 BROUGHTON John Justice, alias Taillor, naif of the lord by blood, pays 2s. for license to marry Agnes, his daughter and naif of the lord, to William Fleschewer, this time.

3120 BROUGHTON (May) Thomas Russell Jr.: one quarter of land in *major censum* recently held by John Clerk and one quarter of land in *minor censum* recently held by Nicholas Turnor Sr., for life, rendering annually in all things as did John and Nicholas., with the first payment at the next feast of St. Andrew. G.: three geese and three capons.

3121 ELLINGTON John West: surrender of one messuage, one virgate of land, one quarter of land once held by his father, John West, to the use of John Baron, and his wife, Alicia, for life, rendering annually in all things as did John. G.: 3s.4d.

3122 BURWELL (27 June: leet) John Blaunteyn and his wife, Beatrix: one tenement of 15 acres once held by John Toys and one tenement of 20 acres recently held by John Wyot Bosom, for 20 years, rendering annually 16s. and suit to court, and all other services and customs rendered by John. G.: 5s.

3123 BURWELL (same leet) John, son of John Rolf, alias Dufhous, and his wife, Agnes: one tenement of 15 acres recently held by John Rolf le Newman, for 30 years, rendering annually in all things as did John, and suit to court and leet. G.: 5s.

3124 BURWELL (same leet) John Pryk Jr.: two tenements of 15 acres with one cotland at le Nesse called Longcroft recently held by Robert Borugh, for 20 years, rendering annually 35s. and suit to court and leet, and all other services and customs rendered by Robert. G.: 5s.

170r **3125** BURWELL (same leet) William Canford and his wife, Helena: one tenement of eight acres once held by John Dery and recently held by Richard Wright, for 20 years, rendering annually 10s.4d. and all other services and customs rendered by Richard, as well as suit to court and leet. G.: two capons.

3126 BURWELL (same leet) Thomas Berker and his wife, Margaret: one croft lying next to the cote once held by Elena Sterne, for 40 years, rendering annually 18d. at the customary times, with the obligation to maintain the croft in enclosures at their own expense, and to repair the King's road at that croft. Further, they will render suit to court and leet. G.: two capons.

3127 BURWELL (same leet) Master John Boys: two crofts recently held by John Pryk Jr. and once held by Thomas Plombe and lying across the rector's lane, for life.

3 JOHN STOWE (1438-1439)

170v **3128** BURWELL (1 October: leet) Robert Wilkyn and his son, John: eight acres of land recently held by Thomas Smyth, for 40 years, rendering annually 9s. at the customary times, *capitagium*, holmsilver and suit to court and leet. G.: 2s. (including a 12d. rent payment).

3129 BURWELL (leet) John Payntor Sr., his wife, Agnes, and his son, John: one tenement of 15 acres and one cote previously held by John Sr., for 40 years, rendering annually in all things as did John Sr., and common fine, holmsilver and suit to court and leet. G.: 3s.4d.

3130 BURWELL (August) John Rolf, son of Thomas Rolf, his wife, Katerina, and his son, John: one tenement of 15 acres previously held by John Rolf Sr., from the next Michaelmas for 30 years, rendering annually 15s. and all other services and customs rendered by John. G.: 5s.

3131 HEMINGFORD ABBOTS (8 October) Thomas Angewyn pays 3s.4d. for license for Agnes, daughter of Robert Brendhous and naif of the lord by blood, to marry whomever, as often as, however, and wherever she wishes during her life.[40]

3132 HEMINGFORD ABBOTS (11 November: leet) John Newman: surrender of one messuage and one virgate of land recently held by William Heyne, to the use of John Sly and his wife, Margaret, for life, rendering annually in all things as did John, with the obligation to repair and rebuild the property. G.: 12d.

3133 HEMINGFORD ABBOTS Note that John Sutton paid the fine to repair his tenement, for 20s. and six cartloads of straw. Pledge: John Almer Jr.

3134 HEMINGFORD ABBOTS (same leet) Edmund Maryot: surrender of one messuage and one virgate of land once held by Thomas Ibbot and afterwards held by John Ibbot, to the use of Walter Lincoln and his wife, Johanna, for life, rendering annually in all things as did Edmund. G.: 40d.

3135 HEMINGFORD ABBOTS (January) Thomas Cadman: surrender of one built up croft recently held by his father, to the use of Walter Murrok, alias Ingall, and his wife, Margaret, for life, rendering annually 12d. and all other services and customs rendered by Thomas, with the obligation to repair and maintain the buildings on that croft. G.: 2s.

171r **3136** HEMINGFORD ABBOTS Thomas Cadman: surrender of one virgate of land once held by his father, to the use of Walter Murrok, alias Ingill, and his wife, Margaret, for life, rendering annually in all things as did Thomas. G.: excused.

3137 HEMINGFORD ABBOTS Robert Bethewater: surrender of one cote with adjacent croft in Estende recently held by John Trappe, to the use of William Herde Jr., and his wife, for life, rendering annually in all things as did Robert, with the obligation to repair and maintain the property at their own expense. G.: 40d.

3138 LITTLE STUKELEY John Skynner Jr. and his wife, Alicia: one messuage built up with one hall, with an annexed *camera*, one grange of posts, and one annexed house

---

[40] The meaning of this entry seems to be that the recipient of the marriage license will not be required in future to pay further fines, nor seek further licenses in the event of the termination of the first marriage.

I am grateful to Professor Michael M. Sheehan for clarification of this question.

recently held by Thomas Gosse and first held by Richard Desburgh, with a half-virgate of land, for life, rendering annually in all things as did Thomas, with the obligation to repair and maintain the property. G.: 6s.8d., which he paid the seneschal, as it appears in the Receipt Roll for the previous year.

3139 St. Ives Agnes Freman: surrender of a half-row in Bridge Street recently held by her husband, William Freman, and once held by Thomas Freman, to the use of William Esex and his wife, Margaret, for life, rendering annually 14s. at the customary times, and all other services and customs rendered by Agnes, with the obligation to repair and maintain the property. *Et non licebit*, etc. Pledge for payments: Thomas Aungewyn. G.: 8s.

3140 St. Ives (January) Thomas Barbor and his wife, Margaret: a ruined half-row in Cheker recently held by John Fletcher and once held by Romburgh, for life. Also: a dove-cote with a parcel of appurtenant garden, for life, rendering 3s.4d. this year and 6s.8d. each year thereafter, in equal portions at Michaelmas and Easter. Further, they will repair and maintain the property. *Et non licebit*, etc. G. excused because of repairs.

3141 St. Ives (April) Thomas Kyngeston and his wife, Agnes: one row recently held by John Prikke lying on the lane leading to the manor, for life, rendering annually 10s. at the customary times, and all other services and customs rendered by John, with the first payment at Michaelmas of 1439. Further, they will build up the row and maintain it thereafter. *Et non licebit*, etc. G.: excused because of repairs.

3142 St. Ives Peter Taillor and his wife: one row recently held by William Pynnok and once held by Robert Salusbury, for life, rendering annually in all things as did William, with the obligation to repair and maintain the property. *Et non licebit*, etc. Further, he will have two wagon loads of undergrowth in Okle for enclosures, by the gift of the seneschal. G.: 2s.

3143 St. Ives Robert Trover and his wife, Margaret: a half-row in Cheker previously held by him and once held by Cristina Chaundeler, with four ruined shops recently held by Thomas Judde and once held by Thomas Baker, for life, rendering annually 6s.8d. for the half-row, which previously rendered 13s.4d., and 7s.4d. for the shops, which previously rendered 11s., at the customary times, with the obligation to repair and rebuild the property wherever necessary within one year, and maintain it thereafter. *Et non licebit*, etc. G.: 40d., and no more because of repairs.

3144 Elsworth (October) Alexander Hobbesson pays 8s. for license to marry Katerina, daughter of John Smyth and naif of the lord by blood, to whomever she wishes, this time.

3145 Graveley (October) William Stongton and his wife, Margaret: one messuage and one virgate of land once held by Poolyard, for life, rendering annually 13s.4d. and all other services and customs rendered by Poolyard, with the obligation to repair and maintain the property at their own expense, with the lord supplying timber in the woods there and at Elsworth, and also the rents of this year and the next two years. G.: two capons.

3146 Graveley John Drew: surrender of one messuage built up with two buildings and a half-virgate of land, to the use of John Baron Jr., for life, rendering annually in all things as did John. Also: a virgate of land recently held by his father, John Baron, for life, rendering annually in all things as did his father. G.: 40d.

3147 Barton (19 November: court) Richard Wodeward: surrender of one messuage and one virgate of land called Roos, to the use of his son, Thomas Wodeward, for life, rendering annually in all things as did Richard. G.: 2s. (paid to the seneschal).

3148 Barton (same court) Agnes, daughter of John Bonde and naif of the lord by blood, pays 3s.4d. for license to marry, the first time.

3149 BARTON (same court) John Martyn: one messuage and one virgate of land recently held by Thomas Colman and seized by the lord for default of repairs, for life, rendering annually in all things as did Thomas, with the obligation to repair the property. G.: 3s.4d.

3150 BARTON (same court) John Davy: one messuage and one croft called Barons recently held by John Carpenter de Faldo and seized by the lord for default of repairs, for life, rendering annually in all things as did John, with the obligation to repair the property at his own expense. Pledge for repairs: Richard Wodeward. G.: 6d.

172r **3151** BARTON (same court) Henry Boriche: one croft in Brokend and another croft called Stoneley croft and one virgate of land recently held by Thomas Stonley, for life, rendering annually in all things as did Thomas, with an allowance of this year's rent and half of next year's. G.: excused because of repairs.

3152 SHILLINGTON (18 November: leet) John Hill: surrender of one messuage and one virgate in Pegsdon, and the sixth part of demesne land recently held by John Atte Hill, to the use of William Atte Hill, and his wife, Justina, for life, rendering annually in all things as did John. G. and heriot: 6s.8d., and no more because *gersuma* was paid for that land the previous year. Further, the *gersuma* is to be paid at the feast of the Purification, under penalty of duplication.

3153 CRANFIELD (21 November: leet) Richard Archer: surrender of one cote with croft once held by Robert Couper, to the use of Robert, son of William Leen, for life, rendering annually in all things as did Richard. G. and heriot: 2s.

3154 CRANFIELD (same leet) Thomas Curteis Jr.: one messuage and a half-virgate of land recently held by Richard Curteis, for life, rendering annually in all things as did Richard with all the demesne land that he now holds, and provided that he observes the terms of the agreements made between him and his sister, Agnes, and pays her accordingly. G.: 5s.

3155 CRANFIELD (21 December) Agnes, daughter of John Alyn Smyth and naif of the lord by blood, pays 6s.8d. for license to marry whomever she wishes, this time. Pledge: the bailiff.

3156 CRANFIELD Margaret, daughter of Thomas DunWode Sr. and naif of the lord by blood, pays 6s.8d. for license to marry whomever she wishes, this time. Pledge: the bailiff.

3157 CRANFIELD Agnes, daughter of Richard Curteis and naif of the lord by blood, pays 6s.8d. for license to marry whomever she wishes, this time. Pledge: the bailiff.

3158 WOODHURST (28 November: leet) John Hunt: one messuage and a half-virgate of land recently held by Thomas Whiston, and a half-virgate of land recently held by John Wyngode, for life, rendering annually 15s. at the customary times and all other services and customs rendered by Thomas and John.

3159 HOLYWELL (28 November: leet) John Hunne and his wife, Margaret: one cote with appurtenances recently held by William Hunne, with one acre of land at Middilfurlong, for life, rendering annually in all things as did William, with the obligation to repair all the buildings on the property within two years, under penalty of forfeit. G.: two geese.

3160 HOLYWELL John Kyng: one acre of meadow at the eastern end of Dichedole near Cotmanmede, for life, rendering annually 2s. at the feast of John the Baptist. Further, he will plant willows in the large parcel of one acre and keep the water from the lord's meadow, at his own expense. G.: three geese.

3161 HOLYWELL William Bryan: one acre of meadow lying next to the aforesaid acre of John Kyng, for life, rendering annually 2s. at the feast of John the Baptist, with the obligation to plant willows on that land and keep the water from the marsh. G.: three geese.

172v **3162** RAMSEY John Beres and his wife, Johanna: from Brother John Swasham, the reversion of one messuage at the eastern end of the Whyte now held by Richard Dewtre, for life, rendering annually in all things as Richard, with the obligation to repair and maintain the property. *Et si predictus redditus*, etc. (distraints after arrears of 15 days). G.: 6s.8d.

3163 RAMSEY (January) Thomas Lancastre, alias Barbor, and his wife, Elena: from Brother John Swasham, sub-cellarer, one cote inside Mechesgate and recently held by John Rasoure and previously held by John Colles and once held by Walter Sporyor, for life, rendering annually 5s. in equal portions at the feasts of the Annunciation and Nativity of Blessed Mary. *Et si predictus redditus*, etc. (arrears of one month). G.: 2s., two capons.

3164 THERFIELD (3 December: leet) William Wynner: surrender of new demesne land recently held by his father, to the use of William Malt, for life, rendering annually in all things as did William. G.: one capon.

3165 THERFIELD (same leet) Thomas Wrighte: one plot and a half-virgate of land at Fynehowsis previously held by him, for life, rendering annually 12s. at the customary times. G.: excused.

3166 THERFIELD John Wyngor and his wife, Agnes: nine acres of new demesne land recently held by John Power and once held by John Ordemar, for life, rendering annually 6s.4d.ob. at the customary times. G.: six pullets.

3167 THERFIELD Richard Gamyn and his wife: the reversion of one messuage and one virgate of land and one cotland once held by Brewir, with 18 acres of new demesne land now held by Thomas Gamyn, for life, rendering annually in all things as Thomas, with the obligation to repair and maintain the property. G.: 6s.8d.

173r **3168** HOUGHTON John Fuller: surrender of one toft with a half-virgate of land recently held by William Fuller, to the use of John Carter, son of Richard Carter, alias Dylemaker, naif of the lord, for life, rendering annually in all things as did John. G.: three capons.

3169 HOUGHTON Note that John Upton will rebuild one grange on his tenement before the feast of the Assumption, with the lord giving him timber and an allowance of half of this year's rent.

3170 HOUGHTON Robert Mason: surrender of one messuage and one virgate of land recently held by Robert Parker, to the use of John Whaplode and his wife, Alicia, for life, rendering annually in all things as did Robert, with the obligation to repair one grange and one bake house within two years, with the lord granting him an allowance of half of this year's rent. G.: 12d.

3171 HOUGHTON Robert Smyth and his wife, Johanna: a half-virgate of land and one quarter in *arentatio* and one croft called Whithronesyerd, one croft called Gomyldesyerd, the Beauraper of one alder-ground called Gosholm, one alder-ground called Ankerholm, six selions of land at Tonnfurlong, which renders 8d. common fine, one croft, one forge at Houghton Cross, a parcel of a croft called Bedeliscroft, one Leighton place at Bedelescroft, and four crofts once held by John Prykke, recently held by his father, William Smyth, for life, rendering annually 21s.4d. at the customary times, and all other services and customs owed therein. G.: 40s.

3172 HOUGHTON William Fown: surrender of one holm with willows growing in it near the village of St. Ives and surrounded by water, to the use of John Bedford and his wife, Margaret, for life, rendering annually 3s.4d. at the customary times and all other services and customs rendered by William. G.: two capons.

3173 HOUGHTON John Fuller: surrender of one croft in *arentatio*, in which William Fuller recently lived, with another croft and a half-virgate of land in *arentatio* recently held by the same William, to the use of William Pynder and his wife, Beatrix, for life, rendering annually 10s.4d. and all other services and customs rendered by John, with the obligation to raise and cover a house on the property at his own expense before the feast of St. John the Baptist. G.: 20d.

3174 HOUGHTON John Whaplode: surrender of one messuage with one house and a half-virgate of land once held by John Cook, to the use of William Dykys, and his wife, Margaret, for life, rendering annually in all things as did John, with the obligation to repair and maintain the property. G.: 12d.

3175 HOUGHTON (20 June) John Fuller and his wife, Agnes: one messuage with appurtenant croft recently held by William Lawe and once held by William Prikke, for life, rendering annually in all things as did William, with the obligation to repair and maintain the property at their own expense. G.: 2s.

3176 HOUGHTON (June) John Preeston: one empty toft and one virgate of land recently held by Robert Andrew, with one parcel reserved to the lord for making a park, for life, rendering annually in all things as did Robert. G.: 2s.

3177 HOUGHTON (July) Robert Barker: surrender of one tenement and one virgate and a half of land once held by John Andrew and Dersson, to the use of Thomas Froxfeld and his wife, Alicia, for life, rendering annually in all things as did Robert, with the obligation to repair the property at their own expense, timber being supplied by the lord. G.: three capons, and no more because of repairs.

3178 HEMINGFORD ABBOTS Thomas Brendhous: a half-virgate of land once held by Fenton with one croft recently held by John Brendhous, for life, rendering annually 6s.2d. for the half-virgate and 12d. for the croft at the customary times, and all other services and customs rendered by John. G.: 12d.

3179 ELLINGTON (10 December) Johanna Bateman, daughter of Thomas Bateman and naif of the lord by blood, pays 3s.4d. for license to marry whomever she wishes, this time.

3180 ELLINGTON (January) William Burgeys, naif of the lord, pays 2s. for license to marry Alicia, his daughter and naif of the lord by blood, to John Jemesson of Hamerton, this time. Pledge: John Holcote.

3181 ELLINGTON Thomas Caus and his wife, Matilda: one plot and three quarters of land once held by William Burgeys, for life, rendering annually in all things as did William, with the obligation to repair and maintain the property at their own expense. G.: 2s.

3182 ELLINGTON John Swyft: surrender of one messuage and one virgate of land once held by William Gymbir, to the use of Thomas Schepperd and his wife, Cristiana, for life, rendering annually in all things as did John, with the obligation to repair and maintain the property at their own expense. G.: 20d.

3183 RAMSEY (January) Robert Brown, alias Tyler, and his wife, Margaret: from Brother John Swasham, sub-cellarer, one messuage next to Mechegate recently held by Richard Wayte and once held by Simon Sege, for life, rendering annually 5s. in equal portions at the feasts of the Annunciation and Nativity of Blessed Mary, with the sub-cellarer responsible for repairs. *Et si predictus redditus*, etc. (arrears of one month). G.: 12d., two capons.

3184 WARBOYS (February) John Croxton and his wife, Johanna: one maltmanland recently *ad opus* and recently held by William Daud, for life, rendering annually 9s. at the customary times, mowing of the meadow in Chevereth, and common fine, with the obligation to repair the property at their own expense within two years, the lord granting them an allowance of this year's rent and that for the next two years. G.: two capons.

173v

174r **3185** WARBOYS (March) Thomas Newman Jr. and his wife, Alicia: half of the lands and tenements once held by Robert Raven and one virgate of land in Caldecote once held by Richard Smyth and recently held by Thomas Newman, his father, for life, rendering annually 22s. at the customary times, which property previously rendered 25s. Further, he will render all services and customs rendered by his father, and he will repair and maintain the property at his own expense. G.: six capons.

3186 WARBOYS (10 July) William Pynder of Houghton, miller: the windmill of Warboys, from the previous feast of the Nativity of John the Baptist for 10 years, rendering annually 40s., in equal portions at Michaelmas, Christmas, Easter, and the feast of John the Baptist. Further, he will repair and maintain the millstones, the entranceway and iron works, with timber being supplied by the lord, and he will dismiss the mill and its appurtenances at the end of his term in as good — or better — condition as when he received it. During the term he will keep, occupy the mill, and serve the customaries and others coming there diligently. If payments are in arrears for 15 days after any term, the lord can impose distraints, and if payments are in arrears for six weeks, in part or in whole, the lord can re-enter the mill and hold it without any contradiction. G.: excused.

3187 WESTON (January) Maria, daughter of Simon Hacon and naif of the lord by blood, pays 5s. and four capons for license to marry Henry Smyth of Clopton, this time. Pledges: William Grymbald and William Flesshewere.

3188 SLEPE (January) William Dryver and his wife, Elena: one messuage and one virgate of land *ad opus,* one quarter of land *ad opus,* one parcel of one virgate called Halydayes recently held by William Ilger and once held by Simon Badewyn, for life, rendering annually 17s.6d. at the customary times, and all other services and customs rendered by William, with the first payment at the next feast of St. Andrew. Further, they will repair the property at their own expense. G.: excused because of repairs.

3189 CHATTERIS (1 April: court) Radulph Tebalde and his wife, Cecilia: half of one tenement of eight acres with half of the meadow in Crowlode and one acre of land in Elmen once held by John Lytholf Sr., for life, rendering annually 6s.2d.ob. and all other services and customs rendered by John. G.: two capons.

174v **3190** CHATTERIS (same court) William Thakestede: surrender of one cotland with meadow in Crowlodmede recently held by Robert Enfeld, to the use of Robert Gravele, for life, rendering annually 2s.10d. and all other services and customs rendered by William, with one *camera* and a parcel of garden are reserved to Alicia Hoberd for life. G.: two capons.

3191 CHATTERIS (same court) John Devell: one cotland recently held by John Clerke, half of one tenement of eight acres with half of the meadow in Crowlodmede recently held by Agnes Enfeld, for life, rendering annually 7d. for the cotland, 4s.7d.ob. for the tenement and meadow, and all other services and customs rendered by Agnes and John. G.: 2s.

3192 BYTHORNE Mariota, daughter of John Wattesson, alias Schepperd, and naif of the lord by blood, pays 2s.6d. for license to marry John Wygyn of Buckworth, this time. Pledge: John Beverich.

3193 BYTHORNE Agnes, daughter of William Randolf and naif of the lord by blood, pays 2s.6d. for license to marry whomever she wishes, this time. Pledge: John Beverich.

3194 WISTOW Robert Russell: one croft called Fen Pithel with adjacent meadow containing five acres, three and a half rods recently held by Robert Nottyng, for life, rendering annually 4s. at the customary times, and all other services and customs rendered by Robert, with the obligation to repair the enclosure of the croft and maintain it. G.: 12d.

3195 Wistow (August) Richard Rede, his wife, Johanna, and their son, Thomas: one empty plot and one quarter of servile land once held by Simon Hacoun and recently held by the same Richard and surrendered back into the lord's hands by him, in bondage for life, rendering annually in all things as he previously did. G.: 12d.

3196 Raveley Cum Wistow (October) Richard Willesson of Raveley pays 40d. for license to marry Anna, his daughter and naif of the lord by blood, to John Walgate Jr., this time.

3197 Woodhurst (April) William Benet, alias Boner, his wife, Agnes, and their son, John: one vacant cote recently held by his father, Benedict Boner, for life, rendering annually 2s.6d., at the customary times, which property previously rendered 4s. Further, they will build a house 40 feet long on the property before Michaelmas of next year, with timber supplied by the lord for posts, sides, beams and spars. G.: two capons.

3198 Raveley Crowche and his wife, Isabella: one messuage and five quarters of land once held by Richard Asplond and recently held by John Sewer, for life, rendering annually 17s.10d. and customs of the vill, with the obligation to repair and maintain the property at their own expense. G.: 2s.

175r

3199 Raveley (August) Thomas Wyllesson and his wife, Agnes: one half-virgate of land once held by John Hyche Sr. and recently held by Richard Crowche, for life, rendering annually in all things as did Richard. G.: 12d.

3200 Raveley John Walgate Sr.: surrender of one messuage with three quarters of land recently held by Thomas Owty, to the use of his son, John, and his wife, Anna, for life, rendering annually in all things as did John Sr. G.: 2s.

3201 Broughton (June) John Cabe, naif of the lord by blood, pays 16d. for license to marry Alicia, his daughter and naif of the lord, to William Keye, this time.

3202 Upwood (June) Thomas Baker: one messuage and a half-virgate of land recently held by Nicholas Hendesson called Schepenesplace, for life, rendering annually in all things as did Nicholas, with the obligation to repair and maintain the property at his own expense, with timber and undergrowth for the enclosure supplied by the lord. G.: two capons.

3203 Holywell (July) John Palmer: surrender of one messuage and one virgate of land with appurtenances in Needingworth once held by Roger Greye, with two acres, three rods of demesne parcelled out of Schepynfurlong once held by the same Roger, to the use of John Asplond Jr. and his wife, Rosa, in bondage for life, rendering annually in all things as did John, with the obligation to repair and maintain the property at their own expense, under penalty of forfeit. G.: 20s.

4 JOHN STOWE (1439-1440)

175v

3204 Graveley (November) Isabella, daughter of William Smyth and naif of the lord by blood, pays 6s.8d. for license to marry whomever she wishes, this time. Pledge: Margaret Edward.

3205 Graveley Elena, daughter of William Smyth and naif of the lord by blood, pays 3s.4d. for license to marry whomever she wishes, this time. Pledge: Margaret Edward.

3206 Graveley (January) Richard Rolf and his wife, Isabella: one messuage and one and a half-virgates of land recently held by Alicia Rolf and previously held by his father, John Rolf, for life, rendering annually in all things as did his father. G.: 6s.8d.

3207 Therfield (November) John Overston: one cotland and four acres of land at Borehill once held by Roger Sewale, for life, rendering annually 10s., with the first payment at the feast of St. Andrew, which property previously rendered 14s. He will repair the property at their own expense, with the lord granting an allowance of last year's rent. G.: excused.

3208 THERFIELD John Wode and John Waryn, son of Thomas Waryn, naif of the lord: all lands and tenements recently held by John Wode, except for two parcels of demesne land, rendering annually 10 marks, with an allowance of this year's rent. G.: excused.

3209 THERFIELD (15 November: court) John Edward and his wife, Elena: one toft with one house and an adjacent croft recently held by John Hatlo, for life, rendering annually 12d. at the customary times, and all other services and customs rendered by John. G.: one goose, one capon.

3210 THERFIELD (same court) Johanna Jankyn: surrender of one tenement of Paynes, with another parcel of land, as found in the Rental, recently held by her husband, John Jankyn, to the use of her son, William Jankyn, for life, rendering annually 40s. at the customary times, which property previously rendered 48s.9d.ob. and all other services and customs owed therein. G.: excused.

3211 THERFIELD (same court) John Marschall of Royston: certain acres of land near Royston called Newlond, with another parcel of land there once held by John Paton and recently held by John Nokys, for life, rendering annually 16s.8d., which property previously rendered 21s. Further, he will render all other services and customs rendered by John. G.: one goose and one capon.

3212 THERFIELD (same court) John Wenham Jr.: surrender of one virgate of land and one croft called Betonswyk and three acres of land once held by Nicholas Adam, to the use of John Sperver, naif of the lord, and his wife, Isabella, for life, rendering annually 25s. at the customary times and all other services and customs rendered by John. G.: 6s.8d.

3213 THERFIELD (same court) Alicia, daughter of John Colle Sr. and naif of the lord by blood, pays, through the hands of Thomas Angtill, 3s.4d. for license to marry whomever she wishes, this time.

3214 THERFIELD (same court) John Colle Sr. and his wife, Johanna: five acres of new demesne land recently held by John Wattes and 13 acres of new demesne land recently held by Robert Prest, for life, rendering annually 10s. at the customary times, and all other services and customs rendered by Robert. G.: two capons.

176r

3215 BURWELL Andrew Moryce: surrender of one messuage and a half-acre of land once held by John Peryng, to the use of Richard Aylwyn, alias Preyntyse, and his wife, Margaret, for life, by the rod, rendering annually 15d. at the customary times, suit to court and leet, and all other services and customs owed therein. G.: 12d.

3216 BURWELL Thomas Goodynche: one cotland in *arentatio* with a parcel of a croft once held by Alexander Sparowe and recently held by John Goodale, the other parcel of which croft is now held by the farmer of the manor, for 30 years, rendering annually in all things as did John and suit to court and leet. G.: 12d.

3217 BURWELL Robert Goodynche: half of one tenement of 24 acres once held by John Wright and recently held by George Burthen, for 24 years, rendering annually in all things as did George, and suit to court and leet. G.: 12d.

3218 BURWELL Thomas Rower: surrender of one cote and one croft held by Adam Alot in North Street with one acre of land, to the use of John Calvysbane, for life, rendering annually all services and customs owed therein, suit to court and leet. G.: two capons.

3219 WISTOW John Helmesle and his wife, Margaret: one messuage with appurtenant demesne land once held by Stephen Aylmar and recently held by John

White, for life, rendering annually 5s. at the customary times, which property recently rendered 7s.6d. Further, they will render all services and customs owed therein, with the obligation to repair the hall and the bake house, timber being supplied by the lord for the first repairs. G.: 20d.

3220 WISTOW (1 October) Robert Hyche of Wistow, naif of the lord, pays 5s. for license to marry Isabella, his daughter and naif of the lord by blood, to Richard Clement of Comberton, this time.

3221 WISTOW (1 October) Richard Hyche will pay 12d. annually at the leet for license for his son, John, naif of the lord by blood, to live off the manor, for as long as it pleases the lord, remaining a naif as before and coming to the leet annually.

3222 WISTOW (1 October) John Barker: two cotes parcelled out of one hidemanland once held by Thomas Botiller and recently held by John Sabyn, and located at the gate of the manor, for life, rendering annually in all things as did John, with the obligation to repair and maintain the property at his own expense, with timber being supplied by the lord, and with the first payment at the feast of All Saints after one year. G.: one capon.

3223 WISTOW (10 December) John Scot of Huntingdon pays 3s.4d. for license to marry Agnes Fraunce, daughter of John Fraunce and widow of Richard Carter of Houghton, naif of the lord by blood.

3224 WISTOW (20 September) John Newman, son of Robert Newman of Upwood, pays 6s.8d. for license to marry Agnes, daughter of John Randolf and naif of the lord by blood.

3225 CRANFIELD (10 October) William Maryson pays 6s.8d. for license to marry Johanna, widow of John Robyn, and for entry into two half-virgates and new demesne land recently held by John Robyn and once held by John Joye and John Atte Pery.

3226 CRANFIELD (9 November: leet) John Hare: one messuage and a half-virgate of land recently held by Robert Baylly and once held by Thomas Aleyn, for life, rendering annually in all things as did Robert. G.: 20d.

3227 CRANFIELD (same leet) William Wodehill Sr.: one messuage called Swaynys and half of one virgate of land with another virgate of land recently held by Isabella Balieswell, for life, rendering annually 28s. at the customary times and all other services and customs rendered by Isabella. G.: 7s.

3228 CRANFIELD John Rede: a half-virgate of land once *ad opus* and recently held by Thomas Of the Made, for life, rendering annually 13s.6d. at the customary times, and all other services and customs rendered by Thomas. G.: 2s.6d., and no more because the land was in the lord's hands, of which the bailiff rendered an account last year.

3229 CRANFIELD William Rede: three acres of demesne land of Cokeslond, two acres of demesne land at Stalipras and one pithel once held by Thomas Of the Made and recently held by John Rede, his father, for life, rendering annually 5s.4d. at the customary times, and all other services and customs rendered by John. G.: 2s.6d., and no more because the land was in the lord's hands, of which the bailiff rendered an account last year.

3230 BARTON (11 November: court) John Gregory: one virgate of land with forland recently held by William Lylly, for life, rendering annually 18s.4d. at the customary times and all other services and customs rendered by William. G.: 2s.

3231 RAMSEY (October) Thomas Wayte Fuller and his wife: from Brother John Swasham, sub-cellarer, one plot in which he lives and once held by John Lyngcoln, for life, rendering annually 8s. in equal portions at the feasts of the Annunciation and Nativity of Blessed Mary, with the sub-cellarer responsible for repairs. *Et si predictus redditus*, etc. (arrears of one month). G.: 6s.8d.

176v

177r

3232 RAMSEY (October) John Keteryng and his wife, Alicia: from the sub-cellarer, one plot in which he lives recently held by John Cooke and once held by John Barbor, for life, rendering annually 12s. in equal portions at the feasts of the Annunciation and Nativity of Blessed Mary, with the sub-cellarer responsible for repairs. *Et si predictus redditus*, etc. G.: 6s.8d.

3233 RAMSEY (October) Richard Wayte and his wife, Johanna, from the sub-cellarer, one plot recently held by Agnes Prykke and once held by William Burton, for life, rendering annually 6s.8d. in equal portions at the feasts of the Annunciation and Nativity of Blessed Mary, with the sub-cellarer responsible for repairs. *Et si predictus redditus*, etc. (arrears of one month). G.: 3s.4d., two capons.

3234 RAMSEY (October) Robert Laborer and his wife: from the sub-cellarer, one plot inside Mechegate recently held by Agnes Rameseye and once held by Simon Sege, for life, rendering annually 5s. at the customary times. *Et si predictus redditus*, etc. G.: 3s.4d.

3235 RAMSEY (October) Richard Tommesson and his wife: from the sub-cellarer, one messuage recently held by John Coupere and once held by Simon Miller, for life, rendering annually 9s. in equal portions at the feasts of the Annunciation and Nativity of Blessed Mary. *Et si predictus redditus*, etc. (arrears of one month). G.: two capons.

177v **3236** RAMSEY (October) William Somerton, *firmarius* of Bodeseye: from the sub-cellarer, one parcel of meadow in Hilke containing 11 acres recently held by Thomas Godfreye, for (*blank*) years, rendering annually 5s.6d. in equal portions at the feasts of the Annunciation and Nativity of Blessed Mary. *Et si predictus redditus*, etc. (arrears of one month). G.: six cheeses.

3237 RAMSEY (October) Robert Tyler and his wife, Margaret: from the sub-cellarer, one empty toft recently burned and lying next to the lane leading to Stokkyngfen next to the tenement of the Sacristy and recently held by John Hardhed, for the whole time that it is vacant and not built up, rendering annually 12d. in equal portions at the feasts of the Annunciation and Nativity of Blessed Mary. *Et si predictus redditus*, etc. (arrears of one month). Further, if they dismiss the property without license, it shall be seized. G.: two capons.

3238 RAMSEY (October) John Clevelok and his wife, Beatrix: from the sub-cellarer, one empty toft at Grene recently burned and recently held by Thomas Clerke and once held by John Wayman, and one cote with one pond once held by Nicholas Orgen-player, for the whole time that it is vacant, rendering annually 2s. *Et si predictus redditus*, etc. (arrears of one month). G.: two tenches.

3239 RAMSEY (October) John Berdewell Jr. and his wife, Johanna: from the sub-cellarer, one empty tenement at Grene recently burned and recently held by John Knapwell, for the whole time that it is empty and not built up, rendering annually 16d. in equal portions at the feast of the Annunciation and Nativity of Blessed Mary. *Et si predictus redditus*, etc. (arrears of one month). G.: two capons.

3240 RAMSEY (October) Richard Berdewell and his wife: from the sub-cellarer, one messuage at Grene recently burned and lying between the two lanes leading to Stokkyngfen and recently held by John Leper, and one cotland recently held by Agnes Waker, rendering annually 16d. in equal portions at the feasts of the Annunciation and Nativity of Blessed Mary. *Et si predictus redditus*, etc. (arrears of one month). Further, they may not dismiss the property without license. G.: two capons.

3241 RAMSEY (October) Thomas Witton Fyssher: from the sub-cellarer, one empty toft at Grene once held by John Wyke and recently burned, held as above, rendering annually 16d. in equal portions at the feasts of the Annunciation and Nativity of Blessed Mary. G.: two fat eels.

3242 RAMSEY (October) John Wayte: from the sub-cellarer, one toft pertaining to the office of the sacristan at Grene and recently burned, held as above, rendering annually 12d. beyond 8d. paid by the sub-cellarer to the sacristan. *Et si predictus redditus*, etc. (arrears of one month). G.: two pullets.

3243 RAMSEY (October) Thomas Botiller: from the sub-cellarer, one messuage pertaining to the office of the custodian of the bank at Grene and recently burned, held as above, rendering annually 12d. at the customary times, beyond 4d. paid by the sub-cellarer to the custodian. *Et si predictus redditus,* etc. (arrears of one month). G.: two capons.

3244 RAMSEY (June) Johanna, widow of Simon Botiller: from the sub-cellarer, one cotland at Cool Lane lying between the tenement of the eleemosynary and that of Nicholas Stucle, with six selions of land recently held by Simon, for life, rendering annually 6s.8d. in equal portions at the feast of the Annunciation and Nativity of Blessed Mary, with the obligation to repair and maintain the property. *Et si predictus redditus*, etc. (arrears of one month). G.: 3s.4d.

178r

3245 RAMSEY (June) John Gymmes Glover and his wife: from the sub-cellarer, one messuage in High Street once held by Henry Overton and recently held by John Sadeler, for life, rendering annually 9s.4d. in equal portions at the feasts of the Annunciation and Nativity of Blessed Mary, with the sub-cellarer responsible for repairs. *Et si predictus redditus*, etc. (arrears of one month). G.: two capons.

3246 RAMSEY (June) John Newman and his wife: from the sub-cellarer, one empty toft between his tenement and that of John Austyn, with three selions of land in a croft recently held by Robert Coupere, for life, rendering annually 20d. at the feast of the Annunciation. *Et si predictus redditus*, etc. (arrears of one month). G.: 12d.

3247 RAMSEY (June) Robert Mory, John Castell and Beatrix, John's wife: from the sub-cellarer, one plot inside Mechegates once held by John Rasour and recently held by Thomas Barbour, for life, rendering annually 5s. at the customary times, with the sub-cellarer responsible for repairs. *Et si predictus redditus,* etc. (arrears of one month). G.: 2s.

3248 SHILLINGTON (13 November: view) Richard Bradyfan: five acres of demesne land at Chirchehill recently held by Thomas Bradyfan, his father, for life, rendering annually in all things as did Thomas. G.: 4s.

3249 SHILLINGTON (same view) John Wenyngham Sr.: surrender of one messuage and one virgate of land recently held by William Waryn, to the use of the same William Waryn, for life, rendering annually in all things as did John. G. and heriot: 13s.4d., to be paid at the next court.

3250 SHILLINGTON (same view) Richard Messanger: one virgate of land recently held by John AtteMede, one lot of demesne land inside the manor, one acre of land of Newmanlond, and one croft called Hary Cokys recently held by the same John, for life, rendering annually 22s.3d., one hen, two cocks and five eggs at the customary times, and all other services and customs rendered by John. G. and heriot: 13s.4d., two capons.

3251 HEMINGFORD ABBOTS (17 November: leet) John Birt and his wife, Cristiana: one cote with croft once held by Ivo Richard and recently held by John Newman, with one other croft once held by the same Ivo and recently held by the same John Newman, for life, rendering annually 2s. at the customary times and all other services and customs rendered by John, with the obligation to repair and maintain the property. G.: 3s.4d.

3252 HEMINGFORD ABBOTS (same leet) Thomas Aungewyn: surrender of one messuage and two virgates of land once held by John Brendhous and one parcel of a certain tenement next to the aforesaid messuage called Clarellis, once held by the same

John, to the use of John Newman and his wife, Beatrix, for life, rendering annually in all things as did Thomas. G.: 5s.

3253 HEMINGFORD ABBOTS Thomas Brendhous: surrender of a half-virgate of land once held by Fenton, to the use of William Herde Jr., for life, rendering annually in all things as did Thomas. G.: 8d.

3254 HEMINGFORD ABBOTS Thomas Brendhous: surrender of one cotland with croft pertaining to the above half-virgate now held by William Herde Jr., to the use of Thomas Aungewyn, his wife, Johanna, and Thomas, son of Johanna, for life, rendering annually 12d. at the customary times, and all other services and customs rendered by Thomas, with the obligation to repair and maintain the property at their own expense. G.: one capon.

3255 HEMINGFORD ABBOTS (January) Thomas Aungewyn and his wife, Johanna: one empty toft recently built up and one virgate of land recently held by John Herde, rendering annually 6s. at the customary times, which property previously rendered 12s.4d., with the first payment at next Michaelmas. In addition, they will render all other services and customs previously rendered by John. G.: one capon.

3256 HEMINGFORD ABBOTS (April) Johanna Lyngcolne and her daughter, Margaret: half of one virgate of land and one cotland recently held by her husband, Walter
178v Lyngcolne, for life, rendering annually 5s.8d. for the virgate and 4d. for the cotland at the customary times, and all other services and customs rendered by Walter. G.: 2s., two capons.

3257 HEMINGFORD ABBOTS (April) Henry Mortemer his wife, Agnes: and their son, Thomas: one messuage called Clarell once held by Richard Botiller, for life, rendering annually 4s. at the customary times, which property previously rendered 4s.4d. Further, they will render all other services and customs rendered by Richard. G.: 6d.

3258 HEMINGFORD ABBOTS (April) Robert Brigge: one messuage and one virgate of land and two half-virgates of land recently held by John Hamond and once held by John Marschall Sr., for life, rendering annually in all things as did John. G.: 2s.

3259 HEMINGFORD ABBOTS (April) John Pope and his wife, Johanna: one virgate of land recently held by John Brigge Sr. and once held by William Bellond, for life, rendering annually in all things as did John. Further, the lord grants them half of this year's rent. G.: 2s.

3260 HEMINGFORD ABBOTS (April) John Feld Sr. and his wife, Johanna: one virgate of land recently held by Robert White, the messuage of which is held by Thomas Aungewyn by copy, and one croft recently held by Richard Botiller for 12d., for life, rendering annually 11s.4d. and all other services and customs owed therein, with the first payment at next Michaelmas. G.: one goose and one capon.

3261 HEMINGFORD ABBOTS (April) Simon Chapman and his wife, Agnes: one cotland recently held by John Brigge and once held by John's father, with a half-virgate of land recently held by John Pope and once held by Thomas Herde, for life, rendering annually 7s.2d. at the customary times and all other services and customs owed therein, with the obligation to repair and maintain the property at their own expense. G.: 20d.

3262 HEMINGFORD ABBOTS (April) William Hyll Smyth and his wife, Alicia: one croft with a cotland once held by Robert Brendhous and recently held by John Brigge atte Crosse, with half of one virgate recently held by Walter Lyngcolne, for life, rendering annually 6s.8d. at the customary times, with the first payment at next Michaelmas, with the obligation to repair and maintain the property at their own expense. G.: 8d.

3263 HEMINGFORD ABBOTS (August) Thomas Aungewyn and his wife, Johanna:

two acres of meadow recently held by Walter Murrok, for life, rendering annually 4s. at the customary times, which property previously rendered 7s. Further, they will plant willows there to preserve the meadow. G.: excused.

3264 WISTOW (20 August) William Pynder of Houghton, miller: the windmill of Wistow, from next Michaelmas for (*blank*) years, rendering annually 20s. in equal portions at the feast of St. Andrew, the Annunciation, the Nativity of John the Baptist, and the Nativity of Blessed Mary, with the obligation to repair and maintain the mill in boards, iron works, mill stones, carpentry, entrance-way, with timber supplied by the lord. He will diligently serve those coming to the mill and if the payments are in arrears for two months, the lord shall take the mill and all the goods and chattels there. G.: excused because of the ruined condition of the mill.

3265 WARBOYS (22 November: leet) John Fyssher: one mondayland recently held by Henry Norborough, for life, rendering annually in all things as did Henry. G.: two capons.

3266 WARBOYS (December) Simon High Sr.: surrender of one tenement from the tenement of Higeney, with two acres of land at Wodecroft, to the use of John Caton Jr., alias Bereford, for life, rendering annually 10s., which property previously rendered 24s. Further, he will render all other services and customs rendered by Simon, and repair and maintain the property, timber and an allowance of next year's rent supplied by the lord. G.: two capons.

3267 WARBOYS (February) John Benson Sr. and his son, William: one maltmanland recently held *ad opus* by William Sande, in *arentatio* for life, rendering annually 6s. for rent, 2s. for works, and customs of the vill, with the obligation to repair the property within the next three years, with the lord granting timber and an allowance of the rents for the next three years. G.: two capons.

3268 WARBOYS Thomas Benet: surrender of one messuage and a half-virgate of land *ad opus*, to the use of Thomas Wroo, for life, rendering annually 6s. for rent and 2s. for works at the customary times, with the obligation to repair and maintain the property at his own expense. G.: 12d.

3269 WARBOYS (May) John Benson, his wife, Agnes, their son, William, and his wife, Agnes: one messuage and a half-virgate of land *ad opus* and another half-virgate of land in *arentatio* once held by Richard Eyr, and a half-virgate of land once held by Thomas Norborough, for life, rendering annually in all things as did Richard and Thomas. Also: one mondayland recently held by William Sande and recently *ad opus*, in *arentatio* for life, rendering annually 8s. and customs of the vill, which property previously rendered 10s. The first payment will be at the feast of St. Andrew after two years, and they will repair the property, timber being supplied by the lord. G.: two capons.

3270 WARBOYS (20 September) John Berenger Jr. pays 3s.4d. for license to marry Agnes, his daughter, to William Filhous of Woodhurst, carpenter, this time.

3271 WARBOYS (August) Richard Laveyn, recently of Stanton: one messuage and a half-virgate of land recently *ad opus* and previously held by William Scut and once held by John Scut, in *arentatio* for life, rendering annually 6s. for rent, 2s. for works, and customs of the vill, with the first payment at the feast of St. Andrew after three years. G.: excused because of repairs.

3272 HOUGHTON (20 November: court) John Whaplode: a parcel of the manor called "le Bury Ilde", for life, rendering annually 6d. at the customary times. He will keep the enclosures at his own expense, and he will not make any waste in the property. G.: excused.

3273 HOUGHTON Robert Owty and his wife, Johanna: one messuage and two virgates of land recently held by William Tyffyn and once held by Robert Roger, for life, rendering annually in all things as did William. G.: excused.

3274 HOUGHTON (16 December) Thomas Robyn, naif of the lord by blood, will pay two capons annually at Christmas for license to live outside the manor, for as long as it pleases the lord, remaining a naif as before. Pledge for payments: John Purdy.

3275 HOUGHTON (March) Robert Andrew: surrender of one messuage and a half-virgate of land recently held by Richard Menor, to the use of William Wyth and his wife, Juliana, for life, rendering annually in all things as did Robert, with the obligation to repair and maintain the property. G.: 2s.8d.

3276 HOUGHTON Thomas Andrewe: surrender of one empty toft and one virgate of land called Snowys, to the use of Richard Atteken and his wife, Margeria, for life, rendering annually in all things as did Thomas. G.: 2s.

3277 HOUGHTON (May) John Aleyn Jr. and his wife, Agnes: one messuage and one virgate of land recently held by Thomas Elyet, for life, rendering annually 10s., which property previously rendered 12s. Further, they will render all other services and customs owed therein, with the first payment at the next feast of St. Andrew, and they will repair the property. G.: four capons.

3278 HOUGHTON (May) John Carter, alias Dylemaker, naif of the lord: one messuage and two cotlands *ad opus* once held by Cranys and recently held by his father, Richard Carter, with one close called Dushousyerd recently held by the same Richard, for life, rendering annually 13s. at the customary times, and all other services and customs owed therein, with the obligation to repair and maintain the property. G.: 13s.4d.

3279 HOUGHTON William Whaplode and his wife, Agnes: surrender of one messuage and a half-virgate of land once held by John Gerard and recently held by John Whaplode Sr., to the use of John Whaplode and his wife, Alicia, for life, rendering annually in all things as did William. G.: 20d., paid to the seneschal.

3280 HOUGHTON (July) William Crosse and his wife, Margaret: one messuage and one virgate of land recently held by him and once held by Matilda Smyth, for life, rendering annually 10s. at the customary times, which property previously rendered 12s. Further, they will render all other services and customs rendered by him. Also: one virgate of land *ad opus* once held by Robert Dylemaker and recently held by John Marchall, and half of the lands and tenements once held by Gilbert de Houghton and recently held by the same John, for life, rendering annually 10s. for the virgate, 5s. for the land of Gilbert, at the customary times, and all other services and customs owed therein, with the obligation to repair and maintain the messuage. G.: 2s., four capons.

3281 UPWOOD CUM RAVELEY (November) Thomas Penyman: one messuage and a half-virgate of land once held by John Hikkesson and one quarter of land once held by Nicholas Alston, with adjacent forland, and a half-virgate of land once held by Richard Payn and recently held by Richard Skynner, for nine years, rendering annually 21s.6d. and all other services and customs rendered by Richard, with the obligation to repair the property, the lord supplying timber, an allowance of this year's rent, half of next year's rent, and two wagon loads of undergrowth for the enclosure. G.: two capons.

3282 UPWOOD (December) Richard Genge: one messuage and one virgate of land and two acres of land once held by Peter Bray and recently held by John Mylys, for life, rendering annually 17s. at the customary times, which property previously rendered 24s. Further, payments will begin at the feast of St. Andrew, and he will repair the property within one year and maintain it thereafter, the lord supplying one quarter of barley, to be restored next year. G.: excused because of repairs.

3283 UPWOOD Thomas Baker: one grange and a half-virgate of land recently held by John Hendesson, for life, rendering annually in all things as did John, with the lord supplying four quarters and two bushels of barley, to be repaid the next year. G.: two capons.

3284 UPWOOD (June) Nicholas Albyn, naif of the lord by blood, will pay 4d. annually for license for his son, William, naif of the lord, to live with Simon Graver of Wisbech and practice the craft of the said Simon, remaining a naif as before. Pledges for payments: Brother John Therfield, monk, and Nicholas Albyn.

3285 WESTON (2 December: leet) John Kyng Sr.: one messuage and one quarter of land recently held by Robert Rukden, for life, rendering annually in all things as did Robert, with the obligation to repair the property before the feast of St. John the Baptist, with timber, 20 feet of beams and six posts, supplied by the lord. Further, the first payment will be at the feast of St. Andrew after one year. G.: two capons.

3286 WESTON John Boncy: surrender of a half-virgate of land and demesne land with another parcel of land recently held by John Carter, to the use of John Felyce and his wife, Mariota, for life, rendering annually 22s., which property previously rendered 33s.10d.ob. Further, they will render all other services and customs owed therein. G.: 2s., six capons.

3287 WESTON Thomas Forster: surrender of a half-virgate and one quarter of land with demesne land and other parcels once held by William Boncy, to the use of John Boncy Jr. and his wife, Johanna, for life, rendering annually 36s., which property previously rendered 37s.9d. Further, they will render all other services and customs owed therein. G.: 2s., six capons.

3288 ABBOTS RIPTON (December) John Gardener Sr.: one messuage and four semi-virgates of land and other lands previously held by him for 26s.8d., for life, rendering annually 22s. at the customary times, and all other services and customs previously rendered by him, with the first payment at the next feast of All Saints. Further, he will repair and maintain the property. G.: three capons.

3289 ABBOTS RIPTON (December) John Gardener Jr.: one messuage and one plot with two semi-virgates of land recently held by Robert Wright and once held by John West, and previously rendering 26s., for life, rendering annually 24s.24d. at the customary times, with the obligation to repair and maintain the property and repair one newly-constructed *camera*, for which he receives an allowance of this year's rent, and hay in the grange. G.: three capons.

180r

3290 ABBOTS RIPTON John Hyche of Estthorp pays 6s.8d. for license to marry Juliana, his daughter and naif of the lord by blood, to whomever she wishes, this time.

3291 ABBOTS RIPTON (August) Thomas Joye and his wife, Agnes: one messuage and one virgate of land recently held by John Lyndeseye and recently *ad opus*, and one messuage and a half-virgate of land *ad opus*, recently held by Thomas Of the Bury, for life, rendering annually 26s.8d. for works and rents, at the customary times, which property previously rendered 24s. Further, they will render all other services and customs rendered by those in *arentatio*, and repair and maintain the property, with four cart loads of undergrowth for the enclosure supplied by the lord. G.: excused.

3292 ABBOTS RIPTON John Crosse Jr.: surrender of one messuage and a half-virgate of land *ad opus* recently held by John Cadman and three acres of land at Catteshegge recently held by the same John Cadman, to the use of William Kelseth, for life, rendering annually in all things as did John, with the obligation to repair the property. Further, by the grace of the lord he will have the goods in the manor which have been arrested. Pledges for holding the land and occupying it according to the above form, as annotated and sworn to in the fifth year of John Stowe: John Catelyn and Richard Smyth. G.: two capons.

3293 LITTLE STUKELEY (December) John Skynner Jr.: surrender of one messuage built up with one hall and a *camera* and one grange, with one *camera* recently held by Thomas Gosse and once held by Richard Desburgh, and a half-virgate of land pertaining to the camera of the abbot, to the use of Thomas Hale, for life, rendering annually in all things as did John, with the obligation to repair and maintain the buildings at his own expense. G.: excused because of repairs.

3294 CHATTERIS John Bate: surrender of one messuage and two acres of land in Horseheath with land in Stokkyng, the ferry on the lord's land, meadow in Crowlodemende once held by John Smyth, to the use of John Smyth Jr., for life, rendering annually in all things as did John. G.: 6s.8d., paid to the lord.

3295 CHATTERIS John Hereforth Bocher: half of one tenement of eight acres with a cote and other parcels recently held by John Hereforth Herde, for life, rendering annually in all things as did John. G.: 3s.4d.

3296 CHATTERIS (May) John Coker: one cotland with appurtenant meadow in Crowlodemede recently held by John Bettesson, for life, rendering annually 2s.5d. and all other services and customs rendered by John. G.: 2s.

3297 CHATTERIS (May) William Poppe: a half-acre of land in Elmen with meadow in Crowlodemede recently held by Alicia Poppe, for life, rendering annually 13s.ob. and all other services and customs rendered by Alicia. G.: 10d. Also: one cotland with other parcels recently held by his father, for life, rendering annually 6s.10d. and all other services and customs rendered by his father. G.: 10d.

3298 CHATTERIS (June) Agnes Peyte: surrender of half of one tenement of eight acres recently held by her husband, Walter, to the use of John Wympool, for life, rendering annually 4s. and all other services and customs rendered by Agnes. G.: 2s.

3299 CHATTERIS (June) John Gere: one long selion of land at Dernhadlond containing a half-acre and 20 perches of land recently held by John Poppe Jr., and one selion of land at Longrave recently held by William Carter, and a half-acre in Elmen recently held by the same William, for life, rendering annually 5d.ob. for the selion at Dernhadlond, 5d. for Longrave, 6d. for the half-acre in Elmen, at the customary times, and all other services and customs owed therein. G.: 12d.

3300 CHATTERIS (June) John Reder: one tenement of eight acres, one acre of land at Medmen, one acre of land in Elmen, with fishpond and meadow in Oldhalf and Crowlodemede recently held by Simon Reder, his father, for life, rendering annually 12s.5d.ob. at the customary times, and all other services and customs rendered by his father. G.: 20d.

3301 CHATTERIS (20 May) John Revesson, bailiff, his son, John Revesson Sr., and John Sempool Atte Brigge: the manor of Hunneye, with all appurtenant meadows, pastures and fishponds, with one hall and camera, from the previous Michaelmas for 10 years, rendering annually four marks in equal portions at Christmas and Easter, with the obligation to repair and maintain the hall, *camera*, ditches, hedges, closes, and keep them in severalty and in their possession. Further, they may cut down undergrowth for fuel and closes, without waste, in 10 parcels, as well as willows, and if the payments are in arrears for two months, or if they fail to observe any of the articles, the lord shall take the property back with all its chattels. G.: excused.

180v

3302 ST. IVES (December) John Elys and his wife, Margaret: one row recently held by William Nicholl, for life, rendering annually 8s. at the customary times, which property previously rendered 13s.4d. Further, they will repair and maintain the property. *Et non licebit*, etc. G.: two capons.

3303 ST. IVES (January) William Judde, his wife, Emma, their son, William, and their daughters, Agnes, Katerina and Alicia and any of their successors: one row reconstructed by them, in which they live, and recently held by John Makesey, from the previous Michaelmas for life, rendering annually 10s. in equal portions at Michaelmas and Easter. Further, they may not sell, will, alienate or assign their status in the property without the license of the lord, and after the death of William and Emma, William, Agnes, Katerina and Alicia will pay the lord 6s.8d. as *gersuma* before 181r entry, under penalty of forfeit, and they will thereafter repair and maintain the property as did William and Emma. *Et non licebit*, etc.

3304 St. Ives (June) John Reedhed and his wife, Avis: one row in Bridge Street recently held by William Purdy, for life, rendering annually 20s. at the customary times, with the obligation to erect one stable in the row, timber being supplied by the lord. *Et non licebit*, etc. G.: 6s.8d.

3305 St. Ives (June) Thomas Stok: surrender of one well-constructed row in Barkersrowe recently held by William Smyth Barker and once held by Richard Eyr, to the use of William Prikke and his wife, Agnes, for life, rendering annually in all things as did Thomas, with the obligation to repair and maintain the property. *Et non licebit*, etc. G.: 6s.8d.

3306 St. Ives (August) William Boys and his wife, Margaret: a half-row in Bridge Street once held by Hugo Lyster and recently held by the said William, for life, rendering annually 12s. at the customary times, which property previously rendered 16s. Further, they will render all other services and customs rendered by William previously, with the obligation to repair and maintain the property, with timber supplied by the lord. *Et non licebit*, etc. G.: 6s.8d.

3307 St. Ives John Tebbe and his wife, Margeria: one row in Bridge Street recently repaired by the lord and recently held by Henry Bocher, for life, rendering annually 20s. at the customary times, and all other services and customs rendered by Henry, with the obligation to repair and maintain the property. *Et non licebit*, etc. G.: 10s.

3308 Broughton (January) Edward Justice and his wife, Johanna: one capital messuage of Dammeslond recently held by Roger Castre, with one selion in a croft, for 181v life, rendering annually 14d. at the customary times, all other services and customs owed therein. G.: two capons.

3309 Hurst (March) John White and his wife, Alicia: one messuage built up with one kiln and a half-virgate of land recently held by John Vycory and once held by Thomas Porters, for life, rendering annually in all things as did John, with the first payment at the next feast of St. Andrew, with the obligation to repair the property, timber to repair the kiln, one cart load of thorns for the enclosure being supplied by the lord. G.: one capon.

3310 Hurst (April) Thomas Hill and his wife, Emma: one messuage and one virgate of land recently held by Reginald Lawman and once held by William Pope, for life, rendering annually 14s. at the customary times, which property previously rendered 16s., with the first payment at the feast of St. Andrew, with the obligation to repair and maintain the property, timber and the yield of a half-acre in Holywell Fen for roofing supplied by the lord. G.: excused.

3311 Hurst (April) Simon Rumburgh and his wife, Margaret: one messuage and a half-virgate of land recently held by John Huntyngdon and previously held by Thomas Whiston, for life, rendering annually 10s. at the customary times, with the first payment at the feast of St. Andrew after one year, with the obligation to repair a bake house on the messuage within one year, timber and one acre of thatch being supplied by the lord. G.: two capons.

3312 Hurst (June) John Nonne: one built up messuage with half of one house and a half-virgate of land recently held by his father, Richard Nonne, and once held by Nicholas Hunney, for life, rendering annually in all things as did Richard, with the obligation to repair and maintain the half-house at his own expense, and with the first payment at the next feast of St. Andrew. G.: two capons.

3313 HURST (June) John Warde: surrender of one messuage built up with an *insathous* and one virgate of land once held by Stephen Canne, to the use of John Huntyngdon and his wife, Margaret, for life, rendering annually in all things as did John. G.: two capons.

3314 HURST (June) William Fylhous: two tofts and a half-virgate of land recently held by William Trover, for life, rendering annually in all things as did William, with the first payment at the next feast of St. Andrew. G.: 12d.

3315 SLEPE (April) William Perney and his wife, Matilda: one messuage and one virgate of land recently held by John Barton, for life, rendering annually in all things as did John, with the obligation to repair and maintain the property, timber being supplied by the lord. G.: 2s.

3316 SLEPE (May) Robert Bernard and his wife, Agnes: one cotland and one selion of land at Howhill recently held by John Burdens and once held by William Herrof, for life, rendering annually in all things as did John. G.: 40d.

3317 KNAPWELL (April) John Reignold and his wife, Margaret: one toft and one quarter of land recently held by John Hopper, called Bereslond, for life, rendering annually 4s. at the customary times, which property previously rendered 4s.4d. Further, they will render all other services and customs rendered by John, with payments beginning at the next feast of St. Andrew. G.: two capons.

3318 ELTON (20 September) Richard Atte Gate pays 20d. for license to marry Alicia, daughter of William Atte Gate Sr. and naif of the lord by blood, to John Clerke of Langtoft, this time.

3319 HEMINGFORD ABBOTS (October) Thomas Aungewyn and his wife, Johanna: one toft and the third part of one virgate of land once held by Walter Ibot and recently held by John Pope, for life, quit, which property previously rendered 4d. G.: one capon.

5 JOHN STOWE (1440-1441)

182r **3320** ST. IVES John Belman: surrender of a half-row once held by Robert Wryghte, to the use of John Cooston, and his wife, Johanna, for life, rendering annually in all things as did John, with the obligation to repair and maintain the property. *Et non licebit*, etc. Pledges for repairs: John Berenger Sr. of Warboys and William Berenger of Warboys. G.: 6s.8d.

3321 ST. IVES (March) Henry Barbor: surrender of three half-rows in Bridge Street once held by Nicholas Hayward, to the use of Richard Alwyn, and his wife, Isabella, for life, rendering annually 26s.8d. at the customary times, and all other services and customs owed therein, with the obligation to repair and maintain the property. *Et non licebit*, etc. G.: 6s.8d.

3322 ST. IVES (September) Laurence Baywell and his wife, Alicia: a half-row once held by John Edenham and recently held by John Valentyne, for life, rendering annually 7s. at the customary times, which property previously rendered 10s. Further, they will repair and maintain the property. *Et non licebit*, etc. G.: 20d., and no more because of repairs.

3323 ST. IVES John Fyssher and his wife, Alicia: a half-row recently held by Thomas Glover, for life, rendering annually 8s. and all other services and customs owed therein, with the obligation to repair and maintain the property. *Et non licebit*, etc. G.: 3s.4d.

3324 ELSWORTH (12 November) William AtteWode, son of John AtteWode and naif of the lord by blood, pays 12d. for license to live off the manor wherever he wishes, for as long as it pleases the lord, rendering 12d. annually at the leet, and suit to court and leet. Pledges: John AtteWode and Alexander Hobbesson.

3325 ELSWORTH (March) John Herry: surrender of one messuage with three quarters of land once held by Grigges, to the use of Walter Owesson and his wife, Alicia, for life, rendering annually in all things as did John, with the obligation to repair and maintain the property. G.: 12d., two capons.

3326 ELSWORTH (March) John Herry: surrender of a half-virgate of land called Cookis, to the use of Thomas Hardyng and his wife, Margaret, for life, rendering annually in all things as did John. G.: 12d., two capons.

3327 ELSWORTH (12 April) Thomas AtteWode, rector of the church, and John Marys: one messuage and one virgate of land recently *ad opus* and recently held by Henry Boner, for life, rendering annually 18s. rent at the customary times, and 6s. for works, with the obligation to enlarge the grange and *camera* by one bay and to rebuild the bake house, and to repair all other houses at their own expense within one year, for which they receive an allowance of 36s. of rent and large timber. G.: 12d.

3328 BROUGHTON William Justice and his wife, Agnes: one messuage built up with one house at the end of the village, with one semi-virgate in *major censum* recently held by Alicia Justice, for life, rendering annually in all things as did Alicia, with the obligation to repair and maintain the messuage, receiving 13 studs from the lord. G.: four capons.

3329 BROUGHTON (January) John Asplond, son of Roger Asplond: one messuage built up with one building and one quarter of land recently held by Thomas Russell, and once held by Thomas Clerke, called Cranys, and previously rendering 3s., and a half-virgate of land recently held by Nicholas Turnor and once held by William Pynchebech, rendering 7s., for life, rendering annually 7s. and customs of the vill, with the first payment at the next feast of St. Andrew, and with the obligation to repair and maintain the property. G.: two capons.

182v

3330 BROUGHTON William Russell: one messuage and a half-virgate of land recently held by Thomas Tiptoft in *minor censum*, and one quarter of land from Cleryvaux land recently held by the same Thomas, for life, rendering annually 8s. and all other services and customs rendered by Thomas. Note further that this property previously rendered 10s. G.: two capons.

3331 BROUGHTON (January) John Tychemersch, rector of the church: one messuage and a half-virgate of land recently *ad opus*, one cotland without mondayland with three butts, and one selion of land, with two quarters of land in *major censum* recently held by John Clerke for 14s.4d. and works, and another half-virgate of land once held by William Pynchebek and recently held by John Crowch in *minor censum* for 6s., for life, rendering annually 14s. and customs of the vill, with the first payment at the next feast of St. Andrew and with the obligation to repair and maintain the property. G.: excused because of repairs.

3332 BROUGHTON (February) Thomas Pulter: one quarter of land once held by William Asplond and recently held by Edward Justice, located next to Pynchebek's Corner, for life, rendering annually 5s. at the customary times, and all other services and customs rendered by Edward. G.: two capons.

3333 WISTOW Robert Russell: surrender of one croft called Fen pithel with adjacent meadow containing five acres and three and a half rods once held by Robert Nottyng, to the use of William Scharp of Warboys and his son, John, for life, rendering annually 5s. at the customary times, and all other services and customs rendered by Robert, with the obligation to repair and maintain the property in enclosures. G.: three capons.

3334 WISTOW (February) John Clerke, parson of the church of Wistow, and William Nottyng: one messuage and a half-virgate of land recently held by William Derworth, for life, with the obligation to build one *insathous* 40 feet long before the next leet, timber being supplied by the lord. G.: six capons.

3335 WISTOW CUM RAVELEY (March) John Owty Jr. and his wife, Alicia: one toft and a half-virgate of land recently held by John Sewer and once held by John Owty Sr., for life, rendering annually in all things as did John. G.: two capons.

3336 HOLYWELL (30 December: leet) Richard Asplond and his wife, Agnes: two acres of demesne land in Netherbrerecroft, for life, rendering annually as do other tenants. G.: two capons.

3337 HOLYWELL John Selde: surrender of one cotland built up with one building and one acre of land at Oxhowe once held by Thomas Pygot, to the use of William Bothe, and his wife, Alicia: for life, with the obligation to repair and maintain the property at their own expense. G.: 12d., for two capons, paid by John Selde.

3338 HOLYWELL Thomas Martyn: surrender of one messuage and one virgate of land with demesne land and two rods of meadow in Salmade and one virgate of land in le Smethe, to the use of John Asplond Jr. and his wife, Margaret, for life, rendering annually in all things as did Thomas. G.: 2s.

183r **3339** HOLYWELL John Fakon: one croft recently held by William Peke and once held by Nicholas Baron, and one other croft with two selions of land in a croft next to Holywell Cross recently held by John Schepperd, with one acre of meadow in Dichefurlong lying next to another acre there dismissed to William Bryan, for life, rendering annually 2s. for the acre of meadow, and for the rest as did William. Peke. G.: excused because of repairs.

3340 HOLYWELL Nicholas Godfrey and his wife, Elena: one messuage and one virgate of land with demesne land and other parcels recently held by William Smyth and once held by Thomas Fecheler, for life, rendering annually in all things as did William. G.: two geese.

3341 HOLYWELL (26 March) John Scot Sr., and his son, John: one demesne meadow called Dryhirst recently held by John Sr. with John Schepperd, deceased, *per copiam*, and surrendered back to the lord by the same John Sr., for life, rendering annually in all things as did John Sr. and John Schepperd. G.: 3s.4d.

3342 HOLYWELL Richard Townesende of Stanton: one messuage and one virgate of land recently held by John Godfrey, for life, rendering annually in all things as did John. G.: 5s.

3343 HOLYWELL (July) William Smyth and his wife, Alicia: one croft in *arentatio* recently held by William Hurleby, with one acre of demesne land in Stonydole, for life, rendering annually 5s. for the croft and for the acre of demesne, nothing, because he holds it in support of the croft, although it previously rendered 12d. Further, they will repair and maintain the croft in splints and plastering this first time, and payments will begin at the next feast of St. Andrew. G.: one capon.

3344 BURWELL (21 January: leet) Robert Wylkyn and Nicholas Wylkyn: one tenement of 20 acres *ad opus* recently held by John Lyne and once held by Thomas Peyer, for 30 years, rendering annually 6s. at the customary times, suit to court and leet and common fine. Further, he will pay the *firmarius* for works and services as agreed between them. G.: two capons.

3345 BURWELL (same leet) Robert Wylkyn: 15 acres of land *ad opus* and recently held by Thomas Rower, the remainder of which is held by William Jaye *per copiam*, for 20 years, rendering annually in all things as did Thomas, and suit to court and leet and common fine. Further, he will pay the *firmarius* for works and customs as agreed between them. G.: two capons.

3346 BURWELL (same leet) Thomas Bole and his son, Richard: one tenement of 20 acres and two crofts next to Fyssher Street and previously held by the same Thomas, for 30 years, rendering annually in all things as did Thomas, suit to court and leet and common fine. G.: 3s.

3347 SHILLINGTON (23 January: leet) Mathew Chambir and his wife, Agnes: four acres of demesne land in Larkenhill and four acres of land in le Croft recently held by John Wenyngham, for life, rendering annually 4s. at the customary times and all other services and customs rendered by John. G.: 2s.

3348 SHILLINGTON (same leet) William Marham: one acre of land in the fields of Gravenhirst recently held by Henry Annsell, for life, rendering annually 8d. at the customary times, and all other services and customs rendered by Henry. G.: excused.

183v

3349 SHILLINGTON (same leet) Thomas Coche and his wife, Alicia, widow of Nicholas Lewyn, will pay 13s.4d., in two installments in the feasts of the Exaltation of the Holy Cross and Christmas for license to take possession of one messuage and one and a half-virgates of land recently held by Nicholas, for 12 years, rendering annually in all things as did Nicholas, with the obligation to repair and maintain the property. Pledges for repairs and payments: Simon Eynysham and John Borough.

3350 SHILLINGTON (same leet) John Gayton Jr.: one messuage and one semi-virgate of land recently held by John Wenyngham Jr., for life, G.: 2s.

3351 SHILLINGTON (same leet) William Chible: surrender of one messuage and one semi-virgate of land, to the use of Thomas Stonle Jr., for life, rendering annually 8s.9d. and all other services and customs rendered by William, with the provision that William and his wife, Alicia, will have one *camera* in the end of the hall, two bushels of wheat and two bushels of malt annually, easement to fire, and free entry and exit for life. G.: 5s.

3352 SHILLINGTON (22 July) John Colman Jr.: one messuage and a half-virgate of land recently held by Thomas Howesson and once held by Nicholas Piers, with the consent of William, son of Thomas Howesson and his next heir, as examined before the seneschal of Ramsey, for life, saving the right of anyone, and rendering annually in all things as did Thomas. G.: 13s.4d., to be paid in two installments of 6s.8d. at Michaelmas this year, and Michaelmas next year.

3353 BARTON (25 January: court) Richard Wodeward and his wife, Johanna: one messuage and one croft called Barons recently held by John Davy, for life, rendering annually in all things as did John, with the obligation to repair the property. G.: 6d.

3354 BARTON (same court) John Colman: surrender one croft once held by William Colman, to the use of John Roger and his wife, Agnes, for life, rendering annually in all things as did John. G.: 5s.

3355 BARTON (same court) Isabella Felmesham: surrender of one croft once held by Robert Stonleye, to the use of Jacob Pope and his wife, Johanna, for life, rendering annually in all things as did Isabella, with the obligation to erect one house on the croft at their own expense. G.: 20d.

3356 BARTON (same court) William Revesson and his wife, Agnes, daughter and heiress of Thomas Martyn: one messuage and a half-virgate of land recently held by Thomas, with a forland, for life, rendering annually in all things as did Thomas. G.: 6s.8d.

3357 BARTON (same court)[41] William Martyn: one messuage and one virgate of land recently held by Simon Fraunceys, for life, rendering annually in all things as did Simon. G.: 13s.4d.

[41] See PRO 179/64 for the death of Simon Franceys. William Martyn is noted as his closest heir.

184r **3358** BARTON William Martyn: surrender of one messuage and one virgate of land recently held by John Wylymot to the use of John Martyn, for life, rendering annually in all things as did William. G. and heriot: 2s., and no more because of repairs.

3359 BARTON (same court) Richard Woodeward Jr. pays four capons for license to move one grange from the tenement of William Revysson in Briggende to his own.

3360 BARTON (same court) William Revesson: surrender of one messuage and one virgate to land, to the use of Thomas Revysson and his wife, Emma, for life, rendering annually in all things as did William. G. and heriot: 20s., six capons, to be paid at Michaelmas and Christmas.

3361 BARTON (same court)[42] Alicia, widow of Thomas Pope: one cotland recently held by Thomas Pope, for life, rendering annually in all things as did Thomas. Fine: 20d.

3362 BARTON (same court) William Revysson: surrender of one cotland to the use of John Swayn, for life, rendering annually in all things as did William. G.: 3s.

3363 BARTON (same court) John Grene: one messuage and one virgate of land recently held by his father, for life, rendering annually in all things as did his father. G.: 6s.8d.

3364 CRANFIELD (27 January: leet) Johanna Robyn: surrender of one messuage and a half-virgate of land recently held by her husband, John Robyn, to the use of Henry Wheler, for life, rendering annually in all things as did Johanna. G.: 3s.4d.

3365 CRANFIELD (same leet) John Warener: surrender of two acres of land at Puryhill, to the use of William Wodehill, for life, rendering annually in all things as did John. G.: 6d.

3366 CRANFIELD William Wodehill Sr.: pays two capons for licence to remove one house from the tenement recently held by Richard Archere of Horley to his own tenement in Cranfield.

3367 CRANFIELD (same leet) Thomas Terry: one cotland once held by William Sautre and recently held by Thomas himself and surrendered back to the lord, to be held with another tenement called Ryngis, fallen into the lord's hands through escheat, for life, rendering annually for the cotland as he previously rendered, and for the rest 10s. and all other services and customs owed therein. Further, he will support one *insathous* on the property. G.: one capon.

3368 WARBOYS (February) William Berenger Jr.: one virgate in Caldecote once held by Thomas Eyr, for life, rendering annually 10s. at the customary times, which property previously rendered 12s. Further, he will render customs of the vill, with the first payment at the next feast of St. Andrew. G.: two capons.

3369 WARBOYS (February) Reginald Tayllor: one dichmanland recently held by William Ravele Jr., for life, rendering annually 4s. at the customary times; and one hen and three eggs, with the obligation to repair the property, timber being supplied the lord. G.: excused because of repairs.

3370 WARBOYS (February) John Horwode: one toft and a half-virgate of land in Caldecote recently held by William Bircher and once held by Richard Berenger, for life, rendering annually 5s. at the customary times and all other services and customs rendered by William, with the first payment at the next feast of St. Andrew. G.: two capons.

3371 WARBOYS (May) John Plombe, son of Richard Plombe and naif of the lord, and his wife, Alicia: half of the lands and tenements once held by Robert Raven and recently held by Thomas Newman, and five acres of demesne land at Lowefurlong

---

[42] See PRO 179/64 for the death of Thomas Pope.

recently held by Thomas, from Michaelmas for life, rendering annually in all things as did Thomas. G.: 6s.8d.

3372   WARBOYS (May) William Berenger, son of John Berenger, bailiff and naif of the lord, and his wife, Emma: half of one virgate of land in Caldecote once held by Richard Hervy, for life, rendering annually 5s. at the customary times, and all other services and customs rendered by Richard, which property previously rendered 6s. Further, the first payment will be at the feast of St. Andrew after one year. G.: two capons.

184v   **3373**   WARBOYS (June) Robert Smyth, son of Roger Smyth: a half-virgate of land in Caldecote in *arentatio* once held by Henry Norborough, for life, rendering annually 5s. at the customary times, and all other services and customs rendered by Henry, with the first payment at the feast of St. Andrew after one year. G.: two capons.

3374   WARBOYS (June) Robert Morell: half of one virgate of land in Caldecote once held by Richard Hervy, the other half of which is now held by William Berenger, for life, rendering annually 5s., which property previously rendered 6s. Further, he will render all other services and customs rendered by Richard, with the first payment at the feast of St. Andrew after one year. G.: two capons.

3375   WARBOYS (June) Robert Raven: one quarter of land parcelled out of three quarters in Caldecote in *arentatio* recently held by Richard Hervy, the other two quarters of which are held by Simon Chapman, in *arentatio* for life, rendering annually 2s.6d. at the customary times, which property previously rendered 3s. Further, the first payment will be at the feast of John the Baptist after one year. G.: two capons.

3376   WARBOYS John Berenger Sr.: one mondayland in *arentatio* recently held by William Shakestaff, for life, rendering annually in all things as did William. G.: two capons.

3377   WARBOYS (July) Johanna, daughter of John Berenger Jr. and naif of the lord, in the presence of the seneschal of Ramsey, pays 20s. for license to marry whomever she wishes, this first time. Pledge: John Caton.

3378   WARBOYS (August) William Hervy: surrender of one maltland and one mondayland recently held by John Hye Milner, to the use of Robert Corbet and John Corbet, for life. Also: one virgate of land in Caldecote recently held by John Dallyng, for life, rendering annually 9s. for the maltland and mondayland and 5s. for the half-virgate, with the first payment for the half-virgate at the next feast of St. Andrew. G.: two capons.

185r   **3379**   WARBOYS Katerina Atte Wode: surrender of two parts of one dichmanland *ad opus*, the third part of which is held by Robert Honyter, to the use of Simon AtteWode and his wife, Margaret, for life, rendering annually in all things as did Katerina. G.: 12d.

3380   HEMINGFORD ABBOTS (January) John Whyn: one messuage and one virgate of land with half of one croft recently held by John Sutton, and once held by William Whyn, for life, rendering annually 10s. and all other services and customs rendered by John, with the obligation to maintain the *insathous* and half of a grange at his own expense, with the lord granting a reduction of the rents for this year and next. G.: one capon.

3381   HEMINGFORD ABBOTS John Est: one tenement and a half-virgate of land recently held by John Marschall Sr., for life, rendering annually 10s., which property previously rendered 12s.4d. Further, he will render all other customs and services rendered by John. G.: two capons.

3382   HEMINGFORD ABBOTS Thomas Aungewyn, his wife, Johanna, and Thomas, son of Johanna: the capital messuage of one virgate of land once held by John Selde and recently held by Robert Wright, and one virgate of land with appurtenant croft at the eastern end of the village, and one vacant plot, two rods of 22 feet of meadow once held by John Webster, four selions of land next to Losebalke, a half-acre of land at Longrumpton, and two selions of land at Gormecestre Barre once held by Thomas Fuller, with two rods of land from the tenement of Thomas Fuller, of which one rod is in Thikkewhatlond, the other at Rompton leading to Cambridge, one toft of the third part of one virgate of land once held by Walter Ibot and recently held by John Pope, and one croft once held by Simon Buntyng and recently held by John Ingyll for 16d., for life, rendering annually 7s., which properties previously rendered 8s.8d. Further, they will render all other services and customs owed therein, with the obligation to repair and maintain the property at their own expense, with two gates and one door supplied by the seneschal. G.: six capons.

3383 HURST (February) Thomas Hyll: surrender of one messuage and a half-virgate of land once held by Thomas Trover, to the use of Robert Cachesoly, for life, rendering annually in all things as did Thomas, with the lord granting an allowance of this year's rent, and timber for repairs, if necessary. G.: two capons.

3384 HURST (April) Thomas Pope and his wife, Margaret: one cotland with appurtenances recently held by John Bolle, for life, rendering annually 2s. at the customary times, with payments beginning at the feast of St. Andrew after one full year, and with the obligation to build one house on the cotland 40 feet long within one year, at their own expense, two oak trees for beams and timber supplied by the lord. Pledge for repairs: John Ferror. G.: two capons.

3385 ABBOTS RIPTON (February) William Lyndeseye and his wife, Juliana: three semi-virgates of land recently held by Richard Wright and recently held by John Gardener Jr., from next Michaelmas for life, rendering annually 24s. at the customary times, which property previously rendered 26s. Further, they will render all other services and customs rendered by John. G.: two capons.

185v   **3386** RIPTON Thomas Michell and his wife, Agnes: one messuage recently held by William Halsham and once held by John Person, for life, rendering annually in all things as did William. G.: two capons.

3387 CHATTERIS (8 March: court) Richard Smyth: one cotland with one horse mill and two selions of land at Muslake recently held by Cristiana Hykkesson, for life, rendering annually 4s.3d.ob. at the customary times, and all other services and customs owed therein, with the obligation to repair and maintain the cotland and supply the mill with two mill stones, to be returned at the end of the term. G.: two capons.

3388 CHATTERIS John Couland: the fourth and fifth parts of one messuage recently held by Thomas Burne and once held by Richard Smyth, with one selion of land at Muslake recently held by Thomas and once held by Richard, for life, rendering annually 2s.6d. at the customary times and all other services and customs rendered by Thomas. G.: 12d.

3389 CHATTERIS Robert Wryght: half of one tenement of eight and a half acres of land in Elmen with meadow in Oldhalf recently held by John Bray Jr. and once held by Thomas Tayllor, for life, rendering annually 4s.10d. at the customary times and all other services and customs rendered by John. G.: 2s.

3390 CHATTERIS Alicia Massely: surrender of one tenement of eight acres with meadow in Crowlode, together with a fishpond called Masselynsdam with forland recently held by John Massely Sr., to the use of her son, John Massely, for life, rendering annually 14s.7d. at the customary times and all other services and customs rendered by Alicia. Further, Alicia will have quit and peacefully one *camera* called Bed chamber, easement in the hall, grange and other buildings, grains and beasts, and food for the said beasts, and a half-acre at Wenneyende, one rod of land beneath the church, one rod at Northdon, and one rod near the mill and two acres of meadow in Crowlode and fuel there as necessary, for life. G.: 6s.8d.

3391 CHATTERIS (8 March: court) John Beche Sr.: surrender of half of one tenement of eight acres with other parcels as found in the Rental, to the use of his son, John Beche, for life, rendering annually 7s.8d. at the customary times, and all other services and customs owed therein, with the obligation to repair and maintain the property. G.: 2s.

3392 HOUGHTON (March) William Crosse: surrender of one messuage and one virgate of land once held by Galfridus Smyth and rendering 12s., to the use of Thomas Elyot Sr. and his wife, Margaret, for life, rendering annually 10s. at the customary times and all other services and customs rendered by William, with the obligation to repair and maintain the property. G.: 3s.

3393 CHATTERIS (March) Thomas Elyot Sr.: surrender of one messuage and a half-virgate of land once held by Robert Morell, to the use of John Yonge and his wife, Juliana, for life, rendering annually in all things as did Thomas, with the obligation to repair and maintain the property at their own expense. Pledge for repairs and payments: Thomas Elyot. G.: 2s.

186r   **3394** CHATTERIS (May) Robert Smyth: one toft and one virgate of land recently held by Thomas Crane and once held by Robert Beton, for life, rendering annually 10s. at the customary times and all other services and customs owed therein. G.: 2s.

3395 CHATTERIS (July) John Stot Piper and his wife, Agnes: one toft and a half-virgate of land recently held by Richard Sampson, for life, rendering annually 4s. and all other services and customs owed therein, with the first payment at the next feast of St. Andrew. G.: 12d.

3396 CHATTERIS (2 August: court) Richard Atte Poole, naif of the lord, pays four capons for license to marry Juliana, his daughter, to John Yonge, this time, and no more in fine because he is a pauper.

3397 BYTHORNE (March) William Wattesson, naif of the lord: one messuage and a half-virgate of land recently held by William Cannard, for life, rendering annually in all things as did William, with the obligation to repair and maintain the property at his own expense, with 40d. and timber supplied by the lord. Further, payments will begin at the feast of St. Andrew after one year. G.: two capons.

3398 ABBOTS RIPTON Thomas Baron and his wife, Agnes: one messuage and two half-virgates of land recently held by Thomas Mychell, for life, rendering annually in all things as did Thomas, with the obligation to repair and maintain the property at their own expense, with the exception that the lord will be responsible for the carpentry of one *insathous*. Pledge for payments and repairs: Thomas Payn. G.: two capons.

3399 ABBOTS RIPTON (August) John Lyndeseye and his wife, Agnes: one vacant toft and a half-virgate of land recently held by Thomas Smyth and once held by Thomas Hawlond, for life, rendering annually 6s.8d., which property previously rendered 10s. Further, they will render all other services and customs owed therein, with payments beginning at the feast of All Saints after three years, and with the obligation to build one *insathous* of eight binding-posts on the toft within three years, timber being supplied by the lord. Pledge for repairs: William Lyndeseye. G.: one capon.

3400 HOUGHTON (April) Simon Thoday: one vacant toft and a half-virgate of land recently held by William Tyffyn, for life, rendering annually in all things as did William, with the first payment at the feast of St. Andrew. Further, he will have eight studs in Okele. G.: two capons.

3401 HOUGHTON (April) Thomas Forster and his wife, Margaret: one vacant toft and a half-virgate of land recently held by Thomas Elyot, for life, rendering annually in all things as did Thomas. G.: two capons.

3402 LITTLE RAVELEY John Walgate: surrender of one toft and one quarter of land called Asplond, to the use of John Wyllesson and his wife, Emma, for life, rendering annually in all things as did John. G.: four capons.

3403 LITTLE RAVELEY Radulph Caly: surrender of one tenement and five quarters of land recently held by John Wyllesson, to the use of John Walgate and his wife, Anna, for life, rendering annually in all things as did Radulph. G.: four capons.

3404 UPWOOD (April) Richard Gretcham of Overedon: one messuage and one virgate of land with appurtenances recently *ad opus* and recently held by John Spenser and once held by John Fox, from next Michaelmas in *arentatio* for 12 years, rendering annually 14s. rents, 4s. for works, and customs of the vill, at the customary times, with the obligation to build up, repair the property within three years, for which the lord grants an allowance of the rent for the next two and a half years, timber, and six cart loads of straw for covering the houses. G.: two capons.

186v

3405 UPWOOD (May) Henry Skynner and his wife, Agnes: a half-cotland of one acre of land, one and a half rods and one acre, and one quarter of one rod of land at Fenhill, and a half-virgate of land in *arentatio* recently held by Nicholas Hendesson, for life, rendering annually 12s. at the customary times, with the obligation to maintain the cotland at their own expense, timber being supplied by the lord. G.: three capons.

3406 RAMSEY (July) John Keteryng Sr. and his wife, Alicia, and John Cobbe and his wife, Johanna: from Brother John Swasham, sub-cellarer, one messuage in High Street recently held by Thomas Wayte Smyth, for life, rendering annually 8s. in equal portions at the feasts of the Annunciation and Nativity of Blessed Mary, with the sub-cellarer responsible for repairs. G.: 6s.8d.

3407 RAMSEY (September) John Keteryng Sr. and John Keteryng Jr.: from the sub-cellarer, all his fishpond in the ditch around the meadow of Newmede, Swonhousmede, Brentmede and Tylehousmede, both within and without, recently held by William Botiller by copy and first held by John Borell, with the fishpond in the adjacent ditch recently held by Thomas Bangold reserved to the sub-cellarer, from the next Michaelmas for 20 years, rendering annually 2s. in equal portions at the feasts of the Annunciation and Nativity of Blessed Mary, with the sub-cellarer responsible for purging and repairing the ditch. *Et si predictus redditus*, etc. (arrears of a half-year). Further, if the pond is given away by them without the lord's license, or if they die before the end of the term, the sub-cellarer shall re-enter and retain the property. G.: 3s.4d.

3408 THERFIELD (12 May) Agreement between the lord and Thomas Wynmer, son of William Wynmer and naif of the lord, that he will hold from next Michaelmas, with his father, all the parcels of land and tenements recently held by his father for 60s.7d.q., rendering annually four marks, with the first payment at the feast of the birth of St. John the Baptist, with an allowance of their arrears from the time of Thomas Angtyll, provided he is a good tenant.

187r

3409 SLEPE (July) Thomas Kyngeston and his wife, Agnes: one cotland recently held by John Barton, for life, rendering annually 8s., which property previously rendered 10s. Further, they will render all other services and customs rendered by John and they are granted an allowance of this year's rent because the land was in the lord's hands. G.: 3s.4d.

3410 CRANFIELD (16 November: leet) William Houghton: surrender of one cote with appurtenances once held by Simon Millebrooke, to the use of William Wodehyll, for life, rendering annually in all things as did William. G. and heriot: 2s.

3411 HOUGHTON (January) Richard Attekyn: one toft and a half-virgate of land recently held by John Apirle and once held by John Style, for life, rendering annually 4s. at the customary times, and all other services and customs rendered by John. G.: two capons.

6 JOHN STOWE (1441-1442)

187v **3412** RIPTON (15 October: leet) Thomas Stookele and his wife, Alicia: one messuage and a half-virgate of land recently held by John Crosse Sr. and two acres of land at Catteshegg recently held by John Howlot, for life, rendering annually 11s. at the customary times, and all other services and customs owed therein, with the lord supplying two quarters of barley, to be returned at the next two Michaelmases. G.: two capons.

3413 RIPTON (same leet) William Birt, son of the *firmarius*, and his wife, Isabella: one messuage and one virgate of land recently held by John Kelseth and once held by John Nicoll, for life, rendering annually 16s. at the customary times, and all other services and customs rendered by John, with the obligation to repair the property within one year at their own expense, timber and two carts of undergrowth and an allowance of rents for two and a half years granted by the lord, because the property is in ruins. G.: two capons.

3414 CRANFIELD Robert Curteys, son of Robert Curteys and naif of the lord, pays the fine for license to live at Merston for as long as it pleases the lord, remaining a naif as before, rendering 4d. annually at the leet, and suit to leet and court. Pledge for payment of the fine: John Curteys.

3415 CRANFIELD (23 December) William Terry, bailiff, pays 2s. for license to marry Alicia of the Mede, daughter of Thomas of the Mede, and naif of the lord by blood, to whomever she wishes, this time.

3416 BARTON (16 November: court) Henry Burrych one cotland and one acre of land recently held by William Sare, for life, rendering annually in all things as did William. G.: 6s.8d., rendering 40d. at the feast of the Purification, and the rest at the next accounting.

3417 BARTON (1 March) William Pekke of Coupeller pays the fine for license to have Johanna Lyllyse, naif and villein of the lord of his manor of Barton, living with and serving John Peke Jr. of Coupeller, for as long as it pleases the lord, remaining a naif as before, and rendering 12d. annually to the lord at Ramsey, to be paid by William Peke.

3418 SHILLINGTON (17 November: leet) Agnes, widow of Thomas Howesson: surrender of one acre, three rods of demesne land in "lee Croft" recently held by Thomas Howesson, to the use of William Sussely, for life, rendering annually in all things as did Agnes. G.: 2s.

3419 SHILLINGTON (same leet) William Howesson, alias Smyth, naif of the lord and his wife, Isabella: one messuage and two virgates of land and three acres of land at Henythorn recently held by John Lambard, for life, rendering annually 32s.6d. and all other services and customs as rendered by John. G.: 53s.4d., payable in three installments, i.e. 20s. at Christmas, 13s.4d. at Easter, and 20s. at the Michaelmas after that.

3420 SHILLINGTON (5 February) John Hyll, son of John Hyll of Pegsdon and naif of the lord by blood, of the manor of Shillington, pays the fine for license from the seneschal of Ramsey to live off the manor for as long as it pleases the lord, remaining a naif as before and rendering 4d. annually at the leet of Shillington. Pledges: Matthew Chambir, bailiff, and Thomas Laurence.

3421 HOUGHTON (March) William Wyth, naif of the lord, and his wife, Juliana: one messuage and two virgates of land with three selions at Sawtreweye and one croft
188r recently held by his father, John Wyth, for life, rendering annually 22s.8d. and all other services and customs rendered by John, with the obligation to rebuild one hall

with annexed *camera* and sheep house at their own expense, and to maintain and repair all other buildings on the property. G.: 6s.8d.

3422 HOUGHTON. William Wyth holds *per copiam*: one cotland recently held by Simon Wyttre for 5s., *in arentatio*; one virgate of land once held by Thomas Elyot called Elyots, *in arentatio*, for 11s., one virgate of land *ad opus* once held by John Gerard for 12s., and one quarter of land with croft recently held by John Whaplode Sr. in *arentatio* for 6s. 8d. Full payments are 57s.4d. Further, he will perform works for two virgates of land above, for the performance of which works and the payment of which rents he is obligated to Walter Tayllard and others to £40, and he will not relinquish any parcel unless he finds a suitable tenant.

3423 HOUGHTON William Whaplode and his wife, Agnes: a half-virgate of land in *arentatio* recently held by Richard Attepooll, for life, rendering annually 4s., which property previously rendered 7s. Further, they will render all other services and customs rendered by Richard, with the first payment at the next feast of St. Andrew. G.: two capons.

3424 HOUGHTON (May) William Bocher and his wife, Johanna: one virgate of land in *arentatio* once held by John Wright, for life, rendering annually 9s. at the customary times, which property previously rendered 12s., with payments beginning at the next feasts of St. Andrew. Further, they will render all other services and customs owed therein.

3425 HOUGHTON (May) William Bocher and his wife, Johanna: half of one virgate of land once held by Peter Andrew for 6s., for life, rendering annually 4s. and all other services and customs owed therein, with payments beginning at the next feast of St. Andrew. G.: 12d.

3426 HOUGHTON (May) Simon Thodaye and his wife, Johanna: one messuage and a half-virgate of land in *arentatio* recently held by Thomas Gryme, alias Pulter, and a half-virgate of land once held by John Hardyng, called Milleslond, for life, rendering annually 5s. for the messuage and half-virgate and 5s. for the other half-virgate, at the customary times, and all other services and customs owed therein, with payments for Milleslond beginning at the next feast of St. Andrew. G.: three capons.

3427 HOLYWELL Richard Townesende of Stanton: surrender of one messuage, one virgate and new demesne land, with a half-acre of land in Malwode once held by Roger Baker and recently held by John Godfreye, to the use of John Baker, son of Roger Baker and naif of the lord, for life, rendering annually in all things as did Richard. G.: 3s.4d.

3428 HOLYWELL (November) Nicholas Baron and his wife, Elena: one cotland next to the bank once held by John Bradenach and afterwards held by William Hunne, one acre of land at Middilfurlong, with the toll ferry pertaining to the cotland, for life, rendering annually 3s.10d. at the customary times and all other services and customs rendered by William. Further, they receive permission to repair and construct one *camera* on the cotland 50 feet long, both in timber and carpentry, with the obligation to repair and maintain all other buildings there at their own expense. G.: two capons.

3429 HOLYWELL (August) Simon Dallyng, cleric: one toft recently held by William Hunne, with adjacent land, one toft with appurtenances recently held by Thomas Arnold, one toft recently held by Katerina Shepperd with appurtenances, and five acres of demesne land at Oxhowe, Overbrerecroft and Stonydole, all of which have been in the lord's hands for many years, for life, rendering annually 2s. at the customary times, and all other services and customs owed therein. G.: excused.

188v **3430** ELSWORTH (November) Richard Parnell: surrender of one messuage and a half-virgate of land recently held by Robert Brawghyng, to the use of John Swynforth and his wife, Johanna, for life, rendering annually in all things as did Richard. G.: 3s.4d.

3431 ELSWORTH (September) John Wryght and his wife, Johanna: one vacant toft and one quarter of land recently held by John Brooke for life, rendering annually 6s.8d. and all other services and customs rendered by John. G.: 12d., two capons.

3432 ELSWORTH (leet) John Bole: surrender of one messuage and one virgate of land recently held by Walter Bole, to the use of John Bangyll and his wife, Margaret, for life, rendering annually in all things as did John, with the road reserved to the *firmarius* and *familia* of the manor. G.: 4s.

3433 ST. IVES (November) Henry Barbor: surrender of a half-row recently held by William Gardener, to the use of Edmund Judde Lyster, and his wife, Alicia, for life, rendering annually 4s. at the customary times, and all other services and customs owed therein, with the obligation to repair and maintain the property. *Et non licebit*, etc. G.: 6s.8d.

3434 ST. IVES (May) John Pope and his wife, Alicia: two half-rows next to the lane leading to the manor once held by John Felyngle, for life, rendering annually 9s. at the customary times, with the obligation to repair and maintain the property. *Et non licebit*, etc. G.: three capons, and no more because of maintenance obligations.

3435 ST. IVES (1 January) William Judde, and his wife, Emma: one cotland built up with one building next to Joseph's Lane at the corner, recently held by John Goodman, with a small adjacent garden, 21 feet in latitude (in the middle) and at each end; and a certain parcel lying next to the said cotland pertaining to a half-row next to the Toll Booth once held by John Goodman, which touches upon the free tenement of the said William at the east, once held by Richard Brabon, containing a length of 21 and a half feet, for life, rendering annually 8d. in equal portions at the customary times, with
189r the obligation to repair and maintain the property. *Et non licebit*, etc. G.: excused.

3436 BROUGHTON (December) Thomas Bonde, naif of the lord: a half-virgate of land in *minor censum* recently held by Nicholas Bocher and once held by Thomas Neele, for life, rendering annually 4s. at the customary times, with payments beginning at the next feast of St. Andrew. G.: three capons.

3437 BROUGHTON (April) John Cabe, son of Richard Cabe, naif of the lord: one messuage and one quarter of land recently held by John Hampton for 3s., one messuage and a half-virgate of land in *minor censum* rendering previously 6s., three quarters of land in *major censum* previously rendering 12s., and one lot of Dammyslond previously rendering 8d. and recently held by John Lete, for life, rendering annually 18s. at the customary times, and all other services and customs rendered by John Hampton and John Lete, with payments beginning at the next feast of St. Andrew, and with the obligation to repair the messuage, timber and 13s.4d. being supplied by the lord. G.: two capons.

3438 BROUGHTON (April) Thomas Phelip, rector of the church: one messuage and one virgate of land *ad opus* and one cotland, or mondayland, with four selions of land and two quarters of land in *major censum* recently held by John Clerke for 14s.4d. and works, another half-virgate of land recently held by John Crowche in *minor censum* for 8s., for life, rendering annually 14s. at the customary times and customs of the vill, with the obligation to repair and maintain the property at his own expense. G.: six geese.

3439 CHATTERIS (January) John Deynes: one tenement of eight acres' with meadow, fishpond, forland, and other appurtenances recently held by Thomas Mason and once held by John Mason, for life, rendering annually 11s.3d. at the customary times and all other services and customs rendered by Thomas, with certain parcels held *per copiam* reserved to Agnes Mason for life. G.: 3s.4d.

3440 CHATTERIS (January) Margaret Massely: surrender of one tenement of eight acres and half of one tenement of eight acres, one acre of land in Elmen with fishpond and meadow in Crowlode recently held by John Massely Jr., to the use of John Balle Jr., for life, rendering annually 10s.4d.ob. and all other services and customs rendered by Margaret. G.: 3s.4d.

3441 CHATTERIS John Beche: half of one tenement of eight acres with meadow in Oldhalf and fishpond at Alyotesmere, one acre and three rods of land at Watergate, one acre of land at Wodegate, and herbage in Wenneye recently held by his father, John Beche, for life, rendering annually in all things as did John, with easement in one camera reserved to Elena Beche for life. Pledge: John Hobkyn. G.: 3s.4d.

3442 CHATTERIS John Lytholf of Wenneyende: one acre of land in Elmen, one and a half acres in Medmen, and two selions outside the western part of the manor recently held by Edmund Cade, for life, rendering annually 2s.6d.ob. and all other services and customs rendered by Edmund. G.: 6d.

189v **3443** CHATTERIS Thomas Egyve: half of one tenement of eight acres with meadow in Oldhalf recently held by Laurence Hykkesson, for life, rendering annually 5s. at the customary times and all other services and customs rendered by Laurence. G.: 3s.4d.

3444 CHATTERIS John Rede Sr.: half of one tenement of eight acres with meadow in Oldhalf and a half-acre of land in Elmen recently held by Robert Wryght, for life, rendering annually 4s.10d. and all other services and customs rendered by Robert. G.: 2s.

3445 CHATTERIS John Berle Jr.: one cotland in Slade Ende recently held by Thomas Berle, for life, rendering annually 23d. at the customary times, and all other services and customs rendered by Thomas. G.: three capons.

3446 CHATTERIS John Mathew, son of John Mathew: one cotland with appurtenances recently held by John Symmesson, for life, rendering annually in all things as did John. G.: two capons.

3447 WARBOYS (February) William Ravele of Warboys pays four capons for license to marry Juliana, his daughter and naif of the lord by blood, to whomever she wishes, this time.

3448 WARBOYS (February) Robert Asshwell and John Brown: half of one virgate of land in Caldecote once held by John Bereford, the other half of which is held by John Shakestaffe, for life, rendering annually 4s.6d. and all other services and customs owed therein, with the first payment at the next feast of St. Andrew. G.: four capons.

3449 WARBOYS (April) William Bradweye pays 20d. for license to marry Johanna, daughter of John Benson of Warboys, naif of the lord, this first time.

3450 WARBOYS (August) Thomas Buntyng: all those lands and tenements recently held by William Bocher for 19s., for life, rendering annually 17s. at the customary times and all other services and customs rendered by William, with the obligation to repair and maintain the property at his own expense, except that the lord will rebuild one grange, in carpentry alone, and grant Thomas two acres of meadow in Holywell and an allowance of this year's rent for covering the grange. G.: excused, because the tenement was burned.

3451 THERFIELD William Yorke of Tempsford pays 6s.8d. for license to have Elena, daughter of William Wyngore and naif of the lord by blood, recently servant of Richard Cok of Therfield, in his service wherever he wishes, for which service the lord will have the full stipend owed by Richard Cok, namely: 20s., for withdrawal from his service. Further, the 20s. will be paid in the following way: 6s.8d. from the sale of straw, 6s.8d. paid to the seneschal at the leet, and 6s.8d. paid by Richard.

3452 THERFIELD (May) William Russell: one messuage and one virgate of land

190r recently held by William Sly and once held by Barcus for 13s.4d., on which property one hall was built by the lord, and one toft with another virgate of land recently held by John Felde for 14s. and called Amprons, for life, rendering annually 18s. at the customary times and all other services and customs owed therein, with the first payment at the next feast of St. Andrew. G.: 3s.4d.

3453 SLEPE (May) William Prikke: surrender of one plot and one virgate of land inside le Garres' and called Pepis, to the use of Thomas Wryght, for life, rendering annually in all things as did William. G.: 3s.4d.

3454 SLEPE (May) John Dryver: one messuage and two cotlands *ad opus* recently held by William Pecok and once held by William Herrof, for life, rendering annually in all things as did William, with the obligation to repair and maintain the messuage. G.: 2s.

3455 RAMSEY (April) Thomas Boteler and his wife, Rosa: from John Swasham, subcellarer, half of one holme, or meadow, next to Hemyng's cote with reeds and willows recently held by Andrew Claxton, from the previous Michaelmas for life, rendering annually 4s.4d. in equal portions at the feasts of the Annunciation and Nativity of Blessed Mary, with the obligation to repair and enclose the property, and with permission to cut down the willows growing there and replace them by planting new willows, as it seems best to them. Further, they may not relinquish or dismiss the property without the license of the sub-cellarer. *Et si predictus redditus*, etc. (arrears of one month). G.: 3s.4d.

3456 RAMSEY (April) William Poolyard and his wife, Margaret: from the subcellarer, one messuage inside Mechegates with appurtenances recently held by John Wayte, from the previous Easter for life, rendering annually 8s. in equal portions at the feasts of the Annunciation and Nativity of Blessed Mary, with the sub-cellarer responsible for repairs. Further, they may not relinquish the property without the license of the sub-cellarer. *Et si predictus redditus*, etc. (arrears of six weeks). G.: 3s.4d., two capons.

3457 RAMSEY (April) Adam Shene and his wife, Isabella: from the sub-cellarer, one messuage recently held by John Keteryng and previously held by John Cooke, from the previous Michaelmas for life, rendering annually 12s. in equal portions at the feasts of the Annunciation and Nativity of Blessed Mary, with the sub-cellarer responsible for repairs. Further, they may not relinquish the property without the license of the sub-cellarer. *Et si predictus redditus*, etc. (arrears of one month). G.: 2s., two capons.

3458 RAMSEY (April) Robert Gyddyng and his wife, Agnes, formerly of St. Neots: from the sub-cellarer, one messuage in Bridge Street recently held by John Gymmys Glover, from the previous Easter for life, rendering annually 9s.4d. in equal portions at the customary times, with the sub-cellarer responsible for repairs, although, if the bay collapses, Robert will effect repairs. Further, they may not relinquish the property without the license of the sub-cellarer. *Et si predictus redditus*, etc. (arrears of one month). G.: 3s.4d., two capons.

3459 RAMSEY (April) Radulph Barbor and John Papworth: from the sub-cellarer, a certain meadow with willows and other appurtenances at Little Hill once held by John Bonde and recently held by William Bernewell, from the feast of the Annunciation for life, rendering annually 2s. at the customary times, with the obligation to repair and maintain the property. Further, they may not relinquish the property without the license of the sub-cellarer. *Et si predictus redditus*, etc. (arrears of one month). G.: two capons.

3460 RAMSEY (May) John Wotton, alias Fyssher, and his son, Thomas: from the sub-cellarer, one meadow with willows, fishponds, reeds and other appurtenances called High Ditch and recently held by John Wotton and once held by John Shirwode, from next Michaelmas for life, rendering annually 26s.8d. in equal portions at the

190v

feasts of the Annunciation and the Nativity of Blessed Mary, with the obligation to repair and maintain the property at their own expense, with the right to cut down willows there for hedges and replace them, without any waste, with the sub-cellarer having the right to sell fish, reeds and willows there. *Et si predictus redditus*, etc. (arrears of six weeks). Further, they may not relinquish the property without the license of the sub-cellarer. G.: a half-mark of eels.

3461 RAMSEY (August) Thomas Clerk, alias Porter, and his wife, Johanna: from the sub-cellarer, one messuage within the great gate recently held by Agnes Marche, from the next Michaelmas for life, rendering 5s. in equal portions at the feasts of the Annunciation and Nativity of Blessed Mary, with the sub-cellarer responsible for repairs. *Et si predictus redditus*, etc. (arrears of one month). G.: two capons.

191r

3462 RAMSEY (August) John Pursse: from the sub-cellarer, one messuage within Mechegates recently held by Agnes Fuller, for life, rendering annually in all things as did Agnes, with the sub-cellarer responsible for repairs. Further, he may not relinquish the property without the license of the sub-cellarer. *Et si predictus redditus*, etc. (arrears of two months). G.: 12d.

3463 RAMSEY CUM UPWOOD (August) William Edward: from the sub-cellarer, one meadow called Tonstede, for life, rendering 3s.10d. each year when the meadow can be mowed, and two capons, at the customary times, which property previously rendered 4s. Further, he may not relinquish or dismiss the property without the license of the sub-cellarer. G.: two capons.

3464 KNAPWELL (September) John Lawe, naif of the lord by blood, pays 5s. for license to marry Agnes, his daughter, to John Fuller of Chesterton, this time. Fine paid through Jacob Hopper.

7 JOHN STOWE (1442-1443)

191v
3465 RIPTON (September) John Mowell of Huntingdon, tailor: one messuage built up with one *insathous*, one grange and one bake house, and a half-virgate of land recently held by William Wolde, for life, rendering annually 8s. and all other services and customs rendered by William, with the obligation to repair the property at his own expense, the lord granting an allowance of this year's rent. Pledges for repairs: Richard Smyth, William Laveyn, and William Wold. G.: one capon.

3466 RIPTON (leet) Agnes Ivell: surrender of one messuage and a half-virgate of land recently held by her husband and located near the rectory, to the use of Thomas Ivell, *ad opus* for life, rendering annually in all things as did Agnes. G.: 20d., two capons.

3467 RIPTON (same leet) Agnes Ivell and her son, John: one messuage and a half-virgate of land once held by John Carter and afterwards held by Robert Ivell, for life, rendering annually in all things as did Robert. G.: excused by the seneschal because of repairs.

3468 RIPTON (30 November) Robert Wryght of Walton pays the fine for license to have John West, son of John West, and naif of the lord by blood, live off the manor for as long as it pleases the lord, rendering 20d. annually and suit to leet, remaining a naif as before, in pledge of which Robert binds himself in writing to the lord for £10.

3469 KNAPWELL (leet at Elsworth). John Ilger: one quarter of land recently held by John Joye, for life, rendering annually in all things as did John, with an allowance of this year's rent because the land is badly cultivated. G.: two capons.

3470 KNAPWELL (October) Thomas Fylhous of Ramsey, blacksmith: license to take Richard Lawe, son of John Lawe and naif and villein of the lord of the manor of

Knapwell, into his service and apprenticeship for learning the art of blacksmithing, from the feast of All Saints for a term of seven years.

3471 BURWELL (7 October) Master John Hygham: one tenement of 24 acres with appurtenances recently held by John Prikke Sr., from the previous Michaelmas for 24 years, rendering annually 22s. at the customary times, and all other services and customs rendered by John. G.: excused.

3472 BURWELL John Prikke Sr. and his son, John: one messuage and 20 acres of land recently held by his father and once held by Robert Wyot Jr., for 30 years, rendering annually 21s. and all other services and customs rendered by his father. G.: (*cut off*).

3473 BURWELL John Hals: one tenement of 20 acres in North Street recently held by John Sparwe, in *arentatio* for 40 years, rendering annually 20s. and all other services and customs rendered by John. G.: 3s.4d.

3474 BURWELL William Cantford and his wife, Elena: one tenement of 15 acres at Wakelynsgate, with parcels of meadow from the tenement of Alota Stetham recently held by John Sparwe, for 40 years, rendering annually 18s. and all other services and customs rendered by John. G.: one capon.

3475 BURWELL John Raven and his wife, Johanna: one messuage and a half-acre of land recently held by Andrew Moryse, for life, rendering annually 15d. at the customary times, the mowing of a half-acre of wheat, and all other services and customs owed therein. G.: 20d.

3476 BURWELL John Barker and his wife, Margeria: one tenement of 12 acres *ad censum* recently held by his father and once held by Radulph Calvesbane, one cotland with a croft, and one and a half acres of land in a croft with three acres of land in the fields called Pymys once held by the same Radulph, for 40 years, rendering annually 15s. at the customary times, with the obligation to rebuild one grange on the land called Prymys within one year, for which repairs they may cut down timber growing on the land, after it has been seen and decided upon by the bailiff. G.: 10s., of which 5s. are paid this time.

3477 BURWELL John Roule: one tenement of eight acres in *arentatio* recently held by Thomas Pury and once held by Thomas Plombe, for 24 years, rendering annually 10s. and all other services and customs rendered by Thomas Pury. G.: 20d.

3478 SHILLINGTON (leet) John of the Abbeye: one messuage and one virgate of land with appurtenances recently held by Henry of the Abbeye, for life, rendering annually in all things as did Henry. G.: 6s.8d.

3479 SHILLINGTON (same leet) Thomas Laurence and his wife, Agnes: one messuage and two virgates of land, four acres of demesne land at Larkenhyll and the third part of meadow called Chaldwell Marsch recently held by John Laurence, for life, rendering annually 42s.3d.ob., one bushel of wheat and two bushels of oats at the customary times, and all other services and customs rendered by John, with the obligation to repair and maintain the property at their own expense. G.: 6s.8d.

3480 SHILLINGTON (same leet) William Whitbred: one semi-virgate, one cotland and two acres of land at Chirchehyll recently held by Robert Waleys, for life, rendering annually 12s. and all other services and customs rendered by Robert. G.: 2s.

3481 SHILLINGTON (same leet) John Hokclyff: surrender of one cote in Bridge Street once held by Dryver, to the use of John Toogoode, for life, rendering annually 2s.1d.ob. and all other services and customs owed therein. G.: 12d.

3482 SHILLINGTON (same leet) John Warde Sr. and his wife, Margeria: one messuage and one virgate of land recently held by Thomas Longe, one vacant toft and one virgate of land once held by John AtteWode, and four acres of land in Newmanlond recently held by Roger Everard, all of which was most recently held by

192r

192v John Warde Sr. and surrendered back to the lord by him, for life, rendering annually 30s.4d. and all other services and customs owed therein, provided that they in no way implead, vex or molest Philip Multon, his wife, or any of their servants for any cause or delict henceforth outside the lord's court, nor that they place themselves under the advocacy or protection of any other lord or person, under penalty of loss and forfeit of their lands and tenements. And they perform fealty. G.: excused.

3483 SHILLINGTON (same leet) Philip Multon and his wife, Isabella: all the lands and tenements previously held and surrendered back by them, for life, provided that they not implead, vex or molest in any way John Warde, his wife, or their servants, for any cause or delict arising between them henceforth, outside the lord's court, nor put themselves under the advocacy or protection of any other lord or person except in the council of the lord abbot, under penalty of loss and forfeit of their lands and tenements, this conveyance not withstanding. And they perform fealty. G.: excused.

3484 SHILLINGTON (27 November) Matthew Chaumbre, his wife, Agnes, and their son, William: the reversion of a certain pasture called Newstokkyng containing 40 acres of land and now held by Master Richard Hethe, rector of the church, for life, rendering annually 16s. at the customary times, which property previously rendered 26s.8d. Further, they will render all other services and customs owed therein. G.: two marks.

3485 BARTON (12 October: court) John Felmesham, son and heir of Isabella Felmesham: with the consent of his brother, William, one croftland with appurtenances recently held by Isabella, for life, rendering annually in all things as did Isabella. And he performs fealty. G.: excused.

3486 BARTON (same court). William Roger Plough Wryght, naif of the lord by blood, pays the fine for license to live off the manor at Lilley in the county of Hartford for as long as it pleases the lord, remaining a naif as before, and rendering to the lord annually 12d. and suit to court. Pledge for payment: Jacob Rogger, his brother.

3487 BARTON (same court) Walter Wodeward and his wife, Johanna: one virgate of land with forland and croftland recently held by William Rogger, for life, rendering annually in all things as did William. G.: 5s. Heriot: 20d.

3488 BARTON (same court) William Martyn: one croftland recently held by Simon Fraunceys, for life, rendering annually in all things as did Simon. G.: 2s.

3489 BARTON (same court) Jacob Roger: one messuage, one virgate of land with forland and two croftlands recently held by Edmund Rogger, for life, rendering annually in all things as did Edmund. G. and heriot: 23s.4d. with 13s.4d. to be paid at the next accounting, and the rest at the next court.

193r **3490** BARTON (same court) Jacob Pope agrees to pay annually the fine and chevage of John Wylymot, naif of the lord, for license to live off the fief at Thaxted for as long as it pleases the lord, remaining a naif as before and coming annually to the general court.

3491 BARTON (same court). Richard Pryor pays 6s.8d. for license to remove one house from the tenement of Walter Revy to his own.

3492 CRANFIELD (14 October: leet) William Wodehill Sr.: surrender of one messuage and a half-virgate of land recently held by Henry Attemede, and four acres of demesne land in Stalyprace and one and a half acres of land Cokkeslond recently held by the same Henry, to the use of Henry Tyler, for life, rendering annually 17s. and all other services and customs rendered by William. Pledges for repairs: William Wodehill Sr. and John Smyth. G.: 8d.

3493 CRANFIELD (same leet) John Robyn: surrender of one messuage and half of one virgate of land in *arentatio* recently held by John Joye, to the use of William Wodehill, son of Thomas Wodehill, for life, rendering annually 10s. and all other services and customs rendered by John, with the provision that he not relinquish any other parcel of land previously received from the lord, under penalty of loss of this copy. G.: 3s.4d.

3494 HEMINGFORD ABBOTS (17 October: leet) John Marschall and his wife, Agnes: one cotland and one croft recently held by Margaret Bartilmewe, for life, rendering annually 13d. at the customary times, and all other services and customs rendered by Margaret, with the obligation to repair and maintain the property at their own expense. G.: two capons.

3495 HEMINGFORD ABBOTS (same leet) William Russell: one messuage recently rebuilt, and one virgate of land recently held by William Sly and one croft with one virgate of land once held by Annpron, for life, rendering annually 18s. at the customary times, and all other services and customs rendered by William, with the obligation to repair and maintain the property, and with payments beginning at the feast of St. John the Baptist. G.: 3s.4d.

3496 HEMINGFORD ABBOTS (same leet) John Thakker and his wife, Johanna: one messuage and a half-virgate of land recently held by John Forest and once held by John Upton, for life, rendering annually 6s.8d. and all other services and customs rendered by John, with the obligation to repair the messuage. G.: (*blank*).

3497 HEMINGFORD ABBOTS Thomas Aungewyn: two acres of meadow rendering 7s. and recently held by Walter Murrok, for life, quit, because of his good service to the lord in the past and in the future, with the obligation to plant willows to save the meadow. G.: excused.

3498 HEMINGFORD ABBOTS (26 May) Beatrix, widow of John Newman and daughter of John Selde, naif of the lord by blood, pays 3s.4d. for license to marry John Page of Long Stanton, this time. And note that John Selde was presented as a naif of the lord in many leets in the time of Abbot Edmund and Abbot Thomas. Pledge for payment: Thomas Aungewyn.

193v   **3499** HEMINGFORD ABBOTS John Clerke: one virgate of land with croft recently held by Marschall for 12s.8d. and two half-virgates of land once held by Alan Ver for 11s.10d., for life, rendering annually 16s. at the customary times, and all other services and customs owed therein. G.: two capons.

3500 HOUGHTON (September) William Gascoyne: one toft and one virgate of land recently held by William Brampton and once held by Walter Bedell, for life, rendering annually 8s. and all other services and customs rendered by William. G.: three capons.

3501 HOUGHTON (September) John Brampton: one toft and one virgate of land recently held by his father and once held by Stephen Marschall for life, rendering annually 8s. and all other services and customs rendered by his father. G.: three capons.

3502 HOUGHTON John Whaplode and his wife Alicia: one toft and croft with 26 acres, one rod of land and meadow in Houghton and Wyton once held by Dyke and recently held by John Aleyne, and once held by Richard Twywell, for life, rendering annually 16s. which property previously rendered 24s. Further, they will render all other services and customs rendered by John. G.: excused.

3503 WESTON (23 October) Johanna, daughter of John Hakon and naif of the lord by blood, pays 6s.8d. for license to marry as often, however, whomever an wherever she wishes, for life.

3504 BYTHORNE John Baron Sr. and his son, John: one messuage and a half-virgate of land recently held by Richard Welles, for life, rendering annually in all things as did Richard. G.: two capons.

3505 BYTHORNE John Barreve and his wife, Margaret: one messuage and a half-virgate of land with other appurtenances recently held by John Randolf, for life, rendering annually in all things as did John. G.: 6s.8d.

3506 BYTHORNE John Hyll: one ruined messuage and a half-virgate of land recently held by William Wattesson, for life, rendering annually 18s., which property previously rendered 22s.2d. because of new repairs. Further, he will render all other services and customs owed therein. G.: four capons.

3507 BYTHORNE Robert Browse and his wife, Alicia: one cotland and a half quarter of land recently held by Richard Wayte, for life, rendering annually in all things as did Richard. G.: 2s.

3508 BYTHORNE John Peek Jr. and his wife, Johanna: one messuage and three quarters of land with other appurtenances recently held by his father, for life, rendering annually in all things as did his father. G.: 2s.

3509 BYTHORNE John Bocher: one cotland with appurtenances recently held by Richard Wayte and once held by John Astyn, for life, rendering annually in all things as did Richard. G.: 2s.

3510 HURST (14 November: leet) (at St. Ives) William Fylhous agrees with the seneschal to repair one *insathous* 30 feet long before Easter, receiving timber (i.e. two beams, eight poles, a board) from the lord, and rents (i.e. 40d.) owed by Thomas Herrof, 20d. from John Warde and 14s. from Thomas Pope owed this year to Michaelmas of 8 John Stowe, with the condition that William will hold one virgate of land with the aforesaid plot.

194r **3511** ST. IVES Richard Pope Miller and his wife: a half-row in the corner recently repaired by the lord and recently held by John Sutton, for life, rendering annually 8s. at the customary times, with the obligation to repair and maintain the property. *Et non licebit*, etc. G.: two capons.

3512 ST. IVES (April) John Roger: surrender of one row recently held by John Maddyngle and once held by Katerina Bysshop, to the use of Robert Herry and his wife, Juliana, for life, rendering annually 13s.4d. at the customary times and all other services and customs owed therein, with the obligation to repair and maintain the property. *Et non licebit*, etc. G.: 26s.8d.

3513 ST. IVES (20 May) Thomas Paye, his wife Emma, and their daughter, Katerina: the reversion of two shops with the garret of one shop with a solar held now by Katerina Martyn for life, rendering annually 20s. in equal portions at the customary times, with the obligation to repair and maintain the property. Further, they will not sell, will, alienate or assign the property to anyone without the lord's license. *Et non licebit*, etc. G.: 5s.

3514 ST. IVES Nicholas Josep: one row once held by William Tychemarssh, for life, rendering annually all services and customs owed therein, and 15s. at the customary times, which property previously rendered 20s. Further, he will repair and maintain the property. *Et non licebit*, etc. G.: one capon.

3515 HOLYWELL Richard Wattes: surrender of one cotland with demesne land and other parcels recently held by Thomas Valentyne, to the use of William Benet, for life, rendering annually in all things as did Richard. G.: 40d., two geese.

194v **3516** UPWOOD (April) Thomas Fylhous: one forge recently held by Thomas Smyth, from Easter for four years, rendering annually 12d. at the customary times, and all other services and customs rendered by Thomas, with the obligation to repair and maintain the forge. G.: excused.

3517 KNAPWELL (April) Jacob Hopper: permission to give *ad firmam* all the lands and tenements he now holds to Thomas Gylot, formerly of Hilton, from Michaelmas for 12 years, rendering annually in all things as did Jacob. Pledge for payments and services: Jacob Hopper. Fine: four capons.

3518 ELTON (22 May) (at Ramsey) Thomas Saldyng Carpenter pays six capons for license to marry Johanna, his sister, daughter of John Saldyng and naif of the lord by blood, to the son of John Denys Wollepakker of Ramsey, this time. Pledge for payment: Thomas Saldyng.

3519 CHATTERIS (9 July: court) John Balle "medius" and his wife, Katerina: surrender and resumption of one messuage and eight acres of land with meadow in Crowlode and other parcels of land once held by his father, for life, rendering annually in all things as did his father. Pledges for repairs, payments and services: John Ravesson and Walter Toye. G.: 2s.

3520 CHATTERIS (same court) William Honte: surrender of one cotland, to the use of John Hunne Jr., for life, rendering annually in all things as did William. Pledge for payments and repairs: his father. G.: 12d.

3521 CHATTERIS (same court) John Hertford Herde: surrender of one tenement of eight acres with meadow in Crowlode and other appurtenant parcels recently held by him, to the use of John Tebaud, for life, rendering annually in all things as did John. Pledge for repairs and payments: his father. G.: 5s.

3522 CHATTERIS (same court) Alicia, widow of John Cok: surrender of one cotland or cote with appurtenances recently held by John Cok, to the use of Hugo Chapman, and his wife, Johanna, for life, rendering annually 23d. at the customary times, and all other services and customs owed therein, with the obligation to repair and maintain the property at their own expense. G.: 12d.

195r **3523** LITTLE RAVELEY (August) Richard Willesson and his wife, Mariota: one cotland recently held by John Owty Sr., rendering nothing this year, because the land was granted to them quit by the lord for his good service, both in the past and future, and which property previously rendered 2s. G.: excused by the lord.

3524 WARBOYS (August) John Cobbe: one vacant toft once a cote of Hochkynsrowe recently held by Thomas Bene, for life, rendering annually 6d. and all other services and customs owed therein. G.: two capons.

3525 BROUGHTON (May) William Webster of Little Raveley pays 2s. for license to marry Margaret, daughter of John Cabe of Broughton and naif of the lord by blood, this time, which payment is listed in the account of the Beadle of Ramsey.

195v *Blank*

8 JOHN STOWE (1443-1444)

196r **3526** RAMSEY (October) John Horwode and his wife, Margaret: from Brother Robert Camebrigg, sub-cellarer, one parcel of meadow of Swonhousmede with appurtenant ditches and willows recently held by Thomas Bangolf, from the previous Michaelmas, for life, rendering annually 6s.8d. in equal portions at the feasts of the Annunciation and Nativity of Blessed Mary, with the obligation to repair and maintain the property in ditches and enclosures, with the right to cut down and plant willows. *Et si predictus redditus*, etc. (arrears of six weeks). G.: four woodcocks.

3527 RAMSEY (April) John Bran Mason and his wife, Anna: from Brother Robert Cambrigg, one messuage in High Street recently held by Nicholas Morell and once held by Thomas Prat, for life, rendering annually 12s. in equal portions at the feasts of the Annunciation and Nativity of Blessed Mary, with the sub-cellarer responsible for repairs. *Et si predictus redditus*, etc. (arrears of one month, with distraints). G.: 13s.4d.

3528 RAMSEY (May) William Medowe and his wife: from Brother Robert Cambrigge, one messuage inside Mechegate recently held by John Clevelok and once held by John Hardhed, from the previous Michaelmas for life, rendering annually 8s. in equal portions at the feasts of the Annunciation and Nativity of Blessed Mary, with the sub-cellarer responsible for repairs and maintenance. *Et si predictus redditus,* etc. (arrears of one month, with distraints). G.: 6s.8d.

3529 RAMSEY (August) Simon Ives Webster and his wife, Johanna: from Brother Robert Cambrigge, one plot in Bridge Street recently held by John Berdewell Sr., for life, rendering annually (*unspecified*) at the feasts of the Annunciation and Nativity of Blessed Mary, which property previously rendered 11s., with Simon and Johanna allowed to have undergrowth from the sub-cellarer, at their own expense, and with the sub-cellarer responsible for repairs. *Et si predictus redditus,* etc. (distraints). G.: 3s.4d.

3530 BURWELL (22 October: leet) Thomas Pury: surrender of one tenement recently pertaining to eight acres of land now held by Thomas Goodale, to the use of Nicholas Rolf, for life, rendering *firmarius* all services and customs owed therein, and suit to court and leet, with the obligation to repair and maintain the property at his own expense. G.: 8d.

196v **3531** BURWELL (same leet) Thomas Goodale: surrender of one rod of land lying against the tenement of William Pury and parcelled out of a tenement of eight acres held by Thomas, to the use of William Pury, as a path to the fields. Also: another rod of land lying against the same tenement, parcelled out of a tenement of eight acres held now by Sibilia Jay, for 40 years as a path to the fields, rendering annually 4d. for the first rod, and reaping, tying and raking of wheat for the second rod. G.: two capons.

3532 SHILLINGTON (26 October: leet) John Toche of Upwood: surrender of one messuage and one toft with two virgates of land, to the use of his son, William and his wife, Margeria, for life, rendering annually 33s.10d. at the customary times, and all other services and customs rendered by John. Further, easement in the hall, kitchen, rooms and all other houses on the property will be reserved to John and his wife, Johanna, for life. G. and heriot: 20s., to be paid at the feast of St. John the Baptist.

3533 SHILLINGTON (same leet) Margaret, widow of John Barfoot: surrender of one cotland and two acres of land at Assyngwell recently held by John, to the use of John Aylmer, his wife, Johanna, and their son, Thomas, for life, rendering annually 4s.10d.ob. at the customary times, with the provision that Margaret will have food and lodging from them for life. Further, John, Johanna and Thomas will repair and maintain the property under penalty of forfeit. G. and heriot: 3s.4d.

3534 SHILLINGTON (same leet) Richard Grave, naif of the lord by blood, and his wife, Elizabet: one croft, one messuage, and one virgate of land with one lot of Burylond in Upnende once held by John AtteMede and recently held by Richard Messenger and seized by the lord for lack of repairs, for life, rendering annually 22s.3d., one rooster, two hens, five eggs, and all other services and customs owed therein. Further, they will rebuild one barn within a year, and repair all other buildings and maintain them thereafter, under penalty of forfeit. G. and heriot: 20s.

3535 SHILLINGTON (November) William Hanto and his wife, Agnes: one tenement in Hanscombe and one semi-virgate once held by Arnold Fawconer Seneschal and recently held by John Hanto and seized by the lord for non-repair after four years of commands and proclamation relative to repairs, for life, rendering annually in all things as did John. G.: 12d., two capons.

3536 SHILLINGTON (November) John Sampson: one messuage and one virgate of land recently held by John Ede and once held by Adam Sparwe, for life, rendering annually 16s.6d. and all other services and customs rendered by John. G.: 12d., two capons.

3537 SHILLINGTON (11 July) Johanna Chible, daughter of William Chible Cannbir, bailiff, and naif of the lord of the manor there, pays 2s. at Ramsey for license to marry whomever she wishes, this time.

197r **3538** BARTON (27 October: General Court) John Prior Jr., naif of the lord by blood, pays 2s. and one capon for license to marry Agnes, his daughter, to Martin Samwell of Hexton, this time.

3539   BARTON (same court) William Prior: one messuage and one virgate of land with adjacent forland recently held by William Prior, his late father, for life, rendering annually in all things as did his father. G. and heriot: 20s., of which 20d. are excused at the request of Matthew Cannbir and others.

3540   BARTON (same court) Simon Golion, alias Bocher, pays 8s. for license to marry Emma, daughter of John Prior Jr. and naif of the lord by blood, and for entry into one messuage and one virgate of land recently held by Thomas Revesson, late husband of Emma.

3541   BARTON (same court) John Prior, son of John Prior, recently bailiff: one messuage built up with one building and one virgate of land with forland recently held by William Revesson and once held by John Scut, for life, rendering annually in all things as did William, with the obligation to repair and maintain the property. G. and heriot: 6s.8d.

3542   CRANFIELD (29 October: leet) Thomas Rydeler, tenant of one messuage with one building and three quarters of land: surrender of the messuage and building of two quarters of the land, to the use of John Whytbroun, for life, rendering annually all services and customs owed therein and 13s.6d., with the obligation to repair and maintain the property. G.: 13s.4d. Heriot: nothing, because Thomas has not yet surrendered all his property, according to the custom of the manor, as they say.

3543   CRANFIELD (13 December) William Terry pays 40d. for license to marry Johanna Terry, daughter of Thomas Terry and naif of the lord by blood, to whomever she wishes.

3544   HOUGHTON (9 November: leet) Philip Thorley and his wife, Agnes: one tenement near the mill called a croft recently held by William Pynder, for life, rendering annually 5s. at the customary times, and all other services and customs rendered by William. G.: 3s.4d.

3545   HOUGHTON (same leet) John Pomys, alias Myller, and his wife, Sara: one messuage and a half-virgate of land recently held by John Yong, for life, rendering annually 6s. at the customary times, and all other services and customs rendered by John. G.: 12d.

3546   HOUGHTON (same leet) John Carter: one vacant toft and a half-virgate of land recently held by John Scot, for life, rendering annually 4s. at the customary times, and all other services and customs rendered by John. G.: 12d.

3547   HOUGHTON (same leet) Thomas Andrewe Carpentar, naif of the lord: one vacant toft and a half-virgate of land in *arentatio* recently held by William Pynder, for life, rendering annually 5s. and all other services and customs rendered by William, with the first payment at the feast of the Nativity of John the Baptist. G.: two capons.

197v   **3548**   WARBOYS (12 November: leet) Robert Honyter: surrender of one toft and a half-virgate of land once held by John Berenger, bailiff, to the use of Thomas Honyter, for life, rendering annually in all things as did Robert. G.: two capons and two woodcocks.

3549   WARBOYS (same leet) Robert Honyter, his wife, Agnes, and their son, Thomas: one parcel of a certain toft held by John Whete and once held by Robert Ravele, as a path to the field called Brachefeld, with hedges, for life, rendering annually 4d. at the customary times. G.: one capon.

3550   WARBOYS (November). John Bonde and his wife, Alicia: a half-virgate of land recently held by Thomas Buntyng and once held by William Smert, for life, rendering annually 5s. and all other services and customs rendered by Thomas. G.: two capons.

3551   WARBOYS (November) John Caton, alias Barford, Jr.: one tenement from the tenement of Hegenys with appurtenances and two acres of land at Wodecroft recently held by Simon Hygh Sr., from Michaelmas for life, rendering nothing for the first four years, because of repairs, and 10s. each year thereafter, at the customary times, which property previously rendered 24s. Further, he will build one bake house and repair all other buildings, timber being supplied by the lord. G.: two capons.

3552 WARBOYS Thomas Buntyng: one maltland, one mondayland once held by William Hervy and recently held by Robert Corbet, half of one virgate of land in Caldecote previously held by him, and another virgate in Caldecote recently held by John Hygh Myller, for life, rendering annually 5s.6d. for the first half-virgate, 8s. for the second half-virgate, and 9s. for the maltland and mondayland, which property previously rendered 12s. G.: (*blank*).

3553 WARBOYS (1 May) John Pomeys, alias Miller: one mondayland built up with one building near Hawegate recently held by Hugo Pulter, and the windmill there, for 10 years, with the obligation to repair in carpentry and iron works, and maintain the property, the lord effecting initial repairs and supplying mill stones, and timber, with its cutting and transport supplied by John. Further, he will render annually 30s. at the feasts of the Annunciation, the Nativity of John the Baptist and the Nativity of Blessed Mary, and he will also support all burdens incumbent upon the mill. At the end of this term, he will dismiss the property, repaired, with iron works and mill stones. And he is sworn. G.: one cake.

3554 WISTOW (November) Richard Skynner and his wife, Oliva: three cotlands and a half-acre at Langheghes, one acre at Brounbryg, one acre at Chesfurlong, one acre at Lowfurlong, eight selions of demesne land at Buriston, and seven selions of demesne land at Little Hill recently held by William Hertwell and once held by Robert Nottyng, for life, rendering annually 7s.8d., one hen and 10 eggs, which property previously rendered 30s.6d.ob. Further, they will render to the lord all other services and customs owed therein. G.: 2s.

198r   **3555** WISTOW (9 December, at Ramsey). Radulph Laly of Covington, of the county of Huntingdon, carpenter, pays the fine for license to have Thomas Atte Gate, son of John Atte Gate, naif of the lord and villein of the lord of the manor of Wistow, in his service and learning his art for six years, rendering annually 8d. at the feast of St. Benedict, at Ramsey, with Radulph obligated by the term of a written agreement to make the payments and return Thomas at the end of the six years.

3556 WISTOW (March) John Atte Gate: surrender of one toft and a half-virgate of land called Benettis, to the use of Thomas Rede and his wife, Margaret, for life, rendering annually in all things as did John, with the obligation to have one *insathous* of eight binding-posts built on the property within four years, timber being supplied by the lord. G.: 2s., two capons.

3557 WISTOW (10 July) Richard Miller, alias Covyngton, and his son, William: the windmill there, from the previous Easter for 12 years, rendering annually 22s., in equal amounts at the feasts of St. Andrew, the Annunciation and the Nativity of John the Baptist and the Nativity of Blessed Mary, with the obligation to repair and maintain the mill, with timber supplied by the lord as deemed appropriate and assigned by the seneschal of Ramsey. Further, the property will be returned at the end of the term in as good — or better — condition as when they received it. G.: one capon.

3558 WISTOW John Rede: surrender of one messuage and one quarter of land recently held by John Helmesle and three quarters of land recently held by William Hyche, to the use of John Atte Chirche and his wife, Emma, for life, rendering annually in all things as did John. Pledge: Richard Skynner. G.: 2s.

3559 GRAVELEY (November) William Smyth, naif of the lord: surrender of one messuage with adjacent croft and a half-virgate of land, to the use of John Smyth and his wife, Agnes, for life, rendering annually 6s.8d. and all other works and customs owed therein, with the obligation to repair and maintain the messuage. G.:2s.

3560 BROUGHTON (November) Thomas Pulter and his wife, Katerina: one messuage and one quarter of land once held by Simon Danneys and recently held by his father, Thomas Pulter, for life, rendering annually 3d. and all other services and customs rendered by his father. G.: six capons.

3561 BROUGHTON (November) Richard Pulter and his wife, Agnes: one virgate of land in *minor censum* once held by John Bigge and recently held by Thomas Pulter, his father, with lands and tenements once held by Simon Bigge and afterwards held by John Wryght, and recently held by the said Thomas and also rebuilt by him, for life, rendering annually 12s. for the virgate and 5s. for the properties of John Wryght, which previously rendered 8s. and sometimes 10s. Further, they will render all other services and customs owed therein. G.: six capons.

3562 BROUGHTON William Owty of Raveley, naif of the lord of Wistow, pays 16d. for license to marry Johanna, daughter of William Cabbe and naif of the lord of Broughton, this time.

198v   **3563** BROUGHTON (November) William Russell: surrender of a half-virgate of land recently held by Thomas Typtet in *minor censum* for 6s., one quarter of land from Cleryvaux land once held by William Smyth for 4s. and mowing of peas for one day. Taken back by him with his wife, Johanna, for life, rendering annually 8s. at the customary times and all other services and customs rendered by Thomas. Also, with their son, Robert: one messuage at the gate of the manor and a half-virgate of land and one lot of Damyslonde recently held by Thomas Clerke and once held by John Cabe for 8s., for life, rendering annually 6s.8d. at the customary times and all other services and customs owed therein, with the first payment at the next feast of St. Andrew. Further, they will repair the property this first time. G.: four capons.

3564 BROUGHTON (March) Thomas Russell Jr. and his wife, Johanna: one messuage, a half-virgate of land and one croft on the other side of the river recently held by John Justice Tayllor and seized by the lord for lack of repairs and default of payments, for life, with the lord obligated to rebuild one *insathous* within two years, including carpentry, roofing, and furnishing timber, its transport, straw, three cart loads of straw for roofing, and plastering for six days. G.: two capons.

3565 HOLYWELL CUM NEEDINGWORTH John Edward Sr.: one messuage and one cotland and certain acres of demesne land and meadow in Salmade recently held by John Shepperd, for life, rendering annually 13s.5d.ob. and all other services owed therein, with the obligation to rebuild one *camera* in the place of one grange, and to repair the grange and two other houses, at his own expense, with the lord supplying ground sills. G.: 40d.

3566 THERFIELD John Gemys Webster his wife, Margaret and their heirs: a parcel of the manor built up with four buildings recently held by Richard Gurney, rendering annually 2s. in equal portions at the customary times, and all other services and customs owed therein. G.: 2s.

3567 THERFIELD (21 July) John Colle Sr., naif of the lord by blood, pays at Ramsey 6s.8d. for license to marry Margaret, his daughter, to John Watte, this time. Because of his poverty, the seneschal reduces the fine to 40d., to be paid before the feast of St. Laurence, under penalty of duplication.

3568 CHATTERIS (December) John Smyth: surrender of half of one tenement of eight acres with forland and meadow in Crowlode and land in Elmen, with a cotland recently held by John Clement, and a fishpond in le Dame, to the use of his son, John, for life, rendering annually 8s.2d. at the customary times, and all other services and customs rendered by John. G.: 12d.

3569 CHATTERIS (December) Radulph Pope: one messuage of four acres with appurtenances recently held by John Clerke, rendering annually in all things as did John. G.: 20d.

199r **3570** CHATTERIS (December) Thomas Fyshher: surrender of one tenement of eight acres with appurtenances once held by Stephen Peyte, to the use of Thomas Hall, for life, rendering annually in all things as did Thomas. G.: 2s.6d.

3571 CHATTERIS (December) Agnes Branncestre: one cotland recently held by Agnes Peyte, for life, rendering annually in all things as did Agnes. G.: 6d.

3572 CHATTERIS (August) Alicia, widow of John Coke: surrender of one tenement of eight acres of land with one quarter and other appurtenances in Old half, half of seven selions of land in Horslade containing one acre and one rod and 30 perches of land recently held by John Coke, to the use of John Curteys of Ely, for life, rendering annually 10s.6d.ob. at the customary times and all other services and customs owed therein, with the obligation to repair and maintain all buildings on the property at his own expense, with half of the yield of the meadow of Oldhalf reserved to the said Alicia for life, in return for 12d. annually. G.: 6d.

3573 CHATTERIS (8 October: court) Galfridus Reygnald: surrender of one cotland once held by John Carter, with meadow, forland and one acre of land in Muslake, to the use of John Berle Sr., for life, rendering annually 3s.6d.ob. at the customary times, and all other services and customs rendered by Galfridus. G.: 20d., to be paid to the seneschal.

3574 CHATTERIS (same court) Agnes, widow of Richard Cokerell: surrender of one cotland with other parcels recently held by Richard, to the use of Richard Barle, for life, rendering annually 4s.10d.ob. at the customary times, and all other services and customs rendered by Agnes, with one acre of meadow in Oldhalf, one selion of land in a croft next to the hedges and easement in the cote at the eastern end of the *insathous* for keeping three animals, a parcel of the garden for herbage with free entry and exit for herbage and fuel and for having water at the well, reserved to Agnes for life. G.: 3s.

3575 CHATTERIS (same court) William Tylney Jr. marries Alicia, widow of John Sant, and enters into half of one tenement of four acres of land and meadow in Oldhalf recently held by John, for life, rendering annually 4s.9d. and all other services and customs owed therein. G.: 18d.

3576 CHATTERIS (same court) John Balle: surrender of one cotland with other parcels of demesne land once held by John Bate in le Hythe, to the use of John Balle Medius, for life, rendering annually 1d. at the customary times, and all other services and customs rendered by John. G.: 16d.

3577 CHATTERIS (same court) William Newman: surrender of half of one tenement of eight acres with meadow in Oldhalf and Crowlode and one acre of land in Elmen, to the use of John Newman, for life, rendering annually 6s.3d. at the customary times, and all other services and customs owed therein. G.: 16d.

3578 CHATTERIS (same court) John Ingram: two cotlands recently held by John South, for life, rendering annually 3s.10d. and all other services and customs owed therein. G.: two capons.

3579 CHATTERIS Richard Fikeys: one acre of land in Elmen and one acre of land in 199v Medmen recently held by John Goodgrene, for life, rendering annually 20d. at the customary times and all other services and customs owed therein. G.: 8d.

3580 HURST (January) William Herrof Jr.: one toft and one virgate of land recently held by John Burton, for life, rendering annually 12s. at the customary times, and the rent of the prior of St. Ives, and all other services owed therein. G.: 12d., two capons.

3581 HURST (January) John Nunne and his wife, Johanna: one tenement and one virgate of land recently held by Simon Longe and once held by Thomas Cutte, for life, rendering annually 14s. at the customary times, and all other services and customs rendered by Simon, with payments beginning at the feast of St. Andrew after one year, with the obligation to repair and maintain the property in carpentry, this time. G.: two capons.

3582 ELSWORTH John Couper and his wife, Emma: a half-virgate of land recently held by Thomas Coo called Muryellislond, for life, rendering annually in all things as did Thomas. G.: 2s.

3583 ELSWORTH John Fermor and his wife, Margaret: one toft next to his free tenement once held by Richard Wymond and a half-virgate of land recently held by Henry Botolf, once held by John Towselond, and another virgate of land recently held by John Alderman, called Cowherdys, for life, rendering annually 6d. for the toft and 20s. for the virgates, and all other services and customs owed therein. G.: 20d.

3584 ELSWORTH Thomas Fermer and his wife, Margeria: one messuage and one virgate of land recently held by his father, William Fermer, for life, rendering annually in all things as did William. G.: 20d.

3585 ELSWORTH John Newman Jr. and his wife, Mariota: one messuage and a half-virgate of land recently held by Walter Howesson, for life, rendering annually 14s. at the customary times, and all other services and customs rendered by Walter. G.: 20d.

3586 ELSWORTH (27 June: court) John Flynt, his wife, Margaret, and their son, Edmund: one cote with adjacent land recently held by Mariota Chircheman, for life, rendering annually in all things as did Mariota, with the obligation to repair and maintain the property at their own expense. G.: two capons, and no more because the cote is in ruins.

3587 ELSWORTH (August) Simon Bateman and his wife, Johanna: one messuage with croft once held by John Sonnyng, for life, rendering annually in all things as did John. G.: 6d.

3588 ELSWORTH (August) Thomas Croft: one plot with land once held by John Swynford and recently held by Robert Kroft (*cut off*), for life, rendering annually 13s.4d. and 15d. to the *firmarius* for works, at the customary times. G.: (*cut off*).

3589 ELSWORTH (August) John Maddy and his wife, Johanna: two messuages and one virgate of land recently held by John Chircheman, for life, rendering annually 22s.6d., and (*unspecified*) to the *firmarius* for works. G.: 2s.

3590 ELSWORTH (August) (at Ramsey) John AtteWode of Elsworth, naif of the lord by blood, pays 2s.8d. for license to marry Alicia, his daughter, to John Smyth of Buckworth.

3591 ELSWORTH John Howlot: surrender of one toft with a half-virgate of land once held by John Newman to the use of Alexander Hobbesson, for life, rendering annually 13s.4d.

3592 HEMINGFORD ABBOTS (February) John Aylmer Jr.: a half-virgate of land recently held by Beatrix Lee and most recently in the lord's hands, for life, rendering annually 3s.4d. at the customary times, which property previously rendered 5s.8d. Further, he will render all other services rendered by Beatrix. G.: 12d.

3593 WOODHURST (February) Johanna Cutte, naif of the lord by blood, pays, through the hands of Thomas Aungewyn, bailiff of St. Ives, 3s.4d. for license to marry whomever she wishes, this time.

3594 WOODHURST (March) John Arneweye and his wife, Alicia: one quarter of land recently held by Simon Romborough, for life, rendering annually 3s.4d. at the customary times, which property previously rendered 4s. Further, the first payment will be at the next feast of St. Andrew, and the reduction of rent is made in support of another quarter of land that he now holds. G.: one capon.

3595 WOODHURST (March) John Tayllor of Woodhurst: one tenement with ap-

200r

purtenances recently held by John Smyth, for life, rendering annually 18s., which property previously rendered 24s. Further, payments will begin at the next feast of St. Andrew, and John will find one laborer for plastering one house there for three days, and the lord will build one *camera*, with John responsible for carpentry and transport of timber and all other things, except splints and thatch. G.: three capons.

3596 UPWOOD (March) John Aleyn: one plot and a half-virgate of land in *arentatio* and a half-virgate of land *ad opus* recently held by John Spenser and one held by John Milys, for life, rendering annually 14s. and all other services and customs owed therein, with the obligation to build one kiln and one oven, with the lord erecting one bake house, John being responsible for splinting and claying. Further, payments will begin at the next feast of St. Andrew. G.: excused, but John will mow for one day in the peas and for one day in the barley, this year.

3597 WOODHURST (March) Robert Cachesoly: one tenement and half of one virgate of land recently held by John Bryngton, for life, rendering annually 8s. at the customary times, with the first payment at the feast of St. Andrew. Further, he receives an allowance of 4s. of this year's rent because of repairs. G.: two capons.

3598 ABBOTS RIPTON (March) Thomas Pye: surrender of one messuage and two semi-virgates of land recently held by John Smyth, one butt of land at Nonnemede, and one toft once held by Henry Schepperd, to the use of William Payn and his wife, Katerina, for life, rendering annually 13s.4d. and all other services and customs rendered by Thomas. G.: (*blank*).

200v **3599** ABBOTS RIPTON (March) William Birt and his wife, Isabella: one plot and one semi-virgate and half of one plot with a half-virgate of land and one selion of land at Angerlond recently held by Thomas Joye and once held by John Hanloie, for life, rendering annually 13s.4d. and all other services and customs rendered by Thomas. Also: one cote with appurtenances recently held by John Bamburg for 2s.4d. and one vacant toft with a half-virgate of land recently held by John Lyndesey and once held by Thomas Haulonde, for life, rendering annually 6s.8d., which property previously rendered 10s. Further, the lord will rebuild one grange of eight binding-posts, with William providing transport of timber, thatch, splinting, claying, roofing and straw. G.: two capons.

3600 ABBOTS RIPTON (June) John Crosse: one vacant plot and a half-virgate of land recently held by William White and once held by John Robbys, for life, rendering annually 7s., which property previously rendered 9s. Further, he will render all other services and customs rendered by John, with the first payment at the next feast of St. Andrew, and he will rebuild one *insathous* on the tenement called Beles in the next year, both in carpentry and roofing. G.: two capons.

3601 THERFIELD Richard Gamyn and his heirs: one plot and one virgate of land with one cotland and 18 acres of new demesne land recently held by his father, Thomas Gamyn, rendering annually 45s. at the customary times and all other services and customs owed therein. Fine: (*blank*).

3602 SLEPE (April) Rosa Payn, widow of Henry Payne: one cote recently held by Henry and once held by Thomas Grenehyll, for life, rendering annually in all things as did Henry. G.: two capons.

9 JOHN STOWE (1444-1445)

201r **3603** KNAPWELL (19 October: leet) Robert Somerby, parson of the church: one toft with one quarter of land recently held by John Reynald, for life, rendering annually in all things as did John. G.: two capons.

3604 KNAPWELL (same leet) Richard Holme and his wife, Johanna: one quarter of land recently held by John Smyth, for life, rendering annually in all things as did John. G.: two capons.

3605 KNAPWELL (same leet) Henry Preste and his wife, Johanna: one quarter of land recently held by John Smyth, for life, rendering annually in all things as did John. G.: 12d.

3606 KNAPWELL (same leet) John Smyth and his wife, Elena: one plot with building and one virgate of land recently held by Henry Preste, for life, rendering annually in all things as did Henry. Pledge for repairs and payments: Jacob Hopper. G.: 2s.

3607 KNAPWELL (same leet) Roger Denyell, naif of the lord, pays the fine for license for his son, Jacob, to live off the manor and practice the craft of tailoring, rendering 4d. and suit to leet annually. Pledge for payment of the fine: Jacob Hopper.

3608 ELSWORTH (same leet). Thomas Shaver and his wife, Margaret: half of one quarter of land recently held by John Swynford, for life, rendering annually in all things as did John. G.: one capon.

3609 ELSWORTH (November) John Howlot his wife, Isabella, and their son, William: one messuage with adjacent croft recently held by his father, John Howlot, and once held by Isabella Hennys, for life, rendering annually 6s. at the customary times and all other services and customs rendered by his father. G.: 12d.

3610 ELSWORTH (November) Thomas Howlot and his wife, Alicia: one messuage with croft recently held by John Chircheman, with six selions of land against Pytden granted quit to him in support of land recently held by his father for 4d., for life, rendering annually 4s. and all other services and customs rendered by John. G.: 8d.

3611 ELSWORTH (November) John Newman, son of Thomas Newman: one plot and three quarters of land recently held by Thomas, for life, rendering annually 19s. at the customary times, and all other services and customs rendered by Thomas. G.: 20d.

3612 BURWELL (21 October: leet) Agnes Plombe, daughter of Thomas Plumbe and naif of the lord by blood, pays two capons for license to marry whomever she wishes this time, and no more (in fine) because she is a servant of Master John Boys, *firmarius*.

3613 BURWELL (same leet) John Maste and his wife, Katerina: one tenement of eight acres *ad opus* recently held by John Jay and once held by Radulph Rower, for 40 years, rendering annually 5s.1d. at the customary times and all other services owed therein. G.: one capon.

3614 BURWELL (same leet) Thomas Prenteys, alias Alwyn: half of one tenement of 24 acres recently held by his father, and half of another tenement of 24 acres recently held by John Kyng, for 30 years, rendering annually 22s. at the customary times and all other services and customs owed therein. G.: 4s.

3615 BURWELL (same leet) Elizabeth Poket: surrender of one toft and one tenement of 20 acres of land recently held by her husband, William Poket, to the use of Thomas Notewyn and his wife, Matylda, for 40 years, rendering annually 21s. at the customary times and all other services and customs owed therein. G.: two capons.

201v **3616** BURWELL (same leet) Robert Wylkyn and his son, Thomas: one tenement of 15 acres of land recently held by Thomas Payman and once held by John Wyot, from Michaelmas for 20 years rendering annually in all things as did Thomas. G.: 5s., to be paid at the next Michaelmas.

3617 BURWELL John Rolf Shypman: half of one tenement of 24 acres with half of a croft at le Nesse recently held by Richard Goodynche, and half of one tenement of 24 acres of land and half of a croft at le Nesse recently hald by George Wylken, for 40 years, rendering annually 24s. at the customary times, and all other services and customs owed therein. G.: one capon.

3618 BURWELL John Calvysban Jr. and his wife, Agnes: one tenement of 15 acres of land recently held by John, son of Cecilia Wyot, and once held by Richard Chapman, for 30 years, rendering annually 23s. at the customary times, and all other services and customs owed therein. G.: two capons.

3619 BURWELL Hugo Sayer and his wife, Margaret: one vacant toft recently held by John Peyer, for 40 years, rendering annually in all things as did John. G.: excused.

3620 BURWELL (13 June: Autumn Court) Thomas Wylkyn and his wife, Matylda: one tenement of 15 acres of land once held by John Rolf and recently held by John Calvysbane, for 30 years, rendering annually in all things as did John. G.: one capon.

3621 BURWELL Robert Wylkyn and his son, John: one messuage with 24 acres of land and appurtenances once held by Thomas Bosome, chaplain, and recently held by Robert himself, for 40 years, rendering annually 26s. and all other services and customs owed therein. G.: 12d., two capons.

3622 SHILLINGTON (25 October: leet) Gilbert of the Hyll, naif of the lord by blood, pays 20d. for license to marry Justiniana, his daughter, to William Pate of Lilley, this time.

3623 SHILLINGTON (same leet) Richard Bradifan: surrender of one built up messuage on the demesne land called Stokynglond, with one cotland and four acres of demesne land in Stokkyng once held by Nicholas of the Abbey, to the use of John Oliver and his wife, Johanna, for life, rendering annually 9s.10d. in equal portions at the customary times, and all other services and customs rendered by Richard. G.: four capons. Heriot: nothing, because he is extremely burdened with rent, as they say.

3624 SHILLINGTON (20 November: at Ramsey) Matthew Chambre pays 12d. and two capons for license to marry Alicia, daughter of John West of Briggende and naif of the lord by blood, to John Whytbred, this time.

3625 SHILLINGTON (1 June: at Ramsey) Robert Gayton pays two capons for license to move one house from the tenement once held by John Barnard in Wodemanende and rebuild it on his own property within one year.

3626 SHILLINGTON (1 June) William Waryn Jr.: surrender of one toft and half of one virgate once held by Robert Pachet, to the use of Robert Gayton, for life, rendering annually in all things as did William G.: 2s.6d. Heriot of Alicia Wynter: one cow.

3627 SHILLINGTON (1 June) Robert Gayton: one semi-virgate of land called Barnard's once held by William Atte Brygge and recently held by John Wenyngham Jr., for life, rendering annually in all things as did John. G.: 2s.6d.

202r **3628** PEGSDON (same leet) Robert Shepperd, son and heir of John Shepperd, and his wife, Alicia: one messuage built up with one house and a half-virgate of land called Grayes and one vacant toft called Ponteris recently held by his father, for life, rendering annually in all things as did his father. G.: 40d., paid through John Cheker. Heriot: one horse, as in the leet.

3629 BARTON (25 January: General Court)[43] Thomas Wodward and his heirs: the built up capital messuage of the forland pertaining to the helf-virgate held by John Hexston and recently held by Alicia Lord, rendering annually in all things as did Alicia. G.: 2s. and one capon. Heriot: one cotland valued at 2s.

3630 BARTON (same court)[44] John, son of John Felmesham: one built up croftland recently held by Isabella Felmesham, for life, rendering annually 19d. at the customary times, and all other services and customs rendered by Isabella. Pledges for repairs during the minority of John: Richard Priour and John Turnour. G.: 2s.

---

[43] See PRO 179/64 for the death of Alicia Lord.
[44] Ibid. The death of John Sr. is recorded. John Jr. is reported to be 11 years old.

3631 BARTON (same court) Matylda, widow of Edmund Chylde: surrender of one croftland recently held by Edmund, to the use of Richard Chyld, for life, rendering annually 23d. at the customary times, and all other services and customs owed therein. G.: 40d.

3632 BARTON (same court)[45] William Burrych, son and heir of Henry Burrych: one virgate of land and a forland with one croft in Brokende and another croft called Stonle Croft recently held by Henry and once held by Richard Stonle, for life, rendering annually 18s.8d. at the customary times, and all other services and customs rendered by Henry. G.: 6s.8d. Heriot: one ox.

3633 BARTON (same court) William Burrych: one cote recently held by his father, Henry Burrych, with certain acres of demesne land recently held by the same Henry, for life, rendering annually 12d. for the cote and 8s. for the demesne land at the customary times, and all other services and customs owed therein. G.: 3s.4d.

3634 BARTON (same court) John Burnard of Barton, son of Edmund Burnard and naif of the lord by blood, pays the fine for license to live off the manor for as long as it pleases the lord, rendering to the lord annually 12d. and suit to the general court. Pledge for faithfully observing the above: Edmund Sampson of Barton.

3635 BARTON (same court) John Burnard, naif of the lord by blood: surrender through the hands of Matthew Chambre, bailiff of Shillington, of one cotmanland with appurtenances once held by his father, Edmund Burnard, to the use of Edmund Sampson, for life, rendering annually in all things as did John, with the obligation to repair and maintain all the buildings on the property at his own expense. G. and heriot: 13s.4d.

3636 CRANFIELD (28 October: leet) William Alyn, naif of the lord: one messuage and a half-virgate of land recently held by Thomas Catlyn, bailiff, and once held by Thomas Fythyon, for life, rendering annually in all things as did Thomas. G.: 8s.

3637 CRANFIELD[46] Thomas Terry: surrender of one tenement and 10 acres of land from the tenement of Rynges, previously rendering 12s., and one cote once held by William Swatre, to the use of William Wodhyll, for life, rendering annually 11s.3d. at the customary times, which property previously rendered 13s.3d. Further, he will render all other services and customs owed therein. G.: 4s. Heriot: determined in the leet.

3638 CRANFIELD (same leet)[47] Thomas Vaus: one messuage and a half-virgate of land recently held by Thomas Catelyn, called Hethewyses, for life, rendering annually in all things as did Thomas. G.: 5s.

202v   **3639** CRANFIELD (same leet) William Baker: surrender of one croft pertaining to the quarter of land he now holds and once held by Thomas Atterode, to the use of Thomas Eyr, for life, rendering annually 12d. at the customary times. G.: 12d.

3640 CRANFIELD (June) William Goodwyn, son and heir of John Goodwyn: surrender of one plot with a half-virgate of land recently held by his father, to the use of Hugo Goodwyn and his heirs, rendering annually in all things as did William, with the provision that Agnes, widow of John, have for her dower dwelling and easement in the properties for life. G.: 6s.8d.

3641 HEMINGFORD ABBOTS (31 October: leet) Robert Marschall: surrender of one messuage and one virgate of land once held by his father, to the use of Robert Lyncolne and his wife, Johanna, for life. Further, easement in one *camera* outside the northern part of the garden, a curtilage, water, free entry and exit, a half-acre of land with

---

[45] Ibid., for the death of Henry Burrych.
[46] Ibid. Thomas Terry's death is recorded. Apparently Thomas died soon after this transaction. William Wodehue pays the heriot of 16d.
[47] Ibid., for the death of Thomas Catelyn.

its crops and use of the property for poultry is reserved to Robert and his wife, Mariota, with Robert obligated to find one roofer in any year for two days' work in roofing the said *camera*. G.: 2s.

3642 HEMINGFORD ABBOTS (same leet) Thomas Conwyne: a half-virgate of land recently held by John Est, for life, rendering annually 6s.2d. and all other services and customs rendered by John. G.: 20d., one capon.

3643 HEMINGFORD ABBOTS (same leet) John Brygges Jr.: one messuage and two virgates of land recently held by his father, William Brygges, for life, rendering annually in all things as did William. G.: 12d., one capon.

3644 HEMINGFORD ABBOTS (same leet) John Tayllour: one messuage and a half-virgate of land recently held by John Forest for life, rendering annually in all things as did John. G.: two capons.

3645 HEMINGFORD ABBOTS (same leet) John Feld Jr. and his wife, Margaret: one messuage and one virgate of land recently held by John Lyncoln and once held by Edmund Mariotte, for life, rendering annually 11s.4d. at the customary times, and all other services and customs rendered by John. G.: 12d., two capons.

3646 HEMINGFORD ABBOTS John Wellys and his wife, Johanna: one cote built up with three houses once held by Adam Tydde, for life, rendering annually 40d. at the customary times, and all other services and customs owed therein, with the obligation to repair and maintain the property at their own expense. G.: 2s.8d.

3647 HEMINGFORD ABBOTS (May) Thomas Angewyn and his wife, Johanna: one toft and one virgate of land one held by Nicholas Bonde and afterwards held by William Herde and recently held by Adam Alcok, because of his good service, rendering annually 6s. at the customary times, which property previously rendered 12s.4d. Further, they will render all other services and customs rendered by Adam. G.: two capons, paid to the seneschal.

3648 HEMINGFORD ABBOTS Robert Brygge: surrender of two virgates and one messuage once held by John Marschall, to the use of John Clerke, his wife, Isabella, and their son, John, for life, rendering annually in all things as did Robert, with the obligation to repair and maintain all the buildings on the messuage, timber for beams for repairing the grange being supplied by the lord. Further, Ribert Brygge will repair a kiln, and John will receive all the fallow land. G.: two capons.

203r

3649 HEMINGFORD ABBOTS (July) Walter Murrok, alias Ingill: surrender of one messuage and two virgates of land once held by William Ingill, to the use of his son, Robert Murrok and his wife, Johanna, for life, rendering annually in all things as did Walter, with a half-acre in Thyk Whatelond and easement in the mill reserved to Walter and his wife, Margeria, for life. G.: six capons.

3650 WARBOYS (1 November: leet) Robert Smyth, son of Roger Smyth: surrender of one half-virgate of land recently held by Henry Norburgh, to the use of John Chyple Thakker and his wife, Elena, for life, rendering annually 5s. at the customary times, and all other services and customs rendered by Robert. G.: three capons.

3651 WARBOYS (June) Richard Bennesson: surrender of one messuage and one virgate of land recently *ad opus* to the use of John Laurence of Stanton, in *arentatio* for life, rendering annually 14s. for the land and 2s. for ploughing works. G.: four capons.

3652 HOUGHTON (8 November: leet) Simon Bryson, chaplain: one messuage built up with one house and one virgate of land recently held by Stephen Marchall for 14s., for 10 years, rendering annually 10s. and all other services and customs owed therein, with the obligation to repair and maintain the house at his own expense, to be returned at the end of his term in good condition and repair. G.: excused, because the land is fallow.

3653 HOUGHTON (same leet) Roger Prestwode, servant of the parson, and his wife, Margaret: one plot with one house recently held by Matylda Carter and once held by Alicia Denton, for life, rendering annually 3s.4d. at the customary times, and all other services and customs rendered by Matylda. G.: two capons.

3654 HOUGHTON Thomas Elyot Jr. and his wife: a quarter of land recently held by Thomas Atkyn, for life, rendering annually 4s. at the customary times and all other services and customs rendered by Thomas. G.: 12d.

3655 HOUGHTON John Hyll of Hartford: one messuage built up with one house and one virgate of land recently held by John Beth and called Pertenaly, for life, rendering annually in all things as did John with the obligation to repair and maintain the property at his own expense, for which he receives an allowance of 5s. of this year's rent and timber for beams and posts from the lord. G.: three capons.

3656 HOUGHTON (1 November) William Wyth, his wife, Juliana, and their son, Robert: one messuage and a half-virgate of land recently held by Simon Thoday and once held by Thomas Gryme, and one toft with a half-virgate of land recently held by Thomas Forster and once held by Thomas Elyot, for life, rendering annually 8s. at the customary times, beginning at the feast of St. Andrew after two years, which property previously rendered 10s. Further, they will rebuild one *insathous* on the tenement once held by Thomas Miller within two years, and also rebuild one grange and one kiln at their own expense, timber for beams and posts being supplied by the lord, with its transport supplied by William. Also: three selions of land at Sawtreweye once held by John Wyth, for life, rendering annually 8d. at the customary times. G.: one capon.

203v **3657** HOUGHTON (November) John Derysson and his wife, Agnes: one toft and a half-virgate of land once held by William Brampton and recently held by John Gascoyn, for life, rendering annually 8s. at the customary times, and all other services and customs rendered by John. G.: 2s.

3658 HOUGHTON (July) William Bocher, alias Rede, and his wife, Johanna: one messuage and a half-virgate of land recently held by John Myller and once held by Thomas Eyr, for life, rendering annually in all things as did John. G.: 12d.

3659 HOUGHTON Robert Smyth: surrender of one virgate of land recently held by Thomas Forester, to the use of William AtteKyn and his wife, Margaret, in *arentatio* for life, rendering annually in all things as did Thomas. G.: (*blank*).

3660 HOUGHTON William Attekyn: surrender of a half-virgate of land recently held by Robert Roger, to the use of Robert Smyth and his wife, Johanna, for life, rendering annually in all things as did William. G.: two capons.

3661 HOUGHTON Robert Smyth: surrender of one virgate of land recently held by Thomas Crane, to the use of Simon Dryson, chaplain, from Michaelmas for life, rendering annually in all things as did Thomas. G.: one capon.

3662 HOUGHTON (June) William Franke and his son, John: one messuage and two cotlands once held by Robert Upton and recently held by the same William Franke and surrendered back by him to the lord, in *arentatio* for life, rendering annually in all things as he did previously, with the obligation to build one *camera* as long and wide as another *camera* recently torn down there, within two years, and to repair and maintain all other buildings on the property under penalty of loss. G.: three capons.

3663 RIPTON William Payn and his wife, Katerina: one messuage and two semi-virgates of land once held by John Smyth and recently held by Thomas Joye, for life, rendering annually 13s.4d. at the customary times, and all other services and customs rendered by Thomas. G.: 20d.

3664 RIPTON John Lyndeseye and his wife, Agnes: one cote once held by John Webster and recently held by Johanna Sewster, for life, rendering annually 2s.6d. at the customary times, and all other services and customs rendered by Johanna. G.: one capon.

3665 R<small>IPTON</small> William Mortimer and his wife, Agnes: one messuage and a half-virgate of land, three acres of land at Cattesheg, and other parcels recently held by John Maggesson and once held by Adam Clerke, for life, rendering annually 8s. at the customary times, which property previously rendered 10s. Further, they will render all other services and customs rendered by John. G.: two capons.

3666 R<small>IPTON</small> Note that Thomas Joye rebuilt one bake house 30 feet long and 16 feet wide, and one stable 22 feet long and 13 feet wide on his tenement, with timber supplied by the lord, and for this the lord allowed the rent of this year, except for 8s. to William Lyndeseye, as found in the account roll of John Frer. and he will receive nothing else from the lord.

3667 R<small>IPTON</small> Matilda, widow of Robert Jurdon: surrender of one messuage with three houses and one quarter of land and four selions of land at Holbrook recently held by Robert, to the use of William Woolle, and his wife, Margaret, for life, rendering annually in all things as did Matilda, with the obligation to repair and maintain the property at their own expense. G.: 2s., two capons.

204r **3668** A<small>BBOTS</small> R<small>IPTON</small> Note that John Weston will render to the lord for the lands and tenements recently held by his father, with a half-virgate of land recently held by Nevys and more recently held by Richard Smyth, the sum of 32s. annually, namely: 27s.8d. for the lands of his father, and 5s. for the half-virgate. Note that the property previously rendered 32s.8d.

3669 A<small>BBOTS</small> R<small>IPTON</small> (May) William Cole and his son, Thomas: one messuage and three semi-virgates of land recently held by William Cabe and once held by Richard Grene, for life, rendering annually in all things as did William, with the obligation to repair and maintain all the buildings and the kiln in carpentry, ramming, splinting and plastering, the lord granting an allowance of next year's rent and timber, splints and two carts of straw. G.: four capons.

3670 A<small>BBOTS</small> R<small>IPTON</small> (June) William Fuller: surrender of one messuage and one semi-virgate of land recently held by John AtteChirche, to the use of William Lyndesey, and his wife, Juliana, for life, rendering annually 8s. and all other services and customs rendered by William. Further, they will rebuild an *insathous* with two rooms of eight binding-posts within one year at their own expense, the lord supplying timber, an allowance of next year's rent, and 23s.4d. from the rents of the time of John Payn, rent collector. G.: four capons.

3671 A<small>BBOTS</small> R<small>IPTON</small> (June) John Lyndeseye and his wife, Agnes: one cotland with two houses in *arentatio* with four butts of land in a croft and two butts in le Londe recently held by John Hawlond, for life, rendering annually 4s. at the customary times and all other services and customs rendered by John, with the obligation to repair and maintain the property at their own expense. G.: three capons.

3672 A<small>BBOTS</small> R<small>IPTON</small> (20 May) Radulph Osberne, his wife, Emma, and their heirs: one messuage with appurtenances near the bridge against the lane leading to Stukeley recently held by Johanna Forester and once held by William Marham, rendering annually in all things as did Johanna. G.: two capons.

3673 H<small>OLYWELL</small> (11 November: leet) Thomas Aungewyn of Hemingford pays 6d. for license to have John Sande, son of John Sande and naif of the lord, in his service for three years, after which term John will be returned to this manor.

3674 H<small>OLYWELL</small> John Elyot Carpenter, naif of the lord, and his wife, Alicia: one messuage, one virgate, new demesne land, one selion of meadow in Saldemade and one acre, a half-rod and a quarter rod of land at Benehill recently held by John Wryght and once held by Nicholas Godfrey, for life, rendering annually in all things as did John, with the obligation to repair and maintain the property. G.: two geese, two capons.

3675 BROUGHTON Richard Cabe: surrender of one messuage and one and a half-virgates of land with three lots of Dammyslond, to the use of his son, Thomas Cabe, and his wife, Johanna, for life, rendering annually 16s.4d. at the customary times, and all other services and customs rendered by Richard. G.: three capons.

3676 WISTOW William Cabe and his wife, Alicia: one cotland and one plot with appurtenant land recently held by Robert Rede and one toft with appurtenances recently held by Stephen Aylmer, and one quarter of land recently held by Thomas Fraunce, for life, rendering annually 8s. for the cotland and plot, 5s. for the quarter, and 5s. for the toft, which property previously rendered 7s.6d. Further, they will render all other services and customs owed therein. G.: 40d., three capons.

204v **3677** WISTOW (20 March) John Owty, son of Thomas Owty and naif of the lord by blood, pays the fine for license to live off the manor for as long as it pleases the lord, remaining a naif as before, and rendering 6d. annually to the rent collector of Wistow at Michaelmas. Pledge for payment: John Collan.

3678 WISTOW (April) Margaret Whyte: surrender of one messuage with adjacent land recently held by John Whyght, to the use of William Nottyng, for life, rendering annually in all things as did Margaret, with the obligation to repair and maintain the property at his own expense. Further, he will pay the rent for this year, and pay Margaret 12d. for her expense in cultivating the land. G.: two capons.

3679 LITTLE STUKELEY (18 February: court) John Skynner: surrender, in the presence of the seneschal of Ramsey, of a half-virgate of land from the land pertaining to the *camera* of the abbot once held by Thomas Gosse, to the use of Richard Denton, for life, rendering annually in all things as did John. G.: 16d., to be paid before Easter.

3680 ELLINGTON (May) John Swasethe and William Cotyngham: one tenement with four cotes and appurtenances recently held by Richard Hykkesson, naif of the lord, and seized by the lord for non-payment of rent and lack of repairs, for life, rendering annually in all things as did Richard, with the provision that Richard will hold two cotes against the rectory, for rents, for life. Further, John will rebuild one grange of eight binding-posts and one bake house within two years at his own expense, with the lord supplying large timber, beams, side pieces, principal posts, and 20 posts, and an allowance of the first year's rents. G.: two capons.

3681 ELLINGTON (20 July: court) Radulph Stanweye Foster: one quarter of land recently held by William Myller, for life, rendering annually in all things as did William. G.: two capons.

3682 ELLINGTON (same court) John Faukes: one toft in Sibthorp with one quarter of land recently held by John Tayllor, for life, rendering annually in all things as did John. G.: two capons.

3683 ELLINGTON (same court) Thomas Isbell: one tenement and one toft with five quarters of land recently held by John Thernyng, for life, rendering annually in all things as did John. G.: 2s.

3684 ELLINGTON (same court) Thomas Beveryche: one messuage and one quarter of land recently held by George Carter, for life, rendering annually in all things as did George. G.: 12d.

3685 ELLINGTON (same court) Thomas Couper: one messuage and one quarter of land recently held by John Skynner, for life, rendering annually in all things as did John. G.: 12d.

205r **3686** WOODHURST (August) John Whyght: one messuage built up with one bake

house and a half-virgate of land recently held by John Vikorye and once held by
Thomas Porter, from Michaelmas for life, rendering annually 6s.8d. at the customary
times, which property previously rendered 8s. Further, he will repair and maintain the
bake house at his own expense, with timber and three cart loads of thorns supplied by
the lord this first time. G.: one capon.

3687 CHATTERIS (24 September: court) Thomas Smyth: half of one tenement of
eight acres of land recently held by John Mathew atte Hythe and once held by William
Wythede, for life, rendering annually in all things as did John. G.: two capons.

3688 CHATTERIS (same court) William Bonyyard: two acres of land in Medmen, one
acre of land in Stokkyng, a half-acre of land in Muslak, one acre at Longgrave once
held by John Fithion Sr., and a half-acre of land in Elmen recently held by John
Hunte, for life, rendering annually 2s.6d. at the customary times, and all other services
and customs rendered by John. G.: two capons.

3689 CHATTERIS (same court) William Hunte: half of one tenement of eight acres of
land, one cotland with meadow in Crowlode, fishpond in Stokkyng, a half-acre in
Medmen, and one messuage once held by Reginald Peryn, and recently held by
Thomas Halle, for life, rendering annually 11s.4d.ob. at the customary times, and all
other services and customs rendered by Thomas, with easement in one *camera* in
which she lives and one Lane in the tenement with free entry and exit, and for a place
to keep hay, reserved to Alicia Peyte for life. G.: 2s.6d.

10 JOHN STOWE (1445-1446)

205v   **3690** ELSWORTH John Swynford and his wife, Johanna: one quarter of land recently
held by John Wryght and once held by John Broke for life, rendering annually in all
things as did John. G.: 12d.

3691 ELSWORTH (10 October: leet) William Howlet and his son, Thomas: one croft
at Gralee and one quarter of land at Matthes recently held by Richard Swynford, and
10 selions of land from the vacant land towards Hilton, for life, rendering annually 5s.
and all other services and customs rendered by Richard, with the obligation to make
ditches around the croft at their own expense within two years. G.: 12d., two capons.

3692 ELSWORTH (October) John Bangyll and his wife, Margaret: one messuage and
a half-virgate of land built up with one kiln recently held by William Burbage, for life,
rendering annually 15s. at the customary times, and all other services and customs
owed therein, with the obligation to enlarge the kiln by 20 feet at their own expense,
and maintain it in good condition thereafter. G.: 2s., two capons.

3693 ELSWORTH Thomas Howesson: surrender of one messuage and one virgate of
land with appurtenances once held by John Aleyn, to the use of Richard Ravene and
his wife, Isabella, for life, rendering annually in all things as did Thomas, with the
obligation to rebuild one kiln of binding-posts at their own expense, large timber being
supplied by the lord. G.: 2s.

3694 ELSWORTH Richard Ravene: surrender of one tenement and a half-virgate of
land once held by Richard Bene, to the use of John Lucas, and his wife, Margaret, for
life, rendering annually in all things as did Richard. G.: 2s.

3695 ELSWORTH (19 October: court) John Hardyng Jr.: a half-virgate of land recently held by John Hardyng Sr., for life, rendering annually 12s. at the customary times,
and all other services and customs rendered by John Sr. G.: 12d. And he swears fealty.

3696 THERFIELD (14 October: leet) William Stoughton and his heirs: a half-virgate
of land recently held by William Caldewell, rendering annually 10s. at the customary
times, and all other services and customs owed therein. G.: two capons.

3697 THERFIELD (same leet) William Somerswayn and his assigns: one messuage built up with three houses, one and a half cotlands containing 15 acres of land recently held by Thomas Frere, one toft with one and a half cotlands containing 15 acres of land once held by Robert Stevens, five acres of new demesne land recently held by Thomas Frere for 26s.6d., with one meadow called Wattesmede, previously rendering 13s.4d., for life, rendering annually 26s.1d. at the customary times, and all other services and customs owed therein, with the obligation to repair and maintain the property at his own expense, for which he receives an allowance of this year's and next year's rents. G.: three capons.

3698 THERFIELD (January) William Peytewyn of Newsell, his wife, Margaret, and their heirs: one messuage and one virgate of land with five acres of demesne land recently held by John Watte and once held by Robert Sparver, rendering 11s. the first year and 22s. each year thereafter, at the customary times, and all other services and customs owed therein, with the obligation to repair and maintain the property. G.: two capons.

206r

3699 THERFIELD (1 January) John Gurneye, alias Evadet, his wife, Johanna, and their heirs: one plot well built up and one virgate of land, 18 acres of land, new demesne land, one meadow called Huntwell Mede and one rod of land in Capulcroft recently held by John Colyn, with half of one virgate of land recently held by Robert Jankyn, rendering annually 47s.2d.ob. at the customary times, and all other services and customs owed therein. G.: two capons. And they swear fealty.

3700 THERFIELD (1 January) John Sperver Jr.: surrender of one plot well built up and one virgate of land with one croft called Betonwyke and three acres of land recently held by John Wenham Jr. and once held by Nicholas Adam, to the use of John Somersham of Newsell and his wife, Elena, and their heirs, rendering annually 23s.4d. at the customary times, and all other services and customs owed therein. G.: four capons. And they swear fealty.

3701 SHILLINGTON (16 October: leet) John Togood: surrender of one cote with appurtenances in Bridge End recently held by John Hokkele and once held by Dryver, to the use of Adam Sparwe, for life, rendering annually 2s.1d.ob. and all other services and customs rendered by John. Further, he will repair and maintain the property, and dwell therein. G.: 12d., two capons. Heriot: nothing, because John Togood has no animals.

3702 SHILLINGTON (same leet) William Whytbred: surrender of one messuage built up with three houses and one semi-virgate with other appurtenances recently held by Robert Waleys, to the use of Richard Leefchyld, for life, rendering annually 12s. at the customary times, and all other services and customs owed therein. G. and heriot: 40d.

3703 SHILLINGTON (same leet) William Waryn: one messuage and one semi-virgate of land recently held by Alicia Wareyn and once held by AtteWelle, for life, rendering annually 8s.8d. at the customary times, and all other services and customs owed therein. G.: 40d. Heriot: one cow.

3704 SHILLINGTON Matthew Chambir: license to move one house from the tenement of John Wyseman. Fine: 6s.8d.

3705 SHILLINGTON (November) John Hantoo: surrender of one messuage and one semi-virgate of land once held by Arnold Fawkener, to the use of John Aylmar, naif of the lord, and his son, Thomas, for life, rendering annually 10s. at the customary times, with the obligation to repair one grange on the property that John Hantoo held *per copiam* before the feast of the Nativity of John the Baptist, and to maintain and repair all other buildings on the property at his own expense. G. and heriot: 2s.

3706 SHILLINGTON (November) John Aylmar: surrender of one cotland built up with two houses in Green End, with two acres of land at Assyngwell recently held by John Berfote, to the use of Nicholas Curlyng and his wife, Alicia, for life, rendering annually 4s.10d.ob. at the customary times, and all other services and customs owed therein, with the obligation to repair and maintain the property at their own expense. G. and heriot: 2s.

3707 SHILLINGTON (November) William Grene: surrender of five acres of demesne land in le Croft, to the use of Robert Geyton, for life, rendering annually 2s.8d. at the customary times, and all other services and customs rendered by William. G.: 2s.

206v

3708 SHILLINGTON (November) William Grene: surrender of four acres of demsne land at Newmanland, to the use of Thomas Laurence, for life, rendering annually 2s. at the customary times and all other services and customs rendered by William; G.: 12d.

3709 SHILLINGTON (November) William Grene, son of John Grene of Wodemanende, naif of the lord: surrender of one toft and half of one virgate recently held by his father and once held by Richard Pachet, the other half of which is held by William Waryn, to the use of Thomas Stonle Jr;, for life, rendering annually 8s.8d. and all other services and customs rendered by William. G. and heriot: 3s.4d.

3710 BARTON (17 October: General Court) Jacob Chyld: surrender of one ruined messuage and one virgate of land with forland, to the use of Thomas Colman, for life, rendering annually 18s.9d. at the customary times, and all other services and customs owed therein, with the obligation to build one barn and one bake house on the messuage within one year, and a new hall within two years, at his own expense, and maintain them thereafter, the lord granting him an allowance of 33s.4d. from his *gersuma* and heriot of 40s. If he should default in these obligations, he shall lose the property and repay the lord 40s. at the end of three years. Pledges: Richard Prior and William Burryche.

3711 BARTON (same court). John Broun: surrender of one messuage and one virgate of land with forland, to the use of John Hyll, for life, rendering annually 19s.6d. at the customary times, and all other services and customs rendered by John. G. and heriot: 13s.4d., to be paid at Easter and the next General Court.

3712 BARTON (same court) John Tayllor: surrender of one cote built up with two houses and two acres of demesne land in Bonstall once held by Agnes Arlyche, to the use of Walter Revysson Sr., for life, rendering annually 5s. at the customary times and all other services and customs owed therein, with the obligation to repair and maintain the houses. G. and heriot: 20d.

3713 BARTON (same court) Walter Revysson Sr.: surrender of one messuage well built up and one virgate with forland, to the use of Richard Chylde, for life, rendering annually 18s.4d. at the customary times, and all other services and customs owed therein. G. and heriot: 10s., two capons, and 12 young doves.

3714 BARTON (same court) John Mattewe, alias Colman, naif of the lord by blood, pays 2s. for license to marry Alicia, his daughter, to Thomas Welle of Offley in the county of Hertfordshire, this time. Pledge: the bailiff.

3715 BARTON (same court) Richard Prior, bailiff, pays 8d. for license for Isabella, daughter of Thomas Stonle of Barton, naif of the lord by blood, to marry Thomas Wodward, this time. And this because she is a servant of the bailiff.

3716 CRANFIELD (18 October: leet) Agnes, widow of Henry Cooke, and her son, Thomas: surrender of one cote and three acres of demesne land recently held by Henry, to the use of Thomas Grene, for life, rendering annually 3s.1d. at the customary times, and all other services and customs owed therein. G.: 40d. Heriot: nothing, because they have nothing.

207r

3717 CRANFIELD (same leet) Roger Dowe: surrender of one cote built up with two houses recently held by Margaret Catelyn, to the use of Robert Baylly, for life, rendering annually 13d. and all other services and customs owed therein. G.: 2s. Heriot: nothing, because he has nothing.

3718 CRANFIELD (same leet) John Terry, son of William Terry: six acres of demesne land at Purydole, three acres of demesne land at Litillhanger, two acres of demesne land at Staliprace and three acres of demesne land at Burisowthewode and one cote in Estende, previously held by Roger Browse and his wife, Margaret, and seized by the lord after their deaths because of the absence of anyone to pay the new heriot, for life, rendering annually 10s.11d. at the customary times, and all other services and customs owed therein. G.: six capons.

3719 CRANFIELD (same leet) Thomas Davy, husband of Elizabeth, daughter of John Skynner, deceased: one messuage and a half-virgate of land recently held by John Skynner, to be held by right of his wife for life, rendering annually 9s.2d. at the customary times and all other services and customs rendered by John. G.: (*blank*). Heriot: one cow worth (*blank*).

3720 HOUGHTON (October) Margaret Andrewe, daughter of Thomas Andrewe and naif of the lord by blood, pays 12d. for license to marry John Beth, freeman and servant of the rector, this time.

3721 HOUGHTON (November) John Beth: surrender of one toft and a half-virgate of land once held by Gilbert Bytherne, to the use of John Upton and his wife, Margaret, for life, rendering annually 6s. et the customary times, and all other services and customs rendered by John. G.: three capons.

3722 HOUGHTON (December) John Carter: surrender of one messuage and two cotlands recently held by Richard Carter *ad opera* and one toft with a half-virgate of land in *arentatio* once held by William Fuller, to the use of William Prykke, and his wife, Margaret, for life, rendering annually in all things as did John. G.: 2s., two capons.

3723 HOUGHTON John Fuller and his wife, Agnes: half of the meadow called Honymede, one acre of meadow next to Damdiche and one parcel of meadow next to Dokkydole called Gore and recently held by Richard Carter, for life, rendering annually 6s. at the customary times, which property previously rendered 7s. Further, they will render all other services and customs rendered by Richard. G.: excused by the bailiff.

3724 HOUGHTON (10 April) Johanna Newman, widow of John Newman, pays the fine for license for her daughter Agnes, naif of the lord by blood, to live off the manor with her for as long as it pleases the lord, rendering to the lord annually two capons in the name of chevage at the vigil of All Saints. Pledge for payment of fine: John Fuller of Houghton.

3725 HOUGHTON (April) John Bethe: surrender of one messuage (i.e. the capital messuage) with half of the land once held by Gilbert de Houghton to the use of John Brampton and his wife, Johanna, for life, rendering annually 10s. at the customary times, which property previously rendered 14s. Further, they will render all other services and customs owed therein. G.: three capons.

207v **3726** HOUGHTON (April) Johanna Newman: surrender of one tenement with cotland and one croft recently held by her husband, John Newman, to the use of Roger Preestwode, and his wife, Margaret, *ad opus*, rendering annually in all things as did Johanna. G.: two capons.

3727 HOUGHTON (April) Philip Thorle: surrender of one built up croft near the mill recently held by William Pynder and one croft once held by William Fuller, to the use of John Miller and his wife, Sarra, for life, rendering annually in all things as did Philip. G.: 20d.

3728 HOUGHTON Philip Goldsmyth and his wife, Cristina: one built up cotland *ad opus* recently held by John Newman and Richard Sovereyn, for life, rendering annually in all things as did John and Richard. G.: two capons.

3729 HOUGHTON (23 June) Anna, daughter of John Gottes, Sutor, alias Belman, son of Thomas Gottys, recently of St. Ives, and who is a servant of Radulph Kerner of Ramsey, naif of the lord by blood, pays three capons for license to marry William Botolf of Ramsey, Sissor. Pledge for payment: John Wyndyll and John Fen. And the fine is so small because of the urging of Radulph Kerner, John Wyndyll and John Fen of Ramsey.

3730 HEMINGFORD ABBOTS (22 October: leet) John Grace Sr.: one cote recently held by John Sutton Sr., for life, rendering annually 18d. at the customary times, and all other services and customs owed therein. G.: 2s.6d.

3731 HEMINGFORD ABBOTS John Almer Jr.: one built up croft once held by Elyas Pope and recently held by Thomas Almer, for life, rendering annually 12d. at the customary times, and all other services and customs rendered by Thomas. G.: four capons.

3732 HEMINGFORD ABBOTS (same leet) Simon Chapman: surrender of one messuage and a half-virgate of land recently held by John Pope and one cote with croft once held by Henry Gamelyn, to the use of John Grounde, for life, rendering annually 7s.2d. at the customary times, and all other services and customs owed therein. G.: 6s.8d.

3733 HEMINGFORD ABBOTS (same leet) Robert Kestvyn, alias Glover: property (*unnamed*) recently held by Thomas Couper and once held by Richard Myller, for life, rendering annually 8d. at the customary times, which property previously rendered 12d. Further, he will render all other services and customs owed therein. G.: one capon.

3734 HEMINGFORD ABBOTS (same leet) John Welles: surrender of one virgate of land without a messuage once held by Thomas Brendhous, to the use of John Grounde, for life, rendering annually 12s.4d. at the customary times, and all other services and customs owed therein. G.: 12d.

208r **3735** HEMINGFORD ABBOTS (October) John Birt and his wife, Cristina: one quarter of land once held by Thomas Carter and recently held by John Whyn for 3s.4d., and one quarter of land with a croft pertaining to the quarter above once held by William Mason and recently held by John Upton for 3s.4d., for life, rendering annually 5s. at the customary times, and all other services and customs owed therein. G.: one capon.

3736 HEMINGFORD ABBOTS (October) Agnes Trappe and her son, William: one half-virgate of land once held by John Brigge and recently held by John Ibot for 5s.8d., for life, rendering annually 4s., with payments beginning at Michaelmas. G.: two capons.

3737 HEMINGFORD ABBOTS (October) John Portos: one messuage recently rebuilt at the abbot's expense and one virgate of land once held by John Osmonde and recently held by Robert Tayllor, for life, rendering annually 8s. at the customary times, beginning at Michaelmas, and which property previously rendered 12s.4d. G.: four capons.

3738 RIPTON (29 October: leet) Thomas Scot and his wife, Johanna: one toft and half of one quarter of land called Lanecroft recently held by John Howlet, for life, rendering annually in all things as did John. G.: one capon.

3739 RIPTON (same leet) Agnes, widow of John Howlet: surrender of one messuage and one quarter of land recently held by John Howlet, to the use of John Wodecoke and his wife, Johanna, for life, rendering annually in all things as did Agnes, with one *camera* in a messuage next to that of Robert Hendesson, easement in another *camera* for keeping straw and cows, and easement in a garden and the well for water, reserved to Agnes for life, in return for which she will pay John 12d. annually. Further, John will maintain all the buildings on the property and repair them at his own expense. G.: two capons.

3740 WISTOW (24 October) (at Ramsey) Margaret, widow of John Whyte and daughter of Robert AtteGate, naif of the lord by blood, pays six capons for license to marry Nicholas Morell of Godmanchester, this time.

3741 WISTOW John AtteGate Jr., son of Robert AtteGate, naif of the lord: surrender of one messuage and a half-virgate of land *ad opus* recently held by John Randolf, to the use of John Asplond of Little Raveley, for life, rendering annually 5s. for rent and 4s. for works, for as long as it pleases the lord, and suit to court and leet, and all other services and customs owed therein, with that reserved to the lord which was renewed in the Rental for December, 10 John Stowe and 23 Henry VI. Further, he will repair and maintain the property at his own expense. G.: 6s.8d.

3742 WARBOYS (November) Emma, widow of Robert Ravyn: surrender, through the hands of John Caton, bailiff, of one quarter of land in Caldecote once held by Richard Berenger, to the use of John AtteWode and his wife, Agnes, for life. Also: one messuage called Mondayland recently held by Henry Norburgh, for life, rendering annually 2s.6d. for the quarter and 4s. for the messuage, at the customary times, and all other services and customs owed therein. G.: three capons.

3743 WARBOYS (December) Robert, son of Roger Smyth, alias Hunte, pays 20d. for license to marry Juliana, daughter of Thomas Benette, alias Herd, naif of the lord by blood, this time.

3744 WARBOYS (December) Robert Asshwell pays 12d. and two capons for license to marry Margaret, daughter of Robert Ravele, widow of William Olyver, naif of the lord by blood, this time.

3745 WARBOYS (December) Thomas Buntyng: surrender of a half-virgate of land in Caldecote once held by John Hygh Miller, to the use of Robert Smyth, alias Hunte and his wife, Juliana, for life, rendering annually in all things as did Thomas. Also: Margaret, widow of William Olyver: surrender to them of one mondayland built up with two houses recently held by William, for life, rendering annually in all things as did Margaret, with the obligation to repair and maintain the property and buildings at their own expense. Pledges for payments and repairs: Roger Smyth, Thomas Buntyng. G.: three capons.

3746 ST. IVES (October) Galfridus Birt and his wife, Johanna: one built up messuage on two half-rows recently held by William Prykke and once held by William Smyth, from the previous Michaelmas for life, rendering annually 12s. at the customary times, and all other services and customs owed therein, with the obligation to repair and maintain the property. *Et non licebit*, etc. G.: 2s.

3747 ST. IVES (1 December) John Wylymot, chaplain, and his mother, Alicia: surrender of a half-row facing west in Bridge Street recently held by William Wilymot, to the use of William Borell and his son, John, for life, rendering annually 5s. at the customary times and all other services and customs owed therein, with the obligation to repair and maintain the property. *Et non licebit*, etc. G.: two salted fish.

3748 SLEPE (December) Robert Wryght: surrender of one cotland and one toft with enclosure from the tenement of Busteler called Fenkilyerd, to the use of Roger atte Chyrche and his wife, Agnes, for life, rendering annually 8s. for the cotland and 5s. for the toft at the customary times, and all other services and customs owed therein. G.: four capons.

3749 Woodhurst (December) Thomas Pope: surrender of one quarter of land once held by his father, William Pope, to the use of John Burne, for life, rendering annually 4s. at the customary times, and all other services and customs owed therein. Pledge for payments: Thomas Pope.

3750 Holywell (December) William Albry, alias Wryght, and William Chapeleyn: one cotland and a half-virgate of land once held by Thomas Hunne, with new demesne land and one acre of land in Middilfurlong and one acre in le Smeteh, recently held by William Albry himself and surrendered back to the lord by him, for life, rendering annually in all things as William previously rendered, with the obligation to build a bake house on the property within one year. G.: 2s.

209r

3751 Graveley (28 December) John Barton Sr. pays 20d. for license to marry Cristina, daughter of Thomas Barton and naif of the lord by blood, to whomever she wishes, this time.

3752 Graveley (28 December) John Barton Jr. and his wife, Mariota: one ruined plot and one virgate of land with one close at the end of the village recently held by John Swon, for life, rendering annually all services and customs owed therein, with the obligation to repair and maintain the property, for which he receives 26s.8d. of his rents. G.: two capons.

3753 Burwell (December) Mariota Hals: surrender of one tenement of 15 acres recently held by her husband, Thomas Hals, to the use of William Roole and his wife, Margaret, for 40 years, rendering annually in all things as did Mariota. G.: 12d.

3754 Burwell William Jay and his wife, Cecilia: one tenement of 15 acres of land recently held by John Plaunteyn and seized by the seneschal for non-payment of rents, for 40 years, rendering annually 12s. at the customary times, and all other services and customs rendered by John. G.: one capon.

3755 Burwell John Powle and his wife, Agnes: one tenement of 20 acres recently held by John Plaunteyn and seized by the lord for non-payment of rent, for 40 years, rendering annually 16s. at the customary times, and all other services and customs rendered by John. G.: two capons.

3756 Elton (13 March) William Deche of Elton, naif and villein of the lord at Elton: license to live off the manor for as long as it pleases the lord, rendering 20d. annually, in person at the leet at Elton, with two capons paid for this license. Further, John, son of the said William, will hold and maintain all the lands and tenements now held by William, rendering all payments and services owed therein, with William giving him chattels and goods sufficient for maintaining and repairing those properties. Pledges for both William and John: William Attegate.

3757 Walsoken cum Popenhoe (1 May) John Hunte Sr., servant of Brother Thomas Chesterton, treasurer of the monastery of Ramsey, naif of the lord by blood, pays two capons for license to have Robert, his son and naif of the lord, living with Richard Towte of Ramsey, taillor, learning his craft as an apprentice for eight years, commencing at the feast of St. Mark. Granted at the request of Thomas Chesterton.

3758 Ramsey (July) Thomas Coke Bocher and his wife, Johanna: from Brother Robert Cammbrygge, sub-cellarer, one plot recently held by Elena Mody, with one shop recently held by John Ryvenale, lying in Bridge Street next to the big bridge at the eastern end, from the previous Easter for 20 years, rendering annually 12s. in equal portions at the customary times, with the sub-cellarer reponsible for repairs and maintenance. *Et si predictus redditus*, etc. (arrears of one month). G.: 5s.

209v

3759 Ramsey (May) John Berforth and his wife, Margaret: from Brother Robert Cammbrigge, one pasture recently enclosed with ditches and willows parcelled out of Swonhousmede, with willows and fishponds in the ditches and with the pasture of

Bramtoe, excepting a fishpond dismissed to John Keening *per copiam*, from the previous Easter for life, rendering annually 12s. in equal portions at the feasts of the Annunciation and Nativity of Blessed Mary, with the obligation to repair and maintain the property in protecting ditches and making hedges, and with permission to cut down and plant willows at the ditch lying at the eastern side of the ditch, at the expense of the sub-cellarer. Further, they may not dismiss the property, nor make waste. *Et si predictus redditus*, etc. (arrears of one month). G.: 6s.8d.

3760 RAMSEY (May) John Hunte Cooke his wife, Juliana and their son, John: from the sub-cellarer, one messuage rebuilt at Grene and recently burned, for life, rendering annually 8s. in equal portions at the customary times, with the sub-cellarer responsible for repairs. *Et si predictus redditus*, etc. (arrears of one month). G.: 40d.

3761 UPWOOD CUM RAVELEY (July) Richard Greecham of Diddington: one messuage and two virgates of land with cotland and forland parcelled out of land pertaining to one virgate once held by William Alcoke, and half of one piece of demesne land at Kyngewelle recently held by John Aubys Sr. and surrendered back to the lord by him, from Michaelmas for six years, rendering annually 46s.10d. for the virgates and cotland and 12d. for the demesne land at the customary times, and all other services and customs rendered by John, with an allowance of 26s.8d. of his rent for the first year because the land is badly cultivated. Further, he will repair and maintain the property at his own expense, with 12 acres of fallow to be granted him after his first repairs, and all the meadow that can be mowed pertaining to the lands and tenements above. Pledges: Walter Baldoke and Thomas Penyman. G.: six capons.

3762 CHATTERIS (3 August: court) Edmund Cade: one messuage and half of eight acres of land with meadow in Oldhalf, demesne land, fishponds and other parcels recently held by Katerina Mathew and once held by John Fithion, for life, rendering annually 13s.10d. and all other services and customs rendered by Katerina. G.: four capons.

3763 CHATTERIS (same court) Anna Thommesson: surrender of one cotland at Pakerell Dole, one cotland once held by John Ase, a half-acre of land in Elmen, one and a half acres in Medmen recently held by John Tommesson Sr., to the use of John Hunte Sr., for life, rendering annually 4s.5d. and all other services and customs rendered by Anna. Pledge for payments and repairs: William Hunte. G.: three capons.

3764 CHATTERIS (same court) John Pekerell: surrender of one cotland and meadow in Oldhalf with fishpond in le Delf, to the use of Richard Pekerell, for life, rendering annually 2s.5d. at the customary times, with half of a solar with a *camera* and easement in the garden with one selion, free entry and exit, quit, reserved to Anna Pekerell for life. Pledge for payments and maintenance: Richard Hobkyn. G.: 8d.

3765 CHATTERIS (same court) Galfridus Royston, alias Tayllour: one messuage, one acre of land in Mademen, four selions in Shepherifen, and four selions outside the northern part of the manor recently held by Thomas Tyllneye, for life, rendering annually 2s.2d. at the customary times, and all other services and customs rendered by Thomas. G.: two capons.

11 JOHN STOWE (1446-1447)

3766 BURWELL (21 October: leet) Mariota Notewyn and her son, Thomas: a capital messuage with croft and three rods of land from one tenement of eight acres presently held by Radulph Edryche *ad opus* and recently held by Robert Edryche, and which messuage and croft and three rods were held by Thomas Notewyn; five acres of demesne land, of which two acres are in Dichefeld, two acres in Estefeld, and one and

210r

210v

a half acres in Bradeweye, to be held by Mariota for life, and after her death by Thomas for 20 years, rendering annually 2s.6d. for the messuage, croft and three rods, at the customary times, and 5s.6d. for the demesne land, the rents for the latter being paid to John Benette, *firmarius*, and after his death, directly to the lord, as determined in a copy drawn up in the fifth year of John Tychemersch. Further, he will render suit to leet and court, common fine and holmsilver. G.: 40d.

3767 BURWELL John Perye Jr. and his wife, Johanna: one tenement of 15 acres recently held by Radulph Calvysbane and once held by William Peyn, for 30 years, rendering annually 7s.6d., works and services to the *firmarius*, and suit to court and leet, *capitagium* and holmsilver, *pro rata*, as do other tenants. G.: excused.

3768 SHILLINGTON (25 October: court) William Shepperd and his wife, Alicia: one messuage, one virgate and one lot of Burilond recently held by John Shepperd, for life, rendering annually (*blank*) in rents and all other services and customs rendered by John. G.: two capons.

3769 SHILLINGTON (same court) Richard Colman and his wife, Margaret: one messuage and one virgate of land recently held by his father, John Colman, for life, rendering annually (*blank*) in rents, at the customary times, and all other services and customs rendered by John. G.: 3s.4d.

3770 SHILLINGTON (same court) Thomas Coche, his wife Alicia, and their heirs: one messuage, one and a half virgates of land recently held by Nicholas Leweyn, for life, and by their heirs, rendering annually (*blank*) in rents and all other services and customs rendered by Nicholas. G.: 13s.4d.

3771 SHILLINGTON (same court) Nicholas May, his wife, Johanna, and their heirs: one cotland containing one acre with a tenement recently held by Adam Sparwe, rendering annually 2s.1d.ob. at the customary times, and all other services, including purging Mylledyke. G.: two capons.

3772 SHILLINGTON (December) John Coche Sr.: surrender of one cotland recently held by Margeria Goberd and once held by John Attestoon, to the use of John Goberd and his wife, Johanna, for life, rendering annually in all things as did Margeria. G. and heriot: two capons.

211r **3773** CRANFIELD (28 October: court) Roger Berne: one cote with a house and recently held by John Lowell, for life, rendering annually 18d. and all other services and customs rendered by John. G. and heriot: 4s.

3774 CRANFIELD (same court) Robert de Leen: one cote with pithel recently held by his father, William, for life, rendering annually 20d. and all other services and customs rendered by William. G.: 12d.

3775 CRANFIELD (January) Elizabeth, daughter of John Skynner: surrender of one messuage and a half-virgate of land once held by John Skynner, to the use of John Curteys Jr., for life, rendering annually 9s.2d. at the customary times, and all other services and customs owed therein. G.: 2s.4d.

3776 CRANFIELD (January) Thomas Ayleyn and his wife, Margeria: surrender of one toft and a half-virgate of land once held by John Ayleyn, to the use of John Terry, for life, rendering annually 13s.6d. at the customary times, and all other services and customs owed therein. G.: six partridges.

3777 CRANFIELD (January) Alicia, daughter and heiress of Thomas Catelyn: surrender of one toft and one quarter of land and another toft next to the aforesaid toft in Horlee, once held by Richard Robyn and recently held by Thomas Catelyn, to the use of William Terry, for life, rendering annually 6s.10d.q. at the customary times, and all other services and customs owed therein. G.: 2s., and no more because he is bailiff.

3778 CRANFIELD (January) Thomas Terry: surrender of one croft recently held by

Thomas Wassyngle and once held by John Atte Crosse, and a half-virgate of land once held by William Faukoner, to the use of William Terry, his wife, Mariota, and their son, Thomas, for life, and after the deaths of William and Mariota to be held by Thomas for life, rendering annually 6s. for the croft and 9s.2d. for the half-virgate, which croft previously rendered 6s.8d. Further, Thomas Jr. also holds the reversion of a parcel of one messuage now held by William Terry — i.e. one *insathous* — half of one pithel, and half of one pond once held by Thomas Coles, for life, rendering annually 6d. at the customary times. G.: six partridges.

3779 GRAVELEY (6 November: court) William Newman Sr., his wife and heirs: four messuages, of which one is built up, four and a half virgates of land recently held by Robert Davenar, rendering annually 26s.8d. and all other services and customs rendered by Robert. G.: 3s.4d. And he swears fealty.

3780 GRAVELEY (same court) John Smyth and his wife, Agnes: one messuage, one and a quarter virgates of land recently held by Robert Stalleworth, and both recently held by John Arnold, rendering annually 15s.10d. and all other services and customs rendered by John. He will receive a cotland of fallow, four acres of land manured with a cart, and 13s.4d. in denarii at the beginning of the term. G.: 2s.

3781 GRAVELEY (8 December) Richard Aleyn of Drayton and his wife, Isabella: one messuage and one and a half virgates of land recently held by Rolf, for life, rendering annually in all things as did Rolf. G.: 10s., half of which is to be paid this year, the other half next year.

211v **3782** GRAVELEY (April) John Smyth, naif of the lord: surrender of one messuage and one adjacent croft, with a half-virgate of land recently held by William Smyth, to the use of John Edward, for life, rendering annually 6s.8d. at the customary times, and all other services and customs rendered by John, with the obligation to repair and maintain the messuage at his own expense. G.: 12d.

3783 GRAVELEY (May) William Stoughton and his wife, Margaret: one messuage and a half-virgate of land recently held by Richard Dyke and a parcel of land containing approximately a half-acre of land from the lands and tenements once held by Richard Baron, called Hallelonde, from Michaelmas for life, rendering annually in all things as did Richard, with the obligation to repair and maintain the *insathous* and to live on the tenement once held by Richard Dyke. Pledge: Edmund Parys. G.: two marks, of which 10s. are excused.

3784 ELTON (4 November: court) Henry Seyn, his wife, Elizabet and their heirs: one messuage and one quarter of land recently held by Henry Carleton, rendering annually 4s.6d. at the customary times, and all other services and customs rendered by Henry. G.: (*blank*).

3785 ELTON (November) William Fayrman and his wife, Margaret: one messuage and a half-virgate of land in Northortown once held by John Clerke and recently held by John Burnet, from next Michaelmas for life, rendering annually 9s. at the customary times, and all other services and customs rendered by John, with payments beginning at the feast of St. Andrew after one year. Further, they will rebuild one *camera* of four beams at their own expense, with two beams supplied by the lord. G.: two capons. Note that the property was seized by the lord for non-payment of rents and lack of repairs by John Burnet.

3786 BYTHORNE (6 November: court — at Weston), Robert Smyth and his wife, Margaret: one cote and one quarter of land recently held by William Spayn, for life, rendering annually (*blank*) in rents, and all other services and customs rendered by William. G.: two capons.

3787 BYTHORNE Robert Smyth: one messuage and one quarter of land recently held by William Spayn, for life, rendering annually in all things as did William. G.: two capons.

3788 BROUGHTON (10 November: court) William Franckeleyn receives from the lord one cote and a half-virgate of land with adjacent meadow recently held by William Wythe, for life, rendering annually in all things as did William. G.: 6d.

212r **3789** BROUGHTON (May) John Fuller, his wife, Agnes, and son, Thomas: one vacant toft lying next to Elmer Street recently held by William Wythe and once held by John Gerard, for life, rendering annually 12d., which property once rendered 2s. Further, they will render all other services and customs rendered by William, with the obligation to rebuild one *camera* at their own expense within three years. G.: nothing, because of repairs.

3790 BROUGHTON (May) Richard Thoday and his wife, Alicia: one messuage and one virgate recently *ad opus* and once held by Thomas Elyot and recently held by John Aleyn Jr. for 10s., and one toft with a virgate of land once held by Thomas Elyot and recently held by William Attekyn, called "Stevenesthereve", in *arentatio* for 12s., for life, rendering annually 11s. for the toft and virgate recently *ad opus*, and 9s. for the other toft and virgate, and all other services and customs rendered by those in *arentatio*, with payments beginning at the feast of St. Andrew, and with the lord responsible for initial repairs. G.: three capons.

3791 BROUGHTON (10 November: court) John Cabe Sr.: one garden recently held by William Pole and once held by William Justice, in exchange for another garden of John's lying at the end of the village towards Raveley, for as long as it pleases the lord for 10 years saving the right of anyone, rendering annually in all things as did William, and one capon. G.: (*blank*).

3792 BROUGHTON (April) Thomas Crowche: surrender of one tenement and a half-virgate of land recently *ad opus*, a half-virgate in *major censum*, one quarter of land called Blassemys, and one cotland once held by William Ivet, to the use of Thomas Pulter and his wife, Katerina, for life, in *arentatio*, from Michaelmas, rendering annually 19s. at the customary times, customs of the vill, and all other services and customs rendered by those in *arentatio*. G.: two capons.

3793 BROUGHTON (April) William Justice: one tenement and a half-virgate of land *ad opus*, a virgate of land in *minor censum*, one quarter in *major censum*, and one quarter of Cleryvaux land recently held by William Poole, from Michaelmas for life, rendering annually in all things as did William. G.: two capons.

3794 RIPTON (20 November) Robert Nottyng: one messuage and a half-virgate of land at Catteshegge recently held by John Cadman, in *arentatio* for life, rendering annually 6s.8d. at the customary times, with payments beginning at the feast of St. John the Baptist. G.: two capons, and raising the height of one (*blank*).

3795 RIPTON (January) William Wangtey: one messuage and three semi-virgates of land recently held by Robert Wryght for 26s., from Michaelmas for life, rendering annually 23s.4d. and all other services and customs rendered by Robert. Further, the lord will build one barn at his own expense before All Saints, except for splints and plastering from William, with William obligated to repair and maintain the property thereafter. G.: one capon.

3796 RIPTON Agreement between the lord and William Birt that the lord will build one barn on his property, in which he lives, before the feast of St. Peter in Chains, supplying timber, carpentry and straw, with William repairing and maintaining the property at his own expense thereafter, and he will also supply transport for timber and straw.

212v **3797** RIPTON (January) Galfridus Lombard and his wife, Agnes: one mondayland at

Hawgate built up with one house recently held by John Wode for 4s., and a half-virgate of land in Caldecote recently held by William Ravele Jr. for 6s., for life, rendering annually 9s. and all other services and customs rendered by John and William, with the obligation to rebuild one *camera* of six binding-posts within one year, with timber and an allowance of this year's rent granted by the lord. G.: two capons.

3798 RIPTON (1 January) Thomas Ware of Hartford: one messuage, one and a half virgates with appurtenances recently held by John Tayllor and once held by John Smyth, for life, rendering annually in all things as did John, with the obligation to repair and maintain all buildings on the property in roofing, raising, plastering, splinting. He will repair the oven and kiln, except for carpentry in le Gabylwall Hall, receiving straw in one stack, undergrowth for the first enclosure, large timber for a cottage in the village and for one pig-house, with an allowance of rent until the feast of St. Andrew. Further, the lord will build one *camera* of eight binding-posts at his own expense, except for ramming, straw drawing and roofing to be performed by Thomas. G.: two capons.

3799 UPWOOD (January) John Gowler: one messuage and three quarters of land in *arentatio* recently held by Nicholas Albyn, for life, rendering annually 12s. at the customary times, and customs of the vill, with carting of five quarters of malt to Ramsey each year at the summons of the bailiff. Further, he receives at the beginning all fallow and reploughed land, four selions in the fields of Botenale, manured with fold, to be returned to the lord at the end of the term. G.: two capons.

3800 WARBOYS (January) John Berenger Sr.: surrender of one messuage built up with three houses and a half-virgate of land *ad opus* recently held by John Plombe, to the use of Thomas Bele and his son, Richard, from Michaelmas, rendering annually 6s. for rent and 2s. for works, and customs of the vill, with the obligation to repair the messuage of their own expense. G.: 3s.

3801 WARBOYS (January) Nicholas Benson and his wife, Emma: one dichmanland *ad opus*, three quarters in *arentatio*, and one acre of demesne land in a croft in Stokkyng recently held by Richard Revysson, for life, rendering annually 9s. at the customary times, which property previously rendered 12s.1d. Further, they will render all other services and customs rendered by Richard. With the obligation to repair and maintain the property. G.: two capons.

3802 WARBOYS (January) Richard Benson and his wife, Johanna: one tenement recently rebuilt and a half-virgate of land *ad opus* and a half-virgate of land in *arentatio* recently held by John Benson and a half-virgate of land in Caldecote recently held by him, rendering annually for the rebuilt virgate 6s. for rent and 2s.8d. for works, and for the half-virgate in *arentatio* 8s. and for the half-virgate in Caldecote 5s. G.: 2s.

3803 WARBOYS (20 September) Richard Baker of Wistow pays six capons for license to marry Alicia, daughter of Thomas Benet, alias Herde, widow of Richard Wilkyn and naif of the lord by blood, this time.

3804 WARBOYS (1 September) John Boleyn Wever and his wife, Alicia: one cotland and one acre of demesne land at Bascroft recently held by Walter Wodeward, for life, rendering annually 4s.2d. at the customary times, and all other services and customs owed therein, with the obligation to repair the cote, for which he receives an allowance of his rent for two years and a quarter, namely, until Easter. G.: two capons.

3805 THERFIELD (September) Johanna Wenham: surrender of one tenement well built up with 18 acres of demesne land, one meadow from the tenement of Peter Branncestre called Crowbroke Mede recently held by her husband, John Wenham, to the use of her son, William, his wife and their heirs rendering annually 36s.8d. at the

213r

customary times, and all other services and customs owed therein, which tenement with demesne previously rendered 33s. and the meadow 7s. G.: four capons.

3806 THERFIELD (15 May) Henry Birt of Warboys and Thomas Stevene, alias Grauntot, of Offord Darcy, pay the fine for license for George Waryn, son of John Waryn and naif of the lord, to live off the manor in the service of Thomas Grauntot, rendering 20d. at Easter. Further, if he withdraws from Thomas' service, he is to be returned to the manor by Thomas. Pledge for payments: Henry Birt.

3807 THERFIELD Note that John Waryn, brother of the aforesaid George Waryn and naif of the lord, lives at Brantfeld without license; Richard Waryn, his brother, lives at Newchepyng without license, learning the craft of blacksmithing; Elizabet, his sister, was married at Godreche to a certain maltman named John Wygge; and Margaret, his sister, was married there to a certain Robert Page, and certain ones of the village say that these were without license.

3808 CHATTERIS (January) John Beche: surrender of one messuage and half of one tenement of eight acres with other parcels, as found in the Rental, to the use of John Hopkyn Jr., for life, rendering annually 7s.8d. at the customary times, and all other services and customs owed therein. G.: 6s.8d.

3809 ELSWORTH (10 January) John Swynford Carpenter, his wife, Johanna, and their sons, Alexander and Jacob: one cote built up with two houses at Brokysbrynke recently held by Alexander Hobbesson and once held by John Pigot, for life, rendering annually in all things as did John. G.: 12d.

3810 ELSWORTH (27 July: court) John Bole: surrender of one cote with croft built up with one *insathous* and one new grange recently held by John Lucas, and one quarter of land recently held by the same John, to the use of William AtWode, naif of the lord, and his wife, Agnes, for life, rendering annually in all things as did John. G.: 12d., two capons.

3811 WISTOW Richard Randolf and his wife, Johanna: one quarter of land in *secunda arentatio* recently held by Richard Picard and once held by William Hyche, for life, rendering annually 4s.6d. for rents and works at the customary times. G.: four capons.

3812 WISTOW (March) Richard Wyllesson: surrender of one plot, a half-virgate of land once held in *arentatio* by his father, a half-virgate of land *ad opus* once held by his father, half of one half-virgate once hald by Thomas Breselaunce in *arentatio*, and one cotland in *arentatio* recently held by John Hyche, to the use of Richard Lyndesey and his wife, Dionisia, from Michaelmas for life, rendering annually 8s. for the plot and half-virgate, and 6s.8d., two capons for the other half-virgates *ad opera*, 3s.6d. for the half of the half-virgate in *arentatio*, and two capons and all services rendered by John Hyche for the two cotlands. Further, they will repair and maintain the property at their own expense. Pledge for payments and repairs: Richard Willesson. G.: 40d., two capons.

3813 WISTOW (April) John Walgate Jr.: surrender of one cote and one quarter of land in *arentatio* recently held by John Walgate Sr. to the use of William Owty Jr., for life, rendering annually 4s. and all other services and customs rendered by John. Same William: one quarter of land once held by Richard Willesson, for life, rendering annually 4s. at the customary times, which property previously rendered 4s.6d. Further, he will render all other services and customs rendered by Richard. G.: three capons.

3814 WISTOW (April) John Aylmar: one cote built up with three houses, namely: one *insathous*, one *camera* in a garden, and one bake house, recently held by Richard Rede and once held by John West, for life, rendering annually 40d., one hen and 10 eggs, and all other services and customs rendered by Richard, with payments beginning at the feast of St. Andrew. Further, he will repair and maintain the property at his own expense. G.: two capons.

3815 WISTOW (1 September) William Pycard: one messuage and a half-virgate of land *ad opus* recently held by John Attegate Sr., for life, rendering annually 5s. in rent and 4s. for works, for as long as it pleases the lord, at the customary times, and all other services and customs reserved to the lord and contained in the Rental and renewed in the 10th year of Abbot John Stowe. Further, he receives all the fallow and reploughed land and hay stored on that messuage at the beginning of the term, to be returned to the lord in the same condition at the end of the term. G.: 6s.8d.

3816 RAMSEY (1 December) Alicia Bagedale, Thomas Fermor, alias Smyth, and his wife, Agnes: from Brother William Bury, sub-cellarer, one plot in Ramsey near the chapel recently held by John Eyer, from Christmas for life, rendering 16s.3d. this year, and 21s.8d. each year thereafter, in equal portions at the feasts of the Annunciation and Nativity of Blessed Mary, with Alicia to effect repairs before Pentecost. *Et si predictus redditus*, etc. (arrears of two months). G.: two capons.

3817 WESTON Robert Thommysson, late of Winwick, pays the fine for license to marry Margaret Ges, daughter of John Carter and naif of the lord by blood. And he proffers six capons, and pays 20s. to remain in the village and wait to hold the lands and tenements recently held by John Bocher.

3818 HEMINGFORD ABBOTS (May) John Barbor: one croft once a cotland recently held by William Hyll, and two half-virgates of land once held by Alan Veer and recently held by John Clerke, for life, rendering annually 10s. at the customary times, which property previously rendered 12s.10d. Further, he will render all other services and customs owed therein. G.: four capons.

3819 HEMINGFORD ABBOTS (May) Robert Almer: one croft and one virgate of land once held by Thomas Everard and recently held by John Clerke for 12s.8d., for life, rendering annually 8s. at the customary times, and all other services ands customs owed therein. G.: four capons.

3820 HEMINGFORD ABBOTS (May) Agnes Heyne, widow of John Heyne, pays heriot for license to hold for life certain lands and meadows recently held by John, in return for the accustomed services, namely: by custom, the rent is doubled, but it is granted to her for 2s.

3821 HEMINGFORD ABBOTS (leet) Robert Pynnoke and his wife, Alicia: one cotland built up with two houses and one croft recently held by Nicholas Fanell, for life, rendering annually 18s. at the customary times, and all other services and customs owed therein. G.: 12d.

3822 ST. IVES (1 August, 10 John Stowe, 23 Henry VI) John Ladde, his wife, Alicia, and their assigns: one plot recently burned and rebuilt by the abbot and once held by John Chamberleyn, from Michaelmas for 80 years, rendering annually 20s. in equal portions at the feasts of the Annunciation and Nativity of Blessed Mary, suit to court and leet, and all other services and customs owed therein. Further, they will repair and maintain the property. *Et non licebit*, etc. G.: excused, this first time. And note that John and Alicia will have this copy in another tenor and in greater freedom than other copies of this vill, because of great repairs effected by them at their arrival, for they came to this plot from St. Neots at the request and strong pleas of the rector of Over. Therefore, this copy is not to be drawn in example.[48]

3823 BROUGHTON (31 December) Thomas Birder: surrender of one plot and three quarters of land in *major censum*, to the use of Richard Waryn and his wife, Agnes, for

214r

214v

---

[48] MS.: "Non trahetur hec copia in exemplum."

life, rendering annually 10s. at the customary times, and all other services and customs rendered by Thomas. Pledges for payments and services: Thomas Birder and Roger Asplond. G.: 2s., two capons.

3824 St. Ives (1 May) John Bocher of King's Lynn: surrender of one tenement built up with one house and one garden once held by John Makesey, to the use of Thomas Judde, his wife, Agnes, and their son, Edmund, from Michaelmas for life, rendering annually 2s. at the customary times, and all other services and customs owed therein, with the obligation to repair and maintain the property. *Et non licebit*, etc. G.: excused by the lord.

12   JOHN STOWE (1447-1448)

215r **3825** Knapwell (20 October: leet at Elsworth) John Hopper: surrender of one messuage and one quarter of land once held by William Geffreye, to the use of Thomas Aunger and his wife, Agnes, for life, rendering annually in all things as did John, with certain easements and profits contained in indentures between Thomas and John Hopper and his wife, Alicia, reserved to the latter for life. Same Thomas and Agnes: one quarter of land recently held by John Hopper and once held by John Arnold, and one toft with one quarter of land recently held by Thomas Gray and once held by William Joy, for life, rendering annually in all things as did John and Thomas. G.: 4s.

3826 Knapwell (same leet) John Reynold and his wife, Agnes: one cote with adjacent croft recently held by John Yntte and once held by Arnold, for life, rendering annually in all things as did John. G.: two capons.

3827 Knapwell (same leet) Thomas Gylot and his wife, Agnes: one messuage and one quarter of land recently held by John Hopper, for life, rendering annually in all things as did John. G.: one capon.

3828 Burwell (22 October: leet) John Wyc and his wife, Florentia: one messuage and a half-acre of land recently held by Andrew Moris, by the rod, for life, rendering annually 15d. at the customary times, and all other services and customs owed therein. G.: 6d.

3829 Burwell (same leet) John Wylkyn, son of Robert Wylkyn: one tenement of 15 acres of land recently held by John, son of John Rolf, and once held by John Fraas, for 20 years, rendering annually 16s. and all other services and customs owed therein. Also: one tenement of 24 acres of land with croft in le Nesse recently held by John Rolf, for life, rendering annually 12s. and all other services and customs owed therein. G.: 12d.

3830 Burwell (same leet) John Rolf, son of John Rolf atte Dufhous: half of one tenement of 24 acres recently held by Robert Goodynche, for 20 years, rendering annually 12s. and all other services and customs owed therein. G.: 6d.

3831 Burwell (same leet) Thomas Role Jr. and his wife, Margaret: one messuage and one tenement of 15 acres recently held by John Pury Jr., and one cote called Gyssher's Plot, for 30 years, rendering annually in all things as did John. G.: 12d.

3832 Burwell (same leet) John Poule and his wife, Agnes: one toft in North Street recently held by John Sparwe, by the rod for 40 years, rendering annually 19d. after the first year at the customary times, and all other services and customs owed therein. G.: one capon.

3833 Burwell Isabella Jay: surrender of one tenement and 24 acres of land and one plot called Puttokys, and one and a half acres of land at the northern end of the village, to the use of Richard Role and his wife, Margaret, for 40 years, rendering annually in all things as did Isabella. G.: 20d.

215v **3834** BURWELL George Burthen and Thomas Purye: one pithel called "Cheste-vynespightill" once held by William Ydeyn and a certain fishpond in le Nesse with meadow and pond recently held by Radulph Lyne, for 20 years, rendering annually 6s. at the customary times and suit to court and leet, which property previously rendered 7s.6d. Payments will begin at Easter, and they will repair and maintain the fishpond at their own expense, and keep the lord and his successors blameless against anyone regarding the fishpond and water. G.: one pike and one tench.

3835 THERFIELD (24 October: leet) Thomas Overston: surrender of one cotland and five acres of new demesne land once held by Robert Sewale, to the use of John Berker his wife, Elena, and their heirs and assigns, rendering annually 13s. at the customary times, and all other services and customs rendered by Thomas. G.: 12d.

3836 THERFIELD (same leet) Richard Watte: surrender of one messuage, one virgate, 18 acres, three rods of new demesne land, one acre of land in Carbeliscroft, and one meadow called Swetewell Mede once held by Thomas Colle, to the use of John Webbe, his heirs and assigns rendering annually 33s.4d. at the customary times, and all other services and customs owed therein. G.: two capons.

3837 THERFIELD (same leet) William Peytewyn: 13 acres of new demesne land recently held by Robert Preeste, for life, rendering annually 6s.6d., with payments beginning at the feast of St. Andrew next year. G.: one capon.

3838 THERFIELD (same leet) Richard Wattes and his heirs: eight acres of land and three rods of demesne land once held by Robert Jankyn, with one curtilage of a capital plot once held by Peter Branncastre lying near Paddokedyche, rendering annually 3s.4d.ob. for the demesne land, and 1d.ob. for the curtilage, at the customary times. Further, the seneschal grants him one old hall on the tenement recently held by Caldewell, with which he will build one house on the curtilage at his own expense, timber and an allowance of rent for the next three years granted by the lord. G.: excused.

3839 THERFIELD (22 December) William Game pays 2s., at this time, for licenses for Agnes and Katerina, daughters of the late John Waryn and naifs of the lord, to marry whomever they wish, this first time.

3840 THERFIELD (December) William Game pays the fines for Richard Waryn, son of the late John Waryn and naif of the lord, living in Newchepyng, and for Johanna Waryn, daughter of the same John and naif of the lord, living in Watton, that they may continue to live off the manor for as long as it pleases the lord, remaining naifs as before, and rendering 4d. annually at the leet, with the first payments due at the next leet. Pledge for payments: William Game.

216r **3841** THERFIELD (December) William Gerveis, his wife, Agnes, and their heirs: one plot and 10 acres of land from Haywardswyke and Tredegoldyswyke, one and a half cotlands, once held by Henry Gerveis, and eight acres, three rods of new demesne land, in bondage rendering annually 34s.ob. at the customary times, and all other services and customs owed therein. G.: two capons.

3842 THERFIELD (December) William Wattes Carpenter, his wife, Isabella, and their heirs: one vacant toft where William Caldewell recently lived, with half of one virgate of land recently held by the same William, in bondage rendering annually 6s.8d., with payments beginning at the feast of St. Andrew, and which property previously rendered 12s. Further, they will render all other services and customs owed therein. G.: two capons.

3843 THERFIELD (December) John Sperver, naif of the lord, pays 12d. for license to live within the village of Therfield and hold no land, rendering to the lord while he holds no land 12d. annually at Easter. Pledge: William Game.

3844 GRAVELEY (31 October: leet) Agnes Buckely: surrender of one tenement and two semi-virgates of land recently held by William Buckely, to the use of John Buckely and his wife, Elyzabet, for life, rendering annually 26s.8d. at the customary times, and all other services and customs rendered by Agnes, with the lord granting at the beginning of the term, 40s., 40 carts of straw, and all the fallow land, which they will return at the end of their term. G.: 2s., one capon.

3845 GRAVELEY (same leet) Nicholas Dyke: surrender of one croft and a half-virgate of land recently held by Nicholas Dyke, to the use of John Mordon and his wife, Margaret, for life, rendering annually 6s.8d. at the customary times, and all other services and customs rendered by Nicholas. G.: 8d.

3846 GRAVELEY (3 December) John Baron Sr. pays two capons for license to marry Margaret, daughter of Thomas Baron and naif of the lord by blood, to John Basely of Papworth Anneys. Note that the fine, originally 3s.4d., was reduced by the seneschal.

3847 ELLINGTON (3 November: leet) John Massy and his assigns: one cote near the church, parcelled out of five cotes recently constructed on the site of the manor there, rendering annually (*blank*) in rents and all other services and customs owed therein, with the obligation to repair and maintain the buildings there at his own expense, with easement in the cottage when necessary for leet and court reserved to the lord. And he swears fealty. G.: (*blank*).

3848 ELLINGTON (December) Elena, widow of Thomas Ponder: one cote recently rebuilt and lately held by Thomas, her husband, lying between the tenement of the lord and that of the parson of Ellington, in bondage for life, rendering annually in all things as did Thomas. G.: 2s., two capons.

3849 HOUGHTON (11 November) John Carter: surrender of one croft and a half-virgate of land, another croft called Dufhomered recently held by Richard Carter, to the use of William Foster and his wife, Agnes, for life, rendering annually 5s. at the customary times, and all other services and customs owed therein. G.: 12d.

216v **3850** SLEPE (December) William Smyth: one tenement with two cotlands recently held by William Pecoke and once held by William Herrof, for life, rendering annually 14s. at the customary times, and all other services and customs rendered by William. G.: 6s., two capons.

3851 SLEPE Rosa Payn: surrender of one cote recently held by Henry Payne and once held by Thomas Grenehyll, to the use of Richard Rameseye and his wife, Alicia. Also: one vacant plot in Cowlane recently held by Henry Payne, for life, rendering annually 2s. for the cotlands and 16d. for the plot at the customary times, and all other services and customs rendered by Henry, with the obligation to repair the cote, under penalty of forfeit of the cote and the plot. G.: 2s.

3852 SHILLINGTON (1 December) Matthew Chambre pays 12d. for license to marry Isabella, daughter of John Hamond and naif of the lord by blood, to whomever she wishes, this time.

3853 SHILLINGTON (1 December) Matthew Chambre pays 12d. for license to marry Johanna, daughter of Thomas Stoonle and naif of the lord by blood, to Thomas Poole, this time.

3854 SHILLINGTON (6 September) Agnes, widow of Robert Halle: surrender of a certain quantity of the manor, namely: a hall with *camera* annexed, chapel, kitchen, bake house, kiln, Abbot's bower with stable, dovecote, garden, another garden, a large grange, three lots of demesne land and other buildings and parcels recently held by her and her husband, to the use of John Goberd, and his wife, Johanna, from the previous Michaelmas for life, rendering annually 6s.8d. for the hall, *camera* and other parcels, and 34s.4d. for the grange, gardens and lots, at the customary times. Further, they will repair and maintain the property at their own expense in carpentry, roofing, enclosing, with timber, splints and rods supplied by the lord according to the judgment of the seneschal or his deputy. They will have *haybote* and *firebote* as necessary from the lord, and they will sustain all other duties and burdens owed by such tenants holding demesne lots. They are prohibited from dismissing any part of those lands or any parcel of the manor without the license of the lord, nor may they put themselves under the protection of any other lord to the harm of the lord or their tenants, under penalty of forfeit. Finally, the seneschal shall have use of the *camerae*, hall, stable, kitchen and other buildings when he comes. G.: 20s. Heriot: found in the leet of this year.

3855 St. Ives (7 December) John Eston and his wife, Isabella: one row built up with one house recently held by John Norton from Michaelmas for life, rendering annually 3s.4d. at the customary times, and all other services and customs rendered by John, with the obligation to repair and rebuild the property with one house within two years.

217r G.: 12d.

3856 St. Ives (1 January) John Bolton, chaplain, Nicholas Bolton, his wife, Agnes, and Katerina, daughter of Thomas Bolton: one row once held by Thomas Erethe and recently held by William Fown, from Michaelmas for life, rendering annually 10s. at the customary times, and all other services and customs rendered by William, with the obligation to repair and maintain the property, receiving from the lord for the first repairs 64 feet of beams, six binding-posts, one beam, one main beam and six posts. *Et non licebit*, etc.

3857 Bythorne John Baron Jr. and his wife, Agnes: one quarter of land recently held by William Cannardis, rendering annually in all things as did William. G.: 12d.

3858 Bythorne Richard Watesson and his wife, Agnes: one messuage and a half-virgate of land and a half-quarter with other parcels recently held by Richard Wayte, and the reversion of a certain cote now held by Agnes Wattesson for life, rendering annually in all things as did Richard. G.: 2s.

3859 Bythorne William Bevereche and his wife, Beatrix: one messuage and a half-virgate of land recently held by his father, for life, rendering annually in all things as did his father. G.: 2s.

3860 Bythorne William Kyng and his wife, Alicia: one messuage and a half-virgate of land recently held by Richard Wallys, rendering annually in all things as did Richard. G.: 2s.

3861 Warboys (December) John Sharpe and his wife, Agnes: one maltland once held by Richard Olyver containing a half-virgate of land, and half of one tenement well built up and once held by Alicia Norys, three acres of land at Calnhyll and one acre of land at Lowfurlong once held by Robert Olyver and recently held by his father, William Sharpe, for life, rendering annually 15s. at the customary times and all other services and customs rendered by William. G.: four capons.

3862 Holywell (December) John Chekker Jr., John Brye, and his wife, Lucia: one messuage and one virgate of land with demesne land and a half acre of land at Malwode and one selion of meadow in Salmade recently held by Thomas Daye and once held by John Asplond, for life. Also: one cote and three rods of land once held

217v by Katerina Shepperd for 10s., one croftland recently held by Thomas Baron for 3s. and one other croftland recently held by William Hunne for 3s.4d. and five acres of demesne land, of which one is in Stonydole, two are in Oxhowe and two are in Overebrerecroft and previously rendering 5s., for life, rendering annually 23s.2d.ob. at the customary times, and all other services and customs owed therein. G.: one capon.

3863 Chatteris (December) Galfridus Reynald: one built up cotland in le Hyth recently held by John Reynald, for life, rendering annually 23d. at the customary times, and all other services and customs rendered by John. G.: 6d.

3864 CHATTERIS (December) John Mathewe: one tenement and eight acres of land with meadow in Oldhalf and with a forland and lands in Medmen, Ellemen and Long Grave recently held by John Hertford Bocher, for life, rendering annually 12s.8d. at the customary times, and all other services and customs owed therein. G.: 3s.4d.

3865 CHATTERIS (31 January: court) Thomas Smyth: surrender of half of one tenement of eight acres of land with other appurtenances recently held by John Mathewe and once held by William Whythed, to the use of William Thaksted, for life, rendering annually in all things as did Thomas. G.: two capons.

3866 CHATTERIS (same court) John Covenaunt: one tenement of eight acres of land recently held by John Hunte and once held by Stephen Cokerell, for life, rendering annually 4s. at the customary times, and all other services and customs rendered by John. G.: 4d.

3867 CHATTERIS (same court) John Matew: surrender of one cotland once held by William Whythede, to the use of John Mychell, for life, rendering annually 23s. at the customary times, and all other services and customs rendered by John. G.: 2s.

3868 CHATTERIS (same court) Agnes Hunte: surrender of half of one tenement of eight acres of land with one acre of land at Shyphernfen, and a half-acre of land in Elmen recently held by William Hunte, to the use of John Gerveys, for life, rendering annually in all things as did Agnes. G.: 6d.

3869 CHATTERIS (same court) John Rede: surrender of one messuage and half of one tenement of eight acres of land with meadow in Oldehalf and a half-acre of land recently held by John Bray in Elmen, to the use of John Bache, for life, rendering annually 4s.10d. at the customary times, and all other services and customs rendered by John. G.: 12d.

3870 CHATTERIS (same court) William Hunte: surrender of one messuage in le Slade Ende recently held by Thomas Halle and once held by John Drynge, to the use of John Hunte, for life, rendering annually 12d. at the customary times, and all other services and customs rendered by William. G.: 12d.

218r **3871** CHATTERIS (same court) John Mathewe: surrender of half of one tenement of eight acres of land with meadow in Crowlode once held by William Whytehede, with one fishpond once held by Simon Braye, to the use of Hugo Cokkesforth, for life, rendering annually 4s.9d. at the customary times, and all other services and customs rendered by John. G.: 2s.6d.

3872 CHATTERIS (same court) Walter Toye: surrender of one vacant toft recently a messuage, with seven acres of land at Keyeslonde and meadow in Horseheath in Crowlode Mede once held by John Bate, to the use of William Gryme, for life, rendering annually 5s.4d. and all other services and customs rendered by Walter. G.: 6d.

3873 CHATTERIS (same court) Simon Alyn: one cotland and a half, with one acre of land in Mademen, two acres in Elmen and other parcels recently held by John Lytholf, with one acre of land in Elmen, an acre and a half in Medemen, and two selions of land at the western part of the manor recently held by Edmund Cade, for life, rendering annually 8s.6d. at the customary times, and all other services and customs rendered by John and Edmund. G.: 20d.

3874 CHATTERIS (same court) Laurence Hykkesson: one cotland in Mylende, two selions of land at Muslake recently held by Cristina Hykkesson, where she occupied one horse mill now in ruins, for life, rendering annually 2s.10d. at the customary times and all other services and customs rendered by Cristina. G.: 6d.

3875 CHATTERIS (same court) Nicholas Clerke: one messuage and one selion of land in a croft in Slade Ende recently held by Agnes Peyte and once held by Walter Peyte, for life, rendering annually 4d. and all other services and customs rendered by Agnes. G.: 20d.

3876 CHATTERIS (same court) John Sempoole Sr.: surrender of one built up cotland, half of eight acres of land, a fishpond with meadow in Crowlode, a forland with meadow in Oldhalf once held by John Balle, to the use of his son, John Sempoole, for life, rendering annually 8s.2d.ob. at the customary times and all other services and customs rendered by John Sr. Further, meadow in Oldhalf and half of the meadow in Crowlode are reserved to John Sr. for life. G.: two capons, and no more, because he is bailiff.

3877 CRANFIELD (January) John Grene, son of Thomas Grene: one plot and three quarters of land once held by John Grene and recently held by Thomas, with three quarters of land once held by Richard AtteRede and recently held by the same Thomas, for life, rendering annually 26s.8d., which property previously rendered 35s.3d.ob.q. Further, he may not relinquish or alienate any of the above, under penalty of forfeit of all his properties. G.: excused.

3878 CHATTERIS (April) John Revesson Jr.: one messuage and one rod of land recently held by Katerina Baxster, one acre of land in Ellemen recently held by Thomas Whythede, for life, rendering annually 7d. for the messuage and rod and 12d. for the acre, at the customary times, and all other services and customs rendered by Katerina and Thomas. G.: excused, because he is a servant of the lord.

218v **3879** CHATTERIS Walter Toye: one tenement of eight acres of land with meadow in Crowlode, three selions of land in Watergate, and five selions and one gore in Stokkyng, with other appurtenances recently held by John Balle in Horseheath, for life, rendering annually 12s.9d. at the customary times, and all other services and customs owed therein. G.: 40d., which the lord grants Walter to repair the tenement the first time.

3880 HURST (January) John Herrof and his wife, Margaret: one messuage built up with one house in ruined condition, one virgate of land recently held by William Boner, for life, in support of another virgate they hold, rendering annually 12s. at the customary times, and all other services and customs rendered by William, with payments beginning at the feast of St. Andrew. Further, they will repair and maintain the house at their own expense, large timber being supplied by the lord. G.: two capons.

3881 HURST (May) John Godman of St. Ives: one tenement with appurtenances recently held by William Waryn, from the previous Michaelmas for life, rendering annually 14s., which property previously rendered 15s.4d. Further, he will repair and maintain the property, both in buildings and walls, hedges and closes, and all other things, for which he receives one acre of thatch in Haliwell Mede, timber for beams, and an allowance of half of this year's rent. G.: not yet determined by the seneschal.

3882 HURST (May) John Herrof and his wife, Margaret: one quarter of land parcelled out of one virgate called Heyn Colle, with a toft pertaining to the virgate, for life, rendering annually 3s.4d. at the customary times, and all other services and customs owed therein, payments beginning as the feast of St. Andrew. G.: two capons.

3883 HURST (May) John Whyte and his wife, Alicia: one tenement with appurtenances recently held by John Tayllor and once held by John Smyth, for life, rendering annually 18s. at the customary times, and all other services and customs rendered by John, with the obligation to rebuild one grange, with John responsible for carpentry, straw with transport, the wages of roofers and all other repairs, and with the lord supplying one carpenter for two days and timber for the Pikwall Hall. Further, payments will begin at the feast of the Annunciation, and John receives four carts of undergrowth and two young trees. G.: two capons.

3884 WISTOW (January) Thomas Aylmar, naif of the lord: one plot with one hidemanland and one quarter of land and a half-quarter, and other parcels recently held by his father, Robert Aylmar, from Michaelmas for life, rendering annually 10s.6d. and all other services and customs rendered by Robert. G.: 2s.

3885 ABBOTS RIPTON (September) John Lyndeseye and his wife, Agnes: one vacant plot at Estgrene and a half-virgate of land with three selions of land in the field and one acre of land abbutting Estthorp Slade recently held by William Halsham, for life, rendering annually 6s. at the customary times, and all other services and customs rendered by William, payments beginning at the feast of St. Andrew after one full year. G.: one capon.

3886 UPWOOD Roger Gryme and his wife, Johanna: a half-cotland of one acre once held by Robert Newman and recently held by Robert Preston, one cotland of one acre with one toft at the end of the village next to Dufhousdole recently held by Robert Preston and certain selions of land at Asplond Dole recently held by John Freston, for life, rendering annually 7s. at the customary times, and all other services and customs owed therein. G.: two pullets.

3887 RAMSEY (20 April) Thomas Filhous Faber and his wife, Margaret: from Brother William Bury, sub-cellarer, one plot in High Street recently held by John Sutton, from the previous Michaelmas for life, rendering annually 6s.8d. in equal portions at the feast of the Annunciation and Nativity of Blessed Mary, with the obligation to repair and maintain the property in enclosures and hedges, receiving thorns and other necessary things from the sub-cellarer. Further, they will perform other repairs and maintenance, and they may substitute any other tenant in their place, provided he render two capons to the sub-cellarer after six days from his entry. Further, the sub-cellarer will repair another plot held by Thomas, with Thomas supplying thorns. *Et si predictus redditus*, etc. (arrears of six weeks). G.: 3s.4d.

3888 RAMSEY (June) Robert Belamy Glover and his wife, Isabella: from Brother William Bury, one plot in High Street on the east now held by Thomas Coke Bocher, from next Michaelmas for life, rendering annually 12s. at the customary times, with the obligation to repair and maintain the property at their own expense in splints, plastering, hedges and enclosures, the sub-cellarer supplying stakes, thorns, splints, clay and transport. G.: 8s.4d.

3889 GRAVELEY (28 August) John Rolf, naif of the lord by blood, pays the fine for license to marry Cristina, his daughter, to John Chapman of Drayton, this time.

3890 RAMSEY (August) John Betecok and his wife, Margaret: from Brother William Bury, sub-cellarer, one messuage with adjacent garden in the Whyte recently held by Robert Lamkyn and once held by Henry Hamond, for life, rendering annually 10s. in equal portions at the feasts of the Annunciation and Nativity of Blessed Mary, and all other services and customs owed therein, with the sub-cellarer responsible for repairs and maintenance, except for closes, for which John and Margaret receive undergrowth and its transport. *Et si predictus redditus*, etc. (distraints after arrears of one month; seizure after arrears of six weeks). G.: 3s.4d.

3891 RAMSEY (August) John Keteryng Jr. and his wife, Sarra: from the sub-cellarer, one plot recently held by John Myssangle and once held by John Tapesere, in High Street, for life, rendering annually 12s. in equal portions at the feasts of the Annunciation and Nativity of Blessed Mary, with the sub-cellarer responsible for repairs and maintenance, except for closes, for which John and Sarra receive undergrowth and its transport. *Et si predictus redditus*, etc. (distraints after arrears of 15 days; seizure after arrears of one month). G.: 6s.8d.

3892 RAMSEY (August) Robert Brampton and his wife, Agnes: from the sub-cellarer, one selion of land lying next to the land of Nicholas Mably, with four acres of land in

219r

219v

one piece, with adjacent meadow recently held by John Ware and once held by John Dalby, for life, rendering annually 4s. in equal portions at the customary times, which property previously rendered 5s.4d. *Et si predictus redditus*, etc. (arrears of one month). G.: 20d., in the account of the sub-cellarer for the preceding year.

3893 HEMINGFORD ABBOTS (August) Thomas Aungewyn: a half-virgate of land recently held by Thomas Whete and first held by William Herde, and once held by William Aylmer, from Michaelmas for life, rendering annually 2s. at the customary times, which property previously rendered 5s.6d. Further, he will render all other services and customs owed therein. G.: excused because of his good service.

3894 LITTLE STUKELEY William Vernon and his wife, Alicia: one toft and a half-virgate of land from the tenement of Veysis recently held by Robert Mokke and once held by Thomas Gylle, for life, without making waste, rendering annually 4s.5d. at the customary times, and all other services and customs owed therein. G.: four capons.

3895 WARBOYS (February) Henry Birt and his wife, Helena: one messuage and a half-virgate of land and one virgate of land in Caldecote recently held by Richard Wilkis, for life, rendering annually 16s. for rent and 2d. for works, at the customary times, and all other services and customs rendered by tenants in *arentatio*. Further, they will repair and maintain the property at their own expense, timber being supplied by the lord. G.: two capons.

13 JOHN STOWE (1448-1449)

3896 CRANFIELD (28 October: leet) Thomas Rede: one quarter of land with one cotland and a half-virgate recently held by John AtteHill and surrendered back to the lord by his widow, Johanna AtteHill, held by him through the right of his wife, Margaret, daughter of John AtteHill, for life, rendering annually 26s. at the customary times, and all other services and customs rendered by John. G.: 3s.4d. Heriot: one sheep valued at 12d. by the bailiff in his account.

3897 WISTOW (11 November) Robert Owty, son of Thomas Owty, living in Hartford next to Huntingdon and naif of the lord, pays the seneschal at Wistow the fine for license to live off the manor with his father at Hartford for as long as it pleases the lord, rendering 12d. annually and suit to leet at Wistow. Pledges: Stephen Marschall of Houghton and William Owty of Little Raveley. Note that the mother of the above Thomas Owty paid the fine this year to John Cheker at Houghton.

3898 ELSWORTH (leet) Richard Ravene: surrender of one messuage and one virgate of land and one cotland recently held by Thomas Howesson, to the use of Thomas Newman, and his wife, Agnes, for life, rendering annually 21s.6d. at the customary times, and all other services and customs rendered by Richard, with the obligation to repair and maintain the buildings already built and to be built on the property at their own expense. G.: 40d.

3899 BURWELL (leet) John Fabbe: one tenement of 20 acres containing Yngoldesslowgh, and one cotland in North Street recently held by Nicholas Attehill, for 30 years, rendering annually (*cut off*) at the customary times, and all other services and customs as did Nicholas. G.: 2s.

3900 WARBOYS (3 December) Agnes Broun: surrender of property back to the lord, to the use of John Gostelowe. G.: two woodcocks. (*Entry is fragmentary*).

3901 WARBOYS (1 December). John Caton Sr., his son, John, William Bonde, John Plombe and John Horwode: the windmill there with the suit pertaining to it, from Christmas for 20 years, rendering to the *firmarius* annually 26s.8d. in four installments of 6s.8d. every quarter, with the obligation to repair and maintain the mill,

221r   receiving at first an allowance of 6s.8d. of rent and timber. Afterwards, they will maintain the mill at their own expense, timber being supplied by the lord, and they will
support other obligations and return the mill at the end of their term in good condition. In addition, they receive at the beginning one new mill stone and one old mill
stone, to be returned at the end of the their term in the same condition and at the same
value. G.: one cake.

3902   Holywell (10 December) William Miller, naif of the lord of the manor of
Weston: surrender of one plot and one rod, one messuage and six acres of land and
one and a half acres of meadow with four gores at Mannesbrigge and one rod of
meadow in Salemade once held by Roger Brayn, to the use of his son, John Miller,
and his wife, Helena, in bondage for life, rendering annually in all things as did
William. G.: 2s.

3903   Shillington cum Pegsdon (leet) William Pate and his wife: one plot, two
virgates of land, one cotland and five acres of servile land recently held by Gilbert Attehill and requested by William through the right of his wife, daughter and heiress of
Gilbert, for life, rendering annually in all things as did Gilbert. Also: one messuage
and one virgate of land recently held by the same Gilbert and once held by William del
Hill, for life, rendering annually in all things as did Gilbert. G.: 26s.8d. Heriot: recorded in the leet of this year.

3904   Shillington (leet) John Stone: all the lands and tenements previously held by
Thomas Porter in Pegsdon and seized by the lord because of felony that Thomas committed resulting in forfeit to the lord, in bondage for life, rendering annually all services and customs owed therein. G.: 3s.4d., to be paid to the lord through the
seneschal.

3905   Shillington (same leet). John Scote of Hitchen pays 4d. for withdrawing
suit to the court of Broughton annually for as long as it pleases the lord for lands and
tenements recently held by Richard Bradyfan in Shillington, which fine, paid to the
seneschal, will be paid by the seneschal to the lord.

221v   **3906**   Bythorne (10 December) William Payne of Bythorne pays 2s. for license to
marry Agnes, daughter of John Kempe and naif of the lord by blood, this time.

3907   Bythorne (10 December) Robert Brewse: surrender of one cotland built up
with one house recently held by Richard Weyte, to the use of William Tomelyn Carpenter and his wife, Katerina, for life, rendering annually 12d. at the customary times,
and all other services and customs rendered by Robert. G.: 12d.

3908   Bythorne William Spayne: surrender of half of one quarter of land with
demesne land, to the use of Thomas Spayne. Same Thomas and his wife, Elena: one
plot and one quarter of land recently held by John Brewster and a half-quarter of land
recently held by William Goodefelowe, for life, rendering annually 19s.9d. at the
customary times, and all other services and customs rendered by John. G.: 20d.

3909   St. Ives (10 December) John Sammes and his wife, Elizabeth: a half-row once
held by John Burneman, a half-row once held by John Revenale and one row once
held by Thomas Ravene and recently held by John AtteWode, for life, rendering annually 40s. at the customary times, with the obligation to repair and maintain all
buildings, both existing and to be built. *Et non licebit*, etc. G.: one pound of pepper
and two ounces of saffron.

3910   St. Ives (10 December) John Bedford: surrender of one row once held by
Robert Elyngton, to the use of Richard Atekyn, and his wife, Margeria, for life, rendering annually 16s. at the customary times, with the obligation to repair and maintain

222r   the property. *Et non licebit*, etc. G.: (*blank*).

3911   Little Stukeley John Dycon: surrender of one croft, once a plot, with adjacent land and meadow once held by William Brekesper, to the use of John Pelle, and his wife, Margaret, in bondage for life, without making any waste, rendering annually 8s. at the customary times, and all other services and customs owed therein, with the obligation to observe all the agreements made between them and John Dycon and his wife, Elena, as contained in certain indentured bills dated 24 November, Henry VI, under penalty of forfeit. G.: 3s.4d. And they swear fealty.

3912 HOUGHTON (10 January) John Upton Sr., who lives in Hemingford Abbots and naif of the lord by blood, pays 3s.4d. for license to marry Agnes, his daughter, to John Barlyman of Stanton, this time.

3913 HOUGHTON (20 March) John Fuller, his wife, Agnes, and their son, Thomas: two parcels of meadow pertaining to the manor of Abbot's Ripton and once held by the prior of Huntingdon and John Maddyngle, from the previous Michaelmas for life, rendering annually 12d. at the customary times, which property previously rendered 6s.8d. Further, they will plant willows around the meadow as seems best to them and according to the discretion of the seneschal of Ramsey within two years, and maintain the ditches and enclosures, and they may cut down willows at an appropriate time and put them to their use without any waste. Further, easement in the two parcels of meadow for grain and other necessities, and carrying of water through and by the two parcels of meadow as often as it pleases him is reserved to the lord for the whole term. G.: two chickens.

3914 HOUGHTON (16 April) John Marschall, naif of the lord by blood, pays two capons for license to marry Alicia, his daughter, to William Mabety of Girton in Cambridgeshire, this time. And the fine is no more because he is a servant of the prior of St. Ives.

3915 CHATTERIS (January) John Amrose receives from the lord two cotlands recently held by John Ingram and once held by John Smyth, for life, rendering annually 3s.10d. at the customary times, and all other services and customs owed therein, with payments beginning at the feast of St. Andrew. G.: two capons.

3916 CHATTERIS (January) John Revesson Sr.: one vacant toft with adjacent croft and willows in le Wyght once held by the sister of Lord Thomas Botirwyke, former abbot, for life, rendering annually 2s. at the customary times, which property previously rendered 13s.4d. Further, he will render all other services and customs owed therein. G.: one capon.

3917 CHATTERIS (January) Thomas Litholf: surrender of one messuage, one rod of land, Burstede with pond and meadow next to Ellemen and meadow at le Grave and land next to the church, two acres of land in Medmen and five selions of land at the western part of the manor, to the use of Richard Broun, for life, rendering annually 12s.4d.ob. at the customary times, and all other services and customs owed therein. G.: 20d.

3918 CHATTERIS (January) Richard Berle: one cotland and meadow in Crowlode with forland recently held by Robert Gravele and once held by Agnes Enfeld, for life, rendering annually 2s.10d. at the customary times, and all other services and customs owed therein. G.: 8d.

3919 CHATTERIS (January) William Hunte: surrender of one (*blank*) and half of eight acres of land with meadow and other appurtenances recently held by Thomas Fisscher, to the use of Thomas Halle, for life, rendering annually 10s.4d.ob. at the customary times, and all other services and customs owed therein. G.: 2s.

3920 CHATTERIS (January) John Clerke: one cotland built up with two houses recently held by John Hikkisson Symmesson, for life, rendering annually 23d. at the customary times, and all other services and customs owed therein. G.: 12d.

222v

3921 CHATTERIS (January) John Poppe Jr.: surrender of half of one tenement of eight acres of land with one built up cotland and meadow in Crowlodemede, to the use of John Revisson, bailiff, for life, rendering annually 6s.11d. at the customary times, and all other services and customs owed therein. G.: two capons.

3922 WOODHURST (11 February) John Catell: one messuage built up with one house and one virgate of land and a half-virgate recently held by Roger Cachesoly and once held by John Vikori, for life, rendering annually 20s. at the customary times, which property previously rendered 24s. Further, payments will begin at the feast of St. Andrew after two complete years, with the lord providing one house from which John will

223r   build one grange. He will move the house beyond the water, and raise, splint and repair the grange; and he receives undergrowth for the enclosure. G.: two chickens.

3923 HURST (11 February) John Huntyngdon: one toft and a half-virgate of land recently held by Richard Nonne, for life, rendering annually 6s. at the customary times, which property previously rendered 8s. Further, he receives the above in support of another half-virgate he previously received from the lord for 7s., with payments beginning at the feast of St. Andrew after one full year. G.: two capons.

3924 KNAPWELL (14 February: Wednesday, St. Valentine) John Lawe, naif of the lord of Knapwell by blood, who lives in Over, pays 12d. and two capons for license to marry Rosa, his daughter, to Thomas Smyth of Over, this time. Pledge: William Mayner of Over.

3925 WARBOYS (February) Thomas Plombe, son of John Plombe: one virgate of land in Caldecote recently held by Nicholas Benson and once held by John Plombe, for life, rendering annually 10s. at the customary times, which property previously rendered 12s. Further, he will render all other services and customs rendered by Nicholas, with payments beginning at the feast of St. Andrew after one full year. G.: two capons.

3926 UPWOOD CUM RAVELEY (March) John Wright: one messuage and two half-virgates with adjacent forland recently held by John Andrewe for 16s.2d., for 12 years, rendering annually 13s.4d. at the customary times, and all other services and customs rendered by John, with payments beginning at the feast of St. Andrew. Further, the lord will build one grange on the property, with John responsible for splints, plastering and roofing, and repairs and maintenance thereafter, at his own expense. G.: two capons.

3927 GRAVELEY John Baron, bailiff, pays 20d. for license to marry Alicia, daughter of Thomas Baron and naif of the lord, to whomever she wishes, this time.

3928 GRAVELEY (1 April) William Stoughton: one messauge built up with one new house called *Insathous*, and a half-virgate of land once held by John Hanle, from Michaelmas for life, rendering annually 13s.4d. at the customary times, and all other services and customs owed therein. Further, the lord will build one grange on the property, in both timber and carpentry, and William will repair and maintain it thereafter and build one bake house on the tenement within two years, in timber and all other things, receiving an allowance of the rents for two years. G.: two capons.

223v   **3929** WISTOW CUM RAVELEY William Owty Jr.: surrender of one messauge and one quarter of land with a cotland recently held by John Walgate, to the use of Richard Plombe, for life, rendering annually in all things as did William. G.: four capons.

3930 SLEPE (May) Richard Morgon: one messauge and one cotland once held by Frederick Skynner and recently held by John Bedford, for life, rendering annually in all things as did John. G.: four capons, two being paid this year and two next year.

3931 ST. IVES (May) William Esex and his wife, Margaret: a half-row recently held by John Cossale and once held by Thomas Glover, from the previous Michaelmas for life, rendering annually 2s. at the customary times, which property previously rendered 6s.8d. Further, they will rebuild one hall at the front of the property before Michaelmas, and repair and maintain it and all other buildings there at their own expense thereafter. *Et non licebit*, etc. G.: 2s.

3932 Sr. Ives (May) John Roger Fuller and his wife, Alicia: one manse of the toll booth recently rebuilt in which he now lives, for life, rendering annually 10s. at the customary times, and all other services and customs owed therein, with the obligation to repair and maintain the buildings already built there and to be built. *Et non licebit*, etc. G.: 3s.4d.

224r   **3933** Wistow (July) William Cabe: surrender of one quarter of land once held by Alicia Fimace, to the use of John Randolf and his wife from Michaelmas for life, rendering annually 5s. and all other services and customs owed therein. G.:16d.

3934 Shillington (25 July) Thomas Stonley: surrender of one messuage and one virgate of land with forland once held by Roger Chible, half of one virgate of land recently held by John AtteStone, one and a half-acres of demesne land at le Croft recently held by Walter Porter, three acres of land recently held by John Kechenere, and six acres of land recently held by Thomas Chible, to the use of Thomas Poole and his wife, Johanna, for life, rendering annually 35s.2d. and all other services and customs rendered by Thomas. G.: 20s. Heriot: to be paid by Thomas at the next leet.

3935 Houghton (7 August) William Wythe, naif of the lord by blood, pays 20d. for license to marry Agnes, his daughter, to whomever she wishes, this time.

3936 Houghton (7 August) William Wythe, naif of the lord, pays 6d. for license for Alicia, his daughter, to serve and live with her sister Agnes at London for as long as it pleases the lord, rendering to the seneschal of Ramsey at Houghton 6d. annually.

3937 Houghton (1 September) William Wythe Jr., son of William Wythe Sr., naif of the lord by blood, pays the fine for license to live with Laurence, the parish chaplain of Therfield, off the manor, for as long as it pleases the lord, rendering 8d. annually. Pledge: Laurence the chaplain.

3938 Ramsey John Bereford: from Brother William Burye, sub-cellarer, one messuage near the bridge called Baxter's Bridge recently held by John Pycard, for life, rendering 7s. at the customary times, and all other services and customs owed therein, with the sub-cellarer responsible for repairs, except for the fortifying of ditches and closes. *Et si predictus redditus*, etc. (arrears of one month). G.: 6s.8d.

3939 Ramsey John Thoday and his wife, Agnes: one plot within Mechegates recently held by William Botiller, for life, rendering annually 5s. at the customary times, and all other services and customs owed therein, with the sub-cellarer responsible for repairs, except for closes. *Et si predictus redditus*, etc. (arrears of one month). G.: 3s.4d.

224v   **3940** Ramsey (August) John Bury: from Brother William Bury, one plot within Mechegates at the north, recently held by Robert Broun Tyler, from Michaelmas for life, rendering annually 5s. in equal portions at the feasts of the Annunciation and Nativity of Blessed Mary, with permission to let the property be occupied by any other tenants during the aforesaid term, provided that repairs be effected at the expense of the sub-cellarer. *Et si predictus redditus*, etc. (arrears of two months). G.: excused.

3941 Hemingford Abbots (August) Thomas Aungewyn and his wife, Johanna: a half-virgate of land recently held by Thomas Whete and once held by William Herde, for life, rendering annually 2s. at the customary times, and all other services and customs owed therein. G.: two capons.

3942 Upwood (1 September) Agnes, daughter of Nicholas Alby, deceased, naif of the lord by blood, and now in service to the rector of Over, pays two capons for license to marry whomever she wishes, this time.

3943 St. Ives (1 September) Thomas Aungewyn and his wife, Johanna: one plot of those two plots newly constructed on one vacant toft one held by Thomas Smythe and next to the tenement of the eleemosynary of Ramsey, from Michaelmas for life, rendering annually 20s. and suit to the mill of the Prior, and all other services and customs owed therein, although the lord pardons the rents because of Thomas' good and laudable service. G.: excused.

14 JOHN STOWE (1449-1450)

225r **3944** Elsworth (9 October: leet) Simon Sparugh: one cotland with croft once held by William Thatcher, and one cotland once held by John Toppe and recently held by William Howlot, for life, rendering annually 4s. at the customary times, and all other services and customs owed therein. G.: 12d., two capons.

3945 Elsworth (same leet) Thomas Croft: one cotland and the sixth part of St. Luke's land recently held by William Howlote, for life, rendering annually 4s. at the customary times, and all other services and customs owed therein. G.: (*blank*).

3946 Elsworth (leet) William Mareys: one cote with appurtenances recently held by John Elyut and once held by John Chircheman Sr., for life, rendering annually in all things as did John. G.: 2s., two capons.

3947 Elsworth (1 January) Thomas Boner, son of Henry Boner and naif of the lord by blood, pays the bailiff 6d. for license to live off the manor for as long as it pleases the lord, rendering 6d. and suit to the leet of Elsworth annually, remaining a naif as before. Pledge: Alexander Hobbesson.

3948 Elsworth (March) John Barker and his wife, Isabella: one messuage built up with one house, and a half-virgate of land recently held by Alicia Coupere, for life, rendering annually 10s. at the customary times, and all other services and customs owed therein. G.: 20d.

3949 Elsworth (March) Alexander Fermor: one quarter of land and one cotland of Gravelond recently held by Alicia Coupere, for life, rendering annually 5s. and all other services and customs rendered by Alicia. G.: four capons.

3950 Elsworth (March) Thomas Fermor: surrender of one built up messuage and one semi-virgate of land once held by William Hobbesson, to the use of Thomas Porter and his wife, Margaret, for life, rendering annually 10s. at the customary times, and all other services and customs rendered by Thomas. G.: two capons.

3951 Elsworth (March) John Elyet: surrender of one plot with two semi-virgates and one quarter of land from Gravelond and one cotland once held by John God, to the use of Thomas Fermor and his wife, Margeria, for life, rendering annually 27s. at the customary times, and all other services and customs owed therein. G.: 3s.

3952 Elsworth (March) John Cristemesse: surrender of one quarter of land once held by Henry Smyth, to the use of Thomas Blakewell and his wife, Johanna, for life, rendering annually 5s. and all other services and customs owed therein. G.: two capons.

225v **3953** Elsworth Thomas Hobbesson, alias Fermer: surrender of one cotland and one quarter of land recently held by William Hobbesson, to the use of John Elyot and his wife, Anna, for life, rendering annually 5s. at the customary times, and all other services and customs rendered by Thomas. G.: 2s.

3954 Elsworth John Eliet, naif of the lord by blood, pays 6d. for license to live on the fief of the parson, for as long as it pleases the lord, rendering suit to court and leet annually.

3955 KNAPWELL (same leet). John Reignald Jr. and his wife, Agnes: one built up messuage with one barn and a half-virgate of land recently held by John Sampson Brewer, for life, rendering annually in all things as did John. G.: 12d.

3956 KNAPWELL (same leet) John Smyth: one quarter of land recently held by John Reignald Jr., for life, rendering annually in all things as did John. G.: 8d.

3957 BURWELL (21 October: leet) John Wylkyn: surrender of half of one tenement of 24 acres with appurtenances recently held by John Rolfe, to the use of Robert Wyot, for 20 years, rendering annually 12s. and all other services and customs owed therein. G.: three capons.

3958 BURWELL (same leet) Nicholas atte Hill: surrender of one tenement of 20 acres of land with one cotland in North Street, to the use of William Fabbe, from the previous Michaelmas for 20 years, rendering annually 20s. and all other services and customs owed therein. G.: 2s., and no more because of repairs.

3959 THERFIELD (23 October: leet) William Colle, son of John Colle atte Wayer, naif of the lord: one tenement and one cotland recently held by Thomas Overston and five acres of demesne land recently held by the same Thomas, for life, rendering annually 13s. at the customary times, and all other services and customs rendered by Thomas. Further, he receives an allowance of half of this year's rent for repairs, and a half-rod of undergrowth. G.: two capons.

3960 THERFIELD (same leet) John Gurney, John Carter and William Gerveys: one meadow called Nastmede nest to the king's road towards Reed, once held by John Roke, from the previous Michaelmas for 20 years, rendering all services and customs owed therein at the customary times, with the obligation to enclose the meadow with hedges and ditches and maintain it at their own expense. G.: (*blank*).

3961 THERFIELD (December) John Edward, his wife, Elena, and their descendants: one cotland built up with one house and adjacent croft in Royston recently held by John Hatlo, in bondage, rendering annually 12d. at the customary times, and all other services and customs owed therein. G.: two capons.

226r

3962 THERFIELD (December) John Evadet, alias Gurney, William Gerveyse and John Carter: one meadow called Nastmede with the yields of the pasture in the field pertaining to it and recently held by John Rooke, from the previous Michaelmas for life, rendering annually 14s. at the customary times, with the obligation to rebuild the enclosure of the meadow along the king's road within one year and maintain it thereafter at their own expense. G.: six capons.

3963 SHILLINGTON (25 October: leet) John Brooke: surrender of one cotland and half of one culture of demesne land in Hanscombe and four acres of land at Chirchehill, to the use of his son, John Brooke, and his wife, Johanna, for life, rendering annually 13s.4d. at the customary times, and all other services and customs owed therein. G. and heriot: blank.

3964 BARTON (26 October: General Court) Emma Bonne: surrender of one cotland recently held by her husband, Thomas Bonne, to the use of her son, Philip Bonne, for life, rendering annually 7s. at the customary times, and all other services and customs owed therein. G.: 2s., two capons. Heriot: paid in the court.

3965 CRANFIELD (28 October: leet) John Sqwyer, and his wife, Johanna, daughter and heiress of Alicia Mowse: three quarters of land and one cotland with one acre of land once held by Thomas Mowse, for life, rendering annually 22s. at the customary times, and all other services and customs rendered by Thomas. G.: 3s. Heriot: paid in the court.

3966 CRANFIELD (same leet) William Wodehill: one messuage and one half-virgate of land recently held by his father, Thomas Wodehill, for life, rendering annually in all things as did Thomas. G.: 6s.8d. Heriot: paid in the court.

3967 CRANFIELD Thomas Rideler: one capital messuage of a half-virgate recently held by William atte Hill and lately held by Thomas Brerele and surrendered back to the lord by him, with one quarter of land once held by Walter Nedeler, for life, rendering annually 3s. for the messuage and 6s.9d. for the quarter, and all other services, and customs owed therein. G.: 12d.

3968 WESTON (7 November: leet) Walter Flesshall pays 12d. for license to marry Beatrix, his daughter, to Thomas Carwold of Brington, this time.

226v **3969** GRAVELEY (November) Richard Dyke: surrender of one messuage and one virgate of land and one parcel of land of Hallelond, to the use of Richard Swane, for life, rendering annually in all things as did Richard. G.: two capons, and no more because of the repairs of a grange in greatly ruined condition and other buildings at his own expense.

3970 ABBOTS RIPTON William Wodeward, alias Fuller and his wife, Margaret: one parcel of demesne land lying in one culture called Frelond recently held by his father, William Fuller, and half of one culture of demesne land called Langlond recently held by the rector, John Gillynge, and one piece of demesne land called Estthorpbriggedole in Millefeld containing nine acres, with one acre of demesne land parcelled out of Shepdole at Haywardishege, and one parcel of pasture once Oxelasne called London Brook, for life, rendering 15s. the first year and 24s. each year thereafter, at the customary times, and all other services and customs owed therein. G.: eight capons.

3971 ABBOTS RIPTON (March) Alan Pollan: one messuage and one semi-virgate of land once held by John Person and recently held by John Crosse, for life, rendering annually in all things as did John, with the obligation to maintain the messuage at his own expense. G.: four capons.

3972 ABBOTS RIPTON (April) Roger Tausley and his wife, Agnes: one cotland and one vacant toft with one semi-virgate and three acres of land called Catteshegelond recently held by Thomas Wattes, for life, rendering annually 11s., one hen and 20 eggs at the customary times, and all other services and customs rendered by Thomas. G.: two capons.

3973 HOLYWELL CUM NEEDINGWORTH (17 November) Adam Hemyngton: surrender of one messuage and one virgate of land with one acre of land in Overebrerecroft and one rod of meadow in Salmade once held by his father, John Hemyngton, to the use of his son, John Hemyngton and his wife, Agnes, daughter of William Gille of Swavesey, for life, rendering annually in all things as did Adam and all other services and customs owed therein. G.: 2s., and no more, at the urging of the seneschal, John Denholt. And they swear fealty.

3974 HOLYWELL CUM NEEDINGWORTH (16 December) (at Ramsey) Simon Tooslond, through his attorney, Roger Cristemesse, pays 20s. for license to marry Johanna, daughter of John atte Well, naif of the lord by blood of Holywell. Further, the original fine of 40s. was reduced to 20s. at the urging of Simon Dallynge, in witness of which the seal of the lord is appended to the present document.

227r **3975** ST. IVES (November) William Tayllor and his wife, Johanna: a half-row at le Barre one held by Alan Smythe and recently held by Laurence Baywell, and a half-row once held by John Edenham and recently held by John Valentine, for life, rendering annually 17s. at the customary times, with the obligation to repair and maintain the property. *Et non licebit*, etc. G.:16s.8d.

3976 WISTOW CUM RAVELEY (6 December) Thomas Bolyon of Brampton: license to have Alicia, daughter of Richard Owty of Little Stukeley and naif and villein of the lord, in his service and living with him, in return for sustenance and an adequate salary, from the present date for one year, at the end of which time he will return her to the manor. Fine for the license: 2s. Pledge for all these matters: William Spycer and Richard Gelan.

3977 WISTOW CUM RAVELEY (December) Richard Benet: surrender of one recently burned plot, two virgates, one quarter of land and half of one quarter, and one acre of demesne land at Lowfurlong, to the use of William Benet, for life, rendering annually 16s.9d. for rent and 8s.2d. for works, at the customary times, for as long as it pleases the lord to receive money for works, with the obligation to repair and maintain the plot, recently rebuilt by the lord, at his own expense. G.: 13s.4d., to be excused if he effects repairs. Further, he will pay two capons.

3978 WISTOW CUM RAVELEY (December) John Chylde and his wife, Isabella: one messuage and one cotland and six acres of demesne land, one acre of land called Hydegorys, a parcel of meadow called Reddyngys, one acre of land called Burysevyn, and six selions of land in Chesfurlong recently held by William Cabe, from the previous Michaelmas for life, rendering annually 13s. at the customary times, and all other services and customs rendered by William, with the obligation to repair and maintain the property at their own expense, under penalty of forfeit, and in consideration for which repairs they receive an allowance of 9s. of this year's rent. G.: two capons.

3979 WISTOW CUM RAVELEY (30 January) John Morton: the windmill, with suit thereto, from the feast of the Annunciation for a term of (*unspecified*) years, rendering annually 20s. at the feast of John the Baptist, the Nativity of Blessed Mary, and the Purification, with the obligation to repair and maintain the mill at his own expense, timber being supplied by the lord, with its cutting and transport supplied by John.

227v

3980 HOUGHTON (December) John Carter Jr., son of Richard Carter of Houghton, alias Richard Harves, naif of the lord by blood, pays the fine for license to live off the manor for as long as it pleases the lord, remaining a naif as before, and rendering 6d. and suit to leet annually. Pledges: Richard Smyth and William Nicholas of Hemingford Gray.

3981 HOUGHTON (April) John Dorson: surrender of one toft and one virgate of land once held by Walter Beddell, to the use of Richard Grene, for life, rendering annually 8s. at the customary times, and all other services and customs rendered by John. G.: 12d.

3982 HOUGHTON Thomas Elyet Jr.: one quarter of land recently held by John Smyth and once held by William Prikke, for life, rendering annually 2s. and all other services and customs owed therein, and in all other things as did John. G.: 8d.

3983 HOUGHTON Richard Attekyn: surrender of one virgate of land once held by Gilbert de Houghton and afterwards held by William Smyth and recently held by John Prikke, to the use of Thomas Brooke, for life, rendering annually 8s., which property previously rendered 10s. Further, he will render all other services and customs rendered by Richard. G.: 12d.

3984 HOUGHTON John Upton Jr.: one toft and one cotland recently held by Richard Attekyn and once held by John Andrewe, for life, rendering annually 5s., which property previously rendered 6s. Further, he will render all other services and customs rendered by Richard, with payments beginning at the feast of St. John the Baptist after one full year. G.: 8d.

3985 HOUGTON William Brampton: one messuage and a half-virgate of land *ad opus* recently held by Emma Andrewe and once held by John Andrewe, for life, rendering annually 6s. at the customary times, and all other services and customs rendered by Emma. G.: 12d.

3986 WARBOYS (1 January) Henry Birt: one parcel of pasture in Caldecote enclosed

228r

with hedges and ditches previously held by the same Henry, and which pasture was built up and utilized by various tenants of the lord, from the previous Michaelmas for life, rendering annually 13s.4d. at the customary times, with the obligation to maintain all the hedges, ditches, and other necessities at his own expense, receiving from the lord the thorns growing there for making the enclosure. Further, he is not to allow anyone to take timber there by cutting down trees or making any waste, under penalty of forfeit. G.: three capons, and no more because of the poor condition of the enclosure.

3987 WARBOYS (1 January) John Caton Sr. and John Caton Jr.: one parcel of pasture in Caldecote enclosed this year by the customaries of the lord and recently built up and utilized by various tenants, from the feast of the Annunciation for life, rendering 6s.8d. for half of this year, and 13s.4d. each year thereafter, at the customary times. Further, they will perform all other services as Henry Birt, above. G.: two capons.

3988 WARBOYS William Strige and his wife, Margaret: surrender of one tenement built up with three houses, called a mondayland, once held by Alicia Wytlesey, to the use of John Shepperd, and his wife, Juliana, for life, rendering annually 4s. at the customary times, and all other services and customs owed therein. G.: 12d.

3989 SLEPE (January) William Atkyn, naif of the lord of Houghton: one plot with two cotlands once held by William Herrof and one plot with one virgate of land recently held by John Barton, from the previous Michaelmas for life, rendering annually 28s. at the customary times, and all other services and customs rendered by John. Further, he will rebuild one *insathous* with annexed stable and *camera* on the tenement once held by John Barton within (*blank*) years, timber being supplied by the lord, and with the obligation to maintain it and all other buildings thereafter, with the lord granting an allowance of the rent for the new repairs. Pledge: Richard Atkyn. G.: 20d.

3990 CHATTERIS (18 March: General Court) John Barle Sr.: surrender of one cotland with meadow in Crowlode, one acre of land in five selions at Muslake, with a forland recently held by Galfridus Reignald and once held by Cartas, and one selion of land in Longrave and one acre of land in Elmen at Slade Ende, to the use of his son, John Barle, for life, rendering annually in all things as did his father. G.: 20d.

228v

3991 CHATTERIS (same court) John Lytholffe atte Corner: surrender of one tenement and eight acres of land with meadow in Oldhalf and fishpond with forland and a half-acre of land in Elmen, to the use of John Rede, for life, rendering annually 9s.4d. and all other services and customs owed therein. G.: 5s., two capons.

3992 CHATTERIS (same court) John Devell: surrender of half of one tenement of eight acres with meadow in Crowlode recently held by Agnes Enfeld, to the use of John Sempool, for life, rendering annually 4s.7d.ob. and all other services and customs owed therein. G.: 20d.

3993 CHATTERIS (same court) Galfridus Roiston, alias Taillor: surrender of one messuage built up with two houses, one acre of land, two selions in Medemen, four selions at Shephernefen, and four selions at the northern part of the manor once held by Thomas Tilneye, to the use of John Reder, for life, rendering annually 2s.2d. at the customary times, and all other services and customs owed therein. G.: 12d.

3994 CHATTERIS (same court) John Hopkyn Sr.: surrender of half of one tenement of eight acres, to the use of John Branncester Sr., for life, rendering annually 4s. at the customary times, and all other services and customs owed therein. G.: 12d., one capon.

3995 CHATTERIS (same court) Hugo Chapman: surrender of one cotland built up with one house recently held by John Coke, and a half-acre in Medemen recently held by John Skynner, and two selions of land in Stokkyng recently held by the same John, to the use of John Branncestre Sr., for life, rendering annually 2s.10d. at the customary times, and all other services and customs owed therein. G.: 20d. And he swears fealty.

3996 UPWOOD (June) Richard Grecham: one messuage, two virgates of land and a cotland and forland and parcels of land pertaining to one virgate of land once held by William Alcoke, with half of one piece of demesne land called Ryngedole, from Michaelmas for six years, rendering annually 42s.10d., which property previously rendered 46s.10d. Further, he will repair the hall and *camera* in splints, plastering, ramming, straw and roofing within three years, and maintain the grange and malt-kiln and other buildings there, with one carpenter for three days supplied by the customaries for the first repairs to Robynsplace, and with timber supplied in any year by the lord through the seneschal, two carts of thorns or undergrowth for the enclosure, wherever he wishes. Further, at the end of the term he will restore 12 acres of fallow land to the lord, granted him in the month of March. G.: excused.

3997 UPWOOD (20 July) William Jonesson of Holme and his wife, Isabella, widow of Thomas Penyman: all lands and tenements recently held by Thomas Penyman, from Michaelmas for six years, rendering annually in all things as did Thomas, with the obligation to make satisfaction to the lord before Easter of six quarters, three bushels of barley, one quarter of wheat, four quarters, four bushels and a half of peas seized from the customaries of the lord on that land. Further, they will repair one *camera* at the end of the hall in splints, plastering and roofing, supplying food for carpenters, with the lord supplying one cart load of straw, and they will maintain all other buildings on the property. G.: excused.

229r **3998** RIPTON (20 August) Richard Weston and his wife, Johanna: one messuage with appurtenances in Ripton next to the bridge at the lane leading to Stukeley recently held by Johanna Forster and lately held by Radulph of Herne and his wife, Emma, and surrendered back to the lord by them, for the lord to do with as he wished, for the life of whoever lives longer, rendering annually in all things as did Radulph. G.: 2s.

3999 ST. IVES (August) Thomas Aungewyn and his wife, Johanna and their heirs: one vacant toft lying at Barkerysrow recently held by Richard Charite and a half-row and buildings once held by Robert Papworth, rendering annually 20d. at the customary times, and all other services and customs owed therein. G.: one goose, one capon.

4000 BARNWELL (at WESTON) Copy of an indenture made at Ramsey, 3 February, 27 Henry VI. Master Richard Dygelon, parson of the church of St. Andrew of Barnwell, co. Northampton: two tenements with lands, meadows and other appurtenances in Bernewell recently held by Richard Graunte, parson of the church, by copy, and which lands pertain to the manor of Weston in Huntingdonshire, for as long as he holds his benefice, rendering annually 20s. at the feasts of the Annunciation and Nativity of Blessed Mary, and acquitting all other obligations and services owed therein. Further, he will repair and maintain all buildings existing and to be built on the property at his own expense, returning the land at the end of his term in as good or better condition than when he received it, both in agriculture and economy, namely waste reploughed and manured. He will not dismiss any of the property to anyone who will cause damage to the lord, his successors or other tenants there, under penalty of loss of his rights in the property, and if the payments, at any term, are 15 days late, the lord and his ministers may effect distraints in the two tenements until the full payments are made, with the right to retain the two tenements if payments are not made after one month, or if Richard fails to meet any of his obligations. Fine: six capons. And he swears fealty.

15 JOHN STOWE (1450-1451)

229v **4001** SHILLINGTON (8 October: leet) John Warde: surrender of one messuage in Stondon and two virgates of land with four acres of land in Newmanlond, to the use of John Berenton and his wife, Johanna, for life, rendering annually 30s.4d., and all other services and customs owed therein. G. and heriot: 10s.

4002 SHILLINGTON (same leet) William Whetele and his wife, Agnes: one messuage with appurtenances in Pegsdon recently held by John Porter and seized by the lord for felony committed by John, for life, rendering annually in all things as did John. G.: 5s., to be paid to the seneschal.

4003 SHILLINGTON (same leet) John Brooke Sr.: surrender of one cotland built up with one house once held by Mileward and four acres of land at Chirchehill and half of one culture of demesne land in Hanscombe, to the use of his son, John Brooke and his wife, Johanna, for life, rendering annually 13s.4d. and all other services and customs rendered by John. G. and heriot: 8s.

4004 SHILLINGTON (same leet) William Goodmar and his wife, Agnes: one messuage and one semi-virgate of land with other appurtenances recently held by Robert Waleys, for life, rendering annually 12s. and all other services and customs owed therein.

4005 SHILLINGTON (same leet) Robert Gayton: surrender of one messuage and one virgate of land recently held by Robert Catelyn, to the use of John Coche, and his wife, Alicia, for life, rendering annually 18s.10d.ob. at the customary times, and all other services and customs owed therein. Also: one semi-virgate of land once held by Bernard, for life, rendering annually 8s.2d. at the customary times, and half of one virgate of land recently held by John Grene, for life, rendering annually 8s.8d. and all other services and customs owed therein. G.: 8d.

4006 SHILLINGTON (same leet) Thomas Stonle Jr. and his wife, Margeria: one messuage and two virgates of land in Cheble and eight acres of demesne land recently held by John Coke, for life, rendering annually 38s.8d. at the customary times, and all other services and customs rendered by John. G. and heriot: 10s., two capons.

4007 SHILLINGTON (same leet) Thomas Stonle Jr.: surrender of one messuage and one semi-virgate of land recently held by William Cheble, to the use of William North, for life, rendering annually 8s.9d. at the customary times, and all other services and customs owed therein. G. and heriot: 2s., two capons.

4008 WESTON (22 October: leet) Walter Kyng, naif of the lord by blood, pays 2s. and six capons for license to marry Margeria, his daughter, to John Bryan, this time.

4009 WESTON (same leet) William Flesshewer, naif of the lord by blood, pays 40d. for license to marry Agnes, his daughter, to John Warenner of Bythorne, this time.

230r **4010** HEMINGFORD ABBOTS (26 October) Robert Marchall, son of John Marchall and naif of the lord by blood, pays the fine for license to live off the manor for as long as it pleases the lord, remaining a naif as before and rendering 20d. and suit to leet annually. Pledge: John Asplond of Holywell.

4011 SLEPE (November) Thomas Boner: one well built up cotland with one cotland recently held by William Herrof, for life, rendering annually 14s. at the customary times, and all other services and customs owed therein. G.: 5s.

4012 WARBOYS (29 October). Johanna, daughter of John Benet of Warboys and naif of the lord by blood, pays 5s. for license to marry Thomas Boner, this time. Pledge: Richard Atkyn, *firmarius* of Slepe. Fine paid to the lord through John Cheker.

4013 WARBOYS (November) Emma Haukyn: surrender of one cote built up with three houses and a half-virgate of land recently held by Robert Ravene, to the use of Thomas Fyssher, and his wife, Katerina, for life, rendering annually in all things as did Emma, with a *camera* and solar reserved to Emma in the eastern end of the cote, if necessary. G.: 20d.

4014 BROUGHTON (9 November) Agnes, daughter of John Cabe Sr., of Broughton, naif of the lord by blood, pays 13s.4d. for license to marry Laurence, son of Laurence Merton of Broughton, this time. Pledge: Richard Willesson of Raveley, Agnes' godfather. The fine is no larger at the request of the said Richard.

4015 RIPTON (November). Thomas Scot: surrender of one messuage and a half-virgate of land in *arentatio*, one quarter of land called Landcroft, and other parcels of land and meadow, to the use of Robert Nottynge, for life, rendering annually in all things as did Thomas. G.: (*blank*).

4016 RIPTON Robert Nottynge: surrender of one messuage and a half-virgate of land *ad opus*, with three acres of land at Catteshegge, to the use of William Baylly Jr., for life, rendering annually in all things as did Robert. G.: six capons.

4017 BURWELL (leet: Thursday, St. Edward the King) Robert Adam: surrender of half of one tenement of 24 acres once held by Thomas Powle, to the use of Thomas Rolf, and his wife, Alicia, for 20 years, rendering annually in all things as did Robert. G.: 6d.

4018 BURWELL (same leet) Thomas Calvesbane: one tenement of eight acres of land recently held by John Calvesbane, for 40 years, rendering annually in all things as did John. G.: 12d.

4019 BURWELL (December) Thomas Godfrey and his wife, Margaret: one messuage with adjacent croft recently held by John Role Jr., for 40 years, rendering annually 5s. at the customary times, and all other services and customs rendered by John. G.: one capon.

230v   **4020** BURWELL (December) John Saxton and his wife, Sibilia: one cote with croft once held by John Pery, for life, rendering annually 20d. at the customary times, and all other services and customs owed therein. G.: one capon.

4021 BURWELL (December) John Prikke Jr.: two crofts once held by Thomas Plombe and recently held by Master John Boyse, for 20 years, rendering annually 3s. at the customary times, and all other services and customs owed therein. G.: one capon.

4022 CHATTERIS (23 March: General Court) John Hertford Bailly: surrender of one and a half acres in Medemen, to the use of John Howesson, for life, rendering annually 12d. at the customary times, and all other services and customs owed therein. G.: one capon.

4022 CHATTERIS (23 March: General Court) John Hertford Bailly: surrender of one and a half acres in Medemen, to the use of John Howesson, for life, rendering annually 12d. at the customary times, and all other services and customs rendered by John. G.: 8d. And he swears fealty.

4023 CHATTERIS (same court) Thomas Gere: one cotland built up with three houses with meadow in Oldhalf and certain lands in Medemen and elsewhere recently held by John Gere, with one selion of land at Longegrave recently held by William Carter, a half-acre of land in Elmen, and a half-acre of land next to the cross recently held by the same William, for life, rendering annually 6s.1d.ob. at the customary times, and all other services and customs rendered by John and William. G.: 3s.4d. And he swears fealty.

4024 CHATTERIS (same court) John Swetemylke: surrender of half of one tenement of eight acres of land, to the use of Thomas Egeve, for life, rendering annually 4s. at the customary times, and all other services and customs owed therein. G.: 20d.

4025 CHATTERIS (same court) John Cade: surrender of one acre of land in Medemen, to the use of John Wympooll, for life, rendering annually 8d. at the customary times, and all other services and customs owed therein. G.: 8d.

4026 CHATTERIS (same court) John Revesson Sr.: one vacant toft with adjacent croft and once a capital messuage of one tenement of eight acres recently held by John Chownesson, for life, rendering annually 6d. at the customary times, and all other services and customs owed therein. G.: two capons.

4027 UPWOOD (19 April) John Waryn of Covington pays 40d. for license to marry Agnes, daughter of John Andrewe and naif of the lord by blood, this time, with 20d. to be paid the next feast of St. John the Baptist, and the remaining 20d. due 15 days after the following Michaelmas.

4028 KNAPWELL (May) William Awbry: surrender of one messuage well and competently repaired, one semi-virgate of land *ad opus* and another semi-virgate in *arentatio* in good culture, to the use of John Hoot and his wife, Leticia, for life, rendering annually 20s. at the customary times, and all other services and customs owed therein, with the obligation to repair and maintain the messuage at their own expense. G.: 40d.

4029 ST. IVES (20 May) Henry Barbour and his wife, Johanna: a half-row in Bridge Street recently held by John Redhed and once held by William Purdy, from the feast of the Nativity of St. John the Baptist for life, rendering annually 13s.4d., which property previously rendered 20s. Further, they will repair and maintain the property. *Et non licebit*, etc. G.: 40d.

231r

4030 KNAPWELL (July) John Pykerell: one messuage and a half-virgate of land recently held by John Hoote, for life, rendering annually in all things as did John. G.: two capons.

4031 RAMSEY (1 August) William Freman and his wife, Isabella: from Brother William Bury, sub-cellarer, one plot lying inside Mechegates in the northern part and recently dismissed by copy to Johanna Bury and previously held by Robert Broun, from Michaelmas for life, rendering annually 5s. in equal portions at the feasts of the Annunciation and Nativity of Blessed Mary, with the sub-cellarer responsible for repairs and maintenance, except for the enclosure. *Et si predictus redditus*, etc. (arrears of one month). G.: (*blank*).

16 JOHN STOWE (1451-1452)

231v

4032 HEMINGFORD ABBOTS (March) Thomas Caythorp and his wife, Agnes: one messuage and two virgates of land recently held by John Clerke, from Michaelmas for life, rendering annually 24s.2d. at the customary times, and all other services and customs rendered by John, with the obligation to repair the messuage at the beginning and maintain it thereafter, receiving an allowance of rent for the first two years, i.e. 4s.2d. G.: two capons.

4033 ELSWORTH (Wednesday, the day after the feast of St. Edward: leet) John AtteWode, naif of the lord by blood, pays 20d. for license to marry Margaret, his daughter, to Robert Tuke, this time.

4034 ELSWORTH (same leet) Laurence Esex: surrender of one messuage and a half-virgate of land recently held by John Lucas, to the use of John Herry and his wife, Alicia, for life, rendering annually 10s. at the customary times, and all other services and customs rendered by Laurence. G.: 20d.

4035 ELSWORTH (same leet) Laurence Esex and his wife, Johanna: one messuage and three quarters of land recently held by Thomas Croft, for life, rendering annually 13s.4d. for rents and works. G.: 20d.

4036 ELSWORTH (same leet) William Howlot Jr.: one cotland and the sixth part of St. Luke's land recently held by William Howlot and once held by John Stapilford, for life, rendering annually in all things as did William. G.: 6d.

4037 ELSWORTH (same leet) Simon Bateman: surrender of one cotland with croft next to Boundryslane once held by John Peeke, to the use of Nicholas Porter and his wife, Alicia, for life, rendering annually 2s.6d. in rent and 6d. for works at the customary times, as did Simon. G.: 6d.

4038 ELSWORTH (same leet) John Newman Sr.: surrender of one messuage and one virgate of land once held by John Phelyp, to the use of Simon Newman and his wife, Margaret, for life, rendering annually 20s. at the customary times, and all other services and customs owed therein. G.: 40d.

4039 ELSWORTH (same leet) John Hardyng: surrender of a half-virgate of land recently held by Richard Dawes and once held by William Touselond, to the use of John Fermor and his wife, Margaret, for life, rendering annually 12s. and all other services and customs owed therein. G.: 20d.

4040 ELSWORTH (December) John Hamond and his wife, Johanna: one messuage and one virgate of land with one cotland once held by John Chircheman and recently held by John Maddy, for life, rendering annually in all things as did John, with the obligation to repair the hall, *camera* and malt-kiln at the beginning, with an allowance of 8s. of rent for the first year. Further, the lord will build a grange, and John will repair and maintain it and all the buildings thereafter. G.: six capons.

4041 GRAVELEY (22 October: leet) John Ralet, naif of the lord: one messuage and one virgate of land recently held by John Wole, for life, rendering annually 13s.4d. at the customary times, and all other services and customs owed therein. G.: 40d.

4042 GRAVELEY (same leet) Margaret Edward: surrender of a half-virgate of land recently held by her husband, to the use of John Smyth and his wife, Agnes, for life, rendering annually 6s.8d.

232r **4043** CRANFIELD (17 October: leet) Thomas Milbroke: surrender of one quarter of land to the use of Thomas Wodehill.

4044 CRANFIELD (same leet) John Smyth: one acre of demesne at Litilhang recently held by John Wodehill Sr., for life, rendering annually 6d. at the customary times, and all other services and customs owed therein. G.: one capon.

4045 CRANFIELD (same leet) William White: four acres of demesne land recently held by John Woodhill Sr., for life, rendering annually 2s. at the customary times, and all other services and customs owed therein. G.: 8d.

4046 CRANFIELD (same leet) William Rynge and his wife, Mariota: one tenement and a half-quarter of land recently held by William Atte Lene and which descends to them by right of Mariota, for life, rendering annually 4s.5d.ob. at the customary times, and all other services and customs owed therein. G.: 20d.

4047 CRANFIELD (January) Thomas Wodehill: from William Wodehill, one quarter of land recently held by Thomas Millebroke, one cotland once held by John Bonbery, one acre of land once held by Margaret Catelyn, and certain acres of demesne land once held by John Webbe, for life, rendering annually 6s. for the quarter, and for the rest as did William. G.: 6s.8d. (?)

4048 CRANFIELD (1 August) (at Ramsey) William Terry pays 3s. for license for Margaret, widow of John Berell and daughter of Thomas Aleyn, naif of the lord, by blood, to marry whomever she wishes.

4049 CRANFIELD (22 October: leet). Thomas Brerell: a half-virgate of land without messuage recently held by his father, Thomas Brerell, for life, rendering annually 10s.6d. at the customary times, and all other services and customs rendered by Thomas. G.: 3s.4d.

4050 BARTON (19 October: General Court) Jacob Childe: one toft and one virgate of land recently held by Henry Burriche and once held by Richard Stonle, for life, rendering annually 16s.8d. at the customary times, and all other services and customs owed therein, with an allowance of this year's rent because of the poor cultivation of the land. G.: 2s.

4051 BARTON (same court) John Roger Jr.: one messuage built up with two houses and two acres of demesne land at Bonstall once held by John Tayllor, for life, rendering annually 5s. at the customary times, and all other customs and services owed therein. G.: 16d.

4052 BARTON (same court) Jacob Pope: one cotland recently held by Thomas Pope, for life, rendering annually 7s. at the customary times, and all other services and customs owed therein. G.: 20d. Heriot for his mother: 6d., as the price of one sheep.

232v **4053** BARTON (same court) John Colman, naif of the lord by blood, pays 2s. for license to marry Johanna, his daughter, to William Edward, this time.

4054 BARTON (December) Jacob Hille: one messuage and one virgate of land recently held by William Bonde, naif of the lord, and seized by the seneschal for default of payments and repairs, for life, rendering annually 18s.9d. at the customary times, and all other services and customs owed therein, with payments beginning at the feast of St. Andrew after one year, and with the obligation to repair and maintain the messuage at his own expense. Pledge for repairs and payments: John Hill, his father. G.: two capons.

4055 BARTON (December) John Burnard, naif of the lord: surrender, outside the court, through the hands of the bailiff, of one cotland built up with four houses once held by John Stonle, and one croftland recently held by the same John, to the use of Richard Priour, for life, rendering annually 9s.3d.ob. at the customary times, and all other services and customs owed therein, with the obligation to repair and maintain the property. G. and heriot: 3s.4d.

4056 SHILLINGTON (20 October: leet) John Grene: surrender of one plot inside the manor with one lot of Burylond and one acre of demesne, to the use of his son, Richard Grene, for life, rendering annually 9s.10d. at the customary times, and all other services and customs owed therein. Same Richard: one cote built up with one house in the common once held by Robert Carter, for life, rendering annually 12d. at the customary times. G.: 10s.

4057 SHILLINGTON (same leet) John Gobert: surrender of one plot within the manor with one lot and one acre of demesne land, to the use of John Draper, for life, rendering annually 10s.4d. at the customary times, and all other services and customs owed therein. G. and heriot: 13s.4d.

4058 SHILLINGTON (same leet) William Grene: one messuage and one semi-virgate of land with one lot and one acre of demesne land recently held by his father, John Grene, for life, rendering annually 17s.1s. at the customary times, and all other services and customs owed therein. G.: 13s.4d.

4059 SHILLINGTON (same leet) Thomas West: surrender of one messuage and two virgates, to the use of Richard Reve, for life, rendering annually 30s.2d. at the customary times, and all other services and customs owed therein. G. and heriot: 13s.4d.

4060 SHILLINGTON (same leet) Thomas Goodmar: four acres of demesne land in le Croft recently held by John Wenyngham, for life, rendering annually 2s. at the customary times, and all other services and customs owed therein. G.: 8d.

4061 SHILLINGTON (same leet) John Olyver: surrender of one messuage recently rebuilt and demesne land containing one acre, with one cotland and four acres of land in Stokkyng once held by Nicholas of the Abbeye, to the use of William Clerk, for life, rendering annually 9s.10d. at the customary times, and all other services and customs owed therein. G. and heriot: 13s.4d.

4062 SHILLINGTON (20 October: leet) Agreement between John Olyver and William Grene, that William concede to John and his wife, Johanna, one plot within the manor with appurtenances recently held by Adam Yonge and five parcels of meadow per-

233r taining to that plot, for life, with William supplying straw sufficient for repairing the plot during their life whenever necessary, as well as transport of wood, thorns, tiles and lime for repairing and enclosing the messuage, and clay for repairing the walls of all the buildings. They will supply rigging at their own expense, pay 4s. annually at the customary times, and repair and maintain the property. Further, after their deaths the plot with appurtenances will return to William Grene. John and William give the lord 20d. for license for this agreement.

4063 THERFIELD (22 October: leet) John Coche: one messuage and one virgate of land with demesne land recently held by John Wenham and once held by William Nicholl, for life, rendering annually 26s.8d. at the customary times, which property previously rendered 33s. Further, they will render all other services and customs owed therein, with the obligation to repair and maintain a *camera* in roofing, splints, plastering, as well as other buildings, at his own expense, timber being supplied by the lord. G.: four capons.

4064 THERFIELD (December) Thomas Stoughton, his wife, Elena, and their assigns: one messuage, one virgate, a half-acre of land in Capulcroft, eight acres and three rods of demesne land recently held by his father, William Stoughton, and half of one virgate of land recently held by William Caldewell, with pasture in the field called Thomasfeld, in bondage for life, rendering annually 36s.9d.ob. at the customary times, and all other services and customs owed therein. G.: 40d.

4065 ELLINGTON (16 November) Richard Mokke, naif of the lord by blood, pays 20d. for license to marry Agnes, his daughter, to John Swyft, freeman, this time.

4066 ELLINGTON (December) Thomas Couper and his successors: two cotes of five cotes built up by the lord on the site of the manor, which two cotes were previously held by Thomas himself without copy, in bondage rendering annually 5s. at the customary times, and all other services and customs owed therein, with the obligation to repair and maintain the cotes at his own expense. Further, if payments are not forthcoming after 15 days after the due date, the lord and his ministers can seize, re-enter and retain the property without contradiction. G.: 20d.

4067 ELLINGTON (December) Thomas Coupere: surrender of one messuage and one quarter of land once held by John Skynner, to the use of William Skynner, for life, rendering annually in all things as did Thomas, with the obligation to repair and maintain the property. Further, if payments are not forthcoming after 15 days after the due date, the lord and his ministers can seize, re-enter and retain the property without any contradiction. G.: 20d.

4068 ELLINGTON (December) John Bateman: one messuage and three quarters of

233v land recently held by Thomas Bateman, his father, for life, rendering annually in all things as did Thomas, with the obligation to repair and maintain the property. Further, if the payments are not forthcoming, etc. G.: 10s.

4069 RIPTON 6s.8d. of the *gersuma* of Robert Nottyng is owed this year because it is not in the bailiff's debts from last year.

4070 RIPTON (December) John Grene: one tenement in Esthorp with appurtenances recently held by John Reed, from Easter in the 13th year of Abbot John for life, rendering annually 20s. at the customary times, and all other services and customs owed therein, with payments beginning at the feast of St. Andrew last year. Further, all the timber growing on the land is reserved to the lord, and John will maintain all the buildings on the property if it pleases the lord to repair them. G.: (*blank*).

4071 RIPTON (10 March) Thomas Joye: surrender of one messuage and one semi-virgate and a half-acre of land lying in Depslape recently held by John Prikke, to the use of Henry Brewer and his wife, Agnes, from Michaelmas, for life, rendering annually for the messuage and semi-virgate as did Thomas, and 4d. for the half-acre at the customary times, with the obligation to repair and maintain the property at their own expense. G.: 40d.

4072 RAVELEY (December) Thomas Willesson and John Willesson: one pasture enclosed with hedges and lying between Stokkyng and the fields of Raveley called Cosley, from Michaelmas for 10 years, rendering annually 14s. at the feasts of the Annunciation and Nativity of Blessed Mary, with the obligation to repair and maintain the enclosures of the pasture, and to eradicate dangerous thorns growing there, receiving thorns for the enclosure. G.: eight capons (?).

4073 ST. IVES (December) John Clynt (Elyut?): the second of three plots at Barker's Row built up anew at the lord's expense, for life, rendering annually 8s. at the feasts of the Annunciation and Nativity of Blessed Mary, with the obligation that he and his wife, Matillis, repair and maintain the property at their own expense. *Et non licebit*, etc. G.: 3s.4d. and no more at the request of the vicar.

4074 ST. IVES (February) Thomas Ravene and his wife, Isabella: a half-row recently held by John Elys and once held by John Chiksande, from Michaelmas for life, rendering annually 12s. at the customary times, and all other services and customs owed therein, with the obligation to repair and maintain the property. *Et non licebit*, etc. G.: 40d.

4075 ST. IVES (February) John Herrof, his wife, Agnes, and their son, William: a half-row recently held by John Tebbe and once held by John Edenham, from Michaelmas for life, rendering annually 6s.8d. and all other services and customs owed therein, with the obligation to repair and maintain the property. *Et non licebit*, etc. G.: 40d.

4076 ST. IVES (February) John Wylymot, chaplain: surrender of a half-row in Bridge Street recently held by his father, to the use of Thomas Barbor, his wife, Margaret, and their sons, John and Thomas, for life, rendering annually 5s. at the customary times and all other services and customs owed therein, with the obligation to repair and maintain the property. *Et non licebit*, etc. G.: 2s.

4077 CHATTERIS (January) Thomas Gere: surrender of one cotland with appurtenances recently held by his father, John Gere, to the use of Richard Smyth, for life, rendering annually in all things as did Thomas. G.: 5s.

4078 CHATTERIS (January) Richard Pikerell: surrender of one cotland with appurtenances recently held by John Pikerell, to the use of Thomas Smyth, for life, rendering annually in all things as did Richard, with use of the cotland reserved to Anna, widow of John Pikerell, as contained in a copy of this year. G.: 12d.

4079 CHATTERIS (January) Alan Kede: surrender of one cotland and half of one tenement of eight acres with appurtenances once held by John Meyke, to the use of John Mathewe Jr., for life, rendering annually 7s.3d. at the customary times, and all other services and customs owed therein. G.: 40d.

4080 CHATTERIS (12 May: court) John Revesson Jr.: surrender of one messuage and half of eight acres of land, one cotland with meadow in Crowlode, to the use of John Halle, for life, rendering annually 6s.3d. at the customary times, and all other services and customs owed therein. G.: 2s.

4081 CHATTERIS (same court) Radulph Tebalde: surrender of one messuage and half of one tenement of eight acres of land, one cotland, one acre in Elmen and meadow in Crowlode, to the use of John Bray, Jr., for life, rendering annually 8s.1d.ob. at the customary times, and all other services and customs owed therein. G.: 40d.

4082 CHATTERIS (same court) John Amrose: surrender of two cotlands recently held by John South, to the use of Richard Turnor, for life, rendering annually 3s.10d. at the customary times, and all other services and customs owed therein. G.: 6d.

4083 CHATTERIS (same court) John Rede: surrender of one messuage and eight acres of land with meadow in Oldhalf and Crowlode, fishpond and one forland in Medemen and Elmen, recently held by Simon Reder, to the use of John Birt, for life, rendering annually 12s.5d.ob. and all other services and customs owed therein. G.: 6s.

4084 CHATTERIS (same court) William Carter: surrender of one messuage and half of eight acres, fishpond and meadow in Oldhalf, to the use of Robert Bette, for life, rendering annually 5s.4d. at the customary times, and all other services and customs owed therein, with one *camera* for dwelling and easement in the other buildings and half of the lands and meadow reserved to William and his wife, Anna, for life, for which they will render to Robert half of the rents and half of the expenses for repairs. G.: 40d.

4085 CHATTERIS (same court) Thomas Pyron: one vacant toft with adjacent land called Holtesplace once held by Robert Benette, for life, rendering annually 6d. at the customary times, and all other services and customs owed therein. G.: one capon.

4086 CHATTERIS (same court) Alicia Sempooll: surrender of four acres of land and meadow in Crowlode recently held by her husband, to the use of William Chasteleyn, for life, rendering annually 4s.7d.ob. at the customary times, and all other services and customs owed therein. G.: 3s.4d.

4087 CHATTERIS (same court) Radulph Pope: surrender of one messuage and half of eight acres of land with fishpond and a half-acre of land in Elmen, to the use of Nicholas Egill, for life, rendering annually 4s.7d. at the customary times, and all other services and customs owed therein. G.: 3s.

4088 CHATTERIS (same court) John Revesson Sr. and his son, John Jr.: eight acres of land once held by John Chownesson, from Michaelmas for life, rendering annually 8s. at the customary times, and all other services and customs owed therein. G.: excused.

4089 CHATTERIS (same court) John Lytholfe Jr.: surrender of one acre, one rod and 20 perches of land at Muslake and one acre of land at Shephernefen and one acre of land in Elmen, to the use of John Household, for life, rendering annually 2s.6d. at the customary times, and all other services and customs owed therein. G.: 12d.

4090 CHATTERIS (1 September) John Clerk: one messuage and half of eight acres of land recently held by John Smyth, and meadow in Crowlode and fishponds in le Dam, for life, rendering annually 5s.4d. at the customary times, and all other services and customs owed therein, with the obligation to repair the messuage and its buildings at the beginning and maintain them thereafter, with an allowance of the first year's rents granted by the lord. G.: 6d.

4091 ST. IVES (1 December) John Ive and his wife, Alicia: a half-row recently built up and held by Peter Cutte, from the previous Michaelmas for life, rendering annually 12s. at the feasts of the Annunciation and Nativity of Blessed Mary, and all other services and customs rendered by Peter, with the obligation to repair and maintain the property. *Et non licebit*, etc. G.: 6d.

4092 ST. IVES (1 December) William Payne and his wife, Margaret: a half-row recently held by John Baker and once held by William Sadeler, for life, rendering annually 12s. at the feasts of the Annunciation and Nativity of Blessed Mary, and all other services and customs owed therein, with the obligation to repair and maintain the property. *Et non licebit*, etc. G.: 40d.

4093 St. Ives (December) Walter Aubry Wever and his wife, Johanna: one row once held by William Lyncolne, for life, rendering 7s.6d. the first year, and 15s. each year thereafter, at the customary times, and all other services and customs owed therein, with the obligation to repair and maintain the property. *Et non licebit*, etc. G.: 6d.

4094 Holywell William Hunne: surrender of one plot and one virgate of land with demesne land and meadow in Salmade once held by John Tayllor, to the use of his son, Robert Hunne, for life, rendering annually in all things as did William. G.: 2s., three capons.

4095 Holywell (February) William Wryght Sr., his son, William, and Agnes, wife of William Jr.: one cotland in which William Sr. lives and one messuage with a half-virgate and other appurtenances recently held by William Sr. and surrendered back to the lord by him, for life, rendering annually in all things as did William Sr. G.: 16d.

4096 Holywell (May) John AtteWell: surrender of one messuage, one cotland and one virgate and one quarter of land with demesne land and meadow in Salmade, to the use of Simon Dallyng and John Shepperd, from the previous Michaelmas for life, rendering annually in all things as did John. Further, a plot and half-virgate recently held by William Palfreyman is reserved to John and his wife, Margaret, for life, with them responsible for payments and repairs. G.: 40d.

4097 Holywell (August) William Elyut, his wife, Katerina, and his son, John: one cotland built up with one house, with a croft once held by William Baron and another vacant croft once held by John Shepperd, for life, rendering annually 4s.10d. at the customary times, and all other services and customs rendered by William and John. G.: 8d.

4098 Holywell Alicia Herle, widow of Nicholas Baron, and her son, William Herle: one cote built up with two houses, and one acre of demesne land at Middilfurlong recently held by Nicholas Baron and once held by William Hunne, for life, rendering annually 3s.10d. at the customary times, and all other services and customs owed therein. G.: 20d.

4099 Ripton Margaret, daughter of William Wattes and naif of the lord, widow of John Payne, pays the fine for license to marry, this time. Fine of 6s.8d. to be paid within the year. Pledge: the same Margaret.

4100 Hurst (December) William Vicori: one toft and a half-virgate of land recently held by Thomas Whiston, for life, rendering annually 7s. at the customary times, and all other services and customs owed therein. G.: (*blank*).

4101 Hurst Thomas Pope: one toft and a half-virgate of land recently held by John White and once held by John Vicory, for life, rendering annually 6s. at the customary times, and all other services and customs owed therein, with payments beginning at the feast of St. Andrew. G.: one capon.

4102 Weston (February) Walter Kyng, son of John Kyng: one messuage with adjacent land and appurtenances recently held by Richard Forstere, from Michaelmas for life, rendering annually (*blank*) and all other services and customs owed therein, with the obligation to repair and maintain the property at his own expense, with an allowance of this year's rents for initial repairs. Pledge for payments and repairs: John Kyng and William Flesshall. G.: four capons.

4103 Weston (January) Walter Kyng, son of John Kyng and naif of the lord: one messuage with three quarters of land and demesne land recently held by Thomas Forster, from Michaelmas for life, rendering annually 28s. at the customary times, which property previously rendered 30s.10d. Further, he will render all other services and

235v

customs owed therein, with payments beginning at the feast of St. Andrew after one full year, and with the obligation to repair and maintain the property. G.: four capons.

4104 BYTHORNE (January) John Brewster: one messuage with appurtenances recently held by John Bocher, from Michaelmas for life, rendering annually in all things as did John. G.: (*blank*).

4105 BYTHORNE (January) John Smyth: one messuage built up recently with one house at the expense of the lord, with appurtenances recently held by John Holcote, for life, rendering annually in all things as did John, with the obligation to build one house within two years at his own expense, timber being supplied by the lord. G.: (*blank*).

4106 BROUGHTON John Justice, son of John Justice Tayllor and naif of the lord, lives at Hoddesdon and practices the craft of carpentry without license.

4107 BROUGHTON (June) Thomas Crowche and his wife, Matillis: one messuage and a half-virgate of land recently held by William Warde and once held by John Crowche, from Michaelmas for life, rendering annually 6s.8d. at the customary times, and all other services and customs owed therein. G.: four capons.

4108 WARBOYS (June) William Shakstaff: surrender of one quarter of land and nine selions of demesne land at Brenfurlong recently held by John Shakstaff, to the use of William Olyver, from Michaelmas for life, rendering annually 2s.6d. as rent and 12d. for works, for the quarter, and 12d. for the nine selions, and customs of the vill, with payments beginning at the feast of St. Andrew after two full years. G.: two capons.

236r **4109** WARBOYS Hugo Fordyngton: surrender of one messuage, one maltland, one mondayland and one and a half acres of demesne land at Bascroft, to the use of his son, Thomas Fordyngton, and his wife, Johanna, daughter of William Sherpe, for life, rendering annually 13s. at the customary times, and all other services and customs owed therein, with the obligation to repair and maintain the property. G.: four capons.

4110 BURWELL (18 May: leet) Agnes Deen: surrender of one messuage and half of 24 acres of land and half of one tenement of 15 acres recently held by John Deen, to the use of William Role, for 40 years, rendering annually in all things as did Agnes. G.: 2s.

4111 BURWELL (same leet) William Tayllor: surrender of one toft and half of one tenement of 24 acres, to the use of Thomas Rolf Carpenter, for 40 years, rendering annually 13s.4d. at the customary times, and all other services and customs owed therein. G.: one capon.

4112 BURWELL (same leet) Radulph Edrich: surrender of one tenement of 15 acres of land to the use of Edmund Wyot, for 30 years, rendering annually 8s.6d. at the customary times, and all other services and customs owed therein. G.: 12d.

4113 BURWELL (same leet) John Waleys Jr.: one tenement of 15 acres of land recently held by John Role Jr., for 30 years, rendering to the lord annually 15s. at the customary times, and all other services and customs owed therein. G.: 16d.

4114 BURWELL (same leet) Thomas Goodwyn: surrender of one messuage and eight acres of land *ad opera* recently held by Radulph Rower, to the use of Thomas Goodale Jr. and his wife, Alicia, for life, rendering annually 5s.ob.q. at the customary times, and all other services and customs owed therein. G.: one capon.

236v **4115** ELLINGTON (3 January, 28 Henry VIII)[49] (at Ramsey) Homage of William

---

[49] This entry occupies an entire half-folio, apparently having been added to a previously blank sheet during the reign of Henry VIII, (1536-37) under the abbacy of John Warboys (II), 1507-39.

Holcott. William Holcott, son and heir of John Holcot, recently of Ellington, deceased, comes before Reverend John Warboys of the abbey of Ramsey and renders homage for the lands and tenements he holds in Ellington for military service. Witnesses: Thomas Love, John Lawrence, Thomas Stevekeley, Robert Gowley, John Burton, Thomas Stokys of Sibthorp, Gabryell Throk, and others (*unnamed*).

17 JOHN STOWE (1452-1453)

237r **4116** ELSWORTH (12 October: leet) Simon Bateman and his wife, Johanna: one house next to the cemetery rebuilt on the waste at the expense of the community of the village, for life, rendering annually one capon at Christmas. G.: two capons.

4117 GRAVELEY (23 October: leet) Robert West, naif of the lord by blood, pays 12d. for license to marry Agnes, his daughter, to John Waltham, tailor, this time.

4118 HOUGHTON (27 October: leet) William Hood of Huntingdon: one cotland recently held by John Newman, for life, rendering annually in all things as did John. G.: 2s., one capon.

4119 HOUGHTON (same leet) William Mustard: one well built up messuage and one virgate, one cotland *ad opus* recently held by Thomas Froxfeld, from the previous Michaelmas for life, rendering annually 19s. at the customary times, and all other services and customs owed therein. G.: 2s., one capon.

4120 HEMINGFORD ABBOTS (1 September) John Heyne: surrender of one cote with appurtenances once held by John Newman, to the use of William Russell, his wife, Agnes, and their daughter, Elena, for life, rendering annually in all things as did John. G.: 12d., two capons.

4121 HEMINGFORD ABBOTS (September) Isabella Marchall: surrender of one messuage and a half-virgate of land recently held by her husband, John Marchall, to the use of John Pope, his wife, Johanna, and their son, Thomas, for life, rendering annually in all things as did Isabella. Further, one house next to the gate and a parcel of the garden for her curtilage is reserved to Isabella for life, together with another parcel next to the house for supplying fuel, and fruits and yields of apple trees and one pear tree, with easement for one rooster and two hens. Further, John, Johanna and Thomas will repair and maintain the house during Isabella's lifetime. G.: 12d., two capons.

4122 HEMINGFORD ABBOTS (September) Thomas Russell: one messuage and one virgate of land recently held by his father, John Russell, and once held by Thomas Whyn, for life, rendering annually in all things as did John. Further, he will build one grange of eight binding-posts at his own expense, the lord granting him an allowance of the rents of his mother, namely 6s. from the time of John Ladde, (*blank*) from the time of Richard Gelen, and 22s.3d. from the time of John Almer. G.: four capons.

4123 HEMINGFORD ABBOTS (November) Robert Kestevyn: surrender of one cote once held by Simon Scot and Richard Miller, to the use of John Upton, blacksmith, for life, rendering annually 12d. at the customary times, and all other services and customs owed therein. G.: 6s.8d.

4124 HEMINGFORD ABBOTS (November) Adam Alcok, his wife, Agnes, and their son, Simon: one cotland in which he lives and which is well built up, one adjacent croft one held by Richard Tayllor, for life, rendering annually 12d. at the customary times, and all other services and customs owed therein. G.: 6d.

4125 HEMINGFORD ABBOTS (June) Thomas Aungewyn: surrender of one croft once held by Walter Ibot, to the use of Adam Alcok and his wife, Agnes, for life, rendering annually 12d. at the customary times, and all other services and customs owed therein. G.: 2s.

4126 HEMINGFORD ABBOTS (June) Thomas Aungewyn: surrender of one cote with croft recently held by Thomas Brendhous, to the use of John Barbor and his wife, Alicia, for life, rendering annually in all things as did Thomas, with three bushels of apples from the garden reserved to Thomas for life. G.: 2s.

4127 HEMINGFORD ABBOTS (June) Thomas Aungewyn: surrender of one messuage and one virgate of land with croft recently held by John Pope, to the use of Thomas Pope and his wife, Katerina, for life, rendering annually 6s. at the customary times, and all other services and customs owed therein. Further, a *camera* at the eastern end of the hall, one *camera* next to "le Cartehous", apples growing on "le Ostdendtre", access to the kitchen, a place for keeping five capons annually, use of the land for keeping four carts of fuel, and free access to the well in the garden and other places, reserved to Thomas and his wife, Johanna, for life. G.: 40d. (*Marginal note*: The rent will be raised, as with other virgates, after the deaths of Thomas and his wife).

237v **4128** WARBOYS (30 October: leet) Richard Berenger, son of John Berenger of Ramsey, pays 12d. for license to marry Mariota, his sister and naif of the lord by blood, to William Dallyng of Ramsey, butcher, this time.

4129 WARBOYS (20 January) Richard Waltham Carpenter, his wife, Agnes, and one of their children: one tenement without buildings, with one mondayland once held by John Dallyng, from Michaelmas for life, rendering annually 12d. at the customary times, customs of the vill, and all other services and customs owed therein, with the obligation to build an *insathous* at least 40 feet long within the next two years, and one bake house, with timber for beams, posts, and sides supplied by the lord. Further, they will maintain the property at their own expense thereafter. In addition, whichever of their legitimate children they choose to take up the land shall pay the lord a *gersuma* of two capons. G.: one capon.

4130 WARBOYS (April) Thomas Berenger: surrender of one mondayland and one messuage with one quarter of well built up land, to the daughter of Thomas Newman and her husband, for life, rendering annually in all things as did Thomas. G.: (*blank*).

4131 BYTHORNE (4 November: leet at Weston) John Wright: one plot rebuilt with one house, one quarter of adjacent land recently held by Thomas Holcote, and adjacent demesne land, from the previous Michaelmas for life, rendering annually 9s.10d.ob. at the customary times, and all other services and customs owed therein, with the obligation to rebuild one house on the property at his own expense, timber being supplied by the lord. G.: (*blank*).

4132 WESTON (leet) William Flesshewer, naif of the lord by blood, pays 40d. for license to marry Margaret, his daughter, to Thomas Mynto of Kimbolton, this time.

4133 CHATTERIS (15 November: court) Alicia Yvet: surrender of one messuage with appurtenances recently held by her husband, John Yvet, to the use of her son, John, for life, rendering annually in all things as did Alicia, with one *camera* in the eastern end of the messuage, three rods of land in the fields, free access to the *camera*, well and garden reserved to Alicia for life, and with John obligated to repair the *camera* during the period. G.: 2s.

4134 CHATTERIS (same court) John Hunte Sr.: one acre of land at Shephernfurlong recently held by Thomas Lytholf, for life, rendering annually 8d. at the customary times. G.: two chickens.

4135 CHATTERIS Note that (*blank*) Gere, naif of the lord by blood belonging to the manor of Holywell, lives at Chatteris, without license.

4136 ST. IVES (November) John Huddesson Mason and his wife: a half-row in Bridge Street recently held by John Reedhed, and which half-row is well built up, for

238r life, rendering annually 13s.4d. at the customary times, and all other services and customs owed therein, with the obligation to repair and maintain the property. *Et non licebit*, etc. G.: 2s.

4137 St. Ives (November) Richard Atkyn and his wife, Margeria: a half-row with appurtenances recently held by John Cayeshoo, for life, rendering annually 14s.4d. at the customary times, and all other services and customs owed therein, with the obligation to repair and maintain the property. *Et non licebit*, etc. G.: 7s.

4138 St. Ives (November) William Smyth and his wife, Agnes: one row recently held by John Malton, for life, rendering annually 10s. at the customary times and all other services and customs owed therein, with the obligation to repair and maintain the property. *Et non licebit*, etc. G.: 6d.

4139 St. Ives (November) John Sammes, his wife, Isabella, and their son, Thomas: two built up half-rows recently held by John AtteWode, for life, rendering 26s.8d. the first year, and 33s.4d. each year thereafter at the customary times, and all other services and customs owed therein. Further, they will repair and maintain the property, receiving from the lord for repairs a 40s. of arrears of rents, timber, and the yield of two acres in Holywell Fen. *Et non licebit*, etc. G.: two capons.

4140 Wistow (September) Richard Godfrey: one messuage with certain acres of land once held by John Tayllour and recently held by John Styward, for life, rendering annually in all things as did John. G.: 2s.

4141 Wistow (16 November) William Asplond Lepe Maker, alias Plough Wright, of Sutton in the Isle of Ely, naif of the lord by blood of the manor of Wistow, in the presence of John Revesson, bailiff, pays the fine for license to live off the manor for as long as it pleases the lord, rendering 6d. annually at the feast of St. Thomas the Apostle. Pledges: (*blank*) Bonyard and (*blank*) Bonyard. In addition, William pays the fine for Reginald, his brother and naif of the lord, to live off the manor. Pledges: the same.

4142 Wistow William Barker and his wife, Johanna: one messuage and one cotland with appurtenances recently held by William Cabe, for life, rendering annually in all things as did William. G.: 4s.

238v **4143** Ellington (December) William Miller and his wife, Agnes: two built up cotes recently rebuilt by the lord on the site of the manor and previously held by the same William, in bondage for life, rendering annually 8s. at the customary times, and all other services and customs owed therein, with the obligation to maintain the property under penalty of forfeit. Further, if the payments are not forthcoming, or are only partially made, at the appointed times, and remain such for one month, the lord or his assigns shall retain the two cotes and dispose of them as he wills. G.: (*blank*).

4144 Ellington John Swasethe: surrender of one messuage and one virgate of land and one quarter of Coton land recently held by Richard Hikkesson, to the use of William Cotyngham and his successors in bondage of the manor, rendering annually in all things as did John, with the obligation to repair and maintain the property. And if the payments are not forthcoming, etc. G.: 6s.8d.

4145 Ellington (January) John Drew: one messuage and one virgate of land with a half-virgate of land of Coton lond recently held by John Mokke, for life, rendering annually all services and customs owed therein, with the obligation to repair and maintain the property. Further, if the payments are not forthcoming, etc. G.: 10s., of which 5s. are excused because of repairs.

4146 Houghton (December) John Wythe Sr., son of William Wythe: one messuage and a half-virgate of land once held by Robert Morell and recently held by John Yonge, one quarter of land recently held by Richard Atkyn and once held by Thomas

Elyot, in *arentatio* for life, rendering annually 6s. for the half-virgate and 2s. for the quarter at the customary times, and all other services and customs owed therein. Further, he will repair and maintain the messuage at his own expense, the lord granting him an allowance of 6s. of this year's rent. G.: two capons.

4147 HOUGHTON Thomas Fuller: one toft and a half-virgate of land once held by Robert Andrewe and recently held by Thomas Andrew, in *arentatio* for life, rendering annually 5s. at the customary times, and all other services and customs owed therein. G.: (*blank*).

4148 SLEPE John Felde and his wife, Agnes: one plot next to les Barres recently held by John Carter, one virgate of land recently held by John Colle and half of one virgate of land recently held by John Freman, and one other plot and virgate of land inside les Barres recently held by William Prikke, for life, rendering annually 27s. for the first plot, virgate and a half, and 14s. for the other plot and virgate, at the customary times, and all other services and customs owed therein. G.: four capons.

4149 SLEPE (24 April) Agnes, widow of Thomas Buk: surrender of one messuage, two cotlands and a half-virgate of land *ad opus*, a half-acre of land at le Howe recently held by her husband, Thomas, and once held by John Roger, to the use of John Syre and his wife, Alicia, from Michaelmas for life, rendering annually in all things as did Agnes, with a third part of the fruit of the trees growing in the messuage reserved to Agnes for life. G.: 13s.4d.

4150 HOLYWELL (December) John Bate: surrender of one cotland once held by John Moryse and built up with one house, with other appurtenances, to the use of his son, John Bate and his wife, Alicia, for life, rendering annually 2s. at the customary times, and all other services and customs owed therein. G.: (*blank*).

4151 HOLYWELL (December) Adam Sewale: surrender of one croftland built up with two houses once held by John Goodsowle, with adjacent land, to the use of John Beaumes, for life, rendering annually in all things as did Adam. G.: (*blank*).

239r **4152** HOLYWELL (June) John Beaumes: surrender of one built up cotland, land and meadow once held by Roger Cachesoly, and once acre of land at Middilfurlong once held by the same Roger, to the use of his son, Richard Beaumes, for life, rendering annually in all things as did John. G.: 2s.

4153 CRANFIELD (February) Thomas Berell: one messuage with three cotes, four acres of demesne land and one pithel once held by Berell, for life, rendering annually 12s.1d. at the customary times, and all other services and customs owed therein. G.: 20d.

4154 CRANFIELD (February) John Mabely: one messuage and a half-virgate of land recently held by Thomas Milbrooke, for life, rendering annually 9s.5d. at the customary times, and all other services and customs owed therein. G.: 2s.

4155 CRANFIELD (February) Katerina Brerele: one cote once held by John Broby and recently held by Thomas Brerele, for life, rendering annually 3s. at the customary times, and all other services and customs owed therein. G.: one capon.

4156 CRANFIELD (September) Matillis, widow of Thomas Catelyn: surrender of one messuage and a half-virgate of land with other appurtenances falling to her by the custom of the manor after the death of her husband, to the use of John Aleyne and his wife, Alicia, daughter of Thomas Catelyn, for the life of Matillis and according to the terms of a bill drawn up between them and turned over into the custody of William Terry, bailiff. Further, John and Alicia may not dismiss the property, in part or in whole, or alienate it during that time to anyone without the license of Matillis, under penalty of loss of the property, and Matillis will pay, at the end of her life, a heriot of 5s. Pledges: William Hyll and Robert Goodwyn.

4157 BRINGTON (20 March) John Bacheler Sr.: one messuage and a half-virgate of land with adjacent demesne land and 12 acres of land at Holwelles recently held by his father, John Bacheler, for life, rendering annually 18s.10d. at the customary times, and all other services and customs owed therein. G.: two capons.

4158 ABBOTS RIPTON (April) George Stockle of Godmanchester and his wife, Isabella: one messuage and two quarters of land recently held by Thomas Coole and once held by John Howlot, with two acres of land at Catteshegg, from Michaelmas for life, rendering annually in all things as did Thomas. G.: two capons.

239v **4159** ABBOTS RIPTON (30 April) (at Ramsey) Margaret, widow of John Hyche of Estthorpe and naif of the lord by blood, pays 13s.4d. for license to marry Agnes, her daughter and naif of the lord, to whomever she wishes, whenever she wishes. Pledges: William Scarlet and William Poolyerd.

4160 ABBOTS RIPTON (30 April) Margaret, widow of John Hyche, pays 13s.4d. for license to marry her other daughter, Alicia, naif of the lord by blood, to whomever she wishes, whenever she wishes. Pledges: William Scarlet and William Poolyerd.

4161 ABBOTS RIPTON (30 April) Margaret, widow of John Hyche, pays 10 marks as fine for waste made by her in the bondage of the lord in Est thorp. This fine, as well as the two marks for marriage fines above, are to be paid in three installments: four marks at the Exaltation of the Holy Cross, four marks at the Nativity of the Lord, and four marks at the feast of the Apostles James and John. Further, this is set down in a sealed obligation. Pledges: William Scarlet and William Poolyerd.

4162 BURWELL (30 July) William Sygar: one cote with appurtenances once held by John Peyer and built up with two houses, and one plot recently held by John Benet, laborer, by the rod, for life, rendering annually 18d. at the customary times, and all other services and customs owed therein. Further, William and his assigns shall repair and maintain all buildings existing and to be built on the property at their own expense, under penalty of loss of the property. Fine: 5s.

4163 RAMSEY (January) William Scarlet: surrender, through the hands of Brother William Bury, sub-cellarer, of one messuage in High Street, to John Baveyne and his wife, Mariota, from the previous Christmas for life, rendering annually 12s. at the feasts of the Annunciation and the Nativity of Blessed Mary, and all other services and customs owed therein, with the sub-cellarer responsible for the repair and maintaining of buildings. Further, they will have undergrowth sufficient for enclosing the messuage, carrying it whenever necessary. If the rent payments are in arrears for three weeks after any due-date, or if John and Mariota put themselves under the protection of any other lord or any attorney which results in prejudice or damage to the lord or his tenants, the sub-cellarer can retain the messuage and dispose of it according to his will, this copy not withstanding. G.: 6s.8d.

18 JOHN STOWE (1453-1454)

240r **4164** HOLYWELL (9 October: leet) Roger Hunne, alias Baker, naif of the lord by blood, pays four capons for license to marry Margaret, his daughter, to John Thurberne, this time.

4165 HOUGHTON (11 October: leet) John Robyn Jr.: one messuage and one virgate of land in *arentatio* and half of one cotland *ad opus* recently held by Thomas Eliet, for life, rendering annually in all things as did Thomas. G.: (*blank*).

4166 HOUGHTON (same leet) John Plumbe: surrender of one messuage and a half-virgate of land once held by Thomas Crane, to the use of Thomas Broun, for life, rendering annually in all things as did John. G.: 8d.

4167   HOUGHTON (same leet) John Plumbe: surrender of one cotland *ad opus* once held by Thomas Crane, to the use of John Mason Sr. and his brother, John Mason, for life, rendering annually in all things as did John. G.: 12d.

4168   HOUGHTON (same leet) Richard Apirle: one messuage and one virgate of land in *arentatio* and one parcel of meadow called Honymede once held by John Andrewson, for life, rendering annually in all things as did John. G.: (*blank*).

4169   HOUGHTON (same leet) John Scot and his wife, Johanna: one messuage and two virgates of land *ad opera*, two half-virgates of land and one cotland in *arentatio* recently held by Robert Plombe, for life, rendering annually in all things as did Robert. G.: 3s.4d.

4170   HOUGHTON (same leet) John Plombe: surrender of half of one virgate of land in *arentatio* once held by John Marchall Jr., to the use of John Tyffyn, for life, rendering annually in all things as did John. G.: (*blank*).

4171   HEMINGFORD ABBOTS (12 October: leet) John Whyn: one messuage and two half-virgates of land recently held by Thomas Whyn, for life, rendering annually 12s.4d. at the customary times, and all other services and customs owed therein. G.: two capons.

4172   HEMINGFORD ABBOTS (same leet) Thomas Feld: one toft and a half-virgate of land recently held by John Est, for life, rendering annually in all things as did John. G.: 2s., two capons.

240v   **4173**   HEMINGFORD ABBOTS (same leet) John Martyn: one messuage and one virgate of land once held by Thomas Herd, and the third part of one cotland and one virgate of land once held by William Ivett and recently held by John Pope, for life, rendering annually in all things as did John. G.: (*blank*).

4174   ELSWORTH (19 October: leet) Thomas Bernard and his wife, Beatrix: one cote built up with one house and with adjacent croft recently held by Simon Sparwe and once held by Thomas Porter, for life, rendering annually in all things as did Simon. G.: 12d.

4175   ELSWORTH (same leet) Isabella Howlet: surrender of one croft and one quarter of land of Gravelond to the use of Thomas Howlet and his wife, Alicia, for life, rendering annually in all things as did Isabella. G.: 8d.

4176   ELSWORTH (same leet) Isabella Howlet: surrender of one quarter of land once held by Stapilford and recently held by Thomas Croft, to the use of Thomas Shaver and his wife, Margaret, for life, rendering annually in all things as did Isabella. G.: 12d.

4177   SHILLINGTON (23 October: leet) John Herberd and his wife, Isabella: one messuage and one virgate of land with appurtenances in Pegsdon recently held by his father, William Herberd, for life, rendering annually in all things as did William. G.: 13s.4d.

4178   SHILLINGTON (same leet) John Ede, languishing unto death: surrender of one quarter and one virgate and a half of land, to the use of Thomas Herberd Sr., and his wife, Isabella, for life, rendering annually in all things as did John. G.: 13s.4d. Heriot: nothing, because it was paid by John.

4179   SHILLINGTON (same leet)[50] John Multon pays 2s. for license to have custody of one messuage and 16 acres of land recently held by John Waryn, deceased, and located in Stondon, until Robert, son of the said John, comes of age, rendering an-

---

[50]   See PRO 179/66, for the death of John Waryn. His land passes to his daughter, Agnes — apparently the wife of John Multon.

nually all services and customs owed therein, with the obligation to maintain both the buildings on the messauge and Robert himself well and competently during the said period.

241r **4180** BARTON (24 October: court) John Child, son of Thomas Child: one virgate of land with adjacent croft recently held his brother, Jacob Child, for life, rendering annually in all things as did Jacob. G.: 3s.

4181 BARTON (same court) William Hille and his wife, Alicia: one messuage and a half-virgate of land with forland recently held by John Broun, for life, rendering annually in all things as did John. G.: 2s.

4182 BARTON (same court) William Kyn and his wife, Johanna: one messuage and a half-virgate of land recently held by John Colman, for life, rendering annually in all things as did John. G.: two capons.

4183 BARTON (same court) John Gregory Jr.: one messuage and one virgate of land and a half-virgate recently held by William Eynysham and earlier held by John Adam, for life, rendering annually in all things as did William. G.: 4s.

4184 ST. IVES (November) William Taillour and his wife, Alicia: a half-row recently held by Richard Charite, for life, rendering annually 10s. at the customary times, and all other services and customs owed therein, with the obligation to repair and maintain the property. *Et non licebit*, etc. G.: 3s.4d.

4185 BROUGHTON (November) John Cabe of Broughton, naif of the lord by blood, pays 6s.8d. for license to marry Johanna, his daughter, to William Rydman of Raveley, draper. Fine to be paid to the lord through the hand of John Cheker.

4186 ST. IVES (November) Thomas Posbrygge and his wife, Katerina: a half-row once held by John Barker and recently held by Thomas Sowle and rebuilt by the lord at his own expense, for life, rendering annually 8s. at the customary times, and all other services and customs owed therein, with the obligation to repair and maintain the property. *Et non licebit*, etc. G.: 40d.

4187 ST. IVES (November) John Carter Smyth and his wife, Agnes: a half-row previously held by John himself and once held by John Raven, for life, rendering annually 13s.4d. at the customary times, and all other services and customs owed therein, with the obligation to repair and maintain the property. *Et non licebit*, etc. G.: two capons.

241v **4188** SLEPE (November) Alicia, daughter of John Grene and widow of Richard Ramsey of St. Ives and naif of the lord by blood, pays two capons for license to marry John Huddesson Mason of St. Ives, this times.

4189 HEMINGFORD ABBOTS (November) Thomas Aungewyn and his wife, Johanna: one virgate of land with pertaining croft once held by William Herde and another half-virgate of land recently held by Thomas Whete and once held by William Herde, for life, rendering annually 6s. for the virgate and 2s. for the half-virgate at the customary times, and all other services and customs owed therein. G.: to be paid after six full years.

4190 ELLINGTON (November) John Illger, husband of Johanna, widow of Thomas Mokke and naif of the lord by blood, pays two capons for license to marry Margaret, daughter of Thomas Mokke, to whomever she wishes, this time.

4191 ELSWORTH (November) Richard Boner, naif of the lord, pays the fine for license to live off the manor for as long as it pleases the lord, rendering 6s. and suit to leet annually. Pledge: John Eliet, bailiff.

4192 BARTON (6 December) Thomas Chyld, son of Thomas Child and naif of the lord by blood, pays the fine for license to live off the manor with Nicholas Curlyng of Shillington, for as long as it pleases the lord, rendering 4d. annually, in person, at the leet of Shillington. Pledge: Matthew Chambyr.

4193 RAMSEY (December) William Sparke Glover and his wife, Isabella: from Brother William Bury, sub-cellarer, one messuage recently held by Robert Belamy Glover, for life, rendering annually 12s. in equal portions at the feasts of the Annunciation and Nativity of Blessed Mary, with the obligation to repair and rebuild all damages by them, their servants or their animals to the buildings, walls, piers, and other necessaries in that messuage, with the sub-cellarer supplying thorns and undergrowth. *Et si predictus redditus*, etc. (arrears of one month). Further, if they do anything in prejudice of the abbot and convent of Ramsey, the property will be seized. G.: 6s. (Paid.)

242r   **4194** RAMSEY (20 December) Robert Benet and his wife, Elizabet: the sub-cellarer, one messuage recently held by John Bryan Mason, from the previous Michaelmas for life, rendering annually 21s. in equal portions at the feasts of the Annunciation and Nativity of Blessed Mary, with the obligation to repair and rebuild all damages to the property committed by them, their servants or animals. G.: 6s.8d.

4195 THERFIELD (20 December) Thomas Wenham and his successors: one messuage, one virgate and one quarter of land with one croft called Hungrycroft recently held by Robert Preest, rendering at the customary times, with the first payment at the next feast of St. Andrew. Further, the lord will make repairs to the barn in carpentry, roofing and straw at the beginning, with Thomas responsible for subsequent repairs in splinting, plastering, ramming, beams, straw, aiding in the roofing, the first time, and all later maintenance. G.: two capons, and no more because of repairs.

4196 ELTON (16 January) William Attegate, *firmarius* of the manor, and naif of the lord by blood, pays two capons for license to marry Margaret, his daughter, to Richard Wodeward, this time, and the fine is no larger because he is both *firmarius* and rent collector of the manor.

4197 UPWOOD (20 January) William Hamond of Diddington: one messuage with the land and meadow pertaining to it recently held by William Jonesson, from the previous Michaelmas for nine years, rendering annually in all things as did William. Further, he receives from the lord the stored hay and the fallow and reploughed land, to be returned at the end of his term, and three quarters of barley, to be returned at the next feast of St. Andrew. G.: four capons.

242v   **4198** HOUGHTON (January) Richard Thoday and his wife, Alicia: one messuage and one virgate in *arentatio* recently held by Thomas Elyot and half of one cotland *ad opus* recently held by the same Thomas, and two quarters of land recently held by Richard Atkyn and parcelled out of one virgate now held by Robert and William Lydonner, for life, rendering annually in all things as did Thomas and Richard, with payments beginning at the feast of St. Andrew. G.: 2s.

4199 CRANFIELD (March) Thomas Ryddeler: one messuage recently *ad opus* and recently held by Thomas Ryddeler, his father, and previously held by Thomas Brerele, which messuage pertains to the half-virgate recently held by the same Thomas Ryddeler, for life, rendering annually 3s. for the messuage and 6s.9d. for the two quarters at the customary times, and all other services and customs owed therein. G.: 2s.

4200 CRANFIELD (March) Rober Goodwyn: a half-virgate of land recently held by John Berell and once held by William Goodwyn, with half of seven acres and one rod of demesne land at Overbercroft, and half of 13 acres and one rod of demesne land at Stokkyng, recently held by the same John Berell, for life, rendering annually 20s.7d.q., and all other services and customs owed therein. G.: (*cut off*).

4201 ST. IVES WITH SLEPE (March) John Fethion and his wife, Cristiana: one row recently held by his father, William Fethion, and once held by Walter Wodeward, and one toft called Balle (*cut off*), opposite the tenement of John Pulter in Slepe and recently held by the same William, for life, rendering annually 13s.4d. for the row and 8s. for the toft, in equal portions at the customary times, with the obligation to repair and maintain the property. *Et non licebit*, etc. G.: 7s.8d., to be paid to the lord through the seneschal.

243r **4202** ELLINGTON (20 April) Thomas Peinell, who lives in Sibthorp, naif of the lord by blood of the manor of Weston, pays six capons for license to marry Margaret, his daughter, to William Marchall, this time.

4203 BROUGHTON (April) Roger Asplond: surrender of one messuage and one virgate and one quarter of land with one pithel to the use of Richard Archer, for life, rendering annually in all things as did Roger. G.: six capons.

4204 BURWELL (24 May: leet) John Rolff Townherde: surrender of one cote with croft and one acre of land lying in the fields, to the use of John Freman and his wife, Elena, for 60 years, rendering annually 4s.6d. at the customary times, and all other services and customs owed therein. G.: one capon.

4205 BURWELL (same leet) Thomas Wylkyn and his son, John: one tenement of 20 acres, of which John Wylkyn recently held one half, the other half of which was held by John Wilkyn, son of the said John Wilkyn Sett and once held by William Berell, for 60 years, rendering annually 10s. at the customary times, and all other services and customs rendered by Wilkyn. G.: 5s.

4206 BURWELL (same leet) John Waleys and his wife, Margaret: one tenement of 15 acres of land *ad opera* next to Scotryde and once held by him, for 40 years, rendering annually 6s.1d. at the customary times, and all other services and customs owed therein. G.: one capon.

4207 BURWELL (same leet) John Spenser, alias Skynner: surrender of one tenement of eight acres in *arentatio*, with croft, recently held by Richard Barker, to the use of William Wylkyn and his wife, Alicia, for 40 years, rendering annually 12s.6d. at the customary times, and all other services and customs owed therein. G.: (*blank*).

4208 HOLYWELL (January) Thomas Arnald, his wife, Alicia, and their son, Roger: one cotland and one acre of land at Oxhowe once held by John Selde, for life, rendering annually in all things as did John, with the obligation to rebuild the cotland within the year with one house at their own expense, timber, transport, carpentry and thatch with its transport supplied by the lord. G.: 8d.

243v **4209** HEMINGFORD ABBOTS (June) Walter Yngyll, alias Murrok, his wife, Margaret, and their son, William: one cote called Clerkescroft and once held by William Ingill, and a half-virgate of land once held by John Osberne, from Michaelmas for life, rendering annually 6s.8d. at the customary times, and all other services and customs owed therein. G.: one capon.

4210 CHATTERIS (12 June: court) Johanna Chapman: surrender of one cotland and meadow on Crowlode and a forland recently held by Hugo Chapman, to the use of John Brancester Jr., for life, rendering annually in all things as did Johanna, with one house and adjacent garden once held by John Coke, and easement for her fuel, reserved to Johanna, quit, for life. G.: 3s.4d. two capons.

4211 CHATTERIS (same leet) John Berle: surrender of half of one tenement of eight acres of land recently held by William Pope, to the use of John Howsson, for life, rendering annually in all things as did John. G.: for himself and John Berle, 4s.

4212 CHATTERIS (same court) Richard Turnour: surrender of two cotlands once held by John South, to the use of Thomas Gere, for life, rendering annually in all things as did Richard. G.: 12d.

4213 CHATTERIS (same court) Richard Tovy: three selions of land next to the marsh, one acre and 20 perches of land in Stokkyng recently held by John Smyth and two selions of land recently held by the same John, for life, rendering annually 17d. at the customary times, and all other services and customs owed therein. G.: 6d.

4214 CHATTERIS (same court) Thomas Pyroun: one cotland and the fishpond of Wolverwere and half of Achynwere and Bed Stychewere recently held by his father, William Pyroun, for life, rendering annually in all things as did William. G.: 4s.

4215 CHATTERIS (same court) John Cokke: the fourth part of one messuage and the fifth part of the same messuage and one selion of land at Muslake recently held by Thomas Burne, and half of one tenement of eight acres of land once held by Stephen Cokerell, for life, rendering annually 6s.6d. at the customary times, and all other services and customs owed therein. G.: 4s.

244r
4216 CHATTERIS (same court) John Howsshold: surrender of three acres, one rod and 20 perches of land once held by John Lytholf, to the use of William Jonson, for life, rendering annually 2s.7d. at the customary times, and all other services and customs owed therein. G. for himself and John Lawe (12d.): 20d.

4217 CHATTERIS (same court) Richard Smyth: surrender of one cotland with meadow, fishpond and land in Medmen, Bernefurlong and Elmen recently held by John Gere, to the use of John Lawe, for life, rendering annually 4s.9d. at the customary times, and all other services and customs owed therein. G.: 5s.

4218 CHATTERIS (same court) Agnes Devyll: surrender of half of a cotland built up with one house recently held by John Devyll, to the use of John Brewster, for life, rendering annually 7d. at the customary times, and all other services and customs owed therein. G.: 2s.

4219 CHATTERIS (same court) William Hunte: half of one tenement of eight acres with meadow in Crowlode Mede, one cotland and forland with a half-acre of land in Medmen and fishpond in Stokkyng once held by Thomas Fyshher and recently held by William Halle, for life, with half the meadow of Crowlode reserved to Thomas Halle. Further, William will render 10s.4d.ob. annually at the customary times, and all other services and customs owed therein. G.: 2s.8d.

4220 CHATTERIS (same court) John Curtes: surrender of one tenement of eight acres of land and meadow in Oldhalf, with one acre and one rod and 30 perches of land in Horslade once held by John Cok, to the use of John Revesson and his son, John, for life, rendering annually 10s.6d. ob. at the customary times, and all other services and customs owed therein. G.: 2s.

4221 ABBOTS RIPTON (May) Freman Umfrey: surrender of two messuages and three semi-virgates of land with four acres of land at Catteshegge, to the use of William Warwyk, for life, rendering annually 26s. at the customary times, and all other services and customs rendered by Freman. G.: four capons.

4222 SLEPE William Prikke and his wife, Emma: one cote, three rods of land and one rod of meadow with a half-acre of land at Howe recently held by Robert Bernard, for life, rendering annually in all things as did Robert. G.: 40d.

19 JOHN STOWE (1454-1455)

244v
4223 ELSWORTH (2 October: leet) Thomas Howlot: surrender of one toft with croft and land pertaining to it and located next to Castlakers and once held by John Chircheman, to the use of Simon Bateman, for life, rendering annually in all things as did Thomas, at the customary times. G.: two capons.

4224 ELSWORTH (29 September) Amicia, daughter of Robert Yntte and naif of the lord by blood, pays 20d. for license to marry William Smyth of Ditton, this time. Pledge for payment: John Elyet.

4225 BURWELL (4 October: leet) Richard Wyet and his wife, Cecilia: one tenement of eight acres recently held by Thomas Smyth and once held by Thomas Goodynch and seized ty the lord's bailiff for lack of repairs, for several years, rendering annually 4s. at the customary times, and all other services and customs owed therein. G.: 40d.

4226 BURWELL (same leet) Thomas Wyet, laborer, and his wife, Mariota: one cotland in *arentatio* with a parcel of a croft recently held by Robert Dene and previously held by John Goodale and once held by Alexander Sparugh, for 40 years, rendering annually in all things as did Robert. G.: one capon.

4227 BURWELL (same leet) William Sygar and his wife, Matilda: one messuage recently held by John Wyot and once held by Andrew Moryce, with a half-acre of land pertaining to it, and one cote with cutilage recently held by John Peyer, and one plot recently held by Mariota Benet, built up with two houses, by the rod for 60 years, rendering annually 15d. for the messuage and half-acre, 13d. for the cote with curtilage, and 5d. for the plot, and all other services and customs owed therein, with the obligation to repair and maintain the two houses and also to rebuild new houses on that messuage within one year. G.: 6s.8d. And they swear fealty.

4228 THERFIELD (6 October: leet) John Eche: surrender of one virgate of land at the end of the village towards Royston, and 18 acres of new demesne land recently held by John Wenham Jr., to the use of Thomas Dane, for life, rendering annually in all things as did John, with the obligation to repair and maintain all buildings already existing or to be built on the property, at his own expense. Pledge: John Geneys. G.: two capons. And he swears fealty.

4229 THERFIELD William Prest: 18 acres of new demesne land recently held by John Webbe and previously held by Elena Angtile and once held by John AtteWode, for life, rendering annually 9s. at the customary times, and all other services and customs rendered by John. G.: one capon.

4230 THERFIELD (January) Richard Colle: one messuage called cotland, with adjacent land and five acres of demesne land once held by Robert Sewale and recently held by William Overston, from the previous Michaelmas for life, rendering annually 13s. and all other services and customs owed therein, with the obligation to repair and maintain the all the buildings on the property. G.: two capons.

4231 SHILLINGTON (8 October: leet) John Grave: surrender of one messuage and one virgate of land once held by Nicholas Grave and a half-virgate of land once held by the same Nicholas, and one lot of Berylond, to the use of Richard Grave and his wife, Elizabeth, for life, rendering annually in all things as did John, with the obligation to repair and maintain the messuage under penalty of loss of their property. G.: 20s.

4232 SHILLINGTON (same leet) John Goberd and his wife, Johanna: a certain quantity of the manor, namely: the hall with annexed *camerae*, the chapel, kitchen, bake house, malt kiln, abbot's bower, stable, dovecote, adjacent garden, another garden, a large grange, four lots of demesne land, and other houses and parcels recently held by the said John and also recently held by Agnes Halle, for life, rendering annually 6s.8d. for the hall and other parcels, 34s.5d. for the grange, garden, and four lots, with the obligation to repair and maintain all the buildings at their own expense, timber, splints and rods supplied by the lord by the judgment of the seneschal of Ramsey. Further, they will have *hayeboot* and *firebote* as much as necessary; they will support all other obligations as performed by those holding demesne lots within the village, and they will provide for the seneschal or his deputy, when he comes, caring for his horses, and providing two beds, jars and cauldrons, with use of all the above reserved to the seneschal at that time. Further, they may not dismiss any part of the land to another without the lord's license, nor shall they put themselves under the protection of any

245r

245v

other lord to the damage or harm of the lord or his tenants, under penalty of loss of the property. G.: two capons, and no more because of the good repairs effected by them in the manor.

4233 SHILLINGTON (same leet) Agnes Stonle, widow of Thomas Stonle: surrender of one plot with one virgate of land once held by John Warde and recently held by her husband, and a half-virgate of land recently held by her husband, with one toft and a forland once held by John Grove and others and recently held by her husband, to the use of Thomas Stonle and his wife, Margeria, for life, rendering annually 32s.10d. at the customary times, and all other services and customs rendered by Agnes, with the obligation to repair and maintain the plot at their own expense, under penalty of forfeit. G.: 20s.

4234 SHILLINGTON (December) Richard Grave: surrender of one messuage and one virgate of land with one croft and one lot of demesne land recently held by John AtteMede, to the use of Robert Gayton and his wife, Alicia, for life, rendering annually 22s.3d., one rooster, two hens and five eggs at the customary times, and all other services and customs owed therein. G. and heriot: 20s.

4235 SHILLINGTON (December) Thomas Herberd and his wife: one messuage and one virgate of land in Pegsdon recently held by John Herberd and once held by William Herberd, for life, rendering annually in all things as did John. G. and heriot: 13s.4d.

4236 SHILLINGTON (December) Thomas Attebrigge and his wife, Johanna: one cotland in Bridge End once held by Dryver and recently held by John Hokelese, for life, rendering annually 2s.1d.ob. at the customary times, and all other services and customs owed therein. G.: two capons.

4237 SHILLINGTON (December) Thomas Stonle: surrender of one virgate of land and eight acres of land at Larkenhyll recently held by John Cooke, to the use of Simon Colyn, for life, rendering annually 21s.4d. at the customary times, and all other services and customs owed therein. G. and heriot: 10s.

4238 SHILLINGTON (December) Matthew Chaumbre: one pasture of demesne land called Colbiesgrene, lying at the gate of the manor towards the south along its length, and between the king's road at the east and Colbyescroft at the west, in width, from Michaelmas for 20 years, rendering annually two capons at Christmas and all other services and customs owed therein, with all the wood and undergrowth growing in the pasture reserved to the lord. He will repair and maintain the pasture at his own expense, and if any damage or harm should come to the lord from this in the future, this copy will be held null. Fine excused because of Matthew's good service.

246r **4239** BARTON (9 October: General Court) Richard Chyld: one messuage and one virgate of land recently held by William Bonde and once held by John Bonde, with a forland, for life, rendering annually in all things as did William, with the obligation to repair and maintain all the buildings existing and to be built on the property, under penalty of forfeit. G.: 4s. Heriot: paid in the court.

4240 BARTON (same court) John Hexton Jr.: surrender of one toft with appurtenant land, to the use of Jacob Wodeward, for life, rendering annually 5s. at the customary times, and all other services and customs owed therein. G.: 12d., one capon.

4241 HOLYWELL (October) John Lanender, his wife, Agnes, his son, Robert, and his wife, Margaret: one messuage and one virgate of land with demesne land pertaining to it once held by Richard Scot and recently held by John himself and surrendered back to the lord by him, for life, rendering annually in all things as before. G.: 6s.8d.

246v *Crossed out*

247r **4242** HOLYWELL (October) John Nicolas: surrender of one cote and two acres of land recently held by John Wodecok and once held by Thomas Edward, to the use of

Simon Nicolas and his wife, Anna, for life, rendering annually in all things as did John. G.: one hen.

4243 Holywell (26 January) John Hunne, alias Baker, pays four capons for license to marry Johanna, daughter of Roger Hunne, naif of the lord by blood, to whomever she wishes, and for license for her to live off the manor.

4244 Holywell (17 February) Margeria, widow of John AtteWelle: surrender of a half-virgate of land with all adjacent demesne land, the yield of that land, recently held by her and her husband *per copiam* and once held by William Palfreyman, to the use of John Elyot and his wife, Alicia, daughter of Margeria and John AtteWelle, for life, rendering annually in all things as did Margeria. G.: 6s.8d.

4245 Slepe (February) William Atkyn: one built up cotland with appurtenant land recently held by Richard Morgon and once held by Thomas White, for life, rendering annually 12s. at the customary times, with the obligation to repair and maintain all the buildings there at his own expense. G.: two capons.

4246 Le Moyne's Manor (November) Thomas Peny and Thomas Gowler of Upwood: the manor called Moyne's Manor, and one piece of meadow called Long medowe, from the previous Michaelmas for life, rendering annually 8s. at the customary times, and all other services and customs owed therein. G.: six capons. And they swear fealty.

4247 Ellington (19 November) William Reynold: surrender, through the hands of John Towslond, bailiff, of one messuage built up with one house on the croft called Ferycroft, and one quarter of land, to the use of John Virly, for life, rendering annually all services and customs owed therein, with the obligation to repair and maintain all the buildings on the messuage at his own expense, under penalty of forfeit. Further, if the payments are in arrears for 15 days after the due-date, either in full or in part, the lord may seize and retain the property without contradiction. G.: 40d.

4248 Ellington (December) John Penyell: surrender of one messuage and three quarters of land in Sibthorp to the use of his son, William Penyell and his successors, in bondage with the obligation to repair and maintain all the houses and buildings on the property under penalty of forfeit. Further, if the payments are in arrears for 15 days, etc. G.: 13s.4d. of which he pays 6s.8d.

4249 Ellington (20 January) William Reignald: surrender of one messuage and three quarters of land once held by John Wysenell, to the use of Henry Loce and his successors rendering annually all services and customs owed therein, with the obligation to repair and maintain all the houses and buildings on the property under penalty of forfeit. Further, if the payments are in arrears for 15 days, etc. G.: 6s.8d.

247v

4250 Brington (25 November) John, son of Thomas Thressher and naif of the lord, pays two capons for license to marry Isabella, daughter of John Bacheler and naif of the lord by blood, this time.

4251 Brington (1 January) William Cusse: surrender of one messuage and three half-virgates of land with forland, one pithel recently held by John Porquey, and a parcel of one virgate once held by William Alcok, to the use of Thomas Buk, and his wife, Lovetta, for life, rendering annually 26s.8d. at the customary times, and one ploughing *precaria*, the supplying of one man for the Great Autumn *Precaria*, suit to court, and customs of the village, except the office of beadle. Further, he will repair and maintain the messuage at their own expense, three wagonloads of undergrowth for the enclosure at the beginning being supplied by the lord. G.: four capons.

4252 Abbots Ripton (January) John Lyndesey: surrender of one cotland built up, with four selions of land recently held by John Hawlond, two selions of land in le Lounde once held by John Webster, and one acre of demesne land at Barbor's Dole, to the use of William Lyndesey and his wife, Juliana, for life, rendering annually 4s. for the cotland and selions and 6d. for the acre of demesne, at the customary times, and all other services and customs owed therein. G.: four capons.

4253 ABBOTS RIPTON (January) William Lyndeseye: surrender of one messuage built up with four houses and one semi-virgate recently held by William Fuller and once held by John AtteChirche, to the use of John Lyndesey. The same John and his wife, Agnes: a half-virgate of land at Estgrene with three selions of land recently held by William Halsham and once held by John Ravenesden, with three acres of demesne land at Barisdole, for life, rendering annually 8s. for the messuage and semi-virgate and 6s. for the half-virgate, and 18d. for the two acres of demesne, at the customary times, and all other services and customs owed therein. G.: three capons.

4254 ABBOTS RIPTON John Crane and his wife, Katerina: one vacant plot lying in Mille Ende, with one semi-virgate of land in *secunda arentatio* once held by William Kelsey and recently held by William Birt, for life, rendering annually in all things as did William Birt. G.: (*cut off*).

4255 WISTOW CUM RAVELEY Thomas Wyllesson, naif of the lord by blood, pays two capons for license to marry Margaret, his daughter, to whomever she wishes, this time.

4256 ST. IVES (March) Robert Bokenham Fuller and his wife, Cristina: two rows with land recently held by John Esex and once held by Robert Takyll, from Michaelmas for life, rendering annually 8s. at the customary times, with the obligation to repair and maintain the property. *Et non licebit*, etc. G.: 12d.

4257 ST. IVES (20 March) Agnes Judde, widow of Thomas Judde, and Johanna, their daughter: a half-row next to the free tenement of Thomas Judde, from Michaelmas for life, rendering annually 4s. at the customary times, and all other services and customs owed therein, with the obligation to repair and maintain the property. *Et non licebit*, etc. G.: 2s.

4258 LITTLE RAVELEY WITH WISTOW (March) John Owty: one toft and a half-virgate of land once held by Richard Baron and recently held by John Asplond Sr., for life, rendering annually 8s. at the customary times, and all other services and customs owed therein. G.: two capons.

4259 CHATTERIS (3 April: General Court) John Swetemelk: surrender of one messuage and half of one tenement of eight acres of land once held by John Wyddon, with meadow in Crowlode, fishpond in Honyholm, and appurtenant forland, three rods of land in Elmen and half of the land in le Slade, to the use of John Berle Jr., for life, rendering annually all services and customs owed therein. G.: 3s.

4260 CHATTERIS (same court) Thomas Gere, son of John Gere and naif of the lord of the manor of Holywell: one cotland with four houses, meadow in Oldhalf, fishpond, and land in Elmen and Medmen, for life, rendering annually in all things as did John Gere. G.: 6d.

4261 CHATTERIS (same court) John Revesson, Jr., alias Sempoll, son of John Revesson Sr.: two perches of meadow in Owse and Owsemor recently held by his father and once held by John Cutt, for life, rendering annually in all things as did John. G.: 12d.

4262 CHATTERIS (same court) John Revesson, bailiff: one acre in Medmen, one cotland of Pakerell dole, one croft once pertaining to a tenement of eight acres once held by John Chownesson, one vacant toft with appurtenances recently held by the sister of Abbot Thomas, and one selion of land recently held by Tromper, for life, rendering annually 4s.4d., and all other services and customs owed therein. G.: 12d.

4263 CHATTERIS (same court) John Dryell: half of one tenement of eight acres of land once held by John Chownesson, for life, rendering annually 4s. at the customary times, and all other services and customs owed therein. G.: 16d.

4264 RAMSEY (1 June) Richard Harpor Mason and his wife, Katerina: one messuage

248r

248v

recently held by John Bryan Mason, from the previous Michaelmas for life, rendering annually 12s. in equal portions at the feasts of the Annunciation and Nativity of Blessed Mary, with the obligation to effect repairs to hedges and closes, with the lord supplying thorns, undergrowth and transport. *Et si predictus redditus*, etc. (arrears of one month). Further, if they do anything prejudicial to the lord, the property will be seized. G.: 8s.

4265 RAMSEY (July) John Halle, chaplain: from Brother William Bury, sub-cellarer, one tenement inside Mechegates in which he lives, from the previous Michaelmas for life, rendering annually 5s. in equal portions at the feasts of the Annunciation and Nativity of Blessed Mary, with the obligation to repair any damages made by him. Further, the sub-cellarer will be responsible for all other repairs, and John may find a tenant for the land if he wishes. *Et si predictus redditus*, etc. (arrears of six weeks). G.: 4s.4d.

4266 RAMSEY (July) William Freman and his wife, Isabella: from the sub-cellarer, one tenement next to Mechgates recently held by Robert Broun Tyler, from the previous Michaelmas for life, rendering annually 5s. in equal portions at the feasts of the Annunciation and Nativity of Blessed Mary, with the sub-cellarer reponsible for repairs. *Et si predictus redditus*, etc. (distraints after arrears of one month). G.: excused.

4267 RAMSEY (July) Richard Mayner and his wife, Johanna: from the sub-cellarer, one tenement in Little Whyte recently held by Thomas Godfrey, from the previous Michaelmas for life, rendering annually 7s. in equal portions at the feasts of the Annunciation and Nativity of Blessed Mary, with the sub-cellarer responsible for repairs. *Et si predictus redditus*, etc. (arrears of six weeks). G.: 3s.4d.

4268 CRANFIELD (July) William Terry, bailiff, pays 2s. for license to marry Isabella, daughter of Thomas Aleyn and naif of the lord by blood, to whomever she wishes. And the fine is no larger at the request of the rector.

4269 ELSWORTH (21 September) Anna, daughter of Robert Yntte and naif of the lord by blood, pays 20d. for license to marry William Smyth of Ditton, this time. Pledge for payment: John Elyot.

249r **4270** ELTON (July) Thomas Saldyng, who lives on the fief of the lord in Ramsey and is a naif of the manor of Elton, pays four capons for license to marry Elena, his daughter, to whomever she wishes, this time.

20 JOHN STOWE (1455-1456)

4271 KNAPWELL (leet) Henry Basse and his wife, Agnes: three cotes recently held by John Gryme, for life, rendering annually in all things as did John. G.: (*cut off*).

4272 KNAPWELL (same leet) John Drew and his wife, Alicia: one plot and one virgate of land recently held by John Smyth, for life, rendering annually in all things as did John. G.: two capons.

4273 KNAPWELL (same leet) John Hogon and his wife, Isabella: one messuage and a half-virgate of land recently held by Thomas Grey, for life, rendering annually in all things as did Thomas.G.: 12d.

4274 KNAPWELL (August) John Smyth: surrender of one quarter of land once held by John Reynald, to the use of John (*blank*) and his wife, Margaret, for life, rendering annually in all things as did Smyth. G.: 4d.

249v **4275** BURWELL (17 October: leet) Thomas Rolfe Carpenter, his wife, Alicia, and their son, Thomas: 15 acres of arable land recently held by his father, John Rolfe, for 30 years, rendering annually in all things as did John. G.: four capons.

4276 BURWELL (same leet) Thomas Hale and John Hale: one messuage with adjacent croft and 15 acres of arable land recently held by Isabella Pocat, for 50 years, rendering annually in all things as did Isabella. G.: two capons.

4277 BURWELL (February) Radulph Wyot and William Coo: the fishpond of le Nesse with meadow and pond pertaining to it, and one pithel called Chastelyn's pithel recently held by Thomas Pury and George Burthen, from the previous Michaelmas for 20 years, rendering annually in all things as did Thomas and George, and all other services and customs owed therein. G.: excused.

4278 SHILLINGTON (21 October: leet) Agnes Reve, widow of Richard Reve: surrender of one messuage and two virgates of land in Hanscombe recently held by Richard and once held by Thomas West, to the use of Walter Swyft, and his wife, Margaret, for life, rendering annually 30s.2d. at the customary times, and all other services and customs rendered by Agnes. G.: 10s., of which 40d. are excused at the request of the rector.

4279 SHILLINGTON (same leet) Agreement between John Olyver and William Grene that William convey to John and his wife, Agnes, one plot inside the manor with appurtenances recently held by Adam Yonge, and five parcels of meadow pertaining to that plot, for life, with William supplying them with straw sufficient to repair the plot whenever necessary, John and Agnes being responsible for transport of undergrowth, thorns, tiles, and lime for repairs and enclosing the messuage, and for clay for repairing the walls and all buildings. Further, John and Agnes will render annually 4s., and after their deaths the property will return to William, and his descendants, rendering all services and customs owed therein. Fine for license: two capons.

4280 BARTON (22 October: General Court) It is determined by an inquisition of the court that Edith AtteWode made waste in one tenement recently held by John Cooke by cutting down trees and not repairing the buildings. Further, she dismissed that tenement and one adjacent croft beyond the term of three years, against the custom of the manor, for which the lord, through his bailiff, seizes the tenement with appurtenances. Afterwards, the lord grants that tenement with adjacent croft to the same Editha, for life, rendering annually in all things as before, with the obligation to repair and maintain the property at her own expense and to enclose the spring there and protect it, under penalty of forfeit. G.: 2s. Fine for waste: 2s.

4281 HEMINGFORD ABBOTS (November) Thomas Yngill, naif of the lord by blood, pays 2s. for license to marry Agnes, his daughter, to Robert Pynnok, this time. Fine paid to the lord by Thomas Aungewyn.

4282 HEMINGFORD ABBOTS (September) Walter Murrok: surrender of one virgate of land recently held by Thomas Cadman and once held by John Bontyng, with one messuage reserved to himself, to the use of Thomas Lyncolne, his wife, Margaret, and their son, John, for life, rendering annually 11s.4d. at the customary times, and all other services and customs owed therein. Also: the capital messuage once held by Reginald de Ayllyngton and recently held by Johanna Lyncolne, for life, rendering annually 3s.4d. at the customary times, and all other services and customs owed therein. G.: three capons.

4283 ST. IVES (November) John Goodman: surrender of a half-row recently held by William Charite, to the use of William Hawes and his wife, Alicia, from the previous Michaelmas for life, rendering annually 8s. in equal portions at the feasts of the Annunciation and Nativity of Blessed Mary, and all other services and customs owed therein, with the obligation to repair and maintain the property. *Et non licebit*, etc. G.: two capons.

4284 ST. IVES (November) William Balle and his wife, Alicia: one row in which he lives, from the previous Michaelmas for life, rendering annually 13s.4d. in equal portions at Michaelmas and Easter, and all other services and customs owed therein, with the obligation to repair and maintain the property. *Et non licebit*, etc. G.: two capons.

4285 ELTON (29 November) Thomas Saldyng, who lives in Ramsey, pays two capons for license to marry Helena, his daughter and naif of the lord by blood, to whomever she wishes.

4286 ELTON (February) John Gebon, alias Smyth, and his daughter, Agnes: one messuage and one virgate of land recently held by William Philyp and once held by Laurence Pokbrook, and one toft once held by Maynard and recently held by William Feryby, from the previous Michaelmas for life, rendering annually as did Laurence for the messuage and virgate, with the obligation to repair the enclosures and maintain the croft with appurtenances at their own expense within one year. G.: two capons.

4287 ELTON (February) John Smyth and his daughter, Agnes: one plot with building now held by him, between his free tenement and the cote once held by John Hych in which he has his forge, from the previous Michaelmas for life, rendering annually 14d. at the customary times, and all other customs and services owed therein. G.: two capons.

4288 ELLINGTON (November) Thomas Buk: surrender of one messuage and one vacant toft and six quarters of land, to the use of William Cutt, for life, rendering annually all services and customs owed therein, with the obligation to repair and maintain the buildings on the property at his own expense, under penalty of forfeit. Further, if the payments are in arrears for 15 days after the due-date, the lord shall seize the property. G.: 2 marks, of which he is allowed 6s.8d.

4289 ELLINGTON (November) John Massy Smyth: one messuage built up on the site of the manor, for life, rendering annually 5s. at the customary times, and all other services and customs owed therein, with the obligation to repair and maintain the property at his own expense, under penalty of forfeit. Further, if the payments are in arrears, etc. G.: 2s., two capons.

4290 ELLINGTON (November) John Mokke, son of Richard Mokke: one quarter recently held by John Skynner, for life, rendering annually all services and customs owed therein. Further, if the payments are in arrears, etc. G.: 4s.

250v

4291 ELLINGTON (1 January) William Myller: two cotes previously held by him, for life, rendering annually 8s. at the customary times, and all other services and customs owed therein, with the obligation to repair and maintain all the buildings on the property at his own expense. If the payments are in arrears for 15 days, etc. Also: a half-virgate of land of a cotland recently held by John Hykkesson, for life, rendering annually all services and customs owed therein. G.: 2s., two capons.

4292 ELLINGTON Henry Sabyn: one messuage and one quarter of land recently held by William Mokke and once held by Laurence Mokke, for life, rendering annually all services and customs owed therein. Further, if the payments are in arrears for 15 days, etc. G.: 4s.

4293 ELLINGTON William Cottyng: surrender of one quarter of land in Coton once held by John Hikesson, to the use of Richard (*blank*), for life, rendering all services and customs owed therein. Further, if the payments are in arrears for 15 days, etc. G.: 2s.

4294 HOLYWELL CUM NEEDINGWORTH (20 February) John Sande and his wife, Alicia: one messuage, one cotland, a half-virgate of land with one croft and demesne land recently held by his father, John Sande, for life, rendering annually in all things as did his father. G.: 20d.

4295 HOLYWELL CUM NEEDINGWORTH (December) John Nicolas: surrender of four acres and a half at Benehill recently held by his father and recently held by William Carter, to the use of Roger Cristemas and his son, John, for life, rendering annually in all things as did John. Also: three acres and the fourth part of one rod in le Brache and three acres in Shepenfurlong and one acre in Netherbrerecroft recently held by Nicholas Baron, for life, rendering annually in all things as did Nicholas. G.: one capon.

4296 HOLYWELL (September) Richard Cristemesse, his wife, Alicia, and their son, Thomas: two messuages and two cotlands with land and meadow of demesne once held by John Bran and recently held by the same Richard and surrendered back to the lord by him, for life, rendering annually 20s.5d.ob. at the customary times, and all other services and customs owed therein. G.: (*missing*).

4297 ELSWORTH (January) John Newman Sr.: surrender of one cote once held by Thomas AtteLane, to the use of Simon Sparugh and his wife, Rosa, for life, rendering annually in all things as did John. G.: three capons.

4298 ELSWORTH (January) William Astyn and his wife, Johanna: one cote and half of one virgate of Gravelond recently held by John Hunne, for life, rendering annually in all things as did John. G.: three capons.

4299 ELSWORTH (22 May) John Wrighte: surrender of one cote with adjacent croft recently held by Margaret Fuller, to the use of John Porter and his wife, Margaret, from the previous Michaelmas for life, rendering annually in all things as did John. G.: 12d., two capons.

4300 CHATTERIS (January) Thomas Smyth, alias Cradwer: surrender of one cotland with meadow and fishpond recently held by John Pykerell, to the use of John Revesson Jr., for life, rendering annually 2s.5d. and all other services and customs owed therein. G.: 6d.

4301 CHATTERIS (January) Simon AtteWode and his wife, Margaret: one messuage and a half-virgate of land with demesne land recently held by William Ber (?), and a half-virgate of land in Caldecote once held by John Dallyng, for life, rendering annually 16s.3d. at the customary times, one ploughing *precaria*, and one carrying service, which property previously rendered 8d. Further, they will render all other services and customs owed therein. G.: four capons.

4302 RAMSEY (February) Thomas Crosse: from Brother William Bury, sub-cellarer, one tenement in Ramsey next to the chapel of St. Thomas the Martyr recently held by John Eyr, for life, rendering annually 20s. in equal portions at the feasts of the Annunciation and Nativity of Blessed Mary, with the obligation to repair all damages to the property committed by him, with the sub-cellarer responsible for other repairs. *Et si predictus redditus*, etc. (distraints after arrears of 15 days; seizure after arrears of two months). G.: excused by the lord.

4303 RAMSEY (August) William Bryngton and his wife, Katerina: from Brother William Bury, sub-cellarer, one messuage next to Carite Bridge recently held by John Carite, from Michaelmas for life, rendering annually 5s. in equal portions at the feasts of the Annunciation and Nativity of Blessed Mary, with the obligation to repair the enclosures, and with the sub-cellarer responsible for other repairs. *Et si predictus redditus*, etc. (arrears of one month). G.: excused because of a rent increase.

4304 RAMSEY (August) John Whitewell and his wife, Johanna: from the sub-cellarer, one messuage inside Mechegate recently held by William Medowe, from the previous Michaelmas for life, rendering annually 8s. in equal portions at the feasts of the Annunciation and Nativity of Blessed Mary, with the obligation to repair all damages made by them, and with the sub-cellarer responsible for other repairs. *Et si predictus redditus*, etc. (arrears of one month). G.: 6s.8d.

4305 RAMSEY (August) John Herwode and his wife, Margaret: from the sub-cellarer, one garden with pond parcelled from and pertaining to a tenement recently held by John Berenger and now held by Thomas Pere, for life, rendering annually 2s. in equal

251r

251v

portions at the feasts of the Annunciation and Nativity of Blessed Mary. Further, Thomas Pere may have undergrowth from the property, and access to the pond for water is allowed to Thomas, his servants and other tenants. *Et si predictus redditus*, etc. (arrears of one month). Further, if they do anything prejudicial to the lord, the property will be seized. G.: (*blank*).

4306 RAMSEY (August) John Gelam and his wife, Johanna: from the sub-cellarer, one messuage recently held by Graunger, from the previous Michaelmas for life, rendering annually 9s. in equal portions at the feasts of the Annunciation and Nativity of Blessed Mary, with the obligation to repair the enclosures and buildings. G.: 5s.

4307 RAMSEY (24 June) Thomas Grene pays two capons for license to marry Elena, daughter of Robert Owty, deceased, and naif of the lord by blood of the manor of Wistow, to Thomas Fuller of Houghton, this time.

21 JOHN STOWE (1456-1457)

252r   **4308** WISTOW CUM RAVELEY (March) Richard Lyndesey: surrender of one messuage and two half-virgates of land and half of one half-virgate recently held by Richard Wyllesson, to the use of Richard Plombe, for life, rendering annually in all things as did Richard, with the obligation to repair and maintain the messuage and rebuild one hall and one *camera* and one Crosseler before Michaelmas at his own expense, with timber and 18s. granted by the lord. G.: four capons.

4309 WISTOW CUM RAVELEY (March) Richard Plombe: surrender of one messuage and one quarter of land recently held by John Walgate Sr. and half of one half-virgate of land recently held by John Plombe, to the use of Thomas, son of John Wyllesson, for life, rendering annually in all things as did Richard. G.: two capons.

4310 WISTOW CUM RAVELEY (March) Richard Plombe: surrender of half of one half-virgate of land recently held by John Plombe to the use of John and Thomas Wyllesson, sons of Richard Wyllesson, for life, rendering annually in all things as did Richard. G.: one capon.

4311 BROUGHTON (December) Thomas Lane and his wife, Agnes: one messuage and one and a half virgates with appurtenances recently held by Roger Asplond, for life, rendering annually 19s. at the customary times, and all other services and customs rendered by Roger, with payments beginning at the feast of St. Andrew after one full year because of repairs to the plot and houses to be effected by the customaries at the expense of Thomas, with timber and undergrowth supplied by the lord the first time. G.: two capons.

4312 BROUGHTON (January) John Of Bury: one quarter of land from the Cleryvaux tenement recently held by John Cabe and once held by William Cabe, from Michaelmas for life, rendering annually 3s.4d. at the customary times, and all other services and customs owed therein. G.: one capon.

4313 BROUGHTON (14 March) Alicia, daughter of John Cabe and naif of the lord by blood and widow of William Keye, through her attorney, John Cullan, pays 6s.8d. for license to marry whomever she wishes, this time.

4314 CRANFIELD (January) John Curteys: surrender of one messuage and a half-virgate of land to the use of Nigel Aleyn, for life, rendering annually in all things as did John. G.: 2s.

252v   **4315** CRANFIELD (January) Thomas Grene Sr.: surrender of one cote and three acres of land, and six acres of a forland, to the use of Robert Grene, for life, rendering annually in all things as did Thomas. G.: 40d.

4316 CRANFIELD (January) Thomas Grene Sr.: surrender of one messuage and one cotland, to the use of his son, Thomas Grene, for life, rendering annually in all things as did Thomas Sr. G.: 4s.

4317 UPWOOD (March) William Freman and his wife, Alicia: one messuage and a half-virgate of land *ad opus* and three quarters of land in *arentatio* recently held by Thomas Hendesson and once held by John Bigge, for life, rendering annually 18s. rent and 6s. for works at the customary times, and all other services and customs owed therein. Also: William, by license of the lord, exchanged four selions of demesne land at Asshenhene and two selions at Henowyk with John Redde for a parcel of a croft abutting his tenement. Further, William and Alicia will repair their properties at their own expense. G.: (*blank*).

4318 GRAVELEY (May) Agnes, daughter of Thomas Baron and naif of the lord by blood, pays two capons for license to marry whomever she wishes, this time.

4319 RAMSEY (1 June) Mariona Crosse, widow, and her son, Thomas Crosse: from William Bury, sub-cellarer, one tenement next to the chapel of St. Thomas the Martyr recently held by John Eyr, for the life of whomever lives longer, rendering annually 20s. in equal portions at the feasts of the Annunciation and Nativity of Blessed Mary, with the obligation to repair and maintain the buildings on the property, with the sub-cellarer responsible for other repairs. *Et si predictus redditus*, etc. (arrears of one month, with distraints; seizure after arrears of two months). G.: one capon.

253r

4320 ST. IVES (June) Radulph Ive and his wife, Anna: one newly-constructed tenement on a parcel of the old toll booth recently held by William Purdy, for life, rendering annually 10s. in equal portions at the feasts of the Annunciation and Nativity of Blessed Mary, with the obligation to repair and maintain the property. Further, if the payments are in arrears for one month, the lord shall seize the property. *Et non licebit*, etc. G.: excused by the seneschal.

4321 ST. IVES (July) John Rogger, his wife, Alicia, and their son, John: a parcel of a tenement once held by Henry Barbor and recently held by Thomas Gentill, for life, rendering annually 8s.10d. at the customary times, and all other services and customs owed therein, with the obligation to repair and maintain the property. *Et non licebit*, etc. G.: two capons.

4322 ST. IVES (July) Isabella Burdy, widow, and her son, John: a half-row recently held by John Cooke, for life, rendering annually 8s. at the customary times, and all other services and customs owed therein, with the obligation to repair and maintain the property. *Et non licebit*, etc. G.: two capons.

22 JOHN STOWE (1457-1458)

253v

4323 CRANFIELD (Thursday after St. Edward the King: leet) John Whitebroun: one cotland with one acre of land recently held by William Pyrye, for life, rendering annually 8d. at the customary times, and all other services and customs rendered by William. G.: 2s.

4324 BARTON (Friday after St. Edward the King: court) Richard Martyn: surrender of one tenement and one virgate of land, to the use of John Child, and his heirs rendering annually 18s. at the customary times, and all other services and customs rendered by Richard. G.: 2s. Heriot: 16d., as the price of one wether.

4325 BARTON (same court) Richard Martyn: surrender of one messuage and one virgate of land called Geffreys, to the use of his son, John Martyn and his heirs rendering annually in all things as did Richard. G.: 20d.

4326 BARTON (same court) Richard Brerele and his heirs: one pithel called Hogespightill recently held by his father, Thomas Brerele, rendering annually in all things as did Thomas. G.: 12d.

4327 Elsworth (20 October: leet) Johanna Boner, naif of the lord by blood, pays 8d. for license to marry John Annger, this time.

4328 Elsworth (same leet) Johanna Herry and her son, William: one messuage recently held by John Hogon, for life, rendering annually rents (*unspecified*) at the customary times. G.: (*blank*).

4329 Elsworth (same leet) Thomas Fermour: a half-quarter of land recently held by John Hogon, for life, rendering annually in all things as did John. G.: (*blank*).

4330 Elsworth (December) Johanna Boole: surrender of one croft at le Grave and one virgate of land with appurtenances, to the use of Simon Sparugh, and his wife, Rosa, for life, rendering annually 13s.4d. at the customary times. G.: two capons.

4331 Elsworth (December) John Hobbesson, alias Fermor, and his wife, Margaret: two tofts once held by Roger Carter and recently held by Alexander Fermor, for life, rendering annually 20d., which property previously rendered 2s. Further, they will render all other services and customs owed therein, with the obligation to build one *insathous* on the two tofts within two years at their own expense. G.: one capon.

4332 Elsworth (January) John Lucas: surrender of one messuage and a half-virgate of land, to the use of Thomas Lucas and his wife, Margaret, for life, rendering annually in all things as did John. G.: 20d.

4333 Hemingford Abbots (December) John Welles: surrender of one cotland built up with three houses once held by Adam Tydde, to the use of Robert Portos, son of John Portos, for life, rendering annually 4d. at the customary times, and all other services and customs owed therein, within the obligation to repair and maintain the three houses under penalty of forfeit. G.: 20s.

4334 Hemingford Abbots (December) Same Robert Portos, son of John Portos: a half-virgate of land recently held by his father, John Est, for life, rendering annually 6s. at the customary times, and all other services and customs owed therein, with Robert prohibited from dismissing any part of that half-virgate to anyone without the license of the lord. G.: one capon.

4335 Hemingford Abbots (May) John Feld Jr. and his wife, Agnes: a half-virgate of land recently held by Richard Botiller, for life, rendering annually 5s.8d. at the customary times, and all other services and customs owed therein, with the first payment at next Michaelmas. G.: one capon.

4336 Hemingford Abbots (May) John Feld Jr. and his wife, Agnes: the capital tenement of a tenement once held by Ayllyngton, one croft and a half-virgate of land recently held by John Ybot, and half of one virgate of land recently held by William Hill, for life, rendering annually 15s.2d. and all other services and customs owed therein. G.: two capons.

4337 Houghton (21 October: leet) Thomas Caus: surrender of one messuage and one virgate of land recently held by William Burgeys, to the use of Hugo Sely, for life, rendering annually in all things as did Thomas. Further, Thomas will have one parcel of the messuage with its houses, the east end of the orchard, easement in the bake house and oven reserved to himself for life, with the obligation to repair and maintain the buildings and orchard at his own expense, and after his death the property will revert to Hugo. G.: 6s.8d.

4338 Chatteris (11 October: General Court) John Brewster: surrender of one cotland built up with two houses recently held by John Devyll, to the use of Alicia Champay, for life, rendering annually 7d. at the customary times, and all other services and customs owed therein. G.: 8d.

4339 Chatteris (same court) John Smyth: surrender of one messuage at Horseheath with certain lands and meadow and le Ferye at Swynshed Wer, called of old a messuage, once held by John Bate, to the use of William Chapell, for life, rendering

254r

annually 13s.11d. at the customary times, and all other services and customs owed therein. Same William: one cotland recently held by John Smyth Jr., for life, rendering annually 23d. at the customary times, and all other services and customs owed therein. G.: 2s.

4340 CHATTERIS (same court) John Ray: one and a half cotlands, one acre of land in Medmen, and two acres of land in Elmen, with other appurtenances recently held by Simon Aleyn, and once held by John Lytholf, for life, rendering annually 5s.11d.ob. at the customary times, and all other services and customs owed therein. Also: one acre of land in Elmen, one and a half acres of land in Medmen, and two selions of land in the western part of the manor recently held by Edmund Cade, for life, rendering annually 2s.6d.ob. at the customary times, and all other services and customs owed therein. G.: 2s., and two capons for the cook.

4341 CHATTERIS (same court) John Skele: surrender of one cotland at le Hithe recently held by John Pyron, to the use of Walter Toye, for life, rendering annually 8d. at the customary times, and all other services and customs owed therein. G.: 40d.

254v **4342** CHATTERIS (same court) John Pyper: surrender of one cotland built up with two houses, with acres in Shephernefen recently held by John Cokerell, one and a half acres in Elmen, and a half-acre of land in Shephernefen, to the use of Thomas Bray, for life, rendering annually 2s.7d. for the cotland and 22d. for the two acres of land, at the customary times, and all other services and customs owed therein. G.: 2s.

4343 CHATTERIS (same court) John Bernard: certain acres of land recently held by John Berle Jr., and one cotland, for life, rendering annually in all things as did John. G.: 20d.

4344 CHATTERIS (same court) John Hopkyn: surrender of one messuage and half of one tenement of eight acres with other parcels of land and meadow recently held by John Beche, to the use of John Brewster Jr., for life, rendering annually in all things as did John. G.: 4s., and four chickens to the cook.

4345 CHATTERIS (same court). Richard Cokkesford: two cotlands in Pakerell dole, a half-acre of land in Elmen, one and a half acres in Medmen recently held by John Hunte and once held by John Tomesson, and one acre of land in Shephernefen once held by Thomas Lytholf Sr., for life, rendering annually 5s.1d. at the customary times, and all other services and customs owed therein. G.: 2s.6d.

4346 CHATTERIS (same court) The jurors present that John Hamond sold all his right and status on one cotland and four selions of land, a half-acre of land in Medmen, and one acre next to the ditch, to John Wympool, which lands were seized by the lord. Afterwards, John came to the court and took up those lands, for life, and he received half of one tenement of eight acres with meadow in Crowlode Mede recently held by John Devyll, for life, rendering annually as did Hamond and Devyll. G.: 4s.

4347 CHATTERIS (same court) Richard Fykeys: eight acres of land recently held by John Lytholf Sr., with forland, cotland and a half-cotland and one acre of land in Medmen, for life, rendering annually 2s.1d. and all other services and customs owed therein. G.: 2s.

4348 CHATTERIS (same court) Nicholas Egyf: half of one tenement of eight acres of land with fishpond of Honyholme recently held by William Thakstede and once held by John Mathew atte Hithe, for life, rendering annually in all things as did William. G.: 8d.

4349 CHATTERIS (same court) Robert Reynold: two cotlands once held by John Sowth and recently held by Richard Turnor, for life, rendering annually 3s.10d. at the 255r customary times, and all other services and customs owed therein. G.: 4d.

4350 CHATTERIS (same court) John Clerke: surrender of one messuage in Horseheath and half of eight acres with meadow in Crowlode and fishpond, and a half-acre of land in Elmen, to the use of John Meyke, for life, rendering annually 5s.5d. at the customary times, and all other services and customs owed therein. Pledge for repairs and payments: John Wympooll. G.: 8d.

4351 CHATTERIS (same court) John Revesson, bailiff: one messuage containing a quarter-rod of land recently held by John Newman and once held by John Bate, for life, rendering annually 12d. at the customary times, and all other services and customs owed therein. G.: two capons.

4352 CHATTERIS (same court) John Revesson, bailiff: surrender of one messuage and eight acres of land with meadow in Oldhalf recently held by John Drynge Bocher, to the use of his son, John, for life, rendering annually 9s.6d. at the customary times, and all other services and customs owed therein, with three selions of land in Harssladefeld and half of the meadow in Oldhalf reserved to John Sr. for life. G.: 2s.

4353 CHATTERIS (same court) Robert Bette: one cotland recently held by William Hunte for 23d., for life, rendering annually 12d. at the customary times, and all other services and customs owed therein. Also: two selions of land at Stokkyng recently held by John Kyng, for life, rendering annually 8d. at the customary times, and all other services and customs owed therein. G.: 4d.

4354 RAMSEY (20 September) Richard (*blank*) and his wife, Juliana: from William Bury, sub-cellarer, a meadow in High Ditch, willows, fishpond, reeds and other appurtenances previously taken up by John Wetton and his son, Thomas, *per copiam*, in the sixth year of the abbot and subsequently seized by the lord for arrears in rents of two years, from Michaelmas for life, rendering annually 30s. in equal portions at the feasts of the Annunciation and Nativity of Blessed Mary, with the obligation to repair and maintain the enclosures, and with permission to cut down willows and replant them, without making waste. The sub-cellarer will have right to reeds and willows, and they may not relinquish the property without the license of the lord. *Et si predictus redditus*, etc. (arrears of one month). Further, if they default in any obligations, the property will be seized.

4355 UPWOOD (6 November: leet with court) Thomas Gowler, naif of the lord by blood, pays two capons for license to marry Agnes, his daughter, to Nicholas Newband, servant of the cellarer of Ramsey, this time.

255v **4356** BURWELL (December) Elena Goodale, widow of Thomas Goodale: surrender, through the hands of John Benet, bailiff: one tenement of eight acres recently held by Thomas, and one tenement pertaining to 20 acres of land once held by John Dene and recently held by Margaret Plombe, to the use of John Kirby, and his wife, Thomesina, for 40 years, rendering annually 11s.1d. at the customary times, and all other services and customs owed therein, with the obligation to repair and maintain the property at their own expense. G.: 12d.

4357 BURWELL (December) William Goodale, alias Wright: one cote in North Street recently held by William (*cut off*) and once held by William Grantham, by the rod for life, rendering annually 1s.11d. for rent, 1d. for tallage, at the customary times, and all other services and customs owed therein, with the obligation to repair and maintain all buildings and houses on the property under penalty of forfeit, and which property previously rendered 4s. G.: 40d.

4358 ABBOTS RIPTON (December) Richard Weston and his wife, Johanna: one messuage recently held by Thomas Mychell, previously held by William Halsham and recently held by John Person, for life, rendering annually 2s. at the customary times, and all other services and customs owed therein, with the obligation to repair and maintain the property at their own expense. G.: two capons.

4359 ABBOTS RIPTON (February) John Burman: surrender of one cotland with appurtenances and one and a half acres of land in Cornercroft once held by Thomas

Swon, to the use of William Wangtey, for life, rendering annually in all things as did John. G.: two capons.

4360 ABBOTS RIPTON (April) John Lyndesey Jr.: one messuage built up on one cotland by Richard Smyth, and one toft with two cotlands and certain adjacent lands recently held by Richard Smyth and once held by John Fletcher, for life, rendering annually 4s. at the customary times. G.: two capons.

4361 ABBOTS RIPTON (1 January) John Weston, his wife, Katerina, and any of their legitimate sons or daughters: the reversion of one tenement recently held by Radulph Osberne and now held by John's father, Richard Weston, for a term of 99 years, rendering annually 12d. at the customary times, and all other services and customs owed therein, with the obligation to repair and maintain the property. Further, they may not will, alienate or assign the property to anyone without the lord's permission, and after the deaths of John and Katerina and their children, no entry may be made into that property until a payment of two capons as *gersuma* has been made. In addition, after the end of the 99 years, the lord may take back the property and dispose of it as he wills. G.: two capons.

4362 HOLYWELL (December) Rosa, widow of John Asplond, her son, Roger Asplond, and Roger's wife, Johanna: one built up croftland in Holywell once held by William Baron and recently held by her husband, John Asplond, together with one messuage and one virgate of land *ad opus* and certain acres of land in Needingworth once held by John Palmer and recently held by John Asplond, for life, rendering annually in all things as did John. G.: 5s.

4363 HOLYWELL (February) John Sande Jr.: surrender, through the hands of Roger Cristemesse, bailiff, of one messuage and a half-virgate of land with cotland and demesne land pertaining to the messuage, to the use of John Bate and his wife, Alicia, for life, rendering annually in all things as did John. G.: two capons.

4364 HOLYWELL (April) John Asplond and his wife, Margaret: one messuage and a half-virgate of land with demesne land an other appurtenances recently held by Thomas Merton and once held by Nicholas Godfrey, for life, rendering annually in all things as did Thomas. G.: 2s.

4365 HOLYWELL Richard Baker, alias Hunne: one messuage and one virgate of land with other appurtenances recently held by his father, Roger Baker, for life, rendering annually all services and customs owed therein. G.: two capons, and no more because of repairs.

4366 HOLYWELL (June) William Herle: surrender of one cote recently held by William Hunne and once held by William Baron, with one acre of demesne land in Middilfurlong recently held by William Hunne, to the use of Richard Beaumes Sr. and his wife, Rosa, for life, rendering annually in all things as did William. G.: 20d.

4367 ELTON (December) Richard Clement and his wife, Margaret: one toft and one virgate of land recently held by his father, John Clement, for life, rendering annually 13s.4d. at the customary times, and all other services and customs owed therein. G.: 12d.

4368 SHILLINGTON CUM PEGSDON (16 October: leet) Thomas AtteWell of Pegsdon: surrender, with the license of the lord, to William Shepperd and Thomas Whitefeld *ad firmam*, of one tenement built up with one hall and annexed *camerae* in ruined condition, with one virgate of land and forland and other appurtenances, from the previous Michaelmas for 12 years, rendering annually all services and customs owed therein, with the obligation to repair and maintain the property at their own expense. Further, they will build one barn 34 feet long and 15 feet wide within two years. In addition, note that the *firmarii* receive the land uncultivated and waste, with no hay at the beginning. But they will receive hay at the end of the term with the consent of

Thomas. Finally, it is agreed that if Thomas AtteWell or any of his blood is unable to occupy the land at the end of the 12 years, William and Thomas will hold it, over the rights of anyone. Fine for the license: two capons.

4369 SHILLINGTON CUM PEGSDON (December) John Draper: surrender of one plot inside the manor with one lot and one acre of demesne land recently held by John Goberd, to the use of William Burgh, for life, rendering annually 10s.4d. at the customary times, and all other services and customs owed therein. G. and heriot: 13s.4d.

4370 SHILLINGTON CUM PEGSDON (December) Matthew Chambre and his daughter, Johanna: the reversion of the hall, kitchen, bake house, malt kiln, stable dovecote, grange, and four lots of demesne land inside the manor, with other parcels and appurtenances held by John Goberd and his wife, Johanna, *per copiam* for life, rendering annually 6s.8d. for the hall, and 34s.4d. for the four lots and other properties at the customary times, with the obligation to repair and maintain the property at their own expense, with the lord supplying timber, splints, rods, *haybote* and *fyrebote*, at the judgment of the seneschal. Further, they will find provisions for the seneschal and his staff, and straw for his horses, when he comes, and if they dismiss any of the property without the lord's license, or perform anything resulting in damage or harm to the lord or his, or if they default in their obligations, the lord shall seize the property.

4371 SHILLINGTON CUM PEGSDON (April) Philip Multon: surrender, through the hands of Matthew Chambre, bailiff, of one virgate, one messuage, a half-virgate of land recently held by John Multon and once held by John Atstyle, and nine acres of demesne land with one meadow recently held by the same John, to the use of William Warde and his wife, for life, rendering annually in all things as did Philip. G.: 10s.

4372 ST. IVES (April) John Roger: surrender of one plot, to the use of John Barbor and his wife, Agnes, for life, rendering annually 10s. and all other services and customs rendered by John, with the obligation to repair and maintain the property. *Et non licebit*, etc. G.: 18d.

FIFTEENTH-CENTURY ABBOTS OF RAMSEY*

Thomas Butterwyk:	1396-1419 (October)
John Tychemersh:	1419 (October)-1434 (14 August)
John Croyland:	1434 (27 August)-1436 (20 March)
John Stowe:	1436 (29 March)-1468 (resigned, *ante* 27 August)
William Witlesey:	1468-1473
John Warboys (I):	1473-1489
John Huntyngdon:	1489-1506
John Warboys (II):	1507-1539

* The sources for this list are: Dugdale's *Monasticon Anglicanum*; the *Chronicon* of Ramsey Abbey; and the *Cartulary* of the Abbey, vol. 3, pp. 171-89.

ACREAGE OF CUSTOMARY UNITS OF LAND
OF RAMSEY MANORIAL VILLAGES*

Village	Virgate	Cotland	Croft
Abbots Ripton	15½		
Barton	23-24	10-12	1-16
Brington	34	5	
Broughton	32		
Burwell	30		
Bythorne	44		
Chatteris	32		1-4
Cranfield	48	16	2-4
Ellington	24		
Elsworth	30		
Elton	24		
Gidding	28		
Graveley	20		
Hemingford Abbots	15-18		½-1½
Holywell	18	10	1-5
Houghton	18	9	1
King's Ripton	24		
Knapwell	40		
Little Raveley	20		
Little Stukeley	24		½-1
Shillington	12		
Slepe	16		
Therfield	64		
Upwood	30		
Warboys	30		
Weston	28	14	1 rod
Wistow	30		
Woodhurst	16		
Wyton	20		

* The sources for the above figures are the extents and surveys in the *Cartulary* of the Abbey, vols. 1-3.

BIBLIOGRAPHY

MANUSCRIPT SOURCES

London: British Library:
  Liber Gersumarum: Harley MS. 445.
  Cellarers' Rolls: Additional Manuscripts 33447, 33448.
  Court Rolls: Additional Rolls 34308, 34322-23, 34368-71, 34779, 34817-31, 34881-
      82, 34909, 34920-21, 39476-82, 39645-46, 39648, 39745-46, 39768-74,
      39861-70.

  Public Record Office:

  Court Rolls: Series SC2, Portfolio 179, nos. 45-68.

PRIMARY SOURCES (edited)

Carte Nativorum: A Peterborough Abbey Cartulary of the Fourteenth Century. Ed. C. N. L.
    Brooke and M. M. Postan. Northamptonshire Record Society 22. Oxford, 1960.
Cartularium Monasterii de Rameseia. Ed. W. H. Hart and P. A. Lyons. 3 vols. Rolls Series 79.
    London, 1884-93.
Chronicon Abbatiae Rameseiensis a saeculo X. usque ad annum circiter 1200. Ed. W. Dunn
    Macray. Rolls Series 83. London, 1886.
Corpus Juris Canonici. Ed. E. Friedberg. 2 vols. Leipsig, 1879-81.
Court Baron, The. Ed. F. W. Maitland and W. P. Baildon. Selden Society, vol. 4. London,
    1891.
Court Rolls of the Abbey of Ramsey and of the Honor of Clare. Ed. W. O. Ault. New Haven,
    1928.
Monasticon Anglicanum. Ed. W. Dugdale. 6 vols. London, 1817-30.
Select Pleas in Manorial and other Seignorial Courts. Ed. F. W. Maitland. Selden Society, vol.
    2. London, 1889.

SPECIALIZED AIDS, ETC.

Catalogue of the Harleian Collection of Manuscripts, 2 vols. London, 1759.
Concise Oxford Dictionary of English Place-Names, The. Ed. E. Ekwall. 4th ed. Oxford, 1960.
Handbook of Dates for Students of English History. Ed. C. R. Cheney. London, 1961.
Medieval Farming Glossary, A. Ed. J. L. Fisher. London, 1968.
Middle English Dictionary. Ed. H. Kurath, S. Kuhn. Ann Arbor, 1956 et seq.
Middle English Dictionary, A. Ed. F. H. Stratmann, rev. H. Bradley. Oxford, 1891.
Place-Names of Bedfordshire and Huntingdonshire, The. Ed. A. Mawer and F. M. Stenton.
    English Place-Names Society, vol. 3. Cambridge, 1926.
Place-Names of Cambridgeshire, and the Isle of Ely, The. Ed. P. H. Reaney. English Place-
    Name Society, vol. 19. Cambridge, 1943.
Place-Names of Hertfordshire, The. Ed. J. E. B. Gover, A. Mawer, F. M. Stenton. English
    Place-Name Society, vol. 15. Cambridge, 1938.
Place-Names of Northamptonshire, The. Ed. J. E. B. Gover, A. Mawer, F. M. Stenton. English
    Place-Name Society, vol. 10. Cambridge, 1933.
Record Interpreter, The. Ed. C. T. Martin. 2nd. ed. London, 1910.
Revised Medieval Latin Word-List. Ed. R. E. Latham. London, 1965.

MONOGRAPHS AND ARTICLES.

Ault, W. O. *Open-Field Husbandry and the Village Community*. Transactions of the American
    Philosophical Society, N.S. 55. Philadelphia, 1965.
DeWindt, Anne Reiber. "Society and Change in a Fourteenth-Century English Village: King's
    Ripton, 1250-1400;" Unpublished Ph. D. thesis, University of Toronto, 1972.
DeWindt, Edwin Brezette. *Land and People in Holywell-cum-Needingworth*. Toronto, 1972.
Donahue, Charles, Jr., and Gordus, Jeanne P. "A Case from Archbishop Stratford's Audience
    Act Book and Some Comments on the Book and its Value." *Bulletin of Medieval Canon
    Law*, 2nd series 2 (1972): 45-59.
DuBoulay, F. R. H. *The Lordship of Canterbury*. New York, 1966.
Hilton, R. H. *A Medieval Society*. London, 1967.
Hogan, Mary Patricia. "Wistow: A Social and Economic Reconstitution in the Fourteenth Cen-
    tury." Unpublished Ph.D. thesis, University of Toronto, 1971.
Homans, G. C. *English Villagers of the Thirteenth Century*. Cambridge, Mass., 1941.
Jones, Andrew "Land and People at Leighton Buzzard in the Later Fifteenth Century,"
    Economic History Review, 2nd ser. 25 (1972): 18-27.
Levett, A. E. *Studies in Manorial History*. Ed. H. M. Cam, M. Coate and L. S. Sutherland. Ox-
    ford, 1938.
May, Alfred N. "An Index of Thirteenth-Century Peasant Impoverishment? Manor Court
    Fines." *Economic History Review*, 2nd ser. 26 (1973): 389-402.
Raftis, J. Ambrose. "Changes in an English Village after the Black Death." *Mediaeval Studies*
    29 (1967): 158-177.
———. "The Concentration of Responsibility in Five Villages." *Mediaeval Studies* 28 (1966):
    92-118.
———. *The Estates of Ramsey Abbey*. Toronto, 1957.
———. "Peasant Mobility and Freedom in Mediaeval England." *Report of the Canadian
    Historical Association*, 1965, pp. 117-130.
———. "Social Structures in Five East Midland Villages." *Economic History Review*, 2nd ser. 18
    (1965): 83-100.
———. *Tenure and Mobility*. Toronto, 1964.
Reaney, P. H. *The Origin of English Surnames*. London, 1967.
Russell, J. C. *Medieval Regions and their Cities*. Bloomington, 1972.
Sheehan, M. M. "The Formation and Stability of Marriage in Fourteenth-Century England:
    Evidence of an Ely Register." *Mediaeval Studies* 33 (1971): 228-263.
Titow, J. Z. *English Rural Society, 1200-1350*. London, 1969.
Wedemeyer (Moore), Ellen. "Social Groupings at the Fair of St. Ives (1275-1302)." *Mediaeval
    Studies* 32 (1970): 27-59.
Wright, Cyril Ernest. *Fontes Harleiani*. London, 1972.

INDEX LOCORUM*

ABBOTS RIPTON (Hunts.): 8-11, 74, 81-2, 95-8, 138-9, 188-9, 225, 267, 346, 360-1, 458, 523, 579-81, 615, 641, 685, 787, 853, 927-8, 1093-4, 1480-1, 1584-6, 2055-9, 2112, 2184-8, 2289-90, 2415-17, 2565-9, 2661-3, 2711-13, 3288-92, 3385, 3398-9, 3598-3600, 3668-72, 3885, 3970-2, 4158-61, 4221, 4252-4, 4358-61. See also: KING'S RIPTON, and RIPTON.
Arlesey (Beds.): 2630.
Ayllyngton. See ELTON.

Barham (Cambs.): 674.
Barnwell (Northants.): 896, 1652, 3100, 4000.
BARTON (Beds.): 18-20, 50-1, 153, 191, 261, 302-5, 385, 491-3, 544-8, 567, 712-13, 791-2, 886-8, 893-4, 907, 1067, 1069-74, 1134-6, 1176-7, 1212, 1288, 1308-9, 1366-7, 1375, 1458-62, 1543-5, 1612-15, 1735-8, 1757-8, 1790-2, 1856, 1888-93, 1979-86, 2117-23, 2195-6, 2226-8, 2313-16, 2392-7, 2535-8, 2582-3, 2620-1, 2722-4, 2763-5, 2896-8, 2949-52, 3004-5, 3036-8, 3147-51, 3230, 3353-63, 3416-17, 3485-91, 3538-41, 3629-35, 3710-15, 3964, 4050-5, 4180-3, 4192, 4239-40, 4280, 4324-6.
Barton (Norhants.): 3101.
BIGGING (Hunts.): 72, 900, 1933; mentioned: 624, 900, 1657, 2736.
Bletchley (Berks.): 2899.
Bluntisham (Hunts.): 1748, 2855.
Bodeseye: 3236.
Brampton (Hunts.): 3976.
Brantfeld: 3976.
BRINGTON (Hunts.): 184, 224, 266, 324, 368-9, 380, 756, 776, 783-4, 918, 925, 1003-5, 1117-18, 1225-8, 1260, 1305, 1339, 1371, 1464-8, 1572, 1767, 1811, 1839, 2002-6, 2113, 2221, 2497, 2539, 2603, 2651-2, 2783-5, 2925-7, 3095-6, 4157; mentioned: 1575, 3968. See also: BYTHORNE, WESTON.

BROUGHTON (Hunts.): 87-8, 134, 190, 196, 217, 233-4, 249, 251-2, 280, 338, 412, 419-20, 467, 482-4, 522, 539, 596, 629, 652, 739, 850-2, 856, 904-6, 1149, 1157, 1192-4, 1221, 1445, 1598-9, 1658-61, 1713, 1763-4, 1813, 1941-8, 2085-7, 2164-77, 2282-8, 2333-4, 2428-30, 2451-3, 2511-14, 2640-7, 2826, 2854, 3120, 3201, 3308, 3328-32, 3436-8, 3525, 3560-4, 3675, 3788-93, 3823, 4014, 4106-7, 4185, 4203, 4311-13; mentioned: 1756, 1779, 3905.
Buckland (Herts.): 2216.
Buckworth (Hunts.): 1468, 2854, 3192, 3590.
BURWELL (Cambs.): 33-5, 43-6, 170-3, 202, 235-6, 277, 311-14, 400-1, 446-8, 495-9, 647-9, 874, 898, 901, 950-3, 1078-81, 1095-6, 1132, 1171, 1229-31, 1346-51, 1421-2, 1529-35, 1623-31, 1696-1702, 1777, 1795-9, 1868-9, 1974-7, 2039-44, 2125-6, 2235-8, 2332, 2379-81, 2499-2500, 2508-10, 2580-1, 2632-3, 2702-4, 2883-90, 2959-60, 3010-12, 3122-30, 3215-18, 3344-6, 3471-7, 3530-1, 3612-21, 3753-5, 3766-7, 3828-34, 3899, 3957-8, 4017-21, 4110-14, 4162, 4204-7, 4225-7, 4275-7, 4356-7.
Bury (Hunts.): 673, 692.
Buryhatle: 1585.
BYTHORNE (Hunts.): 55, 79-80, 149, 182-3, 263, 315-17, 417-18, 454-5, 707, 721-2, 744, 785, 917, 1027, 1469-70, 1669-70, 1838, 2360-1, 3013-14, 3192-3, 3397, 3504-9, 3786-7, 3857-60, 3906-8, 4104-5, 4131. See also: BRINGTON, WESTON.

Caldecote (Hunts.): 774, 932, 1128-31, 1195-6, 1237-40, 1302, 1381-4, 1413, 1416, 1851, 1934, 1939, 2158, 2337-8, 2594, 2917, 2974, 3058, 3185, 3368, 3370, 3372-5, 3378, 3448, 3552, 3742, 3745, 3797, 3802, 3895, 3925, 3986, 4301.

* References are to *entry* numbers, not page numbers. Ramsey villages in caps.

London: 888, 3936.

Mentmore (Berks.): 2208.
Merston (Kent): 3414.
Milford (Suffolk): 1346.
Millbrook (Beds.): 2208.

NEEDINGWORTH (Hunts.): 1854, 1863,
2358; mentioned: 130, 288, 331, 353,
391, 393, 1025, 2031, 3203, 4362. See
also: HOLYWELL-CUM-NEEDING-
WORTH.
Nethstondon: 487.
Newchepyng: 3807, 3840.
Newsells (Herts.): 3698, 3700.
NOVUS LOCUS (Hunts.): 2007.

Offley (Herts.): 3714.
Offord Darcy (Hunts.): 3714.
Oldmol: 1571.
Over (Cambs.): 3924, 3942.
Overedon: 3404.
Overton (Hunts): 1999, 2259.

Papley (Cambs.): 1305.
Papworth Anneys (St. Agnes) (Cambs.):
3846.
PEGSDON (Beds.): 1486-94, 3628, 3757,
3903, 4368-71; mentioned: 154, 273, 488,
796, 1263, 1341, 1617, 1900, 2398,
2955, 3002, 3033, 3152, 3420, 3904,
4002, 4177, 4235, 4368. See also:
SHILLINGTON.
Peterborough: 1016.
Pidley (Hunts.): 388.
POPENHOE: 195, 279. See also:
WALSOKEN.
Pulloxhill (Beds.): 3035.

RAMSEY (Hunts.): 37-41, 70, 287, 398-9,
415-16, 428-30, 618, 623-4, 1146, 1170,
1219, 1264, 1273, 1410-11, 1522-8,
1603-5, 1657, 1746, 1784-7, 1805, 1812,
1827, 1857, 1928-32, 2054, 2124, 2212-
14, 2483-4, 2576, 2609-10, 2679, 2696-
7, 2717-19, 2933-9, 3017-19, 3105-18,
3162-3, 3183, 3231-47, 3406-7, 3455-
63, 3526-9, 3758-60, 3816, 3887-8,
3890-2, 3938-40, 4031, 4163, 4193-4,
4264-7, 4302-7, 4319, 4354; mentioned:
333, 1222, 1244, 1606, 1783, 2430,
3417, 3518, 3537, 3555, 3567, 3590,
3624-5, 3729, 3740, 3757, 3799, 3974,
4115, 4128, 4159, 4270, 4285. See also:
HEIGHMONGROVE.
RAVELEY (Hunts.): 651, 1222, 2111,
2700, 2983-4, 3196, 3198-3200, 3335,

4072, 4255; mentioned: 238, 248, 464,
687, 751, 1100, 1310, 1441, 1601, 2183,
2353, 2701, 2975, 3196, 3562, 3791,
4072, 4185. See also: GREAT RAVE-
LEY, LITTLE RAVELEY, UPWOOD,
WISTOW.
Reed (Herts.): 3960.
RIPTON (Hunts.): 895, 921-4, 926, 949,
969, 997, 1017, 1068, 1139-41, 1234,
1251-7, 1320, 1338, 1356, 1378, 1385-6,
1769, 1828, 1852-3, 1862, 1949-51,
2298, 2450, 2584, 2820-2, 2914-15,
2953-4, 3101-4, 3386, 3412-13, 3465-8,
3663-7, 3738-9, 3794-8, 3998, 4015-16,
4069-71, 4099; mentioned: 1756. See
also: ABBOTS RIPTON, KING'S RIP-
TON.
Royston (Herts.): 164-6, 815-16, 3211,
3961, 4228.

ST. IVES (Hunts.): 12-16, 71, 94, 124-5,
193-4, 239, 241-2, 247, 258-60, 292,
296, 325, 329, 342-3, 356, 395, 397,
479, 500-3, 531-2, 541, 552, 561, 563,
572, 593, 606, 694-5, 825-8, 866-71,
934-8, 1011-15, 1097-9, 1164-8, 1274,
1325-35, 1396-7, 1508-13, 1557, 1634-
51, 1656, 1745, 1773-4, 1781, 1814-22,
1966-73, 2150-2, 2277-8, 2321-6, 2410-
12, 2455-65, 2522-31, 2585-6, 2653-5,
2753-6, 2771-7, 2940, 2985-6, 3015-16,
3073-8, 3087, 3139-43, 3302-7, 3320-3,
3433-5, 3511-14, 3746-7, 3822, 3824,
3855-6, 3909-10, 3931-2, 3943, 3975,
3999, 4029, 4073-6, 4091-3, 4136-9,
4184, 4186-7, 4201, 4256-7, 4283-4,
4320-2, 4372; mentioned: 753, 1739,
2018, 3172, 3510, 3593, 3729, 3881,
4188. See also: GRENE, HURST, SLEPE,
WOODHURST.
St. Neots (Hunts.): 1325, 3458, 3822.
Sandon (Berks.): 2024, 2026.
Shefford (Beds.): 2393.
SHILLINGTON (Beds.): 21-30, 47-9, 154-
63, 273, 306-7, 383-4, 439-42, 487-90,
494, 504, 552, 555-9, 621-2, 681, 715,
793-803, 889-90, 1082-91, 1137-8,
1173-5, 1209-10, 1263, 1284-17, 1307,
1341-5, 1482-5, 1537-42, 1616-22,
1718-25, 1765, 1778-9, 1783, 1824,
1859, 1864, 1895-1902, 1978, 2032-3,
2065-71, 2115-16, 2189-92, 2229-33,
2295-6, 2311-12, 2398-2407, 2476-81,
2540-4, 2601-2, 2622-30, 2721, 2761-2,
2891-5, 2955-8, 2996-3003, 3031-5,
3152, 3249-50, 3347-52, 3418-20, 3478-

ALMAR. See AYLMER.
ALOM, Emma, *Elton*: 2427; Thomas, *Elton*: 2427.
ALOT, Adam, *Burwell*: 647, 2237, 3218; John, *Warboys*: 932, 1237; Margaret, *Warboys*: 932; Maria, *Burwell*: 2237.
ALOUN, Alan, *Elton*: 634; Thomas, *Elton*: 996, 2249.
ALREDE. See ALRETHE.
ALRETHE (Alrede), *Elsworth*: 765, 1705.
ALSON. See ALSOUN.
ALSOUN (Alson, Alfsun), William, *Abbots Ripton*: 928, 1141, 2056.
ALSTON, Nicholas, *Upwood/ Warboys*: 335, 468, 746, 2551, 3281.
ALTHEWERD. See ALTHEWORLD.
ALTHEWORLD (Althewerd, Of the World), Alicia, *Warboys*: 1303; John, *Upwood*: 1906; William, *Warboys*: 598, 736, 1303, 1903, 1947, 2158. See also: WOLD.
ALWYN (Aylwyn, Aylwynne, Ayllewyn), Isabella, *St. Ives*: 3321; John, *Burwell*: 311, 401; Richard (al. Prentyse), *Burwell*: 3215; Richard, *St. Ives*: 3321; Margaret, *Burwell*: 3215.
ALYN. See ALEYN.
ALYNSON. See ALEYNNESSON.
AMERY, Katerina, *Abbots Ripton*: 1378, 1828, 2058; William, *Abbots Ripton*: 1378, 1586, 1828, 2058.
AMPTILL Thomas, *Therfield*: 2436.
AMROSE, John, *Chatteris*: 3915, 4082.
ANABLE, Thomas (Smyth), *Burwell*: 2379.
ANDREW (Andrewe), Agnes, *Houghton*: 1368; Agnes, *Upwood*: 4027; Alan, *Houghton*: 627; Emma, *Houghton*: 3985; John, *Elsworth*: 1002, 1301; John, *Houghton*: 281, 627, 1040, 1206, 1368, 2387, 2468, 2649, 2967, 3177, 3984-5; John, Jr., *Houghton*: 601; John (al. atte Style), *Houghton*: 578, 1039, 1108, 3411; John (Smyth), *Houghton*: 1108, 2320; John, *Upwood*: 282, 1006, 1102, 3926, 4027; John, *Wistow*: 464; Margaret, *Houghton*: 1434, 1960, 2320, 3720; Peter, *Houghton*: 600, 1954, 2842, 2965, 3425; Robert, *Houghton*: 1108, 2318, 3053, 3176, 3275, 4147; Thomas, *Houghton*: 1954, 2239, 3276, 3547, 3720, 4147; William, *Houghton*: 1434, 1954, 1960.
ANDREWSON, John, *Houghton*: 4168.
ANGEWYN. See AUNGEWYN.
ANGTILL (Angetill), Elena, *Therfield*: 2034, 4229; Thomas, *Therfield*: 2034, 3213, 3408; William, *Therfield*: 164.
ANNPROUN, family: *Hemingford*: 3495.

ANNSELL, Henry, *Shillington*: 3348.
ANSLEY, William, *Elsworth*: 2876.
APIRLE (Abirle), John, *Houghton*: 2318, 2650, 3411; Richard, *Houghton*: 4168.
ARCHER (Archere), Richard, *Broughton*: 4203; Richard, *Cranfield*: 1447, 2948, 3366; Richard, *Shillington*: 3153; Thomas, *Cranfield*: 2616.
ARLYCHE, Agnes, *Barton*: 3712.
ARNALD. See ARNOLD.
ARNEWEY (Arneweye), Alicia, *St. Ives*: 2655, 3594; John, *Hurst/ St. Ives*: 2548, 2655, 2756, 3594.
ARNOLD (Arnald), Alicia, *Holywell*: 4208; John, *Knapwell*: 957, 2048, 3825; John, *Graveley*: 2827, 3067-8, 3780; Johanna, *Graveley*: 2827; Oliva, *Burwell*: see WEBSTERE; Petronilla, *Holywell*: 2061; Roger, *Holywell*: 4208; Simon, *Holywell*: 291; Thomas, *Burwell*: see WEBSTERE; Thomas, *Holywell*: 2061, 3429, 4208.
ARTHORNGH, Agnes, *St. Ives*: 936; Hugo (Lystere), *St. Ives*: 936, 1328, 3306; Johanna, *St. Ives*: 1328.
ASCOMB, William, *Houghton*: 670.
ASE. See ACE.
ASPLOND (Aspelond), Agnes, *Holywell*: 3336; Alicia, *Broughton*: 906; Anna, *Wistow*: 2274; Johanna, *Holywell*: 4362; John, *Broughton*: 3329; John, *Holywell*: 2062, 3862, 4010; John, Sr., *Holywell*: 449; John, Jr., *Holywell*: 3203, 4362; John (III), *Holywell*: 3338, 4364; John, *St. Ives*: 1817; John, Sr., *Warboys*: 352; John, *Wistow*: 89, 370, 476, 524, 1100, 1169, 1685, 1872, 1874, 2274, 3741; John, Sr., *Wistow*: 4258; Margaret, *Broughton*: 1763; Margaret, *Holywell*: 3338, 4364; Mariota, *Broughton*: 467; Peter, *Chatteris*: 283; Peter, *Wistow*: 2273; Reginald, *Wistow*: 4141; Richard, *Holywell*: 1222, 2671, 3198; Richard, *Holywell*: 3336; Roger (I), *Broughton*: 1763; Roger (II), *Broughton*: 1763, 3329, 3823, 4203, 4311; Roger, *Holywell*: 4362; Rosa, *Holywell*: 3203, 4362; Thomas, *Warboys*: 345, 387; Thomas (Plouwright), *Wistow*: 275, 2272, 2273-4; William, *Broughton*: 280, 467, 1941, 3332; William (Lepe Maker, al. Ploughwright), of Sutton: 4141.
ASSE. See ACE.
ASSHBY, Margaret, *Elton*: 2928; Robert, *Elton*: 2928.
ASSHWELL, Robert, *Warboys*: 3448, 3744.
ASTY, Robert, *Brington*: 1767.
ASTYN. See AUSTYN.

4305; John, *Warboys*: 271, 466, 1033, 1775, 3372, 3548; John (Wryghte), *Warboys*: 340, 1007, 2154, 2830; John, Sr., *Warboys*: 1408, 1417, 2160, 3056, 3320, 3376, 3800; John, Jr., *Warboys*: 1034, 3270, 3377; Juliana, *Warboys*: 2160, 3056; Katerina, *Warboys*: 481, 754, 963, 1414, 2919, 3058, 3370, 3742; Mariota, *Warboys*: 4128; Richard, *Warboys*: 75, 481, 754, 1414, 2919, 3058, 3370, 4128; Thomas, *Warboys*: 736, 1126, 1936, 4130; William, *Warboys*: 271, 341, 1415, 3056, 3320, 3374; William, Sr., *Warboys*: 2248; William, Jr., *Warboys*: 2158, 2520, 3368; William (son of John), *Warboys*: 3372.

BERENTON, Johanna, *Shillington*: 4001; John, *Shillington*: 4001.

BERES, Johanna, *Ramsey*: 3162; John, *Ramsey*: 3162.

BERKER (Shepherd), Elena, *Therfield*: 3835; Hugo, *Burwell*: 901; John, *St. Ives*: 2323; John, *Therfield*: 3835; Margaret, *Burwell*: 3126; Thomas, *Burwell*: 3126; Thomas, *Elsworth*: 2760.

BERLE (Barle, Berly, Berley), John, *Broughton*: 2644; John, *Chatteris*: 1915, 4211; John, Sr., *Chatteris*: 2748, 3573, 3990; John, Jr., *Chatteris*: 2747, 3445, 3990, 4259, 4343; Richard, *Chatteris*: 3574, 3918; Thomas, *Chatteris*: 2858, 2861, 3445.

BERNARD. See BURNARD.

BERNE, Agnes, *Cranfield*: see FRAY-FELDE; Roger, *Cranfield*: 3040, 3773; William, *Cranfield*: 2304; William, *Elton*: 705.

BERNER, John, *Ramsey*: 1526.

BERNET, John, *Shillington*: 2479, 2762.

BERNEWELL, Alicia, *St. Ives*: 16, 362-3, 1099; Isabella, *St. Ives*: 2586; Johanna, *Broughton*: 420; Johanna, *St. Ives*: 16; John, *Broughton*: 2086, 2173; John, Sr., *Broughton*: 420; John, *St. Ives*: 2586; Margaret, *Slepe*: 362-3; Thomas, *Holywell*: 393; William, *Ramsey*: 1410, 3459; William, *St. Ives*: 16, 362-3, 1099, 1311; Brother William, sub-cellarer of Ramsey: 1657, 2933-5, 2939.

BERONGER. See BERENGER.

BEROUNESSON, Roger, *Brington*: 324.

BERTON, John, *Weston*: 1575; Matilda, *Weston*: 1575.

BERYNGER. See BERENGER.

BESEWORTHE (Beysworth, Beseworth), Johanna, *Elsworth*: 1322, 1479, 1802;

John (al. Peek), *Elsworth*: 1322, 1479, 1802, 4037.

BEST, John, *Elton*: 318, 733, 911, 2428; Richard, *Elton*: 56, 992, 1299, 2834.

BESTON (Beeston), John, *Shillington*: 29, 306, 1082, 1345, 1541, 1621-2.

BET. See BETTE.

BETECOK, John, *Ramsey*: 3890; Margaret, *Ramsey*: 3890.

BETELE, Richard, *Ramsey*: 40.

BETERYNG, Thomas, *St. Ives*: 329.

BETH (Bethe, Bythe), John, *Houghton*: 2844, 2912, 3655, 3721, 3725; Margaret, *Houghton*: see ANDREW.

BETHERE (By the Re), John, *Houghton*: 472, 1426, 1679.

BETHEWATER (By the Water), Agnes, *Hemingford*: 2901; Katerina, *Warboys*: 2156; Robert, *Hemingford*: 2839, 2901, 3137; William, *Warboys*: 2156.

BETON (Betoun), John, *Weston*: 1248; Philip, *Abbots Ripton*: 360; Robert, *Chatteris*: 3394; Robert, *Houghton*: 485, 1963.

BETONSON (Betonsone, Betonsson), John, *Brington*: 1572; William, *Brington*: 1225, 2005.

BETOUN. See BETON.

BETTE (Bet), Johanna, *Ellington*: 1064-5; Johanna, *Knapwell*: 1580; John, *Elsworth*: 1580, 1804; Robert, *Chatteris*: 4084, 4353; Simon, *Ellington*: 1065; William, *Knapwell*: 1668, 2023.

BETTESSON, John, *Chatteris*: 3296.

BEVERECH. See BEVERICH.

BEVERICH (Bevereche, Beveryche), Agnes, *Brington*: 2002; Beatrix, *Bythorne*: 3859; John, *Brington*: 266, 369, 2002; John, *Bythorne*: 3014, 3191-2; Simon, *Brington*: 925, 1004, 1117, 1371, 2652; Thomas, *Ellington*: 3684; William, *Bythorne*: 3859.

BEWBRAY. See BEAUBRAS.

BEYSWORTH. See BESEWORTHE.

BIGGE (Bygge), Agnes, *Upwood*: see PAYN; John, *Broughton*: 1943; John, *Upwood*: 583, 4317; Simon, *Broughton*: 3561.

BIGGYNG, Simon, *Broughton*: 2428.

BILLER (Byllar, Byller), Agnes, *Chatteris*: 684; Jacob, *Chatteris*: 2570; John, *Chatteris*: 283, 1836, 1913, 2010, 2014, 2093; John, Sr., *Chatteris*: 684; John, Jr., *Chatteris*: 684; Margaret, *Chatteris*: 1836.

BILLYNG, John, *Abbots Ripton*: 2568.

BIRCHER (Birchere), Alicia, *Warboys*: 2919; William (al. Barbour), *Warboys*: 2919, 3370.

Shillington: 25, 2032, 3248; William, *Shillington*: 2480.

BRAMPTON (Brantoun), Agnes, *Houghton*: 1679; Agnes, *Ramsey*: 3892; Agnes, *Wistow*: 2734, 3022; Johanna, *Houghton*: 3725; John, *Elton*: 1565, 2727; John, *Houghton*: 3501, 3725; John, *Warboys*: 1032, 2248; Richard, *Elsworth*: 403; Richard, *Wistow*: 2734, 3022; Robert, *Ramsey*: 3892; William, *Houghton*: 1105, 1679, 2648, 3500, 3657, 3985.

BRAN. See BRAYN.

BRANNCASTER (Branncester, Branncestre, Branncetre, Brauncestre, Branceter), Agnes, *Chatteris*: 3571; John, *Chatteris*: 2857; John, Sr., *Chatteris*: 3994-5; John, Jr., *Chatteris*: 4210; Peter, *Therfield*: 169, 549, 1198, 2034, 3805, 3838.

BRANTOUN. See BRAMPTON.

BRAUGHYNG (Brawghyng, Broghyng), Margaret, see SWYNFORD; Richard, see SWYNFORD; Robert, *Elsworth*: 1395, 1705, 2440, 2442, 3430.

BRAY (Braye), John, *Chatteris*: 2860, 3869; John Jr., *Chatteris*: 2991, 3389, 4081; Peter, *Upwood*: 671, 1373, 2181, 2778, 3283; Simon, *Chatteris*: 1360, 2864, 3084, 3871; Thomas, *Chatteris*: 4342.

BRAYN (Bran), Anna, *Ramsey*: 3527; John, *Holywell*: 4296; John (Mason), *Ramsey*: 3527; John, *Warboys*: 526; Roger, *Holywell*: 3902; Thomas, *Holywell*: 290, 480, 790, 2061.

BREDWAN. See BRADYFAN.

BREKEPOT, Richard, *Hemingford*: 135.

BREKESPER, William, *Little Stukeley*: 3911.

BRENDHOUS (Bryndhous), Agnes, *Hemingford*: 3131; John, *Hemingford*: 2008, 3178, 3252; John, Jr., *Hemingford*: 2385; Robert, *Hemingford*: 276, 2008, 3131, 3262; Thomas, *Hemingford*: 3178, 3253-4, 3734, 4126.

BRENHAM. See BROUHAM.

BRENNEWATER (Brynwat, Brynnewater), Alicia, *Warboys*: 132; John, *Warboys*: 132, 1125, 1196, 1235, 2159.

BRERE, Thomas, *Abbots Ripton*: 853.

BRERELE (Brereley, Brerell), Agnes, *Cranfield*: 1610, 2308; Katerina, *Cranfield*: 4155; Richard, *Barton*: 4326; Thomas, *Barton*: 4326; Thomas (al. Newynton), *Cranfield*: 1610, 2308, 2496, 2615, 3967, 4153, 4155, 4199; Thomas (Sr.), *Cranfield*: 4049; Thomas (Jr.), *Cranfield*: 4049.

BRESELAUNCE (Bryselaunce), Johanna, *Wistow*: 1315, 1392; Simon, *Wistow*: see THODAY; Thomas, *Wistow*: 524, 1100, 1224, 1315, 1392, 1514, 1588, 1743, 3812.

BRETON (Bretoun), Peter (al. Cook), *Shillington*: 22, 1174, 2481, 2628.

BRETTENDEN, Richard, *Cranfield*: 367.

BREWER (Brewir), Agnes, *Abbots Ripton*: 4071; Henry, *Abbots Ripton*: 4071; John, *Knapwell*: see SAMPSON.

BREWS (Brewse, Brewys), Robert, *Bythorne*: 1838, 3014, 3907.

BREWSTER, John, *Bythorne*: 3908, 4104; John, *Chatteris*: 2856, 2859, 4218, 4338; John, Jr., *Chatteris*: 4344; Thomas, *Ramsey*: 1857.

BRIGGE (Brigges, Bryge, Bryge, Brygge, at Brigge, atte Brigge), Agnes, *Ramsey*: 1603; Beatrix, *Chatteris*: 107, 845; Johanna, *Shillington*: 4236; John, *Chatteris*: see SEMPOOL; John, *Elsworth*: 1662; John ("Gallicus"), *Elsworth*: 141; John, *Hemingford*: 3261, 3736; John (atte Crosse), *Hemingford*: 3262; John, Sr., 3259; John, Jr., *Hemingford*: 3643; Reginald, *Shillington*: 2895; Robert, *Burwell*: 236, 901; Robert, *Hemingford*: 3258, 3648; Stephen, *Chatteris*: 107, 845, 1271; Thomas, *Ramsey*: 1603, 1930, 1932, 2124, 3108; Thomas, *Shillington*: 2895, 4236; William, *Elsworth*: 142, 1988; William, *Hemingford*: 3643; William, *Shillington*: 3627.

BROBY, John, *Cranfield*: 4152.

BROGHTON (Braughyng, Brawghyng, Broughton, Broghyng), John, *Elsworth*: see SWYNFORD; John, *Slepe*: 929; Richard, *Elsworth*: see SWYNFORD; Robert, *Elsworth*: 389, 1022, 1395, 1705, 2440, 2442, 3430; Thomas, *Broughton*: 852, 1945; William, *Broughton*: 134.

BROK. See BROOK.

BRON. See BROUN.

BROOK (Brok, Broke, Brooke, at, atte), Alicia, *Elsworth*: 141, 550; Gilbert, *Shillington*: 163, 273, 383, 1088, 1089, 2033, 2402; Henry, *Elsworth*: 517; Johanna, *Shillington*: 3963, 4003; John, *Abbots Ripton*: 1828; John, *Elsworth*: 550, 1664, 1803, 3431, 3690; John, *Shillington*: 163, 383, 1089; John, Sr., *Shillington*: 3963, 4003; John, Jr., *Shillington*: 622, 3963, 4003; Lucia, *Shillington*: 383, 1088; Margaret, *Elsworth*: 550, 1803; Thomas, *Houghton*: 3983.

3836; William, *Abbots Ripton*: 3101, 3669; William, *Cranfield*: 2310; William, *Houghton*: 1425; William, *Therfield*: 3959.

COLLES. See COLLE.

COLLESSON, Alicia, *Chatteris*: 2808, 3080; Henry, *Elton*: 421; John, *Chatteris*: see HIKKESSON; John, *Elsworth*: 766, 3091; John, *Shillington*: 681; John, Jr., *Warboys*: 333; Richard, *Chatteris*: 424, 1358; Simon, *Bythorne*: 263, 784; Simon, *Elsworth*: 1002; Thomas, *Chatteris*: 2817.

COLMAN, Alicia, *Barton*: see MATHEW; Isabella, *Barton*: 2122; Johanna, *Barton*: 4053; Johanna, *Shillington*: 3034; John (al. Mathew), *Barton*: 261, 1891, 2227-8, 2722, 2897, 3354, 3714, 4053, 4182; John, *Shillington*: 273, 3034, 3769; John, Jr., *Shillington*: 3352; Margaret, *Shillington*: 3769; Richard, *Shillington*: 1721, 3769; Thomas, *Barton*: 1979, 2896, 3149, 3710; William, *Barton*: 2228, 3354.

COLVILLE (Colvyle), Alicia, *Warboys*: 672; William, *Warboys*: 672, 2519.

COLYN, John, *Elton*: 916, 986, 1296, 1671, 2259; John, Jr., *Elton*: 983, 1199; John, *Shillington*: 2311; John, Sr., *Shillington*: 1537, 2231; John, Jr., *Shillington*: 1537, 2231; John, *Therfield*: 549, 2217, 3699; Simon, *Shillington*: 4237.

CONNYNG, Thomas, *Elsworth*: 1708.

CONQUEST, William, *Cranfield*: 2306.

CONWYNE, Thomas, *Hemingford*: 3642.

CONYENE, Nicholas, *Graveley*: 1444.

COO, Thomas, *Elsworth*: 1476, 3582; William, *Burwell*: 4277.

COOK (Cooke, Kook), Adam, *Chatteris*: 509, 1363; Agnes, *Cranfield*: 2223, 3716; Agnes, *Ramsey*: 2212; Agnes, *St. Ives*: 3015; Alan, *St. Ives*: 2324; Alicia, *Chatteris*: 1551; Alicia, *Ramsey*: 2934; Henry, *Cranfield*: 1611, 2223, 3716; Johanna, *Barton*: see SCOT; John, *Barton*: 544, 1615, 4280; John, *Cranfield*: 54, 620; John, *Elsworth*: 93, 146, 533, 1665; John, *Elton*: 638, 993, 1203; John, *Houghton*: 1429, 1437, 1607, 1962, 3174; John, *Ramsey*: see HUNTE; John, *St. Ives*: 1820, 4322; John, *Shillington*: 2405, 2625-6, 2891, 4237; John, *Therfield*: 2028; Juliana, *Ramsey*: 3760; Katerina, *Shillington*: 2891; Margaret, *St. Ives*: 1820; Nicholas, *Elsworth*: 76, 145; Peter, *Shillington*: 2481, 2628; Reginald, *Elton*: 1561, 1564; Richard, *Elton*: 638; Richard, *Ramsey*: 2212; Robert, *Houghton*: 470; Thomas, *Cranfield*: 3716; Thomas, *Wis-*

tow: 89; Thomas, *St. Ives*: 3015; William, *Cranfield*: 3046; William, *Ramsey*: 1827, 2937; William, *Upwood*: 118.

COOL (Coole), Gloria, *Weston*: see MILLER; Thomas, *Abbots Ripton*: 4158; Thomas, *Weston*: 475.

COOP, Reginald, *Elton*: 1887.

COOSTON, Johanna, *St. Ives*: 3320; John, *St. Ives*: 3320.

COPER, Thomas, *Ellington*: see FOTE.

CORBET, John, *Warboys*: 3378; Robert, *Warboys*: 3378, 3552.

CORBY, John, *Broughton*: 1149; Margaret, *Broughton*: 1149.

CORNER, Robert, *Broughton*: 2086.

CORULMAN, Thomas, *Barton*: 261.

COSSALE, Johanna, *St. Ives*: 3076; John, *St. Ives*: 3076, 3931.

COSTYNE, John, *Chatteris*: 2572.

COTENE, John, *Houghton*: 1680; Matilda, *Houghton*: 1680.

COTON. See CATOUN.

COTTY, Robert, *Wistow*: 3020.

COTTYNG, William, *Ellington*: 4293.

COTYNGHAM, William, *Ellington*: 3680, 4144.

COUCHE (Coucher), Alicia, *Shillington*: 3031; John, *Shillington*: 1091, 1344; John, Jr., *Shillington*: 3031; Margeria, *Shillington*: 1091; William, *Shillington*: 1344; William, Jr., *Shillington*: 1091.

COUHIRD. See COWHERDE.

COULAND, John, *Chatteris*: 3388.

COUPER (Coupere), Adam, *Shillington*: 1489, 1494, 2478, 2629; Adam, *Warboys*: 1007; Agnes, *Broughton*: see CABE; Agnes, *Elsworth*: 3948-9; Agnes, *Shillington*: see SMYTH; Emma, *Elsworth*: 3582; Emma, *Ramsey*: 1146; Henry, *Ramsey*: 1219; Johanna, *Ellington*: see FOOT (Fote); Johanna, *Shillington*: 2478, 2629, 2999; John, *Broughton*: 88, 1943; John, *Elsworth*: 3582; John, *Ramsey*: 2054, 2430, 3235; Nicholas, *Ellington*: see FOTE; Robert, *Cranfield*: 1447, 2224, 3153; Robert, *Ramsey*: 1146, 3246; Robert, Sr., *Ramsey*: 3118; Simon, *Shillington*: 1085; Thomas, *Broughton*: see PECHER; Thomas, *Ellington*: 3685, 4066-7; Thomas, *Elsworth*: 2875; Thomas, *Hemingford*: 3733; William, *Ellington*: 349, 1457; William, *St. Ives*: 1645.

COVENAUNT, John, *Chatteris*: 3866.

COVYNGTON (Covington), John, *Warboys*: 1937; Lucia, *Bythorne*: 1470; Mariota, *Warboys*: 1935; Richard, *Warboys*: 1935;

Richard, *Wistow*: see MILLER; Robert, *Bythorne*: 1470; William, *Wistow*: see MILLER.

COWHERDE (Couhird, Cowhird), Cristiana, *Shillington*: 622; John, *Elsworth*: 144, 763, 960, 1804, 2963, 3030; Richard, *Elton*: 371, 378, 912, 2106; Simon, *Shillington*: 622; William, *Elton*: 378.

COYF, Johanna, *Elton*: see DECHE; William (Carpenter), *Elsworth*: 2669.

CRABBE, Alicia, *Burwell*: 1534; William, *Burwell*: 1534, 1977.

CRANE, John, *Abbots Ripton*: 4254; Katerina, *Abbots Ripton*: 4254; Margaret, *Wyton*: 1850; Thomas, *Chatteris*: 3394; Thomas, *Houghton/Wyton*: 1850, 2470, 3661, 4166-7.

CRANFIELD, rector of: 4268.

CREEK (Crek), John, *Knapwell*: 947, 1579; Margeria, *Knapwell*: 2265; Richard, *Knapwell*: 2265.

CRISP, William, *Elsworth*: 1394.

CRISTEMASSE (Cristemesse, Crystemasse), Agnes, *Holywell*: 2454; Agnes (II), *Holywell*: 2710, 3063; Alicia, *Holywell*: 4296; John, *Elsworth*: 1369, 1707, 2535, 3952; John, *Holywell*: 223, 2710, 4295; John, Jr., *Holywell*: 3063; John, *Slepe*: 571; Katerina, *Slepe*: 571; Katerina, *Warboys/ Holywell*: see HARSENE; Margaret, *Holywell*: 2145; Richard, *Holywell*: 2145, 2710, 4296; Roger, *Holywell*: 2454, 2710, 2787, 3063, 3974, 4295, 4363; Thomas, *Holywell*: 4296.

CRISTEYN, Nicholas, *Houghton*: 1677.

CROBY, John, *Cranfield*: 1076.

CROFT, Thomas, *Elsworth*: 3588, 3945, 4035, 4176.

CROSSE (Cros, at, atte), Alicia, *Abbots Ripton*: 3101; Johanna, *Elton*: 981; John, *Abbots Ripton*: 3101; John (II), *Abbots Ripton*: 3600, 3971; John, Jr., *Abbots Ripton*: 3292; John, Sr., *Abbots Ripton*: 3412; John, *Cranfield*: 1446, 1921, 3778; John, *Elton*: 365, 912, 981; John, Sr., *Elton*: 995, 1047; John, Jr., *Elton*: 365, 981; John, *Hemingford*: see BRIGGE; John, *Houghton*: 137, 1961, 1963; Mariona, *Ramsey*: 4319; Margaret, *Houghton*: 3287; Richard, *Elton*: 365; Thomas, *Ramsey*: 4302, 4319; William, *Chatteris*: 844, 1052; William, *Houghton*: 3287, 3392.

CROWCHE (Crouche), Isabella, *Raveley*: 3198; Johanna, *Broughton*: 1713; John, *Broughton*: 1713, 2169-70, 2284, 2642-3,

3331, 3438, 4107; Margaret/Margeria, *Broughton*: 2170, 2284, 2642; Matilda/-Matillis, *Broughton*: 1445, 2169, 4107; Richard, *Raveley*: 3199; Robert, *Broughton*: 1445; Thomas, *Broughton*: 1445, 2167, 2169, 2452, 3792, 4107.

CROWCHER, Johanna, *St. Ives*: 1014; Thomas, *St. Ives*: 1014, 1510, 2457.

CROWLOND, Richard, *Chatteris*: 2819.

CROXTON, Johanna, *Warboys*: 3184; John, *Warboys*: 3184.

CROY, William, *Therfield*: 1147.

CROYSER, Katerina, *Therfield*: 549, 805; Nicholas, *Therfield*: 444; William, *Therfield*: 549, 805.

CUBATOR, Thomas, *Brington*: 1465.

CUFSE, Johanna, *Upwood*: 2491; William, *Upwood*: 2491.

CULLAN, John, *Broughton*: 4313.

CULPON, Agnes, *Upwood*: 2356; John, *Upwood*: 1755, 2356, 2551.

CURLYNG, Alicia, *Shillington*: 3706; Nicholas, *Shillington*: 3706, 4192.

CURTEYS (Curtes, Curteis), Agnes (I), *Cranfield*: 3154; Agnes (II), *Cranfield*: 3157; Agnes, *Therfield*: 2608; Johanna, *Cranfield*: 2899; John, *Cranfield*: 1401, 2899, 3414, 4314; John, Jr., *Cranfield*: 3775; John, *Chatteris*: 3572, 4220; John, *Therfield*: 2608; Richard, *Cranfield*: 274, 1074, 3154, 3157; Robert, *Abbots Ripton*: 267; Robert, *Cranfield*: 1403; Robert, Sr., *Cranfield*: 3414; Robert, Jr., *Cranfield*: 3414; Thomas, *Cranfield*: 884, 1403; Thomas, Jr., *Cranfield*: 3154; Thomas, *Weston*: 2194; William, *Cranfield*: 1922, 2225.

CUSSE, William, *Brington*: 4251.

CUT (Cutte), Agnes (Felde), *Slepe*: 2266, 2328, 4148; Alicia (Fyscher), *Slepe*: 2018, 3323; Emma, *St. Ives*: 1818; Emma, *Slepe*: 1205, 2301; Johanna, *Woodhurst*: 3593; John, *Barton*: 1134; John, *Chatteris*: 4, 2340; John (of Hythe), *Chatteris*: 110, 1712; John (III), *Chatteris*: 2800, 2861, 4261; John (Taillor), *Chatteris*: 1358; Peter, *St. Ives*: 1818, 4091; Thomas, *Slepe*: 272, 1205, 1549, 2018, 2084, 2266, 2301, 2328, 3581; William, *Ellington*: 4288; William, *Slepe*: 830, 1250, 1521, 2084.

DAGWORTH, Nicholas, *Chatteris*: 2009, 2990.

DAKER, Richard, *St. Ives*: 2772.

DALBY (Dolby), Agnes, *Brington*: see BEVERICH; Galfridus, *Ramsey*: 3017, 3117; John, *Brington*: 2002, 2539, 2785, 3096; John, *Ramsey*: 3892; John, Sr., *Warboys*: 2247; William, *Houghton*: 1434, 1437.

DALLYNG (Dally), Emma, *Warboys*: 891, 1239; John, *Chatteris*: 4301; John, *Warboys*: 592, 698-9, 891, 1028-9, 1239, 3060, 3378, 4129; John, Sr., *Warboys*: 1028, 1935; Mariota, *Warboys*: see BERENGER; Simon (rector of Holywell): 2666, 3429, 3974, 4096; William, *Cranfield*: 1281; William, *Warboys*: 4128.

DALTON, John, *Elton*: 942, 1200; Robert, *Elton*: 1995, 2258.

DAM (Damme), John, *Broughton*: 1941, 2453; John, *Ramsey*: 1603; Peter, *Abbots Ripton*: 895; Simon, *Broughton*: 1943.

DAMMESSON, William, *Holywell*: 1142.

DANE (Danne), Peter, *Abbots Ripton*: 615; Thomas, *Therfield*: 4228.

DANHERD, John, *Chatteris*: 283.

DANNE. See DANE.

DANNEYS, Simon, *Broughton*: 3560.

DANYEL (Danyelle, Denyelle, Dynyell), Agnes, *Graveley*: 966; Beatrix, *Stukeley*: see FOOT; Elena, *Graveley*: 839; Jacob, *Knapwell*: 285, 3607; John, *Graveley*: 434; John, *Stukeley*: 2521; Nicholas, *Knapwell*: 2384; Richard, *Graveley*: 966; Robert (al. Benottis), *Graveley*: 64, 278, 839, 1742, 1780, 3067; Roger, *Knapwell*: 285, 3607; Thomas, *Knapwell*: 2378.

DARBY. See DERBY.

DAUD, William, *Warboys*: 3184.

DAVENAR, Robert, *Graveley*: 3779.

DAVITT, Emma, *Barton*: 1856; John, *Barton*: 1856.

DAVY, Elizabeth, *Barton*: see SKYNNER; John, *Barton*: 3150, 3353; John, *Shillington*: 2479, 2762; Thomas, *Cranfield*: 3719.

DAWES, Richard, *Elsworth*: 4039.

DAWYS, John, *Elsworth*: 1707; Richard, *Elton*: 408.

DAYE. See DEYE.

DECHE, Agnes, *Broughton*: 249; Henry, *Broughton*: 249; Johanna, *Elton*: 2669; John, *Elton*: 102, 103, 981, 3756; Richard, *Broughton*: 249; William, *Brington*: 1464; William, *Elton*: 1188, 2669, 3756; William (Wythe), *Houghton*: 2132.

DECON. See DYCON.

DEEN. See DENE.

DEERSON (Deresson), Alicia, *Houghton*: 2560; John, *Houghton*: 2560, 2649.

DEKENE. See DYCON.

DEKES, Richard, *Graveley*: 2552.

DENE (Deen, Denne), Adam, *Abbots Ripton*: 1951; Agnes, *Burwell*: 2510; 4110; John, *Burwell*: 1976, 2510, 4110; Margeria, *Slepe*: 1823; Peter, *Abbots Ripton*: 969; Robert, *Burwell*: 4226; William, *Houghton*: 1066; and see also: DYCON.

DENEYS. See DENYS.

DENHOLT, John (seneschal), *Holywell*: 3973.

DENTON (Dentan), Agnes, *Wistow*: 1210; Alicia, *Houghton*: 3653; Richard, *Little Stukeley*: 3679; Richard, *Wistow*: 1211; William, *Cranfield*: 1314.

DENYELL. See DANYEL.

DENYS (Deneys, Denyas, Deynes), Custancia, *St. Ives*: 1966, 1973; John, *Bigging*: 900; John, *Chatteris*: 3439; John (Wollepakker), *Elton*: 3518; John, *Ramsey*: 416, 1928, 2938; John, *St. Ives*: 1966, 1973, 2458.

DENYSFORTHE, John, *Graveley*: 2021.

DEPPIS, Johanna, *Weston*: see FLESCHEWER; Richard, *Weston*: 2114.

DERAUNT. See DORAUNT.

DERBY (Darby), Johanna, *Ramsey*: 1604; Laurence (Bocher), *Ramsey*: 1604, 3019.

DERKER, Richard, *Wistow*: 2780.

DERSSON. See DERYSSON.

DERWORTH (Derworthe), Hugo, *Warboys*: 180; Johanna, *Warboys*: 180; Johanna, *Wistow*: 1875; William, *Warboys*: 180; William, *Wistow*: 1875, 3334.

DERY (Derye), John, *Burwell*: 496, 3125.

DERYSSON (Dersson), Agnes, *Houghton*: 3657; John, *Houghton*: 2967, 3657; family, *Houghton*: 3177.

DESBURGH, Richard, *Little Stukeley*: 2198, 3138, 3293.

DETKE, John, *Weston*: 1766; Margeria, *Weston*: see RANDOLF.

DEUTRE. See DEWTRE.

DEVYLL (Devell), Agnes, *Chatteris*: 4218; John, *Chatteris*: 3191, 3992, 4218, 4338, 4346.

DEWTRE (Deutre), Alicia, *Ramsey*: 1746; Richard, *Ramsey*: 1746, 1787, 3162; Richard, *St. Ives*: 1647, 2465, 2772.

DEYE (Daye), Agnes (Schepperd), *Holywell*: 1025, 1507; Hugo, *St. Ives*: 1511-12; John, *Holywell*: 269; Thomas, *Holywell*: 1025, 1507, 3862.

DICON. See DYCON.

DIER, John, *Shillington*: 1089.

DOBYN, Margaret, *Chatteris*: 2013; Richard, *Chatteris*: 2693, 2990; William, *Chatteris*: 109.

DOKE, Edith, *Therfield*: 813; Robert, *Therfield*: 813; Thomas, *Therfield*: see TOTTEHALE.

DOLBY. See DALBY.

DONSTON, John, *Houghton*: 1106.

DONTESON, Roger, *Cranfield*: 1450.

DORAUNT (Deraunt), Johanna, *Hemingford*: 2385; John, *Hemingford*: 2385; Katerina, *Knapwell*: 2294; Thomas, *Slepe*: 1250, 1521; William, *Knapwell*: 2294, 2578.

DORSON, John, *Houghton*: 3981.

DOWE, Roger, *Cranfield*: 3717.

DOWESSON, Roger, *Cranfield*: 1927.

DOWKYS, Elias, *Barton*: 261.

DOWNE, Robert del, *Barton*: 1176.

DRAPER, Agnes, *St. Ives*: 124; Benedict, *St. Ives*: see BAROUN; John, *Ramsey*: 2054; John, *St. Ives*: 124, 1650; John, *Shillington*: 4057, 4369; Margaret, *Ramsey*: 2054; Margaret, *St. Ives*: 1650; Thomas, *St. Ives*: 124, 241; Valentine (Barker), *St. Ives*: 870.

DREW, Agnes, *Graveley*: see ROBAT; Alicia, *Knapwell*: 4272; John, *Ellington*: 4145; John, *Graveley*: 973, 1387, 3146; John, *Knapwell*: 4272.

DRYELL, John, *Chatteris*: 4263.

DRYNGE (Dryng, Dryngs), Agnes, *Chatteris*: 108; Alicia, *Chatteris*: see SUMPTER; John, *Chatteris*: 2348, 2689, 3870; John, Sr. (Bocher), *Chatteris*: 108, 477, 4352; John, Jr., *Chatteris*: 108, 683.

DRYNGESMAN, John, *Chatteris*: 2680.

DRYSON, Simon, *Houghton*: 3661.

DRYVER (Dryvere), Agnes, *Slepe*: 980; Agnes, *Slepe* (II): 2604; Elena, *Slepe*: 3188; John, *Slepe*: 980, 3454; Thomas, *Burwell*: 2499; William, *Elsworth*: 65; William, *Slepe*: 1311, 2604, 3188; family, *Shillington*: 3701, 4236.

DUFHOUS, John, *Burwell*: 3123; and see ROLF.

DUNTON, William, *St. Ives*: 259.

DUNWODE (Dunwud), Alexander, *Cranfield*: 1313; Alicia, *Cranfield*: 2533; Johanna (Barbour), *Barton*: 2756; John, *Cranfield*: 710, 1449, 1989, 2201; Margaret, *Cranfield*: 3156; Thomas, *Barton*: 2756; Thomas, *Cranfield*: 274, 2533; Thomas, Sr., *Cranfield*: 3156.

DYCON (Decon, Dekene, Dicon), Adam, *Abbot's Ripton*: 2055, 2566; Elena, *Little Stukeley*: 3911; John, *Abbots Ripton*: 581, 1951, 2058; John, *Chatteris*: 2862, 2993; John, *Cranfield*: 298; John, *Little Stukeley*: 3911; Margaret, *Weston*: see WRIGHT; Richard, *Weston*: 1652; Richard (II), *Weston*: 2924, 3097.

DYER, John, *Shillington*: 163.

DYGELON, Master Richard, parson of St. Andrew's, Barnwell, *Weston*: 4000.

DYKE (Dykes, Dykys), Elena (Bailly), *Graveley*: 568; John, *Graveley*: 278, 568; Margaret, *Houghton*: 3174; Nicholas, *Graveley*: 3845; Richard, *Graveley*: 2020, 3067, 3069, 3783, 3969; Richard, *Houghton*: see TWYWELL; William, *Houghton*: 3051, 3174.

DYLEMAKER, John, *Houghton*: see CARTER; Richard, *Houghton*: see CARTER; Robert (al. Carter), *Houghton*: 1425, 2197, 3280.

DYNGELE (Dyngley), Johanna, *Weston*: 2591; Thomas, *Weston*: 2591, 2730.

DYNYELL. See DANYELL.

DYRY, John, *Burwell*: 952.

ECHE, John, *Therfield*: 4228.

EDE, Alan, *Houghton*: 964, 1760; John, *Houghton*: 334; John, *Shillington/Pegsdon*: 162, 794, 1486, 1492, 1895, 1898, 2403, 2996, 3536, 4178; John ("Medius"), *Shillington*: 3002; John, Sr., *Shillington*: 3000; Lucia, *Shillington*: 3002; Margaret, *Shillington*: see HAMOND; Margeria, *Shillington*: 2403; Rosa, *Shillington*: 3000; Thomas, *Shillington*: 3002.

EDENHAM, Johanna, *St. Ives*: 14, 572; John, *Chatteris*: 109, 611, 857; John (chaplain), *St. Ives/ Hurst*: 14, 120, 572, 869, 941, 2152, 2972, 3322, 3875, 4075; John, Sr., *Slepe*: 106; John, *Woodhurst*: 660; William, *St. Ives*: 14, 572, 1013.

EDITH, John, Jr., *Shillington*: 504; Roger, *Shillington*: 504.

EDMUND, abbot of Ramsey: 3498.

EDMUND, parish chaplain of Raveley, *Wistow*: 464.

EDRICH (Edryche), Radulph, *Burwell*: 3766, 4112; Radulph, *Elsworth*: 2760; Robert, *Burwell*: 2040, 3766; Robert, *Elsworth*: 2760.

EDWARD (Eduard), Agnes, *Upwood*: 1044; Alicia, *Holywell*: 2668; Alicia, *Needingworth*: 2358; Alicia, *Warboys*: 575; Elena,

EVOT, John, *Elsworth*: 864; John, *Houghton*: 2320; Margaret, (Hobbesson), *Elsworth*: 864.
EYER. See EYR.
EYNESHAM (Eynysham), Agnes, *Shillington*: 1308; Simon, *Shillington*: 3032, 3349; William, *Barton*: 1308, 4184.
EYR (Eeyre, Eyer), Alicia, *Slepe*: 1823; Alicia, *Warboys*: 459, 1158; Johanna, *Upwood*: see SYMOND; John, *Ramsey*: 2939, 3816, 4302, 4319; Richard, *St. Ives/Slepe*: 1823, 3305; Richard (al. Geffreyesson), *Warboys*: 574, 1904, 3269; Roger, *Brington*: 1305; Thomas, *Cranfield*: 2201, 2769, 3639; Thomas, *Houghton*: 3658; Thomas, *Warboys*: 271, 459, 1158, 1195, 1420, 3368; William, *Upwood*: 582.
EYRMONGER. See IRYNMONGER.

FABBE, John, *Burwell*: 648, 3899; John, Sr., *Burwell*: 3011; John, Jr., *Burwell*: 3011; Richard, *Burwell*: 648, 2040, 3011; William, *Burwell*: 3958.
FABER, Agnes, *Broughton*: see BROUN; John, *Broughton*: see BROUN.
FABIAN (Fabyon), John, *Abbot's Ripton*: 1356, 1481; William, *Barton*: 261.
FACOUN (Faucon, Fakon, Fawcon), Agnes, *Elton*: 2833; John, *Holywell*: 3339; Margeria, *Elton*: 2833; William, *Elton*: 915, 1114, 2833; William (II), *Elton*: 1114.
FAKON. See FACOUN.
FALLY (Falley, Falleys), Agnes, *Barton*: 1790, 1983; Agnes, *Shillington*: 2117; Edith, *Barton*: see WODE (Wood, atte); Isabella, *Shillington*: see FELMESHAM; William, *Barton*: 567, 887, 888, 1983, 2118.
FALNON, John, *Abbots Ripton*: 188.
FAN (at, atte), John, *Barton*: 261, 2582, 2621, 2952; Laurence, *Shillington*: see CHYBBELE; Thomas, *Barton*: 2897; William, *Shillington*: see CHIBBELE (Chybbele).
FANELL (Fannell), Margaret, *Hemingford*: 2982; Margeria, *Hemingford*: 2904; Nicholas, *Hemingford/Holywell*: 207, 2904, 3821.
FAREWELL, Robert, *Wistow*: 2368.
FAUCONER (Fawkener, Fawcoiner), Arnold, *Shillington*: 3535, 3705; Thomas, *Elton*: 1843, 1995; William, *Cranfield*: 3778.
FAUKES (Facous), John, *Ellington*: 3682; William, *Brington*: 184, 1225.
FAWCON. See FACOUN.

FAWCONER. See FAUCONER.
FAWKESWELL, Galfridus, *Shillington*: 1537.
FAWNE. See FOUN.
FAYREMAN (Fayrman), Agnes, *Therfield*: see SPARVER; Andrew, *Therfield*: 2034; Margaret, *Elton*: 3785; Thomas, *Therfield*: 2108; William, *Elton*: 3785.
FECHELER. See FYCHELER.
FELD, Agnes, of the, *Cranfield*: see TERRY; Agnes, *Hemingford*: 4335-6; Agnes, *Slepe*: see CUT; Johanna, *Hemingford*: 3260; John, *Hemingford*: 2129; John, Sr., *Hemingford*: 3260; John, Jr., *Hemingford*: 2328, 3645, 4335-6; John, *Slepe*: 4148; John, *Therfield*: 3452; Margaret, *Hemingford*: 3645 Richard, of the, *Cranfield*: 250, 678; Roger, of the, *Cranfield*: 678; Thomas, *Hemingford*: 4172; William, *Hemingford*: 2517.
FELDEW, William, *Abbots Ripton*: 2112.
FELICE (Felis, Felyce, Filice), John, *Weston*: 265, 1355, 2592, 2924, 3286; John, Sr., *Weston*: 2365; Mariota, *Weston*: 3286.
FELMESHAM, Isabella, *Barton*: 2117, 3355, 3485, 3630; Johanna, *Barton*: 1615, 3485; John, Sr., *Barton*: 3630; John, Jr., *Barton*: 3630; William, *Barton*: 3485.
FELYCE. See FELICE.
FELYNGLE. See FYLLYNGLE.
FEN, John, *Houghton*: 3729.
FENORE, Isabella, *Barton*: see REVESSON; Thomas, *Barton*: 1791.
FENTON, family, *Hemingford*: 3178, 3253.
FERMOR (Fermer), Agnes, *Ramsey*: 3816; Alexander, *Elsworth*: 3949, 4331; Anna (Hobbesson), *Elsworth*: 1369, 3089, 3953; John (Hobbesson), *Elsworth*: 3583, 4039, 4331; John, *Hemingford*: 135; Margaret, *Elsworth*: 3583, 4039, 4331; Margeria, *Elsworth*: 3584, 3951; Thomas (Hobbesson), *Elsworth*: 3584, 3950-1, 3953, 4329; Thomas (al. Smyth), *Ramsey*: 3816; William (al. Hobbesson), *Elsworth*: 864, 1369, 1395, 3089, 3092, 3584, 3950, 3953. See also: HOBBESSON.
FERROR (Feror, Ferour), Agnes, *Warboys*: see MARGRETE; John, *Hurst*: 3384; Richard, *Warboys*: 1810; Robert, *Elton*: 320, 371, 421.
FERYBY, Alicia, *Elton*: 2930; William, *Elton*: 988, 2930, 4286.
FETHION. See FYTHION.
FIKEYS (Fykeys), Richard, *Chatteris*: 3579, 4347.
FILHOUS (Fylhous), Agnes, *Warboys*: see

3488; Thomas, *Warboys*: 377; Thomas, *Wistow*: 859, 1880, 3020, 3676; William, *Graveley*: see ESEX.

FRAUNCK. See FRANK.

FRAUNK. See FRANK.

FRAYFELD (Frafeld, Frayfelde), Agnes, *Cranfield*: 2304; John, *Cranfield*: 1729, 2304; family, *Cranfield*: 3040.

FRE, William (Smyth), *Brington*: 1468.

FREESTON. See FRESTON.

FREMAN, Agnes, *Ramsey*: 428, 618; Agnes, *St. Ives*: 3139; Alicia, *St. Ives*: 13; Alicia, *Upwood*: 4317; Alicia, *Warboys*: 271, 1573; Elena, *Burwell*: 4204; Isabella, *Ramsey*: 4031, 4266; Isabella, *Wistow*: 1213; John, *Burwell*: 4204; John, *Slepe*: 2268, 2607, 4148; John, *Wistow*: 1213; Katerina, *Slepe*: 2268; Margaret, *St. Ives*: 13, 1164-5; Richard, *Ellington*: 1453; Thomas, *St. Ives*: 13, 1164-5, 2071, 2326, 3139; William, *Ramsey*: 428, 4031, 4266; William, *St. Ives*: 3139; William, *Upwood*: 4317.

FREMOR. See FERMER.

FRENCH, Agnes, *Cranfield*: see BORELL; Agnes; *St. Ives*: 1637; Stephen (al. Willyam), *Cranfield*: 1178; William, *St. Ives*: 1637, 2069, 2776.

FRENCHEMAN, Janyn, *Elsworth*: 1801.

FRERE (Frer), Alicia, *Therfield*: 2436; Elena, *Therfield*: 2870; John, *Abbots Ripton*: 3666; John, *Houghton*: 3049; John, *Therfield*: 309, 506, 1536, 1866, 2870; John, *Wistow*: 1684, 2672, 2780; Katerina, *Therfield*: 2216; Margaret, *Wistow*: 1684, 2672; Maria, *Therfield*: 2738; Matillis, *Therfield*: 2631; Thomas, *Therfield*: 3697; William, *Therfield*: 309, 1536, 2216, 2436, 2631, 2738.

FRESTON (Freeston), John, *Upwood*: 2181, 3886; Richard, *Upwood*: 90.

FRETTER (Frettere), John, *Elton*: 735; William, *Elton*: 102, 103, 735, 1184, 2257.

FREWET, John, *Chatteris*: 847.

FROST, Johanna, *Cranfield*: 3007; John, *Cranfield*: 148, 274, 885, 1074, 1448; Margaret, *Cranfield*: 148; Maria, *Cranfield*: 1280; Thomas, *Cranfield*: 1280, 2943, 3007; Thomas, *Therfield*: 262; William, *Barton*: 1067; William, *Cranfield*: 814, 2943.

FROXFELD, Alicia, *Houghton*: 3177; Thomas, *Houghton*: 3177, 4119.

FRYER, John, *Therfield*: 262.

FULLER, Adam, *Houghton*: 616, 1431; Agnes, *Broughton*: 3789; Agnes, *Burwell*: see STYWARD; Agnes, *Houghton*: 2319, 2650, 3175, 3723, 3913; Agnes, *Knapwell*: see LAWE; Agnes, *Ramsey*: 3462; Alicia, *St. Ives*: 2458, 2940; Cristina, *St. Ives*: see BOKENHAM; Elena, *Ramsey*: see OWTY; Johanna, *Houghton*: see SAMAN; John, *Broughton*: 3789; John, *Burwell*: 1346; John, *Elsworth*: 2045; John, *Holywell*: see BLOSSOUM; John, *Houghton*: see CLERK; John, *Knapwell*: 3464; John, *St. Ives/Slepe*: see CLERK; Katerina, *Burwell*: 2499; Katerina, *St. Ives*: 1396; Magota, *St. Ives*: 479; Margaret, *Abbots Ripton*: see WODEWARD; Margaret, *Elsworth*: 4299; Matilda, *St. Ives*: 2151; Richard, *Elton*: 2253; Richard, *St. Ives*: 479, 1640, 2151; Robert, *St. Ives*: see BOKENHAM; Stephen, *Hemingford*: 42; Thomas, *Broughton*: 3789; Thomas, *Hemingford*: 2516, 2907, 3382; Thomas *Houghton*: 3913, 4147, 4307; William, *Abbots Ripton*: see WODEWARD; William, *Houghton*: see SAMAN; William, *St. Ives*: 2458, 2940.

FYCHELER (Fecheler), Thomas, *Holywell*. 2413, 3340.

FYCHER. See FYSSHER.

FYCHION, William, *St. Ives*: 2526.

FYKEYS. See FIKEYS.

FYLHOUS. See FILHOUS.

FYLLYNGLE (Felyngle, Fillyngls), John, *St. Ives*: 606, 1643, 3434; Margaret, *St. Ives*: 606.

FYNCHAM, Thomas, *Shillington*: 2232.

FYNE, Alan, *Ramsey*: 70.

FYNYON, John, Sr., *Chatteris*: 1152.

FYSSCHER (Fisscher, Fycher, Fysshere), Alicia, *St. Ives*: see CUT; John, *Ramsey*: see WETTON; John, *St. Ives*: see CHASTEYN; John (of St. Neots), *St. Ives*: 1325; John, *Warboys*: 3265; Katerina, *St. Ives*: 556, 1329, 4013; Simon, *Broughton*: 217, 233; Thomas, *Broughton*: 2172; Thomas, *Chatteris*: 1361, 1916, 3570, 3919, 4219; Thomas, *Ramsey*: see WETTON; Thomas, *St. Ives*: 563; Thomas, *Warboys*: 4013; William, *Abbots Ripton*: 2584; William, *St. Ives*: 247, 292.

FYTHION (Fethion, Fythyon), Cristiana, *St. Ives*: 4201; Elena, *Ramsey*: 3115; Isabella, *St. Ives*: 2526; John, *Chatteris*: 283, 2745, 3762; John, Sr., *Chatteris*: 2796, 3688; John, *St. Ives*: 4201; John, *Ramsey*: 3115;

Katerina, *Chatteris*: 2745; Thomas, *Cranfield*: 3636; William, *St. Ives*: 2526, 4201.

GAGGE, John, *Elsworth*: 66.
GALAPYN. See GALOPYN.
GALLICUS, John: see BRIGGE.
GALOPYN (Galapyn), John, *Upwood*: 1244; Walter, *St. Ives*: 1649; William, *St. Ives*: 2528, 2777; William, *Wistow*: 1589.
GALYOUN, Alicia, *Brington*: see PERYE (Purye); Thomas, *Holywell*: 353; William, *Brington*: 1811.
GAME, William, *Therfield*: 3840, 3843.
GAMEL (Gamele, Gamely), John, *Elton*: 990, 1046; Thomas, *Therfield*: 1161.
GAMELYN, Henry, *Hemingford*: 3732; Thomas, *Slepe*: 150.
GAMYN, Richard, *Therfield*: 3167, 3601; Thomas, *Therfield*: 2034, 3167, 3601.
GANDER (Gandir), Emma, *Brington*: see PYRYE; Matilda, *Brington*: 1839; Thomas, *Brington*: 324, 368, 369, 1227-8, 2539; William, *Brington*: 1839, 2652.
GARDENER (Gardiner, Gardyner), Cecilia, *Abbots Ripton*: 1386; John, *Abbots Ripton*: 2662; John, Sr., *Abbots Ripton*: 3288; John, Jr., *Abbots Ripton*: 3289, 3385; Richard, *Burwell*: 46, 1095; Roger, *Abbots Ripton*: 360, 615, 1386, 1769, 2185; Thomas, *Burwell*: 1095; William, *St. Ives*: 1335, 2462, 3078, 3433.
GARNOUN. See GERNOUN.
GASCOYN (Gascoyne), John, *Houghton*: 3657; William, *Houghton*: 3500.
GATE (Gatte, Ghate, Yatte, at, atte), Agnes, *Elton*: 1571; Alicia, *Elton*: 3318; Henry, *Elton*: 1568, 1571, 1997, 2103, 2252, 2835, 2977; Henry, *Houghton*: 472; Isabella, *Elton*: 2103; Johanna, *Wistow*: 1587; Johanna (II), *Wistow*: 590; John, *Elton*: 264; John, *Houghton*: 835, 1190; John, *Wistow*: 86, 897, 2275, 2733, 3022; John, Sr., *Wistow*: 643, 3815; John, Jr., *Wistow*: 643, 1587, 3741; Katerina, *Wistow*: see OWTY; Margaret, *Elton*: 4196; Margaret (White), *Wistow*: 1883, 2180, 3678, 3740; Richard, *Elton*: 3318; Robert, *Wistow*: 275, 590, 1883, 2178, 3740-1; Stephen, *Wistow*: 2178; Thomas, *Wistow*: 3555; William, *Elton*: 1295, 1997, 2103, 3756, 4196; William, Sr., *Elton*: 3318.
GATTERE, Emma, *Hemingford*: see HEYNE; John, *Hemingford*: 577.
GAUNT, William, *Abbots Ripton*: 3103.

GAWTROUN, John, *St. Ives*: 1637.
GAYTON, Alicia, *Shillington*: 4234; John, *Shillington*: 1286, 2400, 3350; Robert, *Shillington*: 3031, 3625, 3628, 3707, 4005, 4234.
GEBON, Agnes, *Elton*: 4286; John (al. Smyth), *Elton*: 4286.
GEDNEYE, Emma, *Abbots Ripton*: 787; John, *Abbots Ripton*: 787.
GEFFREY, Elena, *Graveley*: see DANYELL; John, *Barton*: 1309, 1985, 2394; John, *Graveley*: 839; John, *Houghton*: 1104; William, *Barton*: 1309; William, *Knapwell*: 3825; William, *Slepe*: 1119.
GEFFREYESSON, Richard, *Warboys*: see EYR.
GELAM, Johanna, *Ramsey*: 4306; John, *Ramsey*: 4306.
GELEN (Gelan), Richard, *Hemingford*: 4122; Richard, *Wistow*: 3976.
GELL (Gelle), William, *Burwell*: 1132, 1231.
GEMYS, John (Webster), *Therfield*: 3566; Margaret, *Therfield*: 3566.
GENEYS, John, *Therfield*: 4228.
GENGE, Richard, *Upwood*: 3282.
GENTILL, Thomas, *St. Ives*: 4321.
GERARD, Alicia, *Houghton*: 2471; John, *Houghton*: 1849, 2132, 2471, 3279, 3422; John, *Broughton*: 3789.
GERE, John, *Chatteris*: 2433, 2485, 3299, 4023, 4077, 4217, 4260; John, *Holywell*: 269; Robert, *Chatteris*: 2485, 2864; Thomas, *Chatteris*: 283, 2746, 4023, 4077, 4212, 4260; Thomas, *Holywell*: 2666; family, *Chatteris*: 4135.
GERMYN (German), Johanna, *Weston*: 3099; John, *Elton*: 319, 422, 635, 996, 2427; William (Tayllor), *Weston*: 3099.
GERNOUN (Gernon, Garnoun), John, Jr., *Wistow*: 554; Thomas, *Broughton*: 2176; Walter, *Wistow*: 58.
GEROLD (Gerowlde), Alicia, *Ellington*: 92; John, *Warboys*: 345, 726, 1123; Thomas, *Ellington*: 92, 268.
GERVEYS (Gervas, Gervais), Agnes, *Therfield*: 2872, 3841; Henry, *Therfield*: 625, 1498, 2872, 3841; Johanna, *Graveley*: 2828; John, *Chatteris*: 3868; John, *Therfield*: 330, 814, 1497; Robert, *Therfield*: 308; William, *Graveley*: 2828; William, *Therfield*: 2872, 3841, 3960, 3962.
GERY, Robert, *Chatteris*: 3084.
GES, Margaret, *Weston*: 3817.
GETTE, Anna, *Wistow*: 1871.
GHATE. See GATE.

GHUTE. See GUTE.

GILDESOWE, Robert, *Warboys*: 345, 461, 1380.

GILLE (Gylle), Agnes, *Holywell*: 3973; John, *Abbot's Ripton*: 895; Thomas, *Little Stukeley*: 3894; William, *Holywell*: 3973.

GILSON, Laurence, *Chatteris*: 2349.

GLOVER (Glovere), Anna, *St. Ives*: 868, 1334; Isabella (I), *Ramsey*: see SPARKE; Isabella (II), *Ramsey*: see BELAMY; John, *Cranfield*: 708; John, *Ramsey*: see GYMMYS (Gymmes); Robert, *Hemingford*: see KESTEVYN (Kestvyn); Robert, *Ramsey*: see BELAMY; Thomas, *St. Ives*: see CLERK; William, *Ramsey*: 4193; and see SPARKE.

GOBALD, Johanna, *Ellington*: see BETTE; Thomas, *Ellington*: 1064.

GOBERD (Gobard, Gobert), Johanna, *Shillington*: 3772, 3854, 4232, 4370; John, *Shillington*: 2401, 3772, 3854, 4057, 4232, 4369-70; Margeria, *Shillington*: 3772; Simon, *Shillington*: 1494, 2401, 2542, 2623.

GOD, John, *Elsworth*: 3951.

GODALE. See GOODALE.

GODARD (Goddard), Johanna, *Shillington*: 155, 157, 273; Richard, *Shillington*: 440, 3003, 3034; William, *Shillington*: 440, 3003.

GODERICH, John, *Slepe*: 1357.

GODESLOW. See GOODSLOW.

GODESWAYN, Adam, *Elton*: 57.

GODEWYN. See GOODWYN.

GODFREY, Agnes, *Holywell*: 2147; Agnes, *Ramsey*: see FREMAN; Agnes, *Warboys*: see BROUNYNG; Alicia, *Holywell*: 2364; Alicia, *Ramsey*: 2697; Elena, *Holywell*: 290, 3340; Emma, *Holywell*: 2064; John, *Holywell*: 2064, 3342, 3427; Margaret, *Burwell*: 4019; Nicholas, *Holywell*: 290, 1365, 1740, 2700, 3340, 3674, 4364; Richard, *Wistow*: 4140; Robert, *Ramsey*: 2697; Roger, *Holywell*: 2147, 2364, 2788, 3063; Thomas, *Burwell*: 4019; Thomas, *Ramsey*: 618, 1170, 3106, 3111, 3236, 4267; Thomas, *Warboys*: 530.

GODMAR. See GOODMAR.

GODWYFF, Agnes, *Elton*: 2929; Robert, *Elton*: 2929.

GOLDSMYTH, Cristina, *Houghton*: 3728; Philip, *Houghton*: 3728.

GOLDYNGTON, Hugo, *Brington*: 2497, 2603.

GOLION, Agnes, *Holywell*: see HOUGHTON; Emma, *Barton*: see PRIOR; Simon (al. Bocher), *Barton*: 3540.

GONNE, John, *St. Ives*: 2529, 2654; Margaret, *St. Ives*: 2529.

GOODALE (Godale), Alicia, *Burwell*: 2580; Alicia (II), *Burwell*: 4114; Elena, *Burwell*: 2041, 4356; John, *Burwell*: 2580, 3216, 4226; Thomas, *Burwell*: 2041, 2508, 2959, 3530-1, 4356; Thomas, Jr., *Burwell*: 4114; William (al. Wright), *Burwell*: 4357.

GOODEFELOWE, William, *Bythorne*: 3908.

GOODESLOW (Godeslow), Helena, *Brington*: 3095; John, *Brington*: 1669, 3095; William, *Bythorne*: 1669.

GOODGRENE, John, *Chatteris*: 3579.

GOODMAN, Agnes, *St. Ives*: 3016, Henry, *St. Ives*: 1645; Johanna, *St. Ives*: 1645; Johanna (II), *St. Ives*: 2461; Johanna (III), *St. Ives*: 2522, John, *Hurst/ St. Ives*: 257, 2522, 3455, 3881, 4283; Robert, *St. Ives*: 2461; William, *St. Ives*: 3016, 3076.

GOODMAR (Godmar), Agnes, *Barton*: see WYLYMOT; Agnes, *Shillington*: 4004; John, *Barton/ Shillington*: 1342, 1460, 1493; Roger, *Abbots Ripton*: 10, 82; Thomas, *Shillington*: 1342, 4060; William, *Shillington*: 4004.

GOODSOWLE, John, *Holywell*: 4151; John, Jr., *Holywell*: 473; William, *Holywell*: 1207.

GOODSPED, John, *Ellington*: 1691.

GOODWYN (Godewyn, Gudwyn), Agnes, *Cranfield*: 1405, 3640; Alicia, *Cranfield*: 875; Hugo, *Cranfield*: 3640; John, *Burwell*: 2704; John, *Cranfield*: 274, 875, 880, 1405, 2944, 3640; John, Sr., *Cranfield*: 883, 2619, 3042; John Jr., *Cranfield*: 2619, 3042; Margaret, *Cranfield*: 876; Margeria, *Cranfield*: 2305; Olyva, *Burwell*: 2704; Robert, *Cranfield*: 4156, 4200; Thomas, *Burwell*: 2890, 4114; Thomas, *Cranfield*: 876, 880, 2305; William, *Burwell*: 2704, 2890; William, *Cranfield*: 2204, 2944, 3640, 4200; William, Sr., *Cranfield*: 880, 883; William, Jr., *Cranfield*: 880.

GOODYNCHE, Cristina, *Burwell*: 1795; Richard, *Burwell*: 3617; Robert, *Burwell*: 3217, 3830; Thomas, *Burwell*: 1795, 3216, 4225.

GOOTHIRD, John, *Abbots Ripton*: 139.

GORBAT, Amya, *Gidding*: see WEST; Thomas, *Gidding*: 457; Robert, *Gidding*: 457.

GORE, William, *Broughton*: 2645.

GORNER, Robert, *Broughton*: 2452.

GORNEYE. See GURNEY.

Hemingford: 975, 2902, 3258; John, *Holy-well*: 2264; John, *St. Ives*: 1635, 2464, 2771; John, *Shillington*: 1485, 1618, 1724, 1859, 3032, 3852; Margaret, *Shil-lington*: 162; Margeria (II), *Shillington*: 1485, 1618, 1724; Nicholas, *Chatteris*: 1693, 2744; Thomas, *Shillington*: 162, 1492, 1620, 2032, 2230; William (of Did-dington), *Upwood*: 4197.

HAMPSON, John (al. Ropere), *Broughton*: 1192.

HAMPTON, John, *Broughton*: 522, 3437; John, *Therfield*: 2738; Maria, *Therfield*: see FRERE.

HAMUND. See HAMOND.

HANLE, John, *Graveley*: 3928.

HANLOIE, John, *Abbots Ripton*: 3599.

HANTO (Hantoo, Hento), Agnes, *Shilling-ton*: 3535; John, *Shillington*: 1090; 3535, 3705; William, *Shillington*: 3535.

HARDHED (Harhed), Johanna, *Ramsey*: 1784; John, *Ramsey*: 1784, 3237, 3528.

HARDY, Nicholas, *Holywell*: 1506.

HARDYNG, John (Smyth), *Elsworth*: 1262, 1705, 1707, 2373, 4039; John, Sr., *Elsworth*: 2443, 3695; John, Jr., *Elsworth*: 1665, 2443, 2635, 3695; John, *Houghton*: 3426; Juliana, *Houghton*: 2242; Margaret, *Elsworth*: 3326; Thomas, *Elsworth*: 3326.

HARE (Har, Here), *Christiana, Cranfield*: see SARE; Helena, *Broughton*: 2826; John, *Cranfield*: 2534, 3044, 3226; Richard (Webster), *Broughton*: 2511, 2642, 2826.

HAREFEYE. See HERVY.

HARHED. See HARDHED.

HARNES, Richard, *Houghton*: see CARTER.

HARPE. See HERP.

HARPER (Harpor, Herper, Herpour), Henry, *Shillington*: 161; John, *Burwell*: 2499; John, *Elton*: 732, 985; Katerina, *Ramsey*: 4264; Richard (Mason), *Ramsey*: 4264; Thomas, *Ramsey*: 1786; William, *Elton*: 1567, 1570.

HARROF. See HERROF.

HARSENE (Hersene), John, *Warboys*: 223, 271, 414, 511-14; Katerina, *Warboys*: 223; William, *Warboys*: 2244.

HARVEYS. See HERVY.

HATLO. See HATTELE.

HATTELE (Hatle, Hatlo), John, *Therfield*: 165-6, 2545, 3209, 3961; Katerina, *Ther-field*: 165-6.

HAUKYN. See HACOUN.

HAULOND. See HAWLOND.

HAUS, Emma, *Barton*: see STONELE; John, *Barton*: 1288.

HAWES, Alicia, *St. Ives*: 4283; William, *St. Ives*: 4283.

HAWKE, Johanna, *Elsworth*: 3090; William, *Elsworth*: 3090.

HAWKYN. See HACOUN.

HAWLER, family, *Slepe*: 1517.

HAWLOND (Haulond, Haylonde), Johanna, *Abbots Ripton*: 2417; John, *Abbots Ripton*: 2417, 3104, 3671, 4252; John, Sr., *Abbots Ripton*: 10; John, Jr., *Abbots Ripton*: 895; Thomas, *Abbots Ripton*: 1769, 3399, 3599.

HAYLONDE. See HAWLOND.

HAYME. See HEYMES.

HAYNE. See HEYNE.

HAYWARDE, John, *Warboys*: 2053; Nicho-las, *St. Ives*: 71, 3321; family, *Abbots Rip-ton*: 1852-3.

HEBBE, Agnes, *Elsworth*: 270, 896; Alan, *Elsworth*: 896; John, *Shillington*: 442; Margeria, *Shillington*: see GRAVE.

HEKKESSON. See HYKKESSON.

HELEWYS, Elena, *Burwell*: 901; family, *Burwell*: 1532.

HELLE. See HALLE.

HELMESLE. See ELMESLEY.

HEMYNGFORD, Margaret, *Slepe*: 1907; Thomas, *Slepe*: 1907.

HEMYNGTON, Adam, *Holywell*: 3973; Agnes, *Holywell*: see GILLE; John, *Holywell*: 61, 393, 1143-4; John, Sr., *Holywell*: 3973; John, Jr., *Holywell*: 3973; Robert, *Abbots Ripton*: 921, 949; Thomas, *Abbots Ripton*: 921; Thomas, *Holywell*: 573, 819, 1144, 1399, 2791; Thomas, *Slepe*: 2143.

HENDESSON, Johanna (of Hemingford Grey): 59; Johanna, *Upwood*: 1373; John, *Elton*: 632; John, *Upwood*: 3283; Nicholas (of Hemingford Grey): 59; Nicholas, *Up-wood*: 1373, 3202, 3405; Robert, *Abbots Ripton*: 1251, 3739.

HENNYS, Isabella, *Elsworth*: 3609.

HENRYSSON, family: 812.

HENTO. See HANTO.

HERBERD, Agnes, *Shillington*: 2998; Isabella (I), *Shillington*: 4177; Isabella (II), *Shillington*: 4178; John, *Shillington*: 2998, 4177, 4235; Thomas, *Shillington*: 4235; Thomas, Sr., *Shillington*: 4178; William, *Shillington*: 273, 2998, 4177, 4235.

HERDE (Hirde, Hurrd, Hyrde), Agnes, *Up-wood*: 1744; Alicia, *Warboys*: see BENET; Anna, *Chatteris*: 2432; Henry, *Broughton*: 482, 539; Johanna (Lyncoln), *Hemingford*: 727, 3256, 4282; Johanna, *Warboys*: see

78, 222, 298, 711, 882, 1402; William, *Burwell*: 1229, 1630, 1701, 2500, 2509, 2883, 3345, 3754; William, *Cranfield*: 274, 328, 882, 1611, 2206, 2303; William, *Knapwell*: 1276, 2554, 3825.

JOYNOR, Cristiana: see MARTYN; John, *Hemingford*: 1556; John, *Knapwell*: 2579.

JUDDE, Agnes, *St. Ives*: 3303, 3824, 4257; Alicia, *St. Ives*: 2411, 3303, 3433; Edmund, *St. Ives*: 3433, 3824; Emma, *St. Ives*: 826, 1648, 2071, 3303, 3435; Johanna, *St. Ives*: 827, 4257; Katerina, *St. Ives*: 3303; Thomas, *St. Ives*: 827, 2070, 2411, 3143, 3824, 4257; William, *St. Ives*: 826, 1648, 2071, 3435; William, Sr., *St. Ives*: 3303; William, Jr., *St. Ives*: 3303.

JURDON, Alicia, *Abbots Ripton*: 2057; John, *Hemingford*: 1808; Matilda, *Abbots Ripton*: 3667; Robert, *Abbots Ripton*: 267, 949, 2057, 3667.

JUSTICE (Justyce), Agnes, *Broughton*: 3119, 3328; Alicia (Pool), *Broughton/ Upwood*: 1945, 2168, 2172, 3328; Edward, *Broughton*: 252, 1945, 2286, 3308, 3332; Emma, *Broughton*: 1764; Johanna (Clerk), *Broughton*: 1948, 2282, 2429, 2640, Johanna (II), *Broughton*: 3308; John, *Broughton*: 252, 412, 904, 2168; John (Taillor), *Broughton*: 3119, 3564, 4106; John, Jr., *Broughton*: 4106; John, *Warboys*: 271; William, *Broughton*: 280, 1764, 1948, 2429, 3328, 3791, 3793.

KEBBE, John, *Houghton/ Wyton*: 101, 1846.

KECHEN, Alicia, *Ramsey*: see TOLY; Robert, *Ramsey*: see TOLY.

KECHENERE. See KYCHENER.

KEDE, Alan, *Chatteris*: 4079.

KEENIG, John, *Ramsey*: 3759.

KELLESHULL, William, *Elsworth*: 121.

KELSEY (Kelsell, Kelseth, Kelsethe, Kelsill), Agnes, *Abbots Ripton*: 2188; John, *Abbots Ripton*: 3413; William, *Abbots Ripton*: 2188, 2298, 2662, 3102, 3292, 4254.

KEMPE, Agnes, *Bythorne*: 3906, John, *Bythorne*: 263, 3906.

KENT, John, *Burwell*: 950, 1230; John (al. Sutbury), *Elton*: 2199; William, *Elton*: 704, 2253, 2422, 2727; William, Sr., *Elton*: 1186; William, Jr., *Elton*: 1186, 1296.

KERNER, Radulph: (of Ramsey), *Houghton*: 3729.

KESTEVYN (Kestvyn), John, *Hemingford*:

2987; Robert (al. Glover), *Hemingford*: 3733, 4123.

KETERYNG (Ketryng), Alicia, *Ramsey*: 3232, 3406; John, *Ramsey*: 3232, 3457; John, Sr., *Ramsey*: 3406-7; John, Jr., *Ramsey*: 3407, 3891; Sarra, *Ramsey*: 3891; Thomas, *St. Ives*: 826.

KEYE, Alicia, *Broughton*: see CABE; John, *Warboys*: 1009; William, *Broughton*: 3201, 4313.

KEYNES, William, *Elton*: 1185.

KEYSE, Matilda, *Chatteris*: 846.

KIRBY, John, *Burwell*: 4356; Thomesina, *Burwell*: 4356.

KIRKEBY (Kyrkeby), Alicia, *Burwell*: 647; Andrew, *Burwell*: 1422; John, *Hemingford*: 2475; William, *Shillington*: 2477, 2602.

KNAPWELL, John, *Ramsey*: 3239.

KNARESBURGH (Knavesbourg), Adam, rector, *Abbots Ripton*: 580, 2712.

KNOP, Alicia, *Houghton*: 2134; John, *Houghton*: see SMYTH.

KNOTTE, Johanna, *St. Ives*: 1822; William (al. Nichol), *St. Ives/ Slepe*: 1822, 2081, 2455, 2751, 3302.

KOKE (Koc), John, *Hemingford*: 136; Matillis, *Hemingford*: 136; Nicholas, *Hemingford*: 136; Simon, *Slepe*: 272; Thomas, Jr., *Hemingford*: 136.

KOKERELL, John (Sr.), *Chatteris*: 1912; John (Jr.), *Chatteris*: 1912.

KOOLE, John, Jr., *Burwell*: 1777; Thomas, *Burwell*: 1974; Thomas, Jr., *Burwell*: 2890.

KROFT, Robert, *Elsworth*: 3588.

KYBATOUR, John, *Elton*: 405.

KYCHENER (Kechenere), John, *Shillington*: 26, 384, 1722, 1724, 2190, 3934; Katerina, *Shillington*: 384.

KYMBLE, William, *Therfield*: 169.

KYMBOLTON, Brother Richard, subcellarer: 1604, 1605; Johanna, *Barton*: 4182.

KYN, Johanna, *Barton*: 4182; William, *Barton*: 4182.

KYNG, Alicia, *Bythorne*: 3860; Alicia, *Chatteris*: 2089; Constancia, *Burwell*: 311-12; Henry, *Holywell*: 473, 778, 2362; Johanna, *Upwood*: 1601; John, *Barton*: 2621; John, *Burwell*: 3614; John, Sr., *Burwell*: 311-12; John, Jr., *Burwell*: 311-12; John, *Chatteris*: 1750, 1776, 2012, 2089, 3086, 4353; John, *Cranfield*: 1406; John, *Ellington*: 2376; John, *Holywell*: 3160;

Nicholas, *Shillington*: 306, 1345, 3352; Richard, *Shillington*: 1345; Robert, *Therfield*: 308; William, *Holywell*: 2363.

PIKELER. See PYKELER.

PIKERELL. See PYKERELL.

PILGRYM, John, *Chatteris*: 2350; William, *Hurst/St. Ives/Woodhurst*: 658, 866, 934, 1204.

PILTON (Pilketon, Pylketon), John, *Elton*: 452, 703, 734, 2249, 2260; Brother Thomas de, sub-cellarer: 37, 39, 70, 72, 428-31, 623.

PIPER (Pyper), Agnes, *Chatteris*: see STOT; John, *Chatteris*: see STOT; Richard, *Chatteris*: 1837; Simon, *Chatteris*: 612, 847.

PIRYE. See PERYE.

PIROUN. See PYROUN.

PLAUNTEYN, John, *Burwell*: 3754-5.

PLOMBE (Plumbe), Agnes, *Burwell*: 3612; Agnes, *Houghton*: 2725; Alicia, *Warboys*: 3371; Johanna, *Warboys*: 1127; Johanna, *Wistow*: see HICHE; John, *Burwell*: 1229, 3012; John, *Houghton*: 2470, 2725, 3048, 4166-7; John, Jr., *Houghton*: 2317; John, *Warboys*: 271, 737, 1127, 1376, 1379, 1383, 1417, 2153, 3371, 3800, 3901, 3925, 4167, 4170; John (Bocher), *Warboys*: 2053; John, Sr., *Warboys*: 737, 2053; John, Jr., *Warboys*: 536, 598; John, *Wistow/ Raveley*: 758, 1873, 2297, 2447, 4309-10; Margaret, *Burwell*: 898, 2041, 4356; Margaret, *Houghton*: 3048; Richard, *Warboys*: 726, 737, 963, 1127, 1376, 3371; Richard, *Wistow*: 758, 3929, 4308-10; Robert, *Houghton*: 2725, 4169; Thomas, *Burwell*: 277, 901, 2959, 3127, 3477, 3612, 4021; Thomas, *Warboys*: 3925.

PLOMER, John, *Ramsey*: 1528.

PLOUGHWRIGHT (Plougwrighte, Plowryte, Plow wryth), John, *Houghton*: see WHITE; Thomas, *Wistow*: see ASPLOND; William, *Barton*: see ROGER; William, *Wistow*: see ASPLOND.

PLUMBE. See PLOMBE.

POCAT. See POKET.

POKEBROOK (Pokbrook), John, *Elsworth*: 403; Laurence, *Elton*: 729, 1199, 4286; William, *Elton*: 408, 2597.

POKET (Pocat), Elizabeth, *Burwell*: 3615; Isabella, *Burwell*: 4276; John, *Burwell*: 1229, 1624; Margaret, *Burwell*: see TAILLOR; William, *Burwell*: see TAILLOR.

POKYS, John, *Slepe*: 272.

POLE, Robert, *Shillington*: 383; William, *Broughton*: 3791.

POLLAN, Alan, *Abbots Ripton*: 3971.

POMERAY, Henry, *Burwell*: 400; Johanna, *Burwell*: see PERYE.

POMYS (Pomeys), John (al. Miller), *Houghton*: 3545, 3727; John (al. Miller), *Warboys*: 3553; Sarra (al. Miller), *Houghton*: 3545, 3727.

PONDE (Poonde), William, *Elsworth*: 121, 213.

PONDER, Elena, *Ellington*: 3848; John, *Ellington*: 1354; Thomas, *Ellington*: 1354, 3848.

POOL (Pooll, Poole), Agnes, *Houghton*: 2969; Alicia, *Broughton*: see JUSTICE; Johanna, *Shillington*: see STONLE; John, *Broughton*: 280, 2167, 2172, 2646; John, *Elton*: 734; John, *Houghton*: 670, 1430, 2037; Juliana (Morell), *Chatteris*: 3393, 3398; Richard, *Chatteris*: 3396; Richard, *Houghton*: 281, 2969, 3423; Robert, *Houghton*: 970, 971, 1206; Thomas, *Shillington*: 3853, 3934; William, *Broughton*: 3793.

POOLYARD (Poleyard, Polyerd, Poolyerd), Agnes, *Graveley*: see DANYELL; Margaret, *Ramsey*: 3456; Thomas, *Graveley*: 278; William, *Abbots Ripton*: 4159, 4161; William, *Graveley*: 966; William, *Ramsey*: 3456.

POONDE. See PONDE.

POPE (Pop, Poppe), Agnes, *Barton*: see WYLYMOT; Alicia, *Barton*: 3361; Alicia, *Chatteris*: 2813, 3297; Alicia, *St. Ives*: 3434; Elyas, *Hemingford*: 3732; Jacob, *Barton*: 2315, 2392, 2722, 3355, 3490, 4052; Johanna, *Barton*: 2392, 3355; Johanna, *Hemingford*: 3259, 4121; John, *Chatteris*: 2092, 2095, 3084; John, Sr., *Chatteris*: 2994; John, Jr., *Chatteris*: 2994, 3299, 3921; John, *Hemingford*: 3259, 3261, 3319, 3382, 3732, 4121, 4127, 4173; John, *Houghton*: 1439, 1681, 2035, 2134, 2137, 2726; John, *St. Ives*: 3434; John, Jr., *St. Ives*: 2776; John, *Upwood*: 282; John, *Wistow*: 2370; Katerina, *Hemingford*: 4127; Margaret, *Hurst/ Woodhurst*: see WALTON; Matilda, *St. Ives*: 825, 1643; Radulph, *Chatteris*: 3569, 4087; Richard, (Miller), *St. Ives*: 3511; Richard, *Wistow*: 2779; Thomas, *Barton*: 545, 1986, 3361, 4052; Thomas, *Chatteris*: 1835; Thomas, *Hemingford*: 4121, 4127; Thomas, *Hurst/Slepe/Woodhurst*: 2598, 2600, 2604, 2658, 3384, 3510, 3749, 4101; Walter (Miller), *St. Ives*: 1397; William, *Chatteris*: 2092, 2741,

John), *Burwell*: 3130, 3829; John (son of
Thomas), *Burwell*: 3130; John (Newman),
Burwell: 3123; John (al. Shipman), *Burwell*: 3617; John (al. Stameryng), *Burwell*:
2332; John (al. Townherde), *Burwell*:
4204; John (atte Dufhous), *Burwell*: 3123,
3830; John, Sr., *Burwell*: 3123, 3130;
John, Jr., *Burwell*: 1171, 1530, 1975,
2885, 3830; John (III), *Burwell*: 2332,
2885; John, *Graveley*: 278, 3206, 3889;
John, Jr., *Graveley*: 2552; Katerina, *Burwell*: 1626, 3130; Nicholas, *Burwell*: 448,
3530; Richard, *Graveley*: 3206; Thomas,
Burwell: 2510, 3130, 4017; Thomas, Sr.
(al. Carpenter), *Burwell*: 4111, 4275;
Thomas, Jr., *Burwell*: 1347, 4275; Tho-
mas, *Upwood*: 747; family, *Graveley*: 3781.
3781.
ROMBURGH (Romborough, Rumburgh),
Margaret, *Hurst*: 3311; Simon (al. Oldich),
Hurst/ Woodhurst: 2548, 3311, 3594;
family, *St. Ives*: 3140.
ROOD. See RODE.
ROODIS. See RODE.
ROOK (Roke, Rooke), John, *Therfield*:
1497, 2631, 3960, 3962.
ROOLE. See ROULE.
ROPERE (Roper), Johanna, *Abbots Ripton*:
1356; John, *Abbots Ripton*: 138;
John, *Broughton*: see HAMPSON; John,
Hurst/Woodhurst: 2074, 2598; Lucia,
Woodhurst: 2074; Richard, (al. Carter),
Abbots Ripton: 1356, 1481.
ROSEBY, John, *Hemingford*: 725.
ROTOR, John, *Slepe*: 2658.
ROULE, (Roole, Roolee), John, *Burwell*:
3477; John, Jr., *Burwell*: 446; Margaret,
Burwell: 3753; William, *Burwell*: 3753.
ROWER, Agnes, *Burwell*: 2886; Agnes
"Bastard", *Burwell*: 2886; Alicia, *Burwell*:
1797; Margaret, *Burwell*: 1629, 2500;
Radulph, *Burwell*: 1629, 2509, 2632,
3613, 4114; Richard, *Burwell*: 3010;
Thomas, *Burwell*: 277, 1230, 1797, 2883,
2886, 3218, 3345; Thomas, *Elsworth*:
2759.
ROYSTON (Roiston), Galfridus, (al.
Taillor), *Chatteris*: 2812, 3765, 3993.
RUKDEN, Robert, *Weston*: 3285.
RUMBOLD (Rumbolde), John, Sr., *Elton*:
379; John, Jr., *Elton*: 379; family, *Elton*:
2425.
RUMBURGH. See ROMBURGH.
RUSSELL, Agnes, *Hemingford*: 4120; Elena,
Hemingford: 4120; Johanna, *Broughton*:

3563; Johanna (II), *Broughton*: 3564;
John, *Hemingford*: 4122; John, *Knapwell*:
1840; Robert, *Broughton*: 3563; Robert,
Warboys: 2921; Robert, *Wistow*: 3194,
3333; Thomas, *Broughton*: 3329; Thomas,
Jr., *Broughton*: 3120, 3564; Thomas,
Chatteris: 1911, 2685; Thomas, *Heming-
ford*: 4122; Walter, *Chatteris*: 1911;
William, *Broughton*: 3330, 3563; William,
Hemingford: 3495, 4120; William, *Ther-
field*: 3452.
RUTLAND, Stephen, *Elton*: 2728.
RYDE, Richard, *Elton*: 1111, 2251, 2255.
RYDELER (Rideler), Agnes, *Cranfield*:
1726; Matilda/Matillis, *Cranfield*: 2, 274,
1407; Thomas, *Cranfield*: 2270, 3542,
3967; Thomas, Sr., *Cranfield*: 4199;
Thomas, Jr., *Cranfield*: 4199; Walter,
Cranfield: 2, 78, 1726; William, *Cranfield*:
2270.
RYDMAN, Ivota, *Ramsey*: 1522; Johanna,
Broughton: see CABE; Robert, *Ramsey*:
1522; William, *Broughton*: 4185.
RYFLEE, John, *Therfield*: 1867.
RYNGGE (Rynge), Isabella, *Cranfield*: 437;
Mariota, *Cranfield*: 4046; William, *Cran-
field*: 437, 4046.
RYVENALE. See REVENALE.

SABBE, Rosa, *St. Ives*: 2067, 2461;
William, *St. Ives*: 2067, 2461.
SABYN, Henry, *Ellington*: 4292; John,
Wistow: 644, 645, 1060, 3222; William,
Wistow: 228.
SACHEBIEN, John, *Bythorne*: 79, 80, 263;
Margaret, *Bythorne*: 79.
SACHELL, John, *Abbots Ripton*: 2184.
SADDE, John, *Burwell*: 901, 1535.
SADELER (Sadiller), Agnes, *St. Ives*: 1819;
John, *Ramsey*: see HERNE; Katerina,
Ramsey: see Herne; William, *St. Ives*: see
HERNE.
ST. IVES, Prior of: 1656, 2586, 2659, 3580,
3914, 3943.
ST. NEOTS, Radulph of, *Graveley*: 1752.
SALDYNG (Saldyn), Elena/Helena, *Elton*:
4270, 4285; Johanna, *Elton*: 3518; John,
Elton: 264, 3518; Thomas, *Elton*: 3518;
4270, 4285.
SALISBURY (Salesbury, Salusbury), Isabella,
St. Ives: 1649; Robert, *St. Ives*: 1649,
2460, 2528, 2655, 2756, 3142.
SALY, John, *Abbots Ripton*: 2186.
SALUSBURY. See SALISBURY.
SAMAN, Johanna (al. Fuller), *Houghton*:

3055; Richard, *Shillington*: 2399; Richard, *Warboys*: 933; Robert, *Pegsdon*: 3628; Roger, *Warboys*: 1418; Thomas, *Ellington*: 3182; Walter (al. Savage), *Abbots Ripton/- Wistow*: 751, 1139, 1169, 1211, 1584, 1685, 1873; William (Savage), *Abbots Ripton*: 523, 1951, 2186; William, *Barton*: 712, 1612, 2537; William, *Holywell*: 2262; William, *Shillington*: 3768, 4368; William, *Therfield*: see MALT.

SHERMAN (Scherman, Shereman), Anna, *Graveley*: see NEWMAN; Beatrix, *Cranfield*: 1733, 3045; John, *Cranfield*: 2203; Laurence, *Graveley*: 435.

SHERPE. See SCHARP.

SHERWODE. See SHIRWODE.

SHILLINGTON, customaries of: 1542; rector of: 4278.

SHIRWODE (Schirwode, Sherwode, Shyrwode), John, *Ramsey*: 37; 399, 1170, 1931, 3460.

SHYPMAN, John, *Burwell*: see ROLF.

SHYRWODE. See SHIRWODE.

SISSOR, William, *Houghton/ Ramsey*: see BOTOLF.

SISTERNE. See SESTERNE.

SIWARD (Seyward), Matilda, *Houghton*: 1433; Thomas, *Houghton*: 605.

SKAKEDALE, John, *Chatteris*: 2009.

SKELE. See SKYLL.

SKENALE, Laurence, *Burwell*: 1231.

SKOT. See SCOT.

SKYBB, John, *Chatteris*: 2693.

SKYLL (Skele), John, *Chatteris*: 2811, 2812, 4341.

SKYNNER (Skynnere), Agnes, *Ellington*: see MOKKE; Agnes, *St. Ives/ Slepe*: 1970, 2016-17; Agnes, *Upwood*: 2736; Agnes (II), *Upwood*: 3405; Alicia, *Little Stukeley*: 3138; Cristina, *Slepe*: 833; Elizabeth (Davy), *Cranfield*: 3719, 3775; Frederick, *St. Ives/ Slepe*: 833, 1970, 2016-17, 2325, 2329, 2410, 3930; Henry, *Upwood*: 3405; Johanna, *Cranfield*: see ALEYN; John, *Burwell*: see SPENSER; John, *Chatteris*: 2350, 2749, 2989, 3995; John, *Cranfield*: 152, 2617, 3719, 3775; John, *Ellington*: 3685, 4067, 4290; John (al. Wright), *Ellington*: 2218; John, *Little Stukeley/ Ellington*: 2596, 3679; John, Jr., *Little Stukeley*: 3138, 3293; John (of Huntingdon), *Warboys*: 1858; Laurence, *Burwell*: 2044; Margaret, *Warboys*: see MOLT; Olyva, *Upwood*: 2551, 3554; Richard, *Upwood*: 2551, 3281; Richard,

Wistow: 3554, 3558; William, *Ellington*: 4067; William, *Upwood*: 2736.

SLEYN, William, *Houghton*: 1677.

SLOGHT. See SLOW.

SLOW (Sloght, Slough), Alicia, *Graveley*: 2836; Custancia, *Graveley*: see NEWMAN; John, *Graveley*: 210, 1633, 2836, 2941; John, *Slepe*: 363; John, Sr., *Slepe*: 2082; John, Jr., *Slepe*: 2078; Robert, *Graveley*: 2836; Robert, *Warboys*: 2335; Simon, *Slepe*: 1608; Walter, *Graveley*: 1633, 2941; William, *Graveley*: 210, 1387.

SLY, Agnes, *Abbots Ripton*: 1068; John, *Abbots Ripton*: 1068; John, *Hemingford*: 725, 3132; Margaret, *Hemingford*: 3132; William, *Hemingford*: 1423, 2903, 3495; William, *Therfield*: 3452.

SMART (Smert), Agnes, *Broughton*: 1661, 2285; Alan, *Elsworth*: 66; John, *Burwell*: 400; Simon, *Elsworth*: 144; Simon, *Warboys*: 466; Thomas, *Elsworth*: 66, 93, 143, 432, 1001, 2276; William, *Broughton*: 1661, 2285, 2514; William, *Warboys*: 181, 1216, 1384, 2049, 2595, 3550.

SMERT. See SMART.

SMUDDYNG, John, *Ramsey*: 39.

SMYGT. See SMYTH.

SMYTH (Smygt, Smyt), Adam, *St. Ives*: 532, 1099, 1972; Adam, *Shillington*: 1287, 1897, 2404; Agnes, *Bythorne*: see HACOUN; Agnes, *Elsworth*: see FLESSHEWER; Agnes, *Elton*: 4286-7; Agnes, *Graveley*: 3559, 3780, 4042; Agnes, *Ramsey*: see FERMER; Agnes, *St. Ives*: see CARTER; Agnes, *Shillington*: 159, 1085; Alan, *St. Ives*: 2412, 3975; Alicia, *Chatteris*: 2012; Alicia, *Elsworth*: see WODE, ATTE; Alicia, *Holywell*: 2413, 2588; Alicia (II), *Holywell*: 3343; Alicia, *Houghton*: see PERSONSMAN; Alicia, *Shillington*: 1484, 1538; Alicia, *Therfield*: 2437, 2547; Amicia, *Holywell*: 289, 291; Andrew, *Wistow*: 854; Elena, *Graveley*: 3205; Elena, *Knapwell*: 3606; Elias, *Cranfield*: 879, 1313, 1728, 2222; Emma, *Barton*: 791; Galfridus, *Houghton*: 42, 101, 205, 1437, 1676, 1956, 3392; Henry, *Elsworth*: 1473, 3952; Henry, *Weston*: 3187; Isabella, *Brington*: 1226; Isabella, *Graveley*: 3204; Isabella, *Shillington*: 1484; Johanna, *Abbots Ripton*: 1852, 2416; Johanna, *Houghton*: 1428, 2131, 2844, 3171, 3660; Johanna, *Shillington*: 1287; John, *Abbots Ripton*: 3102, 3598, 3663, 3798; John, *Barton*: 713, 791, 1889, 2724; John,

SOULTON, Alicia, *Warboys*: see EYR; Robert, *Warboys*: 459.

SOUTH (Sowth), John, *Chatteris*: 2990, 3578, 4082, 4212, 4349.

SOUTHMAN (Sowtheman), Richard, *Burwell*: 1081, 2633.

SOVEREYN (Soverayn), Richard, *Houghton*: 3047, 3728.

SOWER, Thomas, *Hurst*: 3070.

SOWLE, Margaret, *St. Ives*: 2323, 3075; Thomas, *St. Ives*: 2323, 2455, 3075, 4186; William, *St. Ives*: 3075.

SOUTH. See SOUTH.

SOWTHMAN. See SOUTHMAN.

SOWTHWODE, Johanna, *Cranfield*: 1923; Thomas, *Cranfield*: 1782, 1923; William, *Cranfield*: 1782.

SPALDYNG, Agnes, *St. Ives/ Slepe*: see RAVEN; John, *St. Ives/ Slepe*: 1013, 1016.

SPARKE, Isabella, *Ramsey*: 4193; William (Glover), *Ramsey*: 4193.

SPARROW. See SPARWE.

SPARUGH. See SPARWE.

SPARVER, Agnes, *Therfield*: 2108; Felicia, *Therfield*: 2435; Isabella, *Therfield*: 3212; John, *Therfield*: 262, 310, 2108-9, 2215, 2435, 2874, 3212, 3843; John, Sr., *Therfield*: 2109; John, Jr., *Therfield*: 3700; Katerina (Wattes), *Therfield*: 310, 1051; Robert, *Therfield*: 3698.

SPARWE (Sparrow, Sparugh, Sperwe, Sperwer), Adam, *Shillington*: 273, 2232, 2622, 2996, 3536, 3701, 3771; Agnes, *Pegsdon*: 1488; Alexander, *Burwell*: 171, 1533, 2580, 3216, 4226; Helena, *Burwell*: 34; John, *Burwell*: 953, 1535, 3473, 3832; John, Jr., *Burwell*: 202; John, *Shillington*: 273; Rosa, *Elsworth*: 4297, 4330; Simon, *Elsworth*: 3944, 4174, 4297, 4330; Thomas, *Burwell*: 34, 277, 953, 2889; Thomas, *Elsworth*: 822; William, *Shillington/ Pegsdon*: 890, 1488, 1718.

SPAYN (Spaygne, Spayne), Elena, *Bythorne*: 3908; Johanna, *Bythorne*: see BACHELER: Thomas, *Bythorne*: 3908; William, *Bythorne*: 149, 785, 917, 3786-7, 3907.

SPENSER (Spencer), Alicia, *Burwell*: 1627; Henry, *Elton*: 452, 2552; John (al. Skynner), *Burwell*: 4207; John, *Upwood*: 3404, 3596; Richard, *Burwell*: 43; Richard, Sr., *Burwell*: 1627; Simon, *Chatteris*: see THOMESSON.

SPERWE(R). See SPARWE.

SPERYOUR, Edith, *Barton*: see ALEYN; John, *Barton*: 888.

SPICER (Spicher, Spycer), Elena, *St. Ives*: 247; Emma, *St. Ives*: 2527; Henry (al. Okam), *St. Ives*: 247, 2527; John, *Houghton*: 2138, 2467; Petronilla, *Houghton*: 2138; William, *Wistow*: 3976.

SPORYSOR (Sporyor), Walter, *Ramsey*: 3113, 3163.

SPYCER. See SPICER.

SQUYER (Sqwyer), Johanna, *Cranfield*: see MOWSE; John, *Cranfield*: 3965; John, *Weston*: 2592, 2978; William, *Warboys*: 178, 1238.

STABILL (Stable, Stabull), John, *Brington*: 2651-2, 3095; John, Jr., *Brington*: 2603; Margaret, *Brington*: 2652.

STACY, John, *Barton*: 1074; Lucia, *Barton*: see MATHEW.

STALLEWORTH, Robert, *Graveley*: 3780.

STAMERYNG, John, *Burwell*: see ROLF.

STANWEYE, Radulph (Foster), *Ellington*: 3681.

STAPILFORD, John, *Elsworth*: 858, 4036; John, *Warboys*: 73.

STAPILTON, William (Wodeward), *Wistow*: 394, 1290.

STEDMAN, Isabella, *Ramsey*: 3110; William, *Ramsey*: 3110.

STERNE, Elena, *Burwell*: 3126.

STETHAM, Alota, *Burwell*: 3474.

STEUERELEY. See STYVECLE.

STEVEN (Stevene, Stevens), Robert, *Therfield*: 309, 1536, 3697; Thomas (al. Grauntot), *Therfield*: 3806.

STILE. See STYLE.

STODAY, Johanna, *Broughton*: 1658; Simon, *Broughton*: 1658.

STODLE, (Stodele), John, *St. Ives*: 124, 1645.

STOK, Thomas (al. Barker), *St. Ives*: 2986, 3305.

STOKLE, George, *Abbots Ripton*: 4158; Isabella, *Abbots Ripton*: 4158.

STOKKER, Emma, *Cranfield*: 1926.

STOKKIS (Stokys), Johanna, *Ramsey*: 2679; Radulph, *Ramsey*: 2679; Thomas, *Ellington*: 4115.

STOKTON, Felicia, *Therfield*: see WYNMER; William, *Therfield*: 761; John, *Chatteris*: 509.

STOKYS. See STOKKIS.

STONE (Stoon), John, atte, *Shillington*: 3772, 3904, 3934.

STONELD, family, *Barton*: 2951.

STONELE. See STONLE.

STONGHTON (Stongton), Cecilia, *Therfield*: 1499; Elena, *Therfield*: 4064; John,

SWYNEDD, William, *Burwell*: 1171.

SWYTHWYK, Walter, *Elton*: 700.

SYGAR, Matilda, *Burwell*: 4227; William, *Burwell*: 4162, 4227.

SYMME, John, *Hurst*: 2359; John, *Wistow*: 1388.

SYMMESSON, John, *Chatteris*: 2684, 3080, 3446.

SYMOND, Beatrix, *Therfield*: 1161; Johanna, *Upwood*: 582; John, *Houghton*: 1958, 2317; William, *Upwood*: 282, 582, 1102.

SYRE, Agnes, *Houghton*: 628; Alicia, *Slepe*: 4149; Johanna, *Wistow*: see RANDOLF; John, *Slepe*: 4149; William, *Wistow*: 2269.

SYSTERNE. See SESTERNE.

SYWELL. See SEWALE.

TADLOWE (Tadelowe), William, *St. Ives*: 12, 2459, 2531.

TAILLOR of Barton, *Shillington*: 801.

TAILLOR. See TAYLOR.

TAKILL (Takell, Takil, Takyl), Elena, *St. Ives*: 296; John, *St. Ives*: 296; Robert, *St. Ives*: 296, 479, 1640, 1821, 4256.

TAPESERE, John, *Ramsey*: 3891.

TAUSLEY, Agnes, *Abbots Ripton*: 3972; Roger, *Abbots Ripton*: 3972.

TAYLOR (Taillor, Taylard, Tayllor), Adam, *Barton*: 261, 893-4, 1979; Adam, *Chatteris*: 1055; Adam, *Therfield*: 2030; Alan, *Elsworth*: 83, 858; Alicia, *Broughton*: 596; Alicia, *Burwell*: see HURBE; Alicia, *St. Ives*: 4184; Alicia, *Wistow*: 3023; Baldwin, *St. Ives*: 868; Edmund, *Broughton*: 596; Edward, *Elton*: 1845, 2256; Elizabeth, *Burwell*: 2702; Galfridus, *Chatteris*: see ROYSTON; Galfridus, *Cranfield*: 1180, 1611; Hugo, *Woodhurst*: 2075; Isabella, *Burwell*: 1421; Johanna, *St. Ives*: 3975; Johanna, *Wistow*: see GERMAN; John, *Abbots Ripton*: 3798; John, *Barton*: 3712, 4051; John, *Broughton*: see JUSTICE; John, *Burwell*: 2887; John, *Chatteris*: see CUT; John, *Ellington*: 3682; John, *Elton*: 782, 902; John, *Hemingford*: 3644; John, *Holywell*: 742, 790, 872, 902, 2148, 2792, 4094; John, *Hurst/Woodhurst*: 3595, 3883; John, *St. Ives*: see BANDE; John, *Pegsdon*: see COCHE; John (of Royston), *Therfield*: 164; John, *Therfield*: 2546; John, *Warboys*: see LACHE; John, *Weston*: 3100; John, *Wistow*: 3023, 4140; Joseph, *St. Ives*: 342; Juliana, *Wistow*: 1390; Laurence, *Shillington*: 1137, 2761;

Margaret, *Burwell*: 1350; Nicholas, *Abbots Ripton*: 189, 927; Peter, *St. Ives*: 3142; Reginald, *Warboys*: 3369; Reginald, *Weston*: 2590; Reginald, *Wistow*: see GRYM; Richard, *Hemingford*: 4124; Richard, *Warboys*: 133, 2156; Robert, *Elton*: 701, 913; Robert, *Hemingford*: 3737; Roger, *Shillington*: 793; Thomas, *Chatteris*: 2991, 3389; Thomas, *St. Ives*: see MARHAM; Walter, *Houghton*: 3422; Walter, *Warboys*: see ERBY; William, *Broughton*: 2645, 2647; William, *Brington*: see CLEPTON; William, *Burwell*: 1421, 1977, 2887, 4111, and see HURBE; William (al. Poket), *Burwell*: 33, 314, 1229, 1350, 3615; William, Sr., *Burwell*: 2702; William, Jr., *Burwell*: 2702; William, *Chatteris*: 607, 1504, 1695; William, *Ellington*: 1160; William, *Elsworth*: 426; William, *Elton*: 406, 908, 1113, 1999; William, *St. Ives*: 3975, 4184; William, *Wistow*: 848.

TAYNTOR, family, *Elton*: 993.

TEBALDE (Tebaud), Cecilia, *Chatteris*: 3189; John, *Chatteris*: 1010; Radulph, *Chatteris*: 2989, 3189, 4081.

TEBBE, John, *St. Ives*: 1509, 1639, 1646, 3078, 3307; Katerina, *Therfield*: see FRERE; Margeria, *St. Ives*: 1509, 1646, 3307; William, *Therfield*: 2216.

TEMESFORD (Tennysford), family, *Warboys*: 1237, 2520.

TERRY, Agnes, *Cranfield*: 250; Alicia, *Cranfield*: 2767-8; Cristiana, *Cranfield*: 327, 679; Hugo, *Cranfield*: 326-7, 2616; Johanna, *Cranfield*: 3543; John, *Cranfield*: 274, 327, 878, 2200, 2616, 2767, 3718, 3776; Margaret, *Cranfield*: 2496; Mariota, *Cranfield*: 3778; Thomas, *Cranfield*: 54, 326, 884, 1446, 2200, 2496, 3367, 3543, 3637, 3778; Thomas, Sr., *Cranfield*: 620; Thomas, Jr., *Cranfield*: 3778; William, *Cranfield*: 3415, 3543, 3718, 3777-8, 4048, 4156, 4268.

THAKESTEDE. See THAKSTED.

THAKKER (Thacker), Alicia, *Warboys*: 2157; Elena, *Warboys*: see CHIBBELE; Emma, *Therfield*: see WENHAM; Johanna, *Hemingford*: 3496; John, *Ellington*: 1454, 1806; John, *Hemingford*: 3496; John, *Therfield*: 2868; John, *Wistow/Raveley*: see OWTY; John, *Warboys*: see CHIBBELE; Mariota, *Wistow*: see WARENER; Nicholas, *Chatteris*: 1919; William, *Wistow*: see WARENER.

TROWNY, family, *Elton*: 2107.

TRUMPOR (Trinpor), John, *Chatteris*: 113, 1363, 1502, 1550, 2866.

TRYM, Robert, *St. Ives*: 1820.

TRYPPELOWE, Robert, *Wistow*: 248.

TRYVER, George, *Burwell*: 2886.

TUKE, Margaret, *Elsworth*: see WODE; Robert, *Elsworth*: 4033.

TURNOR (Turnour), Alicia, *Ellington*: see GEROLD; John, *Barton*: 2949, 3630; Maria, *Broughton*: 2646; Nicholas, *Broughton*: 2287, 3329; Nicholas, Sr., *Broughton*: 3120; Richard, *Chatteris*: 4082, 4212, 4349; Robert, *Broughton*: 2171, 2283, 2453, 2646; Thomas, *Ellington*: 92.

TURSTER, Emma, *Slepe*: 272.

TWE, John, *Bythorne*: 707.

TWYFORDE, Stephen, *Hurst*: 1364.

TWYNY, Agnes, *Graveley*: 1050; Nicholas, *Graveley*: 1050.

TWYWELL, Richard (al. Dykes), *Houghton*: 205, 2242, 3502.

TYBBEY (Tybey), Agnes, *Cranfield*: 2613, 2946; John, *Cranfield*: 2613.

TYCHEMERSCH (Tychemerssh), John, rector, *Broughton*: 3331; Henry, sub-cellarer: 2054, 2124; William, *St. Ives*: 3514.

TYD (Tydde, Tydy), Adam, *Hemingford*: 3646, 4333; Agnes, *Chatteris*: 1829; John, *Chatteris*: 1829, 2865; John, *Shillington*: 30.

TYFFYN, Alicia, *Houghton*: 2726; John, *Houghton*: 2726, 4170; Matilda, *Houghton*: 2966; William, *Houghton*: 2845, 2966, 2968, 3723, 3400.

TYLER, Andrew, *Wistow*: 2782; Henry, *Cranfield*: 3492; Margaret, *Ramsey*: 3237; Richard, *Ramsey*: 3017; Robert, *Ramsey*: 3237; Simon, *St. Ives*: 1656.

TYLLY, Thomas, *Houghton*: 1190, 1438.

TYLNEY (Tilney, Tyllneye, Tylneye, Tylnye), John, *Chatteris*: 2487, 2796; Nicholas, *Chatteris*: 2344; Thomas, *Chatteris*: 610, 2793, 3765, 3993; William, *Chatteris*: 3575.

TYNKER, John, *Hemingford*: 724.

TYPTOT (Typtet, Typtoft), Margeria, *Hemingford*: see HEYNE; Thomas, *Broughton*: 2174, 2644, 3330, 3563; Thomas, *Hemingford*: 2130.

TYRAAUNT, Emma, *Slepe*: see HERROF; Thomas, *Slepe*: 1038.

ULF, Amicia, *Hurst*: 2550.

UMFREY, Freman, *Abbots Ripton*: 4221.

UNDERWODE, John, *Elsworth*: 2824.

UPTON, Agnes (al. Barleyman), *Houghton*: 3912; Alicia, *Houghton*: 2293; John, *Hemingford*: 2293, 2839, 2905, 3496, 3735, 4123; John, *Houghton/Wyton*: 1430, 1847, 1964, 2910, 3169, 3721; John, Sr., *Houghton*: 3912; John, Jr., *Houghton*: 3984; Margaret, *Houghton*: 1964, 3721; Richard, *Houghton*: 520; Robert, *Houghton/Wyton*: 281, 1680, 1847, 1850, 2293, 3662.

VALE, Alicia, *Elton*: 701; Isabella, *Barton*: 2226; William, *Barton*: 2226.

VALENTINE (Valentyn, Valentyne), John, *St. Ives*: 3322, 3975; Margaret, *Holywell*: see SCOT; Thomas, *Holywell*: 1424, 2146, 3062, 3515.

VAUS (Vauce, Vaux, Vaws), Thomas, *Cranfield*: 3638; William, *Cranfield*: 710, 1547, 2614.

VER (Veer), Alan, *Hemingford*: 2129, 2838, 3499, 3818; Petronilla, *Hemingford*: 2129.

VERNON (Vernoun), Alicia, *Little Stukeley*: 3894; John, *Upwood*: 1906; William, *Little Stukeley*: 3894.

VICORY (Vikori, Vikory, Vikorye, Vycory), John, *Hurst/Woodhurst*: 2292, 2549, 3309, 3686, 3922, 4101; William, *Hurst*: 4100.

VIRLY, John, *Ellington*: 4247.

VYCORY. See VICORY.

WAKE, John, *Abbots Ripton*: 1950.

WAKEFELD, John, *Elton*: 914; William, *Elton*: 371.

WAKER (Wakyr), Agnes, *Ramsey*: 3240; Peter, *Wistow*: 58, 352, 370, 411, 1743.

WALDEN, John, *Burwell*: 170.

WALE, Alicia, *Slepe*: see CARTER; John, *Abbots Ripton*: 2112; John, *Graveley*: 2941; John, *Slepe*: see CARTER; Margaret, *Graveley*: 2941.

WALE FLECHER, John, *St. Ives*: see CARTER; Margaret, *St. Ives*: see CARTER.

WALE SMYTH, Helena, *St. Ives*: 1642; John, *St. Ives*: see CARTER.

WALES, Henry, *Elton*: 2728; Thomas, *Elton*: 2928.

WALESBY, John, *Abbots Ripton*: 1480.

WALEYS (Walis, Wallys), Agnes, *Warboys*: 1413; Alicia, *Elton*: 421; Edmund, *Burwell*: 1095; John, *Burwell*: 4206; John, Jr., *Burwell*: 4113; John, *Elton*: 421, 1046; John, *Graveley*: 1602; John, *Warboys*:

1413, 1903; Margaret, *Burwell*: 4206; Margaret, *Graveley*: see SWON; Margaret, *Shillington*: 1720; Richard, *Bythorne*: 3860; Robert, *Shillington*: 1086, 1720, 3480, 3702, 4004; Thomas, *Elton*: 2421.

WALGATE, Anna, *Wistow/Raveley*: see WILLESSON; John, *Wistow/Raveley*: 2445-6, 2504, 3402; John, Sr., *Wistow/Raveley*: 3200, 3813, 4309; John, Jr., *Wistow/Raveley*: 3196, 3200, 3813.

WALIS. See WALEYS.

WALTER, Roger, *Bythorne*: 454.

WALTHAM, Agnes, *Graveley*: see WEST; Agnes, *Warboys*: 4129; Alicia, *Graveley*: 2220; John, *Graveley*: 2220, 2827, 3067, 4117; Richard, *Warboys*: 4129.

WALTON (Whalton), Margaret, *Woodhurst*: 770, 1716; William, (al. Pope), *Hurst/Slepe/Woodhurst*: 770, 825, 1643, 1715-16, 1861, 2073, 2523, 2600, 3310, 3749; William (al. Pope), *Chatteris*: 2092, 2741, 3297, 4211.

WANGTEY, William, *Abbots Ripton*: 3795, 4359.

WAPPELODE. See WHAPPELODE.

WARBOYS, John (abbot of Ramsey): 4115.

WARBOYS (Wardebusk), John, *Wistow*: 2734, 2750; Thomas, *Upwood*: 1042, 1807, 2182.

WARDE, Agnes, *Holywell*: see HUNNE; Agnes, *Hurst*: 1762; Agnes, *Ramsey*: 2124, 2936, 3105; John, *Brington*: 1305; John, *Cranfield*: 2307; John, *Holywell*: 1036, 1894; John, *Hurst*: 1762, 3313; John, *Ramsey*: 2124, 2936, 3018; John, Sr., *Ramsey*: 3105; John, Jr., *Ramsey*: 3105; John, *Shillington*: 494, 797, 889, 1209-10, 1343, 1619, 2116, 2295-6, 2477, 4001, 4233; John, Sr., *Shillington*: 3482-3; John, *Warboys*: 2053; John (of Barham), *Warboys*: 674; John (of Raveley), *Warboys*: 2975; Katerina, *Brington*: see HOWESSON; Margaret/Margeria, *Shillington*: 1619, 2295, 3482; Margaret, *Warboys*: see MOLT; Thomas, *Hurst/Woodhurst*: 1909, 2705; William, *Brington*: 4107; William, *Cranfield*: 1730, 2307; William, *Elsworth*: 2638; William, *Shillington*: 4371.

WARDEBUSK. See WARBOYS.

WARDON, Richard (al. Revesson), *Warboys*: 1302, 2246, 3801.

WARE, John, *Ramsey*: 3892; Thomas, *Abbots Ripton*: 3798.

WARNER (Warenner, Waryner), Agnes,

Weston: see FLESSHEWER; John, *Cranfield*: 3365; John, *Weston*: 4009; Mariota, *Wistow*: 1687; Robert, *Cranfield*: 1278, 2614; Stephen (al. Cabe), *Hurst*: 1516, 1762; William, *Hurst*: 1233, 1516; William (Thakker), *Wistow*: 1687.

WARTIR, John, *Chatteris*: 219, 2344.

WARWIK (Warwyk), Elena, *Graveley*: see NEWMAN; John, *Graveley*: 2019; William, *Abbots Ripton*: 4221.

WARYN (Wareyn), Agnes, *Broughton*: 3823; Agnes, *Elton*: 2424; Agnes, *Therfield*: 1148; Agnes (II), *Therfield*: 2024; Agnes (III), *Therfield*: 2869; Agnes (IV), *Therfield*: 3839; Agnes, *Upwood*: see ANDREW; Agnes, *Wistow*: 743; Alicia (Wynter), *Shillington*: 441, 3626, 3703; Edith, *Therfield*: 2025; Elena, *Therfield*: 1147; Elizabet, *Therfield*: 3807; Emma, 105; George, *Therfield*: 3806-7; Isabella, *Therfield*: see NOKE; Johanna, *Therfield*: 445; Johanna, *Therfield*: see WODE; John, *Elsworth*: 1019; 2637, John, Jr., *Elsworth*: 1706; John, *Elton*: 983, 1201; John, Sr., *Elton*: 983; John, Jr., *Elton*: 1340; John, *Shillington/Pegsdon*: 27, 1492, 1719, 2032, 4179; John, *Therfield*: 31, 255, 262, 330, 549, 1148, 1198, 1496, 1499, 2110, 2291, 2438, 3208, 3839; John, Sr., *Therfield*: 3806; John, Jr., *Therfield*: 2873, 3807; John, *Upwood*: 4027; John, *Wistow*: 209, 339, 359, 743, 1389; Katerina, *Therfield*: 3839; Margaret, *Therfield*: 2027, 2873, 3807; Richard, *Broughton*: 3823; Richard, *Therfield*: 2110, 2869, 3807, 3839; Robert, *Shillington*: 4179; Robert, *Therfield*: 760; Robert, *Wistow*: 897, 1684; Roger, *Hurst/Slepe*: 570; Roger (of Pidley), *Slepe*: 388; Thomas, *Wistow*: 105; Thomas, *Therfield*: 1147, 3208; William (al. Webster), *Hurst/Woodhurst*: 570, 1855, 2431, 3070, 3881; William, *Shillington*: 441, 803, 1083, 3249, 3703, 3709; William, Jr., *Shillington*: 3626; William (Qwas), *Therfield*: 31, 262, 445, 1374, 1498, 2024-7, 2110, 2291, 2438, 2868; William (of Fynehouses), *Therfield*: 330; William, *Wistow*: 105.

WARYNER. See WARENER.

WASSYNGLE, Johanna, *Cranfield*: 1991; Thomas, *Cranfield*: 3778; William, *Cranfield*: 1991.

WATSON. See WATTESSON.

WATTES (Watte), Agnes, *Graveley*: see

NEWMAN; Anna, *Abbots Ripton*: 2914; Felicia (Wynmer), *Therfield*: 167-8, 1793; Henry, *Graveley*: 1741; Isabella, *Therfield*: 2437, 2869, 3842; John, *Therfield*: 310, 507, 1051, 3214, 3567; Katerina, *Therfield*: see SPARVER; Margaret, *Abbots Ripton*: 2186, 4099; Margaret, *Therfield*: see COLLE; Richard, *Holywell*: 2666, 3062, 3515; Richard, *Therfield*: 3836; Robert, *Therfield*: 549; Thomas, *Abbots Ripton*: 11, 1253, 2914, 3972; William, *Abbots Ripton*: 267, 2186, 2914, 4099; William (Carpenter), *Therfield*: 167, 262, 310, 3842.

WATTESSON (Watson, Wattysson), Agnes (I), *Bythorne*: 3858; Agnes (II), *Bythorne*: 3858; Anna, *Weston*: 786, 809; John, *Abbots Ripton*: see NORTHERNEMAN; John (al. Schepperd), *Bythorne*: 263, 3192; John, *Warboys*: 75; John, *Weston*: 786, 809; John, *Weston*: 265; Mariota, *Bythorne*: 3192; Richard, *Bythorne*: 3858; Roger, *Weston*: 1884; William, *Bythorne*: 3013, 3397, 3506; William, *Weston*: 786, 809, 2383.

WAYER, John, atte, *Therfield*: see COLLE.

WAYNEMAN (Wayman), John, *Ramsey*: 1812, 3238; Margaret, *Ramsey*: 1812.

WAYTE (Weyte), Emma, *Ramsey*: 1524, 2939; Johanna, *Ramsey*: 3233; John, *Ramsey*: 1524, 1526, 1785, 2939, 3242, 3456; Margaret, *Bythorne*: see ROKYSDON; Margaret, *Ramsey*: 2718; Margeria, *Ramsey*: see SMYTH; Richard, *Bythorne*: 744, 3507, 3858, 3907; Richard, *Ramsey*: 3183, 3233; Richard, *Slepe*: 2078; Thomas, *Ramsey*: 39, 2213-14, 2718, 3406, and see SMYTH; Thomas (Fuller), *Ramsey*: 3231.

WEBBE, Agnes, *Cranfield*: see COOK; Agnes, *Shillington*: 2540; Galfridus, *Cranfield*: 2223; John, *Cranfield*: 2494, 2618, 3046, 4047; John, *Shillington*: 2540; John, *Therfield*: 3836, 4229.

WEBSTER (Webbestere, Webstere), Agnes, *Abbots Ripton*: 1320; Agnes, *Warboys*: 1124; Beatrix, *St. Ives*: see GRIGGE; Edmund, *Warboys*: 180; Galfridus, *Elton*: 319, 453; Helena, *Broughton*: see HERE; Hugo, *Warboys*: 181, 377; John, *Abbots Ripton*: 1254, 1320, 2417, 3664, 4252; John (al. Brabon), *Broughton*: 1221, 2085, 2285, 2826; John, *Chatteris*: 1501, 2342; John, *Graveley*: 1050; John, *Hemingford*: 3382; John, *Ramsey*: 415; John, *Slepe*: 2267; John (Gemys), *Therfield*: 3566;

John, *Warboys*: 1124; Katerina, *Broughton*: 2511; Margaret, *Slepe*: 2267; Margaret, *Therfield*: see GEMYS; Nicholas, *Elton*: 704; Oliva, *Burwell*: 1553; Reginald, *Broughton*: 2087; Richard, *Broughton*: see HERE; Richard, *Chatteris*: see MICHELL; Simon, *Ramsey*: 3529; Thomas (al. Arnold), *Burwell*: 1553; Thomas, *Ramsey*: see COK; Thomas, *St. Ives*: see GRYGGE; Thomas, *Warboys*: 599; William, *Abbots Ripton*: 923, 1254; William, *Hurst*: see WARYN; William, *Wistow/Broughton*: 394, 3525.

WEDON (Weddon, WYDDON), John, *Chatteris*: 1711, 2803, 4259; Thomas, *Ramsey*: 3116.

WELLE (Well, at, atte), Johanna, *Holywell*: 117, 1399, 3974; John, *Holywell*: 117, 176, 269, 2063, 3974, 4096, 4244; John, *Shillington*: 154, 1617; Margaret/Margeria, *Holywell*: 2063, 4096, 4244; Richard, *Upwood*: 468, 1825; Robert, *Elton*: 408; Robert, *Holywell*: 176; Roger, *Shillington*: 2295; Thomas, *Shillington*: 154, 1617, 4368; family, *Shillington*: 3703.

WELLES (Welle, Wellys), Agnes, *St. Ives*: 867; Alicia, *Barton*: see MATHEW; Isabella, *Ramsey*: 3116; Johanna, *Hemingford*: 3646; John, *Elton*: 2254; John, *Hemingford*: 2386, 3646, 3734, 4333; John, *Ramsey*: 3116; John, *St. Ives*: 867, 2277; Richard, *Bythorne*: 3504; Thomas, *Barton*: 3714.

WENE (Wyne), Elena, *Ramsey*: 2610; Leonard, *Ramsey*: 2610, 3114; Maria, *Warboys*: 2245.

WENGOODE. See WYNGOODE.

WENHAM, Alicia, *Therfield*: 2874; Emma, *Therfield*: 1865, 2868; Johanna, *Therfield*: 3805; John (Thakker), *Therfield*: 1865, 2868, 3805, 4063; John, Jr., *Therfield*: 3212, 3700, 4228; Thomas, *Therfield*: 4195; William, *Therfield*: 2874, 3805.

WENYNGHAM (Wymyngham, Wyngham), John, *Shillington*: 1082, 1622, 2116, 2762, 3347, 4060; John, Sr., *Shillington*: 3249; John, Jr., *Shillington*: 3350, 3627.

WENYNGTON, John, *Warboys*: 295; John, *Wistow*: 198.

WERNYNGTON, Alicia, *Ramsey*: 1605, 3111; Alicia, *Warboys*: see FREMAN; John (al. de Celar), *Ramsey*: 1605; John, Sr., *Ramsey*: 2697; John, Jr., *Ramsey*: 2697; John, *Warboys*: 1573.

WEST (Weste), Agnes, *Graveley*: 2493;

2501; John, *Woodhurst/Hurst*: 1717, 2502; Margaret, *Brington*: see GANDER; Margaret, *Weston*: 1652; Margaret, *St. Ives/Slepe*: 2653, 2656; Margaret, *Wistow*: see GATE; Radulph, *Wistow*: 2503; Richard, *Abbots Ripton*: 3385; Richard, *Brington*: 1839; Richard, *Burwell*: 1623, 3125; Richard, *St. Ives*: 1329; Richard, *Wistow*: 1876, 1880, 2734; Robert, *Abbots Ripton*: 3289, 3795; Robert (of Huntingdon), *Abbots Ripton*: 2822; Robert (of Walton), *Abbots Ripton*: 3468; Robert, *Chatteris*: 3389, 3444; Robert, *Hemingford*: 2128, 3382; Robert, *St. Ives*: 1781, 2653, 2656, 3320; Robert, *Holywell/Slepe/Woodhurst*: 240, 654, 657-69, 940, 1717, 1761, 1907, 2656, 3748; Robert, *Warboys*: 1236; Robert, *Wistow*: 1878, 2750; Stephen, *Elton*: 56, 992; Thomas, *Houghton*: 964; Thomas, *Slepe*: 256, 833, 2016, 3453; Thomas, *Therfield*: 3165; Thomas, *Warboys*: 460; William, *Brington*: 224; William, *Burwell*: see GOODALE; William, *Holywell*: 449, and see ALBRY; William, Sr., *Holywell*: 4095; William, Jr., *Holywell*: 4095; William, *Houghton*: 1961; William, *St. Ives*: 2653; William, *Slepe*: 232, 2656; William, *Weston*: 1910.

WRO, John, *Slepe*: 272.

WROO, Thomas, *Elton*: 1113; Thomas, *Warboys*: 3268.

WRYGHT. See WRIGHT.

WYAT. See WYOT.

WYC; Florentia, *Burwell*: 3828; John, *Burwell*: 3828.

WYCHE (Wycher), Isabella, *Elton*: 700; John, *Elton*: 453.

WYET. See WYOT.

WYGGE, John, *Therfield*: 3807.

WYGHT. See WHITE.

WYGYN, John, *Bythorne*: 3192; Mariota, *Bythorne*: see WATTESSON.

WYKE, John, *Ramsey*: 3241.

WYLDE, Robert, *Upwood*: 1744.

WYLDEFOWLE (Wildefowll), Amicia, *Shillington*: 21; Johanna, *Shillington*: 2033; John, *Shillington*: 21, 273, 1483, 2033.

WYLKIS. See WILKIS.

WYLKYN. See WILKYN.

WYLLESSON. See WILLESSON.

WYLLYAM. See WILLIAM.

WYLYMOT, Agnes, *Barton*: 1459; Agnes (II), *Barton*: 2315; Alicia, *St. Ives*: 16, 71,

869, 3747; Isabella, *Barton*: 1980; Johanna, *St. Ives*: 16; John, *Barton*: 2582, 3358, 3490; John, *St. Ives*: 16, 869, 1015, 1646, 1816, 2065, 3747; John, Jr., *St. Ives*: 71; John, Sr., *St. Ives*: 71; John, chaplain, *St. Ives*: 3747, 4076; Margaret, *Barton*: 2393; Richard, *Barton*: 1375, 1459, 2392; Thomas, *Barton*: 261, 1375, 1460, 1980, 2315, 2392-3, 3036; Walter, *Barton*: 1459, 1735, 2122, 2195; William, *Barton*: 3036; William, *St. Ives*: 3747; William, *Woodhurst*: 2075; family, *St. Ives*: 1815.

WYMOND (Wymondes), Isabella, *Elsworth*: 806; John, *Elsworth*: 213, 534, 565, 718, 806, 1478, 1803; Margaret, *Elsworth*: 718; Richard, *Elsworth*: 3583; Thomas, *Elsworth*: 534, 716; William, *Elsworth*: 1667, 3093.

WYMONDHAM, John, *Shillington*: 715.

WYMPOOL (Wympooll), John, *Chatteris*: 3298, 4025, 4346, 4350.

WYMYNGHAM. See WENYNGHAM.

WYNDE, John, *Warboys*: 414, 653.

WYNDYLL, John, *Houghton*: 3729.

WYNE. See WENE.

WYNEWYK (Wynnewyk), John, *Chatteris*: 355, 372, 1555.

WYNGHAM. See WENYNGHAM.

WYNGOOD (Wengoode, Wyngode, Wynngoode), John, *Holywell*: 2786; John, *Hurst/Slepe/Woodhurst*: 388, 2852, 2971, 3158; Nicholas, *Cranfield*: 1610; Thomas, *Hurst/Slepe*: 232, 388, 2599; William, *Hurst*: 2932.

WYNGOR (Wyngore, Wynnegore, Wynngor, Wyngord), Agnes, *Therfield*: 3166; Elena, *Therfield*: 3451; Johanna, *Therfield*: see WARYN; Johanna, *Therfield*: see WODE; John, *Holywell*: 940; John, *Therfield*: 3166; Nicholas, *Cranfield*: 1076; Thomas, *Woodhurst*: 1855; Thomas, *Therfield*: 255, 2291; Thomas, Sr., *Therfield*: 17; Thomas, Jr., *Therfield*: 17, 255; William, *Therfield*: 262, 445, 1499, 1867, 3451.

WYNMER (Wymer, Wynner), Felicia, *Therfield*: see WATTE; John, *Therfield*: 262, 267, 761, 1793; Thomas, *Therfield*: 3408; William, *Therfield*: 167, 505, 506, 1793, 2870, 3164, 3408.

WYNNEWYK. See WYNEWYK.

WYNTER, Alicia, *Shillington*: see WARYN; John, *Ellington*: 200, 351; William, *Shillington*: 441.

WYOT (Wyat, Wyet), Cecilia (Rolf), *Bur-*

INDEX RERUM